T0309943

ANGLO-SAXON CHARTERS

SUPPLEMENTARY VOLUMES

ANGLO-SAXON CHARTERS · IV

CHARTERS OF ST AUGUSTINE'S ABBEY CANTERBURY
and
Minster-in-Thanet

EDITED BY

S. E. KELLY

Published *for* THE BRITISH ACADEMY
by OXFORD UNIVERSITY PRESS

*This book has been printed digitally and produced in a standard specification
in order to ensure its continuing availability*

OXFORD
UNIVERSITY PRESS

Great Clarendon Street, Oxford OX2 6DP

Oxford University Press is a department of the University of Oxford.
It furthers the University's objective of excellence in research, scholarship,
and education by publishing worldwide in

Oxford New York

Auckland   Cape Town Dar es Salaam   Hong Kong   Karachi
Kuala Lumpur Madrid Melbourne Mexico City   Nairobi
New Delhi Shanghai Taipei Toronto
With offices in
Argentina Austria Brazil Chile Czech Republic France Greece
Guatemala Hungary Italy Japan South Korea Poland Portugal
Singapore Switzerland Thailand Turkey Ukraine Vietnam

Oxford is a registered trade mark of Oxford University Press
in the UK and in certain other countries

Published in the United States
by Oxford University Press Inc., New York

ISBN 978-0-19-726143-9

To My Parents

FOREWORD

A joint committee of the British Academy and the Royal Historical Society was set up in 1966 to organize the publication of a new edition of the entire corpus of Anglo-Saxon charters, intended to supersede at last J. M. Kemble's *Codex Diplomaticus* (London, 1839–48) and W. de Gray Birch's *Cartularium Saxonicum* (London, 1885–93). Fascicules for the archives of Rochester, Burton and Sherborne and a supplementary volume of *Facsimiles of Anglo-Saxon Charters* have already been published. Another volume, on Shaftesbury, is imminent, while Selsey, Barking and Abingdon will be published shortly; work is progressing on a number of other archives including Christ Church Canterbury, the Old Minster Winchester, Glastonbury, Worcester and Wilton.

St Augustine's Canterbury was the first monastery to be founded in Anglo-Saxon England and seems to have had a continuous existence from the very beginning of the seventh century until the Reformation. Its charters therefore have particular interest and this volume also contains more charters than any of the previous fascicules. Moreover it is unusual in that the bulk of them (38 out of 53) purport to date from the seventh, eighth or ninth centuries, though they only survive in copies preserved in medieval cartularies. Among them are fourteen charters from the archive of the wealthy and important double monastery of Minster-in-Thanet, whose lands and title deeds passed to St Augustine's in the eleventh century. The monks of St Augustine's were intensely interested in their own history and in that of the early Kentish kingdom. Many of the charters can be shown to have been altered to serve changing needs and interpretations at various stages in their transmission. With complex textual histories and acute problems of diplomatic, these charters therefore present more difficult editorial problems than are to be found in the entire Anglo-Saxon series. The Committee is therefore fortunate to have secured Dr Susan Kelly as editor, whose work not only on St Augustine's but across the range of Anglo-Saxon charters equips her to provide as consistent and authoritative a judgement on these fascinating texts as is possible.

The work of the joint editorial committee is a notable example of scholarly collaboration and several of its members have given important assistance to this volume. Membership of the committee has continued to evolve. Mr James Campbell has handed on the chairmanship, but continues as a valued member, as do the secretary, Dr Simon Keynes, Professor Eric Stanley, Mrs Margaret Gelling, Mr Michael Roper and Dr David Dumville. Sadly Professor Michael Lapidge has felt obliged by the pressures of his many commitments to withdraw after notable assistance to this and to earlier volumes. He is replaced by Dr Richard Sharpe and the committee is strengthened by the addition of Mr Patrick Wormald and Dr Susan Kelly. The Committee has been very fortunate to secure five years of generous funding from The Newton Trust and The Leverhulme Trust which has enabled it to employ Dr Susan Kelly to edit charters full-time. Thanks to this support there is now the prospect of a steady stream of important fascicules over the next few years. The Committee is determined that the critical edition of the entire corpus should be achieved by this generation of scholars and that the momentum now gathering should be maintained in coming years.

NICHOLAS BROOKS

CONTENTS

LIST OF PLATES

(between page lxiv and page lxv)

ACKNOWLEDGEMENTS

I should like to express my gratitude to all the members of the Anglo-Saxon Charters committee for their advice and encouragement, and to thank in particular Simon Keynes, Nicholas Brooks, Michael Lapidge, Patrick Wormald and Eric Stanley. I am also indebted to Nigel Ramsay, for advice on aspects of the St Augustine's archive, and to Neil Wright, for instruction in Latin. My work on St Augustine's has extended over many years, and I owe a great deal to the three colleges to which I have been attached during this time – Clare and Newnham in Cambridge, and St Catherine's in Oxford. Over this period I have received generous funding from, at various times, the British Academy, the Rank Foundation, the Leverhulme Trust and the Newton Trust; I am most grateful for the support of all of these bodies, without which I would have been unable to bring my research to its conclusion.

This edition is based on manuscripts preserved in many different libraries. Many thanks are due to the librarians for their help and co-operation, and in particular to the librarians and Fellows of Corpus Christi College and Trinity Hall in Cambridge for permission for reproduce photographs of pages of their manuscripts.

INTRODUCTION

1. ST AUGUSTINE'S ABBEY

St Augustine's Abbey, located just outside the walls of Canterbury, was the first monastery to be founded in England by the Roman missionaries, and one of the very few early foundations to have a continuous existence until the Dissolution.[1] Augustine intended that the Canterbury monastery should serve as an extramural burial-church for the kings of Kent, and for himself and future archbishops of Canterbury.[2] He and his companions had a monastic background, and probably saw the foundation of a contemplative monastery as an important priority; in this respect, St Augustine's provided a religious environment complementary to that of the episcopal community at Christ Church, where the clergy are likely to have participated to a greater degree in evangelization and secular affairs.[3] There may also have been an intention to reproduce, on a small scale, the arrangements for liturgical celebration in the great Roman basilicas, with which the missionaries would have been familiar; it was the custom there for basilican clergy to share responsibility for celebrating the offices with the monks of local monasteries, thus ensuring the regular performance of the liturgical round and freeing the basilican clergy for other duties.[4] Christ Church and St Augustine's also appear to have collaborated in the areas of education and scholarship, and it is possible that the two houses had a common library until the end of the tenth century.[5] There is some evidence from the ninth century that certain

[1] The essential background to the history of St Augustine's in the Anglo-Saxon period is to be found in N.P. Brooks, *The Early History of the Church of Canterbury: Christ Church from 597 to 1066* (Leicester, 1984), to which I am much indebted. Certain aspects are considered in more detail in S.E. Kelly, 'The Pre-Conquest History and Archive of St Augustine's Abbey, Canterbury', unpublished Ph.D. thesis, Cambridge (1986).

[2] Bede, *HE* i. 33. See further, K.H. Krüger, *Königsgrabkirchen der Franken, Angelsachsen und Langobarden bis zur Mitte des 8. Jahrhunderts: ein historischer Katalog*, Münstersche Mittelalter-Schriften 4 (Munich, 1971), pp. 264–87; and Kelly 1986, pp. 8–24.

[3] J.A. Robinson, 'The Early Community at Christ Church, Canterbury', *Journal of Theological Studies* xxvii (1925–6), pp. 225–40, at 231–3; Brooks, *Church of Canterbury*, pp. 87–91.

[4] G. Ferrari, *Early Roman Monasteries*, Studi di antichità cristiana xxiii (Vatican, 1957), pp. 365–75; Brooks, *Church of Canterbury*, pp. 91–3, 156–7.

[5] Brooks, *Church of Canterbury*, pp. 94–9, 277.

abbots of St Augustine's may previously have been members of the episcopal community.[6] The essential interdependence of the monastery and Christ Church is likely to have been an important factor through most of the Anglo-Saxon period, and probably explains the survival of St Augustine's as an independent institution during the vicissitudes of the ninth century. The celebrated rivalry between the two houses may not have developed until the eleventh century and ' may perhaps be connected with the belated transformation of Christ Church into a fully monastic community.[7]

The abbey church was originally dedicated to SS Peter and Paul, and built on an alignment with a smaller (and perhaps earlier) church nearby dedicated to St Pancras; a third church on the same axis, dedicated to St Mary, was erected by King Eadbald (616–40).[8] In charters of the seventh and eighth century, the monastery is usually referred to as St Peter's (see **6, 7, 8, 9, 13**), although sometimes the full dedication to SS Peter and Paul was cited (**11, 12, 14**). During the ninth century the monastery became more closely identified with the cult of St Augustine. In 826 the community is called *sancti Augustini familia* (**17**) and in several private charters of the mid-century the grants are explicitly made to St Augustine (**23A, 24, 25**; S 332, endorsement), although there are continuing references to St Peter's (**18, 20**). In the tenth century the association with St Augustine seems to have become stronger, and was perhaps fixed by Dunstan's rededication of the abbey church to SS Peter, Paul and Augustine in 978.[9] For convenience I shall refer to the monastery throughout as St Augustine's.

[6] Brooks *Church of Canterbury*, pp. 163–4 (but see below, Appendix 4, for qualifications).

[7] Brooks, *Church of Canterbury*, pp. 255–60, 265. See also S.E. Kelly, 'Some Forgeries in the Archive of St Augustine's Abbey, Canterbury', in *Fälschungen im Mittelalter*, MGH Schriften 33.iv (Hanover, 1988), pp. 347–69.

[8] Bede, *HE*, i. 33; ii. 6. Bede refers to the monastery as SS Peter and Paul (*HE* i. 33; ii. 3, 5, 6) and also as St Peter's (*HE* ii. 6, 7; iv. 1; v. 8). For the monastery churches, see Kelly 1986, pp. 13–16, 25–7; H.M. Taylor and J. Taylor, *Anglo-Saxon Architecture*, 3 vols (Cambridge, 1965–78), i. 134–43, 146–8; R.D.H. Gem, 'Reconstructions of St Augustine's Abbey, Canterbury, in the Anglo-Saxon Period', *St Dunstan: his Life, Times and Cult*, ed. N. Ramsay, M. Sparks and T. Tatton-Brown (Woodbridge, 1992), pp. 57–73. For the possible Roman origin of St Pancras: F. J[enkins], 'Preliminary Report on the Excavations at the Church of St Pancras at Canterbury', *Canterbury Archaeology* i (1975/6), pp. 4–5. A fourth church was built on the same axis in the first half of the eleventh century: A.D. Saunders, 'Excavations in the Church of St Augustine's Abbey, Canterbury, 1955–8', *Medieval Archaeology* xxii (1978), pp. 25–63 at 38–44, 51.

[9] The rededication is mentioned by two medieval historians of the abbey, William Thorne and Thomas Elmham (for these, see below, pp. lv–lix, xcvi–xcix). Thorne: *Historiae Anglicanae Scriptores X*, ed. R. Twysden (London, 1652), col. 1780; translated A.H. Davis, *William Thorne's Chronicle of Saint Augustine's Abbey, Canterbury* (Oxford, 1934), p. 38. Elmham: *Historia Monasterii Sancti Augustini Cantuariensis by Thomas of Elmham*, ed. C. Hardwick, RS (London, 1858), p. 22.

The first abbot of the monastery was one of Augustine's original companions, and his next two successors were members of the party of reinforcements which set out from Rome in 601; according to later tradition at St Augustine's, the following three abbots of the house were also Romans (see Appendix 4). The Italian ethos can only have been reinforced by the arrival of Abbot Hadrian in 669 or 670, apparently with a retinue, presumably of Italian monks (Bede, *HE*, iv. 12). Hadrian acted as Archbishop Theodore's assistant and partner in the restructuring of the Anglo-Saxon church, and in the creation of a notable centre of learning and scholarship at Canterbury.[10] In 679 or 680 Hadrian acquired from Pope Agatho a papal privilege for his monastery, which exempted St Augustine's from diocesan control, leaving it subject to the Holy See alone, and guaranteed the community's right to elect its own abbot (BCS 38). This was one of a number of such privileges issued to Anglo-Saxon monasteries in this period.[11] Hadrian ruled St Augustine's for some forty years, and was succeeded by his pupil, Albinus, who ensured that his influence survived for another two decades.

St Augustine's lost its pre-eminence as the principal Canterbury burial-church in the middle of the eighth century. The first blow came when its monopoly of archiepiscopal burial was broken. Archbishop Cuthbert (740–60) built a church dedicated to St John the Baptist at Christ Church, and he and his successors were buried there; the only exception was Archbishop Jænberht (765–92), a former abbot of St Augustine's who insisted on being buried in the monastery. Canterbury accounts of these events, all very much later, suggest that St Augustine's bitterly resented the abrogation of its burial prerogative.[12] The monastery's role as a royal burial-church also evaporated at this time. The ancient Kentish dynasty of the *Oiscingas* disappeared in the early 760s; the last representatives to be buried at St Augustine's appear to have been Æthelberht II (donor of **11**), who died in 762, and his successor, Eadberht II, who was probably dead before 765 (see **12**, **13**, and Appendix 3).

By 785 direct Mercian rule had been imposed on Kent. The surviving muniments do not suggest that St Augustine's enjoyed much special favour

---

[10] Bede, *HE*, iv. 1; Brooks, *Church of Canterbury*, pp. 94–7; M. Lapidge, 'The School of Theodore and Hadrian', *Anglo-Saxon England* xv (1986), pp. 45–72.

[11] The underlying authenticity of BCS 38 is established by W. Levison, *England and the Continent in the Eighth Century* (Oxford, 1946), pp. 187–90; see also H.H. Anton, *Studien zu den Klosterprivilegien der Päpste im frühen Mittelalter* (Berlin and New York, 1975), pp. 66–7. The given date of 675 should be emended to 679 or 680. For the background, see P. Wormald, 'Bede and Benedict Biscop', in *Famulus Christi*, ed. G. Bonner (London, 1976), pp. 141–69 at 146–9.

[12] Brooks, *Church of Canterbury*, pp. 40, 81–3.

from Offa and his successors. A charter of Offa in favour of Abbot Æthelnoth (14) is very unsatisfactory as it now stands and is probably a forgery. An initially promising charter of 804 in which King Coenwulf of Mercia and his brother King Cuthred grant land to their kinsman Abbot Cunred (16) proves disappointing; the original beneficiary of the charter (and the royal kinsman) was a layman, and the abbot's name was substituted at a later date. It is impossible to say whether St Augustine's, like other Kentish minsters connected with the former native dynasty, including Minster-in-Thanet, fell under the control of the Mercian kings. On balance, its close connection with the archbishop and Christ Church makes this unlikely, and it is probably significant that St Augustine's does not seem to be mentioned in documents drawn up by Archbishop Wulfred as part of his campaign to detach the Kentish minsters from Mercian domination.[13] In 826 Wulfred supervised an exchange between Minster-in-Thanet, at that date under his undisputed control, and the St Augustine's community (17). There is an apparent contrast in the treatment of the two houses, for the charter suggests that Wulfred was disposing of Minster land without reference to the titular head of the community, whereas the abbot of St Augustine's is mentioned in the text and also appears in the witness-list.

The West Saxon kings, who ruled Kent from 825 onwards, seem to have been favourably disposed towards the Canterbury monastery. In 836 King Ecgberht granted a small estate to a *clericus* named Ciaba who was living at St Augustine's, apparently with the proviso that it should be passed on to the monastery (18). There are two charters of King Æthelwulf directly in favour of the abbot and community of St Augustine's, dated 838 and 845 (19, 20). In 861 Æthelwulf's son, Æthelberht, gave three sulungs to Abbot Diernoth on condition that he remain loyal to the king's brothers, Æthelred and Alfred (22). The circumstances which prompted this agreement can only be a matter of speculation, but the charter provides good evidence for the continuing importance of St Augustine's as a separate institution in the second half of the ninth century.[14] The monastery also benefited in this period from donations of land and food-rents made by local notables (23A, 24, 25). The archive

---

[13] The dispute over the control of the Kentish minsters is discussed by Brooks, *Church of Canterbury*, pp. 175–206. Two forged privileges were produced in connexion with the dispute (S 22, 90); the first of these lists the disputed minsters and St Augustine's is not included (unless it is to be identified with the mysterious *Upmynster*, dedicated to St Peter, which heads the list; against this identification, see Brooks, *Church of Canterbury*, p. 366 n. 63).

[14] For discussion, see S. Keynes, 'The Control of Kent in the Ninth Century', *Early Medieval Europe* ii (1993), pp. 111–31, at 128; *idem*, 'The West Saxon Charters of King Æthelwulf and his Sons', *English Historical Review* cix (1994), pp. 1111–48, at 1129.

preserves a charter of 850 granting a substantial estate of forty hides at Lenham to Ealdorman Ealhhere (21). Ealhhere and his family were benefactors of both Christ Church and St Augustine's in this period, and it is possible that the ealdorman or one of his immediate heirs gave the land to the monastery.[15]

Viking raids on the coasts of Kent had certainly begun by the first decade of the ninth century, and perhaps even in Offa's reign (see 15). By the middle of the ninth century the Scandinavian pirates were making regular and destructive visits to the province. Canterbury was stormed by a Viking army in 851 and, although there is no firm information about the effects of this attack, the monastery's vulnerable location outside the walls would have left it open to damage and looting. The Kentish countryside was repeatedly ravaged, and it is possible that the food-rents which were granted by lay donors at this time to the St Augustine's and Christ Church communities were needed because supplies from the churches' estates had been disrupted (see 24, 25). In 865 the *Anglo-Saxon Chronicle* records that the people of Kent promised money to the Vikings in an unsuccessful attempt to secure immunity; there were probably other occasions when tribute was paid to the invaders, and this would have put some strain on the resources of even a wealthy monastery. Nevertheless, the St Augustine's community seems to have weathered the difficulties and there is no evidence that disruption was other than temporary. The later historians of the abbey provided a full list of abbots for the ninth century, although this may be partly fictional (see Appendix 4). The charter record also shows continuity until 861, and this can be supplemented by notices of lost charters recording transactions involving the abbey in the later part of the century (see Appendix 1). But there is some evidence that part of the endowment was lost during this difficult period, for in 925 King Athelstan restored to the community a large estate on Thanet that had been unjustly seized many years before (26).

King Athelstan's lawcode issued at Grately between *c.* 926 and *c.* 930 includes a provision which seems to recognise that St Augustine's was a monastery of particular importance. A list of the number of moneyers permitted by the king to operate in the burhs mentions that one was attached to the Canterbury abbot, the only abbot to be so privileged. Athelstan was engaged in ensuring that a common royal coinage was in use throughout the kingdom, and it appears that the privilege accorded to the abbot probably represented a financial interest in the system, rather than a licence to strike

---

[15] For Ealhhere and his family see Brooks, *Church of Canterbury*, pp. 148–9. Ealhburh, donor of 24, may have been his sister. His grandson, Eadweald, granted land at Willesborough to the community (see S 332, and below, p. xxxii n. 57).

a separate coinage. But the archbishops of Canterbury had struck their own coins from at least the eighth century until the early tenth, and it is possible that the abbots of St Augustine's had some interest in this process; thus the privileged position indicated in the Grately code may have been in effect the recognition of an existing customary right.[16]

It was remembered at St Augustine's in the later medieval period that Archbishop Dunstan had rededicated the abbey church in 978. The rededication is probably to be connected with the extension and refurbishment of the church that appears to have taken place at around this time. It has also been suggested that the first cloister at St Augustine's may have been built under Dunstan's influence, perhaps in imitation of one at Glastonbury.[17] It is probable that Dunstan undertook the reform of the Canterbury monastery after he was appointed archbishop in 959, and he may have introduced monks from Glastonbury into the community. Sigeric, abbot from c. 980 to c. 985, was a former monk of Glastonbury, who went on to become bishop of Ramsbury and later archbishop of Canterbury.[18]

[16] II Athelstan 14. 2: edited by F. Liebermann, *Die Gesetze der Angelsachsen*, 3 vols (Halle, 1903–16), i. 159; and translated in Whitelock, *EHD*, p. 420. See P. Grierson and M. Blackburn, *Medieval European Coinage: the Early Middle Ages (5th–10th Centuries)* (Cambridge, 1986), pp. 271–2, for discussion of ecclesiastical coinages; and also Brooks, *Church of Canterbury*, pp. 23–4, 132–3, 215. According to Thorne (Twysden, *Scriptores*, col. 1816; Davis, *Thorne*, p. 94), the abbots of St Augustine's had a mint in Canterbury which was lost on the death of Abbot Silvester in 1161. Another mark of Athelstan's favour was the (probable) grant of a continental gospel-book, BL Royal I. A. XVIII: see S. Keynes, 'King Athelstan's Books', *Learning and Literature in Anglo-Saxon England*, ed. M. Lapidge and H. Gneuss (Cambridge, 1985), pp. 143–201, at 165–70.

[17] For the rededication of the church see above n. 9. The extensions to the church were first linked with Dunstan by C.R. Peers and A.W. Clapham, 'St Augustine's Abbey Church, Canterbury, before the Norman Conquest', *Archaeologia* lxxvii (1927), 201–17, at 210–11. See also Taylor and Taylor, *Anglo-Saxon Architecture*, i. 137, 141; Gem, 'Reconstructions of St Augustine's Abbey', pp. 63–7. For the suggestion about the cloister, see R.J. Cramp, 'Monastic Sites', in *The Archaeology of Anglo-Saxon England*, ed. D.M. Wilson (Cambridge, 1976), pp. 201–52 at 248–9; Gem ('Reconstructions of St Augustine's Abbey', pp. 66–7) points out that there is no firm evidence for the date.

[18] *HRH*, p. 35. Sigeric's Glastonbury origin is mentioned by William of Malmesbury, *De Antiquitate Glastonie Ecclesie*, c. 67: see J. Scott, *The Early History of Glastonbury* (Woodbridge, 1981), p. 137. For highlights of his later career, see V. Ortenburg, 'Archbishop Sigeric's Journey to Rome in 990', *Anglo-Saxon England* xix (1990), 197–246. T.A.M. Bishop (*English Caroline Minuscule* (Oxford, 1971), pp. xx, xxii) has suggested that the type of Anglo-Caroline script being written at St Augustine's in the late tenth century originated at Glastonbury and was indeed borrowed directly, which would reinforce the impression of a link between the two houses in Dunstan's time. But it has recently been pointed out that the grounds for regarding Glastonbury as the source of this script-type are far from strong, and that more attention should be paid to Canterbury as a seeding-ground for script developments: D.N. Dumville, *English Caroline Script and Monastic History: Studies in Benedictinism, A.D. 950–1030* (Woodbridge, 1993), pp. 2–4, 86–110, 143–4. For a provisional list of manuscripts written at St

The surviving muniments provide little information about land-grants to St Augustine's in the tenth century. There is a very difficult charter of King Edgar conveying land at Plumstead to the community, which may have a genuine basis but is more likely to be spurious (29). The lay beneficiary of a small land-grant by King Eadred is said to have subsequently transferred the estate to the monastery, where he hoped to be buried (28). It is impossible to tell when the estates at Sibertswold granted to thegns in 27 and 30 passed into the possession of St Augustine's. Later medieval historians mention several bequests and small gifts made to the monastery in the last decades of the century (see Appendix 1).

From the 990s Kent (and the rest of England) suffered a second wave of Viking assaults, which may have been even more destructive than those of the ninth century. The English response to the crisis involved the frequent payment of huge amounts of nationally-collected geld; some regions made separate payments in an attempt to avert attack. The demand for tribute left even the Canterbury archbishop temporarily impoverished, forcing him to sell a large estate in Buckinghamshire.[19] St Augustine's probably suffered both from the destruction caused by the Viking raiders and from the strain of paying its share of tribute. The culmination of the attacks on Kent was the sack of Canterbury in 1011, which resulted in the capture of a number of ecclesiastics, including Archbishop Ælfheah and the bishop of Rochester. The *Anglo-Saxon Chronicle* says that the invaders allowed Abbot Ælfmær of St Augustine's to escape (possibly because a ransom had been paid). The losses incurred during this period may account for the energy which Abbot Ælfstan ([1023 × 1027] – 1045) directed towards increasing the monastery's endowment. His greatest coup was the acquisition of the relics of St Mildrith, probably in 1030, which gave him an excuse to reconstitute the lands of the decayed monastery of Minster-in-Thanet. Some part of the Minster estates he appears to have acquired already in exchange for land at Folkestone; he may have laid claim to other areas on the ground that the monastery held Mildrith's relics and was therefore her heir. Ælfstan would seem to have been largely responsible for building up the abbey's great manor on Thanet, assessed at forty-eight sulungs in 1066 (see further pp. xxx–xxxi). He also made strenuous but unsuccessful attempts to gain for St Augustine's the

Augustine's in the second half of the tenth century, see T.A.M. Bishop, *Æthicae Istrici Cosmographia Vergilio Salisburgensi rectius adscripta: Codex Leidensis Scaligeranus 69* (Amsterdam, 1966), pp. xix-xx.

[19] See S 882, and Brooks, *Church of Canterbury*, p. 283.

revenues of the port of Sandwich, in competition with Christ Church.[20] At some stage in the reign of the Confessor the monastery came into possession of two-thirds of the burh of Fordwich, the principal port of Canterbury (see **39** and commentary); it is possible that this represents compensation for its disappointment over Sandwich.

Queen Emma was remembered as a benefactor of St Augustine's, and she seems to have had a particular reverence for St Mildrith.[21] Another supporter was Archbishop Eadsige (1038–1050), who made two small land-grants to the monastery (**37**, S 1400), and also gave a psalter, two chalices and one hundred marks for building a tower.[22] A leading Kentish thegn in the Confessor's reign, Æthelric Bigga, made over to St Augustine's two small estates, possibly as part of a dispute settlement (**38**). On the debit side, it was believed in the later medieval period that Earl Godwine had appropriated part of the abbey's estate at Plumstead and given it to his son Tostig, which would be in line with Godwine's depredations on Christ Church (see **29**).[23]

[20] According to S 1467, a highly partisan account, Ælfstan took part in a conspiracy to seize Sandwich from Christ Church, its rightful owner, and bribed King Harold Harefoot's steward to give him the third part of the toll there. Baulked by a sickbed repentance on the part of King Harold, Ælfstan then made an attempt to retain the toll by persuading Archbishop Eadsige to speak on his behalf to the Christ Church community (which suggests that he had some justification on his side). The Christ Church monks would have none of it, and they also refused his request to build a wharf opposite 'Mildrith's field' (and therefore presumably on the mainland near Sandwich); in response Ælfstan tried to have a channel excavated at Ebbsfleet (probably through the northern part of the shingle bank known as the Stonar peninsula), but this proved unfeasible. The dispute must have arisen directly from St Augustine's recent acquisition of Thanet, which Ælfstan seems to have believed entitled him to some measure of commercial control in the eastern Wantsum (possibly based on ancient rights of Minster-in-Thanet, but thwarted by silt-deposition in the area and the development of the Stonar peninsula). S 1467 implies that the dispute faded after Ælfstan's failure at Ebbsfleet, but other documents show that it was more protracted; Sandwich was disputed between Christ Church and St Augustine's until the early twelfth century: see Brooks, *Church of Canterbury*, pp. 292–4; Kelly 1986, pp. 216–23. For the final settlement, see D.M. Stenton, *English Justice between the Norman Conquest and the Great Charter, 1066–1215* (London, 1965), pp. 18–24, 116–23; R. van Caenegem, *English Lawsuits from William I to Richard I*, 2 vols, Selden Society nos 106–7 (London, 1990–1), no. 254 (pp. 216–19).

[21] Emma is said to have made many gifts to St Augustine's and to have provided costly palls for all the saintly tombs in the abbey: see Twysden, *Scriptores*, col. 1784; Davis, *Thorne*, p. 45. She may also be identifiable with the woman named Ælfgifu who in 1019 gave sixty pounds to the community and twenty shillings to each monk (see Appendix 1, no. x). For Emma and St Mildrith, see F. Barlow, 'Two Notes: Cnut's Second Pilgrimage and Queen Emma's Disgrace in 1043', *English Historical Review* lxxiii (1958), pp. 649–56 at 651–5.

[22] Twysden, *Scriptores*, col. 1784; Davis, *Thorne*, pp. 44–5.

[23] In the central decades of the eleventh century the version of the *Anglo-Saxon Chronicle* which was being kept at St Augustine's (now represented by *ASC* E) gives a highly favourable account of the activities of Godwine and his sons, which is difficult to reconcile with this apparent confiscation of one of the monastery's estates. The true history of the Plumstead

In the last decades of the Anglo-Saxon period St Augustine's was an important and successful monastery.[24] Abbot Wulfric (1045–61) was one of King Edward's representatives at the papal synod at Rheims in 1049, where he is said to have received the pope's permission to rebuild the abbey church; on his return he initiated a lavish building programme, which involved an attempt to link the main church with the church of St Mary by means of an octagonal rotunda.[25] According to Goscelin, Wulfric was given a tremendous reception at Rheims, at least in part as the result of a speech previously made in Rome by Bishop Hereman of Ramsbury (and later Sherborne) vaunting the glories of the English church. Hereman supposedly informed Pope Leo that the archbishop of Canterbury and the abbot of St Augustine's had in former times enjoyed the privilege of being seated in prestigious positions when they attended Roman assemblies; the abbot was placed beside the abbot of Monte Cassino. Research into the records supported the claim, and Pope Leo gave his corroboration. Goscelin then goes on to describe an episode which implies even greater papal recognition of the status of St Augustine's. When Wulfric's successor, Abbot Æthelsige, visited Rome in 1063, Alexander II is said to have granted him a very significant honour, the right to wear the pontifical mitre and sandals. Such a concession would suggest a link with a similar privilege granted to abbot of Fulda in June 1049, which involved acknowledgement of Fulda as the leading monastery of Gaul and Germany; it might be thought that Alexander was recognising St Augustine's in a similar way, as the pre-eminent English monastery.[26] It is

---

property may have been more complicated (see further under **29**). For St Augustine's and *ASC* E, see D.N. Dumville, 'Some Aspects of Annalistic Writing at Canterbury in the Eleventh and Early Twelfth Centuries', *Peritia: Journal of the Medieval Academy of Ireland* ii (1983), pp. 23–57.

[24] One manifestation of this, of deeply uncertain significance, is the statement in the *Liber Eliensis* that, from Æthelred's reign until the Conquest, St Augustine's shared with Glastonbury and Ely the honour of providing a representative to perform the duties of a *cancellarius* in the royal court: see discussion in Appendix 5.

[25] For Wulfric's presence at the Rheims synod see *ASC* E, *s.a.* 1049. The rebuilding of the church is described by Goscelin of Saint-Bertin in his *Historia translationis S. Augustini*: see *Acta Sanctorum Maii vi*, ed. G. Henschenius and D. Papebroch (Antwerp, 1688), pp. 432–3 (for Goscelin, see next note). See also H.M. Taylor, 'St Augustine's Abbey', *Archaeological Journal* cxxvi (1969), pp. 228–33 at 229, 232; Gem, 'Reconstructions of St Augustine's', pp. 67–71.

[26] Goscelin, *Translatio S. Augustini*, p. 433. For Goscelin, see F. Barlow, *The Life of King Edward who rests at Westminster*, 2nd edn (Oxford, 1992), pp. 133–49, and R. Sharpe, 'Goscelin's St Augustine and St Mildreth: Hagiography and Liturgy in Context', *Journal of Theological Studies* n.s. xli (1990), pp. 502–16; see also Twysden, *Scriptores*, cols 1784–5 (Davis, *Thorne*, p. 45) and Hardwick, *Elmham*, pp. 26–7. The general significance of the grant of *pontificalia* is discussed by P.P. Hofmeister, *Mitra und Stab der wirklichen Prälaten ohne bischöflichen Charakter*, Kirchenrectliche Abhandlungen civ (Stuttgart, 1928), especially pp. 3–18. For the

a difficulty that there is no independent confirmation of either the recognition of ancient precedence or the grant of the *pontificalia*. The official *acta* of the Rheims synod give no hint that Wulfric had a special status, and Æthelsige's successors did not wear the pontifical mitre and sandals.[27] Yet it seems unwarrantable to conclude that Goscelin had no basis for his claims. Hereman had earlier been his patron,[28] and it is difficult to believe that Goscelin would have attributed to him a wholly fabricated speech to the Roman synod; moreover, the episode is presented as a promotion of the claims of the whole English church, not simply a glorification of St Augustine's. Goscelin was writing within a generation of the supposed grant of the *pontificalia* to Abbot Æthelsige; there would have been men still alive in the 1090s who could have refuted an unfounded claim of this sort. The probability seems to be that the prestige of St Augustine's was indeed given an enormous boost in the last years of the Anglo-Saxon period, and this must have been a potent inspiration for the abbey's subsequent claims of privilege and full independence.

Despite these heady developments on the continental stage, there is some reason to believe that Æthelsige's position in England was badly compromised. In a celebrated passage the *Liber Eliensis* accuses Archbishop Stigand of appropriating certain monasteries and taking their possessions for his own use. St Augustine's is listed among these monasteries.[29] In this context, it seems significant that Æthelsige had previously been a monk at the Old Minster in Winchester, where Stigand was bishop, and there is tenuous evidence to suggest that he may have owed his appointment as abbot to Stigand's patronage. This may point to the establishment by Stigand of a personal dominance over the monastery. It seems to have been Æthelsige's connection with Stigand which led to his downfall after the

---

Fulda privilege, see Anton, *Studien*, pp. 86–8. It may be suspicious that no copy of the St Augustine's privilege has been preserved.

[27] At Rheims squabbles among the bishops about precedence led to them being seated in a circle, with the abbots in an outer circle around them: see. K.J. Hefele, *Histoire des conciles d'après les documents originaux*, transl. and ed. H. Leclercq, 11 vols (Paris, 1907–52), iv. 1018. Hereman's claim for special rights for the Canterbury archbishop and abbot related to Roman synods, so it may be wrong to expect special treatment at Rheims. The wearing of the *pontificalia* by the abbot of St Augustine's is said to have lapsed after the Conquest, in the face of hostility from King William and from the archbishop; it was revived by Abbot Roger I in 1179 (Twysden, *Scriptores*, cols 1785, 1824; Davis, *Thorne*, pp. 46–7, 107–8).

[28] For Goscelin's relations with Hereman, see Barlow, *Life of King Edward*, pp. 133–5.

[29] *Liber Eliensis*, ed. E.O. Blake, Camden Third Series xcii (London, 1962), p. 168 (and see Blake's discussion of this passage, pp. 425–6).

Conquest. He was outlawed and fled to Denmark, probably in 1070, and a Norman abbot named Scotland was imposed on the monks.[30]

The abbey's later historians gave Scotland the credit for regaining certain estates lost during the time of Æthelsige, but his appointment rankled with the community, which was by this time passionately attached to its canonical right to choose its own abbot. A further source of conflict developed when Archbishop Lanfranc, shortly before his death, founded St Gregory's Priory in Canterbury. The pastoral responsibilities given to the new foundation encroached upon those of the ancient monastery, particularly in the profitable area of burial rights. But an even more painful challenge resulted from Lanfranc's transfer to St Gregory's of relics previously culted in the ancient minster at Lyminge. The canons claimed, perhaps with some justification in view of evidence for ancient links between Lyminge and Minster-in-Thanet (see below, pp. xxvii–xxviii), that these relics included those of St Mildrith and her successor at Minster, Abbess Eadburh. St Augustine's had been engaged for the previous half century in promoting itself as the focus of Mildrith's cult, and the challenge was potentially most damaging.[31] These pressures form the background to the violent scenes which occurred after the death of Abbot Scotland in September 1087. Lanfranc appointed as his successor another Norman named Guy (Wido), but the community refused to accept him and cited its canonical right to elect its own abbot. Lanfranc took decisive steps to impose his will, and the prior and other ringleaders of the revolt were imprisoned. Other members of the community, who had been ordered to leave the abbey, took refuge in St Mildrith's church in Canterbury; the more recalcitrant of them were eventually dispersed among other churches. Subsequently a truce was patched up, the exiles were allowed to return and the community accepted Guy. But this was merely a temporary capitulation. When Lanfranc himself died in 1089 the monks incited the citizens of Canterbury to attempt the murder of Abbot Guy and there was

---

[30] For Æthelsige's flight and his relationship with Archbishop Stigand, see Kelly 1988, pp. 365–6. Æthelsige subsequently returned from Denmark and became abbot of Ramsey (*HRH*, p. 62). There is a discussion of his career and its chronological problems by E.A. Freeman, *The History of the Norman Conquest of England, Its Causes and Its Results*, 6 vols (Oxford, 1867–79), iv. 748–52. He is believed to have played a significant part in the development of the cult of the Virgin in England: see R. Southern, 'The English Origin of the Miracles of the Virgin', *Mediaeval and Renaissance Studies* iv (1958), pp. 176–216 at 194–9; M. Clayton, *The Cult of the Virgin Mary in Anglo-Saxon England* (Cambridge, 1990), pp. 46 n. 84, 47–50.

[31] For the foundation of St Gregory's and its consequences for St Augustine's, see M. Gibson, *Lanfranc of Bec* (Oxford, 1978), pp. 186–90; M.L. Colker, 'A Hagiographic Polemic', *Mediaeval Studies* xxxix (1977), pp. 60–108. There is further discussion of the dispute in D. Rollason, *The Mildrith Legend: A Study in Early Medieval Hagiography in England* (Leicester, 1982), pp. 21–5, 62–4.

bloodshed, although the abbot managed to escape. As a consequence the implicated monks were punished by being dispersed once more to other churches, and twenty-four monks from Christ Church, with their prior, were introduced into St Augustine's in their place (the rioting citizens were blinded).[32] Relations between archbishop and abbey remained intermittently stormy until the fourteenth century. The monks claimed that they had always enjoyed the right of free election and total independence from external interference, and bolstered their case by the fabrication of a collection of papal and royal documents detailing the abbey's privileges, most of which were probably in existence by the end of the eleventh century.[33]

The St Augustine's case for independence was intimately linked with the early history of the abbey, since the community's claim to special treatment rested on its early foundation and glorious early history. Generations of St Augustine's monks were inspired to study the pre-Conquest records, and the abbey's historians all made extensive use of the muniments in a sensitive and scholarly way; the culmination of this tradition was the outstanding history written by Thomas Elmham in the early fifteenth century. It is unfortunate that this passionate interest in the records led over the centuries to some contamination of certain of the earlier Anglo-Saxon charters, particularly of their dates, as less scrupulous students tried to integrate the records with a mistaken chronological framework for the period. This characteristic of the archive is discussed below (pp. xcvi–cv).

The abbey was formally dissolved on 30 July 1538, and its deeds and muniments were surrendered to the king's commissioners. Some of the monastic buildings were retained by the king and converted into a royal palace; this was little used, and from Elizabeth's reign it was leased out. The rest of the site, including the abbey church, fell into ruins and was progressively despoiled and demolished.[34] There is some evidence that part

---

[32] These exciting events are described in the *Acta sancti Lanfranci*, edited by C. Plummer, *Two of the Saxon Chronicles Parallel*, 2 vols (Oxford, 1892–9), i. 287–92 (at 290–2). See also Gibson, *Lanfranc*, pp. 189–90.

[33] See **1, 2, 3, 4, 5,** and below pp. lxiv–lxv. For further discussion of these charters and the associated papal privileges, see Levison, *England and the Continent*, pp. 174–233; Kelly 1988. There is a sensitive analysis of the wider background to the claims of St Augustine's by D. Knowles, 'Studies in Monastic History: IV – The Growth of Exemption', *Downside Review* n.s. xxxi (1932), pp. 201–31, 396–436 (at 401–15).

[34] *Calendar of Letters and Papers, Foreign and Domestic: Henry VIII*, ed. J. Gardiner, xiii.1 (London, 1892), no. 1503; Twysden, *Scriptores*, cols 2293–6. For the later history of the buildings and site, see *The History of the King's Works*, ed. H.M. Colvin, 5 vols (1963–82), iv. 59–63; M. Sparks, 'St Augustine's Palace and the King's Park', in *The Parish of St Martin and St Paul, Canterbury: Historical Essays in Memory of James Hobbs*, ed. M. Sparks (The Friends of St Martin's, 1980), pp. 57–9; H. Woods, 'The Despoliation of the Abbey of Saints Peter and Paul and Saint Augustine between the Years 1542 and 1793', *ibid.*, pp. 76–81.

of the abbey's library was still available in the palace buildings in the period between the dissolution and the early seventeenth century, where it was probably subject to the inroads of predatory collectors. The Canterbury school-master John Twyne seems to have acquired his collection of St Augustine's manuscripts (including two important medieval cartularies) from this source, and Dr John Dee probably also paid a visit.[35] In the present century the abbey precincts have been extensively excavated and surveyed.[36]

2. MINSTER-IN-THANET

Minster-in-Thanet was reputedly founded by Æbba or Domneva, a princess of the Kentish royal house, on land given by King Ecgberht (664–73) as compensation for the murders of her two brothers.[37] The house appears to have been a double monastery (see **50, 53**), and it was dedicated to St Mary. Æbba was the first abbess of the community, and is the beneficiary of several royal charters issued between 689 and 697 (**40, 41, 42, 43, 44, 46**); she is almost certainly the Abbess Aeabba who attended a synod in April 699 (**10**). She was succeeded by her daughter, Mildrith, later the focus of a very successful cult, who is the beneficiary of **47, 48, 49** and **50** (as well as the spurious **45**). Mildrith appears to have become abbess at some time in or before 716, for she was present at the Kentish synod of Bapchild, which probably took place in that year or shortly before; the witness-list of the

[35] A.G. Watson, 'John Twyne of Canterbury (d. 1581) as a Collector of Medieval Manuscripts: a Preliminary Investigation', *The Library* 6th ser. viii (1986), pp. 133–51 (pp. 135–6 on the survival of the library).

[36] For a summary of the earlier excavations, see M. Sparks, 'The Recovery and Excavation of the St Augustine's Abbey Site 1844–1947', *AC* c (1985 for 1984), pp. 325–44. The principal excavation reports are: C.F. Routledge, 'Excavations at St Austin's Abbey, Canterbury', *AC* xxv (1902), pp. 222–43; W. St John Hope, 'Recent Discoveries in the Abbey of St Austin at Canterbury', *Archaeologia* lxvi (1915), pp. 377–400 (also published in *AC* xxxii (1917), pp. 1–26); C.R. Peers and A.W. Clapham, 'St Augustine's Abbey Church, Canterbury, before the Norman Conquest', *Archaeologia* lxxvii (1927), pp. 201–17; R.U. Potts *et al.*, 'The Plan of St Austin's Abbey, Canterbury', *AC* xlvi (1934), pp. 179–94; A.D. Saunders, 'Excavations in the Church of St Augustine's Abbey, Canterbury, 1955–8', *Medieval Archaeology* xxii (1978), pp. 25–63; D. Sherlock and H. Woods, *St Augustine's Abbey: Report on Excavations 1960–78*, Monograph Series of the Kent Archaeological Soc. 4 (Maidstone, 1988); M. Sparks, *St Augustine's Abbey, Canterbury* (London, 1988). There is a useful summary of discoveries and conclusions by T. Tatton-Brown, 'The Buildings and Topography of St Augustine's Abbey, Canterbury', *Journal of the British Archaeological Association* cxliv (1991), pp. 61–91.

[37] The traditions surrounding the foundation are examined by Rollason, *Mildrith Legend*, especially chapters 3 and 4 (pp. 33–51). See also *idem*, 'The Date of the Parish Boundary of Minster-in-Thanet', *AC* xcv (1979), pp. 7–17; and comments in Kelly 1986, pp. 171–7.

synod has been preserved because it was used by the forger of S 22 (see p. 42). The latest charter in her favour (**50**) has an implied date of 737 or 738, although there is some possibility that it really belongs to 716 or 717; a date in the later 730s seems incompatible with the traditional identification of Mildrith's successor, Eadburh, with Boniface's correspondent of that name, since the latter is already called abbess in letters datable to the mid 730s.[38] Eadburh is the beneficiary of **51** from 748, which refers to the recent construction by her of a second minster, dedicated to SS Peter and Paul, not far from the original foundation. According to Goscelin, who wrote several works on Mildrith and her cult in the late eleventh century, most of the community of the original minster moved to the new foundation; the implication is that the two houses remained closely connected, under the rule of a single abbess.[39] The fourth abbess was Sigeburh, who is named in two ship-toll privileges from the early 760s (**52, 53**).

The Minster muniments preserved in the archive of St Augustine's all date from the period between 689 and the early 760s, but a casual remark by Goscelin shows that he had access to Minster charters from the early ninth century, so it must be supposed that some part of the archive has been lost since the end of the eleventh century.[40] All but one of the nine Minster charters which can be confidently dated to between 689 and 727 are land-grants in favour of Abbesses Æbba and Mildrith, mostly covering properties on Thanet or in the adjacent mainland region of Sturry; the exception is **45**, an apparent fabrication concerned with the minster's status. The five latest charters in the archive, apparently dating from the 730s to

---

[38] For the identification of Boniface's correspondent with the abbess of Minster-in-Thanet, see Levison, *England and the Continent*, p. 139; Whitelock, *EHD*, pp. 798, 811. Another suggestion is that the former may have been abbess of Wimborne in Dorset: see Patrick Sims-Williams, 'An Unpublished Seventh- or Eighth-Century Anglo-Latin Latter in Boulogne-sur-Mer MS 74 (82)', *Medium Ævum* xlviii (1979), pp. 1–22 (at 22 n. 119).

[39] Goscelin, *Vita Deo dilecte uirginis Mildrethe*, cap. xxviii; edited by Rollason, *Mildrith Legend*, pp. 142–3. Goscelin states that the new house was built because the original foundation was now too small for the community, describes the translation to it of Mildrith's relics, and continues: 'Huc etiam (Eadburga) sacrum collegium filiarum ad ipsam matrem perpetuam transduxit, relicta parte quo primitiue ecclesie sancteque sue memorie iugiter deseruiret. Erat autem utraque domus quasi unum monasterium et una chorea sub una auriga, spacio ad claustri modum tantum bipertita'. Goscelin's description is not necessarily an accurate depiction of eighth-century conditions. In Thomas Elmham's map of Thanet (see p. lvii n. 1), the two foundations are immediately adjacent to one another.

[40] Goscelin, *Translatio S. Mildrethe*, cap. iv; edited by D. Rollason, 'Goscelin of Canterbury's Account of the Translation and Miracles of St Mildrith (*BHL* 5961/4): an Edition with Notes', *Mediaeval Studies* xlviii (1986), pp. 139–210 at 159. Goscelin found his information about the ninth-century abbess *Siledritha* 'in annalibus antiquorum patrum, priuilegiis quoque et cartis monasterii sui . . .'

the 760s (although one of them may actually belong to 716 × 717), are all concerned with the remission of the toll due on Minster ships, generally in the Mercian port of London (**49, 50, 51, 52, 53**). This remarkable group of documents shows that the community accumulated a fleet of at least three ships during this period, one of them purchased in 748 (apparently from a Frank) and another built in the early 760s within the minster itself. The vessels were evidently used for trading purposes, for in **53** the Kentish king insists on his right of pre-emption over the merchandise which the ship carried to Fordwich. Minster was situated on an important shipping route between London and northern France, and this may have inspired the community to exploit the potential for trade. Similar privileges were issued to the minster at Reculver and to the bishops of Rochester, London and Worcester.[41]

There is some evidence that, in the second half of the eighth century and the beginning of the ninth, Minster-in-Thanet was very closely associated with the minster at Lyminge. Goscelin mentions that the abbess at the very beginning of the ninth century, the successor of Sigeburh, was a certain *Siledritha*, apparently a doughty fighter for the community's endowment who contrived to regain estates which had been seized by Archbishop Wulfred.[42] Goscelin is here relying on evidence which he found in documentary sources, including charters from Minster which have since been lost. *Siledritha* can almost certainly be identified with the contemporary Selethryth, who appears as abbess of Lyminge in S 160 (A.D. 804), and was the beneficiary, with her brother, of S 123 (A.D. 785), S 125 (A.D. 786) and S 39 (A.D. 805). A document from 824 (S 1434) describes a dispute over land which Selethryth and her brother had agreed to bequeath to Archbishop Wulfred 'pro eius amabili amicitia', but which was subsequently diverted into the hands of Abbess Cwoenthryth of Minster-in-Thanet, apparently Selethryth's successor; this episode seems to support Goscelin's information about a link between Selethryth and Minster, and is compatible with the suggestion that she came into conflict with Archbishop Wulfred. The implication would seem to be that, by the early ninth century, Lyminge minster and the Thanet community (or communities) were under the rule of a single abbess. Some corroboration is provided by evidence that the relics of Abbess Eadburh had been transferred to Lyminge and culted there before 804 (see S 160). A tendentious account from the later eleventh century,

---

[41] On documents of this type, see further S.E. Kelly, 'Trading Privileges from Eighth-Century England', *Early Medieval Europe* i (1992), pp. 3–27.
[42] Goscelin, *Translation S. Mildrethe*, cap. iv (p. 159).

hostile to St Augustine's and its monopoly of Mildrith's cult, claimed that the Minster community had fled to Lyminge with its relics in the face of Viking attacks.[43]

The association between Lyminge and Minster-in-Thanet perhaps resulted from the Mercian annexation of Kent, which seems to have reached its final stages in the 780s. Both Lyminge and Minster appear to have had a particular connection with the Kentish kings, and Offa may have assumed ultimate control over such royal minsters. It is possible that Selethryth and her brother, who had some connection with the minster at Folkestone, were clients of Offa to whom he delegated the management of several royal minsters in Kent.[44] Offa's successor, Coenwulf, treated Minster-in-Thanet and Reculver as his private property and left them to his daughter, Cwoenthryth, who ruled Minster as abbess; he may also have controlled other Kentish houses. This royal domination was challenged by Archbishop Wulfred, who was concerned to promote episcopal control of minsters. The result was a long-standing feud with Coenwulf and Cwoenthryth, which led to Wulfred's temporary suspension and exile. The archbishop finally achieved his aims in 825, when Cwoenthryth was forced into ignominious surrender and Minster came fully under his control.[45] In the following year Wulfred supervised an exchange of property between Minster and St Augustine's, without reference to Cwoenthryth or any successor as abbess (17).

Virtually nothing is known of the history of Minster after this episode. The continuous existence of a religious community on Thanet through the ninth century seems improbable. It may have been on Thanet that the Vikings over-wintered in England for the first time in 851; the *Anglo-Saxon Chronicle* mentions a battle there in 853 and states that it was used as a Viking base in 865. Destructive Viking raids on the coasts of Kent had begun much earlier, for charters from 811, 814 and 822 refer to the need to destroy Viking fortifications, and **15** implies that the pirates were already a menace at the end of Offa's reign.[46] In 804 Abbess Selethryth was given a

---

[43] For this account see Colker, 'A Hagiographic Polemic'; Rollason, *Mildrith Legend*, pp. 21–5, 62–4.

[44] Brooks, *Church of Canterbury*, pp. 184–5.

[45] See S 1436, and discussion by Brooks, *Church of Canterbury*, pp. 175–206. In this period Minster-in-Thanet seems to have been known as Southminster (**17**, **18**, S 1434, 1436; and see S 22). A tenth-century charter (S 489) concerns a large estate in Thanet known as *North Mynstre*, apparently in the vicinity of Westgate on Sea.

[46] N. Brooks, 'The Development of Military Obligations in Eighth- and Ninth-Century England', *England Before the Conquest: Studies in Primary Sources Presented to Dorothy Whitelock*, ed. P. Clemoes and K. Hughes (Cambridge, 1971), pp. 69–84, at 79–80; and see also S 1264, 168, 177, 186.

small area within the walls of Canterbury to serve as a refuge for her community at Lyminge (S 160). It may be that the Minster community also acquired a Canterbury base, or took sanctuary in the Lyminge refuge. By the eleventh century there was a church dedicated to St Mildrith near the city walls in the extreme south-west of Canterbury, close to the area which had been given to Selethryth in 804, and it has been suggested that this church may have been on the site of a refuge granted to the Thanet community.[47] The present building includes some Anglo-Saxon fabric, which cannot be precisely dated; the dimensions suggest a very substantial building.[48] In the later eleventh century St Mildrith's belonged to St Augustine's, and it was there that part of the community took refuge from Lanfranc in 1087 (see above, p. xxiii).

There is a little evidence from the tenth century for the continued existence of a community of some kind associated with St Mildrith, in the form of references in the boundary clauses of two royal charters from the 940s. S 497 (A.D. 944) is concerned with the grant of land on Thanet in the vicinity of Monkton, just to the west of the site of Minster; the eastern boundary of the estate followed *Mildrythe mearce*, which ran south into the Wantsum Channel. This may indicate that the original site of the Thanet minster was still associated with the cult of Mildrith, and can be linked with evidence from Goscelin's account of the translation of Mildrith's relics from Thanet to Canterbury which suggests that she was still venerated on the island.[49] But it is not very good evidence for the refoundation of a Thanet minster. A more convincing demonstration for the existence of a community is to be found in a second charter dated 948 (S 535), which grants to a religious

---

[47] Gordon Ward ('The Age of St Mildred's Church, Canterbury', *AC* liv (1942 for 1941), pp. 63–8) argued that St Mildred's lies within the area granted as a refuge to Selethryth in S 160; he misinterpreted the bounds (see R.U. Potts, 'St Mildrith's Church, Canterbury: Further Notes on the Site', *AC* lvi (1944 for 1943), pp. 19–22). Brooks (*Church of Canterbury*, pp. 34–5) suggests that St Mildred's church lay within a separate refuge granted to the Minster-in-Thanet community. Both St Mildred's and the land covered in S 160 are situated in the south-western part of the city, an area subject to flooding in the early medieval period and probably only lightly populated (Brooks, *ibid.*, p. 26).

[48] Taylor and Taylor, *Anglo-Saxon Architecture*, i. 145–6. T. Tatton-Brown suggests an eleventh-century date for St Mildred's, and links its construction with the revival of Mildrith's cult after her translation to Canterbury: 'The City and Diocese of Canterbury in St Dunstan's Time', *St Dunstan: his Life, Times and Cult*, ed. N. Ramsay, M. Sparks and T. Tatton-Brown (Woodbridge, 1992), pp. 75–87, at 81.

[49] Goscelin, *Translatio S. Mildrethe*, caps. xiii-xv (pp. 171–3). The underhand abstraction of relics was a popular hagiographical topos: P.J. Geary, *Furta Sacra: Thefts of Relics in the Central Middle Ages*, 2nd edn (Princeton, 1990); and so some of the details of Goscelin's account are probably fictional.

woman land at Wickhambreux, on the mainland opposite Thanet. This estate had an area of appurtenant woodland pasture in Blean Forest, which originally covered a substantial area north of Canterbury. The northern boundary of this den was formed by 'þæs hiredes mearc to sancte Mildryþe', which presumably indicates that a den or other estate in this area was owned by an existing community known as St Mildrith's. This could be a refounded minster on Thanet, but it has also been suggested that the focus of the Minster community may have been transferred to St Mildred's in Canterbury. The female beneficiary of S 535 was not necessarily attached to 'St Mildrith's community'.[50]

The final disintegration of St Mildrith's community may have come about during the second wave of Viking assaults in the reign of Æthelred the Unready. East Kent endured regular attacks of great severity in the 990s and the first decades of the eleventh century. Goscelin appears to have had information that the Thanet house was destroyed at this time and its community massacred.[51] In 1011 Canterbury itself was sacked and Archbishop Ælfheah was captured, together with a number of other ecclesiastics, among them an Abbess Leofrun, identified in one source as abbess of the monastery of St Mildrith.[52] Leofrun may have been connected with St Mildred's in Canterbury, or she could have been a Thanet abbess taking refuge in the city. Her community may not have survived Æthelred's reign, or may have been impoverished by the need to pay a ransom to her captors; certainly, it appears that a number of estates associated with Mildrith and Minster-in-Thanet were available to land-buyers in the reign of Cnut. Around

---

[50] S 535 is one of a number of charters from this period in favour of religious women, only one of them explicitly connected to a named religious house; for their significance, see D.N. Dumville, Wessex and England from Alfred to Edgar: Six Essays on Political, Cultural, and Ecclesiastical Revival (Woodbridge, 1992), pp. 177–8; idem, 'The religiosa femina in the Pre-Reform Generation', in Reformed Englishwomen?, ed. L. Abrams and D.N. Dumville (forthcoming).

[51] Translatio S. Mildrethe, cap. v (pp. 159–62). Goscelin gives no precise date, but implies that the catastrophe took place during Æthelred's reign; he next mentions Cnut's accession under the date 1017. William Thorne (Twysden, Scriptores, col. 1780; Davis, Thorne, p. 38) gives a date of 980 for the destruction, no doubt influenced by the entry in the Anglo-Saxon Chronicle for that year, which mentions that Thanet was ravaged. Thomas Elmham (Hardwick, Elmham, pp. 221–2) puts the episode in the ninth century and speaks of the massacre of Abbess Siledritha and her nuns; he seems here to be misinterpreting Goscelin's account.

[52] Florentii Wigornensis Monachi Chronicon ex Chronicis, ed. B. Thorpe, 2 vols (London, 1848–9), i, s.a. 1011. The Worcester chronicler seems to have had access to additional information about the Canterbury sack, mentioning, for instance, that the Ælmær who betrayed the city was an archdeacon whose life had been saved by Archbishop Ælfheah; the former detail makes it unlikely that the traitor was the contemporary abbot of St Augustine's, who had the same name, and whose escape from the Vikings might seem suspicious.

the year 1030 Abbot Ælfstan of St Augustine's acquired half the Minster lands through an exchange with an unnamed *venditor*, to whom he gave the vill of Folkestone. He subsequently gained possession of the relics of St Mildrith, translating them with some pomp from Thanet to St Augustine's.[53] Thereafter he endeavoured, with some success, to reconstitute the former endowment, apparently basing his case on the abbey's possession of Mildrith's relics. This is certainly the impression given by S 1472 (A.D. 1044 × 1045), which records the settlement of a dispute between the abbot and community of St Augustine's and a priest named Leofwine, over what seems to be described as 'St Mildrith's property'.[54] Leofwine claimed to have bought the property from Cnut, but the abbot countered that Cnut had placed Mildrith's relics at St Augustine's and that therefore her uncles' wergeld passed irrevocably to the abbey. It was decided that St Augustine's should give Leofwine two sulungs and pay him five pounds every year; on his death the land would revert to the abbey and the payment would lapse. Leofwine may perhaps have been a kinsman of Leofstan, remembered for having opposed the removal of Mildrith's relics from Thanet, or of Abbess Leofrun.[55]

The collection of early Minster charters preserved at St Augustine's probably entered the archive in the time of Abbot Ælfstan. By 1066 the abbey's possessions in Thanet amounted to the greater part of the island, and were assessed at forty-eight sulungs, with land for sixty-two ploughs (GDB 12r). The Domesday entry mentions a church with a priest attached to the manor, but this was evidently of minor importance. The eleventh-century list in the *Domesday Monachorum* of churches responsible for collecting the chrism from the archbishop includes the ancient minster churches at St Augustine's, Lyminge, Dover and Folkestone, but not Minster-in-Thanet.[56]

3. THE ARCHIVE AND ITS HISTORY

The St Augustine's archive comprises fifty-three documents of purported pre-Conquest date: thirty-two Latin and five Old English charters associated

---

[53] Goscelin, *Translatio S. Mildrethe*, caps. vi, xii-xvi (pp. 164, 170–6). For the date, see R. Sharpe, 'The Date of St Mildreth's Translation from Minster-in-Thanet to Canterbury', *Mediaeval Studies* liii (1991), pp. 349–54.

[54] '... embe s̄ca Myldryþe are ...': the original is damaged and this is a conjectural reading (see Robertson, *Charters*, p. 190).

[55] Goscelin, *Translation S. Mildrethe*, cap. xv (p. 173), for Leofstan.

[56] Brooks, *Church of Canterbury*, pp. 203–4: see *The Domesday Monachorum of Christ Church, Canterbury*, ed. D. C. Douglas (London, 1944), p. 79. See further, T. Tatton-Brown, 'The

with the monastery itself and its endowment (**1-9, 11-14, 16-39**), two documents recording grants of general privileges to the Kentish churches (**10, 15**) and fourteen Latin charters in favour of the abbesses of Minster-in-Thanet (**40–53**). Post-Conquest sources, including the abbey's historians, a Domesday satellite survey (see pp. cvi–cvii) and a fourteenth-century charter-list (see Appendix 2, and pp. xlvi–xlvii, lii), mention another thirteen early or purportedly early documents which are no longer extant, the majority of them apparently vernacular charters and wills; these are listed and discussed in Appendix 1.

An original ninth-century diploma in favour of a layman (S 332; *OSFacs.*, i. 10), preserved in the Christ Church archive, has a near-contemporary endorsement recording a grant to St Augustine's, which shows that it was in the abbey's possession before the end of the ninth century. The charter and the estate with which it is concerned appear to have been alienated from St Augustine's at some point before the Conquest.[57] The Christ Church archive also contains portions of two eleventh-century chirographs which record transactions relating to the affairs of St Augustine's; one concerns a grant of land by Archbishop Eadsige to the community (S 1400; *OSFacs.*, iii. 43) and the other the settlement of a dispute involving the abbot (S 1472;

Churches of Canterbury Diocese in the 11th Century', *Minsters and Parish Churches: the Local Church in Transition 950–1200*, ed. J. Blair (Oxford, 1988), pp. 105–18 at 109.

[57] S 332 (A.D. 863) records a grant of eight sulungs at Mersham by King Æthelberht of Wessex and Kent to Ealdorman Æthelred. In a vernacular endorsement, added soon after the initial donation, a certain Eadweald transferred 'this land at Willesborough' to St Augustine. A thegn named Eadweald attests Kentish charters from 858 and 859 (S 328, 1196) and is a protagonist in S 1195 (*c.* A.D. 850) and S 1200 (A.D. 867 × 870); he appears to have been the grandson of Ealdorman Ealhhere, beneficiary of **21**, and great-nephew of Ealhburh, donor of **24** (see Brooks, *Church of Canterbury*, pp. 148–9). The bounds in S 332 mention that Eadweald held land to the north and east of Mersham, at Brabourne. In the text of the charter the hidage of the estate has been altered, and this may go some way towards explaining why the land is called Willesborough in the endorsement. Willesborough lies just north-west of Mersham. It is possible that the grant in S 332 was of an area larger than eight sulungs, which incorporated land at Willesborough. At some stage before Eadweald made the grant to St Augustine's, the estate may have been split, with only the Willesborough part of it being transferred to the abbey. The original of Æthelberht's charter was given to St Augustine's, with the hidage altered and an explanatory endorsement; a new charter may have been drawn up for the other part of the split estate. The abbot later sold Willesborough back to Eadweald's son, Eadwulf, for 2000 pence (see Appendix 1, no. ii). S 332, as the title-deed, may have been returned to Eadwulf with the estate, although there is some evidence that this charter (or a copy of it) was still available at St Augustine's in the later tenth or eleventh century (see **29**). The Christ Chuch community acquired an estate at Mersham in the reign of Edward the Confessor, as the gift of lay donors (S 1090); possibly S 332 entered the cathedral archive at this point. There is no separate Domesday entry for Willesborough; Mersham was assessed at six sulungs TRE and listed among the lands of the archbishop (GDB 3v–4r).

OSFacs., i. 23). St Augustine's received a portion of both of these chirographs, but the archive preserves no trace of them. Portions of five other eleventh-century chirographs are known to have been deposited in the abbey, which in these cases was acting as a third-party guarantor (S 1461, 1465, 1471, 1473, 1530), but again no record has survived at St Augustine's.

Only one of the fifty-three documents here edited has been preserved in the form of a single sheet. Wihtred's grant of privileges to the Kentish churches (10) was copied into the abbey's cartularies but also survives as a ninth-century single-sheet copy in the Christ Church archive; it is likely that several copies of the document were made at the time of the initial grant, and that these were distributed to the various minsters. Some of the abbey's single-sheet Anglo-Saxon charters may have been lost in the fire which swept the church in 1168; William Thorne speaks of the destruction of *multae codicellae antiquae* during this disaster.[58] There is later evidence for the continued existence of single-sheet versions of purportedly pre-Conquest charters at St Augustine's. One of the Cartae Antiquae rolls, apparently compiled in the reign of King John, includes copies of a number of St Augustine's charters, including three in the names of Anglo-Saxon kings (3, 33 and 35). The scribe notes that 3 was the only one of these documents which did not have a seal (see further p. xli). In 1326 the abbey submitted a collection of its charters for confirmation by King Edward II, including eight pre-Conquest documents (1, 3, 5, 21, 27, 33, 34, 39). Of these, 21, 27 and 39 are probably authentic. It was normally the rule that charters confirmed in this way had to be available in single-sheet form, and the texts of the enrolled charters seem to be compatible with the suggestion that they were copied from originals. The decision to offer 21 and 27 for enrolment is notable, for they are in favour of laymen. In general pre-Conquest charters submitted for confirmation tend to be direct grants to the church concerned. It is possible that these eight charters represent the portion of the pre-Conquest archive that still survived in single-sheet form in the fourteenth century.

An unknown number of single-sheet charters relating to the Anglo-Saxon period were still available at St Augustine's in the early fifteenth century when they were studied by the historian Thomas Elmham (for Elmham, see below pp. lvii–lix, xcvi–xcvii). The sole medieval manuscript of Elmham's history (Cambridge, Trinity Hall, 1), which may be autograph, contains facsimiles of three forged charters in the name of King Æthelberht (1, 2, 3)

---

[58] Twysden, *Scriptores*, col. 1815; Davis, *Thorne*, p. 94.

and of the celebrated sealed privilege of St Augustine himself (**4**).[59] Elmham had a very great historical sensibility and treated his sources in an admirable fashion. He carefully compared the texts of the *originales* with those of the cartulary copies, and where they were found to differ, particularly in the area of chronology, he gave intelligent reasons for preferring the readings of the former. But it now appears that the chronological details in the cartulary texts are to be preferred, and that the different readings in the *originales* are the result of later contamination. Elmham gives the impression of being an honest historian who would not base his case on single-sheet charters which had obviously been altered, which raises the possibility that earlier St Augustine's scholars had produced 'facsimile' copies of some of the early charters, incorporating the revisions. The four charters reproduced by Elmham himself would appear to have been very skilful forgeries, with scripts based on models from the pre-Conquest period. It may be the case that at some stage in the later middle ages, or perhaps over a protracted period, St Augustine's scribes produced single-sheet copies of charters in the archive in imitative script, possibly to replace damaged or deficient documents, or others which had been lost or destroyed. The textual history of two of the forgeries in the name of King Æthelberht (**2**, **3**) seems to support this suggestion, for it indicates that the single-sheet charters reproduced in facsimile by Elmham may have been 'resurrected' from copies in BL Cotton Vespasian B. xx. See further discussion on pp. 11–12, 17–18.

When John Leland visited the abbey at some point before 1538 he handled single-sheet copies of **4** and **5** and of one of the charters of King Æthelberht, which were then kept *in archivis*.[60] At some point in the sixteenth-century, probably before the dissolution, copies of **1** and **2** were added at the end of BL Add. 53710, a manuscript of William Thorne's history; these may have been taken from the single-sheet versions (see pp. lvi–lvii). It seems likely that the abbey's surviving single-sheet charters were handed over to the king's commissioners when the abbey was dissolved in 1538, for the deed of surrender mentions the transfer of 'omnia et omnimoda cartas, evidentias,

---

[59] See Plates I, II, and M. Hunter, 'The Facsimiles in Thomas Elmham's History of St Augustine's, Canterbury', *The Library* 5th ser. xxviii (1973), pp. 215–20, with reproductions of **1**, **3** and **4**. There is a reproduction of the facsimile of **2** in M. Deanesly, 'The Court of King Æthelberht of Kent', *Cambridge Historical Journal* vii (1942), pp. 101–14, opposite p. 14.

[60] *Johannis Lelandi Antiquarii De Rebus Britannicis Collectanea*, ed. T. Hearne, 6 vols (London, 1770), iv. 8. A collection of monastic foundation charters in BL Harley 358, which includes copies of **1** and **2**, has been wrongly attributed to Leland; it is apparently a copy of the collection compiled by (Sir) John Prise (see below, pp. lix–lx).

obligationes, scripta et munimenta nostra'.[61] Copies of **1** and **2**, probably taken from the single-sheet versions, appear in the collection of monastic foundation charters compiled by John (later Sir John) Prise, who was closely involved in the action against the monasteries and may have had the opportunity to examine monastic documents as they came into the king's possession (see pp. lix–lx). From this point there is no further evidence about the fate of the single sheets from St Augustine's, and the likelihood is that they perished through neglect or deliberate destruction; the more celebrated documents in the archive, such as the forged charters of Augustine and King Æthelberht, are unlikely to have escaped the attention of collectors and scholars had they still been extant as single sheets in the seventeenth century.[62] Clement Reyner states that Sir Henry Spelman at one time owned the original of **4**, the charter in the name of St Augustine, but this is contradicted by Spelman's own statement that he could 'never obtein one Originall'; furthermore, Spelman used Thomas Elmham's facsimile of **4** as the basis for his edition of the charter, and his comments show that he had never seen the purported original.[63] Reyner may have been misled by a copy of the facsimile.

On separate occasions in the tenth century, two vernacular documents (**24, 31**) were copied into a sixth-century gospel-book in the monastery's possession (CCCC 286; see below, pp. xxxviii–xxxix).[64] For the remaining texts in the archive (with the exception of **10**) we are entirely dependent upon post-Conquest copies in cartularies, histories and enrolments. The forged charters and papal privileges relating to the abbey's foundation and 'apostolic' status form something of a special case, for they were very frequently copied in the medieval period; they occur in numerous manuscripts from the early twelfth century onwards.[65] The earliest extant copies of the

---

[61] For the details of the deed of surrender, see above, p. xxiv n. 34. The commisioners seem to have left behind at least some of the abbey's cartularies, for John Twyne of Canterbury came into possession of two registers, now BL Cotton Claudius D. x and BL Cotton Julius D. ii/BL Add. 46352 (see pp. xxiv–xxv).

[62] On the treatment of muniments which fell into the maw of the Augmentations Office, see R.B. Wernham, 'The Public Records in the Sixteenth and Seventeenth Centuries', in *English Scholarship in the Sixteenth and Seventeenth Centuries*, edited by L. Fox (London, 1956), pp. 11–30.

[63] C. Reyner, *Apostolatus Benedictinorum in Anglia* (Douai, 1626), p. 50. For Spelman's lament, see 'Of Antient Deeds and Charters', *The English Works of Sir Henry Spelman*, 2nd edn (London, 1727), pt 2, pp. 233–6 (at p. 236).

[64] For the copying of such records into sacred books in the Anglo-Saxon period, see Keynes 1985, p. 189 n. 216.

[65] The earliest copies are in BL Cotton Vespasian B. xx, written in the first quarter of the twelfth century, and BL Cotton Vitellius A. ii, produced about half a century afterwards (see pp. xxxix–xl). The transmission of **1** was significantly different from that of the other forgeries associated with the foundation.

majority of the St Augustine's charters date from the thirteenth century, from which there are four surviving cartularies, three of them containing significant numbers of pre-Conquest charters.[66] But by far the most important source of early documents is the *Speculum Augustinianum*, compiled by Thomas Elmham in the opening years of the fifteenth century and preserved in a contemporary manuscript, perhaps written by the historian himself.[67] The *Speculum* is a massive but incomplete history of the abbey from its foundation, which contains the full texts of the majority of the seventh- and eighth-century charters from St Augustine's and Minster-in-Thanet. Elmham's charter-texts are usually very good indeed, although there is some chronological contamination (see below, pp. xcvi–cv). For charters later than the early ninth century it is usually necesary to rely on the copies in the thirteenth-century cartularies, which are often abbreviated. Some superior versions can be found in the Charter and Patent Rolls, in copies and confirmations of the Inspeximus charter of 1326 which incorporates several pre-Conquest texts (see below, pp. lx–lxi).

One serious loss from the archive is a manuscript known to Elmham and earlier historians of the abbey as the *Textus S. Adriani*. This volume seems to have been the principal or at least the most venerated source of archival material in the later medieval period. Thomas Elmham states that the *Textus S. Adriani* contained copies of **40** and **41**. He compares these texts to their disfavour with the *originales* in the archive, but in fact the variants noted by Elmham seem to be better readings; the *originales* may have been fairly recent productions (see above). The thirteenth-century historian Thomas Sprott says of the forged privilege of Pope Adeodatus (BCS 31): 'hoc privilegium non habemus sub plumbo sed transcriptum in textu Adriani et in aliis locis'; and in his brief reference to **36** he remarks: 'termini terre in textu sancti Adriani plenius exprimitur'. The volume seems also to have included some historical material, for Sprott referred to it for the incarnation year in which Gregory and Augustine died.[68] The other medieval reference to the manuscript is in the heading added to a survey of St Augustine's estates in PRO E 164/27 which appears to have reached its present form in

[66] BL Cotton Julius D. ii (see pp. xlii–xlvii); PRO E 164/27 (see pp. li–liv); BL Cotton Claudius D. x (see pp. xlvii–li); and BL Cotton Faustina A. i (see p. lxi). The last includes only one pre-Conquest text.
[67] Cambridge, Trinity Hall, MS 1 (see pp. lvii–lix); edited by C. Hardwick, *Historia monasterii sancti Augustini Cantuariensis by Thomas of Elmham*, Rolls Series (London, 1858). For the name of Elmham's history, see F. Taylor, 'A Note on Rolls Series 8', *Bulletin of the John Rylands Library* xx (1936), pp. 379–82.
[68] Hardwick, *Elmham*, p. 237. For Sprott, see pp. xcvii–xcviii. His history is unprinted; the references occur in BL Cotton Tiberius A. ix, 109v, 111v, 119v.

the early twelfth century, but which is ultimately dependent on a compilation made at the time of the Domesday survey: *Extractum de textu sancti Adriani* (for this survey see below, pp. cvi–cvii). The inclusion of Minster charters as well as those directly relevant to the abbey suggests that the *Textus S. Adriani* reflected a systematic attempt at the copying of muniments rather than random additions to an existing manuscript, while the incorporation of an estate-survey and perhaps even a set of annals shows that it was an ambitious and comprehensive volume. Its name indicates that it was fundamentally a gospel-book. The abbey also owned a *Textus S. Mildrede*, a gospel-book with attached canon-tables, kept in the vestry in Elmham's day. Elmham explained its name by reference to a legend that a Thanet peasant had been struck blind after swearing a false oath on it, which suggests that the manuscript was thought to have originated at Minster-in-Thanet.[69] The *Textus S. Adriani* was perhaps an early gospel-book associated, rightly or wrongly, with Abbot Hadrian, to which had been attached at a later date a number of additional quires containing copies of documents relevant to the abbey's Anglo-Saxon past and also other material. There is a parallel for this from Worcester, where it is known that Bishop Wulfstan II (1062–95) arranged for copies of Worcester charters to be added to a bible.[70] It is a great pity that the *Textus S. Adriani* seems to have disappeared without trace after the Dissolution.[71] There is the possibility of a connection with the famous 'St Augustine's Gospels' (CCCC 286), a sixth-century Italian gospel-book which was used in a minor way for copying muniments in the tenth century (see pp. xxxviii–xxxix), but there is no positive evidence that CCCC 286 was ever bound up with a cartulary.[72]

4. THE MANUSCRIPTS

There are four principal manuscript sources for the pre-Conquest archive: three cartularies of the thirteenth and fourteenth centuries (BL Cotton Julius

---

[69] Hardwick, *Elmham*, pp. 97–8. There has been a suggested identification with CCCC 286: see M. Budny, *Canterbury at Corpus: an Exhibition of Manuscripts from St Augustine's Abbey, Canterbury* (Cambridge, 1991), reprinted in the *Old English Newsletter* 24.4 (Summer, 1991).

[70] *Catalogus Librorum Manuscriptorum Bibliothecae Wigorniensis*, ed. I. Atkins and N.R. Ker (Cambridge, 1944), pp. 77–9; S. Keynes, *Anglo-Saxon Charters: Archives and Single Sheets*, Anglo-Saxon Charters, Supplementary ser. ii (forthcoming).

[71] Ussher's remarks about the manuscript, quoted by D. Wilkins (*Concilia Magnae Britanniae et Hiberniae*, 4 vols (London, 1737), i. 43) seem to be based on deduction and do not necessarily imply that he had seen it. Similarly Reyner (*Apostolatus*, p. 52) deduced that the *Textus* was a martyrology on the basis of one of Sprott's comments.

[72] M.R. James, *The Ancient Libraries of Canterbury and Dover* (Cambridge, 1903), p. lxvii n.

D. ii; BL Cotton Claudius D. x; PRO E 164/27), and the single manuscript of Thomas Elmham's great history from the beginning of the fifteenth century (Cambridge, Trinity Hall, 1). Most of the charters here edited survive only in one or more of these sources. But a small number of the pre-Conquest documents, essentially the forgeries purporting to date from the time of the abbey's foundation, were copied very frequently from the twelfth to the seventeenth century, so that there is a total of over forty manuscript sources for the archive. It is neither feasible nor desirable to treat these manuscripts as a chronological continuum, and it is unnecessary to assign sigla to all of them. I have therefore divided them into three groups. The first comprises sixteen manuscripts which do have some textual significance; these range from the tenth-century additions in CCCC 286 to a sixteenth-century transcription. All these manuscripts have been given sigla [B-Q] and are considered in approximate chronological order. In the second group I have placed the various copies and confirmations of Edward II's 1326 Inspeximus charter (incorporating eight pre-Conquest texts), which were added to the Charter and Patent Rolls in the fourteenth to sixteenth centuries; these also have been given sigla [R-W]. To the third group I have assigned the medieval manuscripts and antiquarian transcripts which contain copies of no textual importance.

i. *The principal manuscripts*

a. *CCCC 286* (B)

Copies of two vernacular charters connected with St Augustine's were added in the course of the tenth century to blank folios of a sixth-century Italian manuscript of the gospels (see Plates III, IV). The manuscript was probably in England by the eighth century, for it contains a number of corrections in English uncial and in early Insular minuscule. It may have reached the abbey in the seventh century via the Roman missionaries or Hadrian and his retinue, although this cannot be positively demonstrated.[73] A copy of **24**, the record of a grant of an annual food-rent to the abbey in

---

[73] N.R. Ker, *Catalogue of Manuscripts containing Anglo-Saxon* (Oxford, 1957), p. 95 (no. 55); *Codices Latini Antiquiores: a Palaeographical Guide to Latin Manuscripts Prior to the Ninth Century. Part II: Great Britain and Ireland*, ed. E.A. Lowe, 2nd edn (Oxford, 1972), p. 4 (no. 126); M.R. James, *A Descriptive Catalogue of the Manuscripts in the Library of Corpus Christi College, Cambridge*, 2 vols (Cambridge, 1912), ii. 52–6; F. Wormald, *The Miniatures in the Gospels of St Augustine: Corpus Christi College MS 286* (Cambridge, 1954). There is a remote possibility that CCCC 286 was the *Textus S. Adriani* (see above, p. xxxvii).

the mid ninth century, was added to an originally blank page between the end of Matthew and the *capitula* of Mark (fo. 74v). The scribe wrote an early version of Square minuscule, which can probably be assigned to the 920s.[74] At the end of the tenth or the very beginning of the eleventh century a second document was added to the blank page between the *capitula* and the beginning of Mark. This was a copy of **31**, the record of an agreement between Abbot Wulfric I and a layman; the script of the addition seems roughly contemporary with the apparent date of the agreement, so the copy was probably made soon after the transaction took place. **24** appears to have survived in single-sheet form until at least the thirteenth century; it is mentioned in the charter-list in PRO E 164/27 (Appendix 2, no. xliv), and was known to the post-Conquest historians. The motive for copying it into a gospel-book in the tenth century may have been to guarantee the food-rent after a challenge or a lapse. There is no sign of any post-Conquest awareness of **31**; none of the historians mention it, and there is no entry in the charter-list.

b. *BL Cotton Vespasian B. xx* (C)

BL Cotton Vespasian B. xx was written at St Augustine's by a number of collaborating scribes, probably in the first quarter of the twelfth century.[75] The primary contents are hagiographical works connected with the abbey's early saints, including Augustine, Abbot Hadrian and Mildrith, most of them apparently the work of Goscelin of Saint-Bertin.[76] The final quire (fos 277–84) contains copies of **2** and **3**, and of the associated privileges of Popes Boniface IV, Agatho, Adeodatus and John XII; the whole quire is the work of a scribe writing a round Anglo-Caroline hand, who was also responsible for earlier sections of the manuscript. The layout, illumination and display script show that this quire was an integral part of the manuscript, not a later addition. It begins with an initial of very high quality, incorporating a portrait of King Æthelberht; there is a possibility that this quire was originally intended to stand at the beginning of the manuscript, not the end (but no medieval foliation exists to support this suggestion). The last pages of the quire were left blank, and a later scribe has added on 284v and two inserted leaves a copy of a privilege of Calixtus II from 1120, confirming

---

[74] D.N. Dumville, 'English Square Minuscule Script: the Background and Earliest Phases', *Anglo-Saxon England* xvi (1987), pp. 147–79 (at 171).
[75] N.R. Ker, *English Manuscripts in the Century after the Norman Conquest* (Oxford, 1960), pp. 27, 29 and plate 11; C.R. Dodwell, *The Canterbury School of Illumination* (Cambridge, 1954), pp. 28, 123.
[76] For Goscelin, see works cited p. xxi n. 26.

the earlier papal privileges; this perhaps shows that the first scribe was working before 1120. In the fifteenth century a copy of **34**, a forgery in which Edward the Confessor grants Thanet to the abbey, was added in a blank space at the end of the previous quire (fo. 276rv).

There is an incomplete copy of **4** on fo. 2, which appears to be the second page of an inserted bifolium (the first page was a blank fly-leaf, now containing various titles, notes and a late medieval list of contents). The text breaks off in mid-sentence at the end of fo. 2v. It is written in a Canterbury hand apparently contemporary with the co-operating hands of the main manuscript, but the decoration is cruder, with a more limited range of colours, and the quality of the parchment is not so good. The bifolium probably belonged to another manuscript of around the same date as BL Cotton Vespasian B. xx. It is not clear when it was added to the main manuscript (the foliation is modern).

c. *BL Cotton Vitellius A. ii, fos 3–19* (D)

This is a fragment from a manuscript of the late twelfth century, bound by Cotton into a composite volume which was damaged in the fire of 1731. The parchment is now badly distorted and has been mounted, but little text has been lost. The first part of the fragment is taken up by two Latin works on early Kentish saints and their resting-places. After a gap, the same scribe supplied copies of **2**, **3** and **4**, and of a number of spurious and genuine papal privileges relating to the abbey's status, the latest dated 1146.[77] In his copies of two of the later privileges the scribe has imitated the devices of the original. This practice is not uncommon at St Augustine's, for the thirteenth-century scribe of BL Cotton Claudius D. x treated some papal documents in a similar way, while Thomas Elmham did not merely imitate but actually reproduced in facsimile the devices of certain bulls.[78] The texts of **2** and **3** in BL Cotton Vitellius A. ii are very close to those in BL Cotton Vespasian B. xx, and were probably drawn from the same source (perhaps the pseudo-originals). The incomplete copy of **4** added to BL Cotton Vespasian B. xx is also textually similar to that in the later manuscript.

[77] G.R.C. Davis, *Medieval Cartularies of Great Britain: a Short Catalogue* (London, 1958), no. 191. Davis was probably incorrect in his assumption that the manuscript of which this is a fragment was a register; it is more likely to have been a hagiographical collection with a documentary supplement (and therefore similar to BL Cotton Vespasian B. xx). For the papal privileges, see W. Holtzmann, *Papsturkunden in England*, 3 vols (Berlin, 1930–52), i. 91. The hagiographical texts were edited by F. Liebermann, *Die Heiligen Englands: angelsächsisch und lateinisch* (Hanover, 1889), pp. 2–20; see discussion by Rollason, *Mildrith Legend*, p. 21.
[78] Hunter (1973, pp. 216–19) suggests that Elmham may known BL Cotton Vitellius A. ii, and been directly influenced by its treatment of papal privileges.

d. *Cartae Antiquae Roll 9* (E)

Twenty Cartae Antiquae rolls were produced during the late twelfth and thirteenth centuries.[79] The reason for their compilation remains obscure, but it seems that they may in part have been intended to provide a record, for the use of the royal administration, of the various royal grants and privileges of certain religious houses and members of the laity. They may also represent an unsystematic extension of the practice of copying certain documents involved in litigation onto the Pipe Rolls. The origins of the Cartae Antiquae rolls appear to lie in the Exchequer of Richard I. The twenty rolls can be divided chronologically into two groups. The earlier and larger group seems to belong largely to the reign of John and is connected with Exchequer procedures; the later group, chiefly comprising copies of charters of Henry III, has Chancery characteristics and seems to have provided the basis for confirmations issued by Henry and his two successors.

Roll 9, apparently compiled in John's reign, consists of two membranes containing twenty-one items.[80] Sixteen of these (items 3–18), the work of at least four different scribes, are royal charters from St Augustine's. Most are post-Conquest, in the names of kings from William I to Richard I. The first nine cover specific privileges: the community's rights in Stonar on Thanet, its claim to the churches and tithes at Faversham and Milton, and a grant of toll-exemption by Henry I. Next there are five charters relating to the general judicial and financial rights of the abbey; the first is the vernacular version of the Confessor's grant of these privileges (**35**), while the remainder are confirmations by William I and II, Henry I and Richard. The last two items from St Augustine's are **3**, the most impressive of the abbey's three charters in the name of King Æthelberht, and **33**, Cnut's grant of Mildrith's relics to St Augustine's. The scribe notes that the latter had a seal, while the former did not.

BL Harley 84 and 85 are transcripts of the Cartae Antiquae rolls made for Sir Simonds D'Ewes before 1645. The condition of the originals has since deteriorated, so these transcripts are now of considerable value.[81]

---

[79] L. Landon, *The Cartae Antiquae Rolls 1–10*, Pipe Roll Society, n.s. xvii (1939); J. Conway Davis, *The Cartae Antiquae Rolls 11–20*, Pipe Roll Society, n.s. xxxiii (1957). The following remarks are a summary of aspects discussed in Landon's introduction.

[80] Landon (*Cartae Antiquae Rolls 1–10*, pp. 128–35) calendars the contents of the roll.

[81] For D'Ewes, see *Dictionary of National Biography*, v. 900–3; A.G. Watson, 'Sir Simonds D'Ewes's Collection of Charters, and a Note on the Charters of Sir Robert Cotton', *Journal of the Society of Archivists* ii. 6 (1962), pp. 247–54; *idem, The Library of Sir Simonds D'Ewes* (London, 1966). Other transcripts are discussed by Landon (*Cartae Antiquae Rolls 1–10*, pp. xii-xiii).

e. *BL Cotton Julius D. ii* (F)

BL Cotton Julius D. ii and BL Add. 46352 once formed a very long composite register containing a mass of diverse material: royal charters and papal privileges, details of rentals, leases and private agreements, lists of churches dependent on the abbey, the Benedictine Rule, Magna Carta, various ecclesiastical statutes, and lists of kings, popes, emperors and abbots.[82] Parts of the register appear to date from the 1220s or 1230s, while other sections belong to the later thirteenth and earlier fourteenth centuries. The quires have been rearranged several times, but a fourteenth-century foliation makes it possible to reconstruct an early stage of compilation.[83] At this stage the register began with BL Add. 46352, fo. 94, which has a rubric 'Matricula de camera sancti Augustini Cant.', to which another hand has added 'D[istinctio]. Th. abbatis'. It has been suggested that the register may have been put together from earlier material for use as a handbook, perhaps for Abbot Thomas Fyndon (1283–1309). After the Dissolution the register came into the hands of John Twyne of Canterbury, who also owned another St Augustine's cartulary, BL Cotton Claudius D. x; Twyne probably acquired these and other manuscripts from the remains of the abbey's library, which seems to have been preserved for some time in the former monastic buildings (see above, pp. xxiv–xxv). Twyne passed both cartularies to his son, also John Twyne. There is a partly erased inscription on fo. 94 of BL Add. 46352: 'Liber Johannis Twyne de Grayes Inne ex dono Joannis Twyne patris sui 1578'.[84] The register was split into two parts, of which one (now BL Cotton Julius D. ii) was in the Cotton library by 1621 (see BL Harley 6018, 115v); Sir Edward Dering made an abstract of it in 1628 (BL Stowe 924, 184v–244v). The second part was in Dering's own possession, as shown by an armorial bookstamp on the binding. It passed through various hands (indicated by pressmarks) until it was acquired by Sir Thomas Phillipps *c.* 1830 (Phillipps MS 1085); it was bought by the British Museum in 1946.

---

[82] Davis, *Cartularies*, nos 192 and 200. See also *British Library: Catalogue of Additions to the Manuscripts 1946–50* (London, 1979), pt 1, pp. 44–6. There is an important discussion of this register by J.-P. Genet, 'Cartulaires, registres et histoire: l'exemple anglais', in *Le métier d'historien au moyen âge: études sur l'historiographie médiévale*, ed. B. Guenée (Paris, 1977), pp. 95–138.

[83] Genet (*ibid*, pp. 97–100) has conveniently set out the results of reconstruction in a table. The foliation in his final column is occasionally incorrect.

[84] For John Twyne and his descendants, see: the *Dictionary of National Biography*, xix. 1328–31; A.B. Emden, *A Biographical Register of the University of Oxford A.D. 1501 to 1540* (Oxford, 1974); A.G. Watson, 'John Twyne of Canterbury (d. 1581) as a Collector of Medieval Manuscripts: a Preliminary Investigation', *The Library* 6th ser. viii (1986), pp. 133–51 (with discussion of this manuscript on p. 148, art. 15).

Texts of forty-three apparently pre-Conquest charters appear in one of the earliest sections of the composite register, now fos 24–133 of BL Cotton Julius D. ii, which was written by a single scribe probably in the second quarter of the thirteenth century.[85] A copy of the Benedictine Rule (24r–39r) is followed by Augustine's privilege (**4**) and a collection of papal documents, the latest a bull of Gregory IX (1227–41), with some archiepiscopal letters and a list of indulgences (39v–77r). Fos 77v–83v, the remaining leaves of a quire, were originally left blank; a number of other papal and archiepiscopal documents were added later. Next comes a disorderly collection of royal and private charters, with some leases, agreements and final concords (84r–133v). The first items in this section are **2**, **3** and **5**, the 'earliest' documents in the archive, and these are followed by nine other pre-Conquest charters (**40**, **33**, **9**, **45**, **48**, **53**, **29**, **37**, **35**); these have a vague chronological order, but no particular cohesion as a group, for they include charters in favour of Minster as well as St Augustine's, and a ship-toll charter and grants of privileges as well as land-grants. In the remainder of this section, pre-Conquest charters appear scattered among post-Conquest documents, which themselves have no obvious underlying pattern. The spurious grant of Thanet by the Confessor (**34**) is given with some other Thanet documents; two ninth-century charters (**19**, **16**) appear with other Lenham texts; four Minster charters (**41**, **42**, **43**, **44**) turn up unexpectedly among some final concords and private charters; two tenth-century charters (**27**, **30**) are linked with a single post-Conquest text also relating to Sibertswold; another group of pre-Conquest texts appears in isolation (**26**, **17**, **38**, **36**, **28**, **15**, **10**, **20**, **23**), and the cartulary concludes with a third group (**8**, **11**, **7**, **47**, **49**, **50**, **12**, **18**, **22**, **13**, **14**, **21**)

The scribe has obviously not copied out all the texts at his disposal; he includes at intervals collections of rubrics to charters whose texts he has omitted (see, for instance, 92rv). The reference to the Old English version of **35** on 88v is interesting: 'Eadwardus rex de libertate ecclesie in anglico, sicut continetur in carta que est in cista' (this is followed by a similar

---

[85] The section belongs to Genet's 'Cartulaire I', which was apparently compiled and written in the 1230s. This compilation includes (BL Cotton Julius D. ii, 2rv) a list of archbishops culminating in the pontificate of Edmund Rich (1233–40), with similar lists of kings etc. ending with Henry III, Pope Gregory IX (1227–41), Abbot Robert de Bello (1224–53) and the Emperor Frederick II (1220–50). A chronicle in the form of a table goes up to 1235. For this material, see T.D. Hardy, *Descriptive Catalogue of the Materials Relating to the History of Great Britain and Ireland*, RS, 3 vols (1862–71), iii. 74–5 (no. 142), 244 (no. 437). There are documents concerned with visitations of Bury St Edmunds in 1234 and Westminster in 1236. The selection of royal charters and other documents in the relevant sections of the register seems to be consistent with this implied date.

reference to William I's confirmation of **35**, another vernacular text). There is also a mysterious rubric 'Donacio Ælthelwici (*sic*) Regis in Lenham' (fo. 93v), perhaps a reference to the unrevised version of **21** (the revised version appears in the final group of charters in the cartulary). As well as occasionally reducing a text to a simple rubric, the compiler usually abbreviated the charters he was copying; in the case of the Anglo-Saxon documents, he left out vernacular bounds and sometimes the following dating clause, and either omitted the witness-lists or gave only the first few subscriptions. Post-Conquest documents and papal bulls are also abbreviated.

It seems likely that this section of BL Cotton Julius D. ii is essentially a copy of an existing cartulary, and not an independent compilation. The references in the rubrics to the presence of writs in a *cista* do indeed seem to suggest that the compiler had at least some contact with single-sheet charters; but it must be remembered that such rubrics could be copied from an earlier exemplar. The stray rubrics to absent documents are best explained in terms of reduction from an existing and larger collection. If the St Augustine's community already possessed a full-scale cartulary, then it becomes easier to account for the modest physical dimensions and the radically abbreviated texts of the corresponding section of BL Cotton Julius D. ii. The Julius cartulary may have been produced as a guide to and summary of the larger compilation, perhaps to serve as a handbook for the abbot, an earlier precursor of the more substantial volume put together for Abbot Thomas Fyndon, of which it was later to form a part.

One can only speculate about the hypothetical earlier cartulary. If the order of documents in BL Cotton Julius D. ii is an accurate reflection of the arrangement of its exemplar, then the volume would appear to have had no obvious principles of organisation. The issue is further complicated by consideration of the relationship between BL Cotton Julius D. ii and a later cartulary in the archive, PRO E 164/27 (H), which appears to have been written in the later thirteenth and fourteenth centuries (for a more detailed discussion of this manuscript, see below, pp. li–liv). The two collections have a considerable amount in common in terms of the documents selected for inclusion, both pre- and post-Conquest. They share twenty-two Anglo-Saxon or purportedly Anglo-Saxon charters; BL Cotton Julius D. ii has an additional twenty-one texts which are not found in the PRO cartulary, while the latter has one early charter (**46**) not included in the former. The scribes of the PRO cartulary were not copying from BL Cotton Julius D. ii; often the later compilation has texts which are slightly longer than the abbreviated versions in the Julius cartulary. It is possible that the texts in PRO E 164/ 27 were ultimately dependent upon the hypothetical exemplar of BL Cotton

Julius D. ii, the missing earlier cartulary. Two of the texts found in both manuscripts (**10**, **15**) are essentially the same modified versions of much longer documents; these must ultimately go back to a common exemplar that was not the original charters (it may be significant that these were both general grants of privileges to the Kentish churches, not specific land-grants to St Augustine's). There is a fairly considerable overlap between the charters found in these two early collections and the later selection of documents in Elmham's *Speculum* (Cambridge, Trinity Hall, 1 (N); see pp. lvii–lix); twelve texts occur in all three manuscripts. Elmham is known to have preferred to use single sheets rather than cartulary copies when these were available, and this circumstance would tend to add significance to the instances where the readings in BL Cotton Julius D. ii and the PRO cartulary agree together against those in the *Speculum*; it could be argued that this demonstrates that the two earlier manuscripts relied upon a common exemplar. But the whole question is made infinitely more complex by the fact that at least some of Elmham's 'originals' were pseudo-originals, new single-sheet documents that had been produced since the thirteenth century in order to incorporate revisions, mainly of chronological details (see further, pp. xcvi–cv). And certainly almost all the instances where the Julius and PRO cartularies agree together against the *Speculum* occur where it can be shown that Elmham's texts have been contaminated by later revisors (the other minor points could be accounted for by scribal error on the part of Elmham or the creators of the pseudo-originals). Thus the textual agreements between BL Cotton Julius D. ii and PRO E 164/27 against the *Speculum* could be explained by the fact that they are witnesses to an earlier, less contaminated state of the muniments, and do not necessarily demonstrate reliance on a common exemplar.

The relationship between BL Cotton Julius D. ii and PRO E 164/27 is difficult to establish with absolute confidence. The selection of pre-Conquest charters in the two manuscripts is sufficiently similar to suggest that both drew on an earlier collection of such material. The evidence of textual variants is not conclusive, although it does appear that in both cases the modified texts of **10** and **15** depend ultimately upon a common exemplar. Another problematic factor is the order of the charters in the two manuscripts. As has already been mentioned, there is no obvious underlying principle, such as chronology or topography, governing the arrangement of charters in BL Cotton Julius D. ii. In PRO E 164/27 the majority of the Anglo-Saxon charters are grouped together between fos 76v and 84r. Eight Minster charters in chronological order are followed by eight charters connected with St Augustine's, again in (approximate) chronological order. Taken as a whole, the PRO cartulary is a very miscellaneous volume, with no obvious organisational principles, but its treatment of the Anglo-Saxon charters does have some logical basis, whereas there is none in the arrangement of the corresponding texts in BL Cotton Julius D. ii. If, as I have suggested above, BL Cotton Julius D. ii is essentially a reduced copy of a full-scale cartulary, then the exemplar would not have had a logical arrangement. But if it is accepted that both the Julius and PRO cartularies depend ultimately upon the hypothetical lost cartulary, then the more logical organisation of the Anglo-Saxon texts in the latter requires some explanation. Perhaps there was an intermediary version between the hypothetical early cartulary and PRO E 164/27 which introduced more order into the layout. Or perhaps the arrangement of texts in BL Cotton Julius D. ii has for some reason become confused.

A very murky problem becomes even murkier with the introduction of another piece of evidence. The PRO cartulary contains a separate list of benefactions which seems to be effectively a charter-list (edited in Appendix 2). This refers to forty-four pre-Conquest grants, in addition to some post-Conquest texts. Again there is no obvious principle of organisation, and also no correspondence with the order of the full texts copied into the PRO cartulary. But there is an intriguing (although fairly complex) link with the arrangement of documents in BL Cotton Julius D. ii. Interest focuses on a group of twenty-seven documents which in the Julius cartulary are copied in the following order, with intervening post-Conquest documents: **19, 16, 41, 42, 43, 44, 27, 30, 26, 17, 38, 36, 28, 15, 10, 20, 23, 8, 11, 7, 47, 49, 50, 12, 18, 22, 13**. Twenty-five of these charters (**10** and **15** being excluded) appear in the PRO charter-list, in five groups of between two and nine documents each. In three of these groups the charters are in the same order; in two they are in exactly the reverse order. There is surely some significance in this complicated correspondence, although the explanation is far from clear. The fact that some groups are in reverse order suggests that it is necessary to look to single sheets or at least unbound copies, rather than to a regular cartulary. There may be an ultimate connection with the custody of the original charters in bundles in a muniment chest; when a bundle was examined, the individual charters could easily have been replaced in reverse order. It is possible that this observation is the key to understanding the lack of organisational principles in the Julius cartulary, and in the hypothetical earlier cartulary which it appears to summarise. The compiler of the earlier collection may simply have copied documents as they came to hand from the muniment chest, his purpose being to produce a corpus of transcripts rather than an organised register. The deficiencies of such a volume would soon have become obvious to the St Augustine's community; the next stage would have been the production of more functional cartularies, of which BL Cotton Claudius D. x is an example. Other organised cartularies, now lost, may have been produced at around the same time, and it was perhaps one of these which was used by the compiler(s) of the main part of the PRO cartulary.

It would be gratifying if the hypothetical cartulary lying behind BL Cotton Julius D. ii could be identified with the celebrated *Textus S. Adriani* (for which see pp. xxxvi–xxxvii); the evidence is suggestive, but not conclusive. The *Textus S. Adriani* is known to have contained copies of the privilege of Pope Adeodatus and of at least two Minster charters (**40** and **41**), and some chronological material, at least to the extent that it was consulted for the year in which Gregory and Augustine died (605). BL Cotton Julius D. ii has the texts in question, and also includes a certain amount of chronological data. On 11v, in one such compilation, an entry corresponding to 605 has the note: 'Obiit beatus Gregorius. Eodem anno beatus Augustinus obiit'; this appears to be the same information which Sprott derived from the *Textus S. Adriani*. There is no trace in the Julius cartulary of the survey of St Augustine's estates supposedly extracted from the *Textus S. Adriani* by one of the compilers of the PRO cartulary, but it may have been the case that the compilers of the cartulary in BL Cotton Julius D. ii were simply not interested in such material.

f. *BL Cotton Claudius D. x* (G)

BL Cotton Claudius D. x, known as 'The Red Book of St Augustine's', is a large general cartulary, compiled in the later part of the thirteenth century. After the dissolution of the abbey it passed into the possession of John Twyne of Canterbury, as did the register formed by BL Cotton Julius D. ii and BL Add. 46352.[86] At the top of fo. 123v is a note: 'Liber Johannes Twyne de Grayes Ine ex dono patris sui Johannis Twyne. Teste Humfrido Jurdano Rectore ecclesie de Sturmuthe [Stourmouth, Kent], per me John Twyne'. The same note was also to be found in the lower margin of fo. 9r, the first page of the cartulary proper (Cotton prefixed to it an unrelated quire containing a fourteenth-century chronicle), but it has since been erased. Towards the end of the sixteenth century or in the early seventeenth century a scholar examined the cartulary and made some brief notes on it, now BL Harley 1879, 19v; M.R. James, who first drew attention to these notes, was inclined to identify the hand as that of Dr John Dee (1527–1608), but there

---

[86] Davis, *Cartularies*, no. 193; Watson, 'John Twyne', p. 149, art. 16.

is some reason to think that the author was Sir Robert Cotton himself.[87] It is here stated that that 'This book is now in the hands of Mr Wilford of Kent and (*sic*) old Gentellman being in fetter layn a recusant'. We are also told that the volume was prefaced by a portion in a later hand which consisted of 'an Exemplification and Confirmation of all the charters of the Kinges proinde to Ed. the sonn of Edward mad in the time of Radulphi Abbatis'; this appears to be a reference to a quire containing a copy of Edward II's 1326 Inspeximus charter and other charters of that king, which is an addition to the main cartulary. The quire is now fos 61–73, but the foliation shows that it reached this position at a late stage. When the author of the notes saw the manuscript this quire evidently lay at the beginning of the cartulary; presumably it was Cotton who moved it, at the time when he added the chronicle to the beginning.

M.R. James also suggested a connection between BL Cotton Claudius D. x and another antiquarian note. Among the papers of Brian Twyne (1579? –1644), grandson of John Twyne of Canterbury, is an intriguing reference to a cartulary from St Augustine's: 'Thomas de Thanet (vixit 1272) matricula scil. de variis chartis, libertatibus ac privilegiis et possessionibus monasterii S. Aug. Cantuar. Init: In nomine domini nostri Iesu Christi notum sit omnibus quod ego Adhelbertus etc. This MS was given by John Twyne of Canterbury to Thomas Smyth, high customer of London, and was afterwards in the hands of Richard James of CCC Oxon – a thick 4to with a red cover'.[88] This register would appear to have begun with a copy of **2**, as does the main cartulary of BL Cotton Claudius D. x, and the physical description would fit the 'Red Book'. But the details of its history are somewhat at

---

[87] M.R. James, *Lists of Manuscripts formerly owned by Dr John Dee*, Supplement to the Transactions of the Cambridge Bibliographical Society (Cambridge, 1921), p. 9. Watson ('John Twyne', p. 149, art. 16) attributes the hand to Cotton, correctly in the view of Dr Nigel Ramsay (pers. comm.).

[88] See *The Life and Times of Anthony Wood, Antiquary, of Oxford, 1632–1695, Described by Himself*, ed. A. Clark, Oxford Historical Society, 5 vols (Oxford, 1891–1900), iv. 91. James (*Manuscripts. . .owned by Dr John Dee*, p. 10) suggests identification with BL Cotton Claudius D. x; Tanner earlier made the same connection: *Notitia Monastica* (Cambridge, 1787), under St Augustine's. Clark's edition of Wood states that these comments are to be found in Bodleian, Twyne xxi (at p. 407), while James cites Bodleian, Twyne xvi and the same page-number; neither is correct, and I have been unable to discover in which Twyne manuscript these notes actually occur. Smyth is mentioned in the entry for his son, Sir Thomas Smith (1558?–1625) in the *Dictionary of National Biography*, xviii. 536; he was from Westenhanger in Kent, and was buried at Ashford in 1591 (my thanks to Nigel Ramsay for drawing this to my attention). Richard James was librarian to Sir Robert Cotton: see F. Madden *et al.*, *A Summary Catalogue of Western Manuscripts in the Bodleian Library at Oxford*, ii, pt 2 (Oxford, 1937), pp. 750–1. Twyne's comment is wrongly linked to BL Cotton Julius D. ii and BL Add. 46352 in *British Library: Catalogue of Additions to the Manuscripts 1946–50* (London, 1979), pt 1, p. 46.

odds with *ex libris* inscription of the Cotton cartulary and with the comments in BL Harley 1879. It would be necessary to identify the John Twyne of Brian Twyne's description with John Twyne junior, originally of Canterbury and later of Gray's Inn (that is, Brian Twyne's uncle, rather than his grandfather), and to assume that the manuscript passed first to Thomas Smyth, then to Mr Wilford of Kent, before coming into the possession of Richard James and later of Cotton. This combination of the evidence is not impossible, but an alterative explanation is that there were two manuscripts, the one described in BL Harley 1879 (which was certainly BL Cotton Claudius D. x) and the other associated with a Thomas de Thanet (and since lost). The fifteenth-century library catalogue of St Augustine's mentions Thomas de Thanet as the donor of seven volumes, and he is probably the man of that name who was ordained subdeacon in 1305.[89] The date of 1270 which Brian Twyne associates with Thomas de Thanet seems too early, and may perhaps derive from a mistaken identification with Thomas Sprott, who is regularly given that floruit (see p. xcviii).

BL Cotton Claudius D. x provides a considerable contrast to the haphazard cartulary in BL Cotton Julius D ii. It is meticulously organized, with blank folios left between sections for the addition of new documents, and was originally the work of a single, very competent scribe. At the beginning of the cartulary (now fo. 9) are copies of **2** and **4**, followed without a break by a collection of papal privileges (fos 9–51). In certain instances the scribe has imitated the monograms and devices of the papal bulls, which suggests that he had the originals before him; there is similar imitation of these features in BL Cotton Vitellius A. ii from the twelfth century and in the fifteenth-century manuscript of Elmham's history (see p. xl and n. 78). Some of the papal privileges have been abbreviated, and in certain cases the scribe gives only a rubric, remarking that the privilege follows another document verbatim. After a conclusion 'Summa totius indulgentie tunc temporis concesse et confirmate', the scribe left a gap of six folios, some of which now contain additional material. He recommenced on fo. 57 with a series of royal grants of judicial and financial privileges to the abbey, beginning with those of Cnut and Edward the Confessor (**32**, **35**), and concluding with documents in the name of Henry III. He gives the Latin text of **35**, but notes the existence of a vernacular version.

This section of the cartulary is now followed by a quire containing a copy of Edward II's 1326 Inspeximus charter, with other documents from his

---

[89] For Thomas de Thanet see A. B. Emden, *Donors of Books to S. Augustine's Abbey, Canterbury*, Oxford Bibliographical Soc., Occasional Publications iv (Oxford, 1968), p. 17.

reign. This has an early foliation (xix-xxxvii) which has no connection with
any other foliation in the 'Red Book'; evidently the quire became attached
to the manuscript at a relatively late date. In the early seventeenth century
this quire was located at the beginning of the cartulary (see above); Cotton
probably placed it in its present position. A medieval rubricator has headed
the leaves of the quire with the phrase 'Tempore Radulphi abbatis', a
reference to Abbot Ralph Bourne (1309–34), who procured the Inspeximus
charter from Edward II. The 1326 charter incorporated the texts of eight
pre-Conquest privileges (**1, 3, 5, 27, 21, 33, 34, 39**). The copy in BL Cotton
Claudius D. x is extremely careful and was probably taken from the original
Inspeximus; its readings are generally preferable to the enrolled version.
Because this quire is quite distinct from the rest of the manuscript, which
is otherwise a unified production, I have given it a separate siglum (G*).

The rest of the cartulary has a complex organization based on chronological
and topographical criteria. Some sections cover the documentation of the
estates attached to the various abbey offices, with relevant charters arranged
in topographical subdivisions. The other sections are devoted to the different
manors belonging to the abbey, with the charters being given in chronological
order. Gaps were left after each portion for the addition of new material, and
a number of later scribes have taken advantage of them. Eight pre-Conquest
charters are included in this part of the original cartulary. The first is **25**,
one of the archive's two vernacular grants of food-render from the ninth
century, which heads the section on Nackington. The scribe of the Red
Book has copied it carefully but unhandily, making and correcting many
errors, and the language is modernized; he was probably not using the
original memorandum of the grant. **39** appears in the Fordwich section.
Collected together with other documents related to the manor of Minster
are copies of **33, 34, 26** and **17**; the compiler has ignored the early charters
in favour of the abbesses of Minster-in-Thanet, which had been included in
BL Cotton Julius D. ii. There is a copy of **29** in the Plumstead section and
one of **28** in that relating to Swalecliffe.

The scribe of the Red Book seems in general to have been a careful
copyist, but the quality of his pre-Conquest texts appears to depend largely
on his sources. Elsewhere in the cartulary there is some indication that he
was making use of single sheets, for he imitates the devices of some of the
papal privileges and occasionally remarks in a rubric that a (post-Conquest)
royal diploma was *sigillata* (although in both cases he may have been
reproducing details of an intermediate exemplar). For his pre-Conquest
documents he seems in general to have relied on copies. On of his exemplars
may have been the hypothetical early cartulary lying behind BL Cotton

Julius D. ii (see above, pp. xliv–xlvii); the texts of **2** and **35** in the Red Book are introduced by the same rubrics as those in the Julius cartulary. All the pre-Conquest texts which appear in the Red Book, with the exception of **25** and **32**, also occur in BL Cotton Julius D. ii. Both manuscripts have the same modified text of **26**, which must be some distance from any original. In both versions of **28** the statement of powers is truncated (conceivably this was a mistake by the scribe of the tenth-century original or a later modification when the land was donated to St Augustine's, but it may also represent modification by a copyist). Both manuscripts have a copy of the slightly shorter version of **34**, which seems to have differed from the text confirmed in the 1326 Inspeximus (although this charter is spurious, and it is possible that more than one pseudo-original existed). If the scribe of the Red Book did derive his pre-Conquest charters from the hypothetical lost cartulary, then its texts must have been noticeably good. The copy of **28** in BL Cotton Claudius D. x includes a brief Old English boundary clause, a quite lengthy witness-list (which has probably been abbreviated to a certain extent) and an important passage in the name of the original beneficiary which may have been taken from an endorsement to the original. The text of **39**, an Old English writ, is also very good.

If the scribe of the Red Book did use the hypothetical lost cartulary, then it was not his only source. When he was copying **2** he obviously had more than one exemplar in front of him, for he has erased and rewritten a section of the charter where there is an important variant (see the commentary to **2**). It is possible that he had access to more than one cartulary, and not inconceivable that he consulted single-sheet documents (at least for **28** and **39**, and perhaps also for **2**). Unfortunately, most of the documents he copied were not authentic (**2, 4, 29, 32, 33, 34**).

BL Cotton Claudius D. x was probably the source for the copies of Minster charters in Canterbury, D. & C., Lit. E. 19 (I), which was compiled in the early fourteenth century (see below, pp. liv–lv).

g. *PRO E 164/27* (H)

PRO E 164/27, known as 'The White Book of St Augustine's', was preserved in the Exchequer, one of a series of miscellaneous volumes in the Office of the King's Remembrancer.[90] Five of the cartularies in this series are known to have entered the office between 1579 and 1637 as a result of litigation, and in these cases it appears that they had earlier been transferred to the new owners of monastic estates. The circumstances under which the

---

[90] Davis, *Cartularies*, no. 195. Holtzmann (*Papsturkunden*, i. 44–7) summarizes the contents.

St Augustine's cartulary entered the Exchequer Court are unknown. It may have been in private hands, but it also seems to have been the case that records could be transferred from the Augmentations Office and elsewhere for purposes of litigation.[91]

PRO E 164/27 is a collection of miscellanous documents and statutes with no overall organization. The volume seems to have been compiled over a period of time, partly in the later thirteenth century and partly in the early fourteenth, by a considerable number of scribes, some co-operating and some successive. Up to fo. 150v all the documents copied belong to the reign of Henry III or earlier. Thereafter appear charters of Edward I and Edward II, a number of ecclesiastical deeds and a brief chronicle extending to 1324, with additions down to 1332; the final additions are a few documents from the time of Edward III. This is evidently a cumulative production, but the bulk of the manuscript seems to belong to the late thirteenth century. Three folios have been lost from the beginning since the manuscript was foliated; in his handlist Sawyer took this loss into account, and in all references to charters in this cartulary he gives the true foliation, rather than the actual foliation of the manuscript (for instance, **40** is said to occur on fos 76v–77v, while the actual foliation is 79v–80v). I have followed Sawyer's precedent in this, to avoid confusion.

The first thirty-five folios contain a collection of miscellaneous material, beginning with some inconsequential deeds from the period immediately after the Conquest and a memorandum of some minor estates lost to Normans at this time (see pp. cx–cxi). These deeds and the memorandum are also found together in BL Cotton Julius D. ii, 107v–108r, and may perhaps have been taken from a common exemplar in the form of a lost cartulary (see further, pp. xliv–xlvii). After some notes on rentals and exchange, the PRO cartulary continues with an important list of charters, mostly pre-Conquest, which is edited in Appendix 2. There are similarities between the order of charters in the list and the organisation of pre-Conquest texts in BL Cotton Julius D. ii, which can perhaps be traced back to the custody of documents in bundles in a muniment chest (see pp. xlvi–xlvii). The charter-list is followed by some details of papal privileges, and then by a survey of St Augustine's estates with a later rubric 'Extractum de textu sancti Adriani' (11v–14r); for the *Textus S. Adriani*, see above, pp. xxxvi–xxxvii. This survey is ultimately dependent on material collected at the time of the

---

[91] Holtzmann, *Papsturkunden*, i. 40–7; see Davis, *Cartularies*, nos 225, 462, 527, 788, 979. The transfer of documents between government offices is discussed by W.C. Richardson, *History of the Court of Augmentations, 1536–1554* (Baton Rouge, 1961), pp. 476–7.

Domesday Inquest, but in its present form seems to belong to the early twelfth century (see pp. cvi–cvii). It is associated here with lists of tenants, knight-fees, tithes and so on. Fos 16v–17r contain a shorter survey, headed 'Brevis recapitulacio solingorum', which is followed by a more substantial Domesday satellite survey, with the informative rubric: 'Exce(r)pta de compoto solingorum comitatus Cancie secundum cartam regis, uidelicet ea que ad ecclesiam sancti Augustini pertinent et est in regis Domesday' (17r–25r).[92]

Immediately after this survey come two pre-Conquest texts, records of general grants of privileges to the Kentish churches by Offa (15) and Wihtred (10), which were presumably intended to be associated with the following polemic material on the primacy question and on the injuries that had been visited on St Augustine's by the archbishops. The cartulary proper begins on fo. 49, which has the heading 'Hic notatur antiqua et autentica priuilegia huius monasterii viz. Augustini Anglorum apostoli'. The first document is the spurious charter of Augustine (4), followed by a group of papal privileges; there is the same arrangement in BL Cotton Julius D. ii. The papal privileges are interspersed with a number of ecclesiastical documents and (post-Conquest) royal charters, including material from the early thirteenth century. On fos 76v–84r sixteen pre-Conquest charters are copied together: eight Minster documents in chronological order (40, 41, 42, 43, 44, 46, 48, 47), followed by eight charters with more direct associations with St Augustine's and its estates, arranged on a rather looser chronological basis (8, 12, 18, 14, 27, 30, 38, 20). Next comes a miscellaneous compilation of papal privileges, post-Conquest royal charters and ecclesiastical and private deeds. Three further Anglo-Saxon documents appear in later sections of the register. On fo. 145v there is a copy of Cnut's writ granting Mildrith's relics to the abbey (33), followed by various post-Conquest confirmations; on fo. 147v there is a copy of the Latin version of Edward's grant of sake and soke (35); and, unexpectedly, on fos 150r–151r a copy of Eadberht II's ship-toll privilege for Minster (53) appears among other unrelated post-Conquest charters.

The thirteenth-century scribe who copied most of the Anglo-Saxon charters made frequent errors and had a tendency to modernize place-names and personal names. He almost always omits the bounds and most of the witness-list, but in one instance (27) he has included part of a witness-list

---

[92] The *Excerpta* have been edited, in parallel with Domesday Book and the *Domesday Monachorum*, by Adolphus Ballard: *An Eleventh-Century Inquisition of St Augustine's, Canterbury*, British Academy Records of Social and Economic History iv.2 (London, 1920).

not found in any other copy. The treatment of **53**, which was added in the fourteenth century, is noticeably different; here the charter is carefully copied in full, and the witness-list is uniquely given in the form of a column. A case can be made that the texts of the pre-Conquest charters in the White Book and in BL Cotton Julius D. ii were ultimately dependent upon an earlier cartulary which no longer survives, and of which the Julius cartulary may to be a copy and summary (see full discussion on pp. xliv–xlvii). The selection of Anglo-Saxon charters in the two manuscripts appears to be related; only one charter in PRO E 164/27 does not occur in BL Cotton Julius D. ii (**46**). The texts in the PRO cartulary were certainly not taken directly from the Julius cartulary, for they are usually abbreviated to a lesser degree. The textual evidence for a common exemplar is indecisive, in large measure due to the later contamination of the archive, but it does seem probable that the modified texts of **10** and **15** in the two manuscripts derive from the same source. There is a particular problem in the relative order of the copies of pre-Conquest charters. In BL Cotton Julius D. ii, which probably best represents the arrangement of the presumed lost cartulary, no underlying principle of organisation can be discerned; but the majority of the Anglo-Saxon texts in the PRO cartulary do seem to be grouped on a more logical basis (Minster charters together, with a general chronological arrangement). Since there is no other evidence that the compilers of the PRO cartulary were much concerned to order their royal charters in a regular way, it can be suggested that they made use of an intermediate exemplar which had already imposed a more orderly arrangement on the material.

h. *Canterbury, D. & C., Lit. E. 19* (I)

This is part of a composite register made up of sections from originally separate manuscripts from the thirteenth and fourteenth centuries.[93] The first section (fos 1–31) contains a custumal of deeds relating to St Augustine's possessions on Thanet, including four pre-Conquest charters (**33, 34, 26, 17**), followed by a customary for the manor (headed 'Consuetudines manerii de Menstre'). A contemporary heading reveals that this compilation was put together in 1311, in the first year of Abbot Ralph. It was presumably intended to facilitate the administration of the abbey's pre-Conquest estates

---

[93] Davis, *Cartularies*, no. 196 (the reference here to Minster-in-Sheppey is an error). See also C.E. Woodruff, *A Catalogue of the Manuscript Books in the Library of Christ Church, Canterbury* (Canterbury, 1911), pp. 37–9; *Ninth Report of the Royal Commission on Historical Manuscripts*, Part 1 (London, 1883), Appendix, p. 128.

on the island. Other texts were added subsequently, the latest dated 1527. The text of the pre-Conquest charters were almost certainly copied directly from BL Cotton Claudius D. x, which groups together all the deeds relating to the manor of Minster (and likewise omits all the early charters from Minster-in-Thanet). In a later section of the composite manuscript incomplete copies of **32** and **35** (Latin version), the grants of sake and soke by Cnut and Edward the Confessor, appear among other grants of similar privileges to St Augustine's. Again BL Cotton Claudius D. x was probably the source.

The volume was given to the cathedral library by Dr Farmer, canon of Canterbury from 1782 to 1788.

i. *London, Lambeth Palace, 419, fos 111–60* (J) *and BL Cotton Tiberius A. ix, fos 107–80* (K)

These are the principal manuscripts of the thirteenth-century history of Thomas Sprott (for whom see below, pp. xcvii–xcviii). Both appear to be fourteenth-century, but, in the absence of any proper study of Sprott's work, it is difficult to be certain of their relationship. On the basis of a study of the pre-Conquest section, it is my judgement that the Lambeth Palace manuscript is earlier and represents a better version of the text.[94] BL Cotton Tiberius A. ix, fos 107–80, is the concluding part of a composite manuscript which was damaged in the Cotton fire. The end of the work has been lost, and the remaining pages have been mounted and are somewhat distorted, although the text can generally be made out.[95] Sprott incorporated in his work the texts of **2**, **3** and **4**, and also provided a number of brief summaries of and extracts from other charters, which can be of value for checking dates and beneficiaries (see, for example, **19** and Appendix 1). Sprott's history is an important source for the current state of the texts of the fabricated charters of Æthelberht and Augustine, which underwent some revision between the thirteenth and fifteenth centuries. His work was used and lightly adapted by William Thorne.

j. *CCCC 189* (L) *and BL Add. 53710* (M)

These are the two principal manuscripts of the history of William Thorne, the former perhaps dating from the late fourteenth century and the latter

[94] For discussion of the manuscript, see M.R. James and C. Jenkins, *A Descriptive Catalogue of the Manuscripts in the Library of Lambeth Palace*, 5 parts (Cambridge, 1930–2), pp. 577–9. Hardy (*Cat. Hist. GB*, iii. 61–2) states that the Lambeth text is 'a mere abbreviation' of Thorne and Sprott; but it seems likely that his remarks are based solely on comparison with the text of Thorne's history, as printed by Twysden, and have no bearing on the relationship between the Lambeth manuscript and BL Cotton Tiberius A. ix.

[95] Davis, *Cartularies*, no. 204. See also Holtzmann, *Papsturkunden*, i. 75–6; Hardy, *Cat. Hist. GB*, iii. 125–6 (no. 225)

from the very end of the fourteenth or from the fifteenth century (for Thorne see below, pp. xcviii–xcix). They appear to represent two recensions. In CCCC 189 the history ends in 1375, and the pre-Conquest portion is closer to Sprott's history. The version in BL Add. 53710 goes on to 1397, and has some additions and alterations in the earlier section which seem to reflect further revision of Sprott's chronology and information.[96] According to a note on the first folio, CCCC 189 was given to Matthew Parker, along with other volumes, by Robert Breacher, a former monk of St Augustine's and later chaplain to Queen Elizabeth I; at some previous stage it had been in the hands of Thomas Twyne.[97] The London manuscript has a more complicated history. The historian Roger Twysden bought it from a certain Lawrence Sadler on 15 October 1629 for twenty-five shillings, according to a note on p. 6. While it was in Twysden's possession the manuscript was rather carelessly rebound, and some of the marginal notes were lost as the result of trimming. In 1807 the manuscript was up for sale and was bought by one Weber for twelve shillings. It was sold again in 1836, and purchased by Sir Thomas Phillipps, at a more respectable price of £70 12s. It remained in the Phillipps collection (MS 3138) until it was bought by the British Museum in 1965.[98]

Like Sprott (his main source for the Anglo-Saxon period), Thorne gives the texts of 2, 3 and 4 at the beginning of his history. He also adds, in the relevant place, an abbreviated version of 33, Cnut's grant of Mildrith's relics to the abbey. BL Add. 53710 includes a copy of the 1362 Inspeximus charter of Edward III, which confirmed Edward II's 1326 Inspeximus, and is thus an extra witness to the texts of the eight pre-Conquest charters which were incorporated in the text; the Inspeximus is not included in CCCC 189.

At the end of BL Add. 53710 a sixteenth-century scribe has added incomplete (and error-strewn) copies of 1 and 2. The source for these may have been the pseudo-originals themselves. Like the copies of these two texts in the manuscripts which descend from the Prise-Say register (see below, pp. lix–lx), they are dated to the eighth indiction (a later revisor has once more altered the reading in the first of the texts to six) and 1 is given

---

[96] Sir Roger Twysden based his edition of Thorne on BL Add. 53710: *Historiae Anglicanae Scriptores X* (London, 1652), cols 1757–2207. He collated the manuscript with CCCC 189 and gave the variants in an appendix. Some errors in Twysden's edition are noted by A.H. Davis in his translation: *William Thorne's Chronicle of Saint Augustine's Abbey, Canterbury* (Oxford, 1934).

[97] See James, *Catalogue of Manuscripts in ... Corpus Christi College*, i. 449–51; Watson, 'John Twyne', pp. 144, 147 n. 41. For Breacher see Emden, *Donors*, p. 19.

[98] For the history of the manuscript, see Davis, *Thorne*, pp. xxix–xxx. The final sale took place at Sotheby's on 30 November 1965 (lot 24).

a witness-list; the Prise-Say register was not itself the source, since the copy of **1** in BL Add. 53710 does not have the omission of two words which is a characteristic feature of the text in the Prise-Say register. These transcripts were presumably added to the manuscript of Thorne's history before the suppression of the abbey in 1538, for at the dissolution the single sheets appear to have been given up to the king's commissioners (see pp. xxiv–xxv), while the manuscript itself evidently remained in Canterbury.

k. *Cambridge, Trinity Hall 1* (N)

Thomas Elmham's unfinished history of the abbey survives in a single manuscript, probably autograph and dating from the period shortly before Elmham left St Augustine's in 1414 (for Elmham, see further pp. xcvi–xcvii).[99] It is a very large and most impressive volume, written throughout by a single accomplished scribe, beautifully laid out, and with illuminated initials of high quality. There are several extraordinary illustrations, perhaps the work of Elmham himself: 'facsimile' copies of four of the abbey's 'earliest' charters (**1**, **2**, **3**, **4**), a map of Thanet (42v) and a plan of the High Altar and adjacent shrines in the abbey church (77v).[1] The manuscript was presented to Trinity Hall by the antiquary Robert Hare (died 1611), with the proviso that it should be returned to the abbey in the event of its refoundation.

The manuscript consists of three parts. Prefixed to the history proper (1v–11v) is a complex chronological table, the *Chronologia Augustinensis*, originally extending from 597 until 1414, but carried on to 1418 by another hand; this is followed by a diagram of the solar cycle and a paschal table (12r). Fos 12v–14v are blank. The history proper begins on fo. 15 and breaks off at fo. 73, after reaching the events of the early ninth century. It is possible that Elmham simply abandoned the history when he left the abbey, but the surviving manuscript is clearly a fair copy, and so we might conjecture (if we wish to cling to the idea that the manuscript is autograph) that Elmham had simply found the project too ambitious; it is perhaps significant that the evidence for the abbey's history is at its most complex and confused for the ninth century. After the abrupt end of the history, the

---

[99] Davis, *Cartularies*, no. 198. See M.R. James, *A Descriptive Catalogue of the Manuscripts in the Library of Trinity Hall* (Cambridge, 1907), pp. 1–4.
[1] See Plates I, II, and p. xxxiii n. 59 for reproductions of the charter facsimiles. The plan of the high altar and the map of Thanet have been reproduced many times; see the definitive discussions by W. Urry and F. Hull in *Local Maps and Plans from Medieval England*, ed. R.A. Skelton and P.D.A. Harvey (Oxford, 1986), pp. 107–17 (plate p. 108) and pp. 119–26 (plate p. 120).

scribe left a number of blank folios before continuing with a brief account of events at the abbey in 1087, which is followed by a collection of post-Conquest royal charters and papal privileges from the eleventh and twelfth centuries, with no connecting material.

In the main part of his history Elmham took care to include the texts of all the documents that he could find. From the period before 806 he misses only one charter which has survived elsewhere (**15**); he is the sole witness to **6**, **51** and **52**. Elmham's texts are carefully copied and, as far as it is possible to tell, are usually as complete as possible; this is an important point, for the majority of charters included in the history otherwise survive only in BL Cotton Julius D. ii, where they are generally abbreviated. Elmham appreciated the value of single-sheet charters, pointing out that their readings were to be preferred to those in cartulary texts (see pp. xxxiii–xxxiv); he even reproduced the physical appearance of four of the abbey's most important muniments (**1**, **2**, **3**, **4**). It seems that Elmham also drew on existing cartularies for certain texts. He had evidently studied the documentary contents of the lost *Textus S. Adriani* (see pp. xxxvi–xxxvii). It has been suggested that the collection of post-Conquest material at the end of Elmham's history was copied directly from BL Cotton Julius D. ii.[2] There is also a possibility that Elmham knew BL Cotton Vitellius A. ii, and was influenced by the treatment of the devices of papal privileges in that manuscript.[3] In most respects, Elmham's texts seem superior to those in the earlier cartularies; they are generally more complete, and the spelling of Anglo-Saxon names is usually better. Unfortunately, Elmham was dependent on sources which had in some instances been tampered with by earlier generations of scholars, with the result that in many cases the dates of his texts are not to be trusted; it is especially worrying that in one instance he cites an *originalis* with a contaminated date (see commentary to **40**). The Trinity Hall manuscript itself shows signs of later tampering; in several places dates and regnal years have been erased and rewritten, and there seems to have been some interference with the chronological table. The problems of contamination in the St Augustine's archive are discussed at greater length on pp. xcvi–cv.

The Trinity Hall manuscript was very well-known to antiquarians from the seventeenth century onwards. BL Harley 686 is a seventeenth-century transcript, which omits the chronological table; Birch made extensive use of this manuscript in his editions of the St Augustine's charters, but it has

---

[2] Holtzmann, *Papsturkunden*, i. 69.
[3] Hunter 1973, pp. 218–19.

no independent value. There are also extracts in BL Cotton Vitellius E. xiv (Joscelin), BL Harley 539 (Stowe), BL Harley 692 (Agard from Joscelin), BL Harley 1757, BL Sloane 1301, BL Lansdowne 229, BL Burney 368 and BL Add. 4936. Twysden prints the chronological table (*Scriptores*, cols 2229–2291).

l. *Canterbury, D. & C., Chart. Ant. F. 47* (O)

This is a document consisting of a single membrane, with copies of eight St Augustine's charters relating to Fordwich on the face, and a list of Fordwich customs on the dorse.[4] An early modern endorsement mentions the date 1321, but that seems too early; this is probably a fifteenth-century document. The first two charters on the face are the two writs of Edward the Confessor, **39** and **35**, the latter in both vernacular and Latin versions. These are followed by various Fordwich writs and charters from the reign of William I. The document has been damaged and is rather worn, and the texts of the two pre-Conquest writs have suffered particularly, although they are still largely legible under ultraviolet light.

m. *Bodleian, Tanner 165 (SC 9991)* (P)

The register of William de Molash, prior of Christ Church, Canterbury, dated 1428, has an inserted singleton (fo. 77) with a copy of **2**; this is the only pre-Conquest document in the manuscript, and the hand does not appear elsewhere. This text of **2** has been slightly adapted to emphasize that the grant included the abbey precincts, through the addition of a short phrase to the boundary clause. It is not clear why a version of a St Augustine's charter adapted in this way should have been present in the Christ Church archives. In the sixteenth century this text was used for collation with another version of **2** in CCCC 111 (see below).

n. *Winchester, Cathedral Library, XXB* (Q)

It appears that a register of monastic foundation charters was compiled during the 1530s by (Sir) John Prise, an associate of Thomas Cromwell. Numerous copies of this register were made during the sixteenth and seventeenth centuries, in some of which the contents were reorganised and extra documents added. The relationship of the various copies has not yet been fully elucidated, but it seems that the earliest surviving representative of the register is the version in a manuscript in Winchester Cathedral Library,

---

[4] *Fifth Report of the Royal Commission on Historical Manuscripts* (London, 1876), App. p. 442.

apparently a fair copy made by Prise's secretary, William Say. Other copies are to be found in: CCCC 111, pp. 187–317; BL Harley 358, fos 27–70 (wrongly attributed to Leland); Bodleian, Dugdale 11 (SC 6501); Bodleian, Rawl. B. 252; Bodleian, Eng. hist. c. 241; BL Lansdowne 447; London, Soc. of Antiquaries, 128; and a sixteenth-century manuscript in the possession of Dr Simon Keynes.[5]

Prise would have had the opportunity to examine original charters as they came into the Royal registry. It has not yet been demonstrated whether the majority of the foundation charters in Prise's collection could have been taken from the originals, but this may well have been the case with the two St Augustine's charters which were included (**1, 2**). This point is discussed in the commentaries to the texts. The copies of **1** in the manuscripts derived from the Prise-Say register are distinguished by a particular variant, the omission of the last word of the boundary clause and the first word of the dating clause. In the version of Prise's register in CCCC 111, the text of **2** has been collated with the slightly revised version found in Bodleian, Tanner 165 (P).

ii. Copies on the Charter and Patent Rolls

By the fourteenth century it had become a common procedure for earlier charters to be confirmed by the king in the form of Inspeximus charters, which were issued as separate documents, but also enrolled in the Chancery. In 1326 St Augustine's offered a number of early charters for confirmation, including eight pre-Conquest texts (**1, 3, 5, 21, 27, 33, 34, 39**). The result was an Inspeximus charter which was copied onto the Charter Roll for that year: 20 Edw. II, m. 2 (R). A good contemporary copy of this Inspeximus appears in a quire inserted into BL Cotton Claudius D. x (G*). In 1362 Edward III issued a second Inspeximus, incorporating that of his father: Ch. R. 36 Edw. III, m. 7 (S). A copy of this charter was added to the recension of William Thorne's history in BL Add. 53710 (see above, p. lvi). Edward III's Inspeximus was subsequently enrolled on four occasions: Ch. R. 8 Hen. IV, m. 6 (T); Pat. R. 2 Hen. VI, pt 3, m. 5 (U); Pat. R. 4 Edw. IV, pt 4, m. 29 (V); Pat. R. 14 Hen. VII, pt 1, m. 16 (W). In the last instance a copy of **2** has been incorporated within the Inspeximus; the circumstances

---

[5] For Prise himself see N. Ker, 'Sir John Prise', reprinted in his collected papers, *Books, Collectors and Libraries: Studies in the Medieval Heritage*, ed. A.G. Watson (London, 1985), pp. 471–95. His register of monastic foundation charters was well-known to other antiquaries (*ibid.*, pp. 472–3), but until recently it was not thought to have survived. See the forthcoming discussion of the register and its copies by Simon Keynes, *Anglo-Saxon Charters*.

under which this occurred are mysterious.[6] **35** was offered for enrolment alongside the Inspeximus charter in Henry IV's reign (Ch. R. 8 Hen IV, m. 6 [T]), and was copied with it on the Patent Rolls later in the fifteenth century (U, V).

The Inspeximus charters are chiefly important because they preserve good texts of **21** and **27**. Both are charters in favour of laymen, which were converted into direct grants to St Augustine's in the cartulary versions. In the case of **27** the Inspeximus text has also retained a vernacular boundary clause which was omitted by the cartularists. The charters of Edward II and his son are also useful witnesses to the current state of the fabricated 'foundation' charters, which had a turbulent textual history. It seems to have been normal practice for churches to submit documents for confirmation in the form of single sheets, and so the choice of these eight texts is of some interest, and could be an indication of those pre-Conquest charters which were still available in single-sheet form in the fourteenth century (see p. xxxiii).

iii. *Other manuscripts*

a. *BL Cotton Faustina A. i* ('The Black Book of St Augustine's'). This is a register compiled in the abbey towards the end of the thirteenth century, which is comparable to the contemporary 'Red Book' (BL Cotton Claudius D. x) in its careful organisation, although it is generally a much less impressive volume. It consists of a rental and customary, followed by a collection of charters relating to the abbey's acquisition of minor estates in the post-Conquest period.[7] Only one pre-Conquest document is included, Edward the Confessor's writ concerning Fordwich (**39**), which, together with a similar writ of William I, is prefixed to a Fordwich custumal. The language of the writ has been modernised and the copy here is of no textual importance; an edition is already available.

b. *PRO E 132/1, no. 2*, is a collection of separate membranes with transcripts of monastic charters, probably put together at the end of the thirteenth century. Membrane 12 contains copies of seven writs and charters from St Augustine's, all relating to sake and soke and similar jurisdictions. The

---

[6] See the *Tenth Report of the Deputy-Keeper of the Public Records* (London, 1849), p. 11. I thank Dr Nigel Ramsay for drawing this reference to my attention.
[7] Davis, *Cartularies*, no. 194. The whole manuscript was edited by G. Turner and H.E. Salter, *The Register of St Augustine's Abbey, Canterbury, commonly called the Black Book*, 2 vols, British Academy Records of Social and Economic History ii-iii (London, 1915–24).

collection begins with a copy of **35**, and continues with subsequent confirmations up to the time of Henry III.

c. *Canterbury, D. & C., Reg. A* (s. xv). An incomplete copy of **10** appears
in this Christ Church register.

d. Copies of the *Prise-Say register* (see above, pp. lix–lx), which incorporates
the texts of **1** and **2**: CCCC 111, pp. 310–11 (s. xvi); BL Harley 358 (s. xvi);
MS *penes* S.D. Keynes (s. xvi); Bodleian, Dugdale 11 (s. xvii); Bodleian,
Rawl. B. 252 (s. xvii); BL Lansdowne 447 (s. xvii); Bodleian, Eng. hist. c.
241 (s. xvii); London, Soc. Antiquaries, 128 (s. xvii).

e. *BL Lansdowne 863*, 90rv (s. xvi). Copies of **1** and **2** from CCCC 111.

f. *PRO DL 42/149* (s. xvi/xvii). Collection of drawings of seals and other
items of antiquarian and heraldic interest, mostly in the hand of John
Guillim (died May 1621), with additions by Joseph Holland of Devon. On
107v is a brief summary of **44**, said to have been taken from 'the Legier
book of St Augustine's of Canterbury'. BL Cotton Julius C. vii seems to be
a copy of this collection, with the same summary of **44** on 187v.

g. *Bodleian, Add. C. 296 (SC 27610)*, fos 75–88 (s. xvii). Bishop Ussher's
transcription of BL Cotton Vitellius A. ii, fos 3–19 (D).

h. *Bodleian, Dodsworth 10*, 7rv, 24r (s. xvii). Copies of **10** and **44**, apparently
taken from Spelman's *Councils*, plus a copy of **1** (probably from the Prise-Say
register) and an abbreviated copy of **29**.

i. *BL Dodsworth 120*, 115rv (s. xvii). Copy of **1**, probably from the Prise-Say
register.

5. THE AUTHENTICITY OF THE CHARTERS

The reputation of the St Augustine's archive has for a long time been affected
by the presence of a small number of very notorious and controversial
forgeries, principally relating to the foundation, which have tended to
monopolize discussion and to overshadow the rest of the archive. Certain
other factors have further contributed to the unsatisfactory impression. In
the first place, there are no single-sheet charters and no single reliable

cartulary. The majority of the documents are preserved only as late copies, scattered through a number of generally unsystematic cartularies, frequently shorn of boundary clauses and with curtailed witness-lists. This has made it difficult to appreciate properly the content and quality of the archive. A complication is that St Augustine's monks were prone to tampering with the texts of some of their earliest documents. In three cases (**16**, **21**, **27**) the survival of two versions of a text enables us to see that a charter in favour of a layman was altered to create a direct grant to the monastery; it is possible that other charters were also doctored in this way. More unusual, and of great interest, is the alteration of names and dates in some documents to bring them into line with an incorrect chronological framework for the early Anglo-Saxon period. Such interference seems to have taken place from the thirteenth to the fifteenth centuries, and to have involved in some cases the creation of single-sheet versions of emended texts. As a result, Thomas Elmham used and transmitted contaminated material in painstakingly accurate texts, and later scholars have been badly misled. I discuss this phenomenon in greater detail on pp. xcvi–cv.

Another characteristic of the archive which hampers criticism is the high proportion of very early charters. Even if the five forgeries associated with the foundation are left out of consideration, it is still the case that twenty-four out of forty-eight documents are dated or datable to the later seventh or eighth centuries. Diplomatic discussion of such early charters is handicapped by the relatively small number of originals with which to compare cartulary texts. In this period the diplomatic forms were still very fluid, as the scribes assimilated their models and created their own distinctive types of document. In the absence of sufficient originals it can be difficult to decide whether or not an untypical feature, such as the use of a calendar date in a seventh-century charter, is a reason for suspicion. It is important to be flexible and avoid dogmatism in evaluating early charters, but it is also vital to remember that it is the earliest documents which are most likely to have been revised or interpolated. The particular character of early Kentish diplomatic is considered at length on pp. lxxi–lxxxv.

Behind the smokescreen thrown up by the foundation forgeries and the unsatisfactory transmission, the tampering and the diplomatic difficulties, the St Augustine's archive turns out to be composed, in the main, of quite acceptable documents, many of them of considerable historical importance. A notable feature is the variety of types of charter which have been preserved. As well as royal land-charters, there are several private deeds in which members of the laity make grants of land and food-renders to the monastery. There are two archiepiscopal charters, one detailing an exchange between

St Augustine's and Minster-in-Thanet. There are two royal grants of privileges to the Kentish churches, one of which survives only in this archive. Most intriguing is the collection of five ship-toll privileges from Minster-in-Thanet, a concentration which has no parallel elsewhere.

The following is a summary guide to conclusions about the authenticity of individual documents, which are outlined in more detail in the commentaries.

i. *Charters from St Augustine's*

a. *The 'foundation' forgeries*

The archive contains three charters of Æthelberht I of Kent dated 605 (1–3), and an associated privilege of Bishop Augustine (4). There is also a charter in the name of Æthelberht's son, Eadbald, dated 618 (5). These five documents must be considered in conjunction with five papal privileges, purportedly issued by Boniface IV, Adeodatus, Agatho and John XII, of which only the privilege in the name of Agatho seems to have an authentic basis.[8] These royal charters and papal privileges appear to have been fabricated during the second half of the eleventh century in order to provide documentation for the earliest period of the abbey's history, and to bolster claims about the abbey's 'apostolic' status (for the background, see above, pp. xxi–xxiv). Eight of these ten documents (excluding 1 and 5) survive in copies written in the first quarter of the twelfth century.

In a celebrated study, Wilhelm Levison argued that 1-5 and the papal privileges, together with a charter of the Confessor relating to Mildrith and Thanet (34), were forged around 1070, at the time when Abbot Æthelsige fled the country and the Norman Abbot Scotland was imposed on St Augustine's.[9] He suggested that the forger should be identified with Guerno, a monk of Saint-Medard in Soissons who died between 1119 and 1131, confessing on his deathbed that he had fabricated privileges for a number of houses, including St Augustine's.[10] Levison's arguments are most persuasive, but there are difficulties which suggest that the stages of fabrication may have been more complicated. The chronology seems rather forced,

---

[8] The papal privileges are BCS 11, 31, 38, 915, 916. See H.H. Anton, *Studien zu den Klosterprivilegien der Päpste im frühen Mittelalter*, Beiträge zur Geschichte und Quellenkunde des Mittelalters 4 (Berlin and New York, 1975), pp. 66-7.

[9] Levison, *England and the Continent*, pp. 174–233.

[10] See *Literae Cantuarienses: the Letter Books of the Monastery of Christ Church, Canterbury*, ed. J.B. Sheppard, 3 vols, RS (London, 1887–9), iii. 365–6 (Appendix, no. 21); Levison, *England and the Continent*, pp. 206–23.

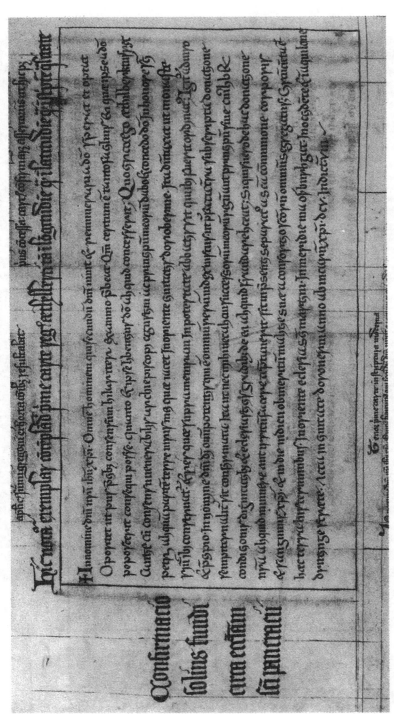

PLATE 1

Cambridge, Trinity Hall, 1, fol. 21v. Thomas Elmham's 'facsimile' of 1 (MS N1)

PLATE 2

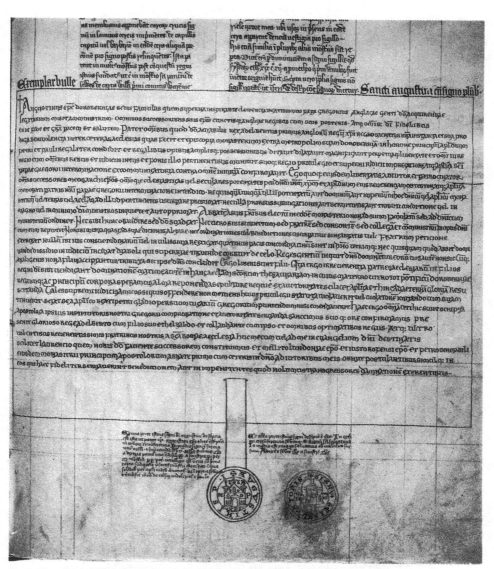

Cambridge, Trinity Hall, 1, fol. 24r. Thomas Elmham's 'facsimile' of 4 (MS N1)

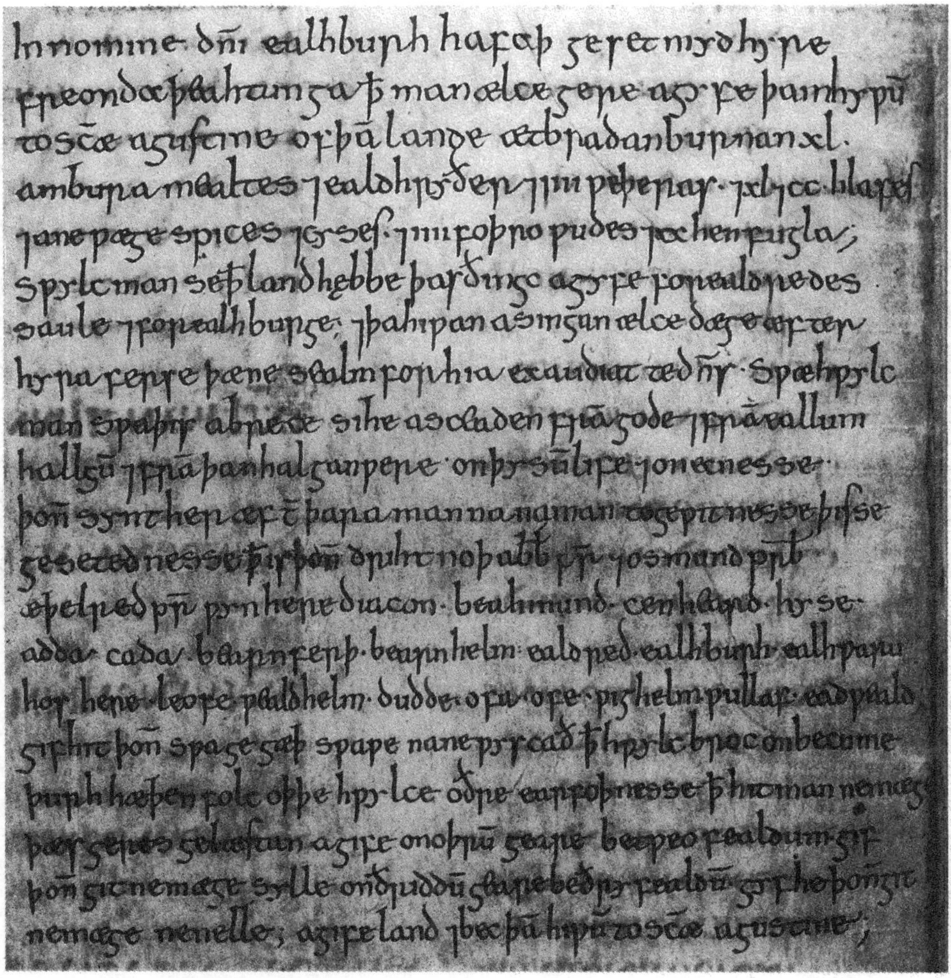

PLATE 3

In nomine· dñi· ealhburh hafaþ geredny ðhy·re
freondæ þeahtam ga þ man ælce gere agyfe þam hy pū
to sce aguſtine of þā lande æt bradan bunnan xl·
ambua mealtes ⁊ ealdhy ðen ⁊ iii pe be nay· ⁊ xl cc blaueſ
⁊ ane pege spices ⁊ g seſ· ⁊ iiii ſob no pudes ⁊ x hennfugla·
ſpyle man seþ land hebbe þay ðinge agy ſe ſon ealdnedeſ
ſaule ⁊ ſon ealhbunge· ⁊ þa hi pan aſ m gun ælce dage oþ ten
hy þa geþe þæne ſealm ſon hia exaudiat æd ñy· ſpæ hpyle
man ſpa þiſ ablende ſihe aſclaðen ſ a ð gode ⁊ þrā vallum
hallg ū ⁊ þrā þan halgan peſe on hyſ ū life ⁊ on ecneſſe·
þon ſyn þeſ cep þ þay a man na ngman ooge pi nedge hiſe
geſetednedge þiſ þon ðyhit noþ alb þū· ⁊ oſmand þrū
eþelued þrū· þyn hene diacon· beahtmund· cenhelard· hyſe
adda· cada· baunſeþþ· beanhelm· ealo ned· ealhbunh· ealhþayu
hoſ· hene· leoſe· pealdhelm· dudde· oſu· oſe· pyhelm pullaſ· eadſealo
ſyhtſe þon ſpa ge geþ ſpaþe nane ſy ſcað þ hyſ lc þ no conbecume
þurh hæþen ſolc oþþe hyſ lce oðne· eaſ ſoſneaoe· þ hio man nomæg
þaſ ſeyeſ ſolæſtan agyſe onoþrū geſe· beþeo ſealdu m giſ
þon ſ it ne mæge ſylle ondyddū ſla pe beð hyſ ſealoū· ſy þ he þoſ y r
ne mæge nenelle· agyſe land ⁊ bec þū hyſ ū to sce aguſtine·

Cambridge, Corpus Christi College, 286, fol. 74v (24)

PLATE 4

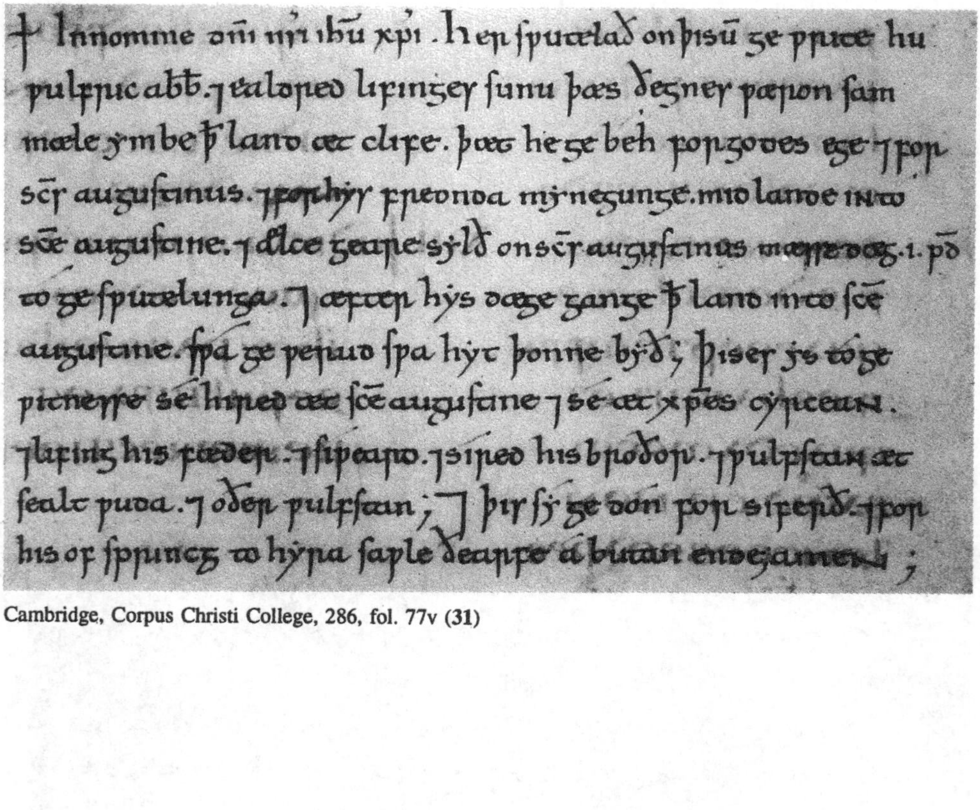

+ In nomine dñi nr̃i ihũ xp̃i . Her er sputelað on þisũ ge write hu
wulfric abb. 7 ealored lifingey sunu þæs ðegner wæron sam
mæle ymbe þ land æt clife. þæt he ge beh for godes ege 7 for
sc̃e augustinus. 7 for þyr freonda mynegunge. mid lande into
sc̃e augustine. 7 ælce geare syld on sc̃e augustinus mæsse dæg .i. pð
to ge sputelunga. 7 æfter hys dæge gange þ land into sc̃e
augustine. swa ge ferud swa hyt þonne byð; þiser ys to ge
witnerre se hired æt sc̃e augustine 7 se æt xp̃es cyrcean.
7 lifing his fæder . 7 siweard . 7 sired his broðor . 7 wulfstan æt
sealt wuda . 7 oðer wulfstan ; 7 þir sy ge don for sireðe . 7 for
his or springe to hyra saule ðearfe a butan endegance ;

Cambridge, Corpus Christi College, 286, fol. 77v (31)

since there is a gap of at least half a century between the time when Guerno is supposed to have been working for St Augustine's and the date of his death. Moreover, there is some reason to believe that these eleven documents were not produced at the same time by a single agency. For instance, there are clear signs of development, and different methods of production, in the three charters attributed to King Æthelberht. **1** was largely modelled on an eighth-century charter, perhaps an original charter of King Æthelberht II which was partly erased and rewritten. **1** in turn formed the model for **2**, which seems to have been intended to supersede it. **3** was almost certainly produced at a later date, for it includes details which suggest that an unsatisfactory 'foundation charter' was already in existence; it was probably forged in association with **4**. **5** and **39** may have been fabricated by different agents, for different purposes. In a separate study I have argued that the forgery of these royal charters and papal privileges took place over a period of time in the second half of the eleventh century. The process of fabrication may have begun as early as the decade 1060–70, and it is possible that the earliest of the forged documents were initially intended to celebrate the abbey's early history and exalted status; they may have been associated with a campaign to promote the abbey's status in the eyes of the pope (see above pp. xxi–xxii). When the climate changed in 1070 and the abbey's independence was seriously assailed by Archbishop Lanfranc and his successors, further documents were produced at intervals for polemical purposes. Guerno's participation in the project may belong to a later stage and, since the documentation concerning him indicates that his forged privileges were exposed and destroyed after his death, it could be the case that none of the extant fabrications represent his work. Subsequently the charters of Augustine and Æthelberht (excluding **1**), and the papal privileges, were treated as a corpus of evidence, but this attitude to them may not have developed until the twelfth century or even later.[11]

b. *The remaining charters from St Augustine's*

After the forgeries in the name of Æthelberht and Eadbald the earliest document in the St Augustine's archive is **6**, a charter in the name of King Hlothhere datable to 675. If genuine, this would be the oldest surviving Kentish charter, comparable in date to S 1164 from Wessex and S 1165 from Surrey, and four years older than S 8 from Reculver, the earliest surviving original charter. But the authenticity of **6** remains uncertain, and a diplomatic case can be made that it was rewritten or fabricated on the basis of an

---

[11] Kelly 1988. There is further discussion in the commentaries to the separate charters.

eighth-century model. **6** has a complex relationship with **40**, a seventh-century charter in the Minster archive, and with two lost charters in the name of Hlothhere (for these see Appendix 1, no. i).

7 is a charter of King Eadric datable to 686. Much of its formulation is acceptably early and, despite a few difficulties, it appears to be genuine. The same seems to be true of charters in favour of St Augustine's issued by Kings Oswine and Wihtred (**8, 9**).

10 is a charter of privileges for the Kentish churches, issued by King Wihtred in 699. A ninth-century single-sheet copy survives in the Christ Church archive, probably based on a text which came to Christ Church from Lyminge or Reculver. **10** appears to be authentic. At St Augustine's the text underwent some interference, and in Elmham's version the regnal year and indiction have been altered.

The next three charters from St Augustine's date from around the year 762. A considerable number of Kentish charters seem to have been issued in the 690s and in the 760s, but relatively few in the intervening years, so the gap in the St Augustine's archive is unlikely to be significant. **11** is an unusual document of 762 recording an exchange of facilities between St Augustine's and the royal vill at Wye, which is ratified by King Æthelberht II. The transaction is unique and the diplomatic is difficult to parallel, but there is nothing overtly suspicious and there seems no reason not to accept it as authentic. **12** is in the name of one of Æthelberht's thegns, and is one of the earliest charters in which the donor is not a king or a royal kinsman. The thegn was preparing to travel to Rome and wished beforehand to signal his intention of granting one of his estates to the abbey, but could not simply hand over the original landbook because it also related to other property; procedures for covering this eventuality had not yet been standardized, and the result was this unique document, a compromise between a will and a land charter. **13** is a straightforward land-grant to St Augustine's in the name of King Eadberht II. The formulation is acceptable for the 760s, which is also the date implied by the witness-list. In Elmham's version the regnal year has been altered as the result of confusion with King Eadberht I (see Appendix 3). Both **12** and **13** seem to be authentic.

14, a charter of King Offa in favour of an abbot of St Augustine's, causes considerable difficulty. The witness-list and some of the formulation seem contemporary, but the inclusion of a vernacular boundary clause is anachronistic in an eighth-century charter and indicates that some reworking has taken place, and the charter is dated by an impossible regnal year. There seems to be good reason to treat **14** as a post-Conquest forgery, partly based on a charter of Offa, rather than a genuine text corrupted in transmission.

Another charter of Offa in the archive is a grant of privileges to certain Kentish minsters (15), which seems acceptable, although it has lost its witness-list and a section in which the minsters themselves were listed.

16 has undergone later reworking. It appears originally to have recorded a joint grant of land at Lenham by Kings Coenwulf and Cuthred to their mutual kinsman, Eanberht. The beneficiary was later altered to Abbot Wernoth, in order to create a direct grant to St Augustine's. There was similar interference in the text of 21, a slightly later charter covering the same estate in favour of an ealdorman, where the name of Abbot Wernoth is again substituted (this may also have been the case with a third Lenham charter, 19, which survives only in a single copy). The emendation of 16 is betrayed because the revisor did not notice a second reference to the beneficiary later in the text and thus failed to change it. Remarkably, Elmham's version shows that 16 was emended a second time, with Wernoth's name being replaced by that of Abbot Cunred. The diplomatic of 16 suggests that it is fundamentally a genuine document of the early ninth century, but there are chronological difficulties with the witness-list, perhaps due to corruption as the result of repeated copying.

There are five further royal land-charters from the ninth century in the St Augustine's archive, all of them apparently authentic, although generally abbreviated. Three are directly in favour of abbots of St Augustine's (19, 20, 22) and one is a grant to a cleric living in the monastery, who may or may not have been a full member of the community (18). The fifth (21) is a charter in favour of an ealdorman, apparently covering the same estate as 16. The thirteenth-century cartularies contain a version of 21 in which Abbot Wernoth is the beneficiary; the name of the true beneficiary has been preserved because the original of 21 was offered for confirmation and enrolled in the fourteenth century.

Four other documents in the archive date from the ninth century. 17 is the record of an exchange of land between St Augustine's and Minster-in-Thanet, conducted under the supervision of Archbishop Wulfred. It seems acceptable, although the witness-list has been abbreviated. The charter is probably from St Augustine's rather than Minster, although it is impossible to be entirely certain of this. In 23 a layman grants land in Romney Marsh to his friend, who subsequently transferred it to St Augustine's (23A). The extant text is abbreviated, but the document seems authentic. In addition, there are two vernacular charters in which members of the laity grant food-renders to St Augustine's; similar and contemporary grants to Christ Church survive as originals. 24 is extant in a pre-Conquest copy in a gospel-book. 25 was copied into one of the thirteenth-century cartularies, in a modernized version.

The St Augustine's archive contains five tenth-century royal diplomas, of which three are grants of land to laymen (**27, 28, 30**). **28** has an addition (perhaps suspicious) in which the beneficiary transfers the land to St Augustine's. The abbey's cartularies preserve a version of **27** in which the beneficiary has been transformed from a thegn into an abbot (who subsequently appeared in the abbey's lists of its abbots, complete with fictional dates; see Appendix 4). These three diplomas seem to be fundamentally authentic. The two royal charters from this period directly in favour of the abbey are less straightforward. **26** records Athelstan's restoration of land in Thanet to St Augustine's. Its form is unparalleled, but the witness-list and some of the internal details seem to be contemporary. The name-forms are unusually corrupt, even for a St Augustine's text. It may perhaps be an unconventional but authentic document or it could be a reworking of some brief memorandum. **29** is even more difficult. This is a charter of Edgar granting land at Plumstead to the abbey; it may be significant that Plumstead was the subject of dispute in the eleventh century. The witness-list, unfortunately curtailed, seems to belong to a genuine charter of Edgar, but the formulation of the main text is largely ninth-century and may indeed be modelled on that of S 332, which is known to have entered the archive in the later ninth century (see above, p. xxxii). This document would appear to have been drawn up at St Augustine's, and is probably a forgery.

From the turn of the tenth century comes a vernacular record of an agreement between the abbot of St Augustine's and a layman (**31**). This was copied into a gospel-book at around the same time as the agreement was made.

Three of the eleventh-century charters in the archive seem to be authentic. **36** is the Confessor's grant of a small estate to Archbishop Eadsige, which he transferred to St Augustine's in **37**, probably a separate document. There is also a brief Latin charter in the name of the Kentish nobleman Æthelric Bigga, in which he grants to the abbey the reversion of two properties after the death of his tenants (**38**). Apart from these we find four writs, two in the name of Cnut and two of the Confessor. Cnut's writs (**32, 33**) survive only in Latin versions, and neither seems acceptable. **32** appears to be based on **35**, the Confessor's grant of similar privileges, while **33** is to be linked with the later controversy over Mildrith's relics. The two writs of Edward (**35, 39**) are preserved in Old English versions which seem to be authentic.

The final charter in the archive is **34**, an elaborate forgery relating to the acquisition of the Minster property. In making the Confessor rather than Cnut the donor, **34** seems to follow an early version of events, and it probably came into existence in the decades immediately after the Conquest, at around the same time as **1-5**, with which it has points of similarity. It may predate **33**, in which Cnut is presented as the donor of the Minster estates.

ii. *The Minster charters*

The St Augustine's archive contains fourteen charters from Minster-in-Thanet. It is possible that three other documents (**10**, **15** and **17**) derive from Minster rather than St Augustine's, but there is not sufficient evidence to argue the point. Eight of the Minster charters record royal land-grants to Abbess Æbba and her successor, Mildrith, and are datable to between 689 and 727. A curious text from 695 purports to transfer jurisdiction of the minster from the king to the abbess. The five remaining charters are all concerned with the exemption of the community's ships from payment of toll at the port of London and elsewhere. The latest of these five toll-privileges belongs to 763 or 764; the oldest are difficult to date, but one may have been issued as early as 716 or 717. Part of the Minster archive appears to have disappeared since the later eleventh century, when the hagiographer Goscelin saw charters relating to the activities of an abbess in the early ninth century (see p. xxvi).

The earliest charters in the archive are in the names of two (or perhaps three) of the obscure kings who ruled Kent in the years after the death of Eadric in 686. **40** was issued by King Suebhardus in 689, and confirmed by Æthelred of Mercia in 691. Suebhardus was probably the same man as the Suabertus who issued **41** (see Appendix 3). Two further charters (**42**, **43**) were issued by King Oswine, who also made a grant of land to St Augustine's at around the same time (**8**). All four Minster charters are concerned with grants of land on Thanet itself and on the mainland opposite the island in the region of Sturry, although **41** also mentions an outlying estate at Bodsham. There can be no doubt that all four documents have an authentic basis, although all are difficult. **41**, **42** and **43** seem fundamentally acceptable, but **40** presents significant problems, and may have been rewritten and reworked on more than one occasion; it was perhaps intended to function as a foundation charter for the community, giving title to the core of the endowment on Thanet. The contradictions in the text of **40** attracted the attention of the revisors of the St Augustine's muniments, who edited out a difficult passage detailing earlier land-grants to Minster; they altered the incarnation date of Æthelred's confirmation to 676, to associate it with the Mercian invasion of Kent in that year, and they altered the indiction to agree with this. Finally they seem to have produced a single-sheet copy of the doctored text, which misled Elmham (see pp. ci–cii).

Considerable problems also attach themselves to **44**, a charter of Wihtred granting land to Minster, datable to 694. The diplomatic of this text seems essentially acceptable. The difficulty lies in its complex relationship with two spurious charters in the Christ Church archive, which throws doubt on certain details in **44**, but a good case can be made that **44** is probably to be accepted as it stands. A second charter of Wihtred granting land to Minster (**46**) is also likely to be authentic, although some of the formulation is unconventional.

The least convincing document in the archive is **45**, in which Wihtred states that Abbess Mildrith and her successors are to have the *defensio* of Minster-in-Thanet as it had previously been held by the kings his ancestors. This seems to reflect a preoccupation with jurisdiction, which would be more appropriate in a document from the late Anglo-Saxon period. **45** exists in two versions, neither diplomatically satisfactory, and its details have a suspicious link with the preamble of Wihtred's lawcode. It seems to be darkly significant that **45** is in favour of Abbess Mildrith, although there is evidence elsewhere that Abbess Æbba was still alive in 695. **45** is surely a fabrication.

The two latest land-charters in the archive are respectively in the names of Æthelberht and Eadberht, sons of Wihtred (**47**, **48**). These two documents are nearly identical. Æthelberht issued **47** before Wihtred's death and with his permission, and the charter is dated by Wihtred's regnal year to 724. **48** appears to belong to 727, three years after Wihtred died and his sons succeeded him as joint-rulers in Kent. There seem to be grounds for accepting both charters as essentially authentic (although the list of dens at the end of **47** is probably an addition). If this is the case, it would indicate that **48** was drawn up at Minster on the model of a charter received a few years previously.

The five ship-toll charters present some difficulties, but it seems likely that all of them are fundamentally authentic. They can conveniently be assessed in three categories. In the first are the two lengthy privileges of King Æthelbald of Mercia in favour of Abbesses Mildrith and Eadburh (**49**, **51**), which are directly comparable to ship-toll privileges in other archives. **49** is very close indeed to S 88, from Rochester, which is dated 734; this similarity could suggest an approximate date for **49**, which has only a very faulty dating clause (perhaps borrowed from **50**). **49** may also have derived its witness-list from **50**, which could imply that the text was in a deficient state at some stage. **51** is in many respects similar to S 1788, an earlier document from St Pauls.

The second category of Minster toll-charters is formed by **50**, Æthelbald's grant to Abbess Mildrith of apparently unrestricted toll-exemption on one ship throughout his kingdom, and **52**, which is Offa's confirmation of **50**. The formulation of these two documents is considerably less elaborate than that of **49**, **51** and their counterparts in other archives, and this has been seen as reason for suspicion. Nevertheless, it is probable that both documents are authentic, and possible that **50** may be datable to 716 or 717.

In a category of its own is **53**, issued by a Kentish king in 763 or 764 and relating to Kentish ports. It is to be compared to S 1612, issued by the same donor to Reculver at around the same time; the two charters seem to represent an imitation of earlier Mercian practice. The regnal year in Elmham's text of **53** has been emended, as was that of **13**, because of confusion between Eadberht I and Eadberht II (see Appendix 3).

6. THE DIPLOMATIC OF KENTISH CHARTERS

Early Kentish charters are considerably easier to analyse than those of any other region of Anglo-Saxon England, due to the preservation of an unparalleled number of original charters in the archive of Christ Church, Canterbury. We have nine apparent originals from Kent from the period before 800, against only five or six from Mercia, one each from the East Saxon and South Saxon kingdoms, and none from Wessex.[12] The disproportion is even more apparent in the ninth century. The archives of Christ Church and Rochester have preserved between them some forty-four apparent originals from the ninth century, most of them dealing with land in Kent, against only three from non-Kentish archives.[13] This munificence

---

[12] From Kent: S 8 (A.D. 679), 19 (A.D. 697 or 712), 23 (A.D. 732), 24 (A.D. 741), 31 (A.D. 748 × 760), 35 (A.D. 778), 123 (A.D. 785), 128 (A.D. 788), 155 (A.D. 799). S 21 is a copy of S 19 with an additional passage, perhaps written in the later eighth century. **10** may be a ninth-century facsimile copy of a charter of 699. From Mercia: S 89 (A.D. 736), 56 (A.D. 759), 106 (A.D. 767), 114 (A.D. 779), 139 (A.D. 793 × 796); it is possible that S 96 (A.D. 757) is also contemporary. S 1171 (c. A.D. 685 × 693) is an East Saxon original; S 1184 (A.D. 780) is the only surviving original from the Selsey archive. S 248 may be a facsimile copy of a charter of Ine of Wessex dated 705: L. Abrams, 'A Single-Sheet Facsimile of a Diploma of King Ine for Glastonbury', *The Archaeology and History of Glastonbury Abbey*, ed L. Abrams and J.P. Carley (Woodbridge, 1991), pp. 97–133.

[13] For ninth-century originals, see Brooks, *Church of Canterbury*, pp. 359–60 nn. 67 and 68. The non-Kentish originals are: S 190, 298 and 1270; plus a fragment (S 1861). S 173 is a Kentish charter preserved in the Worcester archive.

partly offsets the lack of any originals from St Augustine's and makes it possible to discuss with some confidence the defective texts in the archive.

Kentish charters have a distinctive chronological distribution over the pre-Conquest period. The relatively large number of Kentish charters that survive from the ninth century seems to reflect an unusually high rate of production as well as superior conditions of preservation. Responsibility for this can in part be laid at the door of Archbishop Wulfred (805–32), who engaged in large-scale property-transactions and was clearly aware of the importance of comprehensive documentary records.[14] Another contributing factor is likely to have been have been the West Saxon invasion of Kent, which would have led to redistribution of land formerly under Mercian control. In the tenth century also Kent departs from the norm, but in the opposite direction. From 930 onwards, until the turn of the century, the rate of charter-production in southern and central England accelerated to a new level, a development probably to be connected with the unification of the kingdom and and perhaps also with the emergence of a royal secretariat.[15] But relatively few of the royal diplomas issued during this period are concerned with grants of land in Kent; there is a marked contrast with other areas from which charters survive. This can perhaps be seen as the inevitable concomitant of the ninth-century Kentish boom in charter-production; Kent is an area where the amount of cultivable land is limited, so it is possible that most of the land had already been booked in the ninth century, making the production of new diplomas unnecessary (since an existing charter could be handed over when the property changed hands). A similar explanation has been put forward for the apparent steep decline in the production of royal diplomas which is observable throughout England in the eleventh century;[16] Kent would therefore have experienced the phenomenon at an earlier date. However, this is unlikely to be the full explanation for the relatively small number of tenth-century Kentish charters. It may, for example, be significant that Kent, with its limited geographical area, contained two bishoprics and one major monastery in the tenth century, all of them with extensive endowments concentrated in Kent. Land once in ecclesiastical possession tended to stay there, which may have restricted the circulation of land in Kent. The content of the St Augustine's archive is consistent with the local pattern of chronological distribution; the survival

[14] Wulfred's activities are analysed by Brooks, *Church of Canterbury*, pp. 132–42.
[15] The evidence for centralized production in a royal secretariat is marshalled by S. Keynes, *The Diplomas of King Æthelred 'the Unready' 978–1016: a Study in their Use as Historical Evidence* (Cambridge, 1980), pp. 14–83.
[16] Keynes, *Diplomas*, pp. 140–5.

of eight Latin and two vernacular charters from the ninth century contrasts with the preservation of only five Latin diplomas (and perhaps one vernacular document) from the tenth.

The considerable number of original charters surviving from Kent also makes it possible to speculate about the agencies responsible for their production. Brooks's palaeographical and diplomatic analysis of the ninth-century originals from Christ Church has led him to the conclusion that at this time the individual episcopal scriptoria may have had general responsibility for drawing up charters relating to land and beneficiaries within each diocese.[17] During this period distinctive formulas were devised and used at Christ Church, which make it possible to distinguish charters written there from those drawn up in the Rochester diocese, or in Wessex or Mercia. The occasional charter which was produced in unusual circumstances highlights the differences; an example is **21**, which deals with land in Kent but which was issued at Wilton and drawn up in West Saxon formulas. This instance apart, St Augustine's charters from the ninth century are very similar to their counterparts in the Christ Church archive and were presumably drawn up in the archiepiscopal scriptorium or in accordance with model texts supplied from it.

The evidence for production in the period before the ninth century is not so clearcut, in part because proportionately fewer charters survive: the Christ Church archive itself is deficient for the period before 798, and the earlier charters which it preserves are from minsters which later came under archiepiscopal control. Below it is argued that during the seventh and eighth centuries it was usual for the individual Kentish minsters to be involved in the drafting of charters of which they were the beneficiaries. The domination of the archiepiscopal scriptorium in the process of charter-writing perhaps began in the late eighth century. From the tenth century onwards, royal charters dealing with land in Kent generally have no distinctive regional formulation and instead follow the conventions of the central agency responsible for charter-production throughout the kingdom.

i. *Period 1 (to c. 750)*

The earliest surviving land-charters from England date from the 670s. From Kent there is S 8, an apparent original datable to 679 (and also perhaps **6** from 675, although its authenticity is questionable). S 1165 from Chertsey in Surrey, usually given the dating limits 672 × 674, has a genuine

---

[17] Brooks, *Church of Canterbury*, pp. 167–74, 327–30.

basis. S 1164, which covers a Dorset estate, is a slightly revised version of an authentic charter issued between 670 and 676. The archives of Bath, Malmesbury and St Paul's in London have preserved documents which, although not acceptable in their present form, appear to be in part based on genuine charters from the 670s.[18] The evidence superficially appears to suggest that it was this decade which saw the introduction of the practice of charter-writing into Anglo-Saxon England; a possible catalyst would be the arrival of Theodore and Hadrian, and the re-establishment of the English Church. But closer analysis of the surviving seventh-century charters reveals characteristics of formulation which are difficult to reconcile with a relatively recent introduction, and which seem rather to be the result of a longer period of evolution and development. Anglo-Saxon charters from the period share common features of construction, most notably a religious sanction and a form of witness-list in which the autograph element is suppressed. But regional characteristics are already apparent, and there is a considerable variety of formulation; if the practice of charter-writing was inspired by a recent initiative from Canterbury, we might expect to find more uniformity and a reliance on a more limited range of models. It also appears significant that Anglo-Saxon charter-scribes working in the later seventh century had already to a considerable degree assimilated the continental models on which the Anglo-Saxon diploma was ultimately based; formulas and formulation associated with the late Roman private deed can be traced in the early English charters, but they have to a large extent been subsumed into a native diplomatic tradition. The implication of these observations is that charter-writing was no novelty in England in the 670s, but probably goes back to an earlier date, conceivably to the time of Augustine and his fellow Roman missionaries. In this context, it is revealing that one of the models used by the English draftsmen may have been a charter of 587 in which Gregory the Deacon (later Pope Gregory the Great) makes a grant to his

---

[18] For S 1165 see A. Scharer, *Die angelsächsische Königsurkunde im 7. und 8. Jahrhundert* (Vienna, Cologne and Graz, 1982), pp. 133–6. S 1164 and S 1256 form a single document put together in 759 by Bishop Cyneheard of Winchester, who slightly revised the text of a charter of 670 × 676 in the aftermath of a dispute-settlement and appended his own statement about the reasons for this; for an edition and full discussion, see *The Charters of Shaftesbury*, ed. S.E. Kelly, Anglo-Saxon Charters v (forthcoming). From Bath: S 51 (see P. Sims-Williams, 'St Wilfrid and Two Charters dated A.D. 676 and 680', *Journal of Ecclesiastical History* xxxix (1988), pp. 163–83, at 165–74). From Malmesbury: S 1245 (only the witness-list is authentic; see H. Edwards, *The Charters of the West Saxon Kingdom*, British Archaeological Reports (British series) 198 (1988), pp. 85–7). S 5 is a spurious St Paul's charter which incorporates a witness-list from 670 × 676. S 1247 is an episcopal charter of 678 from Chertsey which seems generally acceptable (see also S 1246 from Barking, an adaptation of a similar privilege).

monastery of Saint Andrew on the Caelian, the fount of the missionary effort to the Anglo-Saxons; it seems most likely that a copy of this deed (and perhaps of others in the archive) reached England in the time of Augustine or his immediate successors.[19]

The surviving Kentish charters from the period between the 670s and the mid eighth century tend to share certain common details of formulation, which amount to a recognisable local style. But within this common framework there is considerable diversity of formulation, and this can be taken as evidence for decentralised production within the kingdom, probably within the separate minsters, which would be have been exposed both to local influences and to different external stimuli; for instance, it has been suggested that some of the unusual characteristics of S 19 (A.D. 699 or 712) from the minster at Lyminge can be laid at the door of that community's particular Northumbrian links.[20]

The impression of diversity and decentralised production is reinforced by a consideration of the four Kentish documents from the period which appear to be originals, together with the single-sheet version of 10 which appears to be an early 'facsimile' of a lost seventh-century original. S 8 (A.D. 679) is a charter in favour of Reculver minster, written in uncials, and in the form of a tall rectangle (vertical format); the witness-list was added later (with a narrower pen). The scribe of the Lyminge charter of 699 or 712 (S 19) preferred a horizontal format and a high grade of hybrid minuscule; text and witness-list were written on the same occasion, and the dating clause placed at the end of the document. 10, datable to 699, is apparently a ninth-century copy of an original from Lyminge or Reculver; since this is a grant of general privileges to the Kentish churches, it can probably be assumed that it was orginally produced in multiple copies (perhaps all written in the archiepiscopal scriptorium). In 10 the format is again horizontal, but the witness-list is now arranged in true columns; layout on the page suggests that in the original the dating clause and witness-list may have been added on a later occasion. S 23 (A.D. 732), another charter from Lyminge, returns to the vertical format. It was written in two stages, the first scribe contributing

[19] For discussion of these issues see P. Chaplais, 'Who Introduced Charters into England? The Case for Augustine', *Journal of the Society of Archivists*, iii.10 (1969), pp. 526–42 (reprinted in *Prisca Munimenta*, ed. F. Ranger (London, 1973), pp. 88–107); P. Wormald, *Bede and the Conversion of England: the Charter Evidence*, Jarrow Lecture 1984 (Jarrow, [1985]); S.E. Kelly, 'Anglo-Saxon Lay Society and the Written Word', *The Uses of Literary in Early Medieval Europe*, ed. R. McKitterick (Cambridge, 1990), pp. 36–62. For Gregory's charter see *Gregorii Papae Registrum Epistolarum*, ed. L.M. Hartmann, 2 vols, MGH (Berlin, 1891–9), ii. 437–9
[20] Chaplais 1969, pp. 538–9 (p. 102).

the main text and (after a substantial gap) three subscriptions, while the second scribe added a notice of a secondary donation in the gap and also wrote another four subscriptions; in this case it seems probable that the first scribe drew up the document before the conveyance ceremony and the second scribe completed it afterwards. S 24 (A.D. 741) is likely to be a contemporary charter, although there is a problem with the dating clause. Once more the format is horizontal; although the charter has a holograph appearance, there is a possibility that the dating clause and witness-list were written after horizontal folding (implying two-stage production).

These five Kentish documents from a sixty-year period thus exhibit variations in layout and drafting procedures, which are paralleled by variety and diversity of formulation. They seem to mirror decentralized and dis-organised production, largely (but not exclusively) by the beneficiaries of the charters themselves, and they also provide a warning not to expect too a high degree of consistency and similarity in the formulation of those early charters from other Kentish minsters that are preserved only in copies.

The following is a summary of the characteristic formulation of Kentish charters in the earliest period, and of the particular variants found in the texts from the different minsters.

Pictorial invocation

In the surviving originals this is inevitably a simple cross, the normal form in England until the adoption of the chrismon in the mid tenth century.[21]

Verbal invocation

This is usually a variation upon the formula *In nomine Domini nostri Iesu Christi saluatoris* found in S 8 and in Gregory's charter for St Andrew's in Rome. The changes rung on this simple theme are legion; most of the Minster and St Augustine's charters from this period have a subtle variation of some kind, an early illustration of the characteristic Anglo-Saxon pref-erence for variety of expression over the repetition of fixed formulas.

Proem

In the most reliable seventh-century charters from Kent there is no proem after the verbal invocation and consequently no following exposition; by contrast, proems are commonly found in contemporary charters from

---

[21] There is evidence for some sporadic use of the chrismon in the eighth and ninth centuries: see below, p. xcii.

Wessex, Surrey, Sussex and Essex.[22] More characteristic of Kentish drafting is the inclusion of a statement of pious motivation after the superscription (occasionally before), which to some extent took the place of a proem (see **10**, **41**, **42**, **43**, **44**, and S 19). Proems first appear in Kentish charters in the early eighth century; the earliest surviving examples are in **47** (A.D. 724), **48** (A.D. 727) and S 24 (A.D. 741). But charters continued to be produced in Kent without proems: examples are S 23 (A.D. 732) from Lyminge, which has an anomalous structure, and S 27 (A.D. 738) from Rochester.

Royal style
    The usual style is *rex Cantuariorum*, but *rex Cantie* seems to be a permissible variant; it occurs in **10** and in the witness-list of S 24, as well as in a number of cartulary copies.[23]

Dispositive section:
    i. There is a wide range of *dispositive verbs and phrases*, and no consistency of person or tense: *dono . . . [et] conferimus* (S 8), *donaui et dono* (**7**), *dedi* (**41**), *imperpetuum contuli possidendum* (**8**), *concedo . . . trado* (**42**), *contulimus inperpetuum possidendam* (**44**), *inperpetuo tradimus possidendam* (**9**), *perdonaui* (**46**), *bonum uisum est conferre* (S 19), *dedi et do* (**47**, **48**), *tribuo et dono* (S 23), *donaui, largitus sum* (S 27), *donaui atque dono* (S 24). There is already some sign of the paired dispositive verbs which are characteristic of Kentish diplomatic in the later eighth and ninth centuries.
    ii. The *references to the beneficiary* also vary in form, and to a certain extent seem to be specific to the different minsters. Grants in favour of St Augustine's are made to the *monasterium beati Petri (principis apostolorum)* (**7**, **8**, **9**); in two out of three instances this is qualified by a following oblique reference to the abbot (Hadrian), couched in a formula derived from a continental model.[24] In charters from Minster-in-Thanet, the grant is always

---

[22] See S 71, 73, 100, 227, 231, 234–5, 237, 248, 255, 1164–5, 1169, 1171, 1248. The absolute authenticity of several of these texts can be questioned, but the similarity of the formulas used in contemporary charters from different archives is most striking.

[23] The style *rex Cantiae* also occurs in the text or witness-list of the following charters: **6**, **8**, **9**, **11**, **13**, **40**, **44**; and S 31 (an original), 32, 34, 36, 38–41, 91, 159. See discussion by A. Scharer, 'Die Intitulationes der angelsächsischen Könige im 7. und 8. Jahrhundert', *Intitulatio III: Lateinische Herrschertitel und Herrschertitulaturen vom 7. bis zum 13. Jahrhundert*, Mitteilungen des Instituts für Österreichische Geschichtsforshung, Ergänzungsband xxix (1988), pp. 9–74 at 39–48.

[24] '. . .in quo preesse Adrianus dinoscitur qui a Romana urbe directus est. . .' (**8**). Compare 'sancte ecclesiae catholicae Ravennati, in qua vir beatissimus Petrus archiepiscopus praeese uidetur', from a Ravenna papyrus of 572: J.-O. Tjäder, *Die nichtliterarischen lateinischen Papyri Italiens aus der Zeit 445–700*, 3 vols (Lund, 1954–82), i. 316 (this document is cited by Levison, *England and the Continent*, p. 225).

in favour of Abbess Æbba or Abbess Mildrith, occasionally in conjunction with the Minster *familia*; there is some stress on the personal grant to the abbess. Generally the Minster charters use the third person to refer to the beneficiary; the only instance of the use of the second person is in **44**. Two of the three charters from Lyminge (S 19, 24) are said to be grants to the church (*bassilicae beate Marie*; *ad ecclesiam beatissimi uirginis Marie*). The third, S 23, which has very unconventional formulation (and, it will be remembered, differs from S 19 and S 24 in the adoption of a vertical format), refers to the abbot in the second person, associating him with the *ecclesia beate Marie*. The single charter from Reculver (S 8) is a grant to Berhtwald (evidently abbot) and his *monasterium*; the second person is used (two later Reculver charters, S 31 and 1612, name the abbot and his *familia* as beneficiaries, again using the second person). In the only Rochester land-charter from this period (**27**) the grant is made to the bishopric (*episcopatui beati Andree apostoli ac uenerabile uiro Ealdulfo*). The relative consistency of the different formulas in charters from the individual minsters (admittedly from a small sample) is compatible with the suggestion that ecclesiastical beneficiaries played some role in drafting the texts.

iii. The normal *unit of land-assessment* in Kentish charters is not the hide, as elsewhere in Anglo-Saxon England, but the *aratrum* or sulung; most references in early charters are in the form *(terram) .x. aratrorum* (see **9**, **41**, **44**, **47**, **48**, and S 19, 27). Kent retained its distinctive system throughout the Anglo-Saxon period, and this is usually reflected in the charters.[25] Some royal diplomas issued between the ninth and eleventh centuries dealing with Kentish estates do contain a hidage assessment; this can generally be explained as the result of external influence or drafting by a non-Kentish agency.[26] The only earlier exceptions are four of the seventh-century Minster

---

[25] See discussion by: P. Vinogradoff, 'Sulung and Hide', *English Historical Review* xix (1904), pp. 282–6, 624; H.C. Darby and E.M.J. Campbell, *The Domesday Geography of South-East England*, rev. edn (Cambridge, 1971), pp. 502–7; H.P.R. Finberg, 'Anglo-Saxon England to 1042', *The Agrarian History of England and Wales, I (ii): A.D. 43–1042*, ed. H.P.R. Finberg (Cambridge, 1972), pp. 383–525 at 415–16.

[26] Ninth-century Kentish charters with a hide-assessment: S 40, 161, 169, 178, 286, 350; and **21** (drafted in Wessex). Two dispute settlements from the period (both drawn up in non-Kentish synods) refer to Kentish estates in hides (S 1258, 1436); in both cases the reference is to land ceded by a non-Kentish party to the dispute. S 1414, the will of the priest who was Archbishop Wulfred's heir, also mentions hides. Tenth- and eleventh-century instances: **28** and **30**; S 447, 464, 497, 512, 535, 546, 662, ?859, 885, 1044. Charters in this last group were probably drafted by scribes in a central royal secretariat, who may not have been familiar with Kentish practice. This probably explains why in the tenth century the sulung was occasionally equated with the hide (S 497, 512, 535, 885), although other evidence suggests that it was much larger; for instance, in two ninth-century charters (S 161, 169) the sulung is said to be equivalent to two hides (see Vinogradoff, 'Sulung and Hide', pp. 284–5).

charters, which have a land-assessment expressed in *manentes* (**40**, **42**, **43**, **46**).[27] This may be a reflection of Minster participation in the drafting process. It should be noted that the earliest Kentish charter (S 8) contains no reference to the assessment of the estate, while the next oldest (**7**) mentions the assessment casually at the end of the dispositive section, apparently as an afterthought. It may be that precise land-assessments were not a usual feature of the earliest stratum of Kentish diplomatic. The aberration in the Minster charters could then be a consequence of the lack of an established convention.

iv. The *identification of the estate* is expressed in a number of ways. The use of a simple place-name is fairly tentative in early texts from Kent and from the other Anglo-Saxon kingdoms. Certain charters include them: S 8 (although here the place-name is really a locative description), **9**, **41**, **46**, S 19, S 27. One of the reasons why scribes may have been reluctant to use a place-name is signalled in **44**, which is a grant of land *formerly* called *Humantun*, i.e. 'Huma's enclosure'; the reference is to a previous owner and the name is more of a label than a place-name proper. Generally Kentish charter-scribes in this period simply noted that the land was in Thanet or in a certain lathe, such as Sturry or Eastry, or otherwise referred to the approximate location. But it was often felt necessary to give some further detail that would locate the place a little more closely. One possible solution was to refer to the previous owner of the property (**8**, **43**, **47**, S 24) or to mention the owner of an adjacent estate (**8**). In **7** the estate is defined by reference to the boundaries on two sides, but this is an isolated instance; in general Kentish charter-scribes were uninterested in including boundary clauses. King Hlothhere in S 8 explicitly states that the boundaries of the estate had been 'demonstrated' by him and his officials; this physical demonstration was evidently felt to make explicit description in the charter unnecessary. S 19 speaks of *notissimos terminos* (but does give three boundary marks, a 'way', a path and a wood or clearing). References to 'well-known bounds' are common in Kentish charters until well into the ninth century, and sometimes such a reference is accompanied by a statement that it is unneccessary to set them down (as in **13**). When a boundary clause was included, the preferred form was a simple reference to the most prominent

---

[27] An assessment in *manentes* is also found in S 233, relating to the Kentish minster at Hoo, which is based on some genuine seventh-century documentation (best seen in the witness-list) but which has been completely rewritten at a later date. The hide-assessment in **14** appears to be another indication of its spurious character.

feature at each of the four cardinal points. The earliest example of this in a Kentish context occurs in S 23 (see also the interpolated section in S 21).[28]

v. Many of the earliest Anglo-Saxon charters incorporate a formula referring to the *appurtenances* of the land granted; similar but more detailed formulas appear in Italian and Frankish deeds. A common source evidently lies behind the very similar formulas in S 8 and 7, which share a grammatical error; the unusual word *sationalis* in 7 seems to derive from a Italian model, and also occurs in the corresponding formula in S 65 (A.D. 704) from Middlesex.[29] Similar lists of general appurtenances appear in 42 and 44, and in the related difficult charters 6 and 40; there is an abbreviated version in S 19 (and see 9, 47, 48). The scribe of S 24 did not use a formula to refer to the appurtenances, but named them individually. In the later eighth and ninth centuries it is a feature of Kentish charters that the appurtenances of estates are often individually specified (see, for instance, S 328, 332).

vi. The *statement of powers* in early Kentish charters does not have a consistent pattern of formulation. Some charters (for example, S 19, 24, 27, and 41, 46, 47, 48) do not include a formal statement of powers. When one is incorporated, it generally states that the beneficiary should have full powers to hold the estate and do with it as he wished (S 8, S 23, and 7, 8, 9, 43). Sometimes more detail is given. In 40 the abbess is explicitly permitted to bequeath the estate to any of her successors, and in 42 she can give it to anyone, before or after her death. 44 has by far the most interesting formula of this kind, almost certainly a direct adaptation of an Italian model; the various powers are expressed in a string of verbs, and include permission to give away the land, and to exchange or sell it.[30] It is unlikely that these

---

[28] For the background to the development of boundary-clauses in Anglo-Saxon charters, see M. Reed, 'Anglo-Saxon Charter-Boundaries', *Discovering Past Landscapes*, ed. M. Reed (London, 1984), pp. 261–306 (and p. 267 for examples of continental boundary-clauses mentioning the cardinal points).

[29] For instance: 'cum omnibus ad se pertinentibus campis pascuis meriscis siluis modicis fon[ta]nis piscaris omnibus ut dictum est ad eandem terram pertinentia sicut nunc usque possessa est' (S 8). Compare: 'finibus, terminis, campis, pratis, pascuis, silvis, ṣalectis, sationalibus, vineis, arbustis, arboribus pomiferis, fructiferis et infructiferis diuersisque generibus, ... rivis, fontibus, aquis perennis, liminibus limitibusque suis omnibus . . . sicut a me meaque patrona . . . possessum est atque nunc usque in hanc diem rite possedetur' (Ravenna, c. A.D. 600: Tjäder, *Papryi*, i. 346).

[30] 'teneas, possideas, dones, commutes, uenundes uel quicquid exinde facere uolueris liberam habeas potestatem successoresque tui defendant inperpetuum' (44). Compare: 'habeant, teneant, possedeant, iuri dominioque more, quo voluerit, im perpetuo vindicent atque defendant, vel quicquid ex eadem portionem iuris mei facere maluerint. . .liberam et perpetem in omnibus habeant potestatem' (Ravenna, c. A.D. 600: Tjäder, *Papyri*, i. 346); 'habere, tenere, possidere, vindere, donare, commutare ac suo iuri in perpetuo vendicare permisit' (Ravenna, A.D. 575 × 591: Tjäder, *Papyri*, ii. 116); 'et quicquid de ipsas duas prates facere volueris, abendi, tenendi,

variations in formulation actually reflect any specific differences in the beneficiary's legal powers over the land granted; in general the draftsmen seem variously to be adapting the wording of Italian charters, which were the products of a society with different legal arrangements for land-ownership.[31]

vii. Early Kentish charters commonly include a declaration that the donor and his kinsmen and heirs will not or should not seek to overturn the grant, which seems to represent another borrowing from early Italian models (see S 8, 19, 24, 27, and **7, 10, 44**).[32] A conservative formula of this type is to be found in **7** and **44**, and also in two nearly contemporary charters from Surrey (S 1165, 235) and in two Mercian texts, a charter of King Æthelbald concerning land in Middlesex (S 100), datable only to 716 × 757, and an old-fashioned charter of 756 from the kingdom of the Hwicce (S 56).[33]

viii. Some early Kentish charters include other formulas which reflect late Roman legal ideas. The dispositive sections of several texts incorporate the phrase *a presenti die et tempore* (see **7, 8, 9, 10**; S 23; and **13** from the 760s),

---

donandi, vindendi seu conmutandi . . .. liberam in omnibus abeas potestatem faciendi' (*Formulae Andecavenses*, in *Formulae Merowingici et Karolini Aevi*, ed. K. Zeumer, MGH (Hanover, 1886), p. 25. [no. 58])

[31] Anglo-Saxon land-law is a complex and controversial area: see, for instance, E. John, *Land-Tenure in Early England: a Discussion of Some Problems* (Leicester, 1964); Wormald 1985, pp. 19–23; S. Reynolds, 'Bookland, Folkland and Fiefs', *Anglo-Norman Studies* xiv (1992), pp. 211–27. It is argued that one of the most important characteristics of *bocland* was its alienability; land held by charter could be disposed of freely, without reference to the claims of the owner's kindred. A problem is that this form of tenure is said to have first been devised for ecclesiastical beneficiaries, who could not have been expected to dispose of their estates at will, without reference to the lay donor or to the ecclesiastical authorities. It can probably be assumed that the idea of *bocland* as represented in the charters of the ninth century and later represents a development from the actuality of the seventh century, when notions of land-tenure are likely to have been far more fluid (and may have been influenced by nebulously-understood aspects of Roman law, as imported by the Italian missionaries); the crucial development of the intervening period was the growing lay interest in the holding of land by charter, which is likely to have led to a greater stress on disposability (as opposed to ownership in perpetuity, which was more important to the Church). In this respect the references to alienability in the statements of powers in some early Anglo-Saxon charters may be a red herring; it is possible that these should simply be regarded as formulas, borrowed from continental models and without legal substance.

[32] P. Chaplais, 'Some Early Anglo-Saxon Diplomas on Single Sheets: Originals or Copies?, *Journal of the Society of Archivists* iii.7 (1968), pp. 315–36 at 320–2; reprinted in *Prisca Munimenta*, ed. F. Ranger (London, 1973), pp. 63–87 at 69–72.

[33] '. . .numquam me heredesque meos uel successores contra hanc donationis mee cartulam ullo tempore esse uenturos' (**7**). Compare: 'Contra quam inrevocabilem donationis meae paginam polliceor numquam esse uenturum, neque per me neque per heredes successoresque meos' (Ravenna, c. A.D. 600: Tjäder, *Papyri*, i. 346, 348); '. . .contra quam donationem nullo tempore nullaque ratione me posteros successoresque meos uenturos esse polliceor' (Ravenna, A.D. 553: Tjäder, *Papyri*, i. 304).

which has close parallels in the Ravenna papyri and some Merovingian charters and formularies.[34] Other formulas refer to ideas of jurisdiction: for instance, the statement of powers in **9** has the phrase 'a presenti die et tempore a nostra iurisdictione transferentes' (compare S 1171: 'de meo iure in tuo transcribo').[35]

Sanction

In the seventh century Kentish sanctions are generally a simple anathema, although **42** also has a brief blessing. In the eighth century it becomes increasingly common to find a paired blessing and anathema (see **47, 48,** S 24). The only charter to lack a sanction of any kind is S 23, where the formulation is generally anomalous. The anathema is usually in a standard form, with an initial conditional clause beginning *Quisquis* (or *Quod si* in those charters where the sanction is proceeded by a prohibition), followed by a clause detailing the prospective punishment, usually beginning *nouerit* or *sit*. In Kentish charters the transgressor is generally threatened with separation from the body of believers and exclusion from participation in the eucharist. Threats that the criminal will be actively punished by God or will face a reckoning on the Day of Judgement, which are frequent in West Saxon and Mercian charters, are less common in Kent (but see **46, 47, 48** and S 27).

In Kentish charters from the seventh to the ninth century the sanction is frequently followed by a formula expressing faith that the charter will remain in force; this is a stereotyped phrase in the ablative absolute or accusative absolute, as in S 8: 'manentem hanc donationis chartulam in sua nihilominus firmitate'. Similar formulas are found in Italian and Frankish charters, in the same position after the sanction, which makes it clear that the Anglo-Saxon charter-scribes were in this instance imitating one of their foreign models; in the continental documents the sanction threatens money penalties, and the concluding formula seems to make better sense in this context.[36] During the period from the 670s to c. 750 the formula occurs in Kent in the following charters: **6, 7, 8** and **9** from St Augustine's; S 8 from Reculver; S 88 and 27 from Rochester; **40, 49** and **51** from Minster. There are no examples in the three Lyminge charters, and it should be noted that most of the Minster

---

[34] '..a praesenti die..' (Tjäder, *Papyri*, i. 346, 370); '...ab odierna die' (Zeumer, *Formulae*, pp. 7, 10–11, 16 etc.).

[35] Compare also: '.. ex meo iure in uestro iure dominioque transcribo...' (Gregory the Deacon, A.D. 587: *MGH Epistolae*, ii. 437); '...de iure meo in tua trado potestate uel dominatione' (Zeumer, *Formulae*, p. 138).

[36] Chaplais 1968, p. 323 (p. 72).

land-charters omit this feature (it occurs only in two eighth-century toll-privileges, and in a land-charter which must have been rewritten at some stage). This may be another indicator of beneficiary involvement in the drafting of charters. The formula continued in common use in Kent until the end of the ninth century; later examples are **14, 18** and **20**, and S 30–2, 105, 34–6, 111, 125, 129, 131, 1265, 187, 282, 286–7, 296, 1269, 339, 1204. There are a few non-Kentish instances in early charters from Surrey (S 235, 1247) and Essex (S 1171, 65).

Corroboration

Early Kentish charters usually include a statement by the donor that he has validated the charter by adding the sign of the cross, with a request to other witnesses (sometimes named) to do likewise: for instance, 'et pro confirmatione eius manu propria signum sancte crucis expræssi et testes ut subscriberent rogaui' (S 8). In **10** and **44** the formula begins with the introductory phrase 'ad cuius cumulum affirmationis (firmitatis)', which was probably borrowed from an antique model.[37] Sometimes the formula incorporates a reference to the donor's illiteracy (see S 19, and **8, 9, 44**); the context for this was the Roman provision for illiterate witnesses, who were unable to provide an autograph subscription.[38] In two Minster charters (**43, 44**) the corroboration incorporates a reference to the symbolic placing of sods of earth on the altar, as part of the conveyance ceremony; similar references occur in early charters from other Anglo-Saxon kingdoms.[39]

Dating clause

Kentish charters from the seventh and eighth centuries typically have a dating clause beginning *Actum* or *Actum in*, with no verb, a formula with

---

[37] Compare '...ad cumulum tuae firmitatis..' (A.D. 551; Tjäder, *Papyri*, ii. 100): cited Levison, *England and the Continent*, pp. 231–2.

[38] See also the royal subscriptions in **10** and S (Add.) 103a (the latter is a newly discovered St Paul's charter, edited in Kelly 1992, p. 27, and also discussed below). Compare: '...propter ignorantiam litterarum signa impraessimus' (Ravenna, A.D. 553: Tjäder, *Papyri*, i. 306); '...mano propria propter ignorantia litterarum signum sanctae crucis feci..' (Ravenna, *c*. A.D. 600: *ibid.*, i. 322); '...in qua subter propria manu pro ignorantia litterarum signum venerabilis sancte crucis feci..' (Ravenna, *c*. A.D. 600, *ibid.*, i. 348).

[39] See also S 1164, 239, 1805–6. S 1804 mentions the placing of the charter itself upon the altar as a guarantee, a practice with Italian roots. Compare the statement of a witness to a Ravenna charter of the mid seventh century: '.. et hanc chartulam posita[m] super sancta evvangelia actionariis prefate ecclesie a memorato Gaudiuso sub iusiurandum traditam vidi' (Tjäder, *Papyri*, i. 374); and the statement of the donor in another document of the same date: '...consensi et subscripsi et testis a me rogitis optuli subscrivendum eorumque presentia desuper sancta evvangelia contradidi' (*ibid.*, i. 380). See also *ibid.*, i. 370.

Italian antecedents.[40] Occasionally charters have no dating clause (see, for instance, **41**, **43**); in cartulary copies the dating clause may have been lost, but S 31 from the mid eighth century is an instance of an apparent original with no dating clause. In the seventh century, the chronological indicators were typically the month and the indiction (S 8 and S 19; **7**, **8**, **9**). Other possible factors were the king's regnal year and a precise calendar date, generally using the Roman calendar (**10**, **40**, **42**, **44**, **48**), but sometimes in the simpler form which became the modern usage (S 23). The preference in Minster charters for a precise date contrasts with the simple provision of the month in the St Augustine's texts, and may be further evidence for beneficiary production. The use of the incarnation year appears to be an eighth-century development in Kent. Its first appearance in a surviving Kentish charter is in **48** from 727, and it also occurs in S 27 from 738 and S 24 from 741. Earlier use of the incarnation year in Mercia is indicated by Æthelred's confirmation of **40**, which took place in the Mercian heartland in 691.[41] The dating clause in the Kentish charters is typically placed immediately after the main text and before the witness-list, but it may also be found after the witness-list (S 19) and after the superscription (**6**, **40**, **42**, **46**).

Occasionally the dating clause includes a place-name: Reculver (S 8), *Cilling* near Faversham (**10**), Canterbury (S 23), Lyminge (S 24). In an Italian charter this would have been the place of issue. In an Anglo-Saxon charter, which may have been drawn up separately from the conveyance ceremony (probably before or after), the definition is more complicated; the place mentioned is presumably where the formal conveyance took place, but not necessarily where the charter was written. It does, however, seem significant that in two cases (S 8, 24) the apparent 'place of issue' was the minster that was the beneficiary of the charter; this would be compatible with the suggestion that beneficiaries might take responsibility for drawing up their own charters. There is additional interest in the statement that S 23, although in favour of Lyminge, was 'enacted' at Canterbury, for this might explain why this charter is so very different from the other two Lyminge charters from this period.

---

[40] Chaplais 1968, p. 324 (p. 73). Compare, for instance: 'Actum Ravenna, in domo iuris iugalis donatricis, indictione prima' (Ravenna, A.D. 553: Tjäder, *Papyri*, i. 306).

[41] There is some evidence for the early use of incarnational dating in documents from areas associated with Wilfrid of Northumbria: see K. Harrison, 'The *Annus Domini* in Some Early Charters', *Journal of the Society of Archivists* iv.7 (1963), pp. 551–7; idem, *The Framework of Anglo-Saxon History to A.D. 900* (Cambridge, 1976), pp. 67–75; Sims-Williams 1988. Wilfrid or his followers may also have introduced the practice into Sussex: see S 42, 45, and discussion in *The Charters of Selsey*, ed. S.E. Kelly *et al*, Anglo-Saxon Charters vi (forthcoming).

Witness-list

The earliest Anglo-Saxon charters preserve in a fossilized form the conventions devised in later Roman diplomatic to distinguish between the subscriptions of the literate and the illiterate witness: the former were supposed to be autograph and are in 'subjective' form (+ *Ego N subscripsi*); the latter are in the 'objective' form + *Signum (manus) N*, with the cross supposed to be autograph. While the formulation of the English charters pays lipservice to these conventions, with regular references to subscription *propria manu* and occasional early apologies for the donor's illiteracy (see above), the autograph element had been entirely dropped by the 670s, so that the scribe of the text usually wrote both types of subscription and also supplied all the crosses.[42] In Kentish charters up until the middle of the eighth century the distinction between the two types of subscription is consistently retained; clerics (and frequently also the royal donor) attest subjectively, lay witnesses objectively. The only exception is the first section of S 27 from Rochester, where all subscriptions are subjective; but here there is a strong suspicion that the witness-list has been reworked at a later date, for all the subscriptions echo that of the king and make no sense. After the middle of the eighth century the distinction was gradually abandoned.

ii. *The diplomatic of the ship-toll charters*

Ten charters concerned with the remission of ship-toll have been preserved in five separate archives. Seven of these are in favour of Kentish beneficiaries: five for Minster-in-Thanet (**49, 50, 51, 52, 53**), and one each for Rochester (S 88) and Reculver (S 1612). The others are from Worcester (S 98) and St Paul's in London (S [Add.] 103a, S 1788).[43] The majority of the surviving texts are in the name of Æthelbald of Mercia and seem to belong to the

---

[42] Albert Bruckner has suggested that some of the crosses in some of the subscriptions of a number of the earliest Anglo-Saxon originals may perhaps be autograph: 'Zur Diplomatik der älteren angelsächsischen Urkunde', *Archivalische Zeitschrift* lxi (1965), pp. 11–45 at 38–41; *Ch.L.A.*, iii. 186, 190, 195, 220, 221, iv. 236. He bases his case on minute variations of scale and ink-colour, which seem utterly unconvincing. Comparison with genuine examples of autograph crosses, for instance in the Norman charters of the eleventh century, shows that very much greater variation is to be expected in such cases. The only Anglo-Saxon diploma with arguably autograph crosses in the subscriptions is S 876 from 993, which was evidently a most unusual production; here none of the subscriptions was originally supplied with a cross, but a number were added later, some apparently by different hands (see Keynes, *Diplomas*, p. 101 n. 54).

[43] The background to the toll-privileges is discussed more fully in Kelly 1992, where the two St Paul's texts are edited. My conclusions differ in many respects from those reached by Scharer in an earlier analysis of the group (*Königsurkunde*, pp. 195–211).

730s and 740s; **52** is Offa's confirmation of one of Æthelbald's charters, while **53** and S 1612 were issued by King Eadberht II of Kent in the early 760s, in imitation of Mercian practice. All the charters are in Latin except the Worcester privilege (S 98), which appears to be a vernacular translation of a Latin privilege, probably made in the later ninth or early tenth century.

It appears that charters of this type were issued over a very limited period of time, perhaps because royal policy about such concessions changed. We can only speculate about the way in which these documents were intended to be used. Frankish privileges of a similar type were carried by beneficiaries on trading journeys and shown to the royal agents responsible for tolls. This may have been the case in Anglo-Saxon England as well, although it raises difficult questions about the extent of Latin literacy in the eighth century and the use of writing for administrative purposes.[44] It is clear from the English texts that the toll-exemptions are supposed to apply to particular ships; two of the Minster charters (**51, 53**) identify the ship which is to be immune, while four of the privileges (**51, 53**; S 1788, S 1612) include a clause to the effect that the exemption is to be transferred to another ship if the current vessel is wrecked or falls into decay, which appears to indicate that immunity was felt to reside in the ship, rather than in the document. This characteristic of Anglo-Saxon toll-exemption has no parallel in Frankish practice, and may have been devised specially for English conditions, where royal agents were not accustomed to deal with written records on a regular basis. It is possible that the exempt ships were marked in some way for recognition, perhaps by official branding; the privileges may have been initially submitted to the royal agent to demonstrate toll-immunity, and then stored in the beneficiary's archive until the exemption was challenged. However, the translation of the Worcester example into the vernacular, probably in the later ninth century, does suggest that the toll-privileges might have had a practical function.

It is to be assumed that the ten extant documents are the survivors of a far larger number of English toll-privileges, since their chances of preservation are likely to have been less good than those of formal land-charters; in consequence, it is impossible to decide whether the relatively large number of such texts in the Minster archive is a measure of an unusual level of involvement in trading activity or simply the result of particular circumstances of preservation. There is some difficulty in arranging the surviving toll-privileges in an approximate chronological sequence, for only two of them can be precisely dated (S 88 from 733 and **51** from 748). The dating

---

[44] For the background, see Kelly 1990.

problems of **49** and **50**, the two earliest Minster examples of the genre, are discussed in the commentaries; **49** may belong to the early 730s, while **50** could be as early as 716 or 717 (although its ostensible date is 737 or 738). Neither of the two St Paul's toll-charters (S [Add.] 103a, S 1788) has a dating clause of any kind or a proper witness-list, so they can be placed only in the inconveniently long pontificate of their beneficiary, Bishop Ingwald (716 × 745). S 1788 has links with **51**, issued in 748, and this may suggest that S 1788 belongs to the later part of Ingwald's period of office, perhaps the 740s. S (Add.) 103a is probably earlier than S 1788, and may indeed represent one of the previous toll-concessions to Ingwald to which that charter refers. The Worcester privilege (S 98) also lacks a dating clause. It does have a witness-list, but this causes problems through the presence of two successive bishops of Worcester. A proposed solution is that one bishop was appointed in the other's lifetime, which might suggest that the privilege belongs to the apparent period of overlap, approximately 743 × 745. But this is a dubious conclusion in view of the fact that the extant text is a later translation which may well have been reworked at Worcester. The only fixed point is provided by the subscription of Bishop Ingwald of London; the toll-privilege underlying the Worcester document was issued in or before 745. A possible indicator of the relative chronology of Æthelbald's toll-privileges is the inclusion or omission of the clause transferring the privilege in the case of shipwreck, which is not found in S 88 (A.D. 733) but does appear in **51** (A.D. 748).[45] On this basis, we could identify **49**, **50**, S 88 and S (Add.) 103a as early texts (perhaps from the 730s and before), and assign **51** with S 1788 and S 98 to a later group (perhaps the 740s); but it must be stressed that this is no infallible guide, and there may well have been an overlap.

To the seven charters in the name of Æthelbald can be added three more from the 760s: **52**, which is Offa's confirmation of **50**, and the two charters of Eadberht II (**53**, S 1612). These three documents also lack proper dating clauses, but all refer to Archbishop Bregowine and can thus be placed in his short pontificate (761 × 764). **53** includes a regnal year of the Kentish King Eadberht II, which suggests that it belongs to 763 or 764; the regnal year was altered at St Augustine's in the later medieval period, for the same reasons which led the Christ Church cartularist to provide S 1612 with an impossible incarnation date (see p. ciii).

These toll-charters exhibit considerable diplomatic variety, but there is also an undercurrent of similarity which points to the use of some common models. The most striking instance is the relationship between **49** and S 88,

---

[45] This criterion was suggested by Scharer (*Königsurkunde*, p. 197).

which are almost identical, even though the beneficiaries were respectively abbess of Minster and bishop of Rochester. Various explanations can be suggested for this phenomenon: a common draftsman; the use of one document as the model for the other; access to a common model. The interest of the relationship lies in the fact that diplomatic co-operation has evidently crossed diocesan boundaries. Another important link is between **51** from Minster and the earlier S 1788 from St Paul's in London; the dispositive sections of these two texts have a considerable amount of formulation in common. Since **51** is said to have been issued in London, it might be supposed that both texts were products of the scriptorium of the London bishopric, and that would also be a possible explanation for the link between S 88 and **49**, both of which deal explicitly with an immunity in the port of London. Such a development would contrast with the evidence for beneficiary-production of land-charters, and could perhaps be a consequence of the essentially administrative nature of this type of document.

But further reflection shows it would be unwise to suggest that all Æthelbald's ship-toll privileges had a London origin. **51**, for instance, while it shares some formulation with S 1788, also betrays Minster involvement in its production: it includes information, such as the name of the man who sold the ship to the community and details of the recent building-works of Abbess Eadburh, which could only have been supplied by Minster itself and which is unlikely to have been of interest to a London draftsman. The relationship between **51** and S 1788 is perhaps better explained as the result of the use of a common model; in each case the draftsman has retained the technical formulation in the dispositive section, but has in the remainder of the text succumbed to the general Anglo-Saxon passion for free expression. This solution is underlined by the connection between S 1788 and the other St Paul's toll-charter, S (Add.) 103a; the sanctions of both charters are very close, which suggests a house formula.

Similarly, the formulation of S 88, **49** and the later **51** is more easily understood as deriving from a Kentish background. S 88 and **51** have dating clauses beginning *Actum*, which is characteristic of Kentish diplomatic (the suspect dating clause of **49** begins *Actum est*). All three charters have a very long proem; S 88 and **49** have a sanction composed of both a blessing and an anathema (in **51** the latter is replaced by an idiosyncratic celebration of Christ and St Mary). These features are not characteristic of seventh-century Kentish charters (if we omit **6** and **40** from the reckoning), but can be paralleled to a certain extent in **47** and **48** from the 720s, and in S 24 from 741. By contrast, the two St Paul's toll-charters, which were clearly the product of the London scriptorium, are diplomatically distinct from the three Kentish specimens. S (Add.) 103a has a combined blessing and anathema, but no proem; S 1788 has a very brief proem, but no blessing. Both are relatively modest documents, compared to the verbose Kentish texts. S (Add.) 103a is particularly instructive, in that it is evidently modelled on a land-charter and incorporates none of the formulation characteristic of the other toll-privileges. It is possible that this is the earliest example of a toll-privilege, produced when no existing models were available, but it may also be the case that the London scriptorium had no standard format for documents of this type.

Both S 1788 and S (Add.) 103a survive only in the form of lengthy antiquarian extracts from a lost medieval roll, but in each case the text includes the beginning of a witness-list and so it would be expected that any dating clause preceding the subscriptions would be included. It is possible that such a clause was located after the witness-list (as in **50**), and thus omitted, but it is worth pointing out that the two antiquaries responsible for the extracts did quite often make a note of the dates of the texts they were using, and it is mildly remarkable that none was provided for either of the St Paul's toll-charters. Given the dubious textual background, it is perhaps unwise to stress the apparent omission. But it does seem something of a coincidence that the only other non-Kentish toll-charter, S 98 from Worcester, also appears to lack a dating clause. In this context, it is significant that most of Æthelbald's land-charters seem to have been drafted without dating clauses (see S 94–6, 99, 101–2); the only reliable exception is S 89, on other grounds a rather uncharacteristic document. It can be suggested that there is a significant difference between the Kentish toll-privileges and those for non-Kentish beneficiaries; the former usually included a dating clause (as did Kentish land-charters), while the latter omitted dating material (in line with the current practice of Mercian scribes drawing up land-charters).

This conclusion supports the argument that toll-privileges, like land-charters at this period, were generally drawn up in houses that benefited from the toll-exemptions. Since such documents were a relative novelty, it is not surprising to find that common models seem to have circulated, with the result that some of the toll-privileges share a certain amount of technical formulation; trading journeys to London would account for the contact between distant houses. The exceptionally close relationship between **49** and S 88 was probably due to unusual circumstances, perhaps a direct borrowing of a model or an episode of collaboration. In the case of **50** and S (Add.) 103a, probably the two earliest examples of the type, no specialist model was yet available, so the draftsmen borrowed some of the formulation from land-charters. When the production of toll-charters briefly recommenced in

Kent in the 760s, the Minster community looked to its own archive for models; **52** was based on **50** (which it confirmed), while **53** contains formulation borrowed from both **50** and **51**.

The ten toll-privileges provide a small-scale demonstration of the characteristic methods of Anglo-Saxon charter-scribes in the seventh and eighth centuries. At the heart of their approach to charter-production was the adaptation of existing documents. These could be virtually duplicated, as in the case of **49** and S 88 (a near contemporary parallel is provided by **47** and **48**). Alternatively, the formulation of the models could be partially reproduced, in combination with formulas newly composed by the draftsman or borrowed from different sources (as in S 1788 and **51**). Sometimes radically different documents might be drawn up, perhaps because no guide was available (S [Add.] 103a, **50**). The draftsmen might work by adapting an earlier charter in the archive of the house to which they were attached, but they were also alive to external influences and may have acquired copies of interesting documents from elsewhere. It is possible that among the models circulating in England at this period was a Frankish toll-charter (see commentary to **51**).

iii. *Kentish charters from c. 750 to c. 825*

The second half of the eighth century was a turbulent period in Kentish history, and this is reflected in the charter record. The decline and disappearance of the native Kentish dynasty in the early 760s was accompanied by a sudden acceleration in the rate of charter-production in Kent. There are ten surviving texts datable to between 761 and 765 (**11, 12, 13, 52, 53**; and S 1612, 32, 33, 34, 105), and a further two may have been issued *c.* 760 (S 30, 31). Some are in the names of kings who were probably the last representatives of the native dynasty (Æthelberht II, Eardwulf, Eadberht II); others were issued and confirmed by a series of obscure rulers who passed in rapid succession in these years (see Appendix 3); and there are also two charters in the name of Offa of Mercia, one a confirmation of a ship-toll privilege (**52**), but the other a direct grant of land in Kent (S 105), apparently a reissue of an earlier charter of the Kentish King Sigered in favour of Rochester (S 33). Offa also confirmed another Rochester charter of this period (S 34). The key political development in Kent after the death of Æthelberht II in 762 was the rapid growth of Mercian domination. It is in this period that the first definite Mercian influence on Kentish diplomatic becomes apparent. The draftsmen of an inter-related group of three charters, comprising S 33 and 105 from Rochester and **13** from St Augustine's, may have adapted a single Mercian model. The most significant diplomatic indicators of this Mercian influence are the invocation beginning *Regnante* (rather than the Kentish *In nomine*), found in S 105 and adapted in **13**, and the dating clause beginning *Scripta est* (instead of *Actum*). Eadberht II's toll-privilege for Minster (**53**) also has an invocation of the *Regnante* type.

The spate of charters issued between 762 and 765 was followed by another fairly fallow period, extending to 785. From the two intervening decades there are only three charters of the Kentish king Ecgberht (S 35, 36, 37), one of a King Ealhmund, perhaps a West Saxon (S 38), and two dubious charters of Offa dated 774 in favour of Archbishop Jaenberht (S 110, 111). None of Ecgberht's charters acknowledge Offa's overlordship, and it has been argued from this that Kent enjoyed nominal independence from Mercia domination from the period of the battle of Otford in 776 until the mid 780s. By 785 Offa had taken direct control in Kent, and from that date onwards he issued a series of charters disposing of land in what is often referred to as the *prouincia Cantiae*. Previously, all Kentish charters had been written and ratified within the kingdom, except in the case of the ship-toll privileges. But almost all the surviving Kentish land-charters of Offa, datable to between 785 and 789, seem to have been issued at synodal meetings at Chelsea (S 123, 125, 128, 130, 131); the only exceptions are S 129, apparently not a synodal charter, and perhaps the charter underlying **14**. Offa's grant of privileges to the Kentish churches took place at a *Clofesho* synod in 792 (**15**). Two Kentish charters of Offa's successor Coenwulf (S 153, 155) were also the products of synods; the first probably at *Clofesho*, the second at Tamworth. After this, there was a change of practice, a stronger local role for Kent and Kentish noblemen under Cuthred, who acted as Coenwulf's subking in Kent until his death in 807. During Cuthred's lifetime, he issued charters on his own behalf (S 39, 40, 41) and made a number of joint-grants with Coenwulf (**16** and S 157, 160, 161); there were also occasions when the record of a grant made in Mercia was brought before the Kentish witan at Canterbury for confirmation (S 157; and see also the commentary to **16**). Yet charters granting land in Kent might still be issued or ratified by a non-Kentish synod.[46] After 807 Coenwulf began to rule directly in Kent once more, and it seems significant that all of his Kentish charters

---

[46] S 40 and 161 were issued at the *Aclea* synod of 805, and the witness-list of S 41 shows that it was also issued at a Southumbrian synod (none of which are known to have met in Kent). The truncated witness-list of S 160 includes subscriptions of the bishops of Lichfield and Worcester, so this charter was presumably issued at a Mercian council.

which include a reference to the place of issue derive from meetings and synods held outside Kent.[47]

The charters issued during this period are still recognisably Kentish diplomatic products, but the external contact brought in several alien elements. In the surviving originals, the most visible manifestation of this is the sudden tolerance of writing on the dorse of the charter. Before the imposition of direct Mercian rule in Kent, Kentish charter-scribes had resolutely stuck to the face of the charter, and this is still the case in the two surviving original charters of Offa which deal with land in Kent (S 123, 128). But in S 155 from 799 and in several later Kentish charters from the period before the end of Mercian rule in the province (S 1259, 161, 40, 168, 1264, 169, 1436 MSS 1 and 2; BCS 312) all or part of the witness-list and sometimes even part of the text was written on the dorse, occasionally taking up almost the whole of the available space. Given the lack of Mercian originals from before c. 800, it is not easy to demonstrate that opisthographs were a Mercian speciality, but what evidence there is does seem suggestive. S 89 includes a section on the dorse describing appurtenances, not the work of the scribe of the face, but recognisably coeval. In the case of S 114 most of the witnesses were added on the dorse by a different but contemporary scribe. Part of the witness-list in S 139 is also on the dorse. Together these examples suggest that this was essentially a Mercian habit, which was adopted by some Kentish charter-scribes and used on occasions through the ninth century.[48] Mercian practice also seems to have influenced the pictorial invocation in Kent. Until the beginning of the ninth century, Kentish charters were invariably headed by a simple cross (unless a pictorial invocation was completely omitted). Two of the three surviving Mercian originals from the eighth century include a primitive chrismon, in the form of a capital *P* with a stroke though the stalk (S 114, 139). This chrismon is also found in S 1259, issued by the archbishop of Canterbury (a Mercian), from 805, in S 163 from 808 (issued at Tamworth) and in another archiepiscopal charter written just after 825 (S 1436, MS 2); later examples are S 293, 1194 and 296 (see also S 204 from Mercia and S 298 from Wessex).

The Mercian preference for carrying out land-transactions within synods was probably also responsible for the influence of synodal diplomatic on

---

[47] S 163 (Tamworth, A.D. 808), S 164 (Croydon, Surrey, A.D. 809), S 168 (London, A.D. 811), S 170 (London, A.D. 812), S 178 (Wychbold, Worcs., A.D. 178). For further discussion of this material, and its implications for the nature of Mercian rule in Kent, see S. Keynes, 'The Control of Kent in the Ninth Century', *Early Medieval Europe* ii (1993), pp. 111–31.

[48] See S 1268, 1438 (MSS 1, 2, 3), 287, 296, 332, 338

Kentish land-charters. A characteristic of synodal documents is the provision of a complex dating clause at or near the beginning of the text, usually with a reference to the place where the meeting took place and also to the convening of the meeting.[49] From the early ninth century Kentish charters quite frequently include dating material at the beginning or after the superscription, which could be a throwback to an earlier Kentish practice (see **42**, **46**, and p. lxxxiv, 28), but may also be imitation of synodal diplomatic. Disputes about land were regularly adjudicated at synods and the resulting settlement records couched in a synodal format (see S 1258, 1434, 1436) but from 811 this format was also used on occasion to record land-grants or land-exchanges (see S 168, 169). Under Archbishop Wulfred land-charters in general became far longer and more complex documents, in which the transactions and sometimes the estate history were described in detail. It is possible that this development can in part be attributed to the increasing influence of synodal procedure.

From the second half of the eighth century, charters in favour of lay beneficiaries become increasingly common, and this must have had an effect on the system of charter-production, reducing the role of beneficiaries in the process, and probably promoting the involvement of the local episcopal scriptorium. Certainly from the turn of the eighth century, when charters from the cathedral archives begin to be available, Christ Church can be seen to be playing an important part in charter-production (although there was evidently no fixed procedure, since a charter in favour of Archbishop Wulfred issued in Mercia in 815 (S 178) was drafted in recognisably Mercian formulas). In the central decades of the ninth century the archiepiscopal scriptorium was dominant; the standard formulation which had evolved there was used for charters in favour of the abbots of St Augustine's as well as various laymen, and can be distinguished from the formulation of Rochester charters and of those produced in Mercia and Wessex.

iv. *Kentish charters from c. 825 until 1066*

Kentish charter-production in the ninth century has been very thoroughly analysed by Professor Nicholas Brooks, who has demonstrated that the majority of surviving originals dealing with land in the Cahterbury diocese were probably written by Christ Church scribes, and has analysed the

---

[49] Anglo-Saxon synodal diplomatic is discussed at length in C.R.E. Cubitt, *Anglo-Saxon Church Councils c. 650-c. 850*, unpubl Ph.D. thesis, Cambridge University (1990), pp. 96–113.

distinctive formulas evolved within the scriptorium, which became fossilized after the accession of Archbishop Ceolnoth in 833.[50] These formulas can be seen in several of the mid-century charters preserved at St Augustine's (**18, 19, 20, 22, 23**); three of these documents are directly in favour of the abbot and community, which may show that the cathedral scriptorium was now producing charters on behalf of other religious houses in the diocese (or else was supplying them with diplomatic models). An exception to the general pattern is **21**, a charter in favour of an ealdorman, which was drawn up in Wiltshire in West Saxon formulas.

From the second quarter of the ninth century the level of Latin literacy in Canterbury seems to have plummeted, so that by the beginning of Alfred's reign the archiepiscopal scriptorium could field only one manifestly incompetent scribe capable of drawing up a Latin diploma.[51] Standards of grammar and orthography fell very low, and it is probably no coincidence that charter-scribes in this period increasingly resorted to standardized formulas, which could be copied from a model; those sections of the charter which they were forced to draft from scratch are often unintelligible. Another consequence of poor Latin literacy was an increasing reliance on the vernacular for drawing up private charters, such as the two grants of food-render in the St Augustine's archive (**24, 25**).[52]

Some of the charters produced in Canterbury in the 870s show that the archiepiscopal scriptorium no longer understood the basic diplomatic principles. S 344 (A.D. 873) is a celebrated aberration. Essentially it seems to be an archiepiscopal charter modelled on a standard royal diploma, but a reference to King Alfred has been inconsequentially included at the beginning (perhaps taken from the model), while the witness-list is a miracle of incompetence, for the scribe has copied (twice over) a witness-list of the time of the late King Æthelwulf. A similar horror is S 319, perhaps from 874, where a Canterbury scribe has avoided the need to draw up a new diploma by ingeniously adapting an earlier diploma of King Æthelwulf covering an estate which was subsequently divided; an account of the property's subsequent history has been substituted for part of the dispositive section, the date has been altered, and an extra witness-list has been added after that of the original. To these two Canterbury disasters can be added a suggestive Rochester text (S 321), purportedly a charter of Æthelwulf, but

---

[50] Brooks, *Church of Canterbury*, pp. 167–74, 327–30. See also N. Brooks, 'The Pre-Conquest Charters of Christ Church, Canterbury', unpubl. D.Phil. thesis (Oxford, 1968), pp. 133–92.

[51] Brooks, *Church of Canterbury*, pp. 170–4.

[52] On the use of vernacular records in the ninth century, see Kelly 1990.

dated 880 with the correct indiction and an acceptable witness-list for that date (lacking a royal subscription). This has been seen as a charter of Alfred with the king's name altered (but for what purpose?); comparison with the two slightly earlier Canterbury examples suggests a different interpretation. Very few royal charters indeed have survived from the reigns of Alfred and Edward the Elder, in comparison with the relatively high numbers of extant diplomas issued by Æthelwulf and Alfred's brothers; indeed, there are no acceptable charters at all which can be placed in the last fifteen years of Edward's reign. The evidence suggests that the production of royal charters in the half century between Alfred's accession and his son's death slowed almost to a halt, and may even have stopped altogether.[53] In the Kentish context, the importance of this phenomenon lies in the possible explanation it provides for the aberrant charters of the 870s. If King Alfred was unwilling to issue new landbooks, except in very exceptional circumstances, then the Kentish scriptoria may have seen fit on certain occasions to draw up bastard documents ostensibly in the name of King Æthelwulf and to adapt earlier charters. Whether such procedures were 'official' and had royal sanction is open to question; here the issue of forgery is blurred by the fact that the responsibility for charter-production in normal times lay entirely in the hands of the bodies drawing up these peculiar texts.

The very unusual charter which records a restitution to St Augustine's on the day of King Athelstan's consecration (26) has to be seen against the background of the previous fifteen years, from which no royal diplomas have survived and during which it is possible that none was produced. Such a gap in the tradition of charter-writing may explain why 26 is couched in such an unconventional form, and provides a context for the subsequent developments in the production of royal diplomas throughout the English kingdom. From at least 928 until 934 or 935 all of Athelstan's diplomas, disposing of land in many different shires to various beneficiaries, ecclesiastical and lay, appear to have been drafted and written by a single scribe.[54] From this time onwards centralised production of royal diplomas, probably in a royal secretariat of some kind, seems to have been the norm in England; formulation, layout and script demonstrate that a single agency had responsibility for drawing up the bulk of surviving texts. There is a little evidence for occasional regional production, but generally this seems

---

[53] The reasons for this remain obscure: see D.N. Dumville, *Wessex and England from Alfred to Edgar* (Woodbridge, 1992), pp. 151–3; S. Keynes, 'The Charters of King Æthelwulf and his Sons', *English Historical Review* cix (1994), pp. 1111–48 at 1147 n. 1.

[54] Keynes, *Diplomas*, pp. 42–4; *BAFacs.*, p. 9.

to have been unusual.[55] Like the other episcopal scriptoria, Christ Church was no longer regularly involved in the writing of royal diplomas for its diocese, although its scribes still produced archiepiscopal and private deeds. The surviving royal diplomas from the tenth and eleventh century dealing with land in Kent (relatively few in number, compared with the ninth century; see above, pp. lxxii–lxxiii) seem to be the products of the central agency. In the St Augustine's archive the charters of Edmund and Eadred (27, 28) have formulation linked with that in contemporary charters for non-Kentish beneficiaries. Æthelred's diploma concerning land at Sibertswold (30) is less closely comparable to contemporary texts, but this is not unusual in the very late tenth century, when royal scribes tended to avoid recycling formulas and attempted to strike a novel note; there is no good reason to think that 30 is a local production. A charter of Edward the Confessor for Archbishop Eadsige, extant only in a very truncated form (36), can be related to other charters of that king. It is only Edgar's charter for St Augustine's (29) which seems to depart from the general trend; its formulation is largely based on that of ninth-century Canterbury texts, but it is probable that this text is a forgery based on an earlier model rather than evidence for a fleeting revival of local charter-writing in Canterbury. The scribes of the central agency were also responsible for writing royal writs in the eleventh century; the two examples from St Augustine's which seem to be genuine (35, 39) are acceptable as central products.

7. THE CONTAMINATION OF THE ARCHIVE IN THE POST-CONQUEST PERIOD

In the later middle ages St Augustine's produced no fewer than three house historians. Best known is the last of the three, Thomas Elmham, whose *Speculum Augustinianum* has won the plaudits of modern scholars for its sensitive and progressive use of documentary sources. Elmham was a monk at St Augustine's from 1379 until 1414, when he joined the Cluniac order and was made prior of Lenton. Apart from the *Speculum*, Elmham is known to have been responsible for three other historical works: an undistinguished chronicle, the *Cronica regum nobilium Anglie*, written in 1416 and based to

---

[55] For centralized production and the existence of a royal secretariat, see Keynes, *Diplomas*, esp. pp. 39–83. Some royal diplomas were still being drawn up in the regions; the most celebrated example is that of the so-called 'alliterative' charters, which have strong links with the West Midlands (see Keynes 1985, pp. 156–9).

an uncomfortable degree on Geoffrey of Monmouth; a lost prose life of Henry V, based on the *Gesta Henricii Quinti* (the latter has also been wrongly attributed to Elmham); and a *Libellus metrice de Henricio Quinto*. None of these scaled the heights of the *Speculum*.[56]

Elmham saw himself as heir to a long-standing historical tradition at St Augustine's. In his introduction he mentions his authorities: Bede and William of Malmesbury, but also earlier historians of the abbey, among whom he singles out Thomas Sprott and William Thorne. Sprott has enjoyed a considerable posthumous reputation, based primarily on the respectful citations of his work by Thorne and Elmham, rather than on the true excellence of his history, which is unprinted and was thought until recently to have been lost.[57] Bale had the information that Sprott had written two works, a *Cantuariorum historia* and the *Abbatum suorum uitae*. According to Tanner, there was a manuscript of the former in the library of William Cope in the seventeenth century, and a fragment (covering the period from 1055 to 1111) in BL Cotton Vitellius B. iv, which was lost in the Cotton fire. Tanner also gives an incipit for Sprott's *Chronicon*, presumably to be identified with the *Abbatum suorum uite*, which corresponds with that of a work surviving in London, Lambeth Palace, 419, fos 111–60, and BL Cotton Tiberius A. ix, fos 107–80.[58] These manuscripts can be securely identifed with two of the three volumes containing the *Cronica T. Sport* which are mentioned in the fifteenth-century catalogue of the St Augustine's library.[59] BL Cotton Tiberius A. ix is incomplete, breaking off *c*. 1265 (any continuation was lost when the manuscript was damaged in the Cotton fire); the text of

---

[56] For Elmham, see F. Taylor, 'A Note on Rolls Series 8', *Bulletin of the John Rylands Library* xx (1936), pp. 379–82; A. Gransden, 'Antiquarian Studies in Fifteenth-Century England', *Antiquaries' Journal* lx (1980), pp. 75–97; [repr. in her collected papers, *Legends, Traditions and History in Medieval England* (London, 1992), pp. 299–327]; *eadem, Historical Writing in England c. 1307 to the Early Sixteenth Century* (London, 1982), pp. 206–10, 345–55. For the only surviving manuscript of the *Speculum* (Cambridge, Trinity Hall, 1), see above, pp. lvii–lix.

[57] For the little that is known about Sprott, see J.C. Russell, *Dictionary of Writers of Thirteenth-Century England*, Bulletin of the Institute of Historical Research, Special Supplement iii (London, 1936), p. 170. The disappointing historical miscellany in Cambridge, University Library, Add. 3578, edited by Thomas Hearne as *Thomae Sprotti Chronica* (Oxford, 1719), seems to have been compiled in the later fourteenth century and to have been wrongly attributed to Sprott (in the fifteenth-century St Augustine's library-catalogue the manuscript appears as *Chronica W.T.*, suggesting an alternative identification as the work of William Thorne; see James, *Ancient Libraries*, pp. 296, 518 [no. 925]). W. Bell edited a similar text from a roll in the possession of Joseph Mayer, as *Thomas Sprott's Chronicle of Profane and Sacred History* (Liverpool, 1851).

[58] J. Bale, *Scriptorum Illustrium Maioris Brytanniae Catalogus* (Basle, [1559]), p. 326; T. Tanner, *Bibliotheca Britannico-Hibernica* (London, 1748), p. 685.

[59] James, *Ancient Libraries*, pp. 296, 519 (nos 929–31).

the history in Lambeth Palace 419 ends in 1221 (where there is a change of hand in the copy in BL Cotton Tiberius A. ix). The version in the Lambeth Palace manuscript probably represents an earlier state of the compilation (see further, p. lv). There is an early modern transcript of the history (possibly abbreviated), also ending in 1221, in BL Cotton Vitellius D. xi, fos 39–69; this was damaged in the Cotton fire, but is still mostly legible. Joscelin's epitome of a manuscript of Sprott's history ending in 1221 (possibly Lambeth Palace 419) is now BL Cotton Vitellius E. xiv, fos 237–52. There is a fair copy of this by Arthur Agard in BL Harley 692, fos 75–193.

The extant manuscripts point to a break in composition in 1221, although internal evidence shows that the author was writing after 1238. There is conflicting evidence for Sprott's floruit. Joscelin and other antiquarians associated him with the date 1270. The source for this may well have been William Thorne's statement, in the preface to his own history, that he had relied on Sprott's work until it ended in 1272. It is a complication that elsewhere Thorne indicates that his dependence on Sprott came to an end in 1228.[60] The fifteenth-century library catalogue notes that Thomas Sport or Sprot was the donor of seven volumes, and their content is broadly compatible with the traditional floruit in the second half of the thirteenth century.[61]

William Thorne lived almost a century later. It is known that he was an unsuccessful candidate for the abbacy in 1375, and that he acted as attorney for two abbots; in the course of his duties he spent two years in Italy following the papal court.[62] His history survives in two manuscripts; the version in CCCC 189 (ending in 1375) appears to represent an earlier recension, while that in BL Add. 53710 (ending in 1397) may be a revision by Thorne or a successor (see pp. lv–lvi). Thorne generously acknowledged his very great debt to Sprott, and comparison of his history with that of Sprott shows that he relied almost entirely on his predecessor's work for the pre-Conquest period. On a few rare occasions he does add something from another source, and in places he has tried to correct Sprott's dates where they seem inconsistent.

These three scholars are the only St Augustine's historians to whom we can give a name, but they were not the only post-Conquest members of the

[60] Twysden, *Scriptores*, cols 1757, 1881; Davis, *Thorne*, pp. 2, 196. See comment by Russell, *Dictionary*, p. 170.

[61] James, *Ancient Libraries*, pp. 271, 288, 309, 316, 351, 354, 391 (nos. 718, 859, 1043, 1094, 1300, 1334, 1657). See comment by A.B. Emden, *Donors of Books to St Augustine's Abbey, Canterbury*, Oxford Bibliographical Soc. Occasional Publications iv (Oxford, 1968), p. 16.

[62] For a brief survey of Thorne's life and work, see Davis, *Thorne*, pp. xxxiii–vii.

community who were interested in the abbey's past. For instance, the preliminary version of the register now split between BL Cotton Julius D. ii and BL Add. 46352, probably compiled in the 1230s (see pp. xlii–xliii), incorporates some chronological material, including a list of the kings of Kent and England from Æthelberht to Henry III, with their reign-lengths, and lists of popes, archbishops and Roman Emperors with the same details; there is also a simple list of abbots. The king-list (BL Cotton Julius D. ii, fo. 1rv) is especially interesting, because the compiler has inserted a column with notes about the activities of the kings in question. Some details are taken from Bede and other historical sources (evidently William of Malmesbury), but in a few instances the references are to royal grants to the abbey, information presumably derived from a list of benefactions or even from the abbey's muniments themselves (King Æthelwulf is said to have given Lenham to St Augustine's *per cartam suam*, which is probably a reference to the revised version of **21**). The interests of the compiler were focused entirely on the pre-Conquest period; the last event to which he refers is the Battle of Hastings, and he mentions none of the benefactions of the Norman kings. The chronological material in this register represents an early stage in the historical scholarship that was to culminate in the fifteenth century in Elmham's great chronological table, the *Chronologia Augustinensis* (prefixed to the *Speculum*; see p. lvii), which combines a vast amount of detail about the dates of popes, archbishops, kings and abbots, and about their activities in so far as they related to the history of St Augustine's.

Fixing an exact chronology was an intense preoccupation for all medieval historians, from Bede onwards, and posed particular problems for the scholars whose interests lay in the Anglo-Saxon period, as did those of the St Augustine's community. The great honour of being the first monastery to be founded by the English apostle, the ambitious claims to a special status which were later established on that priority, and the fact that the most important estates were acquired before the ninth century, all served to direct the attention of the abbey's historians to the early Anglo-Saxon period. A basic chronological framework could be built up with material derived from narrative histories, principally Bede and Willam of Malmesbury, which gave details of kings and reign-lengths and of general political events. The post-Conquest historians of St Augustine's had to integrate into this framework the information which they had about the history of their house. It is likely that they had access to some records kept from the very earliest period of the abbey's existence, material such as that with which Abbot Albinus had supplied Bede in the early eighth century, and there may have been collections of annals which have since been lost. The abbey kept records of the sequence and dates of its abbots, although these had become very corrupt by the fifteenth century (see Appendix 4). Some material, especially about Minster-in-Thanet, was derived from earlier hagiographical works, which in certain respects could provide a relative chronology. In addition, and overshadowing all these other sources of information, there was the abbey's rich collection of pre-Conquest charters, the dating clauses of which (especially those that included regnal years) could be used to fix the abbey's history within the general chronology deduced from narrative histories.

The St Augustine's historians worked with great diligence to combine this mass of material into a coherent whole, and in doing so built up skills in the use of muniments which came to fruition in Elmham's sensitive analysis of pre-Conquest charters in the *Speculum*. But the integrated chronology for the abbey's history which was so carefully pieced together had some spectacular flaws, for two principal reasons. In the first place, the historians were unaware that their general chronological framework was in some respects deficient. This is particularly unfortunate for the eighth century, when the sequence of the kings of Kent becomes very complex. The last event of Kentish history which Bede relates is the death of Wihtred in 725 and the succession of his three sons, Æthelberht, Eadberht and Alric (*HE* v. 23). The Anglo-Saxon Chronicle supplemented Bede's information with two obits, one for Eadberht in 748 and one for Æthelberht in 762; it next refers to a king of Kent when it describes the rebellion of 'King' Eadberht Præn in 796–8. Faced with this unpromising material, William of Malmesbury provided a concrete sequence of successive kings: Eadberht (725–48), Æthelberht (748–62), Alric (762–96) and Eadberht Præn (796–8).[63] It is this sequence which is reflected in the thirteenth-century king-list found in BL Cotton Julius D. ii (see above). William's model completely distorts the true picture: Alric probably never ruled, while Æthelberht and Eadberht were joint-rulers for over two decades; in the central decades of the eighth century, particularly the 760s, there was a rapid turnover of joint-kings in Kent, most of whom are known only through their surviving charters (see Appendix 3). The St Augustine's archive contained eighth-century charters, including two of the obscure King Eadberht II (*c.* 762–4), which could not be reconciled with William's regnal framework.

The second factor which impeded the abbey's historians in their quest for a reliable chronology was an early episode of interference with the muniments.

---

[63] *Willelmi Malmesbiriensis Monachi de Gestis Regum Anglorum Libri Quinque*, ed. W. Stubbs, 2 vols, RS (London, 1887–9), i. 17–18.

Already by the first half of the thirteenth century, as the cartulary in BL Cotton Julius D. ii demonstrates, some texts in the archive which were originally in favour of lay beneficiaries had been tampered with to create direct grants to the abbey. In at least two ninth-century documents concerning land at Lenham (**16, 21**), the name of Abbot Wernoth had been substituted for that of the original beneficiary. A tenth-century diploma granting land at Sibertswold to a thegn named Sigeric (**27**) became a direct grant to St Augustine's through the simple transformation of the thegn into an abbot. Such emendation played havoc with attempts to match the muniments with the available information about the sequence and dates of abbots; by the fifteenth century 'Abbot' Sigeric had been integrated into the abbatial list and provided with fictional dates.

The apparent discrepancies between the abbey's muniments and the accepted general chronology for the period appear to have created considerable difficulties for medieval students of the archive. Not only were such inconsistencies worrying in themselves; they also threw a measure of doubt on the authenticity of the abbey's precious ancient records and title-deeds. In order to solve this problem, certain St Augustine's scholars seem to have succumbed to the temptation to alter the dates of some of their Anglo-Saxon muniments. As far as it is possible to tell, the bulk of this interference probably took place at some point between the late thirteenth century and the early fifteenth. There is no trace of this chronological contamination in the texts of the charters contained in the thirteenth-century cartularies, but it is all too evident in the texts in Elmham's history.

The blatant nature of the tampering is immediately clear in **10**, which was preserved in a Christ Church copy as well as at St Augustine's. In the Christ Church single sheet the transaction is said to have taken place in King Wihtred's eighth year and in the twelfth indiction; this is also the dating in the thirteenth-century St Augustine's copy in PRO E 164/27 (another thirteenth-century copy, in BL Cotton Julius D. ii, breaks off before the dating clause). In Elmham's version of the text, Wihtred's grant takes place in his twenty-eighth year and in the second indiction. In this case it is unclear why the dates should have been altered in this way.

One of King Swæfheard's charters in the Minster archive seems to have been emended in order to connect it with the invasion of Kent by Æthelred of Mercia in 676, as mentioned by Bede (*HE* iv. 12). Originally **40** was issued by Swæfheard in March of his second year and the second indiction, and confirmed by Æthelred in Mercia in January 691, the fourth indiction; the use of an incarnation year in Æthelred's confirmation is acceptable in a Mercian context at this period (see p. lxxxiv). This is the reading of the text in PRO E 164/27; the copy in BL Cotton Julius D. ii has the same regnal year and indiction in the first part of the charter, but breaks off before the notice of Æthelred's confirmation. Elmham's version of **40** has very different dating information. Swæfheard's initial grant is said to have taken place in his second year but in the fourth indiction; Æthelred's confirmation is dated to 676, but still in the fourth indiction. This is evidently a deliberate substitution, and rather clumsy since the detail about the indiction makes the document internally inconsistent. The reason for the emendation appears to have been a misunderstanding of the wording of Æthelred's confirmation; the phrase 'dum ille adfirmauerat terram nostram' ('when he confirmed our land') has been taken as a reference to a Mercian invasion of Kent and has thus been connected with Bede's account of Æthelred's ravaging of the kingdom in 676. It is very disturbing that in this case Elmham claims to have been using the 'original' of the charter, explicitly preferring it to the cartulary text. The implication is that an emended single-sheet version of this charter had been created, so convincing that Elmham was deceived.

Another reason to redate **40** was provided by the identification of Swæfheard's sometime joint-ruler, Oswine, with the famous Oswiu of Northumbria. Elmham manfully supports this connection, which causes considerable difficulty in view of the known fact that Oswiu died in 670. In his text he quotes Bede (*HE* iv. 5) on the date of Oswiu's death; in his chronological table he is forced to place Oswine's charters, with Swæfheard's, around the year 675.[64] Scenting discrepancy, a revisor of the Trinity Hall manuscript (possibly Elmham himself) has gone so far as to rewrite Bede, altering Elmham's quotation to shift Oswiu's death to 675. This is an unnerving example of the cumulative error which could result once a text had been altered. The mistaken identification of Oswine with Oswiu and the consequent dating nightmare probably also accounts for the creation of a version of **41** in which Oswine's confirmatory subscription has been dropped; this was another instance where Elmham's 'original' had a reading inferior to that in the cartularies.

It is noticeable that, while Elmham has been terribly deceived by the redated version of **40**, Sprott seems to have used the unemended version; he does not give the incarnation year of the charter, but calmly places the charters of Swæfheard and Oswine into the correct period, between the death of Eadric and the accession of Wihtred. The implication is that the

---

[64] Hardwick, *Elmham*, pp. 6, 231.

emendation took place between Sprott's time and the early fifteenth century. Thorne here simply follows Sprott, so can provide no additional information about the date of tampering.

Other instances of dating discrepancy between the thirteenth-century cartulary texts and those in the *Speculum* occur in three charters of the 760s. Two of these are diplomas of a King Eadberht, in favour of St Augustine's and Minster respectively, both attested by Archbishop Bregowine and thus narrowly datable to between 761 and 764 (**13**, **53**). The only explicit dating information given in these charters is a regnal year. The thirteenth-century texts of these documents date them to the first and second years of King Eadberht, but Elmham puts them both in Eadberht's thirty-sixth year. Elmham identifies the donor of these charters with the son of Wihtred, who began to reign in 725, according to Bede and William of Malmesbury; he quotes these charters as evidence that Eadberht did not die in 748, as some authorities supposed.[65] Elmham is apparently arguing in good faith, but he is wrong; Eadberht I did die in 748 and the charters in the St Augustine's archive were issued by a later king of the same name, perhaps his nephew (see Appendix 3). It is remarkable that the third surviving charter of Eadberht II (S 1612), preserved in the Christ Church archive, has also been equipped with a false date as the result of confusion with Eadberht I.

A charter of Offa appears in the *Speculum* rather incongruously sandwiched between the two diplomas of Eadberht II, and with a regnal year which similarly differs from that in the thirteenth-century cartularies. **14** is dated to Offa's first year in BL Cotton Julius D. ii and PRO E 164/27, but to his fifth year in Elmham's history. The charter itself appears to be a forgery, which is probably why neither regnal year is acceptable; the emendation which is reflected in Elmham's text was presumably prompted by the unsatisfactory original version. The principal reason for emendation here may have been a problem with the abbot. The beneficiary is Æthelnoth, who was not consecrated until 764, according to Sprott's information; Offa's first year may have seemed a little early for a grant to this beneficiary (although his fifth year is not much better).

The attention of the revisor(s) of the archive was usually focused on apparent dating discrepancies, but in one case it was the name of a beneficiary which was changed for historical reasons. The version of **16** preserved in BL Cotton Julius D. ii names as the beneficiary of the royal grant Abbot Wernoth, but a second reference to the beneficiary later in the text unexpectedly mentions a certain Eanberht. It is almost certain that the charter

---

[65] Hardwick, *Elmham*, p. 324.

was originally in favour of a layman named Eanberht, and that Wernoth's name was substituted to create a direct grant to the abbey; the revisor missed the second reference to the beneficiary. But Elmham's text names an Abbot Cunred in both instances. In his chronological table the ostensible date of the grant (A.D. 804) falls into the period assigned to Cunred's abbacy. It appears that Elmham's version represents a second revision of the charter, making it internally consistent and also consistent with the current dating of the abbots. Sprott (followed by Thorne) has Wernoth as the beneficiary of **16**; he was using the text after its first revision, but before the second.

Wernoth's name was also substituted for that a layman in **21**, a charter of 850 again covering land at Lenham (possibly the same estate). The substitution predated the compilation of the register underlying BL Cotton Julius D. ii in the second quarter of the thirteenth century. In this case, we know that the original survived unaltered, for it was submitted to Edward II for confirmation in 1326. But the emended version was known to Sprott and appears in the PRO charter-list (Appendix 2, no. xxv). A charter dated 850 in the name of Abbot Wernoth was problematic to the medieval students of the archive, since Wernoth's traditional dates were 822 to 844. It was perhaps for this reason that the emended text was sometimes associated with the date 840. Sprott puts it in that year, although the PRO charter-list retains the original dating of 850; the copy in BL Cotton Julius D. ii breaks off before the dating clause, so it is unclear which reading was followed by its exemplar. Elmham's chronological table (the *Speculum* proper ends in the early ninth century) refers to the unrevised version of the text under the year 850, but has an erased entry for 840 which is perhaps a reference to the emended version of the text. It is important to note that Sprott seems to have seen a version of the emended text of **21** in which the date had been altered for historical reasons. This is the first indication that scholarly emendation of the muniments may have taken place before the time of Sprott as well as later.

PRO E 164/27 provides further evidence for historical tampering from the later thirteenth or early fourteenth century. In the text of **53**, Eadberht II's charter for Minster, the name of the donor is given as Æthelberht, a significant variant in view of the prevailing confusion about the sequence of Kentish kings in the eighth century; the changed regnal year in Elmham's text of **53** represents a different attempt to deal with the problem of an apparently anachronistic charter of Eadberht I. The entry for **53** in the PRO charter-list ascribes the charter to *Aelbertus* (Appendix 2, no. v). Other entries in the charter-list are incorrect simply through scribal error: charters of Æthelbald, Oswine and Æthelwulf are wrongly said to have been issued by Æthelberht, Edwin and Coenwulf (Appendix 2, nos vii, xiii, xxv). There are further errors in the references to the current archbishop in two entries (Appendix 2, nos vi, xviii). Mistakes of this kind could be as influential in creating chronological distortion as deliberate emendation.

Sprott's reference to the emended and redated version of **21** and the witness of PRO E 164/27 to an early attempt to emend **53** together indicate that St Augustine's scholars were beginning to tamper with their muniments for historical reasons as early as the thirteenth century. By the early fifteenth century the habit of emendation of early documents had become ingrained, and in certain cases the revisions seem to have been supported by the creation of new single-sheet charters. It was this habit of mind which made it possible to create precise but fictional dates for many of the pre-Conquest abbots (see Appendix 4). The difficulty about chronological emendation of muniments was that the changes had an inevitable cumulative effect. This is immediately obvious in the Trinity Hall manuscript of Elmham's history, where the author or a later revisor has erased and rewritten certain dates in an effort to bring about some consistency. The difficulties seem to have been crystallized by the creation of the ambitious chronological table, which painfully exposed dating discrepancies; the table itself shows signs of considerable revision. In the text of the *Speculum* we find that the indictions of **1**, **2** and **5**, and of the privileges of Adeodatus and Agatho, blithely wrong since at least the twelfth century, have been erased and corrected (presumably under the influence of the chronological table); it is amusing to note that Elmham's 'facsimiles' of **1** and **2** have also been corrected in this way. A significant emendation in the manuscript is the regnal year in **49**, which initially seems to have been the donor's first year (as in the earlier cartulary texts); the original reading has been erased and replaced by *xxii*, apparently under the influence of **50**, the next document to be copied (although, since **50** survives only in the Trinity Hall manuscript, it is possible that its regnal year has also been silently emended). In the chronological table, both charters are assigned to 732. Other revisions in the manuscript concern the dates of King Lucius and the obits of Archbishop Wulfred and King Oswiu.

The chronological contamination of the pre-Conquest muniments of St Augustine's is an extraordinary phenomenon. We may deplore the decision to emend the charters, and such revision has sown confusion among modern scholars of the archive, but study of this activity provides some insight into the way that medieval scholars came to grips with the complexities of the Anglo-Saxon past and into their attitudes to pre-Conquest documentation.

8. THE ESTATES OF ST AUGUSTINE'S ABBEY

In 1086 St Augustine's was one of the wealthiest monasteries in England, appearing in fifth place in Knowles's league-table of monastic landholders.[66] In addition to substantial estates, the abbot and monks owned the borough of Fordwich and thirteen burgess-tenements in Canterbury, as well as seventy tenements attached to the Canterbury manor of Langport. More than three-quarters of this endowment, including all the most important estates, was located in the north-east tip of Kent, mostly in four areas flanking the Wantsum Channel: in Thanet; along the Stour below Canterbury and in the marshland to the north; around the mouth and the lower reaches of the Little Stour; and around Northbourne. The rest was to be found scattered elsewhere in Kent: on the formerly-wooded slopes of the Downs, on the fringes of the Weald and in Romney Marsh. The only one of the abbey's Domesday estates that was situated outside the Canterbury diocese was Plumstead, lying in the Woolwich marshes bordering the Thames. The abbey's holdings comprised approximately a tenth of the total Domesday assessment of Kent.

Additional evidence about the abbey's estates in the early post-Conquest period can be drawn from three texts in one of the thirteenth-century cartularies, PRO E 164/27, which seem to derive from a Kentish survey contemporary with Domesday Book.[67] The longest of these texts, which incorporates material not directly connected with the abbey's estates and in its present form dates from the reign of Henry I or later, has been printed in parallel with corresponding sections of Domesday Book and the *Domesday Monachorum*.[68] The other texts, neither of which has been printed, are exclusively concerned with abbey property. The longer of the two begins 'Noticia terrarum sancti Augustini in comitatu de Kent in quo lasco et in quo hundredo' and has a later medieval heading 'Extractum textu sancti Adriani' (11v–13r; for the *Textus S. Adriani*, see above pp. xxxvi–xxxvii). It shares much of its material with the text edited by Ballard, but has a very different order and some variant details. The third and shortest text, headed

---

[66] D. Knowles, *The Monastic Order in England*, 2nd edn (Cambridge, 1963), p. 702.
[67] See discussion of the Kentish satellite surveys by: P.H. Sawyer, 'The "Original Returns" and Domesday Book', *English Historical Review* lxx (1955), pp. 177–97 at 193–4; R.S. Hoyt, 'A Pre-Domesday Kentish Assessment List', *A Medieval Miscellany for Doris Mary Stenton*, ed. P.M. Barnes and C.F. Slade, Pipe Roll Society n.s. xxxvi (1962 for 1960), pp. 189–202; S. Harvey, 'Domesday Book and its Predecessors', *English Historical Review* lxxxvi (1971), pp. 753–73 at 754–9.
[68] See Ballard, *Inquisition*.

'Brevis recapitulatio solingorum', is little more than a list of estates and their assessments, but it has some details which differ from those in the other compilations (16v–17r). The relationships of these documents to each other and to Domesday Book and the *Domesday Monachorum* have not yet been properly studied. In general these surveys have little to add to the Domesday account of the abbey's estates; any significant information which they can provide has been noted in the commentaries.

The concentration of the abbey's Domesday estates within Kent, and indeed within East Kent, calls for some comment. Other great Anglo-Saxon abbeys had a far more widespread endowment; Peterborough, for example, owned property in seven counties in 1086, although its total wealth at that time seems to have been far less than that of St Augustine's. The nature of the St Augustine's endowment is probably a reflection of the abbey's long history and local standing; in the early centuries of its existence it was endowed by the Kentish kings, for whom it functioned as a dynastic burial-place, and subsequently it enjoyed the continuous patronage of local landowners, in contrast to the new foundations and refoundations of the tenth century which tended to build up their endowments quickly from a broader base of patrons in the united English kingdom. However, it is also possible that there was a deliberate policy to restrict the endowment to Kent. Far-flung estates were vulnerable to local encroachment and changes in political circumstances, and it may have been difficult for the monks to manage property that was a great distance away; the abbey's estate at Plumstead, for instance, was partly lost to Earl Godwine in the eleventh century (see commentary to **29**). The community may have found it convenient to concentrate its endowment close to Canterbury, and to this end perhaps solicited donations from this area and disposed of estates further afield.[69] The two most important acquisitions by the community in the later Anglo-Saxon period, when there was a greater scope for gaining possession of lands in other parts of England, were the extensive Thanet property and two-thirds of the borough of Fordwich, both close to the abbey. The archive contains no reference to interests in land outside Kent before the Conquest, but this proves nothing either way since the preservation of charters depended in large part on the continued possession of property.

It is possible to give a very tentative account of the growth of the endowment in Kent, but first a distinction must be drawn between those

---

[69] There is some evidence that Archbishop Wulfred in the early ninth century pursued a policy of retrenchment in respect of the Christ Church endowment (Brooks, *Church of Canterbury*, pp. 138–9).

charters which are in favour of the abbot or the community and those in favour
of laymen, for the time that elapsed between the initial donation and the
transfer of *land and boc* to the church is frequently uncertain, and in some
circumstances it is by no means clear that the property in question ever belonged to the abbey. It is a complication that in some instances it can be shown
that charters in favour of laymen were tampered with to create direct grants
to the abbey (see **16, 21, 27**); when a charter survives only in a single cartulary
copy, it may be impossible to detect or prove such tampering.

St Augustine's was a long-established foundation and we have no evidence
that the continuity of its endowment was ever seriously interrupted. Many
of its more important estates may have been first acquired in the seventh
century, and, as a result, their documentation may have been found deficient
by the later Anglo-Saxon period. It is debatable whether land-charters were
being produced in England as early as the time of Augustine and his
immediate successors (see pp. lxxiv–lxxv). Even if such documents were
being issued from the beginning of the seventh century, they are likely to
have been written on papyrus, which would have quickly decayed in the
English climate. Early land-charters may also have been lost or destroyed
as the result of fires and Viking assaults, or simply mislaid. It is therefore
not surprising that some of the core endowment is not covered by authentic
landbooks. Efforts to repair the deficiency were made in the eleventh century,
through the fabrication of royal diplomas. **1** covered the abbey precincts. **2**
was intended to be a title-deed for the precincts and also the manor of
Langport immediately to the south. The title for the important estate of
Chislet, on the Wantsum to the north-east of Canterbury, was supplied by
a third charter of Æthelberht (**3**), while the manor of Northbourne was
covered by a charter of Eadbald (**5**). It is probable that the community did
acquire some land in the Langport area soon after its foundation, but the
bounds in **2** are likely to represent the accumulation of many smaller
land-grants in the area. Similarly, while Northbourne may well have been
an early acquisition, the thirty hides of the charter are exactly equivalent to
the Domesday reckoning and again are likely to be the result of the
consolidation of a number of smaller properties. There may also be some
truth in the claim that St Augustine's was given land in Chislet in the seventh
century; it has been suggested that the ancient region known as the 'Stour
ge' (Sturry) was split between three minsters in this period, with the northern
part used for the foundation of Reculver, the central part forming the St
Augustine's Chislet estate, and the final section (retaining the name Sturry)
being transferred to Minster-in-Thanet.[70]

[70] Tatton-Brown 1992, p. 85.

The earliest genuine charters in favour of the abbey cover land in the vicinity of Canterbury (**7, 12**), at Littlebourne just to the east (**9**) and at Mongeham near Northbourne (**13**; see also **14**); all these places are situated on the coastal plain, on or close to waterways, in areas of early Anglo-Saxon settlement.[71] **8** and **11** are distinctive in that they transfer facilities, in the first instance an iron mine which was probably located in the Weald, in the second pasture-rights in the same area (in exchange for use of a mill belonging to the monastery); **11** shows that the abbey also already held property in the upland of the Greensand ridge to the south of Holmesdale. **8** and **11** must be seen in the context of other eighth-century Kentish charters which transfer to single owners common rights in the Weald and marshland that had previously been vested in communities.[72]

During the ninth century the abbey's sights moved further afield, to the downlands which were then begining to be exploited and cleared.[73] There is clear evidence of interest in Lenham, in the form of a grant of five sulungs there made to the abbot in 838 (**19**); in addition the archive preserves two ninth-century charters in favour of laymen covering twenty sulungs and forty hides in the same place, both probably referring to the same estate (**16, 21**). Other downland grants were at Lynsore near Bossingham (**20**) and Martin, to the south of Northbourne (**22**). Another focus of interest was around Ashford in Holmesdale. In the later ninth century the abbey acquired estates at Mersham, Willesborough and Hinxhill (see S 332 and discussion on p. xxxii n. 57; S (Add.) 1651a and S 1652, for which see Appendix 1, nos ii, iii). From the early ninth century comes the first evidence that St Augustine's was beginning to acquire land in Thanet (**17**).

Relatively few of the large number of extant tenth-century diplomas deal with land-transactions in Kent (see pp. lxxii–lxxiii). The St Augustine's archive contains only five formal charters from the tenth century. One is a probable forgery in the name of Edgar relating to Plumstead (**29**), another an anomalous but probably credible document recording Athelstan's restoration of land in Thanet to the abbey (**26**). The three remaining diplomas are in favour of laymen. One relates to Swalecliffe on the coast to the north

---

[71] For the history of settlement in Kent, see A. Everitt, *Continuity and Colonization: the Evolution of Kentish Settlement* (Leicester, 1986).

[72] See **47** and commentary. For discussion of the Kentish commons and their break-up, see K. Witney, *The Jutish Forest: a Study of the Weald of Kent from 450–1380 A.D.* (London, 1976). The importance of transhumance in the Kentish economy, the most significant underlying factor in the creation and exploitation of the commons, is considered by Everitt, *Continuity*, especially pp. 32–9.

[73] Everitt, *Continuity*, pp. 135–40.

of Canterbury and has a note of the regrant of the estate to St Augustine's by the beneficiary (28). The other two are concerned with Sibertswold in the downland to the south-west of Northbourne (27, 30), which was in the abbey's possession by the Conquest.

In the eleventh century the St Augustine's endowment was enormously increased as the result of the absorption of estates formerly associated with Minster-in-Thanet; the manor of Minster, reckoned at forty-eight sulungs, made up approximately a third of the abbey's total Domesday assessment. The acquisition was later rationalized as a donation by Cnut, but the true story seems to be more complex, involving purchase, piecemeal acquisition and perhaps arbitrary encroachment, leading to a dispute settled at the beginning of Edward's reign (see pp. xxx–xxxi). At least two royal charters were later forged to cover the Minster lands, a diploma in the name of the Confessor (34) and later a writ attributed to Cnut (33); there is also some evidence for a lost diploma in the name of Cnut (see commentary to 33). The moving force behind the acquisition of the Minster property seems to have been the energetic abbot Ælfstan ([1023 × 1027]-1045), who also made a spirited but ultimately unsuccessful bid to secure toll-rights in Sandwich (see pp. xix–xx). It may have been in compensation for the abbey's disappointment in the Sandwich affair that King Edward ceded to it two-thirds of the borough of Fordwich (39).

The abbey ran into some difficulties in the early years after the Conquest. There is some evidence that Abbot Æthelsige was intimidated into giving up some of the abbey's possessions to the Normans, including its share of Fordwich; his successor, the Norman Abbot Scotland, was credited with regaining most of the lost property.[74] A rather dubious writ of the Conqueror arranges for the restoration of Fordwich and other lands alienated by Æthelsige.[75] It is possible that this represents in part the return of leased estates which had slipped from the abbey's control during the confusion of the Conquest. Such may have been the situation in the case of Badlesmere, where the tenant seems to have changed his allegiance (S [Add.] 1657a; Appendix 1, no. xii). An eleventh-century memorandum preserved in two of the thirteenth-century cartularies lists a number of tiny estates lost to the Normans, some of which had been let to tenants and allegedly stolen by Hugh de Montfort and William de Arques.[76] The Domesday survey indicates

[74] Twysden, Scriptores, cols 1788–9; Davis, Thorne, pp. 50–2.
[75] Hardwick, Elmham, p. 352 (Regesta, i, no. 98).
[76] 'Iste sunt terrule quas ab antiquo tempore et in diebus Eadwardi regis sanctus Augustinus habuit sed sibi potestas diuicium eas contradicentibus fratribus abstulit: unum iugum quod uocatur Suanetun sibi Hugo de Mundfort iniuste usurpauit et .xxx. agros quos Godwine

that the abbey's endowment was not seriously affected as a result of the Conquest. Odo of Bayeux, the main predator in Kent, seems to have been favourably disposed towards the abbey, and in 1075 handed over the remaining third of the borough of Fordwich at William's request.[77] There was some disagreement over Odo's claims to meadowland belonging to St Augustine's, but the community's main grudge appears to have been his tenure of part of their Plumstead manor, supposedly first seized by Earl Godwine.[78] An estate of half a sulung at Garrington was acquired from Odo in exchange for a small part of the manor of Littlebourne (GDB 12r).

The correspondence between the charters in the archive and the abbey's Domesday estates is not particularly close. Only in the case of three forged charters (5, 14, 29) does the land-assessment have some agreement with the Domesday reckoning; generally the two are quite different.[79] For several of the abbey's pre-Conquest estates we know of no Anglo-Saxon charter, extant, lost or forged: Bekesbourne, Ashenfield, Dernedale, Rooting, Ripton (but see 11), Shillingham, Wadholt, Preston, Elmstone and *Lanport* in Stowting hundred. It is possible that some of these were mainland estates of Minster-in Thanet which passed to the abbey (see below). Conversely, a number of the charters in the archive have no apparent connection with the

---

Punterlyn de East Brigge tenebat et unum iugum de Hortone et Hengestelle quod Wilfric Pullchare de sancto Augustino tenebat et terram Alfsicumbe suue de qua sanctus Augustinus solebat habere seruicia. Willelmus de Arces habet dimidium aratrum atte Broke quod Siric habuit.' (PRO E 164/27, 2v: see also BL Cotton Julius D. ii, 108r). For Swanton, see GDB 13v. Sprott (BL Cotton Tiberius A. ix, 115r) mentions the loss of Horton and Hinxhill to Hugh de Montfort, together with the Brabourne food-rent granted in 24 (see also Thorne: Twysden, *Scriptores*, col. 1777; Davis, *Thorne*, p. 33).

[77] GDB 12r; see Hardwick, *Elmham*, p. 351. For Odo and St Augustine's, see N.P. Brooks and H.E. Walker, 'The Authority and Interpretation of the Bayeux Tapestry', *Proceedings of the Battle Conference* i (1978), pp. 1–34, 191–9, at 17.

[78] See 29 for Plumstead. The dispute over meadowland is mentioned in a memorandum edited by F.R.H. Du Boulay, *The Lordship of Canterbury* (London, 1966), pp. 38–9.

[79] Correspondence between assessments in Domesday Book and the hidages mentioned in pre-Conquest charters is often taken as an encouraging sign of the authenticity of the latter. But, except in the case of diplomas issued in the very late Anglo-Saxon period, such correspondence is more likely to be found in spurious charters. Various factors combined to alter the assessments of estates over the centuries, such as fiscal concessions, the break-up of larger land-units and the amalgamation of neighbouring properties. Analysis of large archives such as Abingdon, which preserve series of charters dealing with the same named estates, demonstrate the extent to which assessments changed over the period. Especially when dealing with seventh- and eighth-century charters, it is necessary to be wary when confronted with apparently static assessments. In the Kentish Domesday the main assessment is in *solini* or sulungs, which seem to be a primarily fiscal measure; the subsidiary reference to ploughlands may give a more accurate indication of the extent of the manor: see J. Witney, 'The Period of Mercian Rule in Kent, and a Charter of A.D. 811', *AC* civ (1988 for 1987), pp. 87–113 at 104–9.

abbey's Domesday property. Some of the estates concerned may well be subsumed in another entry (for example, **6**, **7**, **8**, **22**); others cannot be properly identified (**18**, **31**).

9. THE LANDS AND PRIVILEGES OF MINSTER-IN-THANET

The fourteen surviving charters from Minster-in-Thanet probably came into the possession of St Augustine's when it acquired the Minster estates in the eleventh century. The unique feature of the collection, the inclusion of five eighth-century privileges remitting ship-toll which are unlikely to have had any remaining validity in the late Anglo-Saxon period, suggests that the abbey took over Minster's extant archive root and branch, and did not simply acquire the documents as individual titledeeds to specific estates and privileges. Indeed, it is possible that some of the places named in some of the early charters were already obscure. As early as 1044/5 the abbey based its claim to the Minster lands, not on the charters, but on the tendentious proposition that Cnut's grant of the relics of St Mildrith entailed also the grant of her property (S 1472; see pp. xxx–xxxi). When a collection of documents relevant to the Minster manor was put together in the early fourteenth century, the early Minster charters were not included (Canterbury, D. & C., Lit. 19; see above pp. liv–lv).

The eight land-charters in favour of the abbesses of Minster-in-Thanet relate mainly to grants on Thanet itself and in the Sturry area on the mainland. There are two outliers: **41** includes a reference to a grant of land at Bodsham in the centre of the Downland, and **47** disposes of a small area by the River *Limen* in the vicinity of Romney Marsh, probably for use as pasture. It is very unlikely that the surviving documents give an accurate picture of Minster's endowment in its heyday. There are hints that the community held property elsewhere on the mainland. In 826 it acquired a small area at Stourmouth from St Augustine's in exchange for a piece of land the same size near Margate (**17**). An estate at an unidentified place named *Scirdun* granted to a cleric by King Ecgberht in 836 (**18**) was bordered by land belonging to 'Southminster', which was the usual name for Minster-in-Thanet at that date (see p. xxviii n. 45). A charter of 948 granting land at Wickhambreux to a religious woman (S 535) mentions appurtenant woodland in the area of Blean Forest, north of Canterbury, which was bordered on one side by property belong to 'St Mildrith's community' (see pp. xxix–xxx). The estates absorbed by St Augustine's probably represent the rump of the Minster endowment. Some land may have been lost during the travails of the ninth century, and more in the following centuries of apparent decline. Finally, the surviving endowment seems to have been broken up in the reign of Cnut; Abbot Ælfstan of St Augustine's acquired half from an unnamed vendor, and his efforts to reconstitute the whole endowment are unlikely to have been entirely successful (see pp. xix, xxx–xxxi).

The fate of Minster's mainland property is by no means clear. For what it is worth, the forged writ in the name of Cnut granting Mildrith's relics to the abbey mentions the transfer of *tota terra sua infra insulam Tanet et extra* (**33**). Several of the early Minster charters cover land in Sturry (then the name of the region lying north-east of Canterbury). It has been argued that the Sturry region may have been divided in the seventh century between Minster-in-Thanet (which acquired the southern section, retaining the name Sturry), St Augustine's (which received the central portion, representing its later manor of Chislet) and Reculver (established on the northern section).[80] St Augustine's Domesday manor of Sturry, reckoned at five exempt sulungs, with land for twelve ploughs (GDB 12r) could be former Minster land acquired along with Thanet in the eleventh century, but it may equally well have come into the abbey's possession at an earlier date.[81] It is difficult to match the Minster charters relating to other mainland estates with the Domesday endowment of St Augustine's. The sulung at Bodsham held by St Augustine's in 1086 is likely to be the land donated by Æthelric Bigga in the Confessor's reign (**38**). It is possible that some mainland estates acquired with the Minster endowment were reckoned under the Thanet manor of Minster, just as the manor of Chislet included land near Margate on Thanet which the abbey had owned before the eleventh century (see commentary to **17**). One example of this may be Tenterden ('the den of the men of Thanet'), which was accounted part of the manor of Minster in the thirteenth century and has a parish church dedicated to St Mildrith.[82]

The manor of Minster was the essential part of the endowment. Assessed at forty-eight sulungs in 1086 (GDB 12r), it was an enormous consolidated estate extending over the greater part of the island; the remainder of Thanet formed the Monkton manor owned by the Christ Church community and reckoned at eighteen sulungs (twenty TRE; GDB 4v–5r). In Elmham's

---

[80] Tatton-Brown 1992, p. 85.
[81] It is possible that St Augustine's inherited some or all of its land in Sturry from the mysterious *familia Sturensis* mentioned in **17**.
[82] G. Ward, 'Saxon Records of Tenterden', *AC* xlix (1938), pp. 229–46 (at 241–3).

celebrated map of Thanet the division between the two holdings is marked *cursus cerue*, which links it to the Minster foundation legend; King Ecgberht promised to give to Domneva (the founding abbess Æbba) as much land as her pet hind could run around in the course of a day.[83] The route marked on Elmham's map is sufficiently tortuous to give grounds for such a tale. Elmham presumably depicts a boundary that existed in his own day and was believed to be very old. In 1723 Lewis identified Elmham's *cursus cerve* with an existing bank across the island known as St Mildrith's Lynch;[84] the route also agrees quite closely with the nineteenth-century parish boundaries. David Rollason has suggested that the *cursus cerve* of Elmham's map represents the ancient boundary of the Minster property on Thanet and has argued that it was probably in existence at the time of the Domesday survey and perhaps even goes back to the original endowment of the community (as described in the legend of the hind).[85] On balance, a seventh-century date seems improbable. If we jettison the hind theory, the most likely explanation for the strikingly twisted boundary is that it represents the effect of many years of piecemeal acquisition and adjustment of property-boundaries.[86] The surviving Minster charters to some extent support this view. As far as can be determined (admittedly not very far), the Thanet estates with which they are concerned lie in the eastern, 'Minster' part of the island, within the sector which the community apparently claimed to have been granted *in toto* as its initial endowment. In addition, there is evidence that St Augustine's was accumulating property in the 'Minster' part of Thanet from the ninth century. In 826 the abbey acquired land at Dandelion near Garlinge (**17**); this may have formed part of an estate of six sulungs around Margate which seems to have come into the abbey's possession before it acquired the Minster lands. A century later Athelstan restored to St Augustine's fourteen sulungs at *Werburginland*, which is perhaps to be connected with its Margate estates (**26**). This tenurial history makes it unlikely that the land in the 'Minster' sector of the island was treated as a block from the seventh century onwards.

From the 730s, and perhaps as early as 716/17, the Minster abbesses were acquiring toll-privileges from the Mercian kings. The first two examples (**49**

---

[83] See **34**, and Rollason, *Mildrith Legend*, p. 11.

[84] J. Lewis, *The History and Antiquities, Ecclesiastical and Civil, of the Isle of Tenet, in Kent*, 2nd edn (London, 1736), p. 10.

[85] D. Rollason, 'The Date of the Parsh Boundary of Minster-in-Thanet (Kent)', *AC* xcv (1979), pp. 7–17.

[86] This point was made by Canon R.C. Jenkins, 'St Mary's Minster in Thanet and St Mildred', *AC* xii (1878), pp. 177–96 (at 184).

and **50**) seem to relate to a single ship, granted exemption in London and the Mercian kingdom. By 748 Minster had purchased a second ship, which King Æthelbald exempted from half the toll due upon it, probably in the port of London, where the charter was issued (**51**). The latest Minster toll-charter was issued by a Kentish king (**53**). It seems to refer to three ships, two of which were exempted from toll at Sarre and the third, which had recently been built, from toll at both Sarre and Fordwich. The first two ships may be those earlier covered by the Mercian privileges; Minster ships on the way to London would have to pass the toll-station at Sarre, and exemption was presumably highly desirable. If the community's ships went to Fordwich, it must have been to trade goods in the Canterbury market; the reference to pre-emption rights in **53** suggests that these goods were not the monastery's own produce but merchandise acquired elsewhere. Possibly the community played an entrepreneurial role between London and Kent, or between Kent and the Continent. There is no evidence as to what commodities were traded.[87]

---

[87] See Kelly 1992 for more extensive discussion of the purpose and function of these privileges.

ABBREVIATIONS

BL	London, British Library
Bodleian	Oxford, Bodleian Library
CCCC	Cambridge, Corpus Christi College
D. & C.	Dean and Chapter
GDB	Great Domesday Book
PRO	Public Record Office
s.	*saeculo*
TRE	*Tempore Regis Edwardi*

BIBLIOGRAPHICAL ABBREVIATIONS

AC	*Archaeologia Cantiana*
ASC	*Anglo-Saxon Chronicle*
Anton, *Studien*	H.H. Anton, *Studien zu den Klosterprivilegien der Päpste im frühen Mittelalter*, Beiträge zur Geschichte und Quellenurkunde des Mittelalters 4 (Berlin and New York, 1975)
BAFacs.	*Facsimiles of Anglo-Saxon Charters*, ed. S. Keynes, Anglo-Saxon Charters, Supplementary ser. i (London, 1991)
Ballard, *Inquisition*	*An Eleventh-Century Inquisition of St Augustine's Abbey, Canterbury*, ed. A. Ballard, British Academy Records of Social and Economic History iv.1 (London, 1920)
BCS	For 'Birch' in citations of charters
Bede, *HE*	Bede, *Historia Ecclesiastica*
Birch	W. de G. Birch, *Cartularium Saxonicum*, 3 vols (London, 1885–93)
BMFacs.	E.A. Bond, *Facsimiles of Ancient Charters in the British Museum*, 4 vols (London, 1873–8)
Brooks, *Church of Canterbury*	N. Brooks, *The Early History of the Church of Canterbury: Christ Church from 597 to 1066* (Leicester, 1984)
Brooks 1971	N. Brooks, 'The Development of Military Obligations in Eighth- and Ninth-Century England', *England Before the Conquest: Studies in Primary*

	Sources presented to Dorothy Whitelock, ed. P. Clemoes and K. Hughes (Cambridge, 1971), pp. 69–84
Brooks 1988	N. Brooks, 'Romney Marsh in the Early Middle Ages', *Romney Marsh: Evolution, Occupation, Reclamation*, ed. J. Eddison and C. Green, Oxford Univ. Committee for Archaeology, Monograph no. 24 (Oxford, 1988), pp. 90–104
Campbell, *Rochester*	*Charters of Rochester*, ed. A. Campbell, Anglo-Saxon Charters i (London, 1973)
Chaplais 1965	P. Chaplais, 'The Origin and Authenticity of the Royal Anglo-Saxon Diploma', *Journal of the Society of Archivists* iii.2 (1965), pp. 48–61 (repr. in *Prisca Munimenta*, ed. F. Ranger (London, 1973), pp. 28–42)
Chaplais 1966	P. Chaplais, 'The Anglo-Saxon Chancery: from the Diploma to the Writ', *Journal of the Society of Archivists* iii.4 (1966), pp. 160–76 (repr. in *Prisca Munimenta*, ed. F. Ranger (London, 1973), pp. 43–62)
Chaplais 1968	P. Chaplais, 'Some Early Anglo-Saxon Charters on Single Sheets: Originals or Copies?', *Journal of the Society of Archivists* iii.7 (1968), pp. 315–36 (repr. in *Prisca Munimenta*, ed. F. Ranger (London, 1973), pp. 63–87)
Chaplais 1969	P. Chaplais, 'Who Introduced Charters into England: the Case for Augustine', *Journal of the Society of Archivists* iii.10 (1969), pp. 526–42 (repr. in *Prisca Munimenta*, ed. F. Ranger (London, 1973), pp. 88–107)
Colker 1977	M. Colker, 'A Hagiographic Polemic', *Mediaeval Studies* xxxix (1977), pp. 60–108
Davis, *Cartularies*	G.R.C. Davis, *Medieval Cartularies of Great Britain: a Short Catalogue* (London, 1958)
Davis, *Thorne*	A.H. Davis, *William Thorne's Chronicle of St Augustine's Abbey, Canterbury* (Oxford, 1934)
Deanesly 1942	M. Deanesly, 'The Court of King Æthelberht of Kent', *Cambridge Historical Journal* vii (1942), pp. 101–14
DEPN	E. Ekwall, *The Concise Oxford Dictionary of English Place-Names*, 4th edn (Oxford, 1960)
Domesday Monachorum	*The Domesday Monachorum of Christ Church, Canterbury*, ed. D.C. Douglas (London, 1944)
Dumville 1987	D.N. Dumville, 'English Square Minuscule Script: the Background and Earliest Phases', *Anglo-Saxon England* xvi (1987), pp. 147–79
Earle	J. Earle, *A Handbook to the Land-Charters, and Other Saxonic Documents* (Oxford, 1888)

Everitt, *Continuity*   A. Everitt, *Continuity and Colonization; the Evolution of Kentish Settlement* (Leicester, 1986)

Finberg, *Agrarian History*   *The Agrarian History of England and Wales, I.ii :* A.D. *43–1042*, ed. H.P.R. Finberg (Cambridge, 1972)

Gervase, *Opera Historica*   Gervase of Canterbury, *Opera Historica*, ed. W. Stubbs, 2 vols, RS (London, 1879)

Goscelin, *Translatio S. Augustini*   Goscelin, 'Historia Translationis S Augustini', *Acta Sanctorum Maii vi*, ed. G. Henschenius and D. Papebroch (Antwerp, 1688), pp. 411–36

Goscelin, *Translatio S. Mildrethe*   D.W. Rollason, 'Goscelin of Canterbury's Account of the Translation and Miracles of St Mildrith (*BHL* 5961/4): an Edition with Notes', *Mediaeval Studies* xlviii (1986), pp. 139–210

Gough 1992   H. Gough, 'Eadred's Charter of A.D. 949 and the Extent of the Monastic Estate of Reculver, Kent', *St Dunstan: his Life, Times and Cult*, ed. N. Ramsay, M. Sparks and T. Tatton-Brown (Woodbridge, 1992), pp. 89–102

GR   *Willelmi Malmesbiriensis Monachi de Gestis Regum Anglorum Libri Quinque*, ed. W. Stubbs, 2 vols, RS (London, 1887–9)

Haddan and Stubbs   *Councils and Ecclesiastical Documents Relating to Great Britain and Ireland*, ed. A.W. Haddan and W. Stubbs, 3 vols (Oxford, 1869–78)

Hardwick, *Elmham*   *Historia Monasterii S. Augustini Cantuariensis by Thomas of Elmham*, ed. C. Hardwick, RS (London, 1858)

Harmer, *SEHD*   *Select English Historical Documents of the Ninth and Tenth Centuries*, ed. F.E. Harmer (Cambridge, 1914)

Harmer, *Writs*   F.E. Harmer, *Anglo-Saxon Writs* (Manchester, 1952)

Harrison, *Framework*   K. Harrison, *The Framework of Anglo-Saxon History to A.D. 900* (Cambridge, 1976)

Hasted, *History*   E. Hasted, *The History and Topographical Survey of the County of Kent*, 2nd edn, 12 vols (Canterbury, 1797–1801)

Hickes, *Diss. Epist.*   G. Hickes, *De Antiquae Litteraturae Septentrionalis Utilitate sive de Linguarum Veterum Septentrionalium Usu Dissertatio Epistolaris ad Bartholomaeum Shower* (Oxford, 1703)

HRH   D. Knowles, C.N.L. Brooke and V.C.M. London, *The Heads of Religious Houses England and Wales 940–1216* (Cambridge, 1972)

Holtzmann, *Papsturkunden*   W. Holtzmann, *Papsturkunden in England*, 3 vols (Berlin, 1930–52)

Hunter 1973	M. Hunter, 'The Facsimiles in Thomas Elmham's History of St Augustine's', *The Library*, 5th ser. xxviii (1973), pp. 215–20
Kelly, *Shaftesbury*	*Charters of Shaftesbury*, ed. S.E. Kelly, Anglo-Saxon Charters v (London, forthcoming)
Kelly 1986	S.E. Kelly, 'The Pre-Conquest History and Archive of St Augustine's Abbey, Canterbury', unpublished Ph.D. thesis, Cambridge University (1986)
Kelly 1988	S.E. Kelly, 'Some Forgeries in the Archive of St Augustine's Abbey, Canterbury', *Fälschungen im Mittelalter*, MGH Schriften 33.iv (Hanover, 1988), pp. 347–69
Kelly 1990	S.E. Kelly, 'Anglo-Saxon Lay Society and the Written Word', *The Uses of Literacy in Early Mediaeval Europe*, ed. R. McKitterick (Cambridge, 1990), pp. 36–62
Kelly 1992	S.E. Kelly, 'Trading Privileges from Eighth-Century England', *Early Medieval Europe* i (1992), pp. 3–27
Kemble	J.M. Kemble, *Codex Diplomaticus Aevi Saxonici*, 6 vols (London, 1839–48)
Ker, *Catalogue*	N.R. Ker, *Catalogue of Manuscripts Containing Anglo-Saxon* (Oxford, 1957; repr. with addenda, 1990)
Keynes, *Diplomas*	S. Keynes, *The Diplomas of King Æthelred 'the Unready' 978–1016: a Study in their Use as Historical Evidence* (Cambridge, 1980)
Keynes, *Anglo-Saxon Charters*	S. Keynes, *Anglo-Saxon Charters: Archives and Single Sheets*, Anglo-Saxon Charters, Supplementary ser. ii (London, forthcoming)
Keynes 1985	S. Keynes, 'King Athelstan's Books', *Learning and Literature in Anglo-Saxon England: Studies presented to Peter Clemoes*, ed. M. Lapidge and H. Gneuss (Cambridge, 1985), pp. 143–201
Levison, *England and the Continent*	W. Levison, *England and the Continent in the Eighth Century* (Oxford, 1946)
Lewis, *Tenet*	J. Lewis, *The History and Antiquities, Ecclesiastical and Civil, of the Isle of Tenet in Kent*, 2nd edn (London, 1736)
Liebermann, *Gesetze*	F. Liebermann, *Die Gesetze der Angelsachsen*, 3 vols (Halle, 1903–16)
MGH	Monumenta Germaniae Historica
Mon. Angl.	R. Dodsworth and W. Dugdale, *Monasticon Anglicanum*, 3 vols (London, 1655–73)
Mon. Angl. (rev. edn)	W. Dugdale, *Monasticon Anglicanum*, ed. J. Caley, H. Ellis and B. Bandinel, 6 vols in 8 (London, 1817–30)

Morlet, *Noms de personne*   M.-T. Morlet, *Les Noms de personne sur la territoire de l'ancienne Gaul dès vième au xième siècle*, 3 vols (Paris, 1968–85)

O'Donovan, *Sherborne*   *Charters of Sherborne*, ed. M.A. O'Donovan, Anglo-Saxon Charters iii (London, 1988)

OSFacs.   W.B. Sanders, *Facsimiles of Anglo-Saxon Manuscripts*, 3 vols (Ordnance Survey, Southampton, 1878–84)

Pierquin, *Conciles*   H. Pierquin, *Les Annales et Conciles de l'Église d'Angleterre pendant la période anglo-saxonne* (Paris, 1913)

Pierquin, *Recueil*   H. Pierquin, *Recueil générale des chartes anglo-saxonnes: les Saxons en Angleterre 604–1061* (Paris, 1912)

Plummer, *Bede*   *Venerabilis Baedae Opera Historica*, ed. C. Plummer, 2 vols (Oxford, 1896)

Regesta   H.W.C. Davis, *Regesta Regum Anglo-Normannorum 1066–1154. I: Regesta Willelmi Conquestoris et Willelmi Rufi 1066–1100* (Oxford, 1913)

Robertson, *Charters*   *Anglo-Saxon Charters*, ed. A.J. Robertson, 2nd edn (Cambridge, 1956)

Rollason, *Mildrith Legend*   D.W. Rollason, *The Mildrith Legend: a Study in Early Medieval Hagiography in England* (Leicester, 1982)

Rollason 1979   D.W. Rollason, 'The Date of the Parish-Boundary of Minster-in-Thanet', *AC* xcv (1979), pp. 7–17

RS   Rolls Series

S   For 'Sawyer' in citations of charters

S (Add.)   For S. Keynes, 'Addenda to Professor Sawyer's *Anglo-Saxon Charters*', *Anglo-Saxon England* (forthcoming), in citations of charters

Sawyer   P.H. Sawyer, *Anglo-Saxon Charters: an Annotated List and Bibliography*, Royal Historical Society Guides and Handbooks viii (London, 1968)

Sawyer, *Burton*   *Charters of Burton Abbey*, ed. P.H. Sawyer, Anglo-Saxon Charters ii (London, 1979)

Scharer, *Königsurkunde*   A. Scharer, *Die angelsächsische Königsurkunde im 7. und 8. Jahrhundert*, Veröffentlichungen des Instituts für österreichische Geschichtsforschung xxvi (Cologne and Vienna, 1982)

Sims-Williams 1988   P. Sims-Williams, 'St Wilfrid and Two Charters Dated A.D. 676 and 680', *Journal of Ecclesiastical History* xxxix (1988), pp. 163–83

Somner, *Canterbury*   W. Somner, *The Antiquities of Canterbury*, 2nd edn (London, 1703)

Smith, *Bede*   *Historia Ecclesiastica Gentis Anglorum Libri*

	Quinque auctore sancto et venerabili Bæda, ed. J. Smith (Cambridge, 1722)
Smith, *EPNE*	A.H. Smith, *English Place-Name Elements*, 2 vols, English Place-Name Society xxv-xxvi (Cambridge, 1956)
Spelman, *Concilia*	H. Spelman, *Concilia, Decreta, Leges, Constitutiones in Re Ecclesiarum Orbis Britannici*, 2 vols (London, 1639 and 1664)
Tatton-Brown 1992	T. Tatton-Brown, 'The City and Diocese of Canterbury in St Dunstan's Time', *Dunstan: his Life, Times and Cult*, ed. N. Ramsay, M. Sparks and T. Tatton-Brown (Woodbridge, 1992), pp. 75–87
Thorpe, *Diplomatarium*	B. Thorpe, *Diplomatarium Anglicum Ævi Saxonici* (London, 1865)
Tjäder, *Papyri*	J.-O. Tjäder, *Die nichtliterarischen lateinischen Papyri Italiens aus der Zeit 445–700*, 3 vols (Lund and Stockholm, 1954–82)
Turner and Salter, *Black Book*	*The Register of St Augustine's Abbey, Canterbury, commonly called the Black Book*, ed. G. Turner and H.E. Salter, 2 vols, British Academy Records of Social and Economic History, ii–iii (London, 1915)
Twysden, *Scriptores*	R. Twysden, *Historiae Anglicanae Scriptores X* (London, 1652)
Wallenberg, *KPN*	J.K. Wallenberg, *Kentish Place-Names*, Uppsala Universitets Årsskrift (Uppsala, 1931)
Wallenberg, *Place-Names of Kent*	J.K. Wallenberg, *The Place-Names of Kent* (Uppsala, 1934)
Wanley, *Catalogus*	H. Wanley, *Librorum Veterum Septentrionalium...Catalogus Historico-Criticus* (Oxford, 1705)
Ward 1938	G. Ward, 'King Oswin – A Forgotten Ruler of Kent', *AC* l (1938), pp. 60–5
Ward 1947	G. Ward, 'King Wihtred's Charter of A.D. 699', *AC* lx (1947), pp. 1–14
Whitelock, *EHD*	*English Historical Documents, c. 500–1042*, ed. D. Whitelock, English Historical Documents i, 2nd edn (London, 1979)
Whitelock 1976	D. Whitelock, 'Succession among Kentish Kings', in Harrison, *Framework*, pp. 142–4
Wilkins, *Concilia*	D. Wilkins, *Concilia Magnae Britanniae et Hiberniae*, 4 vols (London, 1737)
Witney, *Jutish Forest*	K.P. Witney, *The Jutish Forest: a Study of the Weald of Kent from 450 to 1380 A.D.* (London, 1976)
Witney 1988	J. Witney, 'The Period of Mercian Rule in Kent and a Charter of A.D. 811', *AC* civ (1988 for 1987), pp. 87–113

Woodruff, *Fordwich*   C.E. Woodruff, *A History of the Town and Port of Fordwich* (Canterbury, 1895)

Wormald 1985   P. Wormald, *Bede and the Conversion of England: the Charter Evidence*, Jarrow Lecture 1984 (Jarrow, [1985])

Zeumer, *Formulae*   *Formulae Merowingici et Karolini Aevi*, ed. K. Zeumer, MGH (Hanover, 1886)

LIST OF CHARTERS

CHARTERS OF ST AUGUSTINE'S ABBEY

1. Æthelberht, king of Kent, grants land to the east of Canterbury for the foundation of a monastery in honour of St Peter. A.D. 605

2. Æthelberht, king of the English, grants land to the east of Canterbury to the monastery of SS Peter and Paul. A.D. 605

3. Æthelberht, king of the English, grants land at Sturry, also called Chislet, Kent, to the monastery of SS Peter and Paul. A.D. 605

4. Augustine, bishop of Canterbury, grants privileges to the monastery of SS Peter and Paul.

5. King Eadbald grants thirty sulungs at Northbourne, Kent, to the monastery of SS Peter and Paul. A.D. 618

6. Hlothhere, king of the men of Kent, grants three sulungs in Stodmarsh, Kent, to the abbot and monastery of St Peter. A.D. 675

7. Eadric, king of the men of Kent, grants three sulungs near Stodmarsh, Kent, to the monastery of St Peter. A.D. 686

8. Oswine, king of Kent, grants one sulung on which iron is mined to the monastery of St Peter and Abbot Hadrian. A.D. 689

9. Wihtred, king of Kent, and his wife, Æthelburh, grant five sulungs at Littlebourne, Kent, to the monastery of St Peter. [A.D. 696 or 711]

10. Wihtred, king of Kent, grants privileges to the churches and monasteries of Kent. A.D. 699

11. Æthelberht II, king of Kent, confirms an exchange whereby the monastery of SS Peter and Paul cedes the half-use of a mill to the royal vill at Wye, in return for pasture rights in the Weald for its tenant at Chart, Kent. A.D. 762

12. Dunwald, *minister* of the late King Æthelberht, grants a *villa* near Queningate, Canterbury, to the church of SS Peter and Paul. A.D. 762

13. Eadberht II, king of Kent, grants six sulungs at Mongeham, Kent, to the monastery of St Peter. [*c.* A.D. 762 or 763]

14. Offa, king of the Mercians, grants two hides at Beauxfield, Kent, to Æthelnoth, abbot of [the monastery of] SS Peter and Paul. [A.D. 765 × 792]

15. Offa, king of the Mercians, confirms the privileges granted to the churches of Kent by Kings Wihtred and Æthelbald, and grants exemption from all dues and services to certain Kentish monasteries. [? A.D. 792]

16. Coenwulf, king of the Mercians, and Cuthred, king of Kent, grant twenty sulungs at West Lenham, Kent, and thirteen swine-pastures in the Weald to their kinsman Eanberht. [? A.D. 804]

17. Wulfred, archbishop of Canterbury, supervises an exchange of land between Minster-in-Thanet and the abbot and community of St Augustine's. A.D. 826

18. Ecgberht, king of the West Saxons, grants one sulung *on Scirdun* to Ciaba, a *clericus* living in the monastery of St Peter. A.D. 836

19. Æthelwulf, king of the West Saxons and of the men of Kent, grants five sulungs at Lenham, Kent, to Abbot Wernoth and his *familia*. [? A.D. 838]

20. Æthelwulf, king of the West Saxons and of the men of Kent, grants one sulung at *Lillicesora* (? Lynsore, Kent) to Winehere, priest-abbot of the monastery of St Peter. A.D. 845

21. Æthelwulf, king of the West Saxons, grants forty hides at Lenham, Kent, to Ealhhere, *princeps*. A.D. 850

22. Æthelberht, king of the West Saxons and of the men of Kent, grants three sulungs at Martin, Kent, to Abbot Diernoth and his *familia*. A.D. 861

23. Eadbald grants land at Burmarsh, Kent, to Winemund. [*c.* A.D. 848]

23A. Winemund grants land at Burmarsh and Snavewick, Kent, to St Augustine. [*c.* A.D. 848]

24. Ealhburh grants a food-rent from land at Brabourne, Kent, to the community of St Augustine. [*c.* A.D. 850]

25. Lulle grants a food-rent from land at Nackington, Kent, to the community of St Augustine. [*c.* A.D. 850]

26. King Athelstan restores fourteen sulungs at *Werburginland* in Thanet, Kent, to St Augustine. A.D. 925

27. King Edmund grants two sulungs at Sibertswold, Kent, to Sigeric, *minister*. A.D. 944

28. a. King Eadred grants one and a half hides at Swalecliffe, Kent, to Heresige, his man. A.D. 946.
   b. Heresige transfers the land to the monastery of SS Peter and Paul.

29. King Edgar grants four sulungs at Plumstead, Kent, to St Augustine and his monastery. [A.D. 963 × 971 (? A.D. 963)]

30. King Æthelred grants two hides at Sibertswold, Kent, to Sigered, *minister*. A.D. 990

31. Abbot Wulfric and Ealdred, son of Lyfing, make an agreement about land at *Clife*. [*c.* A.D. 990 × 1005]

32. King Cnut declares that he has granted judicial and financial privileges to St Augustine's.

33. King Cnut declares that he has granted the body of St Mildrith and the estates of her church to St Augustine.

34. King Edward grants the island of Thanet to the church of SS Peter and Paul, and confirms the church's possessions and privileges. [A.D. 1042 × 1045]

35. King Edward declares that he has granted judicial and financial privileges to St Augustine's monastery. [A.D. 1042 × 1050]

36. King Edward grants one sulung at Littlebourne, Kent, to Eadsige, archbishop [of Canterbury]. [A.D. 1042 × 1050, (? 1047)]

37. Eadsige, archbishop [of Canterbury], grants the land at Littlebourne, Kent, to St Peter and St Augustine. [A.D. 1042 × 1050 (? 1047)]

38. Æthelric Bigga bequeaths land at Bodsham and Wilderton, Kent, to St Augustine. [A.D. 1048 × 1050]

39. King Edward declares that he confirms his previous grant of land at Fordwich, Kent, to St Augustine's. [A.D. 1053 × 1066]

CHARTERS OF MINSTER-IN-THANET

40 a. *Suebhardus*, king of the men of Kent, grants forty-four hides *in Sudaneie* in Thanet and twelve hides in Sturry, Kent, to Abbess Æbba. A.D. 689

b. Confirmation by Æthélred, king of the Mercians. A.D. 691

41. *Suabertus*, king of the men of Kent, grants two sulungs in Sturry and three at Bodsham, Kent, to Abbess Æbba. [*c.* A.D. 690]

42. Oswine, king of the men of Kent, grants ten hides in Sturry, Kent, to Abbess Æbba. A.D. 690

43. Oswine, king of the men of Kent, grants eighteen hides in Thanet to Abbess Æbba. [*c.* A.D. 690]

44. Wihtred, king of Kent, grants four sulungs at *Humantun* to Abbess Æbba. A.D. 694

45. Wihtred, king of the men of Kent, grants privileges to Abbess Mildrith. A.D. 696

46. Wihtred, king of the men of Kent, grants forty hides at *Hæg* to Abbess Æbba. A.D. 697

47. Æthelberht, son of King Wihtred, grants one sulung by the River *Limen* and three yardlands at *Hammespot*, Kent, to Abbess Mildrith and her *familia*. A.D. 724

48. Eadberht I, king of the men of Kent, grants a half-sulung *in regione qui dicitur bi Northanuude* to Abbess Mildrith and her *familia*. A.D. 727

49. Æthelbald, king of the Mercians, grants remission of toll on one ship at the port of London to Abbess Mildrith. [*c.* A.D. 716 or 717 (? for *c.* 733)]

50. Æthelbald, king of the Mercians, grants remission of toll on one ship to Abbess Mildrith. [A.D. 737 or 738 (? for 716 or 717)]

51. Æthelbald, king of the Mercians, grants remission of half the toll due on one ship to Abbess Eadburh. A.D. 748

52. Offa, king of the Mercians, grants to Abbess Sigeburh the toll-exemption which King Æthelbald had granted to Abbess Mildrith. [A.D. 761 × 764]

53. Eadberht II, king of Kent, grants to Abbess Sigeburh remission of toll on two ships at Sarre and on a third at Fordwich and Sarre. [*c.* A.D. 763 or 764]

CONCORDANCE OF THIS EDITION WITH SAWYER'S LIST AND THE EDITIONS OF BIRCH, KEMBLE AND OTHERS

	Sawyer	Birch	Kemble	Others
1	2	4	2	
2	3	5	3	
3	4	6	4	
4	1244	7	5	
5	6	13	6	
6	7	36	9	
7	9	67	27	
8	12	73	30	
9	16	90	41	
10	20	99	44	
11	25	191	108	
12	1182	192	109	
13	28	190	107	
14	140	207	119	
15	134	848		
16	159	316	187	
17	1267	851, 1337		
18	279	852		
19	1649			
20	297	853		
21	300	459	1049	
	324	854		
22	330	855		
23	1193/ 1651	837		
24	1198	501		Harmer, *SEHD*, 6
25	1239			
26	394	641		
27	501	755, 797	1132	
28	518	874, 1345	1176	
29	809	1173	502	
30	875		1285	
31	1455		429	Robertson, *Charters*, 62

	Sawyer	Birch	Kemble	Others
32	989		756	Harmer, *Writs*, 36
33	990		1326	Harmer, *Writs*, 37
34	1048		900	
35	1091		831, 902	Harmer, *Writs*, 38
36	1050		1344	
37	1401		1333	
38	1502		1338	
39	1092		854	Harmer, *Writs*, 39
40	10	42	14	
41	11	41	15	
42	13	35	8	
43	14	40	10	
44	15	86	37	
45	17	88, 845	39	
46	18	96	42	
47	1180	141	72	
48	26	846		
49	86	149	97	
50	87	150	84	
51	91	177	98	
52	143	188	112	
53	29	189	106	

NOTES ON THE METHOD OF EDITING

The existence of multiple manuscript sources for most of the charters in the archive has necessitated some tough editorial decisions. In the case of those few charters which survive in a very large number of copies, it is impossible to note all variants; I have edited the text from the best representatives of the principal recensions. The majority of charters are preserved in three or fewer copies; here I have generally collated all the manuscript sources, chosen the best readings, and noted all significant variants in the apparatus.

Punctuation

The majority of texts here edited survive only in one or more late copies and it did not seem profitable to reproduce the manuscript punctuation. I have therefore normalized punctuation and capitalization in order to make the texts as clear as possible. In the case of the two vernacular documents preserved in pre-Conquest copies in CCCC 286, I have tried to respect the manuscript punctuation, adding spacing where necessary to make sense of the text. The ninth-century single-sheet copy of **10** is almost entirely unpunctuated, so I have decided to normalize punctuation in order to assist the reader.

Spelling

Since most of the manuscript sources are late, for the sake of clarity and simplicity I have not noted obviously late spellings among the variants (for example, -h-/-ch-, -ti-/-ci-). The scribe of the Trinity Hall manuscript regularly wrote -ngn- for -gn-; again there seemed little point in noting this in the apparatus.

SIGLA

I have reserved the siglum A for the only single-sheet copy here edited (**10**); this is not an original. The very large number of manuscript sources for the archive makes the assignation of sigla an intractable problem. For practical reasons I have decided not to include manucripts which have no textual significance; these are discussed separately in the introduction (pp. lxi–lxii) and also listed in the commentaries to the individual charters. The more important manuscripts have been divided into two classes: cartularies, histories and transcripts; and enrolments on the Charter and Patent Rolls.

i. *Cartularies, histories and transcripts*

B. CCCC 286 (s. x)
C. BL Cotton Vespasian B. xx (s. xii^1)
D. BL Cotton Vitellius A. ii (s. xii^2)
E. PRO Cartae Antiquae R. 9 (s. xiii^{in})
F. BL Cotton Julius D. ii (s. xiii^1)
G. BL Cotton Claudius D. x (s. xiii^2)
G*. BL Cotton Claudius D. x, fos 61r–73v (s. xiv^1)
H. PRO E 164/27 (s. xiii–xiv)
I. Canterbury, D. & C., Lit. E. 19 (s. xiv^1)
J. London, Lambeth Palace, 419 (s. xiv)
K. BL Cotton Tiberius A. ix, fos 105–68 (s. xiv)
L. CCCC 189 (s. xiv^{ex})
M. BL Add. 53710 (s. xiv^2)
N. Cambridge, Trinity Hall, 1 (s. xv^{in})
O. Canterbury, D. & C., Chart. Ant. F. 47 (s. xv)
P. Bodleian, Tanner 165 (s. xv)
Q. Winchester, Cathedral Library, XXB (s. xvi)

ii. *Enrolments on the Charter and Patent Rolls*

R. PRO Chart. R. 20 Edw. II m. 2
S. PRO Chart. R. 36 Edw. III m. 7

T. PRO Chart. R. 8 Hen. VI m. 6
U. PRO Pat. R. 2 Hen. VI pt 3 m. 5
V. PRO Pat. R. 4 Edw. IV pt 4 m. 29
W. PRO Pat. R. 14 Hen. VII, pt 1, m. 16

THE CHARTERS OF
ST AUGUSTINE'S ABBEY

1

Æthelberht, king of Kent, grants land to the east of Canterbury for the foundation of a monastery in honour of St Peter. A.D. 605

G*. BL Cotton Claudius D. x, 61r: copy of Inspeximus [R], s. xiv[1]
M1. BL Add. 53710, 221v: copy of Inspeximus [S], s. xiv/xv
M2. BL Add. 53710, 253v–254r: copy, s. xvi
N1. Cambridge, Trinity Hall 1, 21v: facsimile, s. xv[1]
   Rubric: Hic notatur exemplar contemplandum prime carte regis Æthelberti tam in longitudine quam in latitudine quam in scripture qualitate.
N2. Cambridge, Trinity Hall, 1, 21v: copy, s. xv[1]
Q. Winchester, Cathedral Library, XXB, 157r: copy, s. xvi
R. PRO Ch. R. 20 Edw. II, m. 2
S. PRO Ch. R. 36 Edw. III, m. 7
T. PRO Ch. R. 8 Hen. VI, m. 6
U. PRO Pat. R. 2 Hen. VI, pt 3, m. 5
V. PRO Pat. R. 4 Edw. IV, pt 4, m. 29
W. PRO Pat. R. 14 Hen. VII, pt 1, m. 16
Ed.: a. Spelman, *Concilia*, i. 118–19, from N
   b. Twysden, *Scriptores*, col. 2123, from M1
   c. *Mon. Angl.*, i. 23, probably from G*
   d. Somner, *Canterbury*, Appendix, p. 6, from ? M1, M2
   e. Wilkins, *Concilia*, iv. 728, from Spelman
   f. Kemble 2 from N
   g. *Mon. Angl.* (rev. edn), i. 126 (no. 1), from 1st edn
   h. Hardwick, *Elmham*, pp. 109–10, from N
   i. Haddan and Stubbs, *Councils*, iii. 54–5, from Kemble etc.
   j. Birch 4 from Kemble, Haddan and Stubbs etc.
   k. Pierquin, *Recueil*, pt 1, no. 2, from Birch
   l. Hunter 1973, plate 1 (reduced facsimile)
Listed: Sawyer 2
Edited from G*, N1 and Q

+[a] In nomine Domini nostri Iesu Christi. Omnem hominem qui secundum Deum uiuit et remunerari a Deo sperat et optat, oportet ut piis precibus consensum hilariter[b] ex animo prebeat, quoniam certum est tanto facilius ea que ipse a Deo[c] poposcerit consequi posse, quanto et ipse libentius Deo aliquid concesserit. Quocirca ego Æthilberhtus[d] rex Cantie,[e] cum consensu uenerabilis archiepiscopi[f] Agustini[g] ac principum meorum, dabo[h] et concedo Deo in honore sancti Petri aliquam partem terre iuris mei quæ iacet in oriente ciuitatis Dorobernie, ita dumtaxat ut monasterium ibi construatur, et res quæ supra memoraui[i] in potestate abbatis sit, qui ibi fuerit ordinatus. Igitur adiuro et precipio in nomine Domini Dei omnipotentis qui est omnium

3

rerum iudex iustus[1] ut prefata terra subscripta donatione sempiternaliter sit confirmata, ita ut nec mihi nec alicui successorum meorum regum aut principum siue cuiuslibet conditionis dignitatibus et ecclesiasticis[j] gradibus de ea aliquid fraudare liceat. Si quis uero de hac donatione nostra aliquid minuere aut irritum facere temptauerit, sit in presenti separatus a sancta communione corporis et sanguinis Christi, et in die iudicii ob meritum malitie suæ a consortio sanctorum omnium segregatus. Circumcincta est hec terra his[k] terminibus: in oriente ecclesia[l] sancti Martini, in meridie uia oþ Burhgat,[m] in occidente et in aquilone Drutingestræte. Acta[n] in ciuitate Dorouerni anno ab incarnatione Christi .dcv., indictione .vi.[o]

+ Ego Æthelbertus rex Cancie[e] sana mente integroque consilio donacionem meam signo sancte crucis propria manu roboraui confirmauique.
Ego Ægustinus[p] gratia Dei archiepiscopus testis consenciens libenter subscripsi.
Eadbald.[q] Hamigils.[r] Augemund referendarius. Hocca. Grafio.[s] Thangil.[t] Pinca.[u] Geddi.

a Cross omitted **G***   _b_ hillariter **G***   _c_ Domino Q
_d_ Æthelbertus **G***; Æthilberktus N1   _e_ Kanc' **G***
_f_ archiepiscopi _altered to_ episcopi Q   _g_ Augustini **G***   _h_ do _added above_ Q
_i_ memraui N1   _j_ eclesiasticis N1   _k_ hiis Q   _l_ eclesia N1   _m_ of burgate **G***
_n_ Act' **G*** (_probably for_ Actum); stræte. Acta _omitted_ Q
_o_ .vi. _altered to_ .viii. N1; .viii. Q. N1 _ends here._   _p_ Augustinus **G***   _q_ Eaðbald Q
_r_ Hamigls **G***   _s_ Grafyo **G***   _t_ Thongl' **G***   _u_ Pynca **G***

[1] Ps. 7: 12: qui est omnium iudex iustus

1 is the most modest and no doubt the earliest of the three spurious charters in the archive attributed to King Æthelberht I. Its main object is to provide title to the abbey precincts, which are defined in a brief boundary clause. These are to be under the control of the abbot, who is to be consecrated in the abbey itself; this last detail is one of the issues on which St Augustine's clashed with the archbishops from the eleventh century onwards (see pp. xxiii–xxiv). The forger appears to have adapted for his purpose a royal charter of the mid eighth century, probably one in the name of Æthelberht II (725–62). The proem appears in other charters of that period (**51** and S 31, 32, 131), and contemporary parallels can be found for the verbal invocation, consent clause, paired dispositive verbs, the corroboration and injunction directed against the donor's successors and other potential challengers, the sanction and the form of the dating clause (compare **53** and S 31–4). The introduction to the boundary clause, and its construction around the four cardinal points, would also be compatible with an eighth-century model (compare S 23, 129 and, for the introduction, **12**; see further, pp. lxxix–lxxx); the details of the boundaries have presumably been changed. The forger's interference with the model seems to lie mostly in the dispositive section and in specific details, such as names; the witness-list appears to have been taken from a different source (see further, below).

The earliest copies of **1** are from the fourteenth century. It was one of the pre-Conquest charters submitted to Edward II for confirmation in 1326; the resulting Inspeximus charter was confirmed and enrolled several times, and a copy also appears in a quire added to BL Cotton Claudius D. x (MS G*). Although **1** was not copied alongside the other forged charters in the name of Æthelberht in the twelfth and thirteenth centuries, there can be little doubt that it was already in existence in that period; it was clearly the model for **2**, a more ambitious production which covered not only the abbey precincts, but also the adjacent territory to the south. It seems probable that **1** was neglected in the twelfth and thirteenth centuries because it was felt to have been superseded by **2**. The mutually exclusive relationship of the two texts is underlined by the fact that **2** was omitted from the group of charters confirmed in 1326, while **1** was included. It is not until the early fifteenth century that the two charters are found copied together, in the Trinity Hall manuscript of Elmham's history, where both appear in allegedly full-size 'facsimiles' and in transcripts. Elmham claimed to have reproduced exactly his single-sheet sources. His 'facsimile' of **1** (see Plate I) measures 133 × 254 mm, and shows that the pseudo-original was written in a clever imitation of eighth-century Anglo-Saxon minuscule, presumably based on the script of the forger's model (the single-sheet version of **2** was apparently written in the same script, which underlines the relationship of the two forgeries; for this see further discussion below, in the commentary to **3**). Both the 'facsimile' and transcript of **1** have suffered from the attentions of a revisor of the Trinity Hall manuscript, perhaps Elmham himself. In **1**, as in several of the other related forgeries, the indiction does not agree with the incarnation year; 605 was the eighth indiction. The revisor has corrected the indiction in both the 'facsimile' and the transcript.

Elmham's 'facsimile' of **1** differs from the enrolled version in one major respect; the latter includes a witness-list (essentially the same as that in **2** and **3**), while Elmham's text does not. This seems to imply that there were two different versions of the charter (indeed, two different pseudo-originals, since Inspeximus confirmations usually only applied to documents in single-sheet form). But it is also possible that Elmham for some reason missed the witness-list in **1**, perhaps because it was written on the dorse of the charter (for Kentish opisthographs, see pp. xcii–xciii). Some support for this suggestion comes from the copies of **1** and **2** found in a number of sixteenth- and seventeenth-century transcripts, all of them ultimately dependent on the copy in a register compiled in the 1530s by Sir William Prise (see pp. lix–lx); they are represented here by MS Q. The copies of the two charters in these manuscripts agree very closely with Elmham's 'facsimiles', and occasionally preserve some better readings. As an agent of Cromwell, Prise could have had the opportunity to examine single-sheet charters from the dissolved monasteries as they came into royal hands, and there is some reason to believe that some if not all of his transcripts were taken from single sheets. In this case, it seems likely that Prise saw the same single-sheet versions of **1** and **2** that were examined by Elmham over a century earlier; it is interesting that in both the indiction is given as eight instead of six, which implies that the revision of the Trinity Hall manuscript led to emendation of the pseudo-originals themselves. Given this possibility, it seems significant that Prise's text of **1** includes the witness-list found in the enrolled version, but absent from Elmham's 'facsimile'. The same is true of an independent sixteenth-century copy, added at the end of a manuscript of William Thorne's history, which may also be based upon the pseudo-original seen by Elmham and Prise (MS M2; see pp. lvi–lvii). It seems probable that the witness-list was a feature of 1 from the beginning. It certainly seems to have been the model for the more elaborate version in 2, where all the witnesses have full-length subjective subscriptions and several of the names have been latinized. Elmham may have been so preoccupied with exactly reproducing the face of the charter that he forgot that there was also material on the dorse.

The witness-list itself is of considerable interest. The formulation of the king's subscription has been adapted from the forger's eighth-century model (compare 13, 53, and S 24, 31, 32 etc.), with the inclusion of the phrase *sano mente integroque consilio*. This is a Roman legal formula (Levison, *England and the Continent*, p. 186 n. 3), and may have been included in the Italian models used by the draftsmen of the earliest English charters; it is also to be found in one of the very earliest Anglo-Saxon charters with some claim to authenticity (S 1165, *c.* A.D. 672 × 674) The forger's use of such a chronologically appropriate formula for a charter of Æthelberht is intriguing. Another early feature may be the spelling of Augustine's name in his subscription in MS Q (and also in the text of Elmham's 'facsimile'); *Ægustinus/ Agustinus* seems to be a pre-Conquest form (compare *scæ Agustine* in 24). The next witness is the king's son, Eadbald; his name was well-known and could easily have been taken by the forger from Bede. But it seems certain that the remaining names in the witness-list derive from an early record of some kind, although some need a little emendation (see Levison, *England and the Continent*, pp. 220–3). *Hamigils* is clearly Hæmgisl; this was the name of a Northumbrian monk and hermit known to Bede (*HE* v. 12), and of an abbot of Glastonbury towards the end of the seventh century (see S 236–8, 1249, 1665–6). Names with the second element *-gisl* are rare after the ninth century. *Augemund* is a very unusual name. Levison suggested emendation to Agemund, which is similar to the unique Agesmundus who attests 46 from 697 (occurrences of Agemund in Cnut's charters relate to a thegn with the Scandinavian name Agmundr: see S 955, 957, 961). But it is possible that no emendation is needed; the element *Auge*, cognate with Gothic *augan-* is found very occasionally in Frankish personal names (see Morlet, *Noms de personne*, i. 46). This Frankish connection seems particularly significant in view of Augemund's style *referendarius*, which is discussed below. Hocca was the name of a reeve in the service of Bishop Wilfrid in the 670s (*The Life of Bishop Wilfrid by Eddius Stephanus*, ed. and transl. B. Colgrave (Cambridge, 1927), p. 41); later occurrences are generally in place-names (see S 726; and *DEPN*, p. 243, Hockenhull, Hockham, Hockley etc.). *Grafio* is more of a problem. Old German *graphio* corresponds to Latin *comes*; it was a word in fairly common use in Francia in the early medieval period, but it does not seem to have been known in early England. The *Dictionary of Latin from British Sources* (iv. 1092) cites only two pre-Conquest instances: a letter of Boniface with a continental context, and a spurious Abingdon charter that was probably forged no earlier than the tenth century (S 183). Levison found it hugely suspicious that *graphio* should apparently be used in this witness-list as a personal name, and erected an extraordinarily elaborate hypothesis to explain why it might have been supplied by the forger. He may have been too critical here; as he admits, there is one instance of *Graffio* as a personal name in a Merovingian charter of the early seventh century (albeit that the copy may not be entirely reliable), and, perhaps more significantly, there is evidence for the later use of an Old Norse derivative of the word, *greifi*, as a byname in the immediately pre-Conquest period (O. von Feilitzen, *The Pre-Conquest Personal Names of Domesday Book*, Nomina Germanica 3 (Uppsala, 1937), p. 274). It does not seem inconceivable that *Graphio* might be found as a personal name in Kent in the early Anglo-Saxon period, especially given the known contact between that kingdom and Merovingian Gaul (see further, below). Alternatively, it may be the case that in 1 *graphio* is not itself a personal name, but rather the style of the preceding witness, Hocca, corresponding to the previous Augemund *referendarius*. Levison did not consider this possibility because he based his commentary on this witness-list on the version in 2, which has a full-blown subjective subscription: *Ego Graphio comes benedixi*. But there is good reason to believe that the simple list of names in 1 is primary, and so it is certainly possible that *graphio* was originally intended as Hocca's style, not as a separate personal name. The punctuation of the surviving copies is not conclusive on this point. Most of the scribes seem to have understood this to be a name, but in Q and in some other versions of the Prise-Say register there was originally no punctuation between *Hocca* and *Grafio*. The next witness is *Thangil* or *Thongl'*, which is evidently another name with the second element *-gisl*. Levison suggested emendation to Eangisl, on the basis of the reading in the witness-list of 2 (*Tangisilus*), but this seems less justified in view of the forms in 1, which was probably the model for the version in 2. The element *Tanc/Thanc* was not uncommon in continental Germanic names in the early medieval period (see P. Piper, *Libri Confraternitatum S. Galli, Augiensis, Fabariensis*, MGH (Berlin, 1884), p. 513). Levison thought that Pinca should probably be Win(e)ca, which is not seen independently but occurs in a number of place-names (*DEPN*, pp. 523–4, Winkburn, Winkfield etc.). This mistake would be dependent upon a scribe misreading *wyn* (*p*) for *p*, which is certainly a common error; but it would require the forger's source to be from the second half of the eighth century or later, since it was not until that period that charter-scribes began (gradually) to use *p* in place of *uu* (Chaplais 1969, pp. 533 n. 58, 538–9 [pp. 96 n. 58, 102–3]). It may be that the reading Pinca is acceptable; a number of minor names seem to include the element (Wallenberg, *Kentish Place-Names*, p. 417), although there is the possibility of confusion here with OE *pynca*, 'point'. Deanesly's suggestion (1942, p. 105) that *pinca* is a scribal misreading of *pincerna* is almost certainly wrong. The name of the final witness, Geddi, should perhaps be emended to Æddi; this was the name of the Kentish singing master invited to Northumbria by Wilfrid (Bede, *HE*, iv. 2), who was probably also the author of Wilfrid's Life (note that a second version of this name, probably referring to a different individual, occurs in *HE* iv. 13, where is is mis-spelt Oiddi). Again it is possible that no emendation is necessary; this may be a hypocoristic version of a name beginning with the element *Gadi-*, which is found in some early Frankish names (Morlet, *Noms de personne*, i. 97).

Although there are problems, the general impression given by this list of names is that it does indeed derive from an early record of some kind. The names of Æthelberht, Augustine and Eadbald may have been supplied by the forger, but the remainder of the list is unlikely to have been constructed piecemeal, and the names themselves seem compatible with a date in the seventh or eighth century (the possible

Frankish affiliations of some of the names seems particularly significant). The first place to look for the source of this list is in the eighth-century charter, probably of Æthelberht II, which seems to have formed a model for the main text of **1**. It can be said at once that none of the names in this witness-list is to be found in the three surviving charters of Æthelberht II (**11**, and S 23, 24; see also **47**), nor in any charter in the name of his joint-rulers Eadberht I (**48**, and S 27) or Eardwulf (S 30, 31), nor in any charter of his predecessor Wihtred or any of his successors (apart from Agesmundus in **46** and an Eangisl in S 105 from 764 and S 37 from 765 × 785). This is not entirely conclusive, given the scarcity of charters from the first half of the eighth century, but it does suggest that the forger did not take the witness-list directly from his model. A radical alternative would be to investigate the possibility that the witness-list does indeed belong to the reign of Æthelberht I. This was a suggestion made by Margaret Deanesly in a series of articles in 1941 and 1942 (see especially Deanesly 1942). Deanesly was especially intrigued by the style *referendarius*, applied here to Augemund. In Merovingian Gaul the *referendarius* was the official connected to the chancery who kept the royal seal and arranged for the drawing up of royal diplomas (G. Tessier, *Diplomatique royale française* (Paris, 1962), pp. 2–3). Æthelberht married a Merovingian princess, the daughter of King Charibert of Paris (Bede, *HE*, i. 25); he may have been subject to Merovingian overlordship (I.N. Wood, *The Merovingian North Sea* (Alingsås, 1983)), and may even have tried to emulate Clovis (Kelly 1986, pp. 17–24); there is some evidence of earlier links between the Merovingians and the Kentish royal dynasty (N. Brooks, 'The Creation and Early Structure of the Kingdom of Kent', *The Origins of Anglo-Saxon Kingdoms*, ed. S. Bassett (Leicester, 1989), pp. 55–74, 250–4, at 64–5). Given this background, it is not entirely farfetched to suggest that Æthelberht's court may have boasted an official with the title of *referendarius* (though it is difficult to believe in the existence of a formal chancery at this time). Levison was entirely dismissive of this point of view. It was his intention to refute Deanesly's defence of the Æthelberht charters (a defence, it must be said, which was largely based on misconceived arguments) and to show that they were eleventh-century forgeries; he was unwilling to concede that the forgeries contained any early material, and was particularly anxious to explain away the reference to a *referendarius*. In an ingenious but ultimately unconvincing argument (*England and the Continent*, pp. 221–2) he focused on France in the eleventh and twelfth centuries, and suggested contexts in which Guerno of St Ouen may have become aware of the word. He is probably wrong in his suggestion that it was Guerno who forged **1** and the other charters in the name of Æthelberht (see pp. lxiv–lxv), and with this plank removed his arguments seem unsubstantial. The term *referendarius* was not in common use in the eleventh and twelfth centuries, but it was well-known in Francia in the sixth to eighth centuries; and that is the period to which the other names in the witness-list seem to belong. In this context, it may also be significant that the style is applied to a man, Augemund, whose name may be Frankish, and that other names in the witness-list may incorporate some Frankish elements. It is difficult to produce any conclusive evidence, but it does not seem to be beyond possibility that that the witness-list found in **1** (and **2** and **3**) could date from a period as early as Æthelberht's reign. The names need not have come from a charter (although a case can be made that charters were being produced in England in the earlier seventh century: see pp. lxxiv–lxxv), but could have been taken from another record of some kind; given its history of continuity from the seventh century, St Augustine's could well have preserved very early documentation into the post-Conquest period. **1** is certainly a forgery, but the forger may have had access to some early material.

The boundary clause locates the land covered by the charter by reference to three features. To the east lay the church of St Martin and to the south the road to Burgate (that is, the Roman road from Canterbury to Richborough). The western and eastern boundary was 'Drutin' street, which has been identified with Old Ruttington Lane; in the twelfth century there was an area known as *Drutintune* in the north-eastern suburbs of Canterbury (see W. Urry, *Canterbury under the Angevin Kings* (London, 1967), pp. 25, 27, 186).

To conclude: **1** is a fabricated foundation charter, which probably came into existence in the eleventh century, at the same time as or shortly before the other charters in the name of Æthelberht and the related forged papal privileges. It could even have been a product of the period immediately before the Conquest (see Kelly 1988). The forger modelled his text on a mid-eighth-century charter, probably of Æthelberht II, and attached to it a witness-list from another source, perhaps from a record of the time of Æthelberht I. The charter seems to have been superseded at an early date by **2**, which would explain why it does not survive in any copies earlier than the fourteenth century.

2

Æthelberht, king of the English, grants land to the east of Canterbury to the monastery of SS Peter and Paul. A.D. 605

C. BL Cotton Vespasian B. xx, 277rv: copy, s. xii[1]
   Rubric: Priuilegium Athelberti regis primi Anglorum gentis Christianissimi.
D. BL Cotton Vitellius A. ii, 6v: copy, s. xii[2]
   No rubric
F. BL Cotton Julius D. ii, 84r: copy, s. xiii[1]
   Rubric: Athelberti regis donatio de terra ubi situm est monasterium apostolorum Petri et Pauli cum terris adiacentibus.
G. BL Cotton Claudius D. x, 9r: copy, s. xiii[2]
   Rubric: Athelberti regis donatio de terra ubi situm est monasterium apostolorum Petri et Pauli cum terris adiacentibus.
K. BL Cotton Tiberius A. ix, 107v–108r: copy, s. xiv
L. CCCC 189, 46rv: copy, s. xiv
M1. BL Add. 53710, 2v–3r: copy, s. xiv/xv
M2. BL Add. 53710, 254r: copy, s. xvi
N1. Cambridge, Trinity Hall, 1, 22r: facsimile, s. xv[1]
   Rubric: Exemplar secunde carte de imitacione fundi amplianda.
N2. Cambridge, Trinity Hall, 1, 22r: copy, s. xv[1]
P. Bodleian, Tanner 165, 97r: copy, s. xv
Q. Winchester, Cathedral Library, XXB, 157rv.: copy, s. xvi
Ed.: a. Spelman, *Concilia*, i. 119, from N
   b. Twysden, *Scriptores*, cols 1761–2, from M1
   c. *Mon. Angl.*, i. 24, ? from C

d. Wilkins, *Concilia*, iv. 728, from Spelman
e. Kemble 3, from N
f. *Mon. Angl.* (rev. edn), i. 110, from P; i. 126–7 (no. 2), from 1st edn
g. Hardwick, *Elmham*, pp. 111–13, from N
h. Haddan and Stubbs, *Councils*, iii. 55–6, from Kemble etc.
i. Birch 5, from G, Kemble etc.
j. Pierquin, *Recueil*, pt 1, no. 3, from Birch
k. Deanesly 1942, facing p. 114 (reduced facsimile)
Listed: Sawyer 3
Edited from C, F, G, N1 and Q

+ In nomine Domini nostri Iesu Christi. Notum sit omnibus tam pręsentibus quam posteris quod ego Æthelbertus*a* Dei gratia rex Anglorum, per euangelicum genitorem meum Augustinum*b* de idolatra*c* factus Christicola, tradidi Deo per ipsum antistitem aliquam partem terrę*d* iuris mei sub orientali muro ciuitatis Dorobernię, ubi scilicet*e* per eundem in Christo institutorem monasterium in honore principum apostolorum Petri et Pauli condidi, et cum ipsa terra et cum omnibus quę ad ipsum monasterium pertinent perpetua libertate donaui, adeo ut nec mihi nec alicui successorum meorum regum nec ulli unquam potestati siue ęcclesiasticę siue seculari quicquam inde liceat usurpare, sed in ipsius abbatis sint omnia libera dicione. Si quis uero de hac donatione nostra aliquid minuere aut irritum facere temptauerit, auctoritate*f* et beati pape*g* Gregorii nostrique apostoli Augustini*h* simul et nostra imprecatione sit hic segregatus ab omni sancte ęcclesię*i* communione et in die iudicii ab omni electorum societate. Circumcingitur hęc terra his terminibus: in oriente ęcclesia*j* sancti Martini, et inde ad orientem be sypenne dune,*k* et sic ad aquilonem be Wykenge mearce,*l* iterumque*m* ad orientem et ad austrum be burnþare mearce,*n* *o*item ad orientem et ad austrum be suth burnþare*p* mearke,*o* et sic ad austrum et occidentem be kynges mearke,*q* item ad aquilonem et orientem be kynges mearce,*q* sicque ad occidentem to riðere ceape,*r* et ita ad aquilonem to druting strǣte.*s*
Actum est hoc in ciuitate Dorouernie,*t* anno ab incarnatione Christi .dcv., indictione .vi.*u*

+*v* Ego Athelbertus*w* rex Anglorum hanc donationem meam signo sanctę crucis propria manu confirmaui.*x*
+ Ego Augustinus*y* gratia Dei archiepiscopus libenter subscripsi.
+ Ego Eadbaldus*z* regis filius*d* faui.
+ Ego Hamigisilus dux laudaui.
+ Ego Hocca comes consensi.
+ Ego Augemundus referendarius approbaui.
+ Ego Graphio comes benedixi.

+ Ego Tangisilus regis optimas confirmaui.
+ Ego Pinca consensi.
+ Ego Geddi corroboraui.

a Æthilberktus N1, Q *b* Agustinum N1, Q *c* ydolatra G, N1, Q *d* *Omitted* Q
e silicet N1 *f* N1 *adds* Dei *g* *Erased* C; episcopi Q *h* Agustini N1 *i* eclesie N1
j eclesia N1 *k* svvendoune F; sivvendoune G, N1; siwendoune Q
l wikenge mearche F, G; uuikenges mærke N1; uuikenges marke Q *m* iterum G
n burhguuare mærke F, N1, Q; bureyare mearke G; *for* burhpare
o '...' *Omitted* G, N1, Q; F *compresses this and the next section of the bounds:* iterum ad
orientem et ad austrum et occidentem be kingesmearche, sicque ad occidentem ...
p *For* burhpare *q* kinges mearche G; kinges mærke N1; kynges merke Q
r riðere sceape F; rithere chepe G; riðæs cæpe N1; riðescępe Q
s drutingstrete F, G; drutingestræte N1, Q *t* Dorouerni F, N1, Q
u .vi. *altered to* .viii. N1; .viii. Q *v* C *has no crosses* *w* Æthelbertus F; Æthilbertus Q
x F *ends here* *y* Agustinus N1; Ægustinus Q *z* Ædbaldus G

2 is a grander version of **1**, intended to provide title to territory lying to the east
and south as well as to the abbey precincts. The forger has jettisoned some of the
old-fashioned diplomatic of **1** (which was constrained by its eighth-century model).
In place of the proem there is a greeting (a sign of post-Conquest influence), and in
keeping with this the dispositive verbs are now in the past tense. A reference to
Æthelberht's conversion has been inserted after the superscription. The dispositive
section has been reworked, in order to show that the privilege applied not only to
the land on which the monastery was built, but also to the abbey itself and everything
belonging to it; all is to be under the control of the abbot. The anathema has been
strengthened with a reference to the authority of Pope Gregory and Augustine; the
boundary clause is now more detailed; the bald witness-list of **1** has been expanded
into a set of full subscriptions, probably modelled on the witness-list of a royal
diploma of the tenth or eleventh century, when it was common for draftsman to
vary the subscribing verbs (compare **28**). It seems probable that **2** was intended to
supersede **1**, and this would explain why the latter was not copied with the rest of
the 'foundation forgeries' in the twelfth and thirteenth centuries. The rubrics to the
copies of **2** in the thirteenth-century cartularies (MSS F, G) show that it was being
treated as the principal title to the abbey precincts. In a copy in a Christ Church
register (MS P) this has been highlighted by adaptation and interpolation of the
introduction to the bounds: 'Circumcingitur hec terra ubi situm est monasterium
apostolorum Petri et Pauli cum terra adiacente his terminibus' (for an edition of
this copy, see *Mon. Angl.* (rev. edn), i. 110).

2 has a complicated textual history, with a major variant in the boundary clause.
The charter was copied repeatedly between the twelfth and fifteenth centuries, and
Elmham supplied a 'facsimile' of the single-sheet version available to him, which
shows that it measured 155 × 285 mm and that it was written in the same imitative
minuscule as **1**, its presumed model (on the script of these pseudo-originals, see
further in the commentary to **3**). The copy of the text in the Prise-Say register (here
represented by MS Q) appears to have been taken from the same pseudo-original
seen by Elmham, and this was probably also the source of the copy added to a

manuscript of William Thorne's history in the sixteenth century (MS M2; see pp. lvi–lvii). The text in these versions differs from that in the two twelfth-century manuscripts (MSS C, D) in one significant respect; it is missing one section of the boundary clause ('item ad orientem et ad austrum be suth burnware mearke'). Since this section is in large part a repeat of the previous phrase, it would be easily omitted by a copyist, but there is also a possibility that the boundary clause was deliberately revised or simplified. There is some evidence that it was during the thirteenth century that this passage dropped out of the received version. MS F, probably dating from the second quarter of the thirteenth century, is a difficult witness, since it appears to compress this part of the bounds; it definitely lacks any reference to the boundary of the *suthware*. The scribe of MS G, writing later in the century, appears to have made use of MS F or its exemplar (note the identical rubric), but he also seems to have had access to a text with a slightly different version of the bounds; his text has the same omission as the version in Elmham's 'facsimile' and the sixteenth-century transcripts, but also has an erasure at the crucial point, indicating that the scribe was choosing between two different readings. The text of 2 in Thomas Sprott's history, written *c.* 1270 but available only in fourteenth-century copies, has the full version of the bounds (see MS K); it is likely that Sprott was here dependent on a text copied into the earlier *Textus S. Adriani*. William Thorne, who otherwise followed Sprott for the pre-Conquest period, has the shorter version (MSS L, M1); this evidently represents deliberate textual revision. Even Elmham, preparing his 'facsimile' of a single-sheet charter, seems to have had his doubts, for there is an erasure at the crucial place in the boundary clause. If Elmham's single-sheet version did, as it appears, lack this particular section of the boundary clause, then it cannot have been the 'original' of the forgery.

In this context, it should be noted that there is some reason to believe that the pseudo-originals of 2 and 3 which were used by Elmham were ultimately based upon the twelfth-century copies in BL Cotton Vespasian B. xx (MS C); in other words, the single sheets was created or resurrected from a manuscript copy. This is most clearly seen in the case of 3, where the text of the charter in MS C has undergone some erasure and reworking which is reflected in Elmham's pseudo-original. But it also seems to be true of Elmham's single-sheet version of 2. In MS C, the section of the bounds missing from the texts of Elmham and others covers a full line, and could easily have been lost through homoeoteleuton; the situation would be unlikely to arise elsewhere, since this part of the manuscript is written in an unusually large script. The implication must be that the pseudo-original of 2 which was available in the fifteenth century was also ultimately based on the twelfth-century manuscript copy. It is impossible to say whether this reflects the loss or destruction of an earlier single-sheet copy, or whether it indicates that 2 was not originally forged in single-sheet form (see further discussion in the commentary to 3).

The boundary clause begins with St Martin's church in the east and ends with 'Drutin' street to the north, as did the simple bounds of 1; it therefore included the abbey precincts, as well as covering a substantial area to the south and south-east which appears to represent the abbey's home farm of Langport. This was beneficially assessed in Domesday Book at one sulung and one yoke, which had always been exempt; it included seventy burgess-tenements in Canterbury (GDB 12r). The bounds are not easy to understand, although Thorne obligingly provides a modern version

(Twysden, *Scriptores*, col. 1762; Davis, *Thorne*, p. 9). Further east from St Martin's church lay *siwenne dune*, which appears to be Thorne's *Mellehelle* or Millhill; Wallenberg (*KPN*, p. 5) suggests that the first element may be a female personal name, *Sigewynn*. The next boundary mark is *wykenge mearce* to the north. This seems to be the boundary of the 'Wic' people, no doubt associated with the area later known as *Wyke*, to the north-east of Canterbury; it has been conjectured that this name originally referred to an early medieval trading emporium stretching along the Stour from Canterbury to Fordwich (M. Sparks and T. Tatton-Brown, 'The History of the Vill of St Martin's, Canterbury', *AC* civ (1987), pp. 200–13). Next, to the east and south, was the boundary with the *burhware*, that is, with land held by the people of Canterbury. On the same orientation was the boundary with the *suth burhware*, whose identity is not clear. From here the St Augustine's estate bordered on an estate belonging to the king; the orientations at this stage are difficult to understand. At the western limit was the cattle market (*hrythera ceap*), which lay outside Newingate and is mentioned in a tenth-century charter (S 1629; see Brooks, *Church of Canterbury*, pp. 32, 336 n. 53).

For the witness-list, see the commentary to **1**.

3

Æthelberht, king of the English, grants land at Sturry, also called Chislet, Kent, to the monastery of SS Peter and Paul. A.D. 605 (9 January)

C. BL Cotton Vespasian B. xx, 277v–279r: copy, s. xii[1]
   No rubric
D. BL Cotton Vitellius A. ii, 7rv: copy, s. xii[2]
   No rubric
E. PRO Cart. Antiq. R. 9, no. 18: copy, s. xiii
   Rubric: Item carta monachorum sancti Augustini Cant' sine sigillo hec sola.
F. BL Cotton Julius D. ii, 84rv: copy, s. xiii[1]
   Rubric: Priuilegium regis Athelberti.
G*. BL Cotton Claudius D. x, 61rv: copy of Inspeximus [R], s. xiv[1]
   Rubric: Carta eiusdem de manerio de Chistelet.
K. BL Cotton Tiberius A. ix, 108rv: copy, s. xiv
L. CCCC 189, 46v–47r: copy, s. xiv
M1. BL Add. 53710, 3rv: copy, s. xiv/xv
M2. BL Add. 53710, 221v–222r: copy of Inspeximus [S], s. xiv/xv
N1. Cambridge, Trinity Hall, 1, 23r: facsimile, s. xv[1]
   Rubric: Exemplar tercie carte Ethelberti regis tam in longitudine quam in latitudine quam in scripture qualitate.
N2. Cambridge, Trinity Hall, 1, 22v: copy, s. xv[1]
R. PRO Ch. R. 20 Edw. II, m. 2
S. PRO Ch. R. 36 Edw. III, m.7
T. PRO Ch. R. 8 Hen. IV, m. 6
U. PRO Pat. R. 2 Hen. VI pt 3, m. 5
V. PRO Pat. R. 4 Edw. IV, pt 4, m. 29
W. PRO Pat. R. 14 Hen. VII, pt 1, m. 16
Ed.: a. Spelman, *Concilia*, i. 120–1, from N

b. Twysden, *Scriptores*, cols 1762–3 from M1, 2123–5 from M2
c. *Mon. Angl.*, i. 24, ? from D
d. Wilkins, *Concilia*, iv. 728–9, from Spelman
e. Kemble 4, from N
f. *Mon. Angl.* (rev. edn), i. 127 (no. 2), from 1st edn
g. Hardwick, *Elmham*, pp. 114–16, from N
h. Thorpe, *Diplomatarium*, pp. 1–3, from G, N
i. Haddan and Stubbs, *Councils*, iii. 56–8, from Kemble etc.
j. Birch 6, from Kemble etc.
k. Pierquin, *Recueil*, pt 1, no 4, from Birch
l. Hunter 1973, plate 2 (reduced facsimile)
Listed: Sawyer 4
Edited from C

*a*Rex Anglorum Æthelbertus,*b* misericordia omnipotentis Dei catholicus, omnibus suę gentis fidelibus et aduentum glorię magni Dei et saluatoris nostri Iesu Christi beata spe expectantibus*c* salutem uitęque ęternae beatitudinem. Largiente summi regis clementia ego Athelbertus,*d* in solio paterno confirmatus paceque diuinitus concessa eo iam per decem quinquennia sceptrigera potestate potitus et per uenerabiles sacrę fidei doctores spiritus sancti gratia irradiatus, ab errore falsorum deorum ad unius ueri Dei cultum toto corde conuersus, ne ingratus beneficiorum appaream illi a cuius sancta sede nobis in regione umbrę mortis sedentibus lux ueritatis emicuit, inter alias quas fabricaui ęcclesias monitu et hortatu beatissimi papę*e* Gregorii et sancti patris nostri Augustini, ipsi beatissimo apostolorum principi Petro et doctori gentium Paulo monasterium*f* a fundamentis construxi*g* illudque*h* terris uariisque possessionum donariis decorare*i* studui inibique monachos Deum timentes aggregari feci et cum consilio*j* eiusdem reuerentissimi archipresulis Augustini ex suo sancto*k* sanctorum collegio uenerabilem uirum secum ab apostolica sede directum Petrum monachum elegi eisque ut ęcclesiasticus ordo exposcit abbatem preposui. Hoc*l* igitur monasterium*f* ad prouectum debiti culminis promouere desiderans suarumque possessionum terminos*m* dilatare gestiens, sana mente integroque consilio cum Eadbaldi*n* filii mei aliorumque nobilium optimatum*o* meorum consensu, ob redemptionem animę meę et spem retributionis ęternę, optuli ei etiam uillam nomine Sturigao alio nomine dictum Cistelet*p* cum omnibus redditibus ei iure competentibus, cum mancipiis, siluis, cultis uel incultis pratis, pascuis, paludibus, fluminibus et contiguis ei maritimis terminis eam ex una parte cingentibus, omnia mobilia uel immobilia in usus fratrum sub regulari tramite et monastica religione inibi Deo seruientium. Missurium*q* etiam argenteum, scapton aureum, iterum sellam cum freno auro et gemmis exornatam, speculum argenteum, armilcaisia oloserica, camisiam ornatam, quod mihi xenium*r* de domno papa[e] Gregorio sedis apostolicę directum fuerat, quae omnia supradicto monasterio[s] gratanter optuli. Quod[t] etiam monasterium[f] ipse seruus Dei Augustinus sanctorum apostolorum ac martyrum reliquiis uariisque ęcclesiasticis ornamentis ab apostolica sede sibi transmissis copiose ditauit seseque in ea et cunctos successores suos ex auctoritate apostolica sepeliri precepit, scriptura dicente, Non esse ciuitatem mortuorum sed uiuorum.[1] Ubi etiam mihi et successoribus meis sepulturam prouidi, sperans me quandoque ab ipso apostolici ordinis principe, cui Dominus potestatem ligandi atque soluendi dedit et claues regni cęlorum tradidit,[2] a peccatorum nexibus solui et ęternę beatitudinis ianuam introduci. Quod monasterium[u] nullus episcoporum, nullus successorum meorum regum in aliquo ledere aut inquietare presumat, nullam omnino subiectionem in ea sibi usurpare audeat, sed[v] abbas ipse qui ibi fuerit ordinatus intus et foris cum consilio fratrum secundum timorem Dei libere eam regat et ordinet, ita ut in die Domini dulcem illam piissimi redemptoris nostri uocem mereatur audire dicentis, Euge serue bone et fidelis, quia super pauca fuisti[k] fidelis, super multa te constituam, intra in gaudium Domini tui.[3] Hanc donationem meam in nomine patris et filii et spiritus sancti largitate diuina, ut mihi tribuatur peccatorum remissio, per omnia cum consilio reuerentissimi patris Augustini condidi idque[w] ad[e] scribendum[x] Augemundum presbiterum ordinaui. De his ergo omnibus quę hic scripta sunt, si quis aliquid inde minuere pręsumpserit, sciat se ęquissimo iudici Deo et beatis apostolis Petro et Paulo rationem esse redditurum. Confirmata est hec[y] donatio pręsentibus testibus, reuerentissimo patre Augustino Dorouernensis ęcclesię archiepiscopo primo, Mellito quoque et Iusto Lundonię[z] et Rofensis[a2] ęcclesię pręsulibus [b2]et religioso famulo Christi Laurentio presbitero, Eadbaldo filio meo, Hamigisilo duce, Augemundo referendario, Hocca et Graphioni[c2] comitibus, Tangisilo et Pinca et Geddi et Aldhuno regis optimatibus aliisque plurimis diuersarum dignitatum personis. Actum sane quadragesimo quinto anno regni nostri sub die .v. idus Ianuarii.

[a] + In nomine sancte et indiuidue trinitatis *inserted here* G*, N1
[b] Athelbertus C, D; Ædelbertus N1 [c] exspectantibus G* [d] Ethelbertus G*
[e] *Erased* C [f] *Erased* C; ecclesiam G*, N1 [g] costruxi D; constuxi N1
[h] *Erased* C; eamque G*, N1 [i] decorari G* [j] *Erased* C; concilio N1
[k] *Omitted* G* [l] *Erased* C; hanc G*, N1 [m] *Erased* C; *omitted* G*
[n] Ædbaldi D; Edbaldi N1 [o] obtimatum N1 [p] Cistelei C, D [q] missurum D, G*
[r] exenium G* [s] -o monasterio *erased* C; supradicte ecclesie G*, N1
[t] *Erased* C; quam G*, N1 [u] aut ecclesiam *added* G*, N1 [v] set G*
[w] id- *erased* C; atque G*, N1 [x] transscribendum G*, N1
[y] est hec *erased* C, *omitted* G*, N1 [z] Londonie G* [a2] Roffensis G*
[b2] *From here* G* *and* N1 *read as follows*: Ædbaldo (Edbaldo N1) filio meo, Hamigisilo,

Augemundo referendario, Hocca, Graphio, Tangil, Pinca, Geddi aliisque plurimis
dignitatum diuersarum. G* *and* N1 *end here, omitting the dating clause*
c2 Graphioni *altered to* Graphione D

¹ See Matt. 22: 32; Marc. 12: 27; Luc. 20: 38. *Non est deus mortuorum sed uiuentium.*
² Matt. 16: 19
³ Matt. 25: 23

3 is the longest and by far the most impressive of the three forged charters in the
name of King Æthelberht. It gives title to a 'vill' named Sturry, which was also
known as Chislet. St Augustine's had Domesday manors at both Sturry and Chislet,
which lie to the north-east of Canterbury, between the Stour and the Wantsum.
Sturry was beneficially assessed at five exempt sulungs, with capacity for twelve
ploughs; the reckoning of twelve sulungs for Chislet also appears to be an un-
derassessment, since it had capacity for thirty ploughs (GDB 12r). The oddity of
providing two different names for one 'vill' can be explained by the earlier application
of the name Sturry to the whole region north-east of Canterbury. It was the 'Stour'
ge, equivalent to the 'Limen' *ge* (Lyminge) and the 'eastern' *ge* (Eastry); the last
element is cognate with German *gau*, with the meaning 'district' or 'territory' (*DEPN*,
p. 158). By the eleventh century all these district names were now applied only to
those settlements which had been their original foci. The apparent confusion in **3**
suggests that the forger was drawing on a record which dealt with the land later
known as the manor of Chislet, but referred to it as part of Sturry; there are parallels
in S 8 from Reculver and in three Minster charters (**40, 41, 42**), where references to
grants of land in Sturry seem to refer to the region rather than to a specific settlement.
The likelihood that the forger of **3** was using an ancient record for the details of the
grant is increased by the archaic spelling of the name Sturry (*Sturigao*): see A.
Campbell, *Old English Grammar* (Oxford, 1959), p. 116, for the diphthong. The
source may have been a list of benefactions, in which Sturry had already been glossed
as Chislet, or perhaps an early charter (not necessarily in the name of Æthelberht).
St Augustine's could well have acquired lands in Sturry in the seventh century, as
did Reculver and Minster (Tatton-Brown 1992, pp. 85–7; and see above, p. cviii),
but there is no guarantee that Æthelberht was the donor, and it is unlikely that
these early acquisitions corresponded very closely with the Domesday manors (which
probably represent consolidations of smaller land-grants).

3 is considerably more discursive than the other Æthelberht charters. After a
general greeting the king refers to his fifty-year reign (a good round figure that is
incompatible with the regnal year in the dating clause) and at length to his conversion
and the foundation and endowment of St Augustine's; we are also told of the election
of Peter as the first abbot. Much of this detail and wording is based on Bede, *HE*,
i. 33 and on the other Æthelberht charters, and no doubt also on historical
compilations and other records which have not survived. A lost source of this kind
presumably underlies the list of gifts here said to have been sent by Pope Gregory
to King Æthelberht and passed on to the abbey (the original inspiration is likely to
have been the reference to *parua exenia* in one of Gregory's letters: Bede, *HE*, i. 32).
The gifts include a silver dish (*missurium* for *missorium*), a gold sceptre or staff
(*scapton*, from a Greek word), a horse-saddle and reins decorated with gold and

jewels, a silver mirror, a silken cloak (*armilcaisia* for *armilausa*) and a decorated robe. It is impossible to say whether these precious objects were still available at the time that **3** was forged, or whether their traditional provenance was correct. Later historians of the abbey were disgruntled to find that these treasures had been lost; Sprott (BL Cotton Tiberius A. ix, 108v) thought that they could have been stolen by the Danes or sold to pay King Richard's ransom. Towards the end of the text, Æthelberht mentions some of the privileges that were to accrue to St Augustine's. There was to be no interference in the abbey by any bishop or any of Æthelberht's successors as king; everything was to be ordered and ruled by the abbot (who was to be consecrated in the monastery), with the advice of the brethren. This is just the kind of unequivocal statement of independence from archiepiscopal and other authority which the St Augustine's community needed in its struggle with Lanfranc and his successors (see pp. xxiii–xxiv).

3 has essentially the same witness-list as **1** and **2** (perhaps derived from a seventh-century record of some kind); it adds Mellitus, Justus and Laurentius (presumably from Bede), and a layman named Aldhun (perhaps from the original source, but omitted in **1** and consequently in **2**). The names are given in a list, in the ablative form, which reflects post-Conquest diplomatic procedures, as does the incorporation of an address at the beginning of the text. The list of appurtenances contains elements such as slaves and coastal privileges which derive from continental formulas; the *rogatio* clause mentioning the priest Augemund is also foreign to the Anglo-Saxon diplomatic tradition (Chaplais 1965, p. 50 [pp. 30–1]). **3** was evidently forged after the Conquest by a scribe with no acquaintance with Anglo-Saxon diplomatic. There is some reason to think that it probably came into existence after **1** and **2**; although it is ostensibly a simple land-charter, it includes elements (such as the explicit references to the abbey's privileges) more appropriate to a foundation charter, and this probably implies that an unsatisfactory foundation charter was already in existence.

The textual history of **3** is complicated. The many texts fall into two groups. In the first, the abbey is throughout described as a *monasterium*; this is the version found in the two twelfth-century copies (MSS C, D) and in the histories of Sprott and Thorne (MSS K, L, M1). In all other copies, including Elmham's 'facsimile', *ecclesia* appears in place of *monasterium*, the subscriptions of Laurentius and Aldhun have been omitted, and the dating clause is missing; a verbal invocation is sometimes included, either at the beginning or after the king's name. One of these versions presumably represents a revision, but it is difficult to be certain which. One reason to suppose that the original read *ecclesia* is the existence in both versions of three feminine pronouns referring to the community (lines 33, 41, 42). On the other hand, the texts with *ecclesia* have at one point the phrase *monasterium aut ecclesiam*, which could reflect the oversight of a revisor. The *ecclesia* version was in existence in the early thirteenth century, when it was copied onto the Cartae Antiquae roll (MS E); the scribe remarked that the document was *sine sigillo*, so he must have seen a single-sheet copy. Probably this was the same single sheet reproduced in facsimile by Elmham, in which case it measured 293 × 486 mm and was written in the same ornate uncial script as **4**.

It is possible that the charter seen by Elmham was not the 'original' of the forgery, for there is some evidence that all the texts with the *ecclesia* version of the charter ultimately descend from the twelfth-century copy in BL Cotton Vespasian B. xx (MS C). Here a revisor has systematically worked through the text, erasing the word *monasterium* and all pronouns agreeing with it (the references to *papa* are also deleted, but more lightly and evidently by a different revisor). It seems significant that the only place where *monasterium* has not been erased is in the instance where the phrase *monasterium aut ecclesiam* appears in the revised copies. This treatment of the text in MS C may have been the preliminary to the creation of the revised single-sheet version of 3. It is possible that the resurrection of the charter was necessary because the 'original' of the forgery had been lost or damaged; it is also possible that 3 was not initially fabricated in single-sheet form. It seems significant that the single-sheet version of 2 used by Elmham also has a major variant which indicates that it was based on the copy of the text in MS C.

A possible context can be suggested for the creation of the single-sheet versions of 2 and 3. It should first be noticed that the script of Elmham's facsimile of 2 resembles that of 1 (imitative Anglo-Saxon minuscule), while the script of 3 is the same as that of 4 (uncial). This implies that the physical appearance of these four documents was based on only two models. 1 was in existence before 2 (which was an adaptation of it); its formulation was apparently based on that of a charter of the eighth-century King Æthelberht II, which was presumably also the model for the script. Thus the script of 2 is probably imitative of the script of 1. In the uncial model, 4 seems likely to have priority; it has a stable textual tradition and the attachment of a lead bull would have impeded the creation of new copies (see further in the commentary to 4). The script of the single-sheet version of 3 was probably based on that of 4. If these observations are correct, it would follow that the single-sheet copies of 1 and 4 were in existence before the creation of the 'originals' of 2 and 3. This suggests a connection with a celebrated episode in the history of the 'foundation forgeries'. In 1181 the St Augustine's community was challenged to submit its privileges for inspection; although it claimed to have many such, it could bring forward only two, the privilege of Augustine and a charter of Æthelberht (see Levison, *England and the Continent*, p. 180; Gervase of Canterbury, *Opera Historica*, i. 296). Hostile commentators reckoned that the first of these looked far too new (they also objected to the leaden bull); the charter of Æthelberht seemed satisfactorily venerable, but appeared to have been tampered with – it was *rasa . . . et inscripta*. This appears to be a description of the pseudo-original of 4 and probably also that of 1; the latter departs very little from its eighth-century model, and the account here suggests that the forger may have proceeded by tampering with the original charter, erasing sections and substituting his own words and phrases. The fact that the monks produced only one and not three charters of Æthelberht in 1181 would be compatible with the suggestion that 2 and 3 were not available in single-sheet form at the time. In that case, the pseudo-originals of these two charters (apparently based on the texts in BL Cotton Vespasian B. xx) must have come into existence at a later stage. Given that 3 was copied onto the Cartae Antiquae Rolls in John's reign, this activity presumably took place soon after the trial of 1181, and was perhaps spurred by the scornful reception of 1 and 4 on that occasion.

4

Augustine, bishop of Canterbury, grants privileges to the monastery of SS Peter and Paul.

C. BL Cotton Vespasian B. xx, 2rv: incomplete copy, s. xii[1]
  No rubric
D. BL Cotton Vitellius A. ii, 7v–8v: copy, s. xii[2]
  Rubric: Priuilegium almi Augustini Anglorum apostoli.
F. BL Cotton Julius D. ii, 39v–40r: copy, s. xiii[1]
  Rubric: Priuilegium beati Augustini Anglorum apostoli.
G. BL Cotton Claudius D. x, 9rv: copy, s. xiii[2]
  Rubric: Priuilegium beati Augustini Anglorum apostoli.
H. PRO E 164/27, 39r–40r: copy, s. xiii
L. CCCC 189, 47rv: copy, s. xiv
M. BL Add. 53710, 3v–4v: copy, s. xiv/xv
N1. Cambridge, Trinity Hall, 1, 24r: facsimile, s. xv[1]
  Rubric: Exemplar bulle sancti Augustini cum signo plumbeo.
N2. Cambridge, Trinity Hall, 1, 23v: copy, s. xv[1]
Ed.: a. Spelman, *Concilia*, i. 121–2, from N
  b. Twysden, *Scriptores*, col. 1763, from N
  c. *Mon. Angl*, i. 25, ? from D
  d. Wilkins, *Concilia*, iv. 729–30, from Spelman
  e. Kemble 5, from N etc.
  f. *Mon. Angl.* (rev. edn), i. 127–8 (no. 3), from 1st edn
  g. Hardwick, *Elmham*, pp. 119–21, from N2
  h. Thorpe, *Diplomatarium*, pp. 3–5, from G, N
  h. Haddan and Stubbs, *Councils*, iii. 58–9, from Kemble etc.
  i. Birch 7, from G, N etc.
  j. Pierquin, *Recueil*, pt 1, no. 5, from Birch
  k. Hunter 1973, plate 3 (reduced facsimile)
Listed: Sawyer 1244
Edited from C, D and N1

+[a] Augustinus episcopus Dorobernię sedis famulus, quem superna inspirante clementia beatissimus papa[b] Gregorius Anglicę genti Deo acquirende legatarium misit amministrum, omnibus successoribus suis episcopis cunctisque Anglię regibus cum suis posteris atque omnibus Dei fidelibus et in fide et gratia pacem et salutem. Patet omnibus quod Deo amabilis rex Aðelbertus,[c] primus Anglorum regum Christi regno sacratus, nostra instantia et sua prodiga beniuolentia inter cęteras ęcclesias quas fecit et episcopia monasterium extra metropolim suam Doroberniam in honore principum apostolorum Petri et Pauli regaliter condidit et regalibus opibus amplisque possessionibus ditauit, dilatauit, magnificauit, perpetuaque libertate et omni iure regio cum omnibus rebus et iudiciis intus et foris illo pertinentibus

muniuit, suoque regio priuilegio et superni iudicii imprecatione atque apostolica sancti pape*b* Gregorii interminatione excommunicatoria contra omnem iniuriam confirmauit. Ego quoque eiusdem libertatis adiutor et
patrocinator omnes successores meos archiepiscopos omnesque ęcclesiasticas
uel seculares potestates per Dominum Iesum Christum et apostolorum eius
reuerentiam obtestor atque apostolica memorati patris nostri pape*b* Gregorii
interminatione interdico ne quisquam unquam ullum potentatum aut do-
minatum*d* aut imperium in hoc dominicum uel apostolicum monasterium
uel terras uel ęcclesias ad illud pertinentes usurpare presumat, nec ulla
prorsus subiugationis aut seruitutis aut tributi conditione uel in magno uel
in minimo Dei ministros inquietet aut opprimat. *e*Abbatem a suis fratribus
electum in eodem monasterio non ad suum famulatum sed ad dominicum
ministerium ordinet, nec sibi hunc obaudire sed Deo suadeat. Nec uero sibi
subiectum sed fratrem sed consortem sed collegam et comministrum in opus
dominicum eum reputet. Non ibi missas quasi ad suę dicionis altare nec
ordinationes uel benedictiones usurpatiue sine abbatis uel fratrum petitione
exerceat. Nullum sibi ius consuetudinarium uel in uilissima re exigat, quatinus
pacis concordia unum sint in Domino utrimque. Nec quisquam quod absit
dominandi dissidio in iudicium incidat diaboli qui superbię tyrannide corruit
de celo. Reges gentium, inquit Dominus, dominantur eorum, uos autem
non sic.[1] Cumque ab alienis*f* non a filiis accipiantur tributa sic ipse Dominus
concludit, Ergo liberi sunt filii.[2] Qua ergo irreuerentia patres ęcclesiarum in
filios regni Dei sibi uendicant dominationem, maxime autem in hanc ęc-
clesiam sanctorum thesaurariam, in cuius materno utero tot pontificum
Dorobernię regumque ac principum corpora speramus alma refouenda*g*
sepulture requie ex auctoritate scilicet apostolica et hinc ad ęternam gloriam
resuscitandam. Tales supremi*h* iudicis amicos si quis offendere non metuens
huius priuilegii statuta uiolauerit uel uiolatorem imitando uim suam tenuerit,
sciat se apostolico*i* beati Petri gladio per suum uicarium Gregorium pu-
niendum nisi emendauerit.

Hec ergo omnia uti hic sunt scripta, apostolica ipsius institutoris nostri
Gregorii comprobatione et auctoritate, seruanda sanccimus suoque ore
confirmamus, presente glorioso rege Aðelberto*j* cum filio suo Æthelbaldo*k*
et collaudante*l* cum ipso et omnibus optimatibus regiis atque ultro
uolentibus*m* reuerentissimis fratribus nostris a sancta romana*n* ecclesia huc
mecum uel ad me in euangelium Domini destinatis, scilicet Laurentio
quem nobis Deo fauente successorem constituimus et Mellito Lundoniae
episcopo et Iusto Rofensi episcopo et Petro uenerabili eiusdem monasterii
principum apostolorum abbate primo, cum cęteris in Domino adiutoribus
meis obnixe postulantibus, simulque in eos qui hec fideliter seruauerint

benedictionem aut in impenitentes, quod nolumus, transgressores dam-
nationem exercentibus.

ᵃ *Cross omitted* C, D   ᵇ *Erased* C   ᶜ Adelbertus C, N1   ᵈ dominium N1
ᵉ *The subject of this and the following sentences is to be understood as* archiepiscopus
ᶠ aligenis N1   ᵍ reponenda N1   ʰ suppremi D   ⁱ a apostolico N1
ʲ Adelberto C, N1   ᵏ Ethelbaldo D, N1. *For* Eadbaldo   ˡ collaudentibus D
ᵐ C *breaks off here*   ⁿ Romae N1

¹ Luc. 22: 25
² Matt. 17: 25

4 is the celebrated document known as the *Bulla Plumbea*, after the lead seal attached
to the single-sheet version. It is the most complete manifesto of the claims of the St
Augustine's community to total independence from all archiepiscopal and royal
control. Augustine addresses all future bishops and kings and informs them of the
exceptional circumstances of the monastery's foundation, before forbidding any
interference whatsoever in the monastery itself or the lands and churches dependent
on it. Next comes a series of instructions intended specifically for the Canterbury
archbishops. The archbishop is to consecrate the abbot (elected by the brethren) in
the monastery itself, for the Lord's service rather than his own, and he is to urge
him to obey God rather than himself. He is to treat the abbot as his colleague and
not as his subordinate. He is not to conduct ordinations or celebrate mass in the
abbey church except at the request of the abbot and brethren, and he must not exact
any customary dues at all. This prescription is bolstered by a series of scriptural
quotations and sanctions.

4 is evidently a product of the post-Conquest period, when issues such as these
were disturbing the relationship between the St Augustine's community and the
Norman bishops (see pp. xxiii–xxiv). It was certainly in existence by the 1120s, for
there is a copy of about that date in a bifolium prefixed to BL Cotton Vespasian B.
xx (MS C); it is incomplete because the text breaks off at the end of the bifolium. 4
was copied again in the second half of the twelfth century (MS D). It was one of
two documents which were submitted by the monks during a trial of their privileges
in 1181; the other was a charter of King Æthelberht, probably 1 (see commentary
to 3). Both privileges met with a hostile reception. Gervase of Canterbury (*Opera
Historica*, i. 296) reports the reaction to 4: 'alia uero scedula multo erat recentior
de qua bulla plumbea cum iconia episcopi noua ualde dependebat'. In addition, it
was pointed out that Cisalpine bishops were not in the habit of using leaden bulls,
and that the language and formulation of the text seemed 'a Romano stilo dissona'.
It seems almost certain that the single-sheet document used in the trial of 1181 was
the same as the one which Thomas Elmham reproduced in 'facsimile' over three
hundred years later; the textual tradition of 4 was remarkably stable from the twelfth
to the fifteenth century, which implies the continuing existence of a reliable exemplar.
Elmham's 'facsimile' measures 257 × 352 mm, and shows that the privilege was
written in an ornate uncial script (as was 3, which was probably based on it). The
circular bull was attached to an inserted tongue, apparently of parchment (see Plate
II). The obverse had a circumscription +AUGUSTINI EPISCOPI surrounding the

representation of a twin-towered gabled church; above the image was *ecclesia*, beneath it *Christi*, to the left *M* (? *monasterium*), to the right *P* (? *Petri*). On the reverse the legend +SIGILLUM SANCTI SALUATORIS surrounded a frontal bust flanked by the words *Iesus Christus*. The whole document must have been a very impressive fabrication, splendidly set off by the bull. The comments of the judges of 1181 on the impression it gave of recent production are probably only relative to its implied age; the single sheet may have been produced at any point between the second half of the eleventh century and 1181. The script of the 'facsimile' seems very similar to that of the Vespasian Psalter (BL Cotton Vespasian A. i), probably written at St Augustine's in the early eighth century and preserved at the abbey until the Dissolution. The forger may have been imitating the script of this or another contemporary manuscript or charter among the abbey's collections.

Having gone to such lengths to fabricate a leaden bull for their document, the St Augustine's monks had to work hard to justify it against criticisms of anachronism, such as that mentioned by Gervase. Sprott (BL Cotton Tiberius A. ix, 109rv) reports that, when Archbishop Richard (1173–84) questioned the authenticity of the St Augustine's bull, 'a certain foreign bishop' gave a similar leaden bull, used by himself and his predecessors, to Philip of Flanders, who passed it on to the abbot of St Augustine's; this was apparently also double-sided, with the legend *Sigillum prothomartyris Stephani* on one side (the other was illegible). Elmham (Hardwick, *Elmham*, pp. 122–3) repeats the anecdote, but confuses the issue by misidentifying the archbishop. If the use of such episcopal seals was a Flemish practice, then it is tempting to make a connection with Guerno, the Flemish monk who admitted forging privileges for St Augustine's (see pp. lxiv–lxv, and Levison, *England and the Continent*, pp. 206–19). Levison argued that Guerno was responsible for four surviving spurious papal privileges (BCS 11, 31, 915, 916), and also for the three charters in the name of Æthelberht and for **5** and **34**. But there are some difficulties in this attribution. Guerno died between 1119 and 1131, although Levison wishes to date the fabrications to the immediate post-Conquest period; the lapse of at least half a century does not make the attribution impossible, but it does make it less likely. The source which mentions Guerno's responsibility for fabricating papal privileges for St Augustine's also says that the offending documents were destroyed; this does not preclude the survival of copies, but would have made it difficult for the abbey to use such privileges in the future. It is likely that the ten documents which Levison identifies as Guerno's work were produced over several decades in the later eleventh and very early twelfth centuries, and that more than one scribe was responsible; the royal charters, in particular, seem to have been fabricated on different occasions, with different techniques and models (see further Kelly 1988, and above, p. lxv). **4**, with its developed version of the abbey's claims, was probably produced late in the sequence; there are particularly close connections with the second of the two privileges in the name of John XII (BCS 916), which may indicate that the two documents were forged at around the same time.

5

King Eadbald grants thirty sulungs (aratra) *at Northbourne, Kent, to the monastery of SS Peter and Paul.* A.D. 618

F. BL Cotton Julius D. ii, 84v–85r: copy, s. xiii[1]
   Rubric: Donacio regis Ædbaldi de Norburne.
G*. BL Cotton Claudius D. x, 61v–62r: copy of Inspeximus [R], s. xiv[1]
   Rubric: Carta Eadbaldi de manerio de Northbourne.
M. BL Add. 53710, 222rv: copy of Inspeximus [S], s. xiv/xv
N. Cambridge, Trinity Hall, 1, 29v: copy, s. xv[1]
   Rubric: Carta Ædbaldi regis de Northbourne.
R. PRO Ch. R. 20 Edw. II, m. 2
S. PRO Ch. R. 36 Edw. III, m. 7
T. PRO Ch. R. 8 Hen. IV, m. 6
U. PRO Pat. R. 2 Hen. VI, pt 3, m. 5
V. PRO Pat. R. 4 Edw. IV, pt 4, m. 3
W. PRO Pat. R. 14 Hen. VII, pt 1, m. 16
Ed.: a. Twysden, *Scriptores*, col. 2125, from M
     b. Smith, *Bede*, p. 694, from N
     c. Kemble 6 from N etc.
     d. Hardwick, *Elmham*, pp. 144–6, from N
     e. Thorpe, *Diplomatarium*, pp. 5–6, from N
     f. Haddan and Stubbs, *Councils*, iii. 69–70, from N
     g. Birch 13 from Kemble etc.
     h. Pierquin, *Recueil*, pt 1, no. 6, from Birch
Listed: Sawyer 6
Edited from F, G* and N

In nomine patris et filii et spiritus sancti. Ego Eadbaldus[a] rex gloriosi regis Æðelberti[b] filius, quem protodoctor[c] et apostolus Anglorum Augustinus cum suo regno ab eternis infernorum[d] cruciatibus eripuit et dealbatum fonte baptismatis sanctorum collegio copulauit, per uenerabilem Laurentium beati Augustini discipulum, quem ipse pater nouelle adhuc Anglorum ecclesie sibi successorem in archiepiscopatum ordinauerat,[e] tandem sermonibus assiduis et signis ac plagis in se ipso pro me passis ac ostensis a uolutabro scelerum lotus et ad agnitionem creatoris omnium creaturarum promotus, Dominum Deum meum recognosco et adoro. Proinde ego Eadbaldus, in solio paterno confirmatus, patris uestigia imitans et ecclesias Dei quas uiriliter instantia patris Augustini fundauit et terris multisque honoribus ditauit augens et confirmans, monasterio apostolorum Petri et Pauli in suburbio Dorouernie ciuitatis fundato et prerogatiuo ecclesiastice libertatis priuilegio munito terris ac uariis honoribus ditato, ad honorem Dei et sanctorum apostolorum sanctique Augustini, pro remedio anime patris mei[f] meeque parentumque meorum, gratanter concedo et amicabiliter do quandam partem terre regni mei, .xxx.^{g} aratrorum nomine Northburne,^{h} in usum monachorum ibidem Deo famulantium, ubi ipse pater Augustinus et pater meus requiescunt,^{i} ubi etiam archiepiscopos et reges sibi succedentes requiescere decreuerunt, ubi et corpus meum sepeliri precipio. Hanc autem prefatam terram in omnibus ad se pertinentibus, pascuis, paludibus, pratis, siluis ac finibus maritimis ita liberam ac quietam dono ac dito, sicut pater meus aut ego unquam liberius habuimus. Huius donationis confirmationem tropheo agie^j crucis +^{k} et carta mea regia consignaui, assidentibus et collaudantibus archiepiscopo, baptista scilicet meo, Laurentio et subscribente cum regina mea Æmma filiisque meis Egfrido ac Ercumberto, cum duobus episcopis Mellito Lundonie^l et Iusto Roffensis^m ecclesie ceterisque multis comitibus et optimatibus^n meis confauentibus et subscribentibus, in huius donationis fautores et auctores uitam eternam optantibus,^{o} in inuidentes seu minuentes Dei omnipotentis et sanctorum apostolorum et patris nostri Augustini terribilem interminationem.^{p}

+^{q} Ego Laurentius gratia Dei archiepiscopus signo sancte crucis sicut regem uidi facere hoc donum confirmo.^{r}

+ Ego Emma Francorum regis filia et^s regis Eadbaldi copula uexillo adorande crucis armaui.

+ Ego Mellitus Lundonie^l episcopus signo sancte crucis que uidi astipulor.

+ Ego Iustus Roffensis^m episcopus laudo et subscribo.

+ Ego Egbertus signo crucis libenter corroboro.^{t}

+ Ego Ercumbertus attestatione^u uenerande crucis gratanter concedo contestor et subscribo.

+ Ego Suueardus^v consensi.

+ Ego Guthardus^w subscribo.

Actum est autem^x anno ^{y}ab incarnatione saluatoris nostri Iesu Christi sexcentesimo octauo decimo,^{y} indictione .iiii.^{z}

---

^{a} Ædbaldus N ^{b} Adelberti G*; Ædelberti N ^{c} prothodoctor G*
^{d} inferorum F, N ^{e} ordinarat F, G* ^{f} mei 'patris' N ^{g} triginta G*
^{h} Nortburne N ^{i} requiescit F, G* ^{j} age F; agye G* ^{k} F omits cross
^{l} Londonie G* ^{m} Rofensis F, N ^{n} obtimatibus N ^{o} obtantibus F
^{p} The draftsman has made the sanction awkwardly dependent on the preceding corroboration. The sense is that all the witnesses are hoping for (optantibus) eternal life for those supporting the grant and punishment for those contravening it
^{q} G* omits the crosses at the beginning of subscriptions and inserts them them in place of the word crucis, except in the subscription of Ercumbertus ^{r} F ends here
^{s} Omitted N ^{t} corrobero G* ^{u} attestante N ^{v} Sueardus N ^{w} Cuthardus G*
^{x} hoc G* ^{y} . . . ^{y} .dcxviii. G ^{z} sexta (written on erasure) N

5 was fabricated to provide a title-deed for one of the abbey's largest estates,

Northbourne in Eastry lathe, which lies on the coastal plain at the head of a stream giving access to the Wantsum. Northbourne was beneficially assessed at thirty sulungs in 1086, with capacity for fifty-four ploughs (GDB 12v). The Domesday manor is likely to have resulted from piecemeal acquisitions; it included a detached property at Beauxfield which clearly came into the possession of St Augustine's at a later date (see **14**). Thus the assessment in **5** probably reflects the situation in the eleventh or twelfth century, when the document was forged. It is by no means impossible that there was a valid tradition that Eadbald had given the abbey land in the Northbourne area, but no reason to think that the forger was relying on any early record for the claim.

Some of the wording of **5** is reminiscent of that in the three charters attributed to Æthelberht, but this may largely be due to common reliance on Bede, *HE*, i. 33 and to the general factor of production at St Augustine's, rather than to the production of Eadbald's charter by the same agent as was responsible for **1**, **2** and **3**. However, **5** does share with **1** and **2** the feature of an indiction incorrect for the regnal year, perhaps because the draftsmen were all relying on the same faulty chronological table, perhaps as the result of later tampering with the dates (as in the case of **1** and **2**, the indiction of **5** was subsequently corrected by the revisor of the Trinity Hall manuscript). The language of **5** is flamboyant and pompous, and seems to reflect the influence of the Anglo-Latin style used in charters and literature from the tenth century; in this respect, it is quite different from the charters of Æthelberht and the privilege of Augustine. The forger may have been modelling his text to a limited extent on a royal diploma of the tenth century (perhaps of Eadmund, Eadred, Eadwig or Eadgar, names with a first element in common with Eadbald). The initial invocation is rare, although it turns up in two charters of Eadwig (S 593 and 666; see also the spurious S 66, 80); it could easily be the forger's own coinage. The formulation of the various subscriptions (with their variety of subscribing verbs) would certainly be consistent with derivation from a mid-tenth-century model (compare, for example, S 495). Also pointing in this direction is a pecularity of the text of **5** which was included in later Inspeximus charters (presumably copied from the single sheet); here a cross is substituted for the word *crucis* in each subscription in which it occurs. This suggests a possible connection with a regular feature of many Anglo-Saxon royal diplomas between *c.* 935 and the reign of Edgar (there are some later examples), namely the provision of a cross above the word *crucis* in every occurrence in a subscription (see S 449, 464 etc.).

If the forger of **5** was influenced by a tenth-century diploma, he made very little use of its formulation in other respects (although the phrase *tropheo agie crucis*, found in the corroboration, is very common in charters of that date). Another source may have been hagiographical and historical material connected with kings buried in the abbey; from this the forger probably derived the names of Eadbald's queen and of an otherwise unknown son of Eadbald (Ecgfrith in the text, Ecgberht in the witness-list). Queen Æmma (or Ymme) is mentioned in several of the texts associated with St Mildrith (Rollason, *Mildrith Legend*, p. 33). According to Sprott (BL Cotton Tiberius A. ix, 111r), she died in 642 and was buried next to her husband in the old abbey church, but was later moved to a place by the altar of St John. Such information must have come from a lost record of burials or a similar St Augustine's document. The names of the ecclesiastics and of Eorcenberht could have been taken from a source of this kind, but more probably derive from Bede. No plausible source suggests itself for the names of the last two witnesses *Suueardus* and *Guthardus*; it is possible that the first is a corruption of *Suebheardus* (Swæfheard), the Kentish king who was the donor of **40** and probably **41**. The forger was probably mixing names and details taken from a variety of different types of document.

6

Hlothhere, king of the men of Kent, grants three sulungs (aratra) *in Stodmarsh, Kent, to the abbot and monastery of St Peter.*

A.D. 675 (1 April)

N. Cambridge, Trinity Hall, 1, 52rv: copy, s. xv[1]
   Rubric: Carta eiusdem regis Lotharii de manerio de Stodemerch'.
Ed.: a. Kemble 9
      b. Hardwick, *Elmham*, pp. 248–9
      c. Birch 36
Listed: Sawyer 7

In nomine Domini Dei et saluatoris Iesu Christi. Ego Lotharius rex Cantuariorum, anno regni nostri primo, indictione tercia, sub die kalendarum Aprilis, cum concilio*a* uenerabilis archiepiscopi Theodori atque consensu primorum meorum, terram trium aratrorum in marisco qui appellatur Stodmerch' iuxta Fordeuuicum, cum pratis, campis, siluis, fontanis, paludibus, fluminibus et omnibus ad eandem pertinentibus rebus in ipsa quantitate sicut antiquitus predecessores mei reges predicta libere tenuerunt, abbati et monasterio beati Petri apostolorum principis quod situm est iuxta ciuitatem Dorouernis in suburbio in sempiterno possidenda concedimus et confirmamus, ita ut nec nobis nec aliquibus successorum nostrorum regum siue principum aut ecclesiasticarum dignitatum gradibus nefario temeritatis ausu aliquando infringere uel diminuere aliquid de donacione nostra liceat, sed pro remedio anime mee et absolucione peccatorum meorum ita ut predixi famulis Dei absque aliqua lesione omnia predicta in euum stabilia permaneant. Quisquis autem heredum successorumque meorum regum Cancie uel si quilibet secularium dignitatum aut etiam ecclesiasticarum de supradicta donacione, quam pro eterna remuneracione anime mee omnipotenti Deo ad utilitatem famulancium ei in ius monasteriale constat esse largitum,*b* aliquid disrumpere aut immutare uel irritum facere tentauerit, sciat se sine dubio omnipotenti Deo fraudem facere et proinde coram eo et sanctis angelis eius eterno anathemate reum. Quicunque uero hec que largita prediximus sub pia proteccione custodierit uel Dei intuitu misericorditer auxerit, sit benedictus in secula audiatque in die nouissimo tremendi examinis ab ipso iudice omnium Christo Domino eterne benediccionis uocem, Venite benedicti patris mei percipite regnum quod uobis paratum est ab origine mundi,[1] manente igitur hac cartula in sua semper firmitate, cum religiosis testibus signo dominice crucis in hoc loco qui dicitur Dorouernis stabiliter in euum confirmamus.

+ Ego Lotharius rex Cancie suprascripta signo sancte crucis per propriam manum roboraui.

+ Ego Theodorus gratia Dei archiepiscopus rogatus a rege subscripsi.

+ Ego Adrianus abbas indignus subscripsi.

+ Signum manus Ecca.

+ Signum Osfridi.

^a *For* consilio   ^b *For* largitam

[1] See Matt. 25: 34

6 is concerned with a grant by King Hlothhere to the monastery of three sulungs in Stodmarsh, near Fordwich; in 686 Hlothhere's successor Eadric transferred to the community a further three sulungs in the same area, said to be adjacent to the land given by Hlothhere (7). 6 is dated 1 April, in Hlothhere's first year as king and in the third indiction. The indiction points to 674–5, but the regnal year is problematic, because it seems to suggest that Hlothhere's reign began rather later than the date given by Bede for his succession (see further discussion below, and in Appendix 3). If authentic, 6 would be the earliest surviving Kentish charter, several years earlier than Hlothhere's charter for Abbot Berhtwald and Reculver (S 8). A date in the mid 670s for the first extant Kentish diploma is quite compatible with evidence from elsewhere (see above, pp. lxv–lxvi, lxxiv), but Scharer (*Königsurkunde*, pp. 63–5) argues that 6 should be treated as a later fabrication, on the grounds that its formulation in part reflects the influence of diplomatic developments in the second half of the eighth century.

Much of the formulation of 6 is completely acceptable in a seventh-century Kentish charter. There is no problem with the invocation, the royal style, the terms of reference to the estate and to the beneficiary, the prohibition against infringement, the characteristic formula which concludes the sanction, or the introduction to the witness-list (see further pp. lxxvi–lxxxv). Archbishop Theodore's subscription has the same form in 42 (compare also the subscriptions of Archbishop Berhtwald in S 19 and 10). The inclusion of the word *indignus* in the subscription of Abbot Hadrian is a contemporary feature, found also in his subscriptions to 10, 42 and 45 (for other instances, see Sims-Williams 1988, p. 166). The two final witnesses both attest other Kentish charters of the period: Ecca subscribes 8, 10, 40, 41, 42, 43 and S 19, 22, 233, while Osfrid's name is found in S 8 and in 8, 40 and 42.

The features which Scharer finds particularly suspicious are: the position of the dating clause after the superscription; the appearance of the word *rebus* in the list of appurtenances, which he considers an eighth-century development; the inclusion of a blessing in the sanction; and the apparently unacceptable form of the king's subscription. He also detects the general influence of the formulation of the mid-eighth-century series of charters granting exemption from ship-toll (see **49, 50, 51, 52, 53**; and pp. lxxxv–xc), for instance in the form of the consent-clause and prohibition. Scharer seems to expect rather too much of consistency in the formulation of early Kentish charters. There are other instances where the dating clause appears in an unusual position, and the late Roman deeds used as models by the earliest Kentish charter-scribes regularly included dating material at or near the beginning of the text. Aside from the word *rebus* the list of appurtenances seems acceptable, with some resemblance to the corresponding formulas in S 8, and in **7** and **42**; it should be remembered that Anglo-Saxon draftsmen were not particularly interested in reproducing formulas verbatim, so this small discrepancy seems unlikely to be significant. Several of the features which in Scharer's opinion reflect the influence of the toll-privileges, such as the blessing, are already present in **47** and **48** from the 720s and in S 24 from 741. Scharer rejects these texts as fabrications, but a good case can be made for their authenticity (see the commentaries to **47** and **48**).

   6 shares much of its formulation, including many of those details which Scharer finds suspicious, with **40**, a charter of King Swæfheard datable to 689, in favour of the abbess of Minster. There can be no doubt that **40** is ultimately based on a genuine seventh-century charter, although the text appears to have been reworked on more than one occasion. If Scharer is correct in his assertion that the formulation which is common to **6** and **40** necessarily represents the influence of mid-eighth-century diplomatic, then in both cases it would appear that an early charter had been partly rewritten at a later date, either independently on the basis of the same model, or serially, with one revised text serving as the basis for the other. The first of these alternatives probably presupposes the revision of the two texts at around the same time. Since **40**, with the other Minster charters, would not have been available at St Augustine's before the reign of Cnut, such a revision could not have been carried out until the eleventh century or later. The same would be true if **6** was revised on the basis of **40**, although the reverse proposition would leave open the possibility that the rewriting of **6** took place before the eleventh century.

   Such conjectures about the reworking of **6** and **40** may be unnecessary. Scharer's case against the present formulation of these charters rests upon the assumption that early Kentish charters would necessarily follow a fairly strict pattern, and that the types of formulation found in the ship-toll privileges and in Kentish land-charters of the 760s must represent a novel development. The first of these points is certainly debatable, and the second argument rests upon the rejection of **47, 48** and S 24, all from the first half of the eighth century and including features found in **6** and **40**. It could be suggested that **6** and **40** represent one strand of seventh-century Kentish diplomatic which was later developed in the course of the eighth century, in which case the two charters could be regarded as supporting each other's authenticity.

   The transmission of **6** is rather unusual, which could be seen as support for Scharer's suspicion. **6** is preserved in the fifteenth-century manuscript of Thomas Elmham's history, one of three pre-Conquest charters to be found only in this manuscript; the others are **51** and **52**, both Minster ship-toll privileges which seem authentic. **6** is omitted from the thirteenth-century cartularies and from the charter-list in PRO E 164/27 (for which see Appendix 2); the only other pre-Conquest royal charter directly in favour of the community which is not included in the list is **14**, an evident forgery. The thirteenth-century historian Sprott probably saw the charter, for he mentions Hlothhere's grant of Stodmarsh in the year 673 (BL Cotton Tiberius A. ix, 111v; followed by Thorne in Twysden, *Scriptores*, col. 1770); his date is probably calculated from the regnal year, without reference to the conflicting indiction. It is possible that **6**, like **51** and **52**, simply escaped the notice of earlier cartularists before being rediscovered by Elmham, a mischance perhaps to be connected with the reference to Hlothhere's grant in **7**, which may have made the earlier charter seem partly redundant. But this apparent neglect of a direct royal grant could indicate that it was felt to be an unsatisfactory text in the thirteenth century, which would support Scharer's doubts about the charter's authenticity in its present form. The restricted transmission may also be significant for the problematic regnal year. It is possible that **6** suffered from the attentions of those St Augustine's scholars who were prone to altering the dates in their muniments (see pp. xcvi–cv); since the charter survives in only one very late copy, such interference would not be detectable. The scholars would have been interested in the date of Hlothhere's accession because they were attempting to insert the reigns of Kings Swæfheard and Oswine after the death of Hlothhere's predecessor, King Ecgberht.

The absolute authenticity of **6** must remain undecided, but the present text probably does represent or at least rely on a genuine seventh-century charter recording a grant by Hlothhere to St Augustine's of land at Stodmarsh. We have the testimony of **7** (where the spelling of Hlothhere's name indicates an early source) that such a grant was made. The name Stodmarsh is now applied to a small village a few miles east of Fordwich, but it probably referred originally to a more extensive area of marshland between the Great and Little Stour. The first element is *stud*, which implies that the marsh was associated with horse-rearing. In **6** the land given by Hlothhere is said to lie in the marsh called Stodmarsh, *iuxta Fordeuuicum*, which (if the charter can be accepted) is the earliest reference to Fordwich. St Augustine's certainly seems to have held land to the east of Fordwich in the middle of the tenth century. A charter of 948 granting six sulungs at Wickhambreux to a religious woman (S 535) states that the land bordered on property belonging to St Augustine's to the south (which was the abbey's estate at Littlebourne) and to the west, which would seem to have been land around Fordwich. The bounds of S 535 next mention a 'plank bridge' (*þæl brycge*), now represented by Elbridge House (TR 203597), and then follow a stream (evidently that flowing north-east from Elbridge House) as far as *hose graf*, where the second element is preserved in Grove (TR 237620). After this, the bounds of S 535 cut west along a stream to the Stour. The boundary formed by the stream between Elbridge House and Grove divided Wickhambreux to the east from Stodmarsh to the west. The bounds can probably be understood as indicating that St Augustine's owned this land to the west of the stream, that is, the Stodmarsh area.

Domesday Book has no separate entry for Stodmarsh. In 1086 St Augustine's controlled the borough of Fordwich, but this represents piecemeal acquisition in the eleventh century (see **39**). The borough was beneficially assessed at a yoke, and consisted in 1066 of one hundred tenements and twenty-four acres of land 'which St Augustine's always held' (GDB 12r). Twenty-four acres is only a fraction of a hide; if the six sulungs of **6** and **7** were attached to Fordwich in the eleventh century then they are hidden in this entry.

7

Eadric, king of the men of Kent, grants three sulungs (aratra) *near Stodmarsh, Kent, to the monastery of St Peter.* A.D. 686 (June)

F. BL Cotton Julius D. ii, 131r: copy, s. xiii[1]
   No rubric
N. Cambridge, Trinity Hall, 1, 52v–53r: copy, s. xv[1]
   Rubric: Carta eiusdem Edrici regis de terra iuxta Stodmerch'.
Ed.: a. Kemble 27 from N
      b. Hardwick, *Elmham*, pp. 251–2, from N
      c. Birch 67 from Kemble and BL Harley 686, a copy of N
      d. Earle, pp. 10–11, from N
      e. Pierquin, *Recueil*, pt 1, no. 15, from Birch
Listed: Sawyer 9
Edited from F and N

In nomine saluatoris, cuius pietate regimen assequti*[a]* sumus, quo etiam gubernante regnamus et omnia que habere cognoscimur ipso largiente habita possidemus. Pro qua re ego Eadricus rex Cantuariorum a presenti*[b]* die et tempore terram iuris mei, quamuis pretium competens*[c]* acciperim hoc est argenti libras decem, in monasterio beati Petri apostolorum principis quod situm est iuxta ciuitatem Dorouernis una cum consensu meorum patriciorum inperpetuum donaui et dono. Que supradicta terra coniuncta est terre quam sancte memorie Clotharius*[d]* quondam rex beato Petro pro remedio anime sue donasse cognoscitur. Que terra determinatur: ex una parte habet uadum quod appellatur fordstreta publica indirectum*[e]* et a parte alia flumen quod nominatur Stur. Omnes terras sationales cum pratis, campis, siluis, fontanis uel mariscum quod appellatur Stodmersch',*[f]* cum omnibus ad supradictam terram aratrorum trium pertinentia,*[g]* beato Petro eiusque familie in qua nunc preesse Adrianus abbas dinoscitur tradidi possidendam,*[h]* et quicquid exinde facere uoluerint utpote Domini liberam habeant potestatem. Sicut donatum est manere decerno, numquam me heredesque meos uel successores contra hanc donationis mee cartulam ullo tempore esse uenturos. Quod si aliquis presumpserit, sit separatus a participatione corporis et sanguinis Domini nostri Iesu Christi, manente hac cartula nichilominus in sua firmitate. De quibus omnibus supradictis ac a me definitis ut ne aliqua*[i]* inposterum sit aduersitas propria manu signum sancte crucis expressi et sanctissimum atque reuerentissimum Theodorum archiepiscopum nostrum ut subscriberet rogaui et alios testes similiter. Actum in mense Iunio, indictione^j .xiiii.

+^{k} Ego Ædricus rex in hanc donationis mee cartulam signum sancte crucis expressi.^{l}

+ Ego Theodorus archiepiscopus gratia Dei subscripsi.

^{a} assecuti F ^{b} presente F ^{c} conpetentem F ^{d} Lotharius N
^{e} *For the meaning of this phrase, see commentary* ^{f} Stodmerse F
^{g} *for* pertinentibus (*see S 8 for the same error*) ^{h} *for* possidendas ^{i} aliquis N
^{j} inditione F ^{k} F *omits cross* ^{l} F *ends here*

Here King Eadric grants to St Peter's minster (St Augustine's) an area of three sulungs said to be adjacent to land at Stodmarsh granted by King Hlothhere, a transaction recorded in **6**. The authenticity of **6** is debatable, but there seems no good reason to question **7**. Its general formulation is closely comparable to that of the two surviving Kentish originals from this period (S 8, 19), and it also incorporates some particular early formulas which occur in contemporary charters from other Anglo-Saxon kingdoms, and which must ultimately be derived from the selection of late Roman private deeds which were used as models by the first draftsmen of Anglo-Saxon charters. The most interesting is the decree that neither the donor nor his heirs shall interfere with the donation; this formula is found also in **44**, in two seventh-century Surrey charters (S 1165, 235) and in two eighth-century Mercian texts (S 100, 56), and it has close parallels in earlier Italian charters (see p. lxxxi). This list of appurtenances is directly comparable to that in S 8 (indeed, the same grammatical error occurs in both texts, which suggests that both ultimately rely on a common model); the rare adjective *sationalis* in the formula in **7** (which also occurs in S 65) may have been taken from a continental exemplar (see p. lxxx).

7 begins with a brief verbal invocation which is also found in **41**, a Minster charter datable to *c.* 690. Here it is extended with a species of creed, which gives a divine imprimatur to the royal position of the donor. This formula can be understood as a statement of the donor's legitimacy, and it is comparable to the more explicit claims of this type in the later charters of Oswine (**8, 42, 43**) and Wihtred (**44**); both these kings began their reigns in disputed circumstances, as did Eadric, whose invasion of Kent with South Saxon backing led to the death of his predecessor, King Hlothhere (Bede, *HE*, iv. 26). The structure of the dispositive section itself is rather muddled, in part because the draftsman has included awkward details about the location of the estate, as well as a primitive boundary clause; but a comparison with the equally confused dispositive section of S 8 shows that this is no reason for suspicion. The terms of the reference to the beneficiary are very similar to those in other early charters in favour of St Augustine's, which may be an indicator of beneficiary production; the formula used to refer to the abbot has Italian antecedents (see p. lxxvii), as does the rudimentary statement of powers (see p. lxxx). The sanction, corroboration and dating clause are all acceptable in a seventh-century text. The witness-list has unfortunately been truncated.

Eadric states that he has accepted ten pounds of silver in return for the land-grant.

Scharer (*Königsurkunde*, p. 69) considers that this is clear mark of fabrication, on the grounds that references of this kind, giving a precise figure for the payment or counter-gift made by the beneficiary, first appear in original charters in the early ninth century; he further notes that even general references to payment, with no precise figure, may be a development of the mid eighth century. On this point Scharer has almost certainly been misled by his strict adherence to the diplomatic principle of basing conclusions strictly on surviving originals, in a period when such originals are very few indeed and from limited provenances. A charter from the kingdom of the Hwicce, dating from the very early eighth century and probably acceptable, refers to the payment of 600 *solidi* in return for land assessed at five hides (S 1177). A Peterborough text, probably based on a seventh-century record of some kind, mentions a payment by the abbot of Breedon of 500 *solidi* (in the form of luxury items including beds, slaves, a brooch, horses and carts) in return for fifteen hides (S 1804). Other early texts confirm that land was effectively being sold in England in the seventh and eighth centuries (see J. Campbell, 'The Sale of Land and the Economics of Power in Early England', *Haskins Society Journal* i (1989), pp. 23–37). References to such payments in early Anglo-Saxon charters are uncommon for the simple reason that the draftsmen of charters did not usually include such details. This was surely a matter of custom rather than a strict diplomatic principle, and the inclusion of details of payment in **9** and S 1177 is more likely to reflect an unusual decision by the original draftsman than a late interpolation or invention (for which the motivation would be unclear).

In the copy of **7** in BL Cotton Julius D. ii, Hlothhere's name appears as *Clotharius*, a spelling which reflects its Frankish origins. Two other purportedly seventh-century documents from England similarly retain the early spelling of the name. BCS 53 is a strange Winchester document purporting to emanate from the synod of Hatfield in 680, in which Hlothhere appears as *Clotherius*. As it stands, this is probably a fabrication (see a forthcoming paper by Catherine Cubitt), but the forger seems to have had access to an early document of some kind (perhaps a copy of the original *acta* of the synod). S 1245 is a spurious foundation privilege for Malmesbury dated 675, which incorporates a genuine contemporary witness-list. In the best and earliest cartulary copy of this charter (Sawyer's MS 5), the name of Bishop Leuthere (a Frankish name essentially equivalent to Hlothhere) was originally spelled *Cleutherius*, although a later revisor has lightly erased the initial letter. These instances indicate that the Frankish spelling of the name was occasionally used in seventh-century England, and suggest that its appearance in **9** is an early symptom. It is probably significant that in the course of the eighth century the initial *C* was gradually dropped from this name in Francia (Morlet, *Noms de personne*, i. 132b, 133b).

The land granted by Eadric is not identified by a place-name, which is also the case in a number of other early charters (see p. lxxix). Instead the draftsman locates it by reference to the previous land-grant of Hlothhere, and also by mentioning the features on two of its boundaries. His use of the word *pars* in this context is similar to that in **8** and **44**. One of the boundaries is easy to distinguish as the River Stour, but the details of the other are more confusing. The text refers to a ford (*uadum*) called *fordstreta publica indirectum*. There would seem to be some corruption here, for a ford cannot be a street. One possibility would to divide *ford* from *streta*, leaving *uadum* and *ford* as equivalents, and qualifying it by the phrase *streta publica* *indirectum*; *streta* would then be a form of Latin *strata*, 'road' (cf. OE *strǣt*, *stret*), and *indirectum* an adjective describing the position of the ford in relation to the public highway. The implication of the prefix would be that the ford was obliquely situated from the highway, which seems unlikely. Alternatively, *ford-streta* could be taken as an unusual inversion of the very common Old English combination, *strǣt-ford*, which would fit the context much better (see B. Cox, 'The Place-Names of the Earliest English Records', *Journal of the English Place-Name Society* viii (1975–6), pp. 12–66 at 21). There is no obvious solution to the problem, but it does seem very likely that the ford in question was in the area of Fordwich, where a Roman road from Canterbury crossed the Stour. Some lost topographical feature may underlie the text. Later evidence for the abbey's landholdings in this area is discussed in the commentary to **6**.

As is the case with many of the very earliest Anglo-Saxon charters, it is difficult to be certain that **7** has not suffered some interference in later years, beyond the abbreviation of its witness-list. A feature which may be suspicious is the reference to a specific appurtenance, the marsh at Stodmarsh; this may be an added detail. There is also the possibility that the confusing boundary clause is an addition, or that it has been reworked. But, on the whole, **7** does seem to be acceptable as a text of the given date.

8

Oswine, king of Kent, grants one sulung (aratrum) *on which iron is mined to the monastery of St Peter and Abbot Hadrian.* A.D. 689 (July)

F. BL Cotton Julius D. ii, 130v: copy, s. xiii[1]
   No rubric
H. PRO E 164/27, 80rv: copy, s. xiii
   Rubric: Carta Oswini regis de terra Liminge.
N. Cambridge, Trinity Hall, 1, 47v: copy, s. xv[1]
   Rubric: Carta regis Oswyni de mina ferri iuxta Lyminge.
Ed.: a. Kemble 30 from N
    b. Hardwick, *Elmham*, pp. 226–7, from N
    c. Birch 73 from Kemble and BL Harley 686, a copy of N
Translated: R.C. Jenkins, *The Chartulary of the Monastery of Lyminge* (Folkestone, [1867]), p. 17
Listed: Sawyer 12
Edited from F, H and N

In nomine Domini Dei nostri et saluatoris[a] Iesu Christi. Ego Oswynus[b] rex Cantie pro absolutione meorum peccatorum de terra iuris mei, que mihi ex propinquitate parentum meorum uenit atque ex confirmatione clementissimi Æthelredi[c] regis collata est, unum aratrum in quo mina ferri haberi[d] cognoscitur, quod pertinebat ad cortem que appellatur Liminge, quod etiam coniunctum est terre uenerabilis presbiteri Brytwaldi[e] abbatis a parte meridiana, a presenti die et tempore monasterio beati Petri apostoli,[f] in quo preesse Adrianus dinoscitur qui a Romana urbe directus est, inperpetuum contuli possidendum,^{g} tam^f ei dum^h aduixerit quam eius congregationi que post eum habitura est, ut prefatam terram unius aratri sibi uendicent ac defendant^i cum omnibus ad se pertinentibus. Quicumque^j uero tam ego quam posteri mei qui in loco meo successerint^k contra hanc largitatis mee cartulam quolibet tempore uenire presumpserint,^{l} sint separati a corpore et sanguine Domini nostri Iesu Christi, manente hac cartula perpetualiter nichilominus donationis mee in sua firmitate, ad cuius etiam confirmationem pro ignorantia litterarum signum sancte crucis expressi et testes ut sub-scriberent rogaui. +^{m} Actum in mense Iulio, indictione secunda.^{n}

+^{m} Ego Oswynus^b rex Cantie donator ad omnia supradicta consensi^o et subscripsi,^{p} + signum sancte crucis feci.
+ Signum manus Ecca.
+ Ego Gabertus^q signum feci.
+ Signum manus Osfridi.
+ Signum manus Uaeba.
+ Signum manus Suydredi.
+ Signum manus Ædilmari.
+ Signum manus Burgredi.
+ Signum manus Frod.
+ Signum manus Eana.

^{a} et saluatoris *omitted* N ^{b} Oswinus F ^{c} Etheldredi H ^{d} habere F, H
^{e} Bertwaldi F; Berthwaldi H ^{f} *Omitted* H ^{g} possidendam H ^{h} eidem H
^{i} deffendant H ^{j} Quicum F ^{k} successerit F ^{l} presumpserit F ^{m} F *omits cross*
^{n} H *ends here* ^{o} concessi F ^{p} F *ends here* ^{q} ? *For* Sabertus (*see commentary*)

Oswine, the donor of this charter and of **42** and **43**, was one of the *reges dubii vel externi* who invaded Kent after the death of Eadric in late 686 (see Appendix 3). **8** shows that he had the support of the Mercian king Æthelred, and that he claimed to have a hereditary right to the kingdom. The insistence on this point, both here and in **42** and **43**, probably indicates that his position was not unchallenged. Similar statements appear in the charter of Eadric (**7**), whose reign began with an invasion of Kent, and in the earliest charter of Wihtred (**44**). It seems to have been thought appropriate to stress that these kings had a valid right to grant land in Kent, which would have been a point of enormous importance to both donors and beneficiaries (see also **15** and **50**).

The formulation of **8** seems entirely compatible with its date. There is particular interest in the use of the adjective *clementissimus* to describe King Æthelred of Mercia. A similar superlative is applied to him in **40** and in two other charters, one preserved at Peterborough and dealing with the minster at Hoo in Kent (S 233), and the other from Malmesbury (S 1169); this appears to reflect the influence of late

Roman honorifics (Edwards, *Charters*, p. 93). The land granted is identified in terms of its previous owner (the vill at Lyminge) and by reference to the owner of adjacent land, the priest Berhtwald. Berhtwald is probably the abbot of Reculver and beneficiary of S 8, who was appointed archbishop of Canterbury in 692; the reference in **8** may indicate that the Reculver community had already been granted an iron-mine in the same area. The corroboration in **8** includes a reference to the donor's illiteracy, a formula derived from antique models and reflecting a vestigial memory of the Roman procedures for autograph subscriptions (see also **9**, **10**, **44** and S 19, and discussion above, pp. lxxxiii, lxxxv).

The copy of **8** in Thomas Elmham's history preserves ten subscriptions, which may represent the full witness-list of the original (S 8 has twelve subscriptions and S 19 has fourteen). All the witnesses appear to be laymen (as in S 8). The subscriptions are all in the objective form, except those of Oswine, the donor, and a certain *Gabertus*. Kemble (followed by Birch) printed this name *Sabertus*, leading to the suggestion that it may be equivalent to *Suabertus*, the name of the donor of **41**, which is attested by Oswine (see Whitelock 1976, p. 143). *Suabertus* is probably the same man as the Swæfheard, donor of **40**, who subscribes the other two charters of Oswine (**42**, **43**); Swæfheard/*Suabertus* and Oswine would appear to have been joint-rulers of Kent in the years around 690 (see Appendix 3). It is a problem that the only manuscript source for the subscription in **8** certainly reads *Gabertus*, but the suggested identification with *Suabertus* may still be valid, given the late date of the manuscript. The lack of a royal style in the subscription presents no difficulty, since such a style is also missing in Oswine's subscription to Swæfheard's charter (**40**) and in Swæfheard's to **42** and **43**. Most of the remaining witnesses in **8** can be identified in contemporary Kentish charters. Ecca appears in **6**, **10**, **40**, **41**, **42**, **43** and S 19, 22, 233, and Osfrid in **6**, **40**, **42** and S 8. Uaeba subscribes **10** and Suydred is perhaps the Scirieard of the same charter. Frod attests S 19. It is possible that Ædilmar and Eana are the abbot and priest with those names who attest **10**; if so, the witnesses to **8** are not all laymen. Burgred's name is not found elsewhere.

This is the only surviving Anglo-Saxon royal diploma to deal with mineral rights. We are told that the iron-bearing land had previously belonged to the vill at Lyminge, which was initially a royal centre but had been the site of a minster since the early seventh century. It is possible that iron was extracted from the subsoil in the Lyminge area, but far more likely that the iron-mine was a distant appurtenance, located in the area of the High Weald which was the centre of an iron industry from prehistoric times (see H. Cleere and D. Crossley, *The Iron Industry of the Weald* (Leicester, 1988), especially p. 87). The seams are near the surface and so mining in this area was predominantly open-cast. It centred around the digging of mine-pits up to twelve metres deep, which were worked out and then refilled with the spoil from a new pit, leaving a pock-marked landscape still visible in some areas (see B. Worssam, 'The geology of Wealden Iron', in Cleere and Crossley, *Iron Industry*, pp. 1–30 [especially pp. 15–19]). This method of extraction required substantial areas of land, which explains why the monastery is granted a full sulung of iron-bearing land. The ore would have been partly processed on the site, and then transported to Canterbury or elsewhere for working into iron implements. It is possible that the grant of a mine to St Augustine's was intended to fulfil the community's own requirements of iron, but surplus iron-bloom or artefacts could have been sold or exchanged. The possession of an iron-mine is not mentioned in any later records of St Augustine's endowment, but it may be hidden in the sources, which do not usually mention mineral rights. Alternatively, the mine may have been alienated or worked out by the eleventh century.

9

Wihtred, king of Kent, and his wife, Æthelburh, grant five sulungs (aratra) *at Littlebourne, Kent, to the monastery of St Peter.*

A.D. 696 or 711 (March)

F. BL Cotton Julius D. ii, 85v–86r: copy, s. xiii[l]
  Rubric: Wyhtredus rex de Littleburne.
N. Cambridge, Trinity Hall, 1, 61v–62r: copy s. xv[l]
  Rubric: Carta eiusdem Withredi regis eodem anno in mense Marcio sequenti die terra quinque aratorum in Littelborne quam donauit presenti monasterio anno regni sui quinto.
Ed.: a. Kemble 41 from N etc.
  b. Hardwick, *Elmham*, pp. 290–1, from N
  c. Birch 90 from Kemble and BL Harley 686, a copy of N
Listed: Sawyer 16
Edited from F and N

Beneficiis Dei et Domini nostri Iesu Christi nobis collatis non immemores,[a] ego Wihtredus rex Cantie et coniunx[b] mea Adelburga pro remedio animarum nostrarum beati Petri apostolorum principis monasterio quod situm est in suburbano huius Dorouernis ciuitatis, in quo preesse dinoscitur Adrianus abbas huc missus ab apostolica sede eiusque familie que nunc et futura est, terram iuris nostri quinque aratrorum que appellatur Litleburne,[c] cum omnibus ad se pertinentibus, a presenti die et tempore a nostra iurisdictione transferentes inperpetuo tradimus possidendam, et quicquid exinde facere uolueritis, uestri erit arbitrii, conditione interposita ut nostri memoriam habeatis tam in missarum solemniis quam in orationibus uestris, incessanter nobis misericordiam a Domino postulantes. Quisquis uero contra hanc largitatis nostre donationem quolibet tempore contraire presumpserit, nouerit se quisquis ille sit a participatione corporis et sanguinis Domini nostri Iesu Christi alienum et a consortio fidelium segregandum, manente hac cartula nostre donationis in sua nichilominus firmitate, ad cuius confirmationem pro ignorantia litterarum signum sancte crucis expressimus et testes ut subscriberent rogauimus. Actum in mense Martio, indictione nona.

+[d] Signum manus Wihtredi regis et donatoris.
+ Signum manus Ethelburge[e] regine et donatricis.
+ Hoc ego Gemundus episcopus expressi.

^a *For* Beneficiorum .... non immemores ^b coniux F ^c Littelb'ne N
^d F *omits all crosses* ^e Adelburge F

9 seems to be an authentic charter. It is unusual in having a statement of pious motivation in place of a verbal invocation, but there is no reason to think this a suspicious feature; there are links with the statement of motivation which appears in a different position in **44**, a slightly earlier charter of Wihtred. Otherwise the formulation follows the usual pattern of Kentish charters of that date, and most of the individual formulas can be closely paralleled. The reference to the beneficiary is expressed in terms which recur in other early charters in favour of St Augustine's, and may be a symptom of beneficiary production (see pp. lxxvii–lxxviii). The formula *a nostra iurisdictione transferentes* reflects the influence of Italian models and ideas about land-tenure (see p. lxxxii); it is comparable to a similar formula in the contemporary S 1171 from Essex (*de meo iure in tuo transcribo*). The brief statement of powers in **9** also seems to depend on an Italian model (compare **7, 44**, S 235; and see pp. lxxx–lxxxi); this reliance on a model probably explains why the draftsman now refers to the beneficiary in the second rather than the third person. A prayer condition is imposed, as in four Minster charters from this period (**41, 46, 47, 48**). The corroboration includes a reference to the donor's illiteracy (compare **8, 10, 44**, and S 19; see p. lxxxiii). The dating clause is in the usual Kentish form, mentioning only the month and indiction (as in S 8 and S 19). Because Wihtred reigned for such a long time the indiction could fit two possible years (696 and 711), although the general chronological distribution of charters in his reign makes the earlier date more likely. The witness-list has been curtailed and cannot help in narrowing the possibilities. The third subscription is that of Bishop Gebmund of Rochester, who was still alive in 699 (**10**). His successor, Tobias, had been appointed by 716, for his subscription appears in the witness-list of a *Clofesho* synod of that year (see S 22).

9 is presented as a joint grant by King Wihtred and his spouse, Æthelburh. It is rare for queens even to attest early Anglo-Saxon charters, and in Kent it is only in Wihtred's charters that the queen is given such a prominent position. Queens in other kingdoms occasionally appear, probably because they enjoyed exceptional status or had a forceful personality. In Wessex another Queen Æthelburh is joint-donor with Ine in two related and rather suspicious charters (S 249 and 251, both dated 725), and Queen Frithugyth is associated with her husband Æthelheard in one charter (S 253 from 729). Frithugyth also attests S 255 (A.D. 739), and S 254 (A.D. 737) is said to have been issued at her request; she was also remembered with appreciation in a series of Winchester forgeries as the donor of Taunton. A queen appears in the witness-list of one Sussex charter dated 714, possibly for 717 (S 42), and the unstyled Eadburh who attests an East Saxon charter of *c.* 700 (S [Add.] 65b) was probably also a queen. Mercian queens attest regularly and prominently from the reign of Offa onwards, but do not appear in earlier charters. The treatment of Wihtred's wife in **9** and elsewhere is therefore remarkable. Æthelburh attests S 19 (A.D. 697 or 712), where her subscription is placed after that of Wihtred, and her consent to a land-grant to Minster-in-Thanet is mentioned in **46** (A.D. 697). She does not seem to have been Wihtred's only queen; in **44** (A.D. 694) Wihtred is joint-donor with his wife *Kinigitha* (Cynegyth), and a Queen Werburh appears in the witness-list to a synod at Bapchild, preserved in the spurious S 22 and probably dating from

716 or shortly before. It seems that Wihtred had three wives, one hopes consecutively: Cynegyth at the beginning of his reign, Æthelburh in the later 690s and perhaps the early eighth century, and Werburh in the later part of his reign (Werburh was probably the mother of Alric, Wihtred's third son, who disappeared soon after his father's death; see Appendix 3). All three women enjoyed an exceptionally high status for Kentish queens.

9 concerns a grant of five hides at Littlebourne, which lies about three miles east of St Augustine's, at the place where the main Roman road between Canterbury and Richborough crosses the Little Stour. It is close to Fordwich and Stodmarsh, where St Augustine's had already received land from Hlothhere and Eadric (6, 7). In 1066 the abbey's manor at Littlebourne was assessed at seven sulungs (GDB 12r). One sulung there had been granted to the community by Archbishop Eadsige in the reign of Edward the Confessor (36, 37).

10

Wihtred, king of Kent, grants privileges to the churches and monasteries of Kent. A.D. 699 (8 April)

A. Maidstone, Centre for Kentish Studies, MS U 140: copy, s. ix[1], 170 × 340 mm (*from the Christ Church archive*)
   Endorsements: (1) *by the scribe of the charter*: + Lib[er] Uuihtredi regis [. . . . .]
   rum in Cantia." (2) *in a hand of s. xii*: Statutum Os[w]ii regis de libertate ecclesiarum Cantie latine.
F. BL Cotton Julius D. ii, 106r: copy, s. xiii[1]
   No rubric
H. PRO E 164/27, 25v–26r: copy, s. xiii
   Rubric: Item Withredus rex de libertatibus ecclesiarum.
N. Cambridge, Trinity Hall, 1, 62v–63r: copy, s. xv[1]
   Rubric: De carta Withredi regis de libertate ecclesiarum concessa ut ab omni exactione publici tributi ac dispendio sint immunes.
Ed.: a. Spelman, *Concilia*, i. 198–9, from Canterbury, D. & C., Reg. A (see commentary)
   b. Wilkins, *Concilia*, i. 63, from Spelman
   c. Kemble 44 from N etc.
   d. Hardwick, *Elmham*, pp. 295–7, from N
   e. Birch 99 from Kemble and BL Harley 686, a copy of N
   f. Pierquin, *Conciles*, i. 198–9, from Birch
   g. Ward 1947, pp. 13–14 from A, with translation, p. 1, and reduced facsimile, plate opposite p. 2
   h. *BAFacs.* 1, facsimile of A
Listed: Sawyer 20
Printed from A, with variants from N

*b*In nomine Domini Dei saluatoris nostri Iesu Christi.*b* Ego Uuihtredus rex Cantie, consulens anime meae in posterum, hanc prouidentiam pro diuersis calamitatibus imminentibus ecclesiis Dei atque monasteriis que in hac Cantia*c*

consistunt, una cum consensu principum meorum quorum nomina sub-
terscribenda sunt, facere curaui ut ab omni exactione publici tributi atque
dispendio uel lesione a presenti die et tempore liberae sint, mihique et
posteris meis talem honorem uel oboedientiam exhibeant qualem exhibuerunt
antecessoribus meis regibus sub quibus eis iustitia et libertas seruabatur,^{d} et
ut tam ego quam posteri mei in hac pia definitione^e permaneant decerno,
nec per quamlibet tergiuersationem que a nobis et a predecessoribus^f nostris
recte indulta sunt concutiantur, sed ita ut iam iamque dictum est inperpetuum
abhinc^g et deinceps Domino^h gubernante custodiantur, ad cuius cumulum
firmitatis manu propria signum sancte crucis expressi et tam^h reuerentissimum
Berhtualdum^i archiepiscopum atque Gemmundum^j sanctissimum episcopum
quam etiam uenerabiles presbyteros et religiosos abbates, ^{k}presentibus itidem
clarissimis abbatissis, hoc est Hirminhilda, Irminburga, Aeaba et Nerienda,^{k}
ut subscriberent rogaui. Actum die .vi. idus Aprilis, anno regni mei .viii.,^{l}
indictione .xii.,^{m} in loco qui appellatur Cilling.^{n}

+ Ego Uuihtredus rex Cantie ad omnia suprascripta et confirmata atque a
me dictata propria manu signum sancte crucis pro ignorantia litterarum
expressi.

+ Ego Berhtuualdus^o archiepiscopus ad omnia suprascripta rogatus a
Uuihtredo rege testis subscripsi.

+ Ego Gemmundus^p episcopus rogatus testis subscripsi.

+ Ego Tobias presbyter rogatus testis^h subscripsi.

+ Ego Aeana^q presbyter rogatus^h testis^h subscripsi.

+ Ego Vinigeld presbyter rogatus testis^h subscripsi.

+ Ego Hadrianus^r indignus monachus rogatus testis subscripsi.

+ Ego Aedilmer^s abbas rogatus subscripsi.^{t}

+ Signum manus Uihtgari.

+ Signum manus Cyniadi.

+ Signum manus Ecca.

+ Signum manus Ueba.

+ Signum manus Headda.

+ Signum manus Headda.^{u}

+ Signum manus Suithbaldi.^{v}

+ Signum manus Scirieardi.^{w}

+ Signum manus Aedilfridi.

+ Signum manus Hagana.

+ Signum manus Beornheardi.^{x}

^{a} *This endorsement is now partly illegible* ^{b} ... ^{b} *Omitted* N ^{c} *Cantica* N
^{d} *For* seruabantur ^{e} diffinicione N ^{f} precessoribus A ^{g} adhinc N

h Omitted N   *i Brihtwaldum* N   *j Gemundum* N
k ... k presentes id idem clarissimas abbatissas, hoc est Hirminhyldam, Irmynburgam, Æbbam et Neriendam N   *l .xxviii.* N   *m .ii.* N   *n Cillinc* N   *o Brihtuualdus* N
p Gemundus N   *q Æna* N   *r Adrianus* N   *s Ailmer* N
t First column of subscriptions ends here A (*note that the last two witnesses in the first and second columns and the final witness in the third column are slightly misplaced because the lower left-hand corner of the parchment is missing*)
u Second column of subscriptions ends here A   *v Suitbaldi* N   *w Surerdi* N
x Third column of subscriptions ends here A

Copies of Wihtred's charter granting privileges to the churches and monasteries of Kent are to be found in two of the abbey's thirteenth-century cartularies and also in Thomas Elmham's history. In addition, the Christ Church archive preserves a single-sheet copy of the document, apparently written in the ninth century (MS A); the exemplar was probably from Lyminge or Reculver (see below). This was copied into a cathedral register in the fifteenth century (Canterbury, D. & C., Reg. A, 77v). A second endorsement was added to the single sheet at Christ Church in the twelfth century. In the seventeenth century it was in the possession of Sir Edward Dering (1598–1644), who probably abstracted it from the Christ Church archive. It was part of the Phillipps collection from 1861 until 1946 (Phillipps MS 31280), and was acquired by the County Museum in 1947 (see *BAFacs.*, p. 3).

Description of A. The single sheet has a horizontal format, comparable to S 19 and 1171 (as opposed to the vertical format of S 8). A rectangular section missing from the lower left-hand corner of the face had been removed before the scribe began writing. At present there are four horizontal folds and ten vertical folds, but there are signs of a different pattern of folding in the past. The contemporary endorsement stretches across the height of the sheet, which indicates that it was originally folded vertically but not horizontally. The script is probably ninth-century; symptomatic features include pointed *a* (note the grossly prolonged ascender to *Actum* in l. 8), pointed *q*, split descenders in *s* (see especially the subscription of Aeana *testis*), disproportionately tall ascenders (see especially the last column of witnesses). Ascenders are sometimes wedge-shaped, and there are very few ligatures and abbreviations. The general aspect of the script is similar to that of S 338 (*BMFacs.*, ii. 37), a Canterbury charter from 867, and it seems possible that the single sheet was written at about this time. The script is stilted and ungainly, perhaps because the scribe had little competence (for the decline of the Canterbury scriptorium in this period, see Brooks, *Church of Canterbury*, pp. 164–74), perhaps because he was imitating the script of his exemplar. Certain aspects of the layout do suggest that the scribe was attempting to produce a faithful copy, in particular the treatment of the witness-list. Here the subscriptions are arranged in columns, but the portion of parchment missing from the lower left-hand corner has forced the scribe to shift to the right the last witnesses in each column. This adaptation indicates that he was reproducing the arrangement of the witness-list in his exemplar. He has spaced the subscriptions in a curious way, leaving a substantial gap between *testis* and *subscripsi* in several of the subscriptions in the first column, while failing to leave a space between the first and second columns; there are also unnecessary gaps in the third column of subscriptions, this time between *manus* and the name of the witness.

Spacing of this kind is compatible with a situation in which the witness-list is added after the charter has been folded verticaly, so that the scribe has to avoid the creases in the parchment. Since the gaps in the single sheet bear no relation to the folding, it is possible that the scribe was here mechanically reproducing the script of his exemplar. The considerable gap between the text of the charter and the witness-list could also reproduce the layout of the exemplar, where it may have been required in order to avoid a horizontal fold. Several other early originals appear to have been produced in two stages, usually with the witness-list being added later (S 8, 1171, 23, 89).

Therefore, although the single-sheet version of **10** is probably ninth-century, it seems to be a copy of an earlier exemplar, quite probably a seventh-century original. It is likely that several contemporary copies of Wihtred's privilege were made, so that versions were available in the all Kentish minsters to which the immunity applied. Since there is some reason to believe that the early Christ Church archives were lost or destroyed during the Kentish rebellion of 796–8 (Brooks, *Church of Canterbury*, p. 121), the exemplar of the ninth-century copy (or the copy itself) probably came from another community, perhaps Lyminge or Reculver, whose archives later passed into the possession of Christ Church, or perhaps even from St Augustine's, if the copy was made simply to supply a gap in the cathedral records. St Augustine's would certainly appear to have had its own text of the privilege, and may also have inherited another from Minster-in-Thanet. Elmham's version of **10** is slightly different from that in the St Augustine's cartularies and in the single-sheet copy. In the first place, the dating has been contaminated, with the alteration of the regnal year and the indiction to produce a date of 719. It is not clear why the St Augustine's scholars who revised the muniments wished to post-date the privilege in this way (see p. ci). Elmham's text also differs from the others in the reference to the presence of the four abbesses at the meeting; this section is in the ablative form in the cartulary copies and in the single sheet, but in the accusative in Elmham's text. It is possible that Elmham and the cartularists were using different versions of the privilege, perhaps from St Augustine's itself and from Minster, of which one had a slight variant. Alternatively, the variant may have crept in when the dating of the privilege was altered, at some point between the thirteenth and fifteenth centuries.

Wihtred states that he is making the grant of privileges in response to certain unspecified disasters (*calamitates*) threatening the churches and monasteries of Kent. Presumably this was an external threat of some kind, perhaps of an otherwise unknown invasion from Wessex or Mercia. Wihtred declares that the religious houses are to be immune from all liability to the payment of public tribute. In return they are to give the same 'honour and obedience' to Wihtred and his successors as they did to his royal predecessors, who for their part ensured them justice and liberty. Wihtred commits himself and his successors to preserve their side of the bargain. The charter seems to be restating an ancient relationship between the Kentish king and the minsters, which may have been been disrupted in the years of foreign invasion between the death of Eadric in 686 and Wihtred's emergence as sole king of Kent in around 694 (see Appendix 3). The statement that the churches owe the king 'honour and obedience' is a reminder that the major religious houses in Kent, including St Augustine's, were closely associated with the native royal dynasty. Wihtred's grant of immunity to the churches is best understood as a confirmation of an existing arrangement, since in his lawcode, datable to 695 (see further below), Wihtred had already stated that the church was to be free from taxation (*gafola*). **10** should be probably be regarded as a formal record of the churches' immunity. Ine of Wessex seems to have issued a similar privilege to the West Saxon churches about five years later (S 245); there is some problem with the dating of this charter, but a genuine document does seem to underlie the extant text (see H. Edwards, 'Two Documents from Aldhelm's Malmesbury', *Bulletin of the Institute of Historical Research* lix (1986), pp. 1–19).

Although it is a grant of immunity, **10** shares some of its formulation with contemporary land-charters and has particularly close links with **44**, a charter of Wihtred in favour of Minster datable to 694. An unusual feature here is the reference to the presence of four abbesses. Hirminhilda, Eormenburh, Æbba and Nerienda appear to have attended the synod, but they do not subscribe the privilege. Women were never regular witnesses in Anglo-Saxon charters. Queens usually attest only in very rare circumstances in the early Anglo-Saxon period and not on a regular basis until the later tenth century (see commentary to **9**). Abbesses do occasionally subscribe early charters (see S 62, 168, 254). The treatment of the four abbesses in **10** suggests that it was not felt proper for them to attest a synodal document; their presence is mentioned prominently and with respect, but they do not subscribe. There is an apparent contrast in the witness-list of the slightly later Bapchild synod in S 22, which has the subscriptions of five abbesses (S 22 is a ninth-century forgery, but it incorporates two apparently genuine witness-lists, emanating from a Kentish synod at Bapchild and from a *Clofesho* synod that met in 716). This may reflect a change of policy, or perhaps simply reworking by the ninth-century forger who made use of the witness-list. Three of the abbesses mentioned in **10** can be identified. Æbba is the foundress of Minster-in-Thanet, beneficiary of six charters (**40–4, 46**) and mother of St Mildrith. Hirminhilda and Eormenburh figure in the hagiographical literature associated with the cult of Mildrith and her sisters (see Rollason, *Mildrith Legend, passim*). Hirminhilda (Eormenhild) was a daughter of King Eorcenberht of Kent (640–64), wife of Wulfhere of Mercia, and mother of St Werburh. In the eleventh century her relics were claimed to be at Ely, together with those of her mother, Seaxburh, and her aunt, the famous St Æthelthryth. If the hagiographical Hirminhilda is to be identified with the abbess mentioned in **10**, then she was presumably in charge of one of the Kentish double minsters. Eormenburh is mentioned in the same literature as a sister of Æbba, like her the daughter of a Kentish prince named Eormenred. Nothing else is known of her and there is no trace of any cult. Nerienda is a woman's name derived from OE *nergend*, 'saviour', and is presumably a religious *alias*, comparable to the name Redemptus attached to a priest in the witness-list of the Bapchild synod (S 22).

The reference to the abbesses is followed by a dating clause in the usual Kentish form, beginning *Actum* with no qualifying word. The dating information consists of a calendar date (instead of a simple reference to the month such as is found in S 8 and 19), a regnal year and an indiction. The calendar date and indiction, in conjunction with the regnal year, give an incarnation date of 8 April 699. Some difficulty arises from the regnal year and its implication for the calculation of the beginning of Wihtred's reign. If 8 April 699 was in Wihtred's eighth year, he must have become king during the year before 8 April 692. A similar conclusion is suggested by the dating clause of **44**, said to have been issued on 17 July, in the seventh indiction and in Wihtred's third year (that is, 17 July 694), which places Wihtred's accession in the year before 17 July 692. But Bede seems to calculate the beginning of Wihtred's reign from a rather earlier date, for he says that Wihtred died in April 725, having reigned for thirty-four and a half years (*HE* v. 23); this points to an accession in the autumn of 690. The *Anglo-Saxon Chronicle* refers to the beginning of Wihtred's reign under the year 694 and gives him a reign length of thirty-three years, which cannot be reconciled with the obit in Bede. The dating evidence of the preface to Wihtred's lawcode is difficult to use. The laws are said to have been issued in the fifth year of Wihtred's reign, in the ninth indiction and on the sixth day of *Rugern*. *Rugern* means 'rye-harvest'; Liebermann equates it with August (*Gesetze*, iii. 25), Whitelock with September (*EHD*, p. 396). The indiction is almost certainly calculated from 1 September, the so-called 'Greek' indiction (see Harrison, *Framework*, pp. 41, 118). Thus, if *Rugern* is September, the laws were issued on 6 September 695, and this was Wihtred's fifth year, which implies an accession date between September 690 and September 691; the earlier dating limit is compatible with Bede, the later with the evidence of **10** and **44**. If *Rugern* is August, the laws were issued on 6 August 696, implying a succession date between August 691 and August 692, compatible with the charters but not with Bede. The conflict between Bede's dating and the charter evidence can perhaps be explained by the ignominious beginning of Wihtred's reign in a period of joint-kingship with the usurper Swæfheard. It is possible that Bede was calculating from the time that Wihtred became king of part of Kent, while the charters celebrate the date when he ousted Swæfheard. See further discussion in Appendix 3.

The privilege was issued at a place called *Cilling*, which Wallenberg (*KPN*, pp. 27–32) wrongly identifies with Selling. It appears to have been a lost place near Graveney in Faversham, mentioned in the bounds of a charter dated 815 (S 177), where it is termed a *portus* (Ward 1947, pp. 5, 12).

Wihtred's subscription incorporates a reference to his illiteracy, and therefore his legal status as a witness, such as is found in **8, 9, 44** and S 19 (see pp. lxxxiii, lxxxv). The rest of the witness-list seems consistent with a date of 699. All the ecclesiastical subscriptions are in the subjective form and all the lay subscriptions (apart from that of Wihtred) in objective form. Gebmund was bishop of Rochester; in the past it has been stated that he died in 693, on the basis of a mistaken reading of the reference to the consecration of his successor in Bede, *HE*, v. 8, but his survival beyond that date is clearly demonstrated by his subscriptions to **9** and **10**. The priest named Tobias who attests after him is probably his successor at Rochester. Aeana is a hypocoristic form of a name beginning Ean- (for example, Eanberht, Eanred); an unstyled Eana appears in **8**. The subscription of Hadrian of St Augustine's incorporates the word *indignus*, a mark of humility which is attached to his name in **7** and elsewhere (see Sims-Williams 1988, p. 166). It is tempting to see this detail as an indication that Hadrian himself drafted the privilege, but this was not necessarily the case; in S 1164 (A.D. 670 × 676) Bishop Leuthhere of the West Saxons is styled *indignus*, but the document is also said to have been written by a priest named Wynberht. Abbot Ædilmer is perhaps to be identified with the unstyled man of that name who attests S 8 and **12**. Several of the lay witnesses attest contemporary charters: Wihtgar (**46**); Cyniadus (**46**); Ecca (S 8, 22, 233, and

6, 8, 40, 41, 42, 43); Ueba (8); Ædilfrid (S 19), Hagana (S 8, 19, and 40), Beornheard (S 8, 19, 233 and 40, 44). Scirieardus is perhaps to be identified with the Suydredus who attests 8.

11

Æthelberht II, king of Kent, confirms an exchange whereby the monastery of SS Peter and Paul cedes the half-use of a mill to the royal vill at Wye, in return for grazing rights in the Weald for its tenant at Chart, Kent. A.D. 762

F. BL Cotton Julius D. ii, 130v–131r: copy, s. xiii[l]
   No rubric
H. PRO E 164/27, 4v: copy, s. xiii
   No rubric
N. Cambridge, Trinity Hall, 1, 69rv: copy, s. xv[l]
   Rubric: Carta de conuentione regis Ethelberti pro terra de Cert.
Ed.: a. Kemble 108 from N etc.
    b. Hardwick, *Elmham*, pp. 325–6, from N
    c. Birch 191 from Kemble and BL Harley 686, a copy of N
    d. Pierquin, *Recueil*, pt 1, no. 49, from Birch
Listed: Sawyer 25
Edited from F, H and N

In nomine Domini nostri Iesu.[a] Possessio quedam est terra in regione que uocatur Cert[b] monasterii scilicet[c] beatorum[d] Petri et Pauli apostolorum quod situm est ad orientem ciuitatis Dorouernis. In hac autem terra habetur molina cuius quippe semis utilitas, id est dimidia pars molendine, a possessoribus prefati monasterii ac terre huius ad uillam regalem que nominatur With[e] tradita est, pro hac uidelicet conditione atque commutatione, ut homo ille qui hanc terram in qua molina est tributario iure teneret unius gregis porcorum pascuam atque pastinationem in saltu Andoredo iugiter haberet. Hanc autem commutationem ego[f] Æthilberhctus[g] rex Cantie ut rata inperpetuum existat signo dominice crucis roborare curaui[h] et testes religiosos ut id ipsum facerent adhibui. Actum in ciuitate Dorouernis, anno incarnationis Domini .dcclxii.

+ Ego Athelbertus[i] rex, ut prefata commutatio atque donatio firma [j]inperpetuo persistat,[j] in nomine Dei omnipotentis quibusque dignitatis ac conditionis hominibus precipio et per crucem dominice passionis adiuro, cuius signum ad cumulum firmitatis in hac paginula descripsi.[k]
+ Ego Bregwynus archiepiscopus testis consentiens canonice subscripsi.
+ Ego Albertus prefectus subscripsi.

^a Iesu Christi H   ^b Cherd H   ^c *Omitted* H; silicet N   ^d beati H   ^e Wyth N
^f *Omitted* H   ^g Ethelbertus H, N
^h curauit. tempore Cuthberti archiepiscopi H. H *ends here*   ⁱ Ethelbertus N
^j . . . ^j perpetuo existat N   ^k F *ends here*

The diplomatic form of **11** is anomalous, but there is no reason to question its authenticity. Relatively few Kentish land-charters survive from the period between the 690s and the early 760s, and this seems to reflect irregular charter-production during that time; the draftsman may simply have been unfamiliar with charter-writing. In addition, the transaction with which **11** is concerned is clearly unusual, and the conventional formulation of land-charters may not have been found appropriate. The text begins with a brief invocation, after which the details of the transaction are set out without elaboration; there is then a brief passage in which King Æthelberht ratifies the exchange, followed by a dating clause and witness-list (in which the king's subscription repeats some elements of the corroboration). The version of the text in the PRO cartulary (MS H) breaks off in the course of the corroboration, where the first-person verb has been altered to the third person. These details are to be linked with the fact that the text does not form part of the main cartulary, but is instead included in a separate list of charters (see Appendix 2); the compiler of the list evidently found some difficulty in summarising the details of the transaction, and so copied out most of the document before him.

There are parallels for the oblique opening of **11** in two nearly contemporary charters, from Lyminge and Rochester, where the transaction involved is also slightly unusual (S 24, 30); but this may be just coincidence. The draftsman seems to have made some use of earlier models, presumably those already available in the St Augustine's archive; the reference to the location of the monastery in relation to Canterbury recalls a similar preoccupation in earlier charters in favour of the monstery (**7, 8, 9**); the formula in Æthelberht's ratification requesting the subscription of witnesses was used in seventh-century land-charters (see **7, 8, 9, 10** etc.). The reference to the double dedication contrasts with the normal usage in the seventh-century charters (where the community is usually called St Peter's), but is the same as that in **12**, also from 762 (see further, p. xiv). The dating clause begins with the word *Actum*, unqualified by a verb, which is the usual formulation in Kentish charters of the seventh and eighth centuries; here the dating information is in the form of an incarnation year, a variety of chronological reckoning which became common in the first half of the eighth century (see p. lxxxiv). Æthelberht's subscription is in an extended form, incorporating a second corroboration with a general injunction to preserve the terms of the exchange. This treatment of a subscription is unusual, but not suspicious when considered within the context of the charter as a whole, where the scribe has departed from the earlier diplomatic models afforded by land-charters. The subscription includes the ancient formula *ad cumulum firmitatis*, found in the corroborations of **10** and **44** (see p. lxxxiii). **11** has two minor features which suggest that the draftsman may indeed have been familiar with **10** (there would probably have been a copy of Wihtred's privilege in the monastery's archive): the phrase *roborare curaui* (which recalls *facere curaui* in **10**), and the inclusion of the word *testis* in the archbishop's subscription. But this is far from conclusive; the phrase *roborare curaui* is also found in S 31 from Reculver (A.D. 748 × 762). The

remaining subscriptions in the curtailed witness-list are those of Archbishop Bregowine (761–4) and a *prefectus*, probably to be identified with the Aldberht *prefectus*
who attests S 24 (A.D. 741).

11 is of considerable interest for the insight which it provides into the monastic
economy in the eighth century. The St Augustine's community cedes to the royal
vill a half share in a mill located on one of their estates in the Chart area; in return,
the tenant of the estate is to be given a swine-pasture in the Weald. This charter
shows that by the middle decades of the eighth century St Augustine's was managing
part of its endowment by leasing or renting it to a tenant, who held the land *tributario
iure*. Worcester was already leasing its property to members of the laity by this date
(S 1254), but this is the earliest indication that similar arrangements were in force
in Kent (in fact, very few formal ecclesiastical leases survive from Kent; the earliest
is S 1288, probably from 905 or 920). There is no way of discovering the terms on
which the tenant held the Chart estate, but it seems from **11** that St Augustine's
retained the right to manage the property by acquiring and disposing of appurtenances.

The reference to a mill is of some significance in the discussion of the community's
relationship with its tenant. Knowledge of water-mill technology is believed to have
diffused from the Mediterranean into northern Europe, and to have reached England
in the Middle Saxon period. Kent, due to its proximity to and close contacts with
the Continent, is likely to have been one of the first areas of England to adopt the
new technology. It has been noticed that that laws of Æthelberht I, from the early
seventh century, refer to the category of royal 'grinding slave', which would indicate
that grain on royal estates was still been ground by hand at that date. **11** suggests
that mills were still a novelty in the mid eighth century, to the extent that the
managers of the royal vill at Wye were prepared to negotiate with St Augustine's
for a share in a mill, rather than build one of their own. From the early ninth
century mills are regularly mentioned among the appurtenances of Kentish estates
(see S 173, 280, 293, 328) and also in non-Kentish charters (see Finberg, *Agrarian
History*, pp. 498–9). The written evidence seems to suggest that water-mill technology
was adopted in southern England in the course of the eighth century and was fairly
wide-spread in the ninth; this pattern conforms to the available information from
archaeological investigation (P. Rahtz and D. Bullough, 'The parts of an Anglo-Saxon
mill', *Anglo-Saxon England* vi (1977), pp. 15–37 at 16–17). **11**, in so far as one
document can be taken as illustrative of a general trend, appears to show that
mill-technology was pioneered on ecclesiastical estates rather than by royal vills. It
is possible that the scattered nature of the ecclesiastical endowment, consisting of
separate estates in different regions (in contrast to the more centralised organisation
of a royal vill and its dependencies), was a factor in the application of technology.
Transport of grain to a central place for processing would not always have been
convenient, and the lack of local labour may have made the application of technology
more economical. The provision of a mill on an estate held by a tenant is perhaps
to be connected with the nature of the rent he paid to the monastery, at this date
more probably a substantial render of local products than a money-rent. Some
grants of food-rents made to St Augustine's and Christ Church in the middle of the
ninth century (see **24, 25**) mention an annual render of large number of loaves. If
the tenant was expected to provide a render of this kind, access to a water-mill

would be a boon. It is possible that the Chart mill serviced several St Augustine's estates in the area, although the arrangement with the vill at Wye indicates that it was not being used to capacity.

Chart is a regional name, applied to a narrow band of hill-country between Holmesdale and the Weald, associated with a ridge of Greensand rocks (see Everitt, *Continuity*, pp. 45, 50–2). It was a wooded region, of limited fertility except in the central regions; in Everitt's opinion it was colonised from primary settlements in Holmesdale. The wording of the charter shows that the St Augustine's estate was situated in the Chartland, but there is no necessity to seek it only in those places where the element has been preserved in a place-name. The estate was presumably in fairly close proximity to Wye. A possible identification is with Ripton, which was located in Chart hundred in the eleventh century, only about four miles from Wye. St Augustine's held a manor there the time of the Domesday survey, obviously under-assessed at one yoke; there was land for two ploughs, which suggests that the manor was at least a sulung in extent, and the value before and after 1066 was a substantial £3, rising to £4 by 1086 (GDB 12r). Among the appurtenances of the Domesday manor is a quarter of a mill. Several of the abbey's Domesday estates have a mill or mills listed among their appurtenances, but this is the only mill-fraction, which might be reason to suggest identification with the Chart estate of **11**. The Ripton manor also included woodland for ten pigs, which could be the Wealden swine-pasture ceded by Wye in 762. There is no evidence as to the date at which Ripton passed into the possession of St Augustine's, but **11** suggests that it may have been an early acquisition.

The swine-pasture in the Weald acquired by the tenant of the Chart estate is likely to have been in the Wealden common attached to the royal vill at Wye; this is the *Weowaraweald* of **47**. There were similar commons associated with Canterbury and Lyminge, which were also been broken up and alienated from the eighth century onwards (see Witney, *Jutish Forest*, chapters 2–4, especially pp. 36, 82–3). According to the list of dens in **47** (probably an addition to the original charter), the *Weowaraweald* included Broombourne in High Halden, which is near Tenterden, about eleven miles from Wye and seven from Ripton (see Witney, *Jutish Forest*, p. 272).

12

Dunwald, minister of the late King Æthelberht, grants a villa near Queningate, Canterbury, to the monastery of SS Peter and Paul. A.D. 762

F. BL Cotton Julius D. ii, 132r: copy, s. xiii[1]
   No rubric
H. PRO E 164/27, 80v: copy, s. xiii
   Rubric: Carta Dunwaldi de terra in Quenegate.
N. Cambridge, Trinity Hall, 1, 69v: copy s. xv[1]
   Rubric: Carta Dunwaldi de terra infra Quengate id est Regine portu.
Ed.: a. Kemble 109 from N etc.
   b. Hardwick, *Elmham*, pp. 326–7, from N
   c. Thorpe, *Diplomatarium*, pp. 36–7, from N

d. Birch 192 from Kemble and BL Harley 686, a copy of N
e. Pierquin, *Recueil*, pt 1, no. 50, from Birch
Listed: Sawyer 1182
Translated: Whitelock, *EHD*, no. 72 (pp. 499–500)
Edited from F, H and N

In nomine Domini nostri Iesu Christi. Ego Dunwald minister dum aduiueret inclite memorie regis Æthelberti,[a] nunc uero pecuniam illius pro anime eius salute ad limina apostolorum Rome cum aliis perferre desiderans, uillam unam post obitum meum, ni[b] forsitan hoc prius me uiuente placeat peragendum, que iam ad Quenegatum urbis Dorouernis[c] in foro posita est, quam nunc Hringuine tenet, quam idem mihi prefatus rex cum aliis terrulis iure proprio cum tributo illius possidendam[d] et cuicumque uoluerim tradendam condonauit; hanc uidelicet ad ecclesiam propepositam beati Petri et Pauli ubi scilicet corpus eiusdem domini mei regis Æthelberti requiescit pro anime illius[e] et [f]mea salute[f] eterna donatione cum tributo illius possidendam[g] attribuo. Et ut nulla esset inposterum de hac contentio hoc ipsum in libello prime donationis mee[h] faciendum descripsi. Et ideo nunc cum consensu uenerabilis archiepiscopi nostri Bregowini[i] hunc libellum huiusce donationis mee describi feci et manu propria roboraui et illum atque alios religiosos testes ut id ipsum faciant adhibeo. Actum anno incarnationis Christi .dcclxii.[j]

+ Ego Bregwinus[k] gratia Dei archiepiscopus signum sancte crucis subscripsi.
+ Ego Dunwald prefatam donacionem meam signum sancte crucis roboraui.
+ Ego Baltheardus[l] dux subscripsi.
+ Ego Kyneardus presbyter consensi et subscripsi.[m]
+ Ego Iambertus abbas testis subscripsi.[m]

Hec terra circumcincta est hiis terminibus, a Quenegatum in meridiem[n] extensas habens .iii. perticas et inde in occidentem rectissima linea diuidit terram regis et istam .xxiii. perticis usque in maceriam que in aquilonali parte ciuitatis muro adiacet uirgas habens .xxxiiii.

[a] Æthelbertu F   [b] nisi F   [c] Dorouerniis F   [d] possedendam F   [e] eius H
[f] ...[f] salute mea N   [g] possedendam F; possidenda N
[h] me F; mee *altered to* me H   [i] Bregwini N   [j] F *ends here*; .dcclx. H
[k] Breogwinus H   [l] Balthardus H   [m] H *omits these subscriptions*   [n] meridie H

12, which is clearly an authentic charter, is important evidence for diplomatic development in Anglo-Saxon England. It was produced under unusual circumstances. Dunwald, a thegn of the late King Æthelberht (II), was on the point of travelling to Rome, taking with him money that was to be dispensed there for Æthelberht's soul. It was Dunwald's wish to bequeath part of his property, a small piece of land in Canterbury, to the nearby church of SS Peter and Paul (St Augustine's), where Æthelberht had been buried. He had been granted this land by Æthelberht, along with other estates. In order to prevent any dispute Dunwald had noted this intention 'in the charter of my first grant' (*in libello prime donationis mee*): now, with the archbishop's consent, he has had drawn up 'the present charter of this grant of mine' (*hunc libellum huiusce donationis mee*), and he asks for witnesses.

Dunwald's wishes are clear, but the account of his documentary activity is much less so. There were evidently two charters, the later of which is the present text. The first charter may have been Dunwald's written will in which this particular bequest was mentioned; the second document would then have been drawn up to strengthen the bequest. Alternatively, it may be that the first charter was the landbook which King Æthelberht had issued to Dunwald as a title-deed for his estates. If this landbook covered several properties, difficulties could have arisen when one of the estates was bequeathed to St Augustine's; this may explain why a notice of the intended bequest was written in (perhaps added to) the first charter and a second document drawn up for St Augustine's. The wording of 12 is not sufficiently precise to confirm either suggestion, but some reason to prefer the latter is provided by a contemporary West Saxon charter (S 1164/1259; Kelly, *Shaftesbury*, no. 1). This was drawn up by Bishop Cyneheard of Winchester in 759, to mark the settlement of a dispute. Between 670 and 676 Cenred, a West Saxon ruler, had granted several estates to Abbot Bectun and his community, and this was noted in a single charter. Bectun's successor had sold thirty hides of this land to the abbot of Tisbury and had drawn up a new charter, possibly an edited version of Cenred's, to cover this land, because the existing title to the estate was inextricably entangled in the documentation for other properties. Subsequently, Bectun's community, which retained the original title-deed, disputed Tisbury's right to the estate. The dispute was resolved in favour of Tisbury, and Bishop Cyneheard drew up the extant document, consisting of an edited version of Cenred's original charter plus his own explanation of the dispute and its settlement. This was given to Tisbury, as title for the thirty hides. The draftsman of 12 may have been aware of the recent West Saxon dispute-settlement and the circumstances behind it. Chaplais (1965, p. 56 [p. 37]) suggests that some of the wording of the Shaftesbury charter reappears in 12. This is rather overstating the case, because there is no real repetition. Nevertheless, the two draftsmen seem to be using similar language to describe the proceedings surrounding the production of documentation; in S 1259 we find references to *libellum alium donationis huius*, *primum libellum* and *presens libellum*, and also the use of the verb *describo* in this context. There is in addition a surprising correspondence between the sanction of Cenred's charter (S 1164), which uses the phrase *a liminibus sanctae ecclesie*, and the reference in 12 to *limina apostolorum Rome*. This does raise the possibility that the St Augustine's draftsman was familiar with the actual record of the West Saxon dispute-settlement, although the extent of the correspondence is too slight for any firm conclusion to this effect. If there is a relationship between the two documents, it would probably indicate that the draftsman of 12 was considering a similar case, in which a charter was the title-deed to several estates, only one of which was to be alienated.

The formulation of 12 is directly affected by the unusual nature of the transaction it records. As in the case of **11** the draftsman has borrowed the frame of the document (invocation, corroboration, dating-clause and witness-list) from the model of a contemporary land-charter, but has replaced the dispositive section with a straight-forward summary of the transaction. Some of the wording of this section is of diplomatic interest. The terms used to describe Æthelberht's grant of this and other estates to Dunwald seem to be a paraphrase of the dispositive section and statement of powers in the original royal charter (perhaps the *libellum prime donationis* mentioned later in the text). The specific statement (repeated later) that this was a grant of land *cum tributo illius* echoes references to tribute in this context in **13** and in S 33, 105, 128 etc. Dunwald's bequest is in favour of the church of SS Peter and Paul. This reference to the double dedication echoes that in **11** and contrasts with the usage in earlier charters in favour of the monastery, where only St Peter is mentioned (see p. xiv). The explicit statement that Æthelberht had been buried at St Augustine's is paralleled by similar references to royal burial in **13**, and demonstrates contemporary anxieties at St Augustine's about the loss of its burial function (see p. xv). In the corroboration the draftsman returns to the regular formulation of the Kentish land-charter; the request for witnesses contains the verb *abhibeo*, also used in this context in **13** and in S 32 from Rochester, both contemporary with **12**. The form of the dating clause, introduced by *Actum* with no verb, is standard in Kentish charters in the seventh and eighth centuries (see pp. lxxxiii–lxxxiv).

The witness-list at present consists of five subscriptions, and has probably been truncated. There is no royal subscription, possibly because the charter was issued immediately after Æthelberht's death and before his successor had established himself, perhaps because a royal subscription was not thought necessary for a document of this type. The first subscriptions are those of Archbishop Bregowine (761–4) and Dunwald himself. There were at least two Baltheards attesting Kentish charters between 727 and 779; two men of that name subscribe S 30 and 36, and single subscriptions of a Baltheard are found in **13**, **48**, **53**, and in S 23, 24, 27, 32–4, 37. The priest Cyneheard does not appear in any other witness-lists in this period. The final subscription is that of Abbot Jaenberht of St Augustine's, who was Bregowine's successor as archbishop.

This is one of the earliest records of a grant by a private individual. Dunwald himself cannot be identified with confidence. The name in the text may be a corruption of Dunwalh, for a Dunuualhus pincerna attests a charter of King Æthelberht in 741 (S 24), alongside another Duunuualla, who also attests a charter of King Eardwulf (S 30, datable to 748 × 760) in association with Æthelberht. One of these men may have been the eponymous owner of *Dunwalinglond* in Eastry, acquired by Archbishop Wulfred from Reculver minster and given by him to the Christ Church community in 811 (S 1264). A Wealden swine-pasture called *dun ualing daenn* is mentioned in S 123 from 785.

Certain details about the Canterbury estate can be retrieved from the main text. It was near Queningate, which was a minor Roman gate in the city wall north of Burgate. It was in the market-place (*in foro*); compare the reference in S 125 from 786 to 'uicum qui dicitur Curringtun in urbe que dicitur Dorouernensi in aquilone parte uenalis loci'. Several ninth-century charters mention small manors or *tunas* just outside the walls of Canterbury, and Dunwald's *villa* and *Curringtun* may have been similar to these; Brooks (*Church of Canterbury*, pp. 26–7) suggests a parallel with aristocratic manors established around cities in the Rhineland. We are also told that Dunwald's *villa* lay close to St Augustine's, and that it was at present held by a certain Hringuine. He may have been Dunwald's kinsman or a friend who was managing the property during Dunwald's projected absence overseas, but it is also possible that he was a tenant.

The charter concludes with a detailed Latin boundary clause, giving the dimensions of the property. It is difficult to decide whether this formed part of the original charter or whether it is a later addition. Its position after the witness-list is suspicious. Kentish charters at this period did not usually include detailed bounds; if a boundary clause was provided, it was brief and simply arranged according to the four cardinal points, in contrast to the very elaborate Latin bounds which were being included in West Saxon charters in the second half of the eighth century (see S 262, 264, 268; and discussion, pp. lxxix–lxxx). But the fact that the estate was located within a town, rather than in the country, may have led to different treatment, for exact dimensions are more important in an area of relatively dense population. A Canterbury charter of 804 which is concerned with a piece of land in the underpopulated southwestern part of the city (S 160) includes a set of bounds and mentions that the land measured fifteen *virgae*. A charter from 823 (S 187) gives the dimensions of a small estate within the walls of Canterbury as sixty feet by thirty. Given these parallels, the similar clause in **12** can probably be accepted as contemporary. The bounds begin at Queningate, and proceed south for three *perticae* (a linear measure here). To the west lay a royal estate, divided from Dunwald's land by a very straight boundary which ran for twenty-three *perticae* as far as a *maceria* (presumably the wall of an enclosure of some kind). The city wall formed the northern boundary; clearly the estate was intramural.

The text of **12** in Bodleian, James 22, p. 55, was copied from PRO E 164/27.

13

Eadberht II, king of Kent, grants six sulungs (aratra) *at Mongeham, Kent, to the monastery of St Peter.* [probably A.D. 762 or 763] (25 July)

F. BL Cotton Julius D. ii, 133rv: copy, s. xiii[1]
  No rubric
N. Cambridge, Trinity Hall, 1, 67v–68r: copy, s.xv[1]
  Rubric: Carta Edberti regis de manerio de Mungeham.
Ed.: a. Kemble 107 from N etc.
  b. Hardwick, *Elmham*, pp. 319–21, from N
  c. Birch 190 from Kemble and BL Harley 686, a copy of N
Listed: Sawyer 28
Edited from F and N

In nomine regnantis inperpetuum Domini nostri Iesu Christi ac cuncta mundi iura iusto moderamine regentis. Quamuis parua et exigua sunt que pro admissis peccatis offerimus, tamen pius Dominus et redemptor noster non quantitatem muneris sed deuotionem offerentium semper inspicit. Qua de re ego Eadbertus Dei dispensatione ab uniuersa prouincia Cantuariorum constitutus rex et princeps, cognoscens initium uite et mortis, quia omni humano generi indifferens est uite cursus et mortis, prouidens ubi corpusculum meum condi deberet, nichil melius arbitratus sum nisi ibi sepulture traderer ubi iam pristino tempore parentes meos sepultos esse omnibus constat, hoc est in monasterio beati apostolorum principis Petri, cui preesse dinoscitur honorabilis abbas Iaenbertus,[a] et quia infructuosus esse non debeo supradicte ecclesie, pro eterna redemptione animarum nostrarum mee uidelicet atque clementissimi regis Æthelberti, et corporum sepulture, necnon et pro missarum solemniis exhibendis, ad augmentum uite[b] inibi famulantium Christo terram aratrorum sex in australi parte uici antiqui qui appellatur Mundelingeham,[c] sicut a regibus Cantie tempore pristino et a nobis usque hactenus[d] concessa et possessa est, interdicens etiam mihi hanc terram meisque successoribus a presenti die et tempore, una cum consensu reuerentissimi archiepiscopi Bregopini aliorumque seruorum Dei et principum meorum, beatissimo clauigero regni celestis eiusque sacre conuersationis familie inperpetuo possidendam optuli, cum campis, siluis, pratis, pascuis et cum omni tributo quod regibus daretur, ut liberam habeant potestatem possidendi uel uendendi[e] uel etiam tradendi cuicumque uoluerint. Terminos uero huius terre ideo non scribimus quia undique ab incolis sine dubitationis scrupulo certi sunt. Et unius carri introitum in silua que appellatur Saenling.[f] Quicumque uero sequentium regum uel episcoporum aut aliquis seculari potestate fretus hec nostre donationis scripta in aliqua parte minuere quod absit uel irrita facere nisus fuerit, inprimis iram Dei incurrat et a cetu omnium sanctorum segregetur et sciat se presumptionis sue ante tribunal Christi in die iudicii rationem esse redditurum. Scripta autem hec est cartula donationis anno primo[g] regni nostri, die .viii. kalendarum Augusti, in ciuitate Dorouerni. Testes uero ad confirmationem infra nominatos adhibui.

+[h] Ego Ædbertus[i] rex hanc donationem meam uolens confirmare propria manu signum sancte crucis expressi.[j]

Ego Bregopinus archiepiscopus consensi et subscripsi.

Ego Iambertus abbas subscripsi.

+ Signum manus Bruni abbatis.

+ Signum manus Escuuald presbyteri.

+ Signum manus Esne comitis.

+ Signum manus Baldhardi.

+ Signum manus Hearedi.

+ Signum Eadberti.

^a Iambertus N   ^b uidelicet *added* F   ^c Mundlingeham F   ^d actenus F
^e uel uendendi *omitted* F   ^f *This phrase may be interpolated (see commentary)*
^g .xxxvi. N *(see commentary)*   ^h F *omits cross*   ⁱ Ægbertus F   ^j F *ends here*

13 is one of two charters in the St Augustine's archive in the name of Eadberht II, successor and probably son of Æthelberht II; the other is a ship-toll privilege in favour of Minster-in-Thanet, issued in the following year (**53**). The identity of the donor was for some time obscured as the result of chronological tampering in the archive. Both charters are dated only by a regnal year, but evidently belong to the period between 762 and 764; they are attested by Archbishop Bregowine (761–4) and Abbot Jænberht (appointed to St Augustine's in *c.* 762), while **13** appears to have been issued after the death of King Æthelberht in 762. In the thirteenth-century cartulary copies, **13** is dated to Eadberht's first year and **53** to his second, which indicates that Eadberht first became king in 762/3. By contrast, the copies of **13** and **53** in the fifteenth-century history of Thomas Elmham both have a regnal year of thirty-six, which seems to reflect deliberate chronological falsification intended to identify the donor with Eadberht I, son of Wihtred, whose succession in 725 is mentioned by Bede; this Eadberht died in 748, according to the *Anglo-Saxon Chronicle*, and so could not have been issuing charters between 762 and 764. For further discussion of chronological contamination in the archive, see pp. xcvi–cv. It is an interesting point that the date of the third surviving charter of Eadberht II, preserved in the Christ Church archives, has also been tampered with for similar reasons. S 1612 is a ship-toll privilege in favour of the Reculver community, which includes a reference to Archbishop Bregowine and is thus datable to between 761 and 764; at some stage the date 747 was attached to the text, apparently in order to associate it with Eadberht I. For further discussion of the identities and dates of these kings, see Appendix 3.

There seems no reason to question the authenticity of **13**. It has very close diplomatic affinities with two charters in the Rochester archive, one in the name of King Sigered and datable to between 761 and 764 (S 33), and the other in the name of King Offa, dated 764 and said to have been issued in Canterbury (S 105). Both S 33 and 105 seem to be concerned with the grant to Rochester of the same twenty-sulung estate at Islingham, and their relationship is rather mysterious. Sigered's charter is probably the earlier, and Offa's may be an effective restatement of the grant; a second charter of Sigered for Rochester (S 32) is associated with a later reissue by Offa (S 131 from 789), while two charters of the Kentish king Ecgberht (S 35, 36) were also capped by a later charter of the Mercian king (S 130 from 789). It has been suggested that these instances of repeated grants to the same beneficiary were necessary because Offa denied that these Kentish kings had any right to grant land without his permission (a position indicated in S 155), but it may also have been the case that Rochester was anxious to acquire new charters from a more powerful overlord to confirm its existing possessions.

13 and the two Rochester charters share much of their formulation, and perhaps depend ultimately on a Mercian model, although they are evidently the work of Kentish draftsmen (perhaps of a single draftsman). The verbal invocation in **13** is in the *In nomine* form typical of early Kentish charters, but it seems to be an adaptation of the Mercian formula beginning *Regnante* which is found in S 105. The short proem in **13** also occurs in S 33. Chaplais (1968, p. 329 [pp. 79–80]) notes that versions of this proem were in use at Fulda at the same period and are found in charters from other Anglo-Saxon foundations on the Continent in the ninth century; this probably reflects the dissemination of an Anglo-Saxon model to the continental missions. The relationship between **13** and the Rochester charters continues in the dispositive section. In both **13** and S 105 the superscription is followed by a statement of pious motivation, a construction familiar in earlier Kentish charters (compare, for instance, **10** and **44**). In **13** this has been adapted to refer to a subject of great importance to the St Augustine's community; Eadberht expresses his intention to be buried in the abbey, where his kindred (including, we are to infer, King Æthelberht II) had previously been buried. This emphasis on St Augustine's role as a royal burial church is found also in **12**, and it seems to reflect current concerns about a challenge to the abbey's ancient burial function (see p. xv). The formula used here to refer to St Augustine's recalls that used in seventh-century charters in favour of the abbey (**7**, **8**, **9**; and see pp. lxxvii–lxxviii). There is great similarity between the formulation of the list of appurtenances and statement of powers in **13** and the corresponding formulas in S 33 and 105. In both **13** and S 105 the dispositive section concludes with a reflection that it is unnecessary to write down the bounds because they are well known to the local people (a similar statement appears in the additional section in S 21, which probably belongs to the second half of the eighth century). Kentish charters frequently refer to *notissimi termini* and there seems to have been in Kent a general inclination to rely on verbal rather than written testimony about estate boundaries (see pp. lxxix–lxxx); the statements in **13** and S 105 are just unusually explicit about this attitude. The first part of the sanction in **13** also occurs in S 105; the second part recalls the wording of some earlier charters (**43**, **44**, **51**), but is also close to the formula in S 34 (A.D. 765). The formulation of the dating clause (beginning *Scripta* rather than *Actum*) shows Mercian influence; again there is a parallel in S 105.

The royal styles in **13** and the two associated Rochester charters are of considerable interest. In **13** Eadberht is, by the dispensation of God (*Dei dispensatione*, a formula found in S 105 and also in **53**), appointed king and ruler by the whole 'province' of the men of Kent. This is a grandiose style in eighth-century terms, and significant in that it refers to Kent as *prouincia Cantuariorum*; the same term is commonly found in charters from the period of direct Mercian rule in Kent (see p. xci), where it seems to reflect a diminution of Kent's status. Eadberht's claim to have been elected by the whole of Kent contrasts with the more modest style of Sigered in S 33: 'rex dimidiae partis prouinciae Cantuariorum'. This seems unusually precise, and again describes Kent as a *prouincia*, rather than a *regnum*. The strangest style in this group is that accorded to Offa in S 105: 'rex Merciorum regali prosapia Merciorum oriundus atque omnipotentis Dei dispensatione eiusdem constitutus in regem.' This is very different from Offa's usual style (the simple *rex Merciorum*) and could be considered suspicious; but comparison with **13** and S 33 shows that the literary bombast was probably the contribution of the draftsman of the charter, not of a later forger.

The Trinity Hall manuscript preserves the subscriptions of eight witnesses apart from that of the king. This may represent the full witness-list of the original charter; S 31 (A.D. 748 × 762), which survives as an apparent original, has only seven witnesses including the king. On the other hand, charters from the 760s preserved in the Rochester archive generally have at least twelve subscriptions, and the second charter of Eadberht II in the St Augustine's archive (53) has thirteen. In 13 the king's subscription is followed by those of Archbishop Bregowine and Jænberht, abbot of St Augustine's, who succeeded him as archbishop. Abbot Brun attests 53 and S 33. The priest named Æscwald also attested S 33. The four lay witnesses also appear in other Kentish charters of the period: Esne (S 32–5, 110–11); Baltheard (11, 48, 53; and S 23–4, 27, 33–4 etc.); Heared (S 34, 37, 110–11); and Eadberht (S 34, 110–11).

13 covers land in the southern part of an ancient *uicus* at Mongeham, probably in the vicinity of the present village of Little Mongeham. St Augustine's held a Domesday manor at Mongeham assessed at two and a half sulungs with land for five ploughs (GDB 12v); part of the estate had never been liable for geld, which may indicate ancient possession. Mongeham is adjacent to Northbourne, which may have been part of the early endowment of the monastery (see 5). The discrepancy between the assessment of six sulungs in the charter and the lower Domesday assessment may perhaps be accounted for by adjustment of the boundaries beween Mongeham and Northbourne. The wording of 13, which locates the six sulungs in the southern part of Mongeham, shows that the place-name was applied to a more considerable area in the eighth century. By the middle of the ninth century, part of Mongeham was in the possession of a religious woman named Lufu or Luba, who granted to Christ Church an annual food-render from her estate there (S 1197). In 974 St Augustine's acquired from a female donor an additional hundred acres at Mongeham, apparently located to the north and west of Little Mongeham (S 1653; see Appendix 1, no. v). Another acquisition in the area was Martin, immediately to the south, granted to the community by the West Saxon King Æthelberht in 861 (22).

Between the statement about the boundaries of the estate and the sanction, a brief note has been inserted concerning a special appurtenance. The note is not integrated with the surrounding text, and could be an interpolation; but it is also possible that the awkwardness is due to the original draftsman. Kentish charters of the later eighth and ninth centuries often mention specific appurtenances (see S 123, 125 etc.; and see 7 for an earlier instance). In this case, the holder of the Mongeham estate is stated to have the right to take a wagon into the king's wood at *Sænling*. *Sænling* survives in the place-name Singledge, now attached to a hamlet in Coldred parish, about four miles south-west of Mongeham (TR 287458). The privilege would have related to the regular collection of firewood in woodland belonging to the king. Other Kentish charters mention similar wood-gathering privileges. The beneficiaries in S 123 (A.D. 785) were given the right to take one hundred loaded wagons (*plaustra*) and two *carras ambulantes* from the wood at Hardres every year. The grant of land at Lenham in 21 from 850 carried with it permission to take three wagons (*carri*) into Blean Wood near Canterbury. A similar privilege in Blean Wood was attached to an estate in Wassingwell in S 328 (A.D. 858), which mentions that the woodland belonged to the king. In S 315 (A.D. 855) there is a reference to the right to take ten wagon-loads of wood *in monte regis*. Some ninth-century charters are more explicit about the terms of such privileges. S 287 (A.D. 839) refers to the king's permission to take two cart-loads of wood in summer from the common woodland, according to ancient custom. In S 332 (A.D. 863) the beneficiary of the charter is allowed to take four wagons into the king's wood six weeks after Pentecost, when the other men take wood. The reference to a wood-gathering privilege in 13 is the earliest of such instances (although the grant in S 23 from 732 includes the right to 120 wagons of wood for salt-making), but it seems acceptable in a contemporary context. 14 also refers to privileges in *Sænling*, this time connected with pasturage, but the charter itself seems to be a fabrication as it stands and the reference to *Sænling* appears to be garbled; it may represent a misunderstanding of a wood-gathering privilege such as that in 13.

14

Offa, king of the Mercians, grants two hides (manentes) *at Beauxfield, Kent, to Æthelnoth, abbot of [the monastery of] SS Peter and Paul.*
[A.D. 765 × 792]

F. BL Cotton Julius D. ii, 133v: copy, s. xiii[1]
  No rubric
H. PRO E 164/27, 81v: copy, s. xiii
  Rubric: Carta Offe regis de Beauuesfeld.
N. Cambridge, Trinity Hall, 1, 70v–71r: copy, s. xv[1]
  Rubric: Carta Offe regis Ethelnotho abbati de terra in Bewesfeld.
Ed.: a. Kemble 119, with bounds in vol. iii, p. 380, from N etc.
    b. Hardwick, *Elmham*, pp. 331–2, from N
    c. Birch 207 from Kemble and BL Harley 686, a copy of N
    d. Pierquin, *Recueil*, pt 1, no. 56, from Birch
Listed: Sawyer 140
Edited from F, H and N

Regnante inperpetuum Domino nostro Iesu Christo. Ego Offa rex Merciorum,[a] anno primo[b] regni mei, do et concedo Æthelnotho[c] abbati[d] apostolorum Petri et Pauli, terram .ii.[e] manentium iuris mei in loco qui appellatur Bepesfeld[f] cum ceteris[g] terminibus, pro expiatione criminum meorum. In ius proprium libenter concedo hoc modo, ut habeat et possideat cum campis et siluis uel omnibus ad se pertinentibus bonis, et ad pascendum porcos et pecora et iumenta in silua regali eternaliter perdono, et unius capre[h] licentiam in silua que uocatur Saenling,[i] ubi mee uadunt. Post obitum uero tuum habeas potestatem tradere eam homini cui tibi placuerit, pro eterna redemptione animarum nostrarum. Si quis uero regum quod non credo seu principum seu[j] quilibet a subiectis eorum hanc nostre[k] munificentie largitatem infringere uel minuere presumpserit, sciat se a participatione Domini nostri Iesu Christi corporis et sanguinis alienum esse in hoc seculo et in districto Dei omnipotentis iudicio coram Christo et angelis eius rationem esse redditurum, manente hac cartula[l] in sua semper nihilominus firmitate.[m]

[n]þon' sind þis þa sutulust an gedere[o] to Beasfeld. Ærest on norþe ƿeasðan[p] east rihte of ellenbeorge .xv. girda, þan on suð rihte sƿa moulman strecte oþ landes ende, þon' ƿest be Æƿille mearce oþ þone cƿichege, suð andlang heges on þane bradan hẹgeƿai, þon' on cingdene on abbudes mearce, of abbudes mearce eft on ellenbeorh.

+[n] Ego Offa rex Merciorum hanc donacionem confirmans propria manu signum crucis Christi infixi.
+ Ego Iambertus archiepiscopus et rector catholice ecclesie consensi et subscripsi.[q]
+ Signum manus Kynedrithe regine.
+ Signum manus Egfridi filii regis.
+ Signum manus Brordan ducis.
+ Signum manus Ædeleardi principis.
+ Signum manus Binnan.
+ Signum manus Berhtuualdi.
+ Signum manus Ædbaldi.

[a] Merciorum rex N [b] quinto N [c] Ædelnotho F; Ethelnoto H
[d] ? *Supply* monasterii [e] duorum F, H [f] Beauuesfeld H
[g] ? *For* certis *or* certissimis; aliis H [h] capree N; ?*error for* carre (see commentary)
[i] Seanling H [j] siue N [k] nostram F [l] H *adds* nostra [m] F *ends here*
[n] . . . [n] *Omitted* H [o] *Corrupt* (*see commentary*)
[p] ? *For* norþeƿest, ðan (*see commentary*) [q] H *ends here*

14 is one of the least satisfactory charters in the archive. In its present form it is certainly not authentic. No genuine Anglo-Saxon charter of this date would include a vernacular boundary clause, so this feature at least would have to be a later addition, and there are difficulties with the implied date. In the two cartulary texts the charter is said to have been issued in the first year of Offa's reign (757–8), while the later Trinity Hall manuscript dates it to Offa's fifth year (761–2). Neither regnal year is compatible with the subscription of Archbishop Jænberht, who was consecrated in February 765; there is also a discrepancy with the dates of Abbot Æthelnoth, who was probably not elected until 764 and may not have been blessed until 766 (see Appendix 4). Kemble, who was using Elmham's text, suggested the insertion of *decimo* before *quinto*, which would shift the charter to Offa's fifteenth year (771–2). But in the other cases where the dating information in Elmham's texts differs from that in the cartulary copies, it is the latter which seem to preserve the earlier reading, apparently because Elmham's sources have been contaminated (see **10**, **13**, **53**; and discussion, pp. xcvi–cv). There seems no reason in this case to prefer Elmham's reading when it would require emendation. We might try to emend the regnal year in the cartulary texts, but it seems a futile exercise. It is easier to accept that in its present form the text of **14** is probably a fabrication and that its regnal year may have been faulty from the beginning. It may be significant that the

charter-list in PRO E 164/27 (see Appendix 2, and pp. xlvi, lii) does not mention
14; the only other direct grant to the monastery which is omitted from the list is 6,
about whose authenticity there is also some suspicion.

A charter of Offa certainly seems to underlie the extant text, but it was probably
not a document in favour of the abbot of St Augustine's. The verbal invocation is
one of the most common formulas in Anglo-Saxon diplomas; its use in a Kentish
document of this period would reflect Mercian influence (see also 13, 53 and S 105).
Offa is given the modest royal style that he has in the vast majority of his authentic
charters. The inclusion of dating information in the form of a regnal year after the
superscription could also be a contemporary feature (compare 15, 53, S 153. 157;
and see also 6, 40, 42, 46); the paired dispositive verbs would also be acceptable in
a Kentish charter of this date. The reference to the beneficiary presents difficulties;
presumably the word *monasterii* has fallen out (or there was not room for the
fabricator to insert it). The use of the double dedication is interesting; although the
monastery is usually referred to as St Peter's in this period, two charters of 762
mention both Peter and Paul (11, 12). The remainder of the dispositive clause
contains formulation which certainly depends upon a contemporary model, but the
strong possibility of interference is signalled by the change from the third to the
second person in the statement of powers. The phrase *cum ceteris terminibus* probably
represents a misunderstanding of *cum certis* (or *certissimis*) *terminibus*; compare
S 31, 37 (and see S 35, 123, 125). The statement of powers and the details of
appurtenances have been combined; for the wording of the former, see S 37, 125.
The permission for the beneficiary to alienate the land after his death would be more
appropriate in a grant to a layman. The general statement about appurtenances
includes the word *bonis*, also found in this context in S 39 from 805. This is followed
by a specific reference to pasture-rights in the king's wood (compare S 186, 286, 296,
328), and then by the curious phrase *unius capre licentiam* in connection with the
wood called *Saenling* (Singledge in Coldred parish). This appears to be a corruption
of *unius carre licentiam* (a copyist must have misread Insular *r*), and to refer to the
right to take one cart (*carra*, an occasional form of *carrus*) into the wood for the
purpose of gathering fuel. 13 refers to a similar privilege in Singledge, this time
attached to an estate at Mongeham; see the commentary to that charter for
other references to wood-gathering rights. The sanction in 14 is acceptable as a
contemporary formula (compare S 30, 37, 39, 108, 123, 125, 129), and the witness-list
certainly derives from a genuine document. The subscription of Archbishop Jænberht
provides the formal dating limits for the model (765 × 792). The inclusion of the
queen's subscription suggests that the witness-list was not compiled before c. 770;
her subscriptions are first found in five spurious or dubious charters of 770 and 774
(S 59–60, 104, 110–11); from the late 770s she attests quite regularly (S 112, 116–18,
120–5, 127, 129, 133). Ecgfrith's subscriptions are generally confined to the last
eleven years of his father's reign, beginning in 785 with S 123; he does make a much
earlier appearance in two charters dated 770 (S 59, 60), but neither of these documents
is authentic. His style here perhaps suggests that the witness-list was compiled before
his consecration as king in 787, although there are instances in charters issued after
that date where he is still styled *filius regis*. The subscriptions of this group of
ealdormen would be most compatible with a date in the later part of Offa's reign
(compare S 114, 123, 125, 1430 etc.).

This analysis suggests that **14** is not a genuine charter of Offa with an inserted boundary clause and a miscopied date. The peculiarities of the present text are most easily explained if it is understood to be a fabrication based on a genuine charter of Offa, probably dating from the later part of his reign and not originally in favour of Abbot Æthelnoth. The forger contributed the erroneous regnal year and the boundary clause, and reworked the dispositive section to a certain extent; the omissions and misreadings may have crept in at this stage. It is not clear whether the forger's model concerned the same estate; the clumsy insertion of the assessment into the formulaic phrase *terram iuris mei* and the use of hides rather than sulungs suggests that this detail at least was an addition.

Bewesfeld survived into the early modern period as Beauxfield, but already by Hasted's day the name was being supplanted by Whitfield (*History*, ix. 394); it is now preserved only as a street-name in the north-eastern part of Whitfield. The first element appears to be a personal name *Beaw*, also occurring in the name of Bewsborough Hundred, in which Beauxfield was physically located (although it was treated as part of the manor of Northbourne in Cornilo hundred). The eponymous Bewsborough also seems to have lain in what is now Whitfield, where it is again represented in street-names; it appears to have been a tumulus situated at a cross-roads (see Wallenberg, *Place-Names of Kent*, pp. 558–9). The second element in *Bewesfeld* is *feld*, which is usually associated with open areas in wooded districts (*DEPN*, p. 177); Beauxfield lay just east of the wood at *Sænling* (Singledge) and also south-east of a formerly wooded area reflected in surviving place-names such as Sibertswold (see **27, 30**), while to the south were the wooded slopes around Temple Ewell. In 1086 a tenant of St Augustine's held land at Beauxfield assessed at one sulung (two ploughs), which would be the approximate equivalent of the two hides of the charter (GDB 12v; for the size of the sulung see pp. lxxviii–lxxix). This land was reckoned as part of the abbey's great manor of Northbourne, from which it is separated by about five miles. The connection between Northbourne and Beauxfield presumably goes back to the pre-Conquest period, but **14** is unlikely to be a trustworthy guide to the date of acquisition.

The vernacular boundary-clause was probably compiled in the tenth century or later (for boundary-clauses in Kentish charters see pp. lxxix–lxxx). The introduction to the clause is unusual and difficult, perhaps corrupt; the correct reading of the central section may be *sutulust angedere*, suggesting a possible translation: 'This is the clearest collection (?) to Beauxfield'. This form of wording is not used in the introduction to any other Anglo-Saxon boundary-clause. The spelling of the place-name here (*Beasfeld*) is probably late (compare the forms in Wallenberg, *KPN*, p. 52). The beginning of the boundary clause itself seems slightly corrupt. Elmham provided his own Latin translation of the clause (Hardwick, *Elmham*, p. 332), which shows that he understood *on norþe weasðan* to mean *ab occidentali aquilone*; if this is correct, it would seem that *west* has been run together with a following *ðan*. The survey would therefore begin in the north-west, and would then proceed eastwards. The first boundary mark is *ellenbeorge*, 'elder-tree hill or tumulus' (*ellen, beorg*). Wallenberg (*Place-Names of Kent*, pp. 561–2) suggests that this may be the place in Temple Ewell later known as Lymborough Bottom, but admits that the identification has little to recommend it; moreover, the boundary-mark should lie further north. After the reference to *ellenbeorge* a measure of distance is provided. This is not the kind of detail that was usually included in an Anglo-Saxon boundary-clause, unless it related to a town-property where dimensions were more important (see 12). Fifteen yards on from *ellenbeorge*, the boundary veered south along *moulman strecte* as far as 'the land's end'. The first element of *moulman* is perhaps *mul*, but the word may be corrupt; this street-name is not found elsewhere. The boundary then turned west along *æpille mearce* (OE *æwiell*, 'spring, source of a river', preserved in Temple Ewell; *mearc*, 'boundary') to a 'living hedge', which it followed south to 'the broad hedge way'. The next boundary-mark is *cingdene*, where the first element is *cyning*, 'king', and the second *denu*, 'valley'. The survey concludes by following 'the abbot's boundary' back to *ellenbeorg*. This may be a reference to a St Augustine's estate at Wadholt, north-west of Whitfield, where the abbey had a manor assessed at a sulung in 1086 (GDB 12v); the date at which Wadholt came into the abbot's hands is unknown, although it was apparently a pre-Conquest possession. The place-name (*wad*, 'woad', and *holt*, 'wood') implies that it was once wooded, and the Domesday entry in fact has the note *ibi silua minuta* (perhaps meaning underwood rather than timber). This would contrast with the neighbouring cleared area or *feld* around Beauxfield.

15

Offa, king of the Mercians, confirms the privileges granted to the churches of Kent by Kings Wihtred and Æthelbald, and grants exemption from all dues and services to certain Kentish monasteries. [? A.D. 792]

F. BL Cotton Julius D. ii, 105v–106r: copy, s. xiii[1]
  No rubric
H. PRO E 164/27, 25rv: copy, s. xiii
  Rubric: Offa rex de libertate ecclesiarum.
Ed.: Birch 848 from F
Listed: Sawyer 134
Edited from F and H

In nomine Iesu Christi saluatoris mundi. Ego Offa rex Merciorum, anno regni mei a Deo concessi .xxxv.,[a] collecta sinodo in loco qui dicitur Clofeshog, cum mihi Deus omnipotens pro sua pietate plus triumphauit in regnum quam antecessoribus meis propinquis, mihi quoque ad[b] augmentum sceptrum regale et gubernacula Cantpariorum[c] concessit, tunc placuit mihi ex petitione [d]et suasione[d] Æþelheardi[e] archiepiscopi necnon cum licentia et consensu omnium episcoporum ac principum meorum, pro honore et[b] amore omnipotentis Dei et intercessione beati patris Augustini seu etiam pro stabilitate regni Merciorum, eandem libertatem ecclesiis Dei intra Cantiam constitutis a nobis iterari atque confirmari fieri condecet, sicut antea fuerat a Þyhtredo[f] rege concessum et constitutum. Iterumque eodem modo[b] ab Æðelbaldo[g] rege in[h] sinodo munitum repperimus. Item ego Offa rex Merciorum libero hec monasteria quorum nomina hic sunt subternotata ab omni grauitate regalium censuum^i seu^b secularium seruitutum uel etiam^b aliorum^j inferiorum personarum, neque in refectione et alimonia regis, nec in operibus ad regales uillulas, nec in susceptione alicuius, id est fæstincmenn,^{k} nec canes aut accipitres,^{l} neque equos uenatoresue et eorum ductores, siue in pascuis camporum siluarumque ab aliquo honere usquam grauentur, nisi expeditione intra Cantiam contra paganos marinos cum classis^m migrantibus uel in australes Saxones si necessitas cogit ac pontis constructionem et arcis munitionem contra paganos iterumque intra fines Cantpariorum,^{c} sed et hec est mea^n petitio atque doctrina ut hec tria consentiatis,^{o} que doceo ut eo stabilior hec mea libertas permaneat, si uestra spontanea uoluntate hoc non negatis.

^{a} .xxv. H ^{b} Omitted H ^{c} Cantuariorum H ^{d}...^{d} Omitted H ^{e} Athellardi H
^{f} Withredo H ^{g} Eadbaldo H ^{h} Omitted F ^{i} sensuum H ^{j} For aliarum
^{k} rastincmen H ^{l} ancipites H ^{m} For classibus ^{n} in ea F ^{o} concenseatis H

This privilege of Offa in favour of the churches and monasteries of Kent survives only in the St Augustine's archive, where it was transmitted alongside a similar privilege of Wihtred (**10**). There are copies in two of the thirteenth-century cartularies, but Elmham does not seem to have known this document. There is no trace of it in the Christ Church archive. This limited transmission is not necessarily a reason to suspect the authenticity of the text. The probable destruction of the Christ Church muniments at the end of the eighth century (see Brooks, *Church of Canterbury*, p. 121) would have meant the loss of any copy of Offa's privilege in the archiepiscopal archive; preservation of the text at Christ Church would then have depended upon its inheritance from the archives of Lyminge and Reculver (which is probably the route by which a copy of **10** entered the Christ Church archive). Elmham's ignorance of the privilege is more surprising, but it could be a simple oversight or it could be connected with the unfinished state of his history, which breaks off at the beginning of the ninth century. Elmham's chronological table does not mention Offa's privilege, but it also omits **10**, the text of which is provided in the history.

The text of **15**, as preserved in the thirteenth-century cartularies, is now deficient. It lacks a witness-list, and it also has an internal reference to a list of monasteries which is now missing. It appears that the compilers of BL Cotton Julius D. ii and PRO E 164/27 were dependent upon a version of the text which had already been abbreviated in this way. In MS F the document is dated to the thirty-fifth year of Offa's reign, which would indicate an incarnation date of 791–2 and is thus just compatible with the reference in the text to Archbishop Æthelheard; he was appointed in 792, although he was technically archbishop-elect until he was consecrated on 21 July 793. The date is significant, because the privilege would seem to have been issued soon after the death of Archbishop Jaenberht, who had attracted Offa's enmity, perhaps because he had supported a Kentish revolt (see Brooks, *Church of Canterbury*, pp. 114–17, and the comment by Offa's successor, Coenwulf, in a letter to Pope Leo III: Whitelock, *EHD*, no. 204). Offa may have been unwilling to ratify the privileges of the Kentish churches during Jænberht's lifetime. Archbishop Æthelheard seems to have been Offa's nominee (Brooks, *Church of Canterbury*, p. 120), which probably led the Mercian king to look more kindly on the issue. In the light of Offa's difficulties with Kent before 792, a passage near the beginning of the document has added relevance. Here Offa appears to boast of the greatness of his royal power, especially in regard to Kent (literally, 'when Almighty God . . . triumphed for me more in the kingdom than for my predecessors, and also granted to me as an increase the royal sceptre and government of the men of Kent'). Although Offa had deposed the local kings and had ruled Kent directly since at least 785 (see S 123), it was probably only after Jænberht's death that he really felt himself master of the kingdom. **15** was issued at a *Clofesho* synod; Offa and his successors usually dealt with Kentish affairs at synodal meetings held outside Kent (see pp. xci–xcii).

In **15** Offa pledges to confirm and uphold the *libertas* which had been granted to the churches of Kent by King Wihtred. This is almost certainly a reference to **10**, in which Wihtred states that the Kentish churches were to be free of all liability to royal dues and services. Offa goes on to refer to a previous confirmation by King Æthelbald *in sinodo*; if genuine, it most likely refers to a confirmation of Wihtred's privilege at a subsequent Southumbrian synod over which King Æthelbald presided, rather than a specific privilege in the name of Æthelbald himself, for there is no reason to believe that Æthelbald would ever have been in a position to exempt Kentish churches from royal dues and services, other than those levied on their trading ships at the Mercian port of London (see **49, 50, 51** and S 88). (An alternative, and uncomfortable possibility is that the reference to a grant of liberty by Wihtred and its confirmation by Æthelbald could be connected with two spurious privileges in the names of those kings, S 22 and 90. These were probably forged at Canterbury in the first quarter of the ninth century, to aid Archbishop Wulfred in his struggle with King Coenwulf over control of the Kentish royal minsters: see Brooks, *Church of Canterbury*, pp. 191–7. But it does seem unlikely that the draftsman of **15** was referring to S 22 and 90, which are more concerned with issues of lordship than with exemption from dues and services. It may be that the references in **15** to privileges of Wihtred and Æthelbald played some part in inspiring the forgery of S 22 and 90.)

15 seems to fall into two sections. In the first part Offa confirms the *libertas* granted by Wihtred, which was to apply to all the Kentish churches. He goes on to refer to a grant of immunity from a number of particular dues and services owed to the king and his household (these include the obligation to entertain the king, to work on royal vills, and to offer hospitality to *fæstingmen* (a class of royal agents) and to various hunting beasts and their keepers); this exemption was apparently to apply only to certain individual minsters, which were originally named in the document. Very similar immunity clauses, with specific references to the obligation of entertaining the king and his followers, appear in a series of ninth-century charters issued by Mercian kings, mostly in favour of religious houses and ecclesiastical beneficiaries (S 186, 188, 190, 197, 198, 1271 etc.). The earliest of these parallels is in S 186 from 822, which is some thirty years later than the date of **15**. This could be interpreted as evidence that **15** in its present state is not contemporary, but Brooks (1971, p. 79 n. 2) suggests instead that this formula in Offa's privilege should be seen as anticipating the formulation of the ninth-century charters. **15** appears to be concerned with lifting this burden of royal taxes and hospitality from a number of specific minsters; their names have been lost, but it seems possible that these were houses which Offa had taken over as his personal property after the conquest of Kent. We know that Offa was interested in acquiring and founding minsters which he dedicated to St Peter, and which he treated as part of his family inheritance (see Levison, *England and the Continent*, pp. 29–31; Whitelock, *EHD*, no. 79; S 158 and 1435). Coenwulf also added minsters in conquered territories to his personal possessions, and both he and Offa acquired papal privileges guaranteeing their rights over family minsters (see Brooks, *Church of Canterbury*, pp. 187–91). Churches which were regarded as hereditary property are likely to have owed certain services and payments to their owners, even when church lands in general were immune from such burdens; a particular service exacted from hereditary minsters is likely to have been the duty to receive and feed their lord, be he king or nobleman, with his entourage, on a regular basis. 15 may have had a double purpose: to confirm the liberty of the Kentish churches in general, and to confirm the immunity from certain dues and services, particularly hospitality, of the individual Kentish minsters which he had come under Offa's personal lordship.

The details of exemption are followed by a clause explicitly excluding from the immunity certain military obligations: namely, military service within Kent against the Vikings (and in Sussex if necessary), and the construction of bridges and fortifications. This clause contains the earliest evidence for Viking attacks on the Kent coast; only twelve years later these had become so serious that the nuns of Lyminge had to be given a refuge within the walls of Canterbury (S 160). From 811 the immunity clauses of Kentish charters mention the Vikings as a present threat (S 168, 1264, 177, 186). Offa asks the minsters to agree to these liabilities, perhaps applying undue pressure with his observation that the immunity will be more stable if they agree. This is the earliest Kentish document to include a clause reserving military obligations, and it may mark the imposition of some or all of these requirements on Kent for the first time (see further Brooks 1971, especially pp. 79–80). In Mercia by this date these three burdens already seem to have been obligatory, and to have applied to church lands. The crucial document in this respect seems to be S 92 (A.D. 749), which set out the immunities of the Mercian churches but specified that they were to be liable to the three military burdens; this seems to have been a codification of current practice in Mercia.

16

Coenwulf, king of the Mercians, and Cuthred, king of Kent, grant twenty sulungs (aratra) at West Lenham, Kent, and thirteen swine-pastures in the Weald to their kinsman Eanberht. [? A.D. 804]

F. BL Cotton Julius D. ii, 93v: copy, s. xiii[1]
  Rubric: Kenewlf rex de Lenheam .xxx.
N. Cambridge, Trinity Hall, I, 73rv: copy s. xv[1]
  Rubric: Carta Kenwlphi regis de Westrelenaham.
Ed.: a. Kemble 187 from N

b. Hardwick, *Elmham*, pp. 341–3, from N
c. Birch 316 from Kemble and BL Harley 686, a copy of N
Listed: Sawyer 159
Edited from F and N

In nomine redemptoris mundi. Ego Kenwlf[n] gratia Dei rex Merciorum et Cuðred[b] rex Cantie diuino ducti amore et consanguinitatis[c] nostro communi propinquo ⟨Eanberto⟩[d] eterna donatione concedimus terram .xx.[e] aratrorum in prouincia Cantie in loco qui uocatur Sepestralenham,[f] cum omnibus scilicet rebus ad eam recte et rite pertinentibus, cum campis, siluis, pratis, pascuis, aquis, iuxta antiquos terminos sicut antecessores eius comites habuerunt, et tresdecim[g] denberende[h] on Andrede ad illam terram antiquo iure pertinentia.[i] Primum scilicet est Mæpulterhirst,[j] secundum[k] Friððingden, tercium Friðesleah, quartum Cumbden, quintum Suattingden,[l] sextum Þiflahirst,[m] septimum alter Mapulterhirst,[j] octauum Babbingden, nonum alter Babbingden, decimum tertia Babbingden, undecimum Tunlafahirst,[n] duodecimum Plussingherst, tercium decimum Friðæleah et Færeden.[o] Sub hac quoque conditione hanc terram[p] predicto Eanberto[q] donabimus uti quamdiu uiuat ipse[r] feliciter perfruatur et post eius obitum cuicumque uoluerit liberum arbitrium habeat [s]ad donandum illam terram inperpetuum possidendam.[s] Et ab omni seculari seruitio regum seu principum uel etiam prefectorum concedimus predictam terram liberam esse inperpetuum, preter[t] his tribus tantummodo rebus, id est expeditione et pontis instructione et arcis munitione. Si quis uero regum uel principum seu[u] prefectorum hanc libertatem infringere uoluerit, sciat se separatum esse in die iudicii a consortio sanctorum nisi digne emendauerit ante reatum suum. Actum est anno aduentus Domini .dccciiii., indictione .xii. et regni regis Coeneuulfi[v] anno .viii. Testium qui hanc predictam donationem consentientes signo[w] sancte crucis munierunt exprimuntur nomina.

+[x] Coeneuulf[y] rex dabo mercedem.[z]
+ Wlfredus archiepiscopus.
+ Cealþard dux.
Wlfheard prepositus.
+ Æðrið regina.
+ Kynhelm dux.
+ Bearnhard prepositus.
+ Cudreð rex.
+ Tiduulf dux.
+ Swyðun comes.
+ Alduulf episcopus.

+ Þicga dux.
+ Sigheard comes.
+ Deneberth episcopus.
+ Ædilhæh comes.
+ Cyga comes.
+ Heaberth dux.
+ Osuulf comes.
+ Beartnoð comes.
+ Beornoð dux.
+ Aedred prepositus.

a Coneuulf F   *b* Cuthreð N   *c* consanguinitatis F, N; *for* consanguinitate
d *Supplied* (*see commentary*); Þernoðo abbati F; Cunredo abbati N   *e* uiginti N
f se þestraleanham F   *g* .xiii. F   *h* OE denbær (pl. denberende), 'swine-pasture'
i *The accusative is used here because the swine-pastures are considered an extension of the*
main grant (*see commentary and compare* 13)   *j* Mepulterhirst F
k *From here F has numerals instead of ordinals*   *l* Suatigden F   *m* Piflahirst F
n Tunlafahyrst F   *o* Fereden F   *p* *Omitted* F   *q* Cunredo N   *r* *Omitted* N
s ... *s* inperpetuum habeat inperpetuum F   *t* exceptis N   *u* se N   *v* nostri N
w et signo F   *x* F *omits cross*   *y* Keneuulf N   *z* F *ends here*

16 provides an interesting demonstration of the repeated emendation of an early
charter by post-Conquest scholars at St Augustine's. In Elmham's text (MS N) King
Coenwulf of Mercia and his brother Cuthred, whom he had made king of Kent,
grant twenty sulungs at Lenham to their common kinsman, Cunred, abbot of St
Augustine's. The relationship seems to be underlined by the alliterating initial of
their names. But in the earlier MS F the charter is said to be in favour of Abbot
Wernoth, while a second reference to the beneficiary in the statement of powers
names a certain Eanberht. This version of the charter seems to indicate that the
original beneficiary was Eanberht, presumably a layman, and that Abbot Wernoth's
name had been substituted for his in order to create a direct grant to the monastery;
the revisor of the text carelessly failed to alter the second reference to the beneficiary,
thus preserving Eanberht's name. A later charter in the archive (**21**), apparently
concerning the same estate at Lenham and in favour of an ealdorman, has been
tampered with in a similar way, for the text in MS F again has Abbot Wernoth's
name substituted for that of the original beneficiary. In both these cases Wernoth's
name may have been chosen by the revisor because he was the beneficiary of a third
Lenham charter, this time covering a separate property (**19**).

Elmham's version of the charter still requires explanation. Here Abbot Cunred is
named in both references to the beneficiary. Cunred occurs in the abbatial lists, and
the chronological table prefixed to Elmham's history gives his period of office as 803
to 822, which is consistent with the apparent date of this charter (although some
dates attached to the list of abbots can be shown to be fictional, and the ninth
century poses particular problems: see Appendix 4). It might seem preferable to
ignore the conflicting evidence of the text in MS F, and to accept Abbot Cunred as
the original beneficiary of the charter. But that would be to ignore the considerable

amount of evidence that some of the documents available to Elmham had been tampered with because they did not agree with prevailing notions of chronology (see pp. xcvi–cv). In the case of **16** it could be suggested that the version of the text available to Elmham (or his immediate predecessors) was that found in MS F, where the references to the beneficiaries are inconsistent, and the naming of Wernoth as abbot would seem incompatible with the current understanding of the chronology of the early abbots. If this were so, Elmham or, more probably, an earlier scholar, may have simply replaced the conflicting references to Wernoth and Eanberht with a simple and consistent reference to Cunred, the appropriate abbot for the date of the charter.

It seems best to assume that the original beneficiary was Eanberht, since otherwise there could be no explanation for the presence of his name in the text in MS F. The supposition that **16** was in favour of a layman, rather than an abbot of St Augustine's, is also easier to reconcile with the fact that **21** seems to be a grant of the same estate in 850, this time to an ealdorman. Eanberht can be tentatively identified with the *dux* of that name who attended a synod in London in 811 and there attested two Kentish charters (S 165, 168) dealing with estates near Rochester and Faversham located less than fifteen miles from Lenham (see also S 167).

In addition to the difficulty with the beneficiary, there are two other sections of the charter which seem to show emendation or rewriting of the text. The first is the very prominent list of thirteen dens in the Weald, all of them meticulously numbered. Later in the ninth century Kentish charters sometimes include within the dispositive section lists of named swine-pastures appurtenant to the estate concerned (see S 173, 293, 331, 332). S 173 from 814, an apparent original, mentions ten swine-pastures in a list which is superficially comparable to that in **16**. But the presentation of the material in **16** seems less than satisfactory; the careful numbering is not paralleled elsewhere. It is also instructive to compare the list of dens here with that in **21**, where many of them recur. In the later charter the dens are given in a simple list, with a brief introduction comparable to that in other contemporary charters. Whereas in **16** place-names are repeated if there was more than one appurtenant swine-pasture in a particular place, in **21** such repetition is avoided by a brief statement that there were so many dens in one place: for instance, three dens at Maplehurst. The evidence is again inconclusive, but there do seem to be grounds for suspecting that the list of dens in **16** has been reworked or even added from another source. The identification of the dens is considered below.

The other section of the charter which indicates that the text may have been reworked is the witness-list. At present the order of the subscriptions is confused, with laymen mingling indiscriminately with bishops. Usually such confusion in a witness-list occurs when a copyist misunderstands the layout of subscriptions arranged in columns. But the witness-list here has a more considerable problem than its confused order. The charter is dated to the incarnation year 804, and this is compatible with the given indiction and the reference to Coenwulf's regnal year. Yet among the witnesses is Archbishop Wulfred, who was elected in July 805 and probably consecrated in October of the same year (Brooks, *Church of Canterbury*, p. 132, n. 7). Wulfred could not have attested a charter of 804, and the occurrence of his name here is a considerable difficulty. A possible explanation is suggested by comparison with a Rochester charter of 801 (S 157), also issued jointly by Coenwulf and Cuthred.

This has a double witness-list; the first section consists of the witnesses to the original grant (which probably took place in Mercia), while the second part relates to a confirmation of the charter in Canterbury later in the year by Archbishop Æthelheard and a number of Kentish noblemen. It is possible that the witness-list in **16** originally had a similar double layout, which has been concealed by the mutilation of the witness-list (see also S 164).

Analysis of the witnesses seems to bear out this hypothesis. These include Coenwulf himself, his wife Ælfthryth and his son Cynehelm; the queen attests several charters between 808 and 821, and there is no reason to believe that she would not have subscribed a charter of 804, while Cynehelm's name occurs in witness-lists between *c.* 800 and 811. The episcopal witnesses are Archbishop Wulfred, with Aldwulf of Lichfield (appointed between 799 and 801, died between 814 and 816) and Deneberht of Worcester (appointed *c.* 800, died in 822). There are five men styled *dux*, apart from Cynehelm. Four of these regularly attest alongside Coenwulf, in charters dealing with land in both Mercia and Kent: Ceolweard between 803 and 811; Wicgga between 798 and 805; Heahberht between 798 and 808; and Beornnoth between 798 and 825. The fifth *dux*, Tidwulf, witnesses two charters from 805 (S 40, 161); both deal with land in Kent, but were issued in a Mercian synod at *Aclea*. The likelihood is that the five *duces* who attest **16** were all Mercians, with no special Kentish connections. By contrast, the six men styled *comes* were probably Kentish noblemen (see S 161 for a similar contrast between Mercian *duces* and Kentish *comites*). Four of these *comites* attest Kentish charters of the period in a context which suggests that they were part of Cuthred's retinue: Swithhun (S 39), Sigeheard (S 1259, 164), Oswulf (S 157, 1259, 39, 41) and Beorhtnoth (S 1259, 39, 41). In S 164 Sigeheard is among a number of men who are explicitly identified as *satrapes Cantuariorum*. The last components of the witness-list are three *prepositi*: Wulfheard, Beornheard and Æthred. The first of these seems to have been beneficiary of S 161 (A.D. 805), where he is said to have been the priest of Archbishop Æthelheard; he attested the *acta* of the 803 synod of *Clofesho* as part of the archbishop's retinue, and subscribed S 1259 and 1265 in association with the Christ Church community (in the second instance with the style *presbyter*). Beornheard *prepositus* attests S 1259 and 161, both from 805; he was also evidently a Kentish ecclesiastic. Æthred's subscription is not found in other charters of this period. The witness-list can therefore be divided into Mercians (the queen and ætheling, two bishops and five *duces*) and Kentishmen (the archbishop, six Kentish *comites* and three priests). If the second group witnessed the charter at a later date (as in the case of S 157), perhaps in Canterbury itself, this could explain the presence of the newly elected or newly consecrated Archbishop Wulfred.

The two major problems with **16**, the list of dens and the subscription of Archbishop Wulfred, can therefore be explained on the assumption that the charter was reworked and repeatedly recopied at a later date, which would be consistent with the indications that the name of the beneficiary was changed on more than one occasion. In general, the formulation of the charter otherwise seems consistent with the given date. The text begins with a brief verbal invocation also found in S 155, an original Canterbury charter from 799; as usual in Kentish charters of this date there is no proem. The two brothers are presented as joint-donors, as in S 160 from 804 and S 161 from the following year; Cuthred appears as the junior partner in S 157 (A.D. 801), while elsewhere he acts alone but with Coenwulf's consent (S 39, 40, 41). The description of the beneficiary in **16** as *nostro communi propinquo* recalls the corresponding phrase in S 157 (*nostro in commune ministro*), while the dispositive verb *concedimus* echoes *concessimus* in S 160. Established Kentish formulation is used for the reference to the land and its assessment, while the stated location of the estate in the 'province' of Kent is typical of Mercian charters dealing with land in the formerly independent kingdom (compare, for instance, S 41). The formula covering the general appurtenances of the estate concludes with a reference to the ancient boundaries, which are to be those held by *antecessores eius comites*. This last detail strongly supports the thesis that the original beneficiary of this land-grant was a nobleman, apparently one with ancestral Kentish connections. It is probably significant that there is a similar formula in S 125 (A.D. 786), which relates to an extensive land-grant to two individuals who may also have been of Kentish noble stock.

After the list of dens, which may not have been a feature of the original charter, the charter continues with a statement of powers, giving the beneficiary full right of posthumous bequest, which again is more appropriate in a grant to a layman than in one to the head of a religious house (the corruption of this clause in MS F may be due to recognition of this fact). There follows an immunity clause, complete with the reservation of the three common burdens. Proper immunity clauses first appear in Kentish land-charters in the first decade of the ninth century; there are early examples in S 41 and 161. In Mercia they occur from a slightly earlier date; there is a full-blown example of an immunity clause with a reservation clause in S 139, an original from the last few years of Offa's reign in favour of a Mercian ealdorman. The wording of the immunity clause in **16** seems acceptable, but the appearance of a reservation clause causes more difficulty, since no other Kentish charter of any reputation includes such a formula until 811 (see discussion in Brooks 1971, pp. 79–80, which does not refer to this charter). However, we learn from **15** that the three military obligations had been imposed on Kent before the end of Offa's reign; it was therefore theoretically possible for them to be reserved in a charter of 804. The Kentish draftsman of **16** could have been influenced by Mercian charters of this period, which did usually include a reservation clause, especially if the original conveyance of the Lenham estate took place in Mercia. For comparison, it is possible to point to the endorsement added to a Middlesex charter *c.* 800 (S 106), which explicitly reserves the military obligations. It is probably also significant that the wording of the reservation clause in **16** resembles that in S 177, an original from 814 and one of the earliest Kentish charters to include such a formula. The reservation clause in **16** can probably be accepted as part of the original charter. The following sanction also seems to be expressed in contemporary language; it reappears almost verbatim in S 173 (A.D. 814): see also S 123, 125, 39. The dating clause departs from the earlier Kentish pattern by inserting a verb after *Actum*; we find the same development in S 163, an original charter from 808. The phrase introducing the witness-list is similar to that in S 1259, a Canterbury charter from 805. It is usual at this date for all witnesses (or at least the more important ones) to be given full subscriptions, but the provision of simple names in **16** is paralleled in S 157 (the Canterbury section) and S 40, both from around the same date.

Diplomatic analysis therefore suggests that a genuine charter of the early ninth century underlies the present text of **16**. This was probably in favour of a royal kinsman named Eanberht. The initial land-grant may have been made in Mercia in 804 and witnessed there by Coenwulf, his family, two Mercian bishops and five Mercian ealdormen. This charter was perhaps later confirmed in Canterbury, by King Cuthred, Archbishop Wulfred, six Kentish noblemen and three Kentish clerics; the theory of a later confirmation could explain the apparently anachronistic subscription of the archbishop. At some stage the charter entered the archive of St Augustine's, and in the post-Conquest period it was transformed into a charter in favour of Abbot Wernoth and thus a direct grant to the abbey. In the course of this transformation the double witness-list may have been corrupted, and the list of thirteen dens was perhaps inserted or rewritten. At a later stage the name of the beneficiary seems to have been altered a second time, with the name of Abbot Cunred being substituted, probably by a scholar concerned with chronology and the dates of the abbots. The witness-list may have been further confused at this stage.

Lenham is situated on the southern slopes of the North Downs, about sixteen miles west of Canterbury. It is probably a very ancient settlement, for it lies on the spring-line of Holmesdale and very close to the prehistoric Greenway (Everitt, *Continuity*, p. 49). Two other charters in the archive are concerned with land at Lenham. **19** records the grant of five sulungs there to Abbot Wernoth in 838; Sprott and Thorne identify this as East Lenham. Later King Æthelwulf granted forty hides at Lenham to Ealdorman Ealhhere (**21**, dated 850); like the present charter, this was subsequently converted into a direct grant to the abbey. **21** includes a brief boundary clause which shows that the forty hides were located at West Lenham. Since forty hides are roughly equivalent to twenty sulungs (see p. lxxviii n. 26), there seems to be a good chance that **16** and **21** refer to the same estate. The listed dens are very similar, although not entirely identical. In 1086 St Augustine's held a manor at West Lenham assessed at five and a half sulungs (GDB 12r). This is probably a beneficial assessment, for there is said to be land for eighteen ploughs. It seems possible that this manor represents some or all of the land covered by **16** and **21**; this West Lenham estate presumably passed into the abbey's possession at some point between 850 and 1066, along with its earlier documentation. It may have been partly broken up and alienated. The history of the estate at East Lenham is more complicated. A small manor of two sulungs at East Lenham was held from the Archbishop by one of his men-at-arms in 1086 (GDB 4v); an unsatisfactory charter of 961 (S 1212, an interpolated version of S 1211) credits Queen Eadgifu, widow of Edward the Elder, with the grant of Lenham and other estates to the archbishop and Christ Church. East Lenham remained an archiepiscopal possession in the later middle ages. The land granted to Abbot Wernoth in **19** would therefore appear to have been lost or alienated before 1066, and perhaps before the mid tenth century.

Most of the dens listed in **16** can be definitely or tentatively identified (see full discussion by Wallenberg, *KPN*, pp. 93–100; Witney, *Jutish Forest*, pp. 246–7). The Lenham swine-pastures seem to have been located in the area of the Weald between Staplehurst and Cranbrook, and thus about twelve miles south-west of Lenham itself. There are two dens at *Mæpulterhirst*, which is Maplehurst in Staplehurst (TQ 798420). *Friððingden* survives as Frittenden (TQ 815410), and *Friðesleah* is the hamlet of Friezley (TQ 773382). *Suattingden* is Swattenden in Cranbrook parish; *Tunlafahirst* is probably to be linked with Tolehurst Farm (TQ 787401); *Plussingherst* is Flishinghurst (TQ 760376). *Cumbden* may have been in the vicinity of Camden Hill

(TQ 792387). The first element of *Wiflahirst* is probably OE *wifel*, 'weevil', which also occurs in the place-name Wilsley, just north of Cranbrook (TQ 780370). Wallenberg suggests a link between *Babbingden*, the location of three swine-pastures, and Babb's Farm in the Cranbrook area. *Færeden* was perhaps connected with the lost *Ferhurst* in Frittenden. See Turner and Salter, *Black Book*, p. 253 (and also p. 275) for a thirteenth-century list of Lenham dependencies which has some similar names.

17

Wulfred, archbishop of Canterbury, supervises an exchange of land between Minster-in-Thanet and the abbot and community of St Augustine's.

A.D. 826 (27 March)

F. BL Cotton Julius D. ii, 105r: copy, s. xiii[1]
    No rubric
G. BL Cotton Claudius D. x, 183v: copy s. xiii[2]
    Rubric: Item donatio Wlfredi Dei gratia archiepiscopus de quodam terra que dicitur Dodingland in Thaneto.
I. Canterbury, D. & C., Lit. E. 19, 2rv: copy (probably of G), s. xiv[1]
    Rubric: Donacio Wlfridi archiepiscopi de Dodyngland in Thaneto.
Ed.: Birch 851 from F, 1337 from G
Listed: Sawyer 1267
Edited from F and G

In nomine Domini nostri Iesu Christi. Ego Wlfredus Christi gratia archiepiscopus eius[a] familie que in Thanet[b] australe nominatur monasterium aliquantulum territorium,[c] id est .vi.[d] iugerum in loco ab incolis ibidem nominatur Doddingland,[e] tribuimus Wernodo[f] uenerabili abbati atque sancti Augustini familie perpetualiter ad fruendum, pro uice mutua illius terre que ab indegenis Ealdanford illic appellatur, eiusdem mensure atque magnitudinis sicut et illa supradicta terra que dicitur Doddingland, id est mensure .vi. iugerum. Et isti termini circumiacentes sunt illius terrule Doddinglande, id est ab aquilone et ab oriente et ab austro [g]ab incolis ibidem nominatis Groenling et Feoðineg. Similiter etiam terrule predicte et Aldanforda hii sunt fines et termini, ab aquilonari[h] parte uia publica, ab oriente et austro agelli adiacent familie Sturensis, ab occasu finem Sturi fluminis habens. Et hec mutatio huius uicissitudinis de particulis agellorum istorum[i] facta[j] cum summo moderamine atque unanimitatis accommoditate et necessitate amborum dominorum familiarumque. Hoc modo constituere et diiudicare absque ullo obstaculo aut contradictione uel aliqua mutatione saluo iure et pace atque unanima concordia partium ambarum atque in nomine Domini nostri Iesu Christi et beati et sancti Petri benedictione perpetualiter perdurare germana et fraterna caritas decreuerunt*^k* atque decernerent hoc modo per omnia ut hic scriptum habetur. Ad huius cartule uicissitudinisque confirmationem testimoniumque unanimo ac bono consensu placuit cum crucis Christi uexillo sacrosanctis manibus partium ambarum in Domino Iesu Christo unanimiter ac perenniter roborare, annuente Christi gratia.*^l*

+ Ego Wlfred archiepiscopus hoc ad firmandum crucis Christi propriis manibus signum impono.

+ Ego Wernoð presbyter*^m* abbas hoc ad firmandum crucis Christi propriis manibus signum impono.

+ Ego Beornþine presbyter*^m* abbas consensi et subscripsi.

+ Ego Feolgeld presbyter*^m* abbas consensi et subscripsi.

+ Ego Ospulf*ⁿ* presbyter*^m* consensi et subscripsi.

Huius rei uicissitudinis actio facta est die uidelicet .vi. kalendarum Aprilis, ⟨anno⟩*^o* dominice incarnationis .dcccxxvi., indictione .iiii., regni uero Beornulfi regis Merciorum*^p* imperii eius anno .iii., in loco autem Dorouernensis ecclesie in communi congregacione et cetu presbiterorum et diaconorum dominisque eorum presentibus et quorum memoria et nomina hic scripta habentur.

^a? *For* illius   *^b* Tenet in F
^c 'some land of (belonging to) the community which is called Southminster in Thanet'
^d sex G   *^e* Doddincland F   *^f* Uuernðo F
^g? *Supply* terris qui ('those lands which are called by the local inhabitants')
^h aquilonali F   *ⁱ* istarum F   *^j*? *Supply* est *or* erat
^k germana et fraterna caritas *is treated as a plural* (*a noun may have been lost after* germana)   *^l* F *ends here*   *^m* pater G   *ⁿ* Ospulȝ G   *^o* Supplied for sense
^p Merc' G

17 is concerned with the exchange of two small estates between the communities of St Augustine's and Minster-in-Thanet. The abbot of St Augustine's is named in the text and his subscription appears in the (curtailed) witness-list. By contrast, Archbishop Wulfred acts as the lord of the Minster community, and its abbess is not mentioned. Wulfred had won at very great cost his right to act for Minster-in-Thanet in this way. As part of a general policy of promoting episcopal control over private minsters, he had challenged King Coenwulf's possession of Minster-in-Thanet and Reculver. He was hounded into exile for some years and finally forced into a humiliating compromise with Coenwulf in 821; he won recognition of his rights over the two minsters, but only by paying a large fine and surrendering a extensive estate. Even this was not a true success, since Coenwulf's daughter and heir, Cwoenthryth, who acted as abbess of Minster-in-Thanet, denied to the archbishop those rents and renders from the two minsters which should have been due to him as their lord. It was not until 825 that Cwoenthryth was forced to give way on this issue and to agree to pay compensation to Wulfred for his tribulations (see S 1436, and the

analysis by Brooks, *Church of Canterbury*, pp. 175–97). It is a mark of Wulfred's final triumph that in **17** he was able to act as the lord of Minster without reference to an abbess.

The collection of documents from Wulfred's time preserved in the Christ Church archive show that he was very actively engaged in land-transactions, both on his own account and on behalf of Christ Church. He seems to have been particularly concerned to concentrate his own holdings and those of the see into large estates, which would be easier to manage and defend than scattered properties. To this end he not only acquired new estates, but also arranged exchanges of land with the king and with the Christ Church community (see Brooks, *Church of Canterbury*, pp. 137–41). Wulfred's keen interest in land-acquisition and management may have been the spur to the transaction recorded in **17**, which adjusted the endowment of his community at Minster. As the result of the exchange, Minster acquired a small area of land at the mouth of the Stour, backed by a road, which may have been of some value for the community's trading activities. St Augustine's gain was of a corresponding piece of land in the north of Thanet, near Margate, where the community may have been building up a more substantial holding (see below).

There seems to be no reason to doubt that **17** is an authentic document, although its witness-list has presumably been abbreviated. The text certainly demonstrates the poor grasp of Latin composition which is characteristic of Canterbury draftsmen in the ninth century (Brooks, *Church of Canterbury*, pp. 164–74). The beginning of the dispositive section is especially confused, to the extent that the meaning is not entirely clear. The word *eius* is a stumbling-block; the scribe may have intended the sense of *illius* (unless he meant to indicate Wulfred's overlordship of the minster, in which case *mee* would be more appropriate). The plural dispositive verb sits uneasily. The clause identifying the present owner of *Doddingland* as 'Southminster' in Thanet is curiously constructed; for references to Minster-in-Thanet as 'Southminster' in this period, see p. xxviii n. 45. The grammatical construction of the two boundary clauses is very shaky indeed, while the sense of the following sentences is sometimes unclear (some words appear to be missing). In two of the subscriptions the formula *propria manu* has been rendered into the plural, which suggests a strange picture (the origin of the mistake may have been a formula such as that in **44**, in which the donor requests several witnesses to subscribe *propriis manibus*). The concluding dating clause is inept; the word *anno* has been omitted from the reference to the incarnation year (either by the draftsman or by a later copyist), the locative clause is awkward, and the draftsman entirely loses his grip at the end.

The slipshod construction is no doubt partly due to the fact that the transaction was not a common one, so that the draftsman was forced to compose the text himself, without recourse to standardized formulas. The closest affinities of the document are with the two contemporary charters which record exchanges of property between Wulfred and the Christ Church community (S 1264, 1266). In the former the dating clause is to be found after the witness-list, as in **17**, while the latter similarly incorporates boundary clauses for both exchanged properties. **17** is said to have been issued in the church at Canterbury, *in commune congregatione*; this wording is probably a reflection of the very close association between St Augustine's and Christ Church that existed in this period (see pp. xiii–xiv). The charter is dated 27 March 826, in the fourth indiction and the third year of King Beornwulf of Mercia. Calendar dates are common in Kentish charters of this period, perhaps because synodal diplomatic was such a potent influence at this time (see pp. xcii–xciii). The regnal year seems to be correct. Beornwulf's reign began in 823; the Anglo-Saxon Chronicle notes his death under the year 825, but the annal seems to cover more than one year and it is likely that he was killed in the course of 826. At about the same time Kent was invaded by the West Saxons, who drove out a King Baldred, probably a Mercian subking. **17** provides the last evidence for Mercian domination of Kent.

The witness-list now contains only five subscriptions, presumably the remnant of a much larger number; the dating clause indicates that the communities of both Christ Church and St Augustine's were present, including or as well as a number of priests and deacons. The first subscriptions are those of Wulfred himself and Wernoth, who was abbot of St Augustine's (see Appendix 4). Two other abbots, Beornwine and Feolgild, also attest, and the concluding subscription is that of a priest named Oswulf. The abbots were originally styled *presbyter abbas*, which is a common style in ninth-century charters (Brooks, *Church of Canterbury*, pp. 162–3); a copyist mistakenly transformed this to *pater abbas*. All three abbots attested S 1264 together in 811. Feolgild was already an abbot when he attended the 803 *Clofesho* synod as part of Æthelheard's retinue (BCS 312); he also subscribed S 1259 (A.D. 805), S 161 (A.D. 805), S 1436 (A.D. 825) and S 1500 (A.D. 805 × 832), and was, with Abbot Wernoth, a witness to the disputed will of Ealdorman Oswulf (S 1434, 1439). His death is mentioned in the Chronicle under 833; he may have been elected archbishop on Wulfred's death (Brooks, *Church of Canterbury*, pp. 142–3). Beornwine attests only S 1264 and the present charter. It is not possible to identify the Kentish houses over which Feolgild and Beornwine ruled. The priest Oswulf seems to have been a member of the Christ Church community; he attests S 1259, 1265, 1266 and 1436, and is probably the archdeacon of that name in a later charter (S 1269).

The six *iugera* which were acquired by St Augustine's as the result of this exchange were at *Doddingland* in Thanet, and were bounded to the north, east and south by *Groenling* and *Feothineg*. The only one of these three places for which an identification has been suggested is *Groenling*, which it is thought may be Garlinge, on the south-western outskirts of Margate (Wallenberg, *KPN*, p. 259; see *grenlinges mearce*, S 489). The suggested etymology for this is *gren-hlinc*, which is some way from the spelling in **17**. If the Garlinge identification is correct, then *Doddingland* may be the lost Dandelion or Dent-de-Lion, a minor place lying just west of Garlinge, now represented by Dent-de-Lion Farm (TR 336693) and a nearby street-name (for medieval references to this place-name, see Wallenberg, *Place-Names of Kent*, p. 595). *Doddingland* incorporates the Old English name Dodda or Dudda. *Feothineg* remains mysterious (see discussion by Wallenberg, *KPN*, pp. 271–2).

17 provides the first indication that St Augustine's was beginning to acquire land in Thanet. The size of the property acquired in the transaction is relatively small, which makes it probable that the community already owned land in the vicinity. In the late eleventh century the St Augustine's manor of Chislet on the mainland included six sulungs at Margate (Ballard, *Inquisition*, p. 17). This land was probably acquired before the community came into possession of the Minster property in Cnut's reign; if it had been a later acquisition, it would presumably have been added to the manor of Minster. **17** suggests that St Augustine's was already building up its holdings in the Margate area in the early ninth century. The monastery had also come into possession of an estate of fourteen hides at *Werburginland* in Thanet by the early tenth century (see **26**); this may have been located in the same area.

Minster acquired by the transaction in **17** an equivalent amount of land at *Ealdanford* on the mainland. To the west lay the 'end' of the River Stour, which is presumably a reference to the place where the Great Stour joined the Wantsum Channel. To the north was a road, while to the east and south was land belonging to the *familia Sturensis*. This last reference is perhaps to an otherwise unknown religious community associated with Sturry. The exact location of the land is difficult to ascertain, because the drainage of the Great Stour and Little Stour has greatly changed since the Wantsum silted up. The probability is that the land lay in the vicinity of the present villages of West and East Stourmouth, which are situated on a spit of dry land in the Stour marshes. The reference to a *via publica* in this area would then seem to support Cecil Knox's case for the existence of a Roman road linking Reculver and Richborough which crossed the Stour ('St Margaret's Bay and the Roman Roads from Richborough to Dover and Canterbury', *AC* liv (1941), pp. 35–40, at 38–40); this was dismissed by Ivan Margary, largely on the basis of the marshy terrain ('Notes on Roman Roads in Kent', *AC* lxi (1948), pp. 126–32, at 132). The first element of the place-name *Ealdanford* is probably the personal name *Ealda*, which also occurs in the Thanet place-name *Ealdingtune* mentioned in a charter of 944 (S 497). *Ealdingtune* seems to have been located in the area of Monkton, and may even have been the earlier name of Monkton itself, which lies directly opposite Stourmouth. This raises the possibility that the ford in question was over the Wantsum. Bede mentions that the Wantsum was three furlongs wide and passable (*transmeabilis*) in only two places (*HE* i. 25). It is not clear whether he means that it could be forded in only two places or whether there were only two crossing points in use. If there was an important ford between Stourmouth and Monkton, it would explain why there should be a *via publica* at Stourmouth. A small area at Stourmouth, close to a ford over the Wantsum, with access to the River Stour and to a road, must have been a desirable possession for Minster, especially if the community was still engaged in commercial activity at this time.

18

Ecgberht, king of the West Saxons, grants one sulung (aratrum) *on Scirdun to Ciaba, a* clericus *living in the monastery of St Peter.* A.D. 836

F. BL Cotton Julius D. ii, 132rv: copy, s. xiii[1]
   No rubric
H. PRO E 164/27, 81rv: copy, s. xiii
   Rubric: Carta Egberti de terra de Scirdune.
Ed.: Birch 852 from F
Listed: Sawyer 279
Edited from F and H

In nomine almo trino diuino. Ego Ægberhtus*ᵃ* rex occidentalium Saxonum, cum consensu et licentia filii mei Æthelwlfi regis Cantuariorum necnon et aliorum sapientum nostrorum, pro Dei omnipotentis amore et pro eius competenti pecunia quam ab eo accepi hoc est .c. mancusas[b] in duabus armillis, dabo et concedo[c] aliquam partem terre iuris nostri Ciaban clerico moranti in monasterio beati Petri apostoli ubi pausat corpus sancti patris nostri Augustini et per eum et post eum fratribus ibidem Deo seruientibus. Hoc autem agellum huius donationis estimatione,[d] id est unius aratri in illo loco qui nominatur on Scirdun,[e] et ante pertinebat ad regalem uillam Dorouernie ciuitatis, his uero notissimis terminibus circumiacentibus: a meridie biscopes snad, ab occidente freoðorices merc,[f] ab aquilone aeschurud[g] ambiente[h] higna lond to suth[i] ministre, et in communione pascua copiosa pecoribus suis et in silua nominamus[j] denbera quae appellatur Hussingden. Hanc autem [k]predictam terram[k] huius donationis huic prenominato clerico Ciaban concedendo donamus perpetualiter habendum, possidendum feliciterque in dies eius perfruendum, cum omnibus utilitatibus intus et foris ad eam rite ac recte pertinentibus, et post dies eius Deo et sancto Augustino derelinquendum liberam per omnia habeat potestatem. Hoc idemque agellum ab omnibus difficultatibus secularium seruitutum liberabo, nisi his tantum tribus causis, hoc est expeditione et arcis pontisque constructione. Si quis autem hanc nostram suprascriptam donationem quod non optamus alicuius persone homo diabolica instigatus temeritate surrexerit qui hanc nostre munificentie traditionem[l] istius agelli frangere aut[m] minuere uel in aliud uertere quam a nobis constitutum est temptauerit, sciat se ante tribunal eterni iudicis rationem esse redditurum, nisi antea digna satisfactione emendare uoluerit, manente hac cartula in sua nichilominus firmitate. Actum est autem anno dominice incarnationis .dcccxxxvi., indictione .xiiii., his[n] autem testibus consentientibus et signo sancte crucis Christi confirmantibus quorum hic nomina subterius in cedula[o] continentur.[p]

Ego ⟨Egbertus⟩[q] gratia Dei rex occidentalium Saxonum cum signo sancte crucis Christi confirmaui et subscripsi.

+ Ego Ethewlfus[r] rex hanc eandem donacionem cum signo sancte crucis Christi roboraui et subscripsi.

---

[a] Egbertus H   [b] manc' F, H   [c] concede H
[d] *A verb is required here, although the sense is clear*   [e] Scirdon H
[f] *Or* mere F; foeoðrices merk H   [g] *Or* æschurnd F; aescburnd H; ? *for* æschurst
[h] ? *For* ab oriente   [i] sud F   [j] ? *For* silua nostra una   [k] ... [k] terram predictam H
[l] traditioni H   [m] au H   [n] hiis H   [o] F *adds* probabiliter   [p] F *ends here*
[q] *Supplied* (H *omits the king's name*)   [r] *For* Ethelwlfus

18 is the record of a grant of land by King Ecgberht, in association with his son Æthelwulf, to a cleric living in St Peter's minster (St, Augustine's), conditional on the reversion of the estate to the brethren. It is not clear from the wording of the text whether the beneficiary was actually a member of the community. In a strictly regular monastery the monks should not have owned private property, but the beneficiary is explicitly a *clericus* rather than a monk; there is also no evidence as to whether or not St Augustine's was conducted as a regular monastery at this date. Furthermore, the wording of the clause specifying reversion to the *fratres* suggests that they might have access to the land before Ciaba's death. Possibly Ciaba was being prepared for admission into the St Augustine's community and the land at *Scirdun* was vested in him in order that he might give it to the monastery on his admittance.

The formulation of **18** seems to be contemporary, with especially close links to S 293 from 843. The invocation was used in three other Canterbury charters of the ninth century (S 39, 1196 and 344). Ecgberht similarly acts in association with Æthelwulf in a Rochester charter of 838 (S 280; Campbell, *Rochester*, 19). In a second charter of that year (S 286) Æthelwulf is the principal protagonist, but Ecgberht's consent is mentioned in a formula similar to that used in **18**. Kentish charters of this date normally lack a proem. Other charters of the period mention a counter-payment for a royal grant in the form of a precious object valued in mancuses (for instance, S 186, 187, 196). The reference to the presence of Augustine's relics in the monastery is expressed in the same terms in **20**, and there are similar references to Paulinus in two Rochester charters (S 129, 271; Campbell, *Rochester*, 12, 18). The paired dispositive verbs are standard for ninth-century Canterbury charters of the ninth century. The description of the estate is unremarkable; there is a near-contemporary instance of the alienation of land belonging to a royal vill in S 286 (A.D. 838). The statement of powers, the immunity and reservation clauses and the anathema are again in standard Canterbury formulas, and especially close to those in S 293 (A.D. 843). The formulation of the dating clause is acceptable, and the indiction agrees with the incarnation year. Only two subscriptions survive; Æthelwulf's subscription is in the same form in S 286. In general, the grammatical construction of the text is far better than that in **17**, probably because the draftsman was here able to make greater use of standard formulas. The string of gerundives in the statement of powers should be feminine to agree with *hanc ... terram*; conceivably, the original scribe may have used an open *a*, characteristic of ninth-century script, which was misread by a later copyist.

Scirdun has not been securely identified. Its location was already obscure in the thirteenth century, for Sprott noted: 'que ista sit terra de Scirdun nullus modernorum commemorat eo quod vicissitudo temporum nomina locorum antiqua non tam corrupit quam mutavit' (BL Cotton Tiberius A. ix, 115r). In Kent the element *scir* is often associated with upland pasture or marshland (Everitt, *Continuity*, pp. 160–1). Wallenberg (*KPN*, pp. 272–3) suggests a possible connection between *Scirdun* and Sheerland in Pluckley (TQ 935453), which is in the Charing area and also close to Rooting, where St Augustine's held a pre-Conquest manor assessed at half a sulung (GDB 12r). This identification must be regarded as extremely tenuous. The bounds are not helpful. The southern boundary was *biscopes snad*. This may be a reference to the bishop of Rochester, but in this locality is more likely to refer to the archbishop of Canterbury; compare Bishopsbourne, which was an archiepiscopal estate. *Snad* means 'clearing' or perhaps 'woodland', which is the sense it has in S 293. To the west was 'Frithuric's boundary'. The northern boundary was *æschurud* (or *æschurnd/ æscburnd*), where the first element is certainly *æsc*, 'ash', but the second is obscure and apparently corrupt; Wallenberg suggests a connection with OE *hryding*, 'clearing', but an easier emendation would be *hurst, hyrst*, 'wood'. The boundary clause concludes with a statement that the property was surrounded by land belonging to the community at Minster-in-Thanet (Southminster). The *Scirdun* estate carried rights in common pasture and was associated with a swine-pasture called *hussingden*, which Wallenberg identifies with Housendane Wood in Charing. The passage introducing the name of the den is not at all satisfactory as it stands. A possible emendation for *in silua nominamus* would be *in silua nostra una (denbera)*. There is an added complication in the PRO charter-list, where the relevant entry includes the passage: 'cum siluis que appellantur Daiborne et Hussingdenn' (Appendix 2, no. iii). Presumably the first name was also derived from the charter text.

19

Æthelwulf, king of the West Saxons and of the men of Kent, grants five sulungs (aratra) *at Lenham, Kent, to Abbot Wernoth and his* familia.
[? A.D. 838 (9 March)]

F. BL Cotton Julius D. ii, 93rv: copy, s. xiii[1]
    Rubric: Aeþelwlfus Rex de Leanham .xxix.
Not previously edited
Listed: Sawyer 1649

In nomine saluatoris Dei Iesu Christi conditoris nostri. Ego Aþeluulf rex occidentalium Saxonum et Cantuariorum, cum consensu ac licentia meorum seniorum, dabo et concedo Þernoðo abbati eiusque familie, pro eius humili obedientia competentique pecuniam*ᵃ* quam ab eo accepi, hoc est .c. mancas*ᵇ* et duo milia argenti, aliquam partem terram*ᶜ* iuris mei id est .v. aratrorum in loco qui nominatur Leanham, ad habendam, possidendam, feliciterque in dies eius perfruendum*ᵈ* iure hereditario in perpetuam possessionem tradendo illi concedo, seu etiam post dies eius quacumque ei conditione placuerit derelinquendum,*ᵉ* semper in posterum liberam per omnia habeat potestatem, cum campis, siluis, pratis, pascuis, montanis, uenationibus omnibusque utilitatibus, intus et foris, rite ac recte ad eum*ᶠ* pertinentibus. Istis uero terminibus circumiacentibus, ab oriente Scælf et iterum in oriente et meridie sua.

ᵃ For pecunia   *ᵇ For* mancusas   *ᶜ For* terre   *ᵈ For* perfruendam
ᵉ For derelinquendum   *ᶠ For* eam

19 has not previously been printed, apparently because it was confused with another charter in the archive, in which Abbot Wernoth was granted a different estate at

Lenham; this was a version of **21** in which the name of the lay beneficiary had been altered to create a direct grant to the abbey. In S 324 the source of **19** is cited as MS 2, and the altered version of **21** as MS 1.

The text of the charter has been abbreviated by the compiler of MS F, following his normal practice. It now breaks off after the exiguous boundary clause, and lacks a sanction, dating clause and witness-list. The charter is presented as a grant by Æthelwulf, king of the West Saxons and the men of Kent, to Abbot Wernoth of St Augustine's and the community, in return for a money payment. The land granted at Lenham is assessed at five sulungs, and is thus a considerably smaller property than the twenty sulungs of **16** and the forty hides of **21**, which are the two other charters in the archive covering land at Lenham (both may refer to one and the same estate). Thomas Sprott knew a more complete version of **19**, for he mentions the grant of five sulungs to Wernoth and continues with the information that: 'hec donatio facta fuit in villa de Faversham quinto idus Martii sub anno .dcccxxxviii.' (BL Cotton Tiberius A. ix, 114v). He also says that the land concerned was at East Lenham. This last statement agrees with the boundary information. We are told that to the east, and also to the east and south (? to the south-east) lay *scælf*. OE *scylf* has the topographical sense of 'hill', 'ledge' and so on: see M. Gelling, *Place-Names in the Landscape* (London, 1984) pp. 186–7. The name is preserved in Old Shelve (TQ 924512) and New Shelve Farm (TQ 917515), which are situated east and south-east of East Lenham. There were three small Domesday manors at Shelve, all held by tenants of Odo of Bayeux (GDB 8r); in Hasted's day (*History*, v. 430–6) there were still three manors, known as Old Shelve, West Shelve and Cobham *alias* East Shelve (see Cobham Farm, TQ 932515). This seems to confirm that **19** was concerned with a grant of land at East Lenham, whereas the estate or estates in **16** and **21** definitely lay in West Lenham. St Augustine's held a Domesday manor at West Lenham, but East Lenham belonged to the archbishop in 1066; it may have been given to the archbishop and Christ Church in the mid tenth century by Queen Eadgifu, widow of King Edward the Elder (see S 1212 and the commentary to **16**). Therefore, if **19** is a genuine record of a contemporary grant, the estate with which it was concerned no longer belonged to St Augustine's in the eleventh century and may indeed have been alienated before the middle of the tenth century.

Some suspicion attaches to the date which Sprott provides for the charter. If it was issued in 838, then King Ecgberht would still have been alive. Æthelwulf was then king only of Kent, so it would be inappropriate for him to have been styled king of the West Saxons as here; a reference to Ecgberht's consent to the grant would also be expected. In S 286, for instance, another Kentish charter from 838, Æthelwulf makes the grant as king of Kent and refers to the consent of his father Ecgberht, king of the West Saxons. It is possible that Sprott misread the incarnation year, omitting a minim from 839 (*dcccxxxviiii*). Elmham inserts a reference to this grant in his chronological table under the year 838; this could be an independent witness to the dating of the charter, but it is also possible that Elmham was here simply following Sprott and Thorne.

The formulation of the charter seems contemporary with the given date. The verbal invocation is not paralleled exactly elsewhere, but its form is consistent with contemporary practice in Kent. After his father's death in 839 Æthelwulf is regularly styled king of the West Saxons and of the men of Kent in the Kentish charters issued in his name (**21** is an exception); this practice was continued by his sons until Alfred pioneered the styles *rex Saxonum* and *rex Angol Saxonum*. The grant is made in return for the beneficiary's 'humble obedience' (compare S 293) and also in recognition of a money payment; the formulation used here is the same as that in **18** and S 287 (839). In **18** the payment or countergift for land assessed at a sulung was one hundred mancuses in the form of two armlets; here a larger estate attracted the sum of one hundred mancuses and 'two thousands of silver', presumably meaning two thousand silver coins. In S 287 the beneficiary handed over *.iiii. argenti*; something seems to have been omitted here, perhaps the word *milia*, which would correspond to the similar phrase in **19**. The remainder of the dispositive section, with the statement of powers and the list of appurtenances, and the introduction to the boundary clause, are couched in the standard formulas which were devised and used in Canterbury at this period (see Brooks, *Church of Canterbury*, p. 328). **19** can be compared especially to the contemporary examples of S 286 and 287.

The two other charters in the archive concerning land at Lenham (**16** and **21**) were both originally in favour of laymen, but were tampered with at a later date to create direct grants to the monastery. In both instances the name of Abbot Wernoth was substituted for the name of the original beneficiary in the version of the charter in MS F. This substitution can be detected in the case of **16** because a second reference to the beneficiary was not altered and in the case of **21** because the original charter was enrolled. It is possible that Wernoth's name was also substituted for that of the original beneficiary in **19**, but this cannot be demonstrated in the absence of another copy of the charter. The statement of powers, which gives the beneficiary full rights of posthumous bequest, would seem more appropriate in a land-grant to a layman than in one to an abbot and his community, but it may be that here the draftsman was simply using standard formulation which was not adapted to the particular circumstances of this transaction.

20

Æthelwulf, king of the West Saxons and of the men of Kent, grants one sulung (aratrum) *at* Lillicesora *(? Lynsore, Kent) to Wynhere, priest-abbot of the monastery of St Peter.* A.D. 845 (16 November)

F. BL Cotton Julius D. ii, 106rv: copy, s. xiii[1]
   No rubric
H. PRO E 164/27, 83v–84r: copy, s. xiii
   Rubric: Carta Ethelwlfi de Lynchesore.
Ed. Birch 853 from F
Listed: Sawyer 297
Edited from F and H

In nomine altitroni regis eterni. Ego*ᵃ* Æðeluulf*ᵇ* gratia Dei rex occidentalium Saxonum necnon et Cantuariorum, pro spe remunerationis eterne atque competenti pecunia quam ab eo accepi hoc est .lxx. mancusis, cum consensu

ac licentia meorum optimatum libenti animo dabo et concedo Winhere*
presbytero abbati monasterii sancti Petri apostoli, ubi pausat corpus beati
patris nostri Augustini, aliquantulam partem terre iuris mei in orientali parte
Cantie, id est unum aratrum in illo loco qui ab incolis Lillicesora* nominatur,
cum campis et siluis omnibusque rebus intus ei et foris ad se rite ac
recte pertinentibus habendam et possidendam feliciterque in diebus eius in
quacumque ei conditione perfruendum et post dies eius cuicumque* heredi
derelinquendum placuerit liberam per omnia habeat potestatem. Istis notissimis terminibus circumcinctis, *ab oriente tafinguueg, a meridie hælgarda,
ab occidente cornuug,* ab aquilone norðhommis.* Hanc eandem donationem
meam cuius supracripsi* agelli ab omnibus secularium difficultatum seruitiis
liberabo, hoc idemque omnibus successoribus meis in nomine omnipotentis
Dei obseruandum precipio. Si autem quod non optamus alicuius persone
homo diabolica temeritate instigatus surrexerit, qui hanc nostram mu-
nificentiam confringere uel mutare* aut in aliud conuertere quam a nobis
constitutum est temptauerit, sciat se a Deo et ab omnibus sanctis eius
alienatum nisi ante digna satisfactione Deo et hominibus emendare uoluerit,
manente* hac cartula* in sua nichilominus firmitate roborata. Actum est
autem anno dominice incarnationis .dcccxlv., indictione .viii., die .xvi. kalendarum Decembris, in illa famosa uilla que dicitur æt Uuie,* his testibus*
consentientibus et signo sancte crucis Christi confirmantibus quorum hic
nomina infra in cedula caraxata continentur.

+ Ego Ethelwlf rex hanc meam donationem cum signo crucis Christi
roborabo et subscribo.
+ Ego Ethelstan rex et cetera.

---

a ege H   *b* Ethelwlfus H   *c* Winehere H   *d* Lyncesore H
e Omitted H; eiuscuicumque eius F   *f* H omits boundary clause   *g* ? For cornuueg
h ? For norðhammas   *i* ? For illius suprascripti   *j* presumpserit (added and deleted) H
k Omitted H   *l* hanc cartulam H   *m* at Wi H   *n* F ends here

---

This charter was issued on the same day and in the same place (the royal vill at Wye
in Kent) as a charter in favour of a layman which was preserved at Christ Church
as an original (S 296). The beneficiary is Abbot Wynhere, who attests S 296. There
are problems with the dates of Wynhere's period of office. Sprott and the chronological
table in Elmham's history both indicate that he was abbot for only two or three
years, from 863 or 864 until 866; this is incompatible with the evidence of **20** and
S 296. The later medieval lists of St Augustine's abbots and the implied dates in the
works of the abbey's historians are difficult to reconcile with the ninth-century
charter evidence, and it seems likely that they are in part fictional, or a reconstruction

of deficient material. The problems are discussed in Appendix 4. Wynhere's sub-scription to S 296 shows that he was indeed abbot (presumably of St Augustine's) in 845, so there is no difficulty in accepting him as beneficiary of **20**.

The charter is composed in the standard Canterbury formulas of this period (see Brooks, *Church of Canterbury*, pp. 327–30). The same verbal invocation was used in S 1268 (A.D. 825 × 832) and close variants appear in S 164, 168–9, 1264 and 293. Æthelwulf's style is of the type regularly applied to the West Saxon kings in Kentish charters between 839 and 868. As in S 296, and in a number of other charters of the period (see **18**, **19**), the draftsman mentions the amount which the beneficiary had given in return for the land-grant, in this case seventy mancuses for one sulung (in **18** one hundred mancuses were handed over in exchange for a similar area of land). Abbot Wynhere is decribed as priest-abbot, a common style in ninth-century Kentish charters (see **17**, and Brooks, *Church of Canterbury*, pp. 162–3); the reference to St Augustine's is in the same words as in **18**. There is nothing remarkable about the standard formulation of the remainder of the dispositive section and the sanction; these sections of **20** can be directly compared with contemporary texts such as S 286, 287, 293, 296 etc. The dating clause in expressed in exactly the same words as S 296.

Birch printed his text from the copy in BL Cotton Julius D ii, which breaks off at the beginning of the introduction to the witness-list. The later copy in PRO E 164/27 continues a little further, and includes the subscriptions of King Æthelwulf and his son, King Æthelstan, whom he had set over Kent, Sussex, Surrey and Essex in 839. It is likely that the original witness-list would have been almost identical to that in S 296. There the subscriptions of the two kings are followed by that of Bishop Tatnoth of Rochester; Archbishop Ceolnoth did not attest for some reason. S 296 is also subscribed by Ealdorman Ealhhere, beneficiary of **21**, by an Abbot Degberht, whose name does not occur elsewhere, by the priest-abbot Wynhere, who would probably not have attested the charter of which he was beneficiary, and by nine unstyled laymen. In **20** the witness-list is said to be written *infra in scedula*; S 296 has the phrase *in scedula*, but then advises the reader to turn to the dorse for the witness-list. **20** is the shorter of the two texts, and it would seem that the scribe managed to fit some or all on the witness-list on the face, while the scribe of S 296 was compelled to make use of the dorse (for ninth-century Kentish opisthographs, see p. xcii).

The two cartulary copies have different versions of the name of the estate granted: *Lillicesora* (MS F) and *Lyncesore* (MS H). Thomas Sprott (BL Cotton Tiberius A. ix, 115r) refers to this as a grant of a place anciently called *Lylhcesora*, but more recently known as *Lyncesore*, which suggests that the reading in MS F may be closer to the reading of the charter, although Sprott's distinction between the old and the new name for the place may simply be based on the difference between the charter-reading and the place-name with which the charter was in his day associated. The relevant entry in the PRO charter-list (Appendix 2, no. xli) and the reference to the charter in Elmham's chronological table (Hardwick, *Elmham*, p. 15) both have *Linchesore*. Wallenberg (*KPN*, pp. 273–4) was inclined to treat *Lillicesora* as a corruption of an original name place-name *hlincesora*, 'the border or bank of the lynch'. It is difficult to see how such corruption could have occurred. An alternative possibility is that a charter covering a forgotten *Lillicesora* was later associated with a different place with a similar name. In *Lillicesora* itself the first element would appear to be an otherwise unknown personal name Lillic; this might be connected with the better-evidenced Lilla or Lill, found in a number of place-names including Lillchurch in Kent (note also that a Lulluc attests S 291 and 293, both nearly contemporary with **20**). The land-grant in **20** has been connected at least since Hasted's day with Lynsore Court (TR 165489) and Lynsore Bottom (TR 163496) near Bossingham (*History*, ix. 306). St Augustine's is not known to have held any property in this area at the time of the Domesday survey.

The brief bounds are not of much assistance in locating the estate. To the east lay *tafinguueg*, where the second element is *weg*, 'way' and the first element appears to derive from an unknown OE personal name **Tafa*. Wallenberg (*KPN*, p. 275) suggests a connection with Tappington Farm, about three miles south-east of Lynsore (see Tappington Hall near Wootton, TR 210462), which would entail a corruption from *tapingweg* to *tafingweg*; the underlying personal name would then be *Tappa* or *Tæppa*. It should be noted that *f* and *p* in ninth-century Anglo-Saxon minuscule could easily be confused by a later reader. The southern boundary of the estate was *hælgarda*, from *heall*, 'hall', or *healh*, 'angle, corner', and *geard*, 'yard, fence, enclosure'. To the west was *cornuug*. It is probable that the second element is a corruption of *uueg*: thus 'corn way'. The northern boundary was formed by the 'north meadows' (*north*, *hamm*).

21

Æthelwulf, king of the West Saxons, grants forty hides (cassati) *at Lenham, Kent, to Ealhhere, princeps.* A.D. 850

F. BL Cotton Julius D. ii, 133v: copy, s. xiii[1]
  No rubric
G*. BL Cotton Claudius D. x, 62v–63r: copy of Inspeximus [R], s. xiv[1]
  Rubric: Carta regis Adeluulfi de manerio de Leanham.
M. BL Add. 53710: copy of Inspeximus [S], s. xiv/xv
R. PRO Ch. R. 20 Edw. II, m. 2
S. PRO Ch. R. 36 Edw. III, m. 7
T. PRO Ch. R. 8 Hen. IV, m. 6
U. PRO Pat. R. 2 Hen. VI, pt 3, m 5
V. PRO Pat. R. 4 Edw. IV, pt 4, m. 29
W. PRO Pat. R. 14 Hen. VII, pt 1, m. 16
Ed.: a. Twysden, *Scriptores*, cols 2126–7, from M
      b. Kemble 1049 from G*
      c. Birch 459 from G*, 854 from F
      d. Pierquin, *Recueil*, pt 3, no. 48, from Birch
Listed: Sawyer 300 (see also 324 MS 1)
Translated: Davis, *Thorne*, pp. 569–71, from M
Edited from F and G*

Regnante inperpetuum Domino nostro Iesu Christo, cum cuius *"imperio hic"* labentis seculi prosperitas in aduersis successibus sedulo permixta et conturbata cernitur et omnia uisibilia atque desiderabilia ornamenta huius mundi cotidie ab ipsis amatoribus transeunt, ideo beati quique ac sapientes cum hiis fugitiuis seculi diuitiis eterna et iugiter permansura gaudia celestis patrie adipisci properant. Quamobrem ego Ætheluulf[b] occidentalium Saxonum rex cum consensu et licentia episcoporum ac principum meorum etiam pro remedio anime mee et pro expiatione facinorum meorum aliquam partem terre iuris mei 'Alher meo principe pro eius humili obedientia[c] in perpetuam hereditatem libenter largitus sum, in uilla que nuncupatur Leanham, id est .xl. cassatos, ut habeat et perfruatur quamdiu sub astrifero[d] celo uitam duxerit, cum omnibus utilitatibus ad eam pertinentibus, campis, siluis, pratis, pascuis, piscariis, et loco[e] in quo sal adipisci potest, et cum gressu[f] trium carrorum in silua que dicitur Blean, et post finem uite illius heredi cuicumque placuerit eternaliter relinquat. Terra hec[g] predicta secura et immunis omnium rerum permaneat regalium et principalium tributorum et ui exactorum operum furisque comprehensione simulque et omni populari grauedine, nisi expeditione et pontis factione et arcis munitione.[h]

Hec sunt territoria prefate telluris. 'Wiltuman ninhinga[i] pest merc, ðaræ hina land to Scaepege[j] norð mearc, East Leanaham east mearc, Cyningessnade to Feferesham suð mearc, 7 his teares les[k] on cyningesdune to teninge faledun 7 his ceares les[k] to beringtune on cyningesfirhðe suie to ðeon lond belimpe, 7 pidumga[l] on cyningessnade suie to ðiam londe belimpe. 7 Ðis sind[m] ða dænbæra[n] ðes londes, Ninsila herst, Rusting den, þornden, on Mapolder herst[o] ðrio den, Friððingden tþa, on Friðesleas .iiii., on Tun laf hirste .iii., on Haðdune suðan an, be suðan Stan ea an.

Et qui[p] hanc meam donacionem augere et amplificare uoluerit, multiplicet Dominus partem eius hic et in futuro seculo. Si quis autem hoc infringere uel minuere temptauerit, sciat se separatum a consorcio beatorum spiritum et racionem in tremendo die iudicii coram Christo et angelis eius redditurum nisi ante satisfaccione emendauerit. Scripta est hec[g] huius donationis cartula anno dominice incarnacionis .dcccl., indictione uero .xiii., in uilla regali que nominatur Wiltone coram idoneis testibus quorum nomina subtus annexa notantur.

+ Ego Aedeluulfus rex hanc meam donationem manu proprio[q] cum signo sancte crucis Christi roborando confirmandoque subscripsi.

+ Ego Alhstan episcopus consensi et subscripsi.

+ Ego Aedelbaldus dux filius regis consensi et subscripsi.

+ Ego Aedelstan rex hoc consentiens signum crucis imposui.

... hic imperio F (' ... Christ, with whose governance the prosperity of this transient world ...')   *b* Adeluulfus G*
c ...* c* apostolorum principum Petri et Pauli ministro Ꝑernoðo abbati F   *d* astrigero F
e locus F   *f* ? *For* ingressu   *g* *For* autem (*misreading of insular abbreviation*)
h F *ends here*   *i* ...* i* *Corrupt* (*see commentary*)   *j* Scaerege G*
k *Corrupt* (*see commentary*)   *l* *For* pudunga   *m* sinti G*   *n* dænhæra G*
o hest G*   *p* *For* quicumque   *q* *For* propria

21 exists in two versions. The original charter was in favour of Ealdorman Ealhhere. It was one of eight Anglo-Saxon diplomas presented to Edward II in 1326 for confirmation; the texts were preserved in Edward's Inspeximus charter, which was enrolled and confirmed on several occasions, and which was also copied into a quire added to BL Cotton Claudius D. x (MS G*; see pp. xlix–l). In the second version, preserved only in BL Cotton Julius D. ii (MS F), the name of Abbot Wernoth has been substituted for that of the ealdorman. It is this revised version of the charter which is mentioned in the charter-list in PRO E 164/27, where it has the date 850 (see Appendix 2, no. xxv). Sprott also knew this revised text, which he associated with the date 840 (BL Cotton Tiberius A. ix, 114v). In the chronological table prefixed to Elmham's history a reference to this grant under the year 840 has been deleted, and under the year 850 there is a note of the grant to Ealhhere (Hardwick, *Elmham*, p. 15).

This is one of several pre-Conquest charters in the archive which have been tampered with to create a direct grant to the abbey (see also 16, 27). The revised version was apparently already in existence in the first half of the thirteenth century. Since the original diploma was still available to be submitted for confirmation in 1326, we must conclude that either the revision of the text involved the creation of a new single sheet or the emended version existed only as a cartulary copy. Abbot Wernoth's name was substituted for that of a layman in a second charter concerned with land at Lenham (16), which was probably the title-deed to the same estate as 21 (see below). There is a third Lenham charter in the archive, again in favour of Wernoth (19); since this survives only in a single manuscript copy, we cannot tell whether this also reflects tampering with a grant to a layman. If 19 is genuine, it may have inspired the revisor(s) of 16 and 21. At some stage the revised version of 21 seems to have become associated with the year 840, rather than 850, perhaps because the abbey's historians recognised that the later year was not compatible with the received dates for Wernoth's period of office (see p. civ, and Appendix 4). The fact that Elmham noted the fabricated version of the charter under 840 and then deleted this notice may indicate that he found that the date could not be supported by the archive evidence.

Since the fabricated version of 21 represents only a mild modification of the original text, as represented in the Inspeximus charter, it has not been treated as a separate document. In Sawyer's handlist the fabricated version is given a separate entry (S 324). It is S 324 MS 1; the second manuscript reference in the entry is to another of the charters linking Wernoth and Lenham (19).

The original beneficiary of 21 was the Ealdorman Ealhhere who fought against the Vikings at Sandwich in 851 and met his death at their hands in Thanet in 853, as noted in the *Anglo-Saxon Chronicle*. Æthelwulf made him a second land-grant in

850, this time of a small area outside Rochester (S 299). In the middle years of the ninth century Ealhhere and members of his family arranged to give food-rents from some of their estates to Christ Church and St Augustine's (see S 1195, and Brooks, *Church of Canterbury*, pp. 148–9); the donor of **24** was probably his sister. It is possible that Ealhhere or an immediate heir gave to St Augustine's the Lenham estate covered in **21**. In 1086 the abbey held a manor beneficially assessed at five and a half sulungs at West Lenham, which may represent at least part of the property granted to Ealhhere (GDB 12r). There is further discussion in the commentary to **16**, which seems to be an earlier title-deed to the estate granted in **21**.

21 was issued at the royal vill at Wilton in Wiltshire, and its formulation indicates that it was drafted by a West Saxon rather than a Canterbury scribe; this is unusual in the ninth century, when charters in the name of the West Saxon kings dealing with land in Kent were normally drawn up by Kentish draftsmen (see pp. xciii–xciv). It seems possible that the charter underlying S 301 from the Malmesbury archive was drawn up on the same occasion as **21**. The Malmesbury charter is spurious as it stands, for the dispositive section has been rewritten to create a direct grant to the monastery, but the invocation, proem and the beginning of the dispositive section were apparently based on the formulation of a genuine charter, which also supplied the date and the witness-list. S 301 was issued in 850, as was **21**. The two charters have the same invocation, of the *Regnante* form, common in Wessex and Mercia but rare in Kentish charters. They have the same proem, which also occurs in a charter of 860 preserved at Shaftesbury (S 326); Kentish charters at this period do not usually include proems. Æthelwulf is simply styled king of the West Saxons in **21** as well as in S 301, although Kentish charters normally refer to him as king of both the West Saxons and the men of Kent. The consent-formula of **21** is the same as that in S 298 (846), the first surviving West Saxon original; the formulation of this section and the following statement of motivation are also very similar in S 301. **21** and S 301 share the dispositive verb *largitus sum* (see also S 292); in the ninth century West Saxon charter-scribes showed a fondness for verbs in the past tense, while their Canterbury counterparts preferred to use a pair of verbs, one in the present tense and one in the past (Brooks, *Church of Canterbury*, p. 328). Also characteristic of West Saxon charter-writing is the use of the hide (*cassatus*) as the unit of assessment in place of the Kentish sulung. The statement of powers and immunity clause are formulated on the West Saxon rather than the Kentish model: compare S 326, 329, 334–5, 336, 341, 539. There is a particularly close parallel in S 202, a difficult Abingdon charter dated 852 in the name of Berhtwulf of Mercia; this appears to be a fabrication modelled on a West Saxon charter, perhaps of 842, which was issued in the same place as S 290 (O'Donovan, *Charters of Sherborne*, no. 3). The sanction consists of a blessing and an anathema; the latter is very different from the standard formula used in Canterbury charters at this period (for this see **18**, **20**, **22**, **23**). The formula in **21** is similar to those found in contemporary West Saxon texts (compare 326, 329, 334–6, 340, and the sanction of the 'Decimation charters' of 854). The dating clause begins *Scripta*, in contrast to the usual Kentish formula beginning *Actum* or *Actum est*; for the formulation of this section of the charter, compare S 202 and 335, both issued at royal vills.

Four subscriptions have been preserved. After Æthelwulf attest Bishop Ealhstan of Sherborne and the king's second son Æthelbald, as *filius regis*; the last subscription is that of King Æthelstan, Æthelwulf's oldest son, whom he had appointed king of south-eastern England in 839 (see **20**). The relative order of the subscriptions suggests that King Æthelstan may have confirmed Æthelwulf's grant at a later time, perhaps in Kent. Usually Æthelstan attests Kentish charters after his father, but **21** was evidently drawn up in Wessex in unusual circumstances; Æthelstan may not have been present at the meeting, so that his subsequent consent and confirmation were required.

The draftsman was influenced by Kentish diplomatic in two respects. The formulaic list of abstract appurtenances is here interrupted by two specific references, the first to a saltern and the second to wood-gathering privileges in Blean Wood, which lay north of Canterbury (and was thus an odd appurtenance for the fairly distant estate at Lenham). The identification of particular appurtenances is very much a Kentish feature at this date. An instructive comparison is with the Wassingwell charter of 858 (S 328), which mentions a saltern and wood-gathering privileges in Blean as well as many other appurtenances, including rights over marshland which had previously belonged to Wye, Lenham and Faversham. Also recognisably Kentish is the formulation of the bounds in **21**. By this period West Saxon charters regularly include detailed Old English surveys (see S 298, 304, 308, 317, 326, 329 etc.). In Canterbury in the mid ninth century charter-scribes usually provided only brief Latin bounds, based on the four points of the compass (see **20**, **22**, **23**, and S 287, 316, 328 etc). In **21** the bounds are in Old English, but they differ from the normal West Saxon bounds in conforming to the compass-format (compare also S 286). The West Saxon charter-scribe was evidently given a Latin record of the Lenham bounds which he translated into the vernacular. Some of the corruption of the boundary clause may be due to his unfamiliarity with the place-names, rather than later scribal error. The boundary clause is followed by details of other appurtenances of the estates and a list of swine-pastures in the Weald. These details of appurtenances, the basis of the boundary clause and the list of Wealden dens must have been supplied to the West Saxon scribe before he drew up the text. Some of this information may have been derived from the original text of **16**, which as it stands has been considerably reworked.

The western boundary of the forty-hide estate of **21** is the corrupt *Wiltuman ninhinga*; the form of the first part has probably been influenced by the subsequent reference to Wilton. There is probably a connection with the church called *Welcumeweye* which is mentioned in the *Domesday Monachorum*, and which was situated between Lenham and Hollingbourne; Wallenberg (*Place-names of Kent*, p. 212) identifies this with the church of Harrietsham, the village immediately west of Lenham, which lay on an ancient route known as the Greenway (Everitt, *Continuity*, pp. 49, 84–5). The church at Harrietsham seems to have been dedicated to St John the Baptist; a street in its vicinity is now called St Welcume's Way, but this may be a recent christening. The basis of the name in the *Domesday Monachorum* seems to be a feminine personal name *Wilcume* or OE *wilcuma*, 'welcome guest', with *weg*, 'way'. The second part of the boundary mark, *ninhinga*, is obscure; perhaps it is a corruption of OE *niming, 'land taken into cultivation' (Smith, *EPNE*, p. 50). The remaining bounds are relatively straightforward. To the north was land belonging to the community on (the isle of) Sheppey; this is the last reference to Minster-in-Sheppey, which seems to have disappeared in the course of the ninth century (the Vikings over-wintered on the island in 855/6). The eastern boundary was with East Lenham, the estate previously granted to an abbot of St Augustine's in **19**. To the south lay the king's *snad*, probably here meaning 'wood' (see **18** and S 293), belonging to the royal vill at Faversham. The name survives in that of the hamlet of Kingsnoad, a few miles south-west of Lenham (TQ 856479).

Between the boundary clause and the list of dens are references to three appurtenant privileges attached to the estate. The first two relate to something called *his teares les* or *his ceares les* in two different places. The final element is probably *læs*, meaning 'pasture', but *his teares/ceares* is apparently corrupt (there may be a connection with *hyrst*, 'woodland'). The first of these pastures lay at a place called 'king's hill', and appears to have been attached to *teninge faledun*; Wallenberg (*KPN*, p. 191, and *Place-Names of Kent*, p. 227) identifies these with Kingsdown and Timbold Hill. In *teninge faledun* the second element is *falod*, 'fold', while the first may be *Tæningas*, based on a personal name **Tena*, a short form of names in *Tun-*. The name recurs in Teynham, a settlement between Sittingbourne and Faversham, about eight miles north of Lenham; Ekwall (*DEPN*, p. 464) interprets the reference in **21** as 'the fold belonging to the Teynham people'. The second area of pastureland lay *on cyningesfirthe*, 'in the king's wood' (*fyrhth*), and was associated with a settlement called *beringtune*. Wallenberg's suggestion (*KPN*, pp. 190–1) that the latter is a mistake for Pivington seems unfounded; the first element is likely to derive from a personal name *Bære*. The owner of the Lenham estate was also entitled to woodgathering rights (*wudung*) in the king's wood, probably that which lay on the southern boundary and was attached to Faversham (for privileges of this kind, see **13**).

There were seventeen Wealden swine-pastures appurtenant to the estate, all of them probably located in the area between Staplehurst and Cranbrook. There is a high level of correspondence with the thirteen dens listed in **16** (precise details of the locations are given in the commentary to that charter). There were three dens at Maplehurst, two at Frittenden, four at Friezley and three at Tolehurst (Farm). Wallenberg (*KPN*, pp. 190–1) considers that *ninsila herst* is a corruption of the *wiflahirst* of **16**, which has a probable connection with Wilsley, and that *rustingden* is a corruption of Plusshenden, a lost manor in Headcorn. See also Witney, *Jutish Forest*, pp. 246–7.

22

Æthelberht, king of the West Saxons and of the men of Kent, grants three sulungs (aratra) at Martin, Kent, to Abbot Diernoth and his familia.

A.D. 861

F. BL Cotton Julius D. ii, 132v–133r: copy, s. xiii[1]
Ed.: Birch 855
Listed: Sawyer 330

In nomine Domini Dei summi saluatoris Iesu Christi. Quamuis igitur sermo solus catholicorum Dei seruorum ad testimonium rebus rite peractis fideliter sufficere possit ac debeat, iuxta sacre scilicet scripture assertionem quia in ore duorum inquit uel trium testium stabit omne uerbum,[1] attamen ob incertam futurorum temporum conditionem manifestissimis auctorum cirographis necnon et firmissimis testium plurimorum adstipulationibus ac subscriptionibus sunt roboranda, ne quando labentibus annis atque incerto quippe statu aduenientium hominum inscius quis quomodo se res haberet aut inprobus et*a* auarus aduersus ueritatem aditum quomodo repperire causando et inuidendo ualeant.*b* Quoniam sepe ex ignorancia, sepe quoque quod est execrabilius ex inprobitate contingit ut de negotio rerum uere et bene gestarum nascatur.*c* Et quia omnem hominem qui secundum Deum uiuit et remunerari a Deo sperat et optat, oportet ut piis precibus assensum ex animo hilariter prebeat, quoniam certum est tanto facilius ea que ipse a Deo poposcerit consequi posse, quanto et ipse libentius hominibus recte postulata concesserit; quod tunc bonorum omnium larcitori Deo acceptabile fit, cum pro eius amore et utilitate famulantium ei peragitur. Quocirca ego Æthelbertus occidentalium Saxonum necnon et Cantuariorum rex dabo et concedo Diernoðo abbati eiusque familie pro expiatione facinorum meorum aliquam partem terre iuris mei hoc est tria aratra illa*d* loco qui nominatur Merecum*e* in orientali parte regionis Cantie. Hoc feci pro eius humili obedientia et quia mihi meoque patri semper fidelis atque obedibilis permansit simulque 'pro eius placibili atque competenti pecunia quam ab eo accepi, hoc est .lx. mancusas auri optimi, sibi habendum et possidendum feliciterque in dies eius in sempiternam hereditatem perfruendum liberam per omnia habeat potestatem, cum omnibus utilitatibus rite ac recte ad eandem terram pertinentibus. Hanc autem terram supranominatam ego Æthelbertus rex ab omni difficultate secularium seruitutum regali operis*f* intus et foris, magnis et modicis, notis et ignotis, eternaliter liberabo nisi sola expeditione. Isti sunt termini circumiacentes, ab oriente terra regis ad Roedligpealda, a meridie ad abbates land to Langandune, ab occidente et ab aquilone Elpealdes*g* land regis ministri. Si quis uero heredum successorumque meorum regum, principum, ducum, optimatum siue extraneorum hanc meam donationem uel libertatem seruare uoluerit, augeat omnipotens Deus dies eius prosperos hic et in futuro. Quod si alicuius persone homo diabolica temeritate instagatus*h* surrexerit, qui hanc meam donationem uel libertatem infringere uel diminuere in aliquo*i* re temptauerit, sciat se ante tribunal summi et eterni iudicis rationem esse redditurum nisi ante digna et placabili satisfactione Deo et hominibus emendare uoluerit. Hac uero conditione composita inter Æthelbertum regem et Diernoðum abbatem.*j* Si mihi meisque karissimis fratribus humilis ac 'fidelis Ethelredo et Æluredo permanere uoluerit, nobisque obtemperare non desiuit, tunc ista omnia uerba supradicta fixa permaneant sicut a nobis nunc concessa sunt. Actum est autem anno dominice incarnationis .dccclxi., indictione .ix., in loco preclaro qui nominatur Fregetburna an hsuðrium,[k] his testibus consentientibus ac conscribentibus et cum uexillo sancte crucis Christi confirmantibus quorum hic nomina infra hac in scedula karaxata adnotantur.

[a] For aut   [b] For ualeat
[c] This sentence appears to lack a subject (the formula has the same deficiency in S 327)
[d] For illo   [e] For Meretun (see commentary)
[f]? Read (et) regalis operis (a standard formula has been poorly adapted)   [g] Elpealdes F
[h] For instigatus   [i] For aliqua   [j] This sentence may be an intrusive gloss
[k] Probably a corruption of in Suðregum

[1] See Deut. 19: 15; Matt. 18: 16

In **22** King Æthelberht grants land to the abbot of St Augustine's in return for a payment of sixty mancuses of gold. The background to the transaction is of considerable interest for an assessment of the realities of West Saxon rule in Kent. Æthelberht states in the dispositive section that he is making the grant on account of the abbot's humble obedience and because he had always been loyal to himself and to his father. More detail is given in a unique passage after the sanction: the land-grant will stand only if the abbot remains humble and loyal to the king and his two younger brothers, Æthelred and Alfred. This seems to show Æthelberht soliciting the support of an important Kentish religious house for the continuation of West Saxon overlordship in Kent. The date of the grant is of some importance in this context. It had previously been the regular practice of the West Saxon kings, from the time of Ecgberht, to divide their greatly enlarged realm and to place the south-eastern part, comprising Kent, Surrey, Sussex and Essex, into the hands of a subordinate ruler, generally their eldest son. This was the position assumed by Æthelwulf in relation to his father after the initial conquest of Kent, and when he succeeded Ecgberht as king in Wessex in 839 he placed his own son Æthelstan over the south-eastern provinces. Æthelstan seems to have died before his father, for he is last heard of in 851, and his place was taken by his brother Æthelberht, who subscribed two Kentish charters of 853 and 855 as rex (S 315, 316). When Æthelwulf died the West Saxon realm was divided between Æthelbald and Æthelberht, with the latter retaining his position in the south-east and the former taking the western part of the kingdom. The importance of this arrangement was that it gave the conquered territories, of which Kent was the most important, their own ruler and thus some sense of a continued existence as independent units. But there was a change of policy after Æthelbald's death in 860. When Æthelberht took charge of the whole kingdom he did not appoint one of his two surviving brothers as subordinate ruler in the south-east; instead, according to the account in Alfred's will (S 1507), all three brothers came to an agreement designed to keep together their patrimony, and by implication the realm, according to which the survivors were to inherit the whole. It is possible that Æthelberht expected some trouble from Kent as the result of this change of policy, and that to circumvent it he took pains to make sure that the leaders of Kentish society supported the move. The urgent need for un-compromised loyalty was underpinned by the increasing seriousness of Viking attacks.

The sequence and dates of the ninth-century abbots of St Augustine's are horribly confused. In the first half of the century there was an Abbot Wernoth, with traditional dates of 822 to 844. An Abbot Dryhtnoth attests 24 from the middle of the century, and the spelling *Diernodus* in 22 may represent a Latinized version of this name. The abbey's later historians believed that *Diernodus* succeeded *Wernodus*, but badly confused the two, attributing charters variously to either. There is also the difficulty of inserting into the chronology the Abbot Wynhere of 20, who flourished in 845; he was supposed to have been the successor of *Diernodus*. I have considered the problems of abbatial succession in Appendix 4. There is no especial difficulty in accepting that *Diernodus* was an appropriate beneficiary for a charter of 861.

The diplomatic of the charter seems contemporary, and it was evidently drafted by a Canterbury scribe. The verbal invocation is not precisely paralleled elsewhere, but it follows the normal Kentish pattern. The very long proem is not usual in a ninth-century Kentish charter, but its presence here may be linked with the serious underlying purpose of the grant, which was to bind the abbot to the West Saxon interest. The theme of the first part of the proem is the need to record transactions in writing and to have them properly witnessed, in order to prevent future disruption. This is a common preoccupation of Anglo-Saxon proems, although here expressed at unusual length; there is a close parallel in S 327, a Rochester charter of 860 (in which a later revisor has altered the date and tampered with the beneficiary). The second part of the proem is a standard formula on the joys of generosity, first found in a Minster ship-toll privilege of 748 (51) and then in a charter for Reculver (S 31, 748 × 762) and two related texts from Rochester (S 32 from 762 and S 131 from 789); it was also in the eighth-century model used by the forger of 1. The draftsman of 22 had to turn back to the charters of the previous century to find inspiration for his proem because ninth-century Kentish charter-scribes had eschewed such formulas.

The formulation of the remainder of the text generally follows contemporary Canterbury norms. Æthelberht is styled king of the West Saxons and the men of Kent, which was the style usually given to his father in Kentish charters and also to his own successor, Æthelred. The paired dispositive verbs *dabo et concedo* are standard in Canterbury charters of the period. The land is said to be located in *orientali parte regionis Cantie*; there is a parallel for this in 20, where the estate is said to lie *in orientali parte Cantie*. The formula in which the king expresses his motives for the grant is an adaptation of that found, for instance, in S 332 (A.D. 863), where only the beneficiary's obedience and money-payment are cited; in 22 an additional phrase about loyalty to the king and his father has been inserted. The statement of powers is a reworking of the standard Canterbury formula of the mid century, with the omission of the right of free alienation (inappropriate for a grant to a religious house): for the more usual form see 18, 19, 20, 23. The formulation of the list of appurtenances and the immunity clause is also standard (compare, for instance, 20). The reservation clause is unusual in that it mentions only military service, and not bridge-building and fortress-work; this peculiarity is shared with S 329 (Kelly, *Shaftesbury*, no. 4), a charter granting land in Wiltshire to a layman, which was issued in Somerset in 860. It is difficult to explain why two documents drafted in different parts of the West Saxon realm should have this unusual feature in common. The boundary clause is expressed according to the cardinal points, which is the normal form in Kentish charters in this period. The sanction consists of a blessing and a sanction, both standard formulas (compare S 316, 332), and the formulation of the dating clause and the following introduction to the witness-list is typical of Canterbury practice at this time (compare S 328, 332). The charter is said to have been issued at a place named *Fregetburna*, apparently in Surrey; this may be a corruption of *Freoricburna*, a royal vill in Surrey mentioned in a charter of Offa (S 144) and again in a charter of King Ecgberht (S 280). None of the subscriptions has been preserved.

22 records the grant of three sulungs at Martin, which lies south of Mongeham, where St Augustine's was granted land by King Eadberht II in 762 or 763 (**13**), and also south of Northbourne, which may have been part of the monastery's early endowment (see **5**); it is close to Beauxfield, supposed to have been given to St Augustine's by Offa (**14**). The simple boundary clause is easily interpreted. To the east lay a royal estate at Ringwould; to the south was the abbot's land at (East) Langdon; while to the west and north were lands belonging to a king's thegn named Elweald. It would appear that the abbot of St Augustine's already owned a neighbouring estate at East Langdon. In 1044 or 1045 a dispute between St Augustine's and a priest named Leofwine over 'St Mildrith's property' was settled in favour of the monks, but the abbot agreed to pay the priest a yearly pension and to give him for his lifetime one sulung at Langdon and one at Ileden, to revert to St Augustine's after his death (S 1472; see p. xxxi). Neither Martin nor Langdon is given a separate entry in Domesday Book. They may have been reckoned under another St Augustine's manor, most probably Northbourne (which certainly incorporated at least one outlying estate, at Beauxfield); the Northbourne manor was assessed at thirty sulungs, with capacity for fifty-four ploughs, and a large part of it was held in small parcels by tenants (GDB 12v). There was a later connection between the parish of Langdon and the minster at Northbourne (Everitt, *Continuity*, p. 157), and Martin may already have been treated as part of East Langdon parish at an early date. Martin is likely to have been originally a peripheral settlement, for *Meretun* means 'boundary *tun*' (from *(ge)mære*). The manor of Langdon was one of those assigned to supply the monks' clothing by Abbot Hugh II in the twelfth century (Twysden, *Scriptores*, col. 1799).

23

Eadbald grants land at Burmarsh, Kent, to Winemund. [*c.* A.D. 848]

F. BL Cotton Julius D. ii, 106v: copy, s. xiii[1]
Ed.: Birch 837
Listed: Sawyer 1193

In nomine trino diuino Dei celi. Ego Ædbaldus[a] do et concedo Winemundo amico meo aliquam partem terre agelluli mei contra eius pecuniam quam ab eo accepi, hoc est .viii. hund pendinga, in loco qui dicitur Burparamers halfsæta. Necnon et illud agellum his terminibus circumcincta[b] est, in oriente Suþsaxa lond, in meridie terra Folcanstaninga, in occidentale regis terra, in aquilone Limenaea.[c] Necnon et illud agellum ego illi dabo in sempiternam hereditatem illi habendum et possidendum feliciterque in dies eius perfruendum et post dies eius cuicumque heredi placuerit derelinquendum. Hoc ipsum agellum ab omni seculari difficultate et aduersitatibus intus et foris, notis et ignotis, maioribus minoribus, quamdiu Christiana fides in terra seruetur eternaliter permaneat liber, hoc ipsumque omnibus successoribus nostris in nomine omnipotentis Dei obseruare precepimus. Et si quis hoc seruare uoluerit, seruet illum omnipotentis Dei benedictio hic et in futuro. Si autem sit quod non optamus ut alicuius persone homo diabolica temeritate ausus surrexerit qui hanc donationem nostram infringere uel minuere uel in aliud conuertere quam constitutum est a nobis temptauerit, sciat se rationem esse redditurum in die iudicii, nisi ante digna satisfactione Deo et hominibus emendare uoluerit et cetera.

[a] ÆDBALB F   [b] *For* circumcinctum
[c] *The boundary clause seems intrusive in the dispositive section, but this may simply be due to incompetent adaptation of a model*

23A

Winemund grants land at Burmarsh and Snavewick, Kent, to St Augustine's.
[*c.* A.D. 848]

M. BL Add. 53710, 19rv: copy, s. xiv/xv
Ed.: Twysden, *Scriptores*, col. 1776
Listed: Sawyer 1651 (and see 1650)
Translated: Davis, *Thorne*, p. 33

In nomine Dei celi. Ego Wymundus amicus Edwolphi do et concedo Deo sanctoque Augustino terram de Borewarmers cum terra de[a] Wyk inperpetuum liberam sicut predictus dominus meus michi donauit pro redempcione ipsius anime et mee parentumque nostrorum ubi sepulture requiem michi elegi. Si quis hoc infregerit, anathema sit.

[a] del M

23 is a private charter, recording a sale of land in Romney Marsh by Eadbald to his friend Winemund. The transaction is mentioned by Sprott, who says that Eadbald was the *nepos* of King Æthelwulf (BL Cotton Tiberius A. ix, 115r). There is an entry in the charter-list in PRO E 164/27 (see Appendix 2, no. xlii), which gives the additional information that the grant was made with the consent of King Æthelwulf and Archbishop Ceolnoth, details probably drawn from the lost witness-list. Sprott implies that Eadbald's charter dated from around the same time as the previous charter which he mentions, **20** from 845. In both Sprott's history and the charter-list the reference to Eadbald's grant is followed by a notice that Winemund subsequently gave the estate to St Augustine's; this information may perhaps have been taken from an endorsement, such as those added to S 287 and 332. The chronological table prefixed to Elham's history has an entry under the year 848 for Winemund's grant to St Augustine's (Hardwick, *Elmham*, p. 15), but this may actually have been the date of Eadbald's charter. These three references to Winemund's regrant of the Burmarsh estate are listed as S 1650. One of the manuscripts of William Thorne's history (BL Add. 53710) incorporates a brief extract from a supposed charter of Winemund in favour of St Augustine's, concerning the grant of land at Burmarsh and also at *Wyk* (Snaves or Snavewick, also in Romney Marsh). This has been listed as S 1651, and is printed above as **23A**. It is suspicious that this extract was written by a revisor on an erasure of a longer passage, presumably the description of **18** which appears in this position in CCCC 189, the earlier recension of Thorne's history (see pp. lv–lvi), and that it is firmly identified as a grant of Snaves (Snavewick), which was the object of a long-running dispute (see Twysden, *Scriptores*, cols 1917, 2113; Davis, *Thorne*, pp. 252, 550). As it stands, **23A** appears to be a fabrication.

    23 is one of several surviving private charters produced in the Canterbury diocese in the middle years of the ninth century; it is very similar indeed to S 1196 (A.D. 859), 1199 (A.D. 858 × 866) and 1204 (A.D. 868) in the Christ Church archive. All of these are Latin charters recording land-sales in which the protagonists are laymen and the prices paid for the land are expressed in pence. In each case the charter is attested by the king at a major gathering, usually attended by the archbishop, several ealdormen and a number of thegns and ecclesiastics. The formulation in these documents, as in **23**, is essentially the same as that of the royal diplomas produced in the Canterbury scriptorium at the same period. In **23** the statement of powers, immunity clause and sanction are all standard formulas; the dispositive phrase *do et concedo* is close to the usual *dabo et concedo*, and the wording of the reference to the payment is also characteristic (compare, for instance, **20**). The invocation of **23** is a variant of a common Kentish type, found in S 1196 as well as **18** and S 39 and 344 (see also S 315, 332).

    The extract printed as **23A** is less prepossessing. The invocation appears to be an abbreviation of that used in **23**, and the dispositive phrase is also the same. Winemund describes himself as the *amicus* of Æthelwulf and ascribes the initial grant to *predictus dominus* rather than to Eadbald. The land is 'terram de Borewarmers cum terram de Wyk', which is not contemporary wording. Winemund says that he is making the grant for the souls of Æthelwulf, himself and his kinsmen, and that he intends to be buried at St Augustine's, and the extract concludes with a remarkably brief anathema. There is no good reason to believe that the surviving text was derived from an existing Latin charter, but it may have been built up from some record of Winemund's grant of Burmarsh to the monastery. There are contemporary grants to St Augustine's explicitly made for the soul of the donor and his or her kinsmen and friends (see **24**, **25** and the endorsement to S 332). It is possible that Winemund may indeed have arranged to be buried at the monastery (compare the beneficiary's endorsement to **28**), though this might be an addition connected with later medieval preoccupation with cemetery rights (see p. xxiii, and also the commentary to **28**). It is possible that Winemund's regrant of Burmarsh to St Augustine's was recorded as a vernacular endorsement to his charter, comparable to the endorsement to S 332. The present text of **23A** would then be a fabrication based on the endorsement, with some borrowing from **23**; the intention may have been to incorporate a reference to another Romney Marsh estate supposedly given by Winemund, or to create a document to be used in the dispute with the rector of Snaves.

Neither Eadbald nor Winemund can be positively identified in the witness-lists of contemporary charters (unless Winemund is the Wynna who appears in the witness-list of S 1439, a Canterbury charter of 844).

Burmarsh lies on the northern fringes of Romney Marsh. Its name indicates that it was formerly an area of marshland allocated to the people of Canterbury, the *burhware*, who would have used it for winter-pasture for their flocks (see Everitt, *Continuity*, pp. 58–61). The word *halfsæta* in **23** probably means 'half-pasture'. By the ninth century Burmarsh had evidently passed from common into private ownership, which was also the case with other areas of woodland and marsh in Kent which had formerly been held in common (see **47**, and p. cix). Over the course of the Anglo-Saxon period, land in this area probably became less marshy, as more silt built up on the seaward side of the marsh, so that the area became suitable for cultivation as well as pasture; the Domesday manor of Burmarsh supported forty-four villagers and there was land for twelve ploughs (GDB 12v). For the exploitation and colonization of the marsh during the Anglo-Saxon period see Brooks 1988. The bounds in this charter have been studied and plotted by Ward ('The Saxon Charters of Burmarsh', *AC* xlv (1933), pp. 133–41 at 137–9) and Brooks (1988, p. 96 and fig. 8.5). To the east lay *Suthsaxa lond*, which was a piece of territory belonging to the South Saxons rather than Sussex itself. To the south was land associated with the people of Folkestone; this is also mentioned in the bounds of another Romney Marsh estate located south-west of Burmarsh (S 510). The king held the land to the west, and to the north lay the River *Limen*, which was the name of the eastern section of the River Rother. The deposition of silt in Romney Marsh has completely altered the drainage patterns of the Rother, but references to the *Limen* in charter-boundaries makes it possible to discover its course in the Anglo-Saxon period (see Brooks 1988, pp. 95–8).

In 1086 the abbot's manor of Burmarsh was assessed at two sulungs and three yokes, probably an beneficial assessment since there was capacity for twelve ploughs (GDB 12v). This may have been the land covered in Eadbald's charter, but it is also possible that the abbey had acquired additional holdings in the same place. Part of a marriage agreement made between 1016 and 1020 involved the transfer between the parties of 150 acres at Burmarsh (S 1461). In 1086 St Augustine's also held a manor of four sulungs at Kennington near Ashford, far inland from the Marsh, which is said to have lain in the lands of Burmarsh before the Conquest (GDB 12v). Kennington is likely to have been a fairly late acquisition, for the abbey had a royal charter of 1045, now lost, covering land at Selling and Kennington (S 1657; see Appendix 1, no. xi).

24

*Ealhburh grants a food-rent from land at Brabourne, Kent, to the
community of St Augustine. [c. A.D. 850]*

B. CCCC 286, 74v: copy, s. x[1]
Ed.: a. Thorpe, *Diplomatarium*, pp. 479–80, with translation
   b. Birch 501
   c. Harmer, *SEHD*, pp. 9–10 (no. 6), with translation, pp. 44–5
Listed: Sawyer 1198

In nomine Domini Ealhburh hafaþ geset mid hyre freonda þeahtunga þ
man ælce gere agyfe þam hyþum to scæ Agustine of þam lande æt Bra-
danburnan xl. ambura mealtes 7 eald hryðer 7 iiii peþeras . 7 xl 7 cc hlafes
7 ane pæge spices 7 cyses . 7 iiii foðro þudes 7 xx henfugla ; Spylc man se
þ land hebbe þas ðingc agyfe for Ealdredes saule 7 for Ealhburge ; 7 þa
hiþan asingan ælce dæge æfter hyra ferse þæne sealm for hia Exaudiat te
Dominus . Spæ hpylc man spa þis abrece si he asceadan fram Gode 7 fram
eallum hallgum 7 fram þan halgan pere on þysum life 7 on ecnesse . þon'
synt her æfter þara manna naman to geþitnesse þisse gesetednesse þ is þonne
Drihtnoþ abb' pr' 7 Osmund presbyter Æþelred pr' Þynhere diacon .
Beahmund . Cenheard . Hyse . Adda [.] Cada . Bearnferþ . Bearnhelm .
Ealdred . Ealhburh . Ealhparu . Hoshere . Leofe . Þealdhelm . Dudde .
Ofa . Ofe . Þighelm . Þullaf . Eadpeald . Gif hit þon' spa ge gæþ spa þe na
ne þyscað þ hpylc broc on becume þurh hæþen folc oþþe hpylce oðre
earfoþnesse þ hit man ne mæge þæs geres gelæstan agife on oþrum geare
be tþeofealdum . Gif þon' git ne mæge sylle on ðriddum geare be
ðryfealdum . Gyf he þon' git ne mæge ne nelle ; agife land 7 bec þam hiþum
to scæ Agustine.

24 was one of two vernacular documents copied in the tenth century into CCCC
286, a sixth-century gospel-book (see also **31**). The document was almost certainly
drawn up in the middle of the ninth century, but the present copy belongs to a later
date, probably the 920s (see Plate III and Dumville 1987, p. 171). **24** must have
existed in a separate form for some time before it was added to CCCC 286; by
contrast, the script of **31** seems very close to the apparent date of the transaction
recorded, which suggests that it may perhaps have been copied directly into the
gospel-book. It seems significant that **24** is mentioned in the charter-list in PRO E
164/27 (Appendix 2, no. xliv) and was known to Sprott and Elmham, while there is
no reference in any of these sources to **31**; the implication is that a separate copy of
24 was available. This may have been copied into CCCC 286 at a later date as the
result of a dispute or other problem. The document envisages that subsequent owners
of Brabourne may renege on the agreement, and specifies penalties for that eventuality;

some hitch may have transpired, which prompted the monks to provide the agreement with an extra religious sanction by associating it with a venerated ancient gospel-book.

This is one of a number of ninth-century Canterbury documents concerned with the grant of specified annual food-rents to religious houses. The earliest is S 1188 (probably A.D. 805 × 810) in which arrangements are made for the payment of an annual render from an estate at *Stanhamstead* to Christ Church, in order to celebrate the anniversary of Ealdorman Oswulf and his wife with a general refection of the community and charitable doles; in return, the community pledge liturgical intercession for the souls of the donors. One of the provisions in the will of the Kentish reeve Abba (S 1482) involved a payment of an annual render from an estate in Folkestone; Abba's wife added to this a food-rent from an estate at Challock. Two documents very similar to **24** are preserved as originals at Christ Church. S 1197 is in the name of Lufu or Luba, described as *ancilla dei*, who promised to Christ Church an annual render from her estate at Mongeham (for Mongeham see also **13**). S 1195 is a composite document; in the first part Ealhburh (also the donor of **24**) and Eadweald arrange for the annual payment of a food-rent from an estate at *Burnan* to the Christ Church community, while the second part records an injunction by (Ealdorman) Ealhhere (see **21**) to his daughter to pay a money-rent from an estate at Finglesham. Another document of this type is **25**, a grant by Lulle to St Augustine's of a food-render from an estate at Nackington.

In **24** Ealhburh makes over to St Augustine's an annual food-rent from her estate at Brabourne. This was to consist of forty ambers of malt, a full-grown bullock, four wethers, 240 loaves, a wey of lard and cheese, four fothers of wood and twenty hens (an 'amber' was the equivalent of four bushels of dry weight, a 'wey' was a measure for dry goods which varied with different commodities, and a 'fother' was a cartload). The range of agricultural products is essentially the same as in the other Kentish documents which detail food-renders. Whoever holds the land in the future is to continue to make the render, for the souls of Ealdred and Ealhburh. In return for the food-rent, the community is to sing Psalm 20 daily on her behalf. The sanction and witness-list are followed by a most interesting provision. If the food-rent is not paid, because of the depredations of the Vikings or for some other reason, it is to be doubled in the following year. Continued failure was to bring upon the land-holder an obligation to pay threefold the next year, and a third default would result in the land and the title-deeds being given to St Augustine's (for similar instances of incremental punishment, see S 509, 1417). This rather harsh arrangement gives some insight into the economic damage which might be the result of Viking raids. It seems that the final penalty was never put into effect. According to Sprott (BL Cotton Tiberius A. ix, 115r), the *redditus* was usurped after the Conquest by Hugh de Montfort, who also deprived the abbey of a yardland at Horton and an estate at Hinxhill (see pp. cx–cxi). Before the Conquest Brabourne and Horton were both held by Godric of Bishopsbourne, one of the most important Kentish nobles (GDB 10v, 13v; and see 1r). It is not entirely clear why the charter-list in PRO E 164/27 speaks of **24** as an English charter 'de Braburne id est Hortune' (see Appendix 2, no. xliv); perhaps the fact that both places belonged to a single owner before the Conquest resulted in adjustments being made to the arrangements for the St Augustine's render. An estate at Brabourne was one of those forfeited by the

notorious Wulfbald in the reign of Æthelred the Unready and granted to the king's
mother in 996 (S 877).

The survival of a number of private charters from the ninth century in the Christ
Church archive makes it possible to recognise the relationships of several of the men
and women who are mentioned in them (see Brooks, *Church of Canterbury*, pp.
147–9). Ealhburh seems to have been the sister of two successive ealdormen of Kent,
Ealhhere (841–53) and Æthelmod (853–9). The Ealdred who is mentioned in **24** was
probably her husband; he is also mentioned in the grant of render which Ealhburh
made to Christ Church (S 1195). Eadweald, with whom Ealhburh is acting in S 1195,
seems to have been her great-nephew, the grandson of Ealdorman Ealhhere; he was
the donor of an estate at Willesborough to St Augustine's (S 332 endorsement; see
p. xxxii n. 57). Ealhburh, Ealdred and Eadweald appear among the witnesses to **24**.

The inter-relationships of these donors and documents confirm that the historians
were correct to treat this as a grant of the mid ninth century. In Elmham's
chronological table it is entered under the year 850 (Hardwick, *Elmham*, p. 15); this
could well be a guess, since vernacular documents of this date were not usually dated
(although Elmham may have had access to supplementary information, such as a
list of benefactions with dates). The document is witnessed by Abbot Dryhtnoth, by
two priests and a deacon, and by nineteen others, some of them women. Dryhtnoth
was abbot of St Augustine's, but the dates of his period of office are a matter of
debate (see Appendix 4). He may be the same man as the Abbot *Diernodus* who is
the beneficiary of **22** from 861. At least some of the other witnesses may be members
of the communities of St Augustine's and Christ Church.

The extant text has only one distinctive Kentish spelling, *hia* (l. 6), although *hebbe*
(l. 5) could also be a Kentish symptom (see A. Campbell, 'An Old English Will',
Journal of English and Germanic Philology xxxvii (1938), pp. 132–52 at 146). Vernacular Canterbury documents from the middle of the ninth century preserved as
originals in the Christ Church archive are usually written in a Kentish dialect (see
Harmer, *SEHD*, pp. 128–9). The orthography of **24** seems to represent a later stage
in the development of Old English; Harmer (*ibid.*, p. 85) points to the use of *y* for
i, and forms such as *wudes* and *pæne*. The spelling of the document would appear
to have been modernised when it was copied into CCCC 286.

25

*Lulle grants a food-rent from land at Nackington, Kent, to the community
of St Augustine. [c. A.D. 850]*

G. BL Cotton Claudius D. x, 104r: copy, s. xiii²
  Rubric: Donacio Lulle manerio de Natindone.
Ed.: *Mon. Angl.* (rev. edn), i. 140 (no. 44)
Listed: Sawyer 1239

In nomine Domini. Ic Lulle ꝛeckeᵃ þa hisetnesse þam hiƿm to sc̄e Augustine
for hi ꝛ for hire bearn libbinde, ꝛ for hire freond, ꝛ for alle þa þe hi forþingie.
þanne is þis seo isetnesse of Natindone .xxx. hambre clenes meltes ꝛ tƿa

foðæ þodes 7 .iiii. peþeres 7 a þeimel cheses 7 a sester huniges 7 .v. gys 7 .x. henfugeles. 7 .i. c. hþetene sura lhafa. 7 .xx. clanra hlafa. Ðonne is þis þara gode lean, þ þa hiþen don scealon þat hi agan ealle to cyrican 7 gesingan hore psaltere sealme elce dage þe hia þa god þicgen 7 ælce messe prest ane messe 7 ælce dage hire pater noster 7 se þe þis healde[b] god hine healde.

<ul>
<li>[a] For andette   [b] heade G</li>
</ul>

In the name of the Lord. I Lulle promise this food rent to the community at St Augustine's, for myself (her) and for my (her) living children and for my (her) friends, and for all those who intercede for me (her). This is the render from Nackington: thirty ambers of pure malt and two fothers of wood and four wethers and a wey of cheese and a sester of honey and five geese and ten hens and (? one hundred) loaves of fermented wheat and twenty loaves of pure wheat. This is the reciprocation for the benefits, that the community shall arrange that on each day that they receive the render they shall all go to church and sing their psalter-psalm and each mass-priest shall say a mass and each day they shall say their paternoster. May God preserve whoever preserves this arrangement.

25 is undated and has no witness-list, but it almost certainly belongs to the middle years of the ninth century. Its affinities are with 24, another grant of a food-render to St Augustine's, and with S 1195 and 1197, which are similar grants to the Christ Church community (see further under 24). 25 is preserved only in BL Cotton Claudius D. x, where it is copied at the head of a section referring to Nackington. It does not seem to have been known to the abbey's historians. Presumably a record of the grant of render was kept with other Nackington documents and was not recognised as a pre-Conquest charter. The language of the text has been partly modernized. The scribe of BL Cotton Claudius D. x had difficulty with the text, for he has several times had to erase and rewrite words, but he seems to be making an effort faithfully to reproduce his source, which probably implies that the orthography of the exemplar had been altered. It is possible that the original included a witness-list, similar to those of 24 and S 1197; however, S 1195 is unwitnessed and the same may have been true of 25.

Lulle evidently was or had been married (the lack of any reference to her husband or her husband's soul is remarkable). A *matrona* named Lulle appears in the witness-list of a Worcester charter of 897, apparently an associate of Winchcombe minster (S 1442); she is unlikely to be the same woman as the Nackington donor. In ninth-century Kent the masculine name Lulla (sometimes Lulle) was very common; three men of that name attest S 332 (A.D. 863), a Lulla owned land at Horton and Chartham, just west of Nackington (S 319, A.D. 844 × 874) and another bought property in Canterbury in Alfred's reign (S 287, addition).

The manor of Nackington was held by Odo of Bayeux in 1086 and previously by the burgesses of Canterbury (GDB 9r). A note relating to Nackington has been added to the copy of William Thorne's history in CCCC 189; in the revised version of the history in BL Add. 53710 the note has been incorporated into the text. This states that in 1046 the manor of Nackington was given to Turstin, the abbot's *domicellus*, and afterwards lost to the abbey (Twysden, *Scriptores*, col. 1784; Davis, *Thorne*, p. 44). It is possible that the basis of this story was the alienation of the food-rent rather than of the estate itself. There is no other indication that St Augustine's held land at Nackington before the Conquest. In the reign of Æthelred an estate at Nackington was among several properties forfeited by Wulfbald for his many crimes and given to the king's mother in 993 (S 877); another of Wulfbald's estates was Brabourne, which also owed an annual food-render to St Augustine's (24). In the thirteenth century the abbey was still receiving a rent from Nackington, by now converted into a money-payment. In 1274 part of the rent (5 marks) was assigned for the celebration of the anniversary of the late Abbot Roger (Twysden, *Scriptores*, cols 1921–2; Davis, *Thorne*, pp. 259–60). Fourteen years later St Augustine's was given royal permission to exchange a number of properties with Christ Church, including a rent of thirty-two shillings and eight pence halfpenny from Nackington; the abbey subsequently entered into litigation for the return of six shillings and three pence of the Nackington rent illegally collected by the prior of Christ Church (Twysden, *Scriptores*, cols 1950, 1958–9; Davis, *Thorne*, pp. 302, 316).

26

King Athelstan restores fourteen sulungs (aratra) *at* Werburginland *in Thanet, Kent, to St Augustine.* A.D. 925 (4 September)

F. BL Cotton Julius D. ii, 104v: copy, s. xiii[1]
   No rubric
G. BL Cotton Claudius D. x, 183rv: copy, s. xiii[2]
   Rubric: Item donacio regis Athelstani de quadam terra in Taneto.
I. Canterbury, D. & C., Lit. E. 19, 1v–2r: copy (probably of G), s. xiv[1]
   Rubric: Carta regis Athelstani de Werburginland in Thaneto.
Ed.: a. Birch 641 from G
   b. J. A. Robinson, *The Saxon Bishops of Wells*, British Academy
   Supplementary Papers iv (London, 1918), p. 31, from G
Listed: Sawyer 394
Edited from F and G

Anno ab incarnatione Domini .dccccxxv., indictione .xiii., primo anno regni regis Adalstani,[a] die consecrationis eius, pridie nonas Septembris, rex Saxonum et Anglorum Adalstan terram quatuordecim aratrorum dedit sancto Augustino, que terra in insula Tanet[b] habetur nomine Werburginland, pro remedio anime sue, que etiam rapta fuerat iniuste a sancto Augustino per multos annos sed Deo annuente rex Adalstanus restaurauit iterum illam terram sancto Augustino cum consensu episcoporum octo et principum duorum quorum nomina hec sunt. [c]Adlem archiepiscopus. Alla episcopus.[d]

Siglem episcopus. Wlflem episcopus. Wlbred episcopus. Berneth episcopus. Eatolp episcopus. Winsige episcopus. Ordgar princeps. Aelwald princeps, et Odda minister regis, et Cened abbas, et Alfeth sacerdos, et alius Alfeth sacerdos et monachus.

a Adalstan F   *b* Thanet G
c *For the corrupt names in the witness-list, see commentary.*   *d* F *ends here*

26 records the restoration by King Athelstan to St Augustine of fourteen hides in Thanet, of which the saint had been deprived for many years. The restoration is said to have taken place on the day of Athelstan's consecration, 4 September 925, and a list of witnesses is provided, headed by the archbishop of Canterbury and seven bishops. The form of the charter is anomalous, with no parallel among earlier or later royal diplomas, and it has been suggested that **26** may be a memorandum compiled from a lost charter or perhaps a document originally copied into a gospel-book, rather than a regular royal diploma.

There are two reasons for thinking that a contemporary record underlies the present text. In the first place, the charter seems to contain accurate information about the date of Athelstan's consecration. In two versions of the West Saxon regnal table Athelstan is given a reign-length which seems to have been calculated from 4 September 925 (D.N. Dumville, 'The West Saxon Genealogical Regnal List: Manuscripts and Texts', *Anglia* civ (1986), pp. 1–32 at 29). Two charters of Athelstan which were issued on 16 April 928 (S 399, 400) are assigned to Athelstan's third regnal year, which implies that the draftsman was calculating from a date after 16 April 925. After this there seems to have been a change of policy, for in later diplomas of Athelstan the regnal year was apparently reckoned from a date at the beginning of 925. The explanation for this perhaps lies in the circumstances of Athelstan's accession. After the death of Edward the Elder on 17 July 924 his kingdom was divided between his two sons, Ælfweard and Athelstan, the latter being elected king by the Mercians. Ælfweard survived his father by barely a fortnight, dying on 1 August 924. It is possible that Athelstan was not accepted as king in Wessex until early 925 (implying a five-month inter-regnum in the South), and that this date was later taken as the benchmark for the beginning of his reign; this difficulty in Wessex perhaps explains the postponement of his consecration until September 925, over a year after the deaths of his father and brother (see Keynes 1985, pp. 186–7). According to the Mercian Register, Athelstan was consecrated at Kingston-on-Thames in Surrey, as were most other tenth-century kings of England (see Keynes, *Diplomas*, pp. 270–1).

The witness-list also seems to have been taken from a contemporary source, although the name forms are now corrupt (a fact which is of some importance for evaluating the history of the text). The first witness is Archbishop Athelm, or Æthelhelm, who had previously been bishop of Wells. His attestation of **26** helps to fix the dates of his brief tenure of the Canterbury see. Plegmund, his predecessor, probably died on 2 August 923. The death of Athelm himself was commemorated at Canterbury on 8 January, while *ASC* E and other post-Conquest sources place the succession of the next archbishop, Wulfhelm, in the year 925. But if Athelm died on 8 January 925, he could not have consecrated Athelstan in September of that year. The implication of **26** that it was Athelm and not Wulfhelm who consecrated Athelstan finds support in a statement to this effect by Adelard of Ghent, writing in the early eleventh century (*Vita S. Dunstani auctore Adelardo*, ed. W. Stubbs, in *Memorials of St Dunstan*, RS (London, 1874), pp. 55–6). It seems to have been the case that Athelm's death did not take place until January 926 (see Brooks, *Church of Canterbury*, pp. 214–16).

The seven bishops who attest **26** can be all identified, with a certain amount of confidence. Alla is Ælfwine (known as Ælle) of Lichfield ([903 × 15] – [935 × 941]); Sigelm is Sigehelm of Sherborne (c. 909 or [918 × 925] – [932 × 934]); Wlflem is presumably Wulfhelm, Athelm's immediate successor at Wells and then at Canterbury; Wlbred is probably Wilferth of Worcester (922 or [915 × 922] – [928 × 929]); Berneth is Beornheah of Selsey (*c.* 909-[930 × 931]); Eatolw is perhaps Eadwulf of Crediton (c. 909–934); Winsige is Wynsige of Dorchester ([909 × 925] – [934 × 945]). These bishops had presumably gathered at Kingston for the coronation. Ealdorman Ordgar attests charters of Edward the Elder between 900 and 909 and makes a final appearance in the witness-list of S 396 from 926; Aelwald is the Ealdorman Ælfwald who subscribes several times between 903 and 938. A thegn named Odda attests regularly between 901 and 943. The abbot is Cynath of Evesham (see J.A. Robinson, *The Times of St Dunstan* (Oxford, 1923), pp. 36–40). The final witnesses are two priests named Alfeth (for Ælfheah), the second also identified as a monk. The first Ælfheah is probably the mass-priest of that name who witnessed a manumission by Athelstan, the record of which was entered into a blank space in an eighth-century gospel-book, BL Royal I. B. vii (Keynes 1985, p. 185). The manumission is said to have taken place when Athelstan first became king, and there has been speculation that it was on this gospel-book that Athelstan swore his coronation-oath; in extension, the gospel-book has been associated with St Augustine's and with the transaction recorded in **26**. This connection is questioned by Keynes (1985, pp. 185–9), who points out that the manumission related to the affairs of the royal household and suggests that it was copied into a manuscript which at that time belonged to the king himself. The priest Ælfheah who attests both **26** and the manumission may have been the man of that name appointed to Wells in succession to Wulfhelm in 926; it has been suggested that the second Ælfheah of **26**, the monk-priest, was Ælfheah 'the Bald', who was appointed to Winchester *c.* 934 (see Robinson, *Saxon Bishops of Wells*, pp. 32–3; Keynes 1985, p. 182 n. 186). Both men were presumably priests attached to the king's household.

It seems therefore that the dating clause and the witness-list of **26** almost certainly belong to a record which was made on the day of Athelstan's consecration, but it remains to be seen whether the document in its present form can be considered a contemporary record. A factor of some importance is the degree of corruption in the personal names, which is far more pronounced than is usually the case in documents preserved in the thirteenth-century cartularies from St Augustine's. Both manuscript copies have this feature, and this suggests that they were drawing on a common source which was already several stages removed from any contemporary record. This feature has to be considered against the diplomatic peculiarities of **26**. The extant text has no diplomatic links with charters of Edward the Elder or with later charters of Athelstan. The only formula that is really suitable for comparison with regular land-charters of the period is the royal style, which is unique. Edward the Elder was most commonly styled *rex Angul Saxonum*, and this style is also accorded to Athelstan in two charters of 926 (S 396–7); Athelstan was otherwise styled *rex Anglorum* or a close variant. It is not possible to compare **26** with immediately preceding charters because, for reasons which are now unclear, very few diplomas indeed survive from Edward the Elder's reign, and none at all from the period between 909 and 925 (see p. xcv). The reasons for this development are unclear, but it does suggest that the production of royal charters declined and may even have come to a halt during these years. This could perhaps explain the unusual form of **26**; the scribe may simply have had no practice in drafting diplomas. However, an apparently genuine charter in a conventional form was issued for a Mercian beneficiary in 925 (S 395; Sawyer, *Burton*, no. 2), and it would seem probable that the eminent ecclesiastics who convened for Athelstan's consecration could have mustered at least one scribe capable of drafting a conventional Latin charter, if one were required. It has been suggested, on the basis of the spelling of the king's name, that **26** was drafted by a continental scribe resident in England (M. Lapidge, 'Some Latin poems as evidence for the reign of Athelstan', *Anglo-Saxon England* ix (1981), pp. 61–98 at 77 n. 74). This could account for the peculiarities of form, but it seems unwise to put too much stress on the orthography of this text, given the fact that all the name-forms are so poor (unless these too are to be attributed the scribe's unfamiliarity with Anglo-Saxon names).

Alternatively, it may be that the extant text of **26** represents reworking, and perhaps repeated reworking, of an early record; this would explain the degree of corruption in the personal names. One possibility is that original record was in Old English and that it was translated into Latin after the Conquest. In a pre-Conquest context, the provision of witnesses as a simple list running on in the text is associated with vernacular documents rather than Latin diplomas, where the norm is full subscriptions in columns; examples of Old English texts with witness-lists in this form are **24** and S 204, 1281. But this is hardly a conclusive argument, in view of the possibility of influence in this area from the post-Conquest writ-form; moreover, the form of the dating clause and the reference to *aratra* in the text are perhaps best attributed to a Latin source. It is difficult to reach a firm conclusion on the original form of **26**. It may even be the case that the present document represents a later fabrication where the forger has made use of a charter of 925 to provide certain details, although it is not obvious why St Augustine's should wish to forge a record of this particular transaction.

If we accept that this account of the restoration to St Augustine's is based on a contemporary record of some kind, it is of particular interest in showing that the monastery was already accumulating land on Thanet. The first indication of this came in 826, when St Augustine's acquired a tiny area in the Margate area, probably as an addition to an existing estate in the vicinity (see **17**). **26** suggests that the community held at least fourteen sulungs on the island by the turn of the ninth century. The precise location of *Werburginland* cannot be identified with any confidence. The first element incorporates the female name Werburh (the original form was probably *Werburgingland*). St Werburh of Hanbury and later Chester, the daughter of King Wulfhere of Mercia, had Kentish connections in that she was the grand-daughter of

King Eorcenberht of Kent and thus a cousin of Æbba and Mildrith of Minster-in-Thanet; her cult had a fringe connection with that of Mildrith (see Rollason, *Mildrith Legend*). The obscure Kentish minster at Hoo was apparently dedicated to a St Werburh, according to a note in the *Textus Roffensis* (see G. Ward, 'The Forgotten Saxon Nunnery of Saint Werburg at Hoo', *AC* xlvii (1935), pp. 117–25). This may be the Hanbury Werburh, but there is an alternative Kentish candidate. In the genuine witness-list to the Council of Bapchild preserved in the spurious S 22, which probably dates from 716 or shortly before, a Queen Werburh attests alongside King Wihtred and is identified as the mother of his third son, Alric; she was probably Wihtred's third wife (see commentary to 9). It is possible that Queen Werburh was buried and culted at Hoo, and she may previously have retired there after Wihtred's death. The St Werburh of Hoo may perhaps be associated with *Werburginland* in Thanet; alternatively, the place-name may refer to a completely unknown woman of the same name. It may be noted that between 844 and 852 King Burgred of Mercia confirmed the Rochester ship-toll charter (S 88) at a place named *Werburgewic*; this was almost certainly not in Kent, which was by that time controlled by the West Saxon kings.

Wallenberg (*KPN*, p. 237) could suggest no identification for *Werburginland*, but A.H. Davis (*Thorne*, p. 35 n. 3) proposed Way, a tiny hamlet situated about half a mile east of the village of Minster, which appears as Wayborough on eighteenth-century maps. It seems unlikely that St Augustine's already owned a substantial property in the close vicinity of Minster as early as the ninth or early tenth century, and it is difficult to see how the medieval place-name could have become Wayborough. It seems more likely that the fourteen sulungs lay in the vicinity of Margate, where the monastery was acquiring land in the early ninth century (17).

27

King Edmund grants two sulungs (aratra) *at Sibertswold, Kent, to Sigeric, minister.* A.D. 944

F. BL Cotton Julius D. ii, 104r: copy, s. xiii[1]
   No rubric
G*. BL Cotton Claudius D. x, 62rv: copy of Inspeximus [R], s. xiv[1]
   Rubric: Carta Edmundus regis de Sybrighteswealde.
H. PRO E 164/27, 82rv: copy, s. xiii
   Rubric: Carta Eadmundi regis de Siberdeswelde.
M. BL Add. 53710, 222v–223r: copy of Inspeximus [S], s. xiv/xv
R. PRO Ch. R. 20 Edw. II, m. 2
S. PRO Ch. R. 36 Edw. III, m. 7
T. PRO Ch. R. 8 Hen. IV, m. 6
U. PRO Pat. R. 2 Hen. VI, pt 3. m. 5
V. PRO Pat. R. 4 Edw. IV, pt. 4, m. 29
W. PRO Pat. R. 14 Hen. VII, pt 1, m. 16
Ed.: a. Twysden, *Scriptores*, cols 2125–6, from M
      b. Kemble 1132 from F, 1149 from G*

c. Birch 755 from F, 797 from G*
d. Pierquin, *Recueil*, pt 3, no. 98, from Birch
Listed: Sawyer 501
Edited from F, G* and H

*a*In nomine sancte trinitatis. Quamuis decreta pontificum et uerba sacerdotum uelut*b* fundamenta montium in districtis ligaminibus fixa sint,*c* tamen plerumque tempestates*d* et turbines secularium rerum etiam religio sancte Dei ecclesie maculis reproborum dissipabitur*e* ac rumpitur. Idcirco incertum futurorum temporum statum*f* prouidentes posteris succedentibus profuturum esse decreuimus ut ea que communi tractu salubri*g* consilio diffiniuntur, sertis*h* litterulis roborata confirmentur. Quapropter ego Eadmundus*i* rex Anglorum ceterarumque gentium in circuitu persistentium gubernator et rector cuidam mihi fidelissimo ministro nomine Sigerico,*j* deuotionis eius solertia*k* eiusdemque placatus obsequio, dignatus sum impertiri duas aratras in illo loco ubi iamdudum solicole*l* illius regionis nomen imposuerunt *m*æt Spyðbrihtespealde.*m* Tali autem tenore hoc prefate munificentie munus tradendo concessi ut possideat et firmiter teneat usque ad ultimum uite sue cursum, cum omnibus utensilibus que Deus celorum in ipsa telluris gramine creauerit,*n* tam *o*in notis*o* causis quam*p* et ignotis, in modicis et in magnis, campis, pascuis, siluis, omnino donans donabo libertatem. Et postquam humani generis fragilitatem*q* deseruerit et ad*r* desiderabilem iocunditatis uiam per gratiam superni iudicis adierit, *s*succedentium sibi cuicumque libuerit*s* eternaliter derelinquat, ceu*t* superius prenotaui. Sit autem predictum rus liber ab omni fiscali tributo seculariumque seruitutum exinanitum, sine expeditione et pontis arcisue instructione,*u* precipioque in nomine Dei summi tam nobis uiuentibus tam etiam diuina precepta predicantibus huius libertatis statuta ad irritum deducere minime quispiam presumat. Quisquis beniuola mente meam donationem amplificare satagerit in hoc presenti seculo, uita illius amplificetur feliciter longiturneque uite gaudia teneat. Si quis autem propria temeritate uiolenter inuadere presumpserit, sciat se proculdubio ante tribunal districti iudicis titubantem tremebundumque*v* rationem redditurum ni prius digna satisfactione emendare maluerit.

Istis terminibus predicta terra circumcincta esse uidetur.*w* *x*Of cymesing on otpunes*y* hyldan ufepyrde, ⁊lang ricges oð ða*z* stret, niðer ⁊lang strete ⁊ spa norð on aggint beorgas, of hagging beorgan on brynessole, of brynessole ⁊lang Colredinga gemercan oð helfesdene, oð*a2* helfesdene oð lectan æcer, oð*a2* leccan æcere oð Þiccham, ut on ðone feld oð bealdessol, of bealdessole þest oð Stylfing*b2* on ðone kalepanstoce, of ðam kalepanstocce on beodune oð ðone ealdanþeg, ⁊lang þeges eft ongean*c2* cymesing.*x*

Acta est hec prefata donatio anno ab incarnatione Domini nostri Iesu Christi
.dcccc.xliiii., indictione .ii.^{d2}

Ego Eadmundus rex Anglorum prefatam donationem meam cum signo
sancte crucis confirmaui +.
Ego Edred eiusdem regis frater consignaui +.
Ego Edgifa eiusdem regis ⟨mater⟩^{e2} consensi +.
Ego ⟨Oda⟩^{e2} Dorouernensis ecclesie archiepiscopus eiusdem regis donationem
cum tropheo agye crucis consignaui +.
Ego Wlstan archiepiscopus predictum donum subarraui + etc.

^{a} Inspeximus etiam carta Edmundi quondam regis Anglie in hec uerba G*
^{b} uelud H ^{c} sunt H
^{d} *The sense requires* per *or an equivalent before* tempestates (*there is the same deficiency in
the other examples of this formula*) ^{e} discipatur F; dissipatur H ^{f} *Omitted* F
^{g}? *Read* salubrique ^{h} certis H ^{i} Edmundus G*, H
^{j} Si'gi'rigo abbati F; Sirigo abbati H ^{k} sollercia F ^{l} cilicole H
^{m} . . . ^{m} at Sibrighteswealde G*; Siberdeswalde H ^{n} creauit G* ^{o} . . . ^{o} ignotis H
^{p} *Omitted* G* ^{q} *Omitted* H ^{r} *Omitted* F, H
^{s} . . . ^{s} succedentibus sibi (filii F) abbatibus et sanctis apostolis famulantibus F, H
^{t} seu G*, H ^{u} constructione H ^{v} tremebundamque F, G*, H ^{w} F *ends here*
^{x} . . . ^{x} H *omits bounds* ^{y}? *Or* otþunes (*see commentary*) ^{z} da G* ^{a2} *For of*
^{b2} *For* Scylfing ^{c2} ong' G* ^{d2} secunda G*. G* *ends here*
^{e2} *Supplied* (*these words are omitted in* H, *the only source for the witness-list*)

27 exists in two versions. In Edward II's Inspeximus charter the beneficiary is a
thegn named Sigeric, who is given full powers to dispose of the estate. But in the
thirteenth-century cartulary copies (and also in the relevant entry in the PRO
charter-list; see Appendix 2, no. xxvii) Sigeric has been transformed into an abbot
and the statement of powers has been amended to refer to the abbot's successors
and the community. It appears that, as in the case of 16 and 21, the cartularies
contain a version of the diploma which had been tampered with in order to create
a direct grant to St Augustine's; here the revisor simply converted a thegn into an
abbot and altered the statement of powers. Since the Inspeximus charter contains
an unrevised version of the text, it would appear that the original itself had not been
tampered with and was still available in the early fourteenth century to be submitted
for confirmation (see also 21). It is an added complication that by the fifteenth
century the fictitious Abbot Sigeric had been added to the list of St Augustine's
abbots, complete with fictitious dates (Hardwick, *Elmham*, p. 20; see further Appendix
4).

The copy of the text in MS F concludes with the introduction to the bounds. In
MS H the bounds are omitted, but the dating clause and the first five subscriptions
of the witness-list are provided; these have not previously been printed. The version
of 27 in the Inspeximus charter (MS G*) gives the boundary clause and dating
clause, but omits the witness-list.

There can be no doubt that the unrevised version of 27 is authentic. It has very close diplomatic links with a small group of charters with nearly identical formulation issued between 944 and 947 (S 497, 506, 525, 528; and see S 507). These typically have the same brief invocation (found also in two other contemporary charters, S 500 and 510), the same proem on the theme of the necessity for recording decrees in writing (also in S 493), the same royal style (the one most commonly applied to Edmund and Eadred), very similar formulation in the dispositive section, the same elaborate statement of powers (for which see also S 493, 513, 530, 532–3), the same immunity clause (also in S 493, 530, 532, 535) and the same common sanction (S 528 has a different sanction). In only one respect does 27 differ from the group formed by S 497, 506, 525 and 528; three of these four charters, those which most probably survive in their original form (the exception is S 506), give a vernacular translation of the Latin unit of assessment, but this is not the case in 27. The formulation of the dating-clause is the same as in the majority of Edmund's charters. The forms of the surviving subscriptions in 27 are paralleled in S 497, a Christ Church original from the same year. S 497 is the first surviving example of a diploma written by the scribe known as 'Edmund C', who seems to have been the principal scribe of royal charters between 944 and 949 (see Keynes, *Diplomas*, pp. 16–17). He was also responsible for S 510, 528, 535 and 552; the only surviving originals from this six-year period which he did not write are S 495 and 546 (the latter may not be original). The balance of probability is that the lost original of 27 was the work of 'Edmund C'. He is most likely to have been a scribe attached to a central royal secretariat (see Keynes 1985, p. 150).

The thegn who was the beneficiary of 27 cannot be positively identified in contemporary witness-lists, although he may perhaps be the Sigeric who attested a Canterbury lease which was probably issued in 905 or 920 (S 1288). It is remarkable that the Sibertswold estate seems to have been particularly associated with men whose names began with the same letter. The place-name itself means 'Swithbeorht's wood' (*DEPN*, p. 421). The beneficiary of 27 is Sigeric. A further grant of land at Sibertswold was made by King Æthelred to a thegn named Sigered (30). This Sigered can be perhaps be identified with a Kentish thegn known as Sired who regularly attests Kentish charters at the turn of the tenth century alongside his brother Siweard (see Keynes, *Diplomas*, pp. 132–4). It is possible that all these men were members of the same family, whose male offshoots were generally given names alliterating in *S*.

Sibertswold, also known as Shepherdswell, lies on the northern slopes of the Kent Downs, in an area where the many of the Anglo-Saxon place-names refer to woodland or wood-pasture. Everitt (*Continuity*, pp. 127–8) suggests that Sibertswold was one of a number of estates here that began as wood-pastures colonized from the longer-established settlements on the coast and in the lower parts of the river valleys. The second Sibertswold charter in the archive records the grant of two hides there to Sigered in 990 (30). No bounds have survived for the later diploma, but it seems probable that it referred to an additional estate. In 1086 St Augustine's held a manor at Sibertswold assessed at two sulungs, with land for four ploughs (GDB 12v); three other small estates there, with a total assessment of rather less than two sulungs, were listed among the lands of the canons of St Martin's at Dover (GDB 1v). Sprott mentions the two pre-Conquest charters relating to Sibertswold and then complains that the lands to which they gave title were alienated by the first Norman abbot,

Scotland; he promises to relate the circumstances in the appropriate place, but in the event he simply says that the land was farmed out for an annual rent (BL Cotton Tiberius A ix, 115v, 122rv).

The boundary clause preserved in the Inspeximus charter is difficult to follow on the ground. It probably begins at a point on the north-eastern boundary of the estate, the usual starting-point in Anglo-Saxon charter-bounds. *Cymesing*, which is the same name as Kemsing near Otford in West Kent, seems to incorporate a personal name *Cymesa* and to mean 'Cymesa's place' (*DEPN*, p. 271). Next comes a slope (*h(i)elde*), defined by a personal name in the genitive which is perhaps Ohtwyn or Ohthun;. From the upper part of the slope the boundary follows a ridge and a street to *(h)agging beorgas*. Here *beorg* probably means 'tumulus', while the first part of the name may be associated with the personal name *Hæcga* or with OE *hag(g)a*, 'haw, fruit of hawthorn' (Smith, *EPNE*, p. 222); Wallenberg (*KPN*, p. 264) suggests a connection with Haynes Farm, north-east of Sibertswold (TR 274485). The next boundary mark is *brynnesole*, probably 'Bryni's pond or muddy place' (OE personal name Bryni, *sol*). Several surviving place-names in the vicinity of Sibertswold incorporate the element *-sole* (Sole's Farm, Newsole Farm, Claysole Wood), but none of these can be positively identified with this boundary mark; the survey also mentions a *bealdessol* at a later point. From this the boundary marched with that of the people of Coldred (a settlement south-east of Sibertswold) as far as *helfesdene*; here the first element may be OE *ælf*, 'elf', or *hielfe*, 'handle', and the second element is *denu*, 'valley' (the reference may be the the steep valley in which lies Lydden, just south of Coldred). *Leccan* (or *lectan*) *æcer* would have been a particular field; the first element is perhaps OE **læc(c)e*, 'stream, bog' (Smith, *EPNE*, p. 10). The next boundary mark is preserved in the modern place-name Wickham Bushes (TR 246457). From here the survey proceeds out into a *feld* or clearing (see *Bewesfeld* in **14**) to 'Bald's pond or muddy place' and then to Shelvin (TR 225475); the name *Scylfing* contains the topographical element *scylf*, 'shelf, ledge', which occurs also in Old and New Shelve to the east of Lenham (see **19**). The next boundary mark is 'the bare stump' (*calu*, *stocc*); from here the boundary touches on 'bee hill' (*beo*, *dun*), and then follows 'the old way' back to *cymesing*.

28

a. *King Eadred grants one and a half hides* (mansae) *at Swalecliffe, Kent, to his man Heresige.* A.D. 946

b. *Heresige transfers the land to the monastery of SS Peter and Paul.*

F. BL Cotton Julius D. ii, 105v: copy, s. xiii[1]
   No rubric
G. BL Cotton Claudius D. x, 307r: copy, s. xiii[2]
   Rubric: Carta regis Eadredi de manerio de Suualecliue.
Ed.: a. Kemble 1176 from G
   b. Birch 874 from F, 1345 from G
   c. Pierquin, *Recueil*, pt 3, no. 16, from Birch
Listed: Sawyer 518
Edited from F and G

Regnante inperpetuum Domino nostro Iesu Christo. Imminentibus*a* uite caducis terminis qua in*b* nos sceleris licet onere pressi nutu diuino statuti,*c* tamen dominica prosequentes monita prout quimus secundum illud euangelii ubi dicitur, Date et dabitur uobis.[1] Quapropter ego Eadredus rex Anglorum ceterarumque gentium in circuitu persistentium gubernator et rector cuidam meo homini uocitato nomine Heresige mansam et dimidiam concedo ubi ruricoli antiquo usu nomen imposuerunt æt Spaleþanclife, eatenus ut hoc diebus suis possideat tramitibusque uite sue, et post se.*d* Maneat prout iam predixeram donum istud ab omni seculari seruitio exinanitum cum omnibus ad se rite pertinentibus, campis, pascuis, pratis, siluis, *e*excepto istis tribus, expeditione pontis arcisue constructione.*e* Si quis autem quod non optamus hanc nostram diffinitionem elationis habitu incedens infringere temptauerit, perpessus sit gelidis glaciarum flatibus et pennino exercitu*f* malignorum spirituum, nisi prius inriguis penitentie gemitibus et pura emendatione emendauerit.

Istis terminibus predicta terra circumgirata*g* esse uidetur.*h* *i*Hec fynteali mearc.*i* þis sindon Spaleþanclifes land gemero. Ærest of þære se to þam burnan, of þam burnan be þere east mearke, spa to ælfþoldes*j* mearke, of ælþoldes*k* mearke to kynges mearke to se, et seo þudureden þe þer mid rihte to gebirede et þ dændere*l* Cæthærst hatte, 7 þ sealttærn steal æt Here pic.*m*

Acta est prefata donacio anno ab incarnacione Domini nostri Iesu Christi .dccccxlvi., indictione quarta.

+ Ego Ædredus rex Anglorum prefatam donationem cum sigillo sancte crucis consignaui.
+ Ego Oda archiepiscopus cum sigillo sancte crucis confirmaui.
+ Ego Ælfheah episcopus cum signaculo sancte crucis impressi.
+ Ego Cenþald episcopus consensi.
+ Ego Ælfric episcopus consignaui.
Æþelstan dux.
Ædric dux.
Ælfstan minister.
Þulfric minister.
Ælfsige minister.
Þistan abbas sancti Augustini.
Sifreð minister.
Ældred minister.

Heresi[n] minister Anglorum regis Eadredi dito monasterium beatorum apostolorum Petri et Pauli eorumque seruos sibi inhibi seruientes predicta ditacione qua me dominus meus prefatus rex ditauit, ubi michi locum sepulture meisque successoribus eidem tenature dominantibus elegi, rege Ædredo eiusque regina cum regni eius optimatibus uolente. Ualeant omnes hiis fauentes.

[a] iminentibus G   [b] *Read* in qua
[c] *A verb is needed here, perhaps* sumus (*this is a common standard formula, and always deficient in this respect*)
[d] *The remainder of the statement of powers has been omitted in both F and G, probably deliberately. The missing text can be supplied from S 500 and 510:* cuicumque sibi placuerit post hoc tradat hereditario eternaliter ceu predixi illi.   [e] *...* [e] *Omitted* G
[f] excercitu G   [g] circumgyrata F   [h] *F ends here*
[i] *...* [i] *Corrupt (probably for* Hec synt eal imare)   [j] ælfpoldes G   [k] ælpoldes G
[l] *For* dænbere   [m] pic G   [n] [ ]eresi G

[1] Luke 6: 38

The better version of this text is that in BL Cotton Claudius D. x, where it is copied with other documents relating to Swalecliffe. The scribe has carefully reproduced the boundary clause (obviously with some difficulty) and what may be the whole of the witness-list, together with an addition in the name of the beneficiary transferring the land to St Augustine's, which may have been an endorsement to the original charter. The compiler of BL Cotton Julius D. ii, in accordance with his usual practice, has abbreviated the text, breaking off after the introduction to the boundary clause.

The formulation of **28** aligns it with two contemporary texts, S 500 (A.D. 944) from Abingdon, dealing with an estate in Berkshire, and a second Kentish charter from 946 (S 510), preserved as an original at Christ Church. The latter was written by the royal charter-scribe known as 'Edmund C' (see further under **27**), who seems to have been responsible for the majority of royal charters issued between 944 and 949, and who probably wrote the original of **28**. The text begins with a common invocation. The proem, on the theme of generosity, is shared with S 500 and 510; it recurs in three charters of Edgar (S 704, 770 and 794). Eadred's royal style here is the one most commonly applied to him and to his predecessor. The wording of the disposition in **28** is closely comparable to the corresponding sections in S 500 and 510. The three diplomas also share a unique statement of powers, which is deficient in **28**, lacking the reference to the right of posthumous bequest in both surviving manuscript copies. The omission of this significant formula is unlikely to be the result of a simple error on the part of a copyist. It is possible that the original draftsman modified the formula because Heresige had already made known his intention to pass on the estate to St Augustine's, but the probability is that this is a later emendation, either made (with a degree of legitimacy) at the time of Heresige's grant to the abbey or carried out subsequently in the St Augustine's archive. It is important that both cartulary copies of the diploma have this omission; ultimately both go back to a common source, either an original diploma with this feature or a modified text in a lost cartulary (see further, pp. l–li).

The close relationship between **28** and S 500 and 510 continues in the immunity clause, which is found in all three texts and also in S 580 (A.D. 946 × 955), 704 (A.D. 962), 770 (A.D. 969); see also S 951 (A.D. 1018). The anathema of **28** is a common formula condemning the malefactor to perpetual refrigeration instead of the more usual hell-fire; this was in regular use between 938 and 947, and also occurs in S 510 (the anathema in S 500 is rather different). The wording of the introduction to the bounds is standard for this period, as is that of the dating clause. The form of the subscriptions of the principal witnesses is rather more restrained than is usually the case in the 940s, but this need not be significant. The witnesses are headed by King Eadred and Archbishop Oda. The other three bishops are Ælfheah of Winchester, Cenwald of Worcester and probably Ælfric of Ramsbury. The two ealdormen are Æthelstan 'Half-King' of East Anglia and his brother Eadric, who governed part of Wessex. The remaining witnesses are thegns, apart from a certain Wigstan who is identified as abbot of St Augustine's. It is not usual for an abbot to be identified in the witness-lists of charters at this period; indeed, it is not usual for abbots to attest at all in the pre-Reform period. Wigstan does not appear in the lists of abbots of St Augustine's, although the significance of this is not clear-cut, since the lists appear to be defective and partly fictitious (see Appendix 4) and are obviously not definitive for the 940s. It is possible that a later scribe supplied the identification, not necessarily on good grounds.

The formulation of **28** links it with other contemporary royal diplomas, as well as the two with which it is most closely aligned, and there can be no doubt that it is a product of the central writing-office. The note recording Heresige's regrant of the estate may have been added as an endorsement. There is little material with which to compare its wording, for it was not usual for tenth-century royal diplomas to be endorsed in this way. The nearest parallel is **23A** from the ninth century, in which the beneficiary of **23** transfers his estate to St Augustine, with a similar statement about his wish to be buried in the monastery. **23A** appears to have been interpolated, and there is perhaps some reason to believe that the extant text has been constructed at a later date, partly on the basis of **23** and perhaps also of a lost vernacular endorsement. The wording of Heresige's addition has some details in common with that of **23A**. It is possible that both these passages are of pre-Conquest origin, and that St Augustine's had a particular interest in endorsing original charters which came into its possession; alternatively, the particular interest may have been shown by post-Conquest scribes. The formulation of the passage in **28** does not really seem contemporary, and suspicion certainly arises from the use of the word *tenatura*, attested in England only in post-Conquest contexts. A noticeable feature of this section is the reference to the abbey as the minster of SS Peter and Paul. The double dedication is rare in St Augustine's charters, although it was technically correct until 978, when Dunstan rededicated the church to SS Peter, Paul and Augustine; in the ninth and tenth centuries (and thereafter) the abbey was usually known as St Augustine's (see p. xiv). In surviving charters the double dedication occurs only in two mid-eighth-century texts (**11**, **12**), in a spurious text of the same period (**14**), and in the series of post-Conquest forgeries supposed to date from the seventh century; its use here reinforces suspicion of the passage. Surprisingly, the entry for **28** in the PRO charter-list states that Heresige gave the land to SS Peter and Paul and also to St Augustine (see Appendix 2, no. xxxiii).

28 is one of a number of tenth-century diplomas in which the beneficiary is described as the king's man, rather than by the usual term *minister* (thegn); other examples are S 510, 522, 552, 580, 628, 653, 669 etc. This may be simply a variant introduced by charter-scribes, but it is possible that the status of these men differed from that of the usual king's thegn, although it is not clear that they were less important; Wulfric, described as the king's man in S 552 (A.D. 949), was an extremely wealthy man with extensive estates in three shires in 960 (S 687). Heresige is not mentioned elsewhere. He was presumably a Kentishman.

28 is concerned with the grant of one and a half hides at Swalecliffe, which lies on the north coast of Kent, just east of Whitstable and some six miles north of Canterbury. For the use of a hide-assessment in tenth-century Kentish charters see pp. lxxviii–lxxix. The only Swalecliffe manor mentioned in the Domesday survey was one assessed at half a sulung, held by Vitalis of Canterbury from Odo of Bayeux and previously by Edward Snoch from King Edward (GDB 10r). However, it seems to have been the case that in the eleventh century St Augustine's held land at Swalecliffe which was reckoned under its manor of Sturry; the estate-survey in PRO E 164/27 headed *Extractum de textu S. Adriani*, which seems to draw on material contemporary with the Domesday Inquest (see pp. cvi–cvii), has an entry 'in Stureie hundredo Storeie et Swalclive quinque solinos (PRO E 164/27, 11v). This indicates that there was land in Swalecliffe which was treated as a detached portion of the Sturry manor, just as the abbey's lands at Margate in Thanet were associated with the mainland manor of Chislet at the time of the Domesday survey (see **17**). But the association between Sturry and Swalecliffe in the estate-survey suggests that it may be incorrect to identify the Swalecliffe property with that in **28**. There is good reason to believe that the Sturry manor represents part of the mainland property of Minster-in-Thanet, inherited by St Augustine's in the eleventh century (see further under **41**). Moreover, it seems almost certain that the Swalecliffe outlier of the Sturry manor is to be identified with the small estate in the area called *bi Northanuude* granted to Minster by King Eadberht I in 727 (**48**); the link between Sturry and the detached property at Swalecliffe would therefore seem to predate the acquisition of the Minster estates by St Augustine's. It is difficult to see how **28** fits into this picture. It is possible that the one and a half hides at Swalecliffe granted to Heresige and acquired at some stage by St Augustine's were subsequently combined with the former Minster property in the area, and that both were reckoned together under the Sturry manor. In the twelfth century Abbot Hugh II assigned the abbey's land at Swalecliffe to provide clothing for the brethren (Twysden, *Scriptores*, col. 1799).

Between the Latin and vernacular introductions to the bounds appears a corrupt phrase, partly in Latin and partly in Old English, which seems to be an interpolation, perhaps an interpolated gloss (*Hæc sunt eal gemære*); it is not found elsewhere. The survey begins at the sea, and then follows a stream past 'the east mark'. The remaining boundaries were with an estate belonging to Ælfwold (probably to the south) and a royal estate (probably to the west); the latter is perhaps to be identified with the small manor held by Edward Snoch from King Edward in 1066. The survey concludes with notices of appurtenances belonging to Swalecliffe. These included 'wood-rights' (*wuduræden*) and a wood-pasture called *Cæthærst*. The second element of the latter is presumably OE *hyrst*, 'hill, woodland', but the first is British *ceto-* ('forest'), also found in the Kentish place-names Chatham and Chattenden (see

DEPN, p. 97). Wallenberg (*KPN*, p. 308) notes a reference in the thirteenth-century register BL Cotton Faustina A. i to an appurtenance of Swalecliffe called *Hagenilde Chetterste ad Merestune* (Turner and Salter, *Black Book*, p. 150), and suggests that *Merestune* may have been the lost Merston near Shorne; Shorne is north-west of Rochester, and thus close to Chatham and Chattenden. It seems unlikely that an estate at Swalecliffe would have an appurtenant woodland pasture beyond Rochester; a more appropriate location for *Cætherst* would be in the nearby Blean Forest. The final appurtenance of the estate is a salt-works (*sealtern, steall*) at *here wic*. There is a similar reference in S 332 (A.D. 863), relating to an inland estate at Mersham, which mentions 'unam salis coquinariam hoc est .i. sealternstall et ðer cota to in illa loco ubi nominatur herewic'. Wallenberg (*KPN*, pp. 217, 308) argues for a link with Harwich Street in Whitstable; his further suggestion that *sealternsteall* is Seasalter itself is clearly incorrect.

29

King Edgar grants four sulungs (aratra) *at Plumstead, Kent, to St Augustine and his monastery.* [A.D. 963 × 971 (? A.D. 963)]

F. BL Cotton Julius D. ii, 86v–87r: copy, s. xiii[1]
  Rubric: De quatuor solinis de Plumstede.
G. BL Cotton Claudius D. x, 222r: copy, s. xiii[2]
  Rubric: Carta regis Eadgari feofantis Deum et beatum Augustinum Anglorum apostolum ac fratres in monasterio sancti Augustini Cantuarie seruientes cum terra quatuor aratrorum que nominatur Plumstede.
Ed.: a. J. Thorpe, *Registrum Roffense* (London, 1769), pp. 520–1, from G
    b. Kemble 562 from G
    c. *Mon. Angl.* (rev. edn), i. 144 (no. 58), from G
    d. Birch 1173 from G
    e. Pierquin, *Recueil*, pt 4, no. 16, from Birch
Listed: Sawyer 809
Edited from F and G

In nomine trino diuino, regi regnanti inperpetuum Domino Deo Sabaoth, cui patent cuncta penetralia cordis et corporis terrestria simul et celestia, necnon super ethera regnans in sedibus altis ima et alta omnia sua dicione gubernans. Cuius amore et eternis premiis,[a] ego Eadgarus rex Anglorum do et concedo sancto Augustino Anglorum apostolo et fratribus in illo sancto cenobio conuersantibus terram quatuor aratrorum que nominatur Plumstede. Hanc ergo terram cum consensu archiepiscopi Dunstani optimatumque meorum libenti animo concedo pro redemptione anime mee ut eam teneant perhenniterque habeant. Si quis uero heredum successorumque meorum hanc meam donationem seruare uel amplificare studuerit, seruetur ei desuper benedictio sempiterna. Si autem sit quod non optamus quod alicuius persone homo diabolica[b] temeritate instigatus surrexerit, qui hanc meam donationem infringere in aliquo temptauerit, sciat se ante tribunal summi et eterni iudicis rationem esse redditurum, nisi ante digna et placabili satisfactione Deo et sancto Augustino fratribusque emendare uoluerit.

+[c] Ego Eadgar[d] Anglorum monarchus hoc donum agie crucis taumate roboraui.[e]

+ Ego Dunstanus archiepiscopus consensi.

+ Ego Osketel Eboracensis archiepiscopus consensi.

+ Ego Athelstan Lundon' episcopus consensi.

+ Ego Atewolf Herefordensis episcopus consensi.

+ Ego Alfric abba.

+ Ego Osgar abba.

+ Ego Oslac dux subscripsi.

+ Ego Ælfere dux subscripsi.

> [a] *The exposition requires a participle for sense, but in this case has been borrowed directly from a ninth-century model (see S 332, and commentary below)*   [b] dyabolica G   [c] *F omits cross*   [d] *Ædgar F*   [e] *F ends here*

29 purports to be a grant by King Edgar to St Augustine, Apostle of the English, and to the brethren of the monastery. There is no boundary clause or dating clause, although part of a witness-list has been preserved. This is almost certainly a forgery.

The formulation of the charter has largely been borrowed from a ninth-century exemplar. The elaborate extended invocation is also found in S 332 (A.D. 863), an original charter preserved at Christ Church, which has an endorsement showing that in the late ninth century it was at St Augustine's (see p. xxxii n. 57); indeed, it seems possible that S 332 itself was the draftsman's model. The blessing and anathema are based on standard Canterbury formulas of the mid ninth century, and these could also have been derived from S 332; the anathema has been reworked to include a reference to St Augustine and the monks. The dispositive verbs *do et concedo* can be associated with the standard formula *dabo et concedo* of S 332 and other ninth-century Canterbury diplomas. The dispositive section departs from the ninth-century model, but does not conform to tenth-century usage, although Edgar is given a contemporary royal style. The attached witness-list appears to derive from an authentic diploma of the period. The king's subscription is essentially the same as that in S 690, a original from 961, and the associated S 688 and 689. The other subjective subscriptions are much less elaborate than is usual in Edgar's diplomas, perhaps as a result of the influence of the ninth-century exemplar. Both archbishops attest. The name of the bishop of London is given as Æthelstan instead of Ælfstan; for such mistakes by copyists see Keynes, *Diplomas*, p. 235. The second bishop is Athulf of Hereford. The identification of Athulf's see is very unusual. In charters of the central decades of the tenth century the subscriptions of bishops of London and Winchester identify their sees on some occasions, especially in the 940s, but there is no parallel for this reference to Hereford; it was not until Æthelred's reign that other episcopal sees were identified on a regular basis (see Keynes, *Diplomas*, pp. 24 n. 32, 119–20). Yet it is most unlikely that a later forger would have known that Athulf was bishop of Hereford, which suggests that the source for the witness-list may have been slightly unorthodox. The next two subscriptions are those of abbots. Ælfric was probably the contemporary abbot of St Augustine's (see Appendix 4). Osgar succeeded Æthelwold at Abingdon in 963; he was blessed on 28 December in that year, and does not attest charters until 964. The remaining subscriptions are those of Ealdormen Oslac of Northumbria and Ælfhere of Mercia. It is generally believed that Oslac was not appointed until 966 (D. Whitelock, 'The Dealings of the Kings of England with Northumbria in the Tenth and Eleventh Centuries', *The Anglo-Saxons*, ed. P. Clemoes (London, 1959), pp. 70–88 at 78).

Thus the witness-list of **29** seems to be acceptable in a charter of Edgar, presumably one dating from the period between Oslac's appointment (? in 966) and Osketel's death in 971 (and perhaps drawn up in unusual circumstances, as suggested by the identification of the see of Hereford). The text of the charter itself was evidently written at St Augustine's and was probably modelled in part on a ninth-century charter in the archive. It remains to be decided whether **29** is to regarded as a St Augustine's fabrication with a genuine witness-list appended or as an authentic but unorthodox charter of Edgar. A possible reason for taking the latter view is the parallel presented by S 1215 (A.D. 968). This is a private charter, which survives as a Christ Church original, but it is attested by Edgar and Dunstan and by a motley body of Kentish witnesses, including a number of *rustici* and the communities at Christ Church and St Augustine's. Here again the draftsman has gone back to a ninth-century model for the statement of powers and the sanction. It may be that **29** was a similar local production, drafted by a scribe well out of the diplomatic mainstream, but written with royal permission and attested by the king.

But there are far more potent reasons for considering **29** to be a forgery. One is the date of 963 which Elmham offers for the charter in his chronological table, and which was presumably derived from or associated with the text of the charter (Hardwick, *Elmham*, p. 21). Since this is exactly a century later than the date of S 332, which probably served as the draftsman's exemplar, it suggests that the date of the charter (suitably emended) was also taken from the model; this would be an unusual proceeding if the charter was an unorthodox but contemporary production. A date of 963 is incompatible with the subscriptions of Abbot Osgar and Ealdorman Oslac.

If S 332 itself was the draftsman's model, certain difficulties arise concerning its whereabouts and history. It covers an estate at Mersham, but has an endorsement in which Eadweald grants 'this land at Willesborough' to St Augustine's. The circumstances in which the endorsement was added and its meaning remain mysterious (see p. xxxii n. 57), but there can be no doubt that the charter was at the abbey in the later ninth century. Willesborough was sold back to Eadweald's son for 2000 pence (see Appendix 1, no. ii). In theory the abbey should have returned the title-deed to him, but it is possible that a new document was drawn up, or that the abbey retained a copy. An estate at Mersham was given to Christ Church by Sigweard and his wife, probably in the period between 1053 and 1061 (see S 1090); it seems likely that S 332 entered the Christ Church archive at this time. The easiest reconstruction would be to suppose that S 332 was given back to Eadweald's son in the late ninth century, and that it remained in lay possession until it passed into the hands of the Christ Church community in the Confessor's reign. In that case the use of the charter by the draftsman of **29** would be impossible; he would have to have seen either a copy or another document altogether.

Further reason to be wary of **29** is provided by the fact that it covers an estate which was disputed in the eleventh century. In 1086 St Augustine's held a manor at Plumstead answering for two sulungs and one hide; the number of ploughs is not given (GDB 12r). A contemporary estate-survey provides the additional detail that this estate was held by Sorag TRE (Ballard, *Inquisition*, p. 1); it is not clear whether he was a tenant. Among the estates of the bishop of Bayeux was another Plumstead manor, also assessed at two sulungs and a yoke (five ploughs); before the Conquest it was held by Brihtsige Cild from King Edward, and in 1086 by the abbot of St Augustine's from Odo (GDB 6v). The later medieval historians of the abbey claimed that this second estate rightly belonged to St Augustine's, but had been seized by Earl Godwine and given to his son Tostig, then restored by King Edward, subsequently claimed and stolen by Odo of Bayeux, and finally confirmed by King William (BL Cotton Tiberius A. ix, 116r; Twysden, *Scriptores*, col. 1779; Davis, *Thorne*, p. 37); the spurious charter of William concerning Plumstead is included in Elmham's history (Hardwick, *Elmham*, pp. 350–1; see *Regesta*, i, no. 88). A final detail that seems relevant appears in the estate-survey in PRO E 164/27 which is said to have been taken from the *Textus sancti Adriani* (see pp. cvi–cvii) and which is probably early-twelfth-century in its present form: 'Alia pars de Plumsted quam diu tenuit (sanctus Augustinus) et *per cartas suas* iuste possedit sed modo inuste ei ablata est' (fol. 11v).

It is difficult to know what to make of this involved story. An aspect which is hard to reconcile with other evidence is the nefarious behaviour of Earl Godwine towards St Augustine's. During the middle decades of the eleventh century the version of the Anglo-Saxon Chronicle which was being kept at St Augustine's (the prototype of *ASC E*) gaves a consistently favourable account of the activities of Godwine and his sons, which seems an unlikely attitude if Godwine had indeed appropriated part of the abbey's endowment; similarly, relations between Odo and St Augustine's seem to have been generally good (see p. cxi). It is possible that the later tale of confiscation and restoration conceals a more complex dispute about ownership of Plumstead, and that St Augustine's did not have a clearcut title to both estates (the fact that the two Plumstead manors have exactly the same assessment perhaps indicates that a larger property had been at some stage split in two, perhaps as part of a dispute settlement). This situation provides an adequate context for the fabrication of **29**. The four sulungs of the charter approximately correspond with the total Domesday assessment of the two Plumsteads (four sulungs and two yokes). **29** was probably fabricated before the early twelfth century, since it is likely to have been one of the *cartae* on which the abbey based its claim to the 'other Plumstead', according to the estate-survey taken from the *Textus S. Adriani* (see above).

30

King Æthelred grants two hides (cassati) *at Sibertswold, Kent, to Sigered,*
minister. A.D. 990

F. BL Cotton Julius D. ii, 104v: copy, s. xiii[1]
  No rubric
H. PRO E 164/27, 82v–83r: copy, s. xiii
  Rubric: Item carta Ethelredi de eadem terra.
Ed.: Kemble 1285 from F
Listed: Sawyer 875
Edited from F and H

Fortuna uolubilis infortunii fallax sibi iugiter aggeratim*ᵃ* dum plus aliquan-
tisper solito fauet, nectarea plerisque in sui certaminis palestra ap-
plaudentibus deceptatoriaque*ᵇ* fraudulenter famulantibus conficiendo
odoramina florum, quibus plerumque ignauos ubi ad maiora quam necessaria
sunt inhiare, suapte illiciendo proterueque instigando prouocat, nequaquam
uerso pollice sine meroris grauissima permittit abire acrimonia quos mundi
istius maxima pellexerat illecebra.*ᶜ* Quapropter, cogitando instantis*ᵈ* temporis
lubrica et futuri apud*ᵉ* superos gaudia regni, ego Æðelredus*ᶠ* rex Anglorum,
anno a passione Domini .dccccxc., regno uero mihi commissi*ᵍ* .xi., indictione*ʰ*
.iii.,*ⁱ* per eiusdem pantocratoris*ʲ* idumam totius Britannie solio sublimatus,
condonaui quandam mihi ab eo telluris particulam mirabiliter concessam
meo fideli ministro Sigeredo, id est duorum cassatorum in loco quem solicole*ᵏ*
Spyðbeortespeald*ˡ* uocant, cum pratis, pascuis omnibusque ad eam rite
pertinentibus, ut possideat liberaliter usque ad extremum uite sue tramitem,
deinceps*ᵐ* autem sibi succedenti cuicumque placuerit heredi in eternam
relinquat hereditatem, ab omni re seculari liberam exceptis tribus, hoc est
expeditione, pontis arcisue constructione. Tellus quidem prescripta his*ⁿ*
terminis circumcingitur*ᵒ* et cetera. Si quis autem ut non optamus hanc me*ᵖ*
donacionis cartulam cupiditatis liuore depressus uiolari satagerit, agminibus
tetre caliginis implicitur, uocem audiat examinationis in die magni arbitris
dicentis, Discedite a me maledicti in ignem eternum,[1] nisi digna satisfactione
sinon*ʳ* penituerit ante.

Ego Ethelredus rex Anglorum proprie manus impressione signaui +
Ego Sigericus Dorobernensis archiepiscopus subscripsi + et cetera.

ᵃ agregatim H   *ᵇ* deceptoriaque H   *ᶜ* illicebra H   *ᵈ* instanti H
ᵉ aput H   *ᶠ* Ethelredus H   *ᵍ* concessi H   *ʰ* indirectione F
ⁱ *Omitted* H   *ʲ* pantocratonis H   *ᵏ* celicole H   *ˡ* Siberdeswelde H

m de deinceps F   *n* hiis H   *o* F *ends here*   *p For* mee   *q* uiolari H
r implicitur H   *s Corrupt* (? *read* suum reum)

¹ Matt. 25: 41

The beneficiary of **30** is perhaps the Kentish thegn usually known as Sired, who together with his brother Siweard attests a number of royal diplomas issued between 995 and 1005 (S 878, 885, 893, 899, 904–5) and two Kentish private charters, **31** and S 1456 (see Keynes, *Diplomas*, pp. 132–4). The archive contains an earlier charter concerning Sibertswold, which records a grant of two sulungs there to a thegn named Sigeric (**27**). It is possible that the repeated initial indicates a family relationship between the earlier and later beneficiary, and perhaps also with the eponymous Swithbeorht of Sibertswold. The history of the abbey's estate at Sibertswold is discussed in the commentary to **27**. .

The text of Æthelred's charter is preserved only in an abbreviated form. Both manuscripts omit the boundary clause and most of the witness-list has been lost; the anathema and the two subscriptions preserved in PRO E 164/27 have not previously been printed. There is no diplomatic reason to suspect the authenticity of the charter, although it has some unusual features. The draftsman has evidently been influenced by the formulation of diplomas from the earlier tenth century, particularly the elaborate charters issued in the name of Athelstan between 930 and 934 and associated with the scribe known as 'Æthelstan A' (for these see Keynes, *Diplomas*, pp. 42–4); the recycling and adaptation of earlier formulas is very characteristic of Æthelred's charters issued between his accession and 990 (*ibid.*, pp. 85–7). The proem of **30** is reminiscent of, although not verbally close to, that beginning *Fortuna fallentis seculi*, found in charters of Athelstan issued between May 934 and December 935 (S 407, 425–6, 458; ands see S 434–6, 1166). The royal style (here split by a dating clause) is an elaboration of the already elaborate style applied to Athelstan in charters of 'Æthelstan A' (for this see S 416, 425). The position of the dating clause may also be due to influence from a model of the same period (see S 399, 400). The regnal year in **30** appears to be calculated from the king's coronation on 4 May 979, and not from his accession on 18 March 978 (Keynes, *Diplomas*, p. 233); this is one of several charters in which this was the case (see also S 842, 869, 873, 875, 886). The wording of the reference to the regnal year also displays the influence of the complex dating clauses of 'Æthelstan A'; there is further correspondence in the reference to the estate as *telluris particulam* and the wording of the introduction to the (lost) boundary clause. For other sections of the charter the draftsman has turned to slightly later models. The statement of powers is an adaptation of a standard formula in regular use between 940 and 962, while the sanction represents a reworking of another common formula in use over approximately the same period and indeed often found alongside the same statement of powers (see S 465, 474–5, 502, 536, 585, 587, 674, 679; and S [Add.] 517a, 517b). It appears that the draftsman of **30** was adapting formulas derived from at least two models (a diploma of 'Æthelstan A' and another slightly later charter) and perhaps more. The surviving subscriptions are those of King Æthelred and Archbishop Sigeric, who was transferred from Ramsbury to Canterbury in 990; he had been abbot of St Augustine's (*HRH*, p. 35; and see p. xviii n. 18).

31

Abbot Wulfric and Ealdred, son of Lyfing, make an agreement about land at Clife. [c. A.D. 985 × 1006]

B. CCCC 286, 77v: copy s. x/xi
Ed.: a. Hickes, *Dissertatio Epistolaris*, p. 10
    b. Wanley, *Catalogus*, p. 151
    c. Kemble 429
    d. Robertson, *Charters*, p. 128 (no. 62), with translation, p. 129
Listed: Sawyer 1455

+ In nomine Domini nostri Iesu Christi . Her sputelað on þisum geƿrite hu Ƿulfric abb' . 7 Ealdred Lifinges sunu þæs ðegnes pæron sammæle ymbe þ land æt Clife. þæt he gebeh for godes ege 7 for sc̄s Augustinus . 7 for hys freonda mynegunge . mid lande into sc̄e Augustine . 7 ælce geare sylð on sc̄s Augustinus mæssedæg .i. pund to gesputelunga . 7 æfter hys dæge gange þ land into sc̄e Augustine . spa geƿerud spa hit þonne byð ; þyses ys to geƿitnesse se hired æt sc̄e Augustine 7 se æt Cristes cyrcean . 7 Lifing his fæder . 7 Siƿeard . 7 Sired his broðor . 7 Ƿulfstan æt Sealtpuda . 7 oðer Ƿulfstan ; 7 þis sy gedon for Siferð . 7 for his ofsprincg to hyra saple ðearfe a butan ende ; Amen ;

31 is one of two vernacular documents copied into CCCC 286, a sixth-century gospel-book belonging to St Augustine's (Plate IV; see also **24** and pp. xxxviii–xxxix). It records an agreement between Wulfric, abbot of St Augustine's, and Ealdred, son of Lyfing, about land at *Clife*. Ealdred has commended himself and the land to St Augustine's, and has promised to pay one pound every year; on his death the land is to pass to the monastery. The verb used here is *(ge)bugan*, 'to bow', employed elsewhere for the act of voluntary submission to lordship (see R.P. Abels, *Lordship and Military Obligation in Anglo-Saxon England* (Berkeley, Los Angeles and London, 1988), p. 82). Commendation seems to have been an important process in later Anglo-Saxon England and is a constant theme in Domesday Book, although it is rarely noted in the pre-Conquest sources (for discussion see F.M. Stenton, *Anglo-Saxon England*, 3rd edn (Oxford, 1971), pp. 490–2, 518; F.W. Maitland, *Domesday Book and Beyond* (Cambridge, 1897), pp. 67–74; Abels, *Lordship and Military Obligation*, p. 150; S. Reynolds, *Fiefs and Vassals* (Oxford, 1994), pp. 29–30, 338–40). One exception is S 1081, a writ of the Confessor from Bury St Edmund's, which gives a thegn named Ælfric Modercope permission to commend himself to two lords, the abbots of Bury and Ely.

    31 belongs to the time of Abbot Wulfric I, the successor of Sigeric (*HRH*, p. 35). Sigeric was made bishop of Ramsbury in 985, but he may have remained abbot of St Augustine's until he was transferred to Canterbury in 990. Wulfric attests charters between 993 and 1005 (see Keynes, *Diplomas*, Table 6); his successor, Ælfmær, does not subscribe any of Æthelred's charters, so the date of his election cannot be

ascertained. In Elmham's chronological table Wulfric's period of office is assigned
to the years 989–1006 (Hardwick, *Elmham*, p. 23), but there is little reason to believe
the dates in the table at this point. The dating limits for **31** are those of Wulfric's
period of office. Among the witnesses are the brothers Siweard and Sired, Kentish
thegns who attest several royal charters between 995 and 1005 (Keynes, *Diplomas*,
pp. 132–4); Sired may be the beneficiary of **30**. Lyfing, Ealdred's father, is perhaps
Lyfing of Malling, who attests S 1456, a document drawn up at Canterbury between
995 and 1005, which concerns a dispute over land at Snodland, near Malling. S 1456
is also attested by Siweard, Sired and Wulfstan of Saltwood; these three men, with
Lyfing, subscribe S 905 from 1002, which records a lease of land in Canterbury, with
reversion to Christ Church. There can be little doubt that **31** belongs to the end of
the tenth or the beginning of the eleventh century.

The script of the copy in CCCC 286 seems roughly contemporary with the date
of the transaction (see Ker, *Catalogue*, no. 55), and it is possible that the record was
entered directly into the gospel-book. There is no evidence that **31** was widely known
in the later medieval period. It is not mentioned in the charter-list in PRO E 164/
27, nor by any of the medieval historians. This neglect contrasts with the treatment
of **24**, the other vernacular document copied into CCCC 286, which certainly appears
to have existed as a separate document and was not added to the gospel-book until
over half a century after the benefaction had been made. But **31** may not have
received attention for some other reason, perhaps because the connection between
St Augustine's and the estate had been subsequently broken. It is unfortunate that
Clife cannot be properly identified. One suggestion is that it was Cliffe (Cliffe at
Hoo), which lies some four miles to the north of Rochester. There were two Domesday
manors there, one assessed at three and a half sulungs (two and a half TRE) and
held by Christ Church before and after the Conquest, and the other assessed at half
a sulung and held by two brothers from King Edward and later by a tenant of Odo
of Bayeux (GDB 4v, 9r). There is no sign that St Augustine's had pre-Conquest
interests in this area. Closer to other St Augustine's estates are St Margaret's-at-Cliffe
and West Cliffe, near Dover and adjacent to land held by the abbey at Martin and
Langdon (see **22**), and at no great distance from Northbourne, Mongeham and
Sibertswold. West Cliffe was held by the Bishop of Bayeux in 1086 and had previously
belonged to King Edward (GDB 11r); St Margaret's-at-Cliffe was among the
possessions of St Martin's at Dover (GDB 1v). An original charter datable to
between 1042 and 1044 (S 1044) records the grant to a layman of two hides *æt Clife*,
apparently in the vicinity of West Cliffe. Ealdred's estate may have been located in
this area, and not at Cliffe at Hoo. Alternatively, another *Clife* may have been
intended, perhaps even Swalecliffe (see **28**).

32

*King Cnut declares that he has granted judicial and financial privileges to St
Augustine's.*

G. BL Cotton Claudius D. x, 57r: copy, s. xiii[2]
 Rubric: Rex Cnutus de libertate ecclesie sancti Augustini Cantuar'.

I. Canterbury, D. & C., Lit. E. 19, 94r: incomplete copy, s. xiv[1]
Ed.: a. Kemble 756 from G
    b. *Mon. Angl.* (rev. edn), i. 139 (no. 36), from G
    c. Thorpe, *Diplomatarium*, p. 336, from G
    d. Harmer, *Writs*, pp. 197–8 (no. 36), from G
Listed: Sawyer 989
Printed from G

Ego Cnut per Dei misericordiam basileus Ægelnodo archiepiscopo et omnibus episcopis, abbatibus, comitibus, uicecomitibus et omnibus fidelibus tocius Anglie salutem et amiciciam. Sciatis me dedisse Deo et sancto Augustino et fratribus ut habeant eorum saca et socna, et pacis fracturam, et pugnam in domo factam, et uie assaltus, et latrones in terra sua captos latronumque suscepcionem uel pastionem super illorum proprios homines infra ciuitatem et extra, theloneumque suum in terra et in aqua atque consuetudinem que dicitur theames*a* et super omnes allodiarios quos eis habeo datos. Nec uolo consentire ut aliquis in aliqua re de hiis se intromittat, nisi eorum prepositi quibus ipsi hec commendauerint, quia habeo has consuetudines Deo datas et sancto Augustino pro redempcione anime mee et successorum meorum, ita ut eas libere et pleniter habeant et possideant inperpetuum. Et qui hanc donationem meam infringere uel irritam facere temptauerit a Deo omnipotente et omni sancta ecclesia excommunicatus sit. Amen.

a For teames

32 is almost certainly a post-Conquest fabrication, largely based on **35**, a writ of the Confessor granting the same privileges. The greeting and concluding sanction were apparently modelled on those of **33**, an equally suspicious writ of Cnut concerning the Minster property, while the central section is borrowed from the Latin version of **35** (see Harmer, *Writs*, pp. 190–1). The Confessor's writ may be authentic in its vernacular form (although it is not without difficulties), but **32** is best regarded as a spurious concoction, rather than as a translation of a lost English writ. The forger was probably inspired by the statement in **35** that St Augustine's was to enjoy its privileges as it had done in the reign of Cnut.

32 appears to have had little circulation in the later medieval period, and may not have come into existence until the later thirteenth century. It seems particularly significant that it was not added to the Cartae Antiquae Roll alongside **35** and the series of post-Conquest writs covering similar privileges. The other three writs in the archive (**33**, **35**, **39**) were submitted for confirmation and enrolment in 1326, and were much copied; all three are mentioned together in the charter-list in PRO E 164/27 (Appendix 2, nos xlvi–viii) and were known to the later historians, but there is no reference at all to **32**, although it should have been regarded as an important document. It would appear that the fabrication had little currency. The only time at which it does seem to have been put to use is in 1313, when the community used a *carta regis Knutty*, together with **35**, to prove their rights to jurisdiction and the related privileges (Harmer, *Writs*, p. 191 n. 1).

33

King Cnut declares that he has granted the body of St Mildrith and the estates of her church to St Augustine.

E. PRO Cart. Ant. R. 9, no. 19: copy, s. xiii[1]
  Rubric: Carta eorundem [*sc.* monachorum sancti Augustini] cum sigillo.
F. BL Cotton Julius D. ii, 85v: copy, s. xiii[1]
  Rubric: Donacio regis Knuti de Taneto.
G. BL Cotton Claudius D. x, 183r: copy, s. xiii[2]
  Rubric: Donatio regis Knuti de Menstre cum corpore beate uirginis Mildrede.
G*. BL Cotton Claudius D. x, 63r: copy of Inspeximus [R], s. xiv[1]
  Rubric: Carta regis Cnud de donacione corporis sancte Mildrede.
H. PRO E 164/27, 145v–146r: copy, s. xiii/xiv
  Rubric: Donacio sanctissimi regis Cnuth de Thanet.
I. Canterbury, D. & C., Lit. E. 19, 1r: copy (probably of G), s. xiv[1]
  Rubric: Carta regis Knuti de manerio de Menstre.
J. London, Lambeth Palace, 419, 122r: copy, s. xiv
L. CCCC 189, 53v: copy, s. xiv
M1. BL Add. 53710, 14r: copy, s. xiv/xv
M2. BL Add. 53710, 223v: copy of Inspeximus [S], s. xiv/xv
R. PRO Ch. R. 20 Edw. II. m. 2
S. PRO Ch. R. 36 Edw. III m. 7
T. PRO Ch. R. 8 Hen. IV m. 6
U. PRO Pat. R. 2 Hen. VI. pt 3, m. 5
V. PRO Pat. R. 4 Edw. IV, pt 4, m. 29
W. PRO Pat. R. 14 Hen. VII, pt 1, m. 16
Ed.: a. *Mon. Angl.*, i. 84, from F
    b. Twysden, *Scriptores*, cols 1783 from M1, 2127 from M2
    c. Kemble 1326 from R
    d. *Mon. Angl.* (rev. edn), i. 449 (no. 2), from 1st edn
    e. Harmer, *Writs*, p. 198 (no. 37) from F
Listed: Sawyer 990
Edited from E and F

Ego Knut[a] per Dei misericordiam basileus Ægelnoðo[b] archiepiscopo et omnibus episcopis, abbatibus, comitibus, uicecomitibus et omnibus fidelibus tocius Anglie salutem et amicitiam. Notum sit uobis omnibus me dedisse sancto Augustino patrono meo corpus sancte Mildryþe[c] gloriose uirginis cum tota terra sua infra insulam Tænæt[d] et extra, cum omnibus consuetudinibus ad suam ecclesiam pertinentibus. Hec omnia ita libera et quieta reddo Deo et abbati Ælfstano et fratribus loci sicut ego ea unquam melius[e] habui, tam in terra quam in mari et in litore,[f] ut habeant et[g] possideant inperpetuum. Et qui hanc donationem meam infringere uel irritam facere temptauerit, a Deo omnipotente et omni sancta ecclesia excommunicatus sit. Amen.

^a Cnud E   ^b Ægelnodo F   ^c Mildriþe F   ^d Tenet F   ^e *Omitted* E   ^f littore E
^g *Omitted* F

33 is a writ supposedly associated with Cnut's grant to St Augustine's of Mildrith's relics and of the estates associated with her community. The abbey certainly seems to have gained possession of the relics and of at least part of the Minster endowment in the course of Cnut's reign (see pp. xxx–xxxi), but the writ itself is probably a post-Conquest fabrication, rather than a Latin translation of a genuine vernacular document. When **33** was copied onto a Cartae Antiquae roll, probably in the early thirteenth century, the scribe noted that it was equipped with a seal (*cum sigillo*), which indicates that the Latin text was a pseudo-original, not an innocent translation. Harmer (*Writs*, pp. 196–7) considered that some of the wording recalled that of the more celebrated forged charters in the name of King Æthelberht, but the correspondence is not strong and the details may have been drawn independently from the common stock of Anglo-Saxon diplomatic.

In his account of Mildrith's translation, written between 1087 and 1091, Goscelin mentions that Cnut gave to St Augustine's all the lands and privileges which had previously belonged to Minster-in-Thanet, and that he confirmed this with a royal charter ('regio testamento et priuilegio'), which was attested by all the bishops and important men ('omnium ... pontificum et magnatum regni subscriptione astipulatum'): see Goscelin, *Translatio S. Mildrethe*, pp. 166–7. This can hardly be a reference to **33**. It is possible that the primary record of Cnut's grant (not necessarily an authentic document) was a Latin diploma in the traditional Anglo-Saxon form, which was later superseded by a fabricated writ with a forged seal, a diplomatic type more consistent with post-Conquest practice. The writ may have derived some of its wording from the diploma. Goscelin uses the phrase *intra et extra insulam* in connection with Cnut's charter, and there is a corresponding phrase in **33**. Cnut's royal style in the writ could have been taken from a diploma; he is styled *basileus* in several originals (S 956, 961, 963, 971, 977). The relationship of this lost charter of Cnut with the extant fabrication in the name of Edward granting Thanet to St Augustine's is not clear (see further under **34**). It may be significant that **33** and, on Goscelin's account, the Latin charter of Cnut, were particularly concerned with the grant of Mildrith's relics and not simply with the Minster property, while Edward's charter simply assumes that the relics are at St Augustine's and deals primarily with the land. It is possible that the documents in Cnut's name were intended to support the abbey's claim to possess the relics, which was challenged by St Gregory's Priory in the later eleventh century (see p. xxiii).

It seems likely that **33** came into existence in the course of the twelfth century, between the time of Goscelin and the compilation of Cartae Antiquae Roll 9, probably in John's reign. From the thirteenth century onwards it was frequently copied, and was one of the documents confirmed by Edward II in his Inspeximus charter of 1326. It appears to have been used as a model by the forger of **32**.

34

King Edward grants the island of Thanet to the church of SS Peter and Paul, and confirms the church's possessions and privileges. [A.D. 1042 × 1045]

C. BL Cotton Vespasian B. xx, 276r: copy, s. xv
   Rubric: Confirmacio sancti Edwardi regis et confessoris Westmonasterii [. . . . .]ᵃ
F. BL Cotton Julius D. ii, 90rv: copy, s. xiii¹
   Rubric: Confirmatio regis Edwardi de Tenet.
G. BL Cotton Claudius D. x, 183r: copy, s. xiii²
   Rubric: Item confirmacio sancti Edwardi regis Anglie de manerio de Menstre.
G*. BL Cotton Claudius D. x, 63rv: copy of Inspeximus [R], s. xiv¹
   Rubric: Carta regis Edwardi de manerio de Menstre.
I. Canterbury, D. & C., Lit. E 19, 63rv: copy (probably of G), s. xiv¹
   Rubric: Confirmacio regis Edwardi de ecclesia sancti Augustini et super Menstre.
M. BL Add. 53710, 223v–224r: copy of Inspeximus [S], s. xiv/xv
R. PRO Ch. R. 20 Edw. II, m. 2
S. PRO Ch. R. 36 Edw. III, m. 7
T. PRO Ch. R. 8 Hen. IV, m. 6
U. PRO Pat. R. 2 Hen. VI, pt 3, m. 5
V. PRO Pat. R. 4 Edw. IV, pt 4, m. 29
W. PRO Pat. R. 14 Hen. VII, pt 1, m. 16
Ed.: a. *Mon. Angl.*, i. 84–5, from F
      b. Twysden, *Scriptores*, cols 2127–8, from M
      c. Kemble 900 from C, F and G*
      d. *Mon. Angl.* (rev. edn), i. 450 (no. 3), from 1st edn
      e. Thorpe, *Diplomatarium*, pp. 425–6, from C, F and G*
      f. Pierquin, *Recueil*, pt 6, no. 53, from Kemble
Listed: Sawyer 1048
Edited from C, F and G*

Conditor celi terreque Deus, uniuersitate totius creature de nichilo perfecta, primum hominem de limo formauit eumque ad imaginem suam configurauit, cui et omnium operum suorum dominari precepit, ea uidelicet ratione ut homo rationabilis irrationabili uteretur creatura,ᵇ per quam ipse Deo seruiens obediret et obediendo creatorem honoraret. Deinde, succedente generatione in generationem, templa et ecclesias fieri constituens, de primitiis et decimis ac de substantia sue largitionis eas in nomine suo honorari precepit. Insuper et per euuangelium nos instruens ait, Thesaurizateᶜ uobis thesauros in celo et reliqua.¹ Quapropter ego Eadpeardusᵈ regis regum gratia rex et Anglorum princeps, post longam exiliationem solius miserentis Dei nutuᵉ in regno meo reuersus et in solio patrum meorum residens, ecclesiam quam hortatu beati Augustini rex Æthelberhtᶠ in honore apostolorum Petri et Pauli a fundamento constituit diuersisque donis ditauit, in qua ipsius regis et omnium episcoporum Cantie ac regum corpora poniᵍ possent, cum omnibus appenditiis uel adiacentiis*h* suis liberam esse annuo et statuto. Quoniam quidem in eadem ecclesia supradictus rex conditus iacet eiusque stirpis progenita Deo dilecta requiescit uirgo Mildryþa,*i* ego etiam eiusdem regis stemmate*j* ortus et regno eius Deo iuuante*k* potitus, Tanatos insulam trado, quam Hegberctus*l* rex iure hereditario concessit uenerabili regine Domneue, matri scilicet sancte Mildrythe,*m* quantum cerua cursu suo lustrauerat, pro interemptione duorum fratrum eius Æþelredi atque Æþelberti,*n* quos iussu eiusdem principis Deo odibilis Thunur iniqua strauit morte, quem mox celestis ultio terribiliter subsecuta est ipsum perimendo. Sed et omnes donationes possessionum uel facultatum quas prisco siue moderno tempore predecessores mei reges eidem ecclesie contulerunt, et ego regia potestate contrado atque firma astipulatione, cum consensu et testimonio episcoporum, ducum, principum et satellitum meorum, abbati Ælfstano ac monachis ibidem sub regula beati Benedicti abbatis Deo militantibus ad habenda et perfruenda sibi perpetua libertate constituens attribuo.*o* Si cui uero hec largitio displicet uel si quis quod absit hanc *p*minuerit, percutiat*p* eum Deus amentia et cecitate ac furore mentis omnique tempore calumpniam maledictionis Dei sustineat, nec sit qui eum liberet nisi penitens*q* resipiscat et digna emendatione satisfaciat. Hec autem traditio regalis in eodem loco seruetur inconuulsa et incontaminata, Deo teste qui dixit, Michi uindicta,*r* ego retribuam,[2] contradicentibus uero ad ruinam et ad condempnationem in die furoris*s* Domini, cum eos qui dixerunt Domino Deo, Recede a nobis, scientiam*t* uiarum tuarum nolumus.[3]

---

a Rest of rubric illegible C   *b* creature F, G*   *c* thesaurizare G*
d Eadpardus C; Edwardus G*   *e* intuitu G*   *f* Ædelbrit F; Adelbright G*
g corpora poni (*with transposition marks*) C; poni corpora F   *h For* adiacentibus
i Mildrytha *altered to* Mildretha C; Mildrida G*   *j* stemate C   *k* adiuuante G*
l Hegbertus C, G*   *m* Mildrytha *altered to* Mildretha C; Milbrythe F; Midrihe G*
n Æthelbryti C   *o* attributo G*
p . . . *p* donationem zelo ductus diaboli quoquo ingenio infringere temptauerit, iram Dei et omni sanctorum maledicta incurrat et subita morte intereat sicut predictus 'Dei' inimicus Thunur interiit percutiatque G*   *q* penites F   *r* uindictam C, F, G*
s die ire furoris C   *t Omitted* G*

[1] Matt. 6: 20
[2] Rom. 13: 19; Heb. 10: 30
[3] Job 21: 14

There are two versions of **34**, distinguished by one major variant. The shorter version is that preserved in two thirteenth-century cartularies (MSS F, G), in a fourteenth-century copy derived from one of these (MS I), and in a fifteenth-century addition to BL Cotton Vespasian B. xx (MS C). The text of **34** incorporated into the Inspeximus charter of Edward II in 1326, which was subsequently enrolled and confirmed on several occasions, includes an extra passage in the sanction referring to the divine punishment of the villain Thunur, who opposed the foundation of Minster-in-Thanet (see MS G*). It is impossible to be certain whether the cartulary text or the Inspeximus represents the primary version of the charter. Since it is probable that the charter submitted to Edward II was in the form of a single sheet, it could be argued that the longer version was primary and should be preferred; but, against this, there is some evidence that St Augustine's was producing fake originals in this period, sometimes apparently derived from cartulary copies (see commentaries to **2**, **3** and **40**).

34 is almost certainly a fabrication, and perhaps a very early one. It has a two-fold purpose. Edward is made to confirm the abbey's liberties and estates, in terms which stress its ancient foundation and long history; he also grants to St Augustine's the island of Thanet, as it had previously been granted to the mother of St Mildrith. There is no dating clause or witness-list in any of the surviving manuscripts, but it is clear that the charter is supposed to belong to the very beginning of Edward's reign; the king refers to his long exile and his accession, and there is also a reference to Abbot Ælfstan, who resigned in 1045 and died in 1046. It was Ælfstan who acquired Mildrith's relics, in rather dubious circumstances, and it may be significant that he subsequently became involved in a dispute about 'Mildrith's property' with a priest named Leofwine; this was settled in 1044 or 1045, with a compromise that suggests that Leofwine has some justification in his claims (S 1472). The abbot's case in this dispute seems to have rested entirely upon the possession of Mildrith's relics, which were reckoned to attach the Minster property ineluctably to St Augustine's (see further, pp. xxx–xxxi). The same argument seems to underlie **34**; Edward gives Thanet to the abbey simply because Mildrith is buried there. In both **34** and the record of the dispute settlement some attempt is made to exploit the legends about Minster's original foundation; S 1472 refers obliquely to 'her uncles' wergeld', while the draftsman of **34** goes into detail about the story. The two documents seem to provide a similar justification for the abbey's tenure of the Minster property, and also agree in their implication that the early years of Edward's reign were a significant period in respect of this issue. There is something of a contrast with the emphasis in the later hagiographical material, and in **33** (probably forged in the twelfth century), on Cnut as the unquestioned donor of the Minster estates to the abbey. It does seem important here that S 1472 stresses that Cnut gave Mildrith's relics to St Augustine's, but says nothing about him actively donating the lands (indeed, the evidence strongly indicates that Cnut had been selling off the Minster estates without reference to St Augustine's); similarly, **34** presents Edward as the donor of Thanet, with no suggestion that he was actually confirming a grant by Cnut. S 1472 and **34** seem to represent an earlier stage in the abbey's claims about its Minster property, and to belong to a period when St Augustine's could not successfully argue that Cnut had made over the Minster estates along with Mildrith's relics. By the later eleventh century the exact circumstances of the abbey's acquisition of Thanet had been forgotten, and the story could be simplified, with the whole credit for the donation given to Cnut.

It is important to consider whether **34** could be regarded as a genuine document of the 1040s, perhaps produced after the settlement with Leofwine and intended as a title-deed for the abbey's Thanet property. The eccentric formulation of **34** is not necessarily an obstacle to such a conclusion, since the draftsmen of Edward's diplomas appear to have been allowed a wide degree of latitude in this respect; there is also evidence that decentralized production by bishops and beneficiaries was by no means unknown (see S 1067, 1105, 1115), which might account for unorthodox texts. The proem and the sanction (in its shorter form) would not seem out of place in a contemporary charter; the Creation theme of the former is shared by a number of apparently authentic charters from the early years of the reign (see S 1004, 1019, 1021). The royal style, although not precisely paralleled, would not seem unacceptable in a charter of the Confessor. It would, of course, be very much easier to evaluate the document if it included a dating clause and witness-list; the lack of these features in both versions of the diploma and in its many copies could be seen as a possible reason for suspicion, although it could be accounted for by deficiencies in transmission. Sprott (BL Cotton Tiberius A. ix, 119r) and Elmham's chronological table (Hardwick, *Elmham*, p. 25) date Edward's charter to 1043, which is compatible with the internal reference to Abbot Ælfstan (see above); the source for the date may have been a more complete version of the diploma, or perhaps a separate document, such as a list of benefactions.

One reason to reject **34** is its occasional similarity to the forged charters relating to the foundation (**3, 4, 5**), and the associated spurious papal privileges. The choice of scriptural quotation to support the theme of the proem echoes the reference to St Augustine's as a treasury of saints in **4**. After the superscription in **34** comes a passage in which the king mentions his return from exile and installation *in solio patrum meorum*; **3** and **5**, the supposed charter of Eadbald, have a corresponding phrase *in solio paterno confirmatus*. In the reference to the abbey the draftsman of **34** has used the double dedication to SS Peter and Paul, which is mentioned by Bede and occurs in the forgeries concerned with the foundation (**2, 3, 4, 5**) and the associated papal privileges, but was rarely used in genuine pre-Conquest documents (see p. xiv). It is possible that the draftsman was here simply influenced by Bede, since in this passage he has drawn much of his wording from the account of the abbey's foundation in *HE* i. 33. The correspondence between **34** and the foundation forgeries is not sufficient to justify the argument that they were all produced by the same agency at the same time (as suggested by Levison); it may even be the case that the foundation forgeries were influenced by **34**. But the link does not help the case for this difficult charter. Against this background, it is impossible to view charitably the second part of the dispositive section, with its excursus on the legendary history of Minster-in-Thanet. There is also some difficulty with the nature of the supposed grant, here equated with the island of Thanet, even though the Minster properties only covered part of the island. Such imprecision in a royal diploma is unacceptable. Many of the texts associated with the legend of St Mildrith do give a (varying) estimate of the amount of land initially granted to Æbba; in Goscelin's *Vita S. Mildrethe* this corresponded with the Domesday assessment (Rollason, *Mildrith Legend*, pp. 23, 48, 66). The vagueness of **34** in this respect (and the lack of any reference to the Minster property on the mainland which is mentioned explicitly in **33**) perhaps show that Edward's diploma was not intended as a formal title-deed; its function seems to have been to define the fact of the abbey's tenure in suitably grand terms.

It seems best to consider **34** a fabrication produced in the abbey itself at some point in the second half of the eleventh century. By the time that Goscelin was writing the *Translatio S. Mildrethe* (*c.* 1091) St Augustine's was basing its claims to Thanet on a diploma in the name of Cnut, which is now lost (see commentary to **33**); this diploma seems to have superseded **34**. If **34** were forged for any practical purpose (and it may simply have been intended for the satisfaction of the community), it can hardly have come into existence during the Confessor's reign. This suggests that **34** was produced at some point between 1066 and 1087, probably earlier rather than later in that span; this seems to have been the period during which the foundation forgeries were being created (see pp. lxiv–lxv, and Kelly 1988).

35

King Edward declares that he has granted judicial and financial privileges to St Augustine's monastery. [A.D. 1042 × 1050]

a. *English*

E. PRO Cart. Ant. R. 9, no 12: copy, s. xiii
O. Canterbury, D. & C., Chart. Ant. F. 47; copy, s. xv
T. PRO Ch. R. 8 Hen. IV, m. 6
U. PRO Pat. R. 2 Hen. VI, pt 3, m. 5 (art. 12)
V. PRO Pat. R. 4 Edw. IV, pt 4, m. 29 (art. 11)
Ed.: a. Kemble 831, from a copy of E in BL Harley 84, 99v
      b. H. Adams, H. C. Lodge *et al.*, *Essays in Anglo-Saxon Law* (Boston, 1876), pp. 46–7, from Kemble
      c. Harmer, *Writs*, p. 199 (no. 38) from U
Listed: Sawyer 1091
Edited from E and U

+ Eadþard king gret Eadsige arceb'[a] 7 Godþine eorl 7 ealle mine þegnas[b] on Kent frendlice[c] 7 ic kyðe eop þ ic hæbbe geunnen sc̄e Augustine 7 þam gebroðran þe þær to hyrað[d] þ hi[e] beon heora saca þurðe 7 heore socna 7 griðbrices[f] 7 hamsocne 7 forstealles 7 infangenes þiofes[g] 7 flymæne fyrmðe ofer heore agene menn binnan burh 7 butan tolles 7 teames on strande 7 on streame[h] 7 ofer spa feole þegna spa ic hiom[i] habba to gelæten 7 ic nelle þ æni mann[j] æni þing þær on teo buton heom 7 heore picneres[k] þe hi hit betæcen[l] þillan for þam ic habbe forgefen sc̄e Augustine þas gerihte[m] minre saple to alesednysse[n] spa full[o] 7 spa forð[p] spa hi[e] hit fyrmest hæfden on Cnudes dægge[q] cinges[r] 7 ic nelle geþafyan[s] þ æni mann[j] þis abrece be minan freondscipe.[t] God eop gehealde.

   [a] Ealsige archeb' E   [b] þegnes E   [c] freondliche E   [d] hyrad U   [e] hie E
   [f] gridbrices U   [g] infangene þieofes E   [h] strama U   [i] hem E   [j] man E
   [k] pitnesse E; picnefer U   [l] bitæche E   [m] gerithe E   [n] alesnesse E   [o] ful E
   [p] ford E   [q] dagie E   [r] kinges E   [s] geeþafian U   [t] freonscipe E, U

b. *Latin*

F. BL Cotton Julius D. ii, 87r: copy, s. xiii[1]
   Rubric: Eadwardus rex de libertate.
G. BL Cotton Claudius D. x, 57r: copy, s. xiii[2]
   Rubric: Edwardus rex de libertate.
H. PRO E 164/27, 147v–148r: copy, s. xiii/xiv
I. Canterbury, D. & C., Lit. E. 19, 94r: incomplete copy, s. xiv[1]
J. London, Lambeth Palace, 419, 122v: incomplete copy, s. xiv
K. BL Cotton Tiberius A. ix, 119r: incomplete copy, s. xiv
O. Canterbury, D. & C., Cart. Ant. F. 47: copy, s. xv
Ed.: a. W. Somner, *A Treatise of Gavelkind* (London, 1660), pp. 207–8, from Sprott (MS J)
      b. Kemble 902 from G
      c. *Mon. Ang.* (rev. edn), i. 139 (no. 37), from G
      d. Thorpe, *Diplomatarium*, p. 420, from G
      e. H. Adams, H. C. Lodge *et al.*, *Essays in Anglo-Saxon Law*, (Boston, 1876), pp. 46–7, from G
      f. Harmer, *Writs*, p. 199 (no. 38), from G
Listed: Sawyer 1091
Edited from F and G

Ego Ædpardus[a] Dei gratia rex Anglorum Eadsio archiepiscopo et Godpino[b] comiti et omnibus suis baronibus Cantie salutem. Sciatis me dedisse Deo ac sancto Augustino et fratribus ut habeant eorum saca et socna et pacis fracturam et pugnam in domo factam et uie assaltus et latrones in terra sua captos latronumque susceptionem uel pastionem super eorum proprios homines, infra ciuitatem et extra, theloneumque suum in terra et in aqua atque consuetudinem que dicitur teames, et super omnes allodiarios quos eis habeo datos. Nec uolo consentire ut aliquis in aliqua re de iis se intermittat, nisi eorum prepositi quibus ipsi hec commendauerint,[c] quia habeo has consuetudines Deo datas et sancto Augustino pro redemptione anime mee ita pleniter et libere, sicut melius habuerunt tempore predecessoris mei Knuti regis. Et nolo consentire ut aliquis hec infringat sicuti meam amicitiam uult habere.[d]

[a] Eaduuardus G   [b] Godino G   [c] commendauerit F
[d] Idem rex Eaduuardus confirmat illud idem quod prius per cartam suam in anglico G

Edward here informs Archbishop Eadsige, Earl Godwine and the thegns of Kent that he has granted to the community of St Augustine's a range of privileges, including jurisdiction over its own men and over all the thegns that he has permitted it to have; this last reference is probably to men who had committed themselves to the lordship of the abbot, as did Ealdred in **31**. Only the community and its officers are to take anything from men covered by the abbey's jurisdiction. These privileges are to be enjoyed as fully and completely as they were in the time of Cnut.

The vernacular version of **35** may be authentic. It was copied onto a Cartae

Antiquae roll in the reign of John, along with a series of post-Conquest writs granting similar privileges, followed by **3** and **33**. The scribe notes that **3** was not sealed and that **33** was; he does not comment explicitly on the state of **35**, but the implication is that it was in the form of a regular sealed writ, like the Norman writs which follow it. **35** probably still existed as an original writ in the fifteenth century, for in 1407 it was submitted separately for confirmation; it was copied onto the Charter Rolls and later onto the Patent Rolls. There is a fifteenth-century copy of both the English and the Latin versions of the writ in Canterbury, D. & C., Chart. Ant. F. 47 (MS O), a compilation of documents put together in the fifteenth century and primarily relating to the abbey's rights in Fordwich. The Latin translation alone appears in the main thirteenth-century cartularies (MSS F, G: in MS G the scribe refers to the vernacular version but does not reproduce it). The PRO charter-list mentions both the Latin and English versions (Appendix 2, no. xlvii).

Two writs recording grants of judicial and financial privileges very similar to those outlined in **35** are preserved in the Christ Church archive. One is a vernacular writ of Cnut, datable to 1020 (S 986), which was shortly afterwards copied into the MacDurnan Gospels and seems to be acceptable. This is a personal grant to Archbishop Æthelnoth, who had just been consecrated, of the privileges which are given generally to St Augustine's in **35**. There is also a second Christ Church writ (S 1088), which grants the same privileges to Archbishop Stigand and the Christ Church community. This survives as an original sealed writ, but most of the text has been erased and rewritten in a different hand, probably in the twelfth century. Presumably the original text of the writ has been altered and perhaps partly replaced by other material. Harmer (*Writs*, p. 173) suggests that the substituted text may derive from another genuine writ of the Confessor; alternatively, it may have been taken from a copy of Cnut's writ for Archbishop Æthelnoth. It could be argued that the Christ Church writ and **35** support each other, although S 1088 is clearly a shaky prop; furthermore, S 986 shows that writs with such formulation were indeed being issued before the Conquest. In view of the relationship between S 986 and S 1088, there does seem to be some possibility that **35** is a reissue of a lost writ of Cnut; certainly the text implies that Edward was simply confirming privileges enjoyed in Cnut's day. But the extant Latin writ of Cnut (**32**) appears to be a fabrication, not simply a translation of a lost vernacular document.

36

King Edward grants one sulung (aratrum) *at Littlebourne, Kent, to Eadsige, archbishop [of Canterbury].* [A.D. 1042 × 1050 (? 1047)]

F. BL Cotton Julius D. ii, 105rv: copy, s. xiii[1]
  No rubric
Ed.: a. Kemble 1344
    b. Pierquin, *Recueil*, pt 5, no. 55
Listed: Sawyer 1050

Sacre nos catholicorum patrum per quos Dei spiritus est locutus admonent scripture,[a] ut despicientes terrena concupiscamus celestia, dum transeuntis seculi uicissitudo per dierum incrementa crescendo decrescit et ampliando minuitur et nil penitus prodecere homini lucrare mundum, nisi per temporalia commutauerit eterna, quoniam uelut umbra presens computatur uita ad futuram que in nobis reuelabitur gloriam. Quapropter ego Ædwardus regis regum Dei predestinatione Anglorum rex et dominium habens dilecto mihi archiepiscopo Ædzino quandam hereditatis mee tradidi partem in plaga orientali, terram uidelicet unius aratri cui incole eiusdem prouincie ab antiquo Lytleburnan nomen indiderunt, ut habeat et possideat ac secundum proprium libitum [. . .]atur*b* et fruatur, postque ipsius uite discessum cui sibi placuerit heredi in perhenni possessione derelinquat. Sit etiam eadem terra ab omni seruitutis obstaculo libera, excepto quod in regali contra hostes expeditione uel pontis constructione siue in arcis reedificatione exhibeat supplementum. Si quis autem quod absit uesana mente tumidus huic*c* nostre donationis emulator existens eam infringere temptauerit, multiplicentur in eo omnes plage quas Dominus intulit Egiptiis ac perpetuis subiciatur maledictionibus nisi penitens resipiscat et emendauerit. Istis terminis predicta terra circumgirata.

> *a Read* Sacre scripture . . . nos admonent . . .   *b MS damaged* (? utatur)
> *c ? For* huius

36 is the record of a grant by Edward the Confessor to Archbishop Eadsige of land at Littlebourne which Eadsige subsequently gave to St Augustine's (**37**). The text survives only in BL Cotton Julius D. ii, and has been abbreviated, so that it lacks not only bounds but also dating clause and witness-list. In Sprott's history (BL Cotton Tiberius A. ix, 119v) and Elmham's chronological table (Hardwick, *Elmham*, p. 26) the date 1047 has been attached to the grant to Eadsige and the regrant to St Augustine's. This detail may have been taken from a more complete version of Edward's diploma. The suggested date would be appropriate for a charter in favour of Eadsige, who was already in office when Edward came to the throne and who died in October 1050. Sprott also mentions here that a copy of the bounds was available in the lost *Textus S. Adriani* (see above p. xxxvi).

The formulation of the charter is consistent with a date in the 1040s. The draftsmen of eleventh-century royal diplomas were increasingly less inclined to use standardized wording, often preferring instead to create fresh formulas for each document, while conforming to the general conventions for royal diplomas and often adapting the formulation of earlier texts. **36** fits this pattern. Like many charters of this period it lacks a verbal invocation and begins directly with the proem. The proem itself is unique, but the draftsman seems to have been aware of an earlier formula, extant in two variant forms: one beginning *Sacre autem scripture*, which appears in five extant texts spread over the period 944 to 1013 (S 504, 619, 834; S [Add.] 517a, 1013a); and a shorter version beginning *Quoniam quidem transeuntis*, found in two charters of 944 (S 495, 498) and reused in 964 (S 724). The royal style in **36** has no precise parallel, but unusual royal styles incorporating a present participle, as in this instance, appear in several other charters of Edward (see S 1003, 1024, 1033, 1038). There is nothing suspicious about the terms of the disposition, although it is remarkable to find the land described as lying *in plaga orientali*; the draftsman evidently intended to indicate that the estate was located in the eastern part of Kent. The wording of the statement of powers and immunity clause has no exact equivalent, but it follows the general pattern for such formulas; the draftsman is again trying to find a fresh turn of phrase for stereotyped material. In the sanction he has certainly succeeded in being original, invoking the plagues of Egypt on any malefactor. Biblical themes are noticeable in the sanctions of other diplomas from the Confessor's reign, which are inhabited by the like of Dathan and Abiron (S 1003, 1028), Beelzebub (S 1003, 1026), Herod (S 1026), Pilate (S 1012, 1017, 1026) and Caiaphas (S 1017), but the draftsman of **36** has certainly hit on a fresh new image.

For the abbey's estates at Littlebourne, see **9**.

37

Eadsige, archbishop [of Canterbury], grants land at Littlebourne, Kent, to St Peter and St Augustine. [A.D. 1042 × 1050 (? 1047)]

F. BL Cotton Julius D. ii, 87r: copy, s. xiii[1]
    Rubric: Eadzinus archiepiscopus de Litleburne.
Ed.: Kemble 1333
Listed: Sawyer 1401

Hanc terram id est Litleburne*ᵃ* ego Ædzinus gratia Dei archiepiscopus sicut dominus meus rex mihi tradidit, ita Deo et sancto Petro apostolorum principi et sancto Augustino nostrae gentis apostolo donatione perpetua trado et tumulo illius libellum impono, cum consensu eiusdem regis, episcoporum, ducum, abbatum aliorumque multorum nobilium seu ignobilium, pro re- demptione anime domini regis et nostre. Quam donationem si quis infringere temptauerit seu rex seu episcopus seu dux seu abbas*ᵇ* seu clericus seu laicus sit, auctoritate patris et filii et spiritus sancti a consortio sancte Dei ecclesie separetur et anathema a sancta uirginum uirgine Maria et a sancto Petro celestis regni clauigero et a sancto Augustino et ab omnibus sanctis iudicetur. Amen.

    ᵃ Litleb' F   *ᵇ* abba F

This appears to be the record of Archbishop Eadsige's transfer to St Augustine's of the land which he had been granted by King Edward in **36**. The present document may have originated as an endorsement to **36**. Pre-Conquest originals rarely have additional notices of later changes of ownership, for it was usual simply to hand over the existing charter when the estate was alienated, but there is some sign that the St Augustine's community favoured the addition of endorsements: see **23/23A**,

28 and S 332 (p. xxxii n. 57). **36** and **37** are widely separated in BL Cotton Julius D. ii, the only manuscript source, and this suggests that the latter had an independent existence of some kind; the two documents have therefore been edited separately.

The text of **37** is likely to have been drawn up at St Augustine's itself. There are repeated references to Peter and Augustine, the principal saints of the monastery, and the interesting detail that the charter was placed on the latter's tomb, a symbol that the grant was to the saint himself. A similar practice seems to have obtained at Crowland, which was also closely associated with a single saint; the Guthlac Roll shows charters being offered by benefactors to Guthlac's shrine (*The Guthlac Roll*, ed. G. Warner (Roxburghe Club, 1928), pl. xviii; see M. Clanchy, *From Memory to Written Record: England 1066–1307* (London, 1979), p. 127). In the eleventh century Augustine's tomb seems to have been a rather magnificent affair. It was destroyed when the saint was translated during the rebuilding of the abbey church by the first two Norman abbots, but Goscelin gives us a brief glimpse of it when he describes how the archiepiscopal tombs were miraculously preserved when a masonry wall accidentally collapsed on them: 'omnes illae illorum sepulcrales aedificiulae, cum essent fractiles et lateritiae, sed et sculpture et imagines angelicae cum Dominica maiestate super tumbam magnifici Augustini mirifice formatae . . . illaesae apparuere' (Goscelin, *Translatio S. Augustini*, p. 413). It has been tentatively suggested that Augustine's tomb may have been a reused Roman marble sarcophagus, with a carving of a bust supported by Victories (C.R. Dodwell, *Anglo-Saxon Art: a New Perspective* (Manchester, 1982), pp. 122–8).

This was not Eadsige's only gift to St Augustine's. He also gave to the community two small pieces of land outside Canterbury, consisting of five acres outside Ridingate and a meadow near Worthgate (S 1400). This was recorded in a bipartite chirograph, of which portions were given to Christ Church and St Augustine's; the former survives as an original, but there is no trace of the document at St Augustine's. It is not mentioned in the PRO charter-list (Appendix 2). Eadsige seems to have been very favourably disposed towards the St Augustine's community, to the extent of taking the part of Abbot Ælfstan in his dispute with Christ Church over the Sandwich tolls (S 1467). Conversely, he had a poor posthumous reputation at Christ Church, where he was blamed for permitting the alienation of property to Earl Godwine (Brooks, *Church of Canterbury*, pp. 300–2).

38

Æthelric Bigga bequeaths land at Bodsham and Wilderton, Kent, to St Augustine's. [A.D. 1048 × 1050]

F. BL Cotton Julius D. ii, 105r: copy, s. xiii[1]
   No rubric
H. PRO E 164/27, 83rv: copy, s. xiii
   Rubric: De Bodesham et Wilrintone.
Ed.: a. Kemble 1338 from F
        b. Thorpe, *Diplomatarium*, p. 586, from F
Listed: Sawyer 1502
Edited from F and H

Hic notatur quod Ægelricus Bigga concedit sancto Augustino post obitum suum, consensu*a* domini sui Ædwardi regis, terras Bodesham et Wilrintun,*b* eo pacto quod Wade eius miles sedeat dies suos in*c* Bodesham et Lifwine Feireage*d* sedeat dies suos in Wilrinton.*e* Et post obitum amborum*f* terre remaneant sancto Augustino et abbas procuret terras ad opus monasterii sicut amorem Dei habere*g* uelit et sancti Petri et sancti Augustini. Et Dei odium habeat quisquis hanc donationem infregerit,*h* nisi citius emendauerit erga Deum et sanctos ibi quiescentes. Huic donationi sunt testes Eadsinus*i* archiepiscopus et conuentus Christi ecclesie et Rodbertus*j* episcopus London' *k*et Godwinus episcopus sancti Martini etc.*k*

a concessu F   *b* Wilrintone H   *c* de H   *d* Limine Fairege H   *e* Wilrintun' H
f eorum F   *g* habere Dei F   *h* fregerit H   *i* Eadzinus F   *j* Robertus F
k ... k et multi alii cum eis. H

Æthelric Bigga was a prominent Kentish thegn under Cnut and the Confessor. He attests S 1465 (A.D. 1032), 1473 (A.D 1044 × 1048) and 1400 (A.D. 1038 × 1050). S 1471 (*c*. A.D. 1045) is the record of an elaborate agreement between Æthelric and Archbishop Eadsige which resolves a disputed claim to Little Chart by giving Æthelric a lifetime tenure, and also notes arrangements for the future disposition of land at Stowting and Milton and of a *haga* in a *port* (? Canterbury), which are to pass to the archbishop after the lifetimes of Æthelric and his son Esbearn (see Brooks, *Church of Canterbury*, pp. 302–3). Esbearn Bigga figures as a privileged landowner in Domesday Book. He was one of a select group of Kentishmen whose heirs would not owe heriot to the king and in whose lands the king did not have full jurisdiction (GDB 1r, 2r). Presumably as a result of this immunity, the present holdings of these men are not listed in the Domesday survey; there are only notes of property which they had held before the Conquest in their own right or as royal tenants and subsequently lost. Esbearn had, for instance, lost to the bishop of Bayeux eleven *hagas* at Canterbury and lands at Keston, Birling, Thurnham, Fairbourne and Pivington which he had held from King Edward (GDB 2r, 7r, 7v, 8r, 10v). Moreover, he had lost his own land at Garrington to Odo, and a manor at Postling to Hugh de Montfort (GDB 12r, 13r).

38 appears to be a memorandum of a post-obitum bequest of a small part of Æthelric's property. It is probably a translation of a vernacular document; the introductory phrase corresponds with the formula *Her swutelaþ on þysan gewrite* common in Old English charters, and it would certainly be more usual in the late Anglo-Saxon period for a private charter of this type to be couched in the vernacular. The form of the witness-list would also be more appropriate in an Old English charter. None of the formulation is comparable to that used in royal diplomas in this period. The document was probably drawn up at St Augustine's. It was witnessed by Archbishop Eadsige and the Christ Church community, Bishop Robert of London and Godwine, bishop of St Martin's in Canterbury, who acted as an auxiliary for Eadsige in the last years of his pontificate (for the bishops of St Martin's see Brooks, *Church of Canterbury*, pp. 295–6, 300). Godwine was appointed after the resignation

of the previous holder of the post, Abbot Siward of Abingdon, in August or September 1048. The record underlying **38** must belong to the period between that date and the death of Archbishop Eadsige on 29 October 1050.

Although **38** in its present form may be a translation, there is no reason to think the transaction anything but authentic. It is a particularly interesting detail that Æthelric provides for the continued occupation of the estates by the two men whom he has settled on them, presumably as military tenants who acknowledged his lordship. It is unusual in a document of this type to find no reference to a request for prayers, or at least some kind of spiritual benefit for the donor, and this might suggest that the transaction here was not a simple bequest to a religious house but rather a negotiated agreement, perhaps over disputed property. Bodsham figures in a seventh-century grant to Minster-in-Thanet (**41**), and it is possible that the abbot of St Augustine's had laid claim to it in his capacity of St Mildrith's heir and as part of the quest to reconstitute the Minster endowment. The fact that Æthelric had settled his men on the land does suggest that he had not originally intended to leave it to a religious house after his death, and the wording of the document implies that the abbot was expected to pay relief of some kind in order to gain possession of the land. Such an agreement would be comparable to the one which Æthelric reached with Archbishop Eadsige about Chart, to which there was a ninth-century Canterbury claim, and other properties in Kent (S 1471).

Bodsham and Wilderton are some ten miles apart and in different lathes. The former lies in the heart of the Downland, near Hastingleigh, while the latter is just south of Faversham. In 1086 the abbot of St Augustine's held manors in both places, each assessed at a sulung (GDB 12r, 12v).

39

King Edward declares that he confirms his previous grant of land at
Fordwich, Kent, to St Augustine's. [A.D. 1053 × 1066]

G. BL Cotton Claudius D. x, 175r: copy, s. xiii[2]
    Rubric: Donatio domini Eadwardi regis de Fordwico.
G*. BL Cotton Claudius D. x, 63v: copy of Inspeximus [R], s. xiv[1]
J. London, Lambeth Palace, 419, 123r: incomplete copy, s. xiv
M. BL Add. 53710, 224r: copy of Inspeximus [S], s. xiv/xv
O. Canterbury, D. &. C., Cart. Ant. F 47: copy, s. xv
R. PRO Ch. R. 20 Edw. II, m. 2
S. PRO Ch. R. 36 Edw. III, m. 7
T. PRO Ch. R. 8 Hen. IV, m. 6
U. PRO Pat. R. 2 Hen. VI, pt 3, m. 5
V. PRO Pat. R. 4 Edw. IV, pt 4, m. 29
W. PRO Pat. R. 14 Hen. VII, pt 1, m. 16
Ed.: a. Twysden, *Scriptores*, col. 2128, from M
    b. Kemble 854 from G
    c. *Mon. Angl.* (rev. edn), i. 142 (no. 49), from G
    d. Woodruff, *Fordwich*, p. 25, from Kemble
    e. Turner and Salter, *Black Book*, i. 144 , from BL Cotton Faustina A. i

f. Harmer, *Writs*, p. 200 (no. 39), from G etc., with translation
Listed: Sawyer 1092
Edited from G and O

Eadþard cyng gret Stigande*a* arceb' 7 Harold*b* eorl 7 Ospeard 7 ealle mine þegenas*c* on Cent freonlice,*d* 7 ic cyðe eop þ ic eom þæs gecnaþe þ ic geuðe Criste 7 sce Augustine 7 þan halgan þær binnan spa*e* micel landes binnan Fordþic*f* for*g* minre saule spa ic me sylf þer hafde, spa full 7 spa forð spa it me sylfan*h* on honde*i* stod on eallan þingan. Nu þille ic þat hit licge into þan halgan minstre, eall*j* spa ic hit ær þider*k* in geuðe, 7 ic*l* nelle geþafian þat ænig man mine gyefe*m* geutige, 7 ic þille habban fullne dom of þam menn þe mine sputelinge*n* apængnian*o* þolde þe ic þer to gegyefen hafde.

a Stigan O   *b* Haroldus O   *c* þegnas O   *d* frenlice G; *for* freondlice   *e* sua G
f Forðþic G   *g* ford G   *h* selfan O   *i* handa O   *j* eal O   *k* Omitted G
l 7 ic *omitted* O   *m* gif O   *n* spatelinge G   *o* apegnian O

The best witnesses to **39** are the copies in the Red Book (MS G) and in a brief fifteenth-century compilation of St Augustine's documents relating to Fordwich (MS O). In the version of the writ which was offered for confirmation in 1326 and later enrolled on several occasions, the language has been modernized; this version was also copied into BL Cotton Faustina A. i (fo. 84v) in the late thirteenth century (see p. lxi).

39 appears to be an authentic writ of the Confessor, datable to the period after Harold's appointment to the earldom of Wessex and Kent in April 1053. The king informs the members of the shire-court that the St Augustine's community is to hold the land at Fordwich just as he had previously granted it; the implication is that an earlier grant of Fordwich to the abbey had for some reason been thwarted or reversed. There are no strong objections to the language and formulas of the writ. The *gecnawe* clause is paralleled in a Bury writ of the Confessor (S 1084); for the formula *licgan in to*, see Harmer, *Writs*, pp. 64. We learn from Domesday Book that the royal share of Fordwich which passed to St Augustine's amounted to two-thirds; the remaining third, which belonged to the earl of Kent, was transferred to the abbey by Odo of Bayeux after the Conquest (GDB 12r). The collection of post-Conquest charters at the end of Elmham's history includes Odo's writ granting his share of Fordwich to the abbey, as well as the Conqueror's writ of seisin concerning Fordwich, which relates that Abbot Æthelsige, *fugitivus meus*, had alienated the borough and that it was presently in the hands of the sheriff, Haimo (Hardwick, *Elmham*, pp. 351, 352; *Regesta*, i, no. 98); the chronological table prefixed to the history places these documents under the years 1075 and 1076 respectively (Hardwick, *Elmham*, p. 28). Sprott gives a date of 1055 for Edward's grant of Fordwich (BL Cotton Tiberius A. ix, 119v) and the chronological table mentions a *carta de Fordwico* in the same year (Hardwick, *Elmham*, p. 26). These may be references to the present writ, or to an earlier document recording Edward's initial grant.

Fordwich lay at the head of the Stour estuary and was the port serving Canterbury. Ownership of the borough presumably entitled St Augustine's to levy toll on ships and merchants using the wharfs. A customal of 1272 describes a Fordwich 'liberty' that comprised the territory surrounding the borough and extended up the Stour as far as its mouth, and included the land on both banks as far inland as a man standing in a boat could throw an axe weighing seven pounds called a taper-axe (Woodruff, *Fordwich*, pp. 280–1). A very similar liberty accruing to the port of Sandwich is described in an early forgery, ostensibly dated 1023, which survives in a version written in the second half of the eleventh century (S 959; see Brooks, *Church of Canterbury*, pp. 292–4). This document purports to record Cnut's grant to Christ Church of the port of Sandwich and the right to all revenues of Sandwich haven between *Peppernesse* and *Mearcesfleote*. The liberty included the rights of ferrying and salvage and the right to all tolls levied on ships using the haven, and it extended as far inland as a man standing on a floating boat could toss a taper-axe. The points of similarity between the eleventh-century description of the Sandwich liberty and the thirteenth-century description of the Fordwich liberty may indicate that the latter also had an early origin.

St Augustine's already owned land in the Fordwich area before Edward granted to the community his share of the borough. The two earliest charters in the archive (6, 7) seem to be grants of land in the vicinity of Fordwich, and the monastery certainly held property there in the reign of Eadred, for it is mentioned in the bounds of a neighbouring estate (S 535). A further donation was made by a certain Bruman, described as *portreve*, probably in Edward's reign; he gave Abbot Wulfric a life-interest in two tenements and a meadow at Fordwich, with reversion to the monastery (S 1654; see Appendix 1, no. vi). Domesday Book also mentions that the abbey had 'always' held twenty-four acres with six burgesses at Fordwich (GDB 12r).

THE CHARTERS OF
MINSTER-IN-THANET

40

a. Suebhardus, *king of the men of Kent, grants forty-four hides* (manentes) in Sudaneie *in Thanet and twelve hides in Sturry, Kent, to Abbess Æbba.* A.D. 689 (1 March).

b. *Confirmation by Æthelred, king of the Mercians.* A.D. 691 (8 January).

F. BL Cotton Julius D. ii, 85rv: copy, s. xiii[1]
    Rubric: Suabertus rex de Taneto et Stureie.
H. PRO E 164/27, 76v–77r: copy, s. xiii
    Rubric: Carta terre beate Mildrethe.
N. Cambridge, Trinity Hall, 1, 48v–49r: copy, s. xv[1]
    Rubric: Carta regis Suabherti de Thaneto et Sturigao.
Ed.: a. Lewis, *Tenet*, pp. 56–7, from N
    b. Kemble 14 from N
    c. Hardwick, *Elmham*, pp. 232–4, 237, from N
    d. Birch 42 from N
Listed: Sawyer 10
Edited from F, H and N

In nomine Domini nostri Iesu Christi saluatoris. Ego Suebhardus[a] rex Cantuariorum, anno secundo[b] regni nostri, indictione secunda,[c] sub die kalendarum Martis, cum consilio uenerabilis archiepiscopi Theodori atque consensu [d]primorum meorum sed et cum consilio quoque ac consensu[d] patris mei Sebbe regis, terram que dicitur in Sudaneie[e] intra insulam Tenet,[f] que et continet antiquo iure .xliiii. manentes, quibus modo addimus curtem .xii.[g] manentes habentem ultra insulam in loco qui dicitur Sturgeh,[h] cum siluis et paludibus, cum fluminibus et fontibus, cum pratis et pomariis, cum domibus cunctisque utensilibus et omnibus ad eandem pertinentibus rebus, in ipsa quantitate sicut antiquitus principes a regibus sibi perdonatam habuerant,[i] Æbbe[j] abbatisse iure ecclesiastico ac monasteriali et quibuscumque successoribus ipsa uoluerit derelinquere tantum in domino[k] in sempiternum possidendam perdonamus, ita ut nec nobis nec aliquibus successorum nostrorum regum siue principum aut etiam ecclesiasticarum dignitatum gradibus nefario temeritatis ausu aliquando infringere uel deminuere[l] aliquid de ea liceat, sed pro remedio anime mee et absolutione peccatorum meorum ita ut predixi famulis Dei perdonata absque aliqua lesione in euum permaneat.

[m]Hec autem terra antea per Hlotharium[n] et Edricum reges Cantuariorum tantum accommodata sub dominio famulantium Deo iacebat.[o] Postea autem a Mulo rege regnum Cantie[p] optinente perdonata est in ius ecclesiasticum Æbbe[q] abbatisse[r] .xliiii. manentes, comparante ab eo ipsa sua pecunia digna,[s]

139

ex quibus sunt intra insulam Tenet^t .xliiii.^u manentes, extra autem eam insulam .x. manentes sunt, in his regionibus que hoc modo nominatur, id est in Sturige et ut nos solemus dicere ad aquilonis siluam ubi dicitur Maeccanbrooc.^m

Igitur hanc terrarum prescriptarum largitionem,^v non solum pro pecunia quadam siu^w propinquitate sed mercede quoque ab omnipotente Deo, Eabbe abbatisse eternaliter possidendam contradimus et confirmamus. Hanc autem donationem^x meam cum consensu et uoluntate precellentissimi regis Edilredi^y fecimus. Quisquis^z autem heredum successorumque meorum regum Cantie uel si quilibet^{a2} secularium dignitatum aut ecclesiasticarum de supradicta donatione, quam pro eterna remuneratione anime mee omnipotenti Deo ad utilitatem famulantium ei in ius monasteriale constat esse largitam, aliquid disrumpere^{b2} aut immutare uel irritum facere temptauerit, sciat se sine dubio omnipotenti Deo fraudem facere et proinde coram eo et sanctis angelis eius eterno anathemate reum. Quicumque uero hec que largita prediximus sub pia protectione custodierit uel pro Dei intuitu misericorditer auxerit, sit benedictus in secula audiatque in die nouissimo tremendi examinis ab ipso iudice omnium Christo Domino eterne benedictionis uocem, ¹Uenite benedicti patris mei, ^{c2}percipite regnum quod uobis paratum est ab origine mundi,^{c2} manentem igitur hanc cartulam in sua semper firmitate, cum religiosis testibus signo dominice crucis in hoc loco qui dicitur Dorouernis stabiliter in euum confirmamus.

+ ^{d2} Ego Sueaberdus^{e2} rex Cantie suprascripta signo sancte crucis per^{f2} propriam manum roboraui.^{g2}

^{h2}+ Signum manus Gumbercdi.

+ Signum Gebredi.

+ Signum Osfridi.

+ Signum Verbaldi.

+ Signum Hagona.

+ Signum Egisan.

+ Signum Bernhardi.^{h2}

+ Signum Sebbe regis.

+ Signum Ecce.

ⁱ²+ Signum Raban.

+ Signum Albercti.

+ Signum Gudhardi.ⁱ²

+ Theodorus gratia Dei archiepiscopus subscripsi.

+^{j2} Ego Adrianus abbas subscripsi.

+ Ego Osuuini^{k2} propria manu subscripsi.

+ Signum manus Ædilredi^{l2} regis Merciorum^{m2} dum ille adfirmauerat terram nostram in hoc loco erat qui dicitur Mirafeld^{n2} atque Stapulford, anno ab incarnatione Christi .dcxci.,^{o2} indictione .iiii., .viii. die mensis Ianuarii, prima feria.

^{a} Suebardus F; Swabertus H ^{h} .ii. N ^{c} .iiii. N (see commentary) ^{d} ... ^{d} Omitted H
^{e} Sudanei F ^{f} Thanet H, N ^{g} duodecim F ^{h} Sturegh H ^{i} habuerat F
^{j} Eabae F; Eabe H ^{k} domino F, H, N; for dominio ^{l} diminuere H
^{m} ... ^{m} Omitted by one source of N (see commentary) ^{n} Lotarium H; Lotharium N
^{o} adiacebat N ^{p} Kancie H ^{q} Aette F; Aete H; Æbba N ^{r} abatissa F, N
^{s} 'she procuring (the land) from him with her worthy payment' ^{t} omitted H; Thanet N
^{u} Perhaps a corruption of .xxxxiiii. (see commentary) ^{v} largitioni F
^{w} siu F, H, N; for seu ^{x} confirmationem H ^{y} Eldredi altered to Elredi H
^{z} si quis H ^{a2} quislibet H ^{b2} dirumpere H ^{c2} ... ^{c2} Omitted H
^{d2} Cross omitted F, H ^{e2} Suehaerdus F; Swabertus H ^{f2} Omitted F
^{g2} F ends here ^{h2} ... ^{h2} Omitted H ^{i2} ... ^{i2} Omitted H ^{j2} Omitted H ^{k2} Oswyn H
^{l2} Edredi H; Ædilredis N ^{m2} Mercionum N ^{n2} Wrafeld H
^{o2} .dclxxvi. N (see commentary)

[1] Matt. 24: 34

40 is apparently the earliest and certainly the most difficult of the surviving Minster charters. Its textual history is bizarre, its dates have been tampered with, and there is a strong suspicion that it has been extensively reworked, but there can be little doubt that **40** is based on genuine seventh-century documentation. The donor can be identified with the King Swæfheard (Suæbhardus) who was ruling with Wihtred in Kent in July 692 (Bede, HE, v. 8), and who was evidently one of the reges dubii uel externi who invaded Kent after the death of King Eadric in 686 (Bede, HE, iv. 26). According to **40** he was the son of King Sebbi of Essex; he is also associated with Sebbi in S 233, a charter relating to the Kentish minster at Hoo, which is not genuine in its received form but seems to be based on several lost seventh-century documents. Swæfheard may have predeceased his father, who died in or after 693. It is not clear whether he can be identified with the Suabertus who is the donor of **41**, another grant to Minster. Both **40** and **41** are attested by Oswine, the donor of **8** to St Augustine's and **42** and **43** to Minster. The latter two charters are in turn attested by Suebhardus, while the witness-list of **8** contains the subscription of a Gabertus, who may be a corruption of Suabertus. It appears that Oswine and Suebhardus/Suabertus were joint-kings of Kent (see further, Appendix 3).

Much of the discussion about **40** and the other four charters in the names of these two (or three) kings has centred on their dates. The dating information in these texts usually consists of a regnal year and indiction, sometimes with a calendar date. But **40** also includes an incarnation year, in a concluding section where Æthelred of Mercia confirms Swæfheard's grant. In Elmham's text this confirmation is dated to 8 January 676, in the fourth indiction, which is internally consistent but difficult to reconcile with the dating information for Swæfheard's original grant, said to have been made on 1 March, also in the fourth indiction. A grant made in March 676 can hardly have been confirmed in January 676. It is also difficult to believe that the charters of Swæfheard/*Suabertus* and Oswine belong to a period as early as the 670s. In a brief survey of the issues involved, Professor Whitelock (1976, p. 142–4) concluded that the initial indiction and the incarnation year of the confirmation had both been altered by a later copyist and suggested a revised dating of 1 March 690 for Swæfheard's original grant to Minster and 8 January 691 for Æthelred's confirmation. The copy of the charter in PRO E 164/27, which has not previously been printed, demonstrates that this hypothesis is substantially correct. It has an incarnation date of 691 for Æthelred's confirmation, and it also puts the original grant by Swæfheard in the second indiction rather than the fourth, which indicates that Swæfheard's charter was issued on 1 March 689. The version of **40** in BL Cotton Julius D. ii also puts the original grant in the second indiction (it breaks off before Æthelred's confirmation, so it does not bear witness to the incarnation year). The copies of **40** in the two thirteenth-century cartularies do not therefore present any dating difficulties; it is only Elmham's text which contains the discrepancies. Evidently the dates of **40** were tampered with before Elmham's time, presumably in order to associate the charter with Æthelred's invasion of Kent in 676, as mentioned by Bede (*HE*, iv. 12). This is only one of several instances of chronological manipulation in the early charters of the St Augustine's archive: see further discussion on pp. xcvi–cv.

The fact that the dates in Elmham's text of the charter seem to have been altered has some disturbing implications. It was in the context of **40** and **41** that Elmham made his celebrated observation on the superiority of the readings of original charters over those of cartulary copies (Hardwick, *Elmham*, pp. 237–8). He states that he has taken his copies of **40** and **41** from the originals, because the cartulary versions of these texts were clearly faulty. He does not mention the discrepancy of the date in **40**, but he does say that the cartulary texts incorporated a passage relating to the earlier history of the estate which was not found in his 'original', and to which he objects on (mistaken) chronological grounds. This raises considerable problems. The dating of the cartulary texts is clearly preferable to that of Elmham's 'original'. Elmham was acute enough to notice if the dates in his single-sheet copy had been tampered with, so the possibility arises that his 'original' in this case was a pseudo-original, a single-sheet version fabricated between the thirteenth and fifteenth centuries which incorporated the revised dating and omitted the passage on the earlier history of the estate (which mentioned kings who were presumed to have been Swæfheard's successors). This is certainly the implication of Elmham's discussion of **41**, where his 'original' omitted the subscription of King Oswine found in the cartulary text, although this was almost certainly an authentic part of the original charter. In view of the doubts about Elmham's 'originals', the testimony of the cartulary texts has generally been preferred in this edition, not only in the matter of dating but also in the incorporation of the passage about the earlier history of the estate. This passage is unlikely to have formed part of Swæfheard's original charter, but it is based on an early record and (as shown below) it was probably inserted at the stage when Swæfheard's charter was revised to create the extant text.

40 is considerably longer than other seventh-century charters from Kent, and it is also surprisingly repetitive and has an odd construction. After a verbal invocation of the usual Kentish type and an unremarkable superscription, there is a dating clause and a consent formula naming Archbishop Theodore and King Sebbi (for the position of the dating clause, see p. 28). The dispositive section proper mentions a grant of forty-four hides in Thanet, to which the donor (the use of a plural verb here and elsewhere may associate Sebbi in the grant) adds a vill of twelve hides on the mainland in Sturry. Next comes an extended list of general appurtenances, and then the beneficiary is named and her powers over the estate described. The structure of the disposition is a little confusing, especially the delay in supplying the main dispositive verb; this could well be due to incompetence or inexperience on the part of the draftsman, but it is possible that there was some rewriting here (perhaps in order to insert the reference to the additional grant in Sturry). The king then forbids anyone to interfere with the grant, which is to remain in perpetuity in the possession of God's servants. At this point the passage about the earlier history of the estate intervenes. After this the disposition is recapitulated and the beneficiary named a second time, and the donor mentions that he is making this grant with the permission of King Æthelred. The charter concludes with a blessing and anathema, a cor-roboration, the witness-list to Swæfheard's grant and then Æthelred's confirmation.

Early Anglo-Saxon charters should not be judged with over-rigid expectations, but here there seems to be some justification for considering that the present text is not a straightforward seventh-century charter. One of the many surprising features is the change of allegiance in the course of the text. The reference to Æthelred's consent comes towards the end of the charter, although it would have been more appropriate in the consent-formula at the beginning, where Sebbi of Essex is named as the higher authority. It may be that the present document is a conflation of two charters of Swæfheard, one of a slightly later date, which might explain some of the repetition. Of interest in this context is the form of Æthelred's confirmation, where the objective subscription is continued with a third-person statement. We are told that Æthelred subscribed the charter 'when he confirmed our land at the place called *Mirafeld* atque *Stapulford*' on the given date. The meaning of this sentence has been obscured by Kemble's misreading (or possibily emendation) of *infirmauerat* for *adfirmauerat*. The use of *infirmo* in this context was thought to refer to Æthelred's ravaging of Kent, so that 'our land' became Kent itself; originally this was understood as a reference to the invasion of 676, but the emendation of the incarnation year in **40** to 691 has raised the ghost of a second invasion of Kent in that year (Brooks, *Church of Canterbury*, p. 77). In fact, the only manuscript reading is *adfirmauerat*, and the reference is to Æthelred's confirmation of Minster estates. The phrase 'our land' in this context can only have been used by a Minster scribe; indeed, the whole sentence now reads as a Minster gloss on the confirmation. This should probably be connected with the internal passage on the earlier history of the estate, which tells how the land was first made available to the servants of God by Hlothhere and Eadric, then given *in ius ecclesiasticum* by the interloper Mul. The whole charter should perhaps be seen as a composite text, built up from more than one charter and incorporating additional material on the previous history of the land and on its confirmation by Æthelred.

The reason for such unusual treatment may have been that this document was regarded, or intended to be regarded, as the title-deed for the core of Minster's early endowment. The forty-four hides granted by Swæfheard are said to be *in Sudaneie* on Thanet. The meaning of this place-name is unclear, as is the corresponding *westan ae* in S 8, a charter granting land on Thanet to Reculver. The first elements of the two names are presumably *suðan*, 'from or in the south', and *westan* 'from or in the west'. S 8 probably gives the best version of the second element, which appears to be *ea* 'river'. Unfortunately there is no convenient river on Thanet which might have given rise to these place-names; in references to this area, *ea* generally means the Wantsum Channel, and any areas west or south of the Wantsum would be on the mainland and not on Thanet. The (much) later form in **40** points to a derivation from *ieg*, 'island'; it is more likely to be corrupt than the spelling in S 8, but it does have the advantage of offering a slightly more satisfactory prospect of explaining the place-names. The Reculver property on Thanet appears to have been located in the western part of the island, where the Canterbury archbishops (the heirs of Reculver minster) were later to hold land (see Rollason 1979, pp. 14–15). Similarly, Æbba's foundation on Thanet was situated in the extreme south of the island. Problems remain, but it does seem possible that *in Sudaneie* was thought to refer to an area in the south of the isle of Thanet, surrounding Æbba's minster, while *Westan ae* was an area in the west. Thus the donation in **40** might be understood to apply to the immediate vicinity of the minster.

Certainly the historical passage in **40** suggests that the estate was of more than ordinary importance. This tells us that the land was first placed under the control of the servants of God by Kings Hlothhere and Eadric. The suggestion here that these were joint-kings of Kent is consistent with the evidence that they issued a joint lawcode (Liebermann, *Gesetze*, i. 9–11; Whitelock, *EHD*, no. 30); the information in the charter surely derives from a seventh-century record. Later the land was given to Abbess Æbba by Mul, the brother of Cædwalla of Wessex, who was briefly king in Kent between 686 and 687. Mul gave Æbba the land *in ius ecclesiasticum*, which perhaps here indicates a different type of tenure from that granted by Hlothhere and Eadric; it may have been the case that the earlier kings simply gave the land to the church, whereas Mul issued a royal charter for it. Æbba apparently paid Mul for the privilege; see S 1177 for a similar, slightly later, example of an religious woman handing over money to local rulers in return for land. Mul's reign was short, and his overthrow may have made it necessary to seek another charter from the new ruler of Kent, Swæfheard, also an intruder into Kent. Subsequently the abbess applied for further confirmation to Æthelred of Mercia, perhaps belatedly acknowleged by Swæfheard as his overlord. Certainly this activity implied that the land in question was important to Minster. There is a parallel with the series of charters apparently covering the central endowment of the minster at Hoo, which was supposedly granted by Cædwalla and confirmed by Sighere of Essex, Swæfheard and his father Sebbi of Essex, Wihtred of Kent and Æthelred of Mercia (see S 233). Land first provided by an invader needed all possible guarantees.

The passage on the early history of the estate gives some details about the size of the property. The figures have become corrupt, but the general outlines of the statement are fairly clear. The land consisted of forty-four hides, of which forty-four (? thirty-four) were in Thanet, and ten on the mainland, in the area known as Sturry and in a place named *Maeccanbrooc* (the lost Makenbrook in Herne, also mentioned in the bounds of S 546; see Gough 1992, pp. 92–3, and map pp. 98–9); the phrase *ad aquilonis siluam* can be connected with the region called *bi Northanuude* in **48**. The information in the historical passage does not correspond well with the details in the dispositive section, except in so far as it shows that the charter was understood to relate both to land in Thanet and to property on the mainland. What the discrepancies may show is that the text was seen as the title-deed to an accumulation of property, rather than to one or two discrete estates. This seems consistent with the argument that **40** as it stands is a composite document rather than a single charter.

At some stage versions of **40** and **41** were produced in the name of King Hlothhere (S 1648, S (Add.) 1648a; see further discussion in Appendix 1, no. i). It is not clear when these texts came into existence. The motive for their creation may have been the desire to attribute such important early title-deeds to the well-attested Hlothhere, instead of an obscure interloper. The charters of Oswine do not appear to have received the same treatment, perhaps because he was identified with King Oswiu of Northumbria at an early date (see p. cii). It may be significant that in the historical passage in **40** Hlothhere is identified as the initial donor of the property, along with Eadric.

The formulation of **40** raises several difficulties. Its closest affinities are with **6**, a charter of Hlothhere in favour of St Augustine's datable to 675. The correspondence between the two texts begins with the dating clause, in both cases inserted after the royal style and consisting of a regnal year, indiction and calendar date expressed in the same wording (1 April in **6**, as opposed to 1 March in **40**). They have a similar consent clause, the reference to Sebbi being of course missing in **6**, and the lists of appurtenances are clearly related. In both charters the dispositive verbs are plural and in the present tense; *possidendam concedimus et confirmamus* in **6** corresponds to *possidendam perdonamus* (and later *possidendam contradimus et confirmamus*) in **40**. Both charters have the same formula promising that there shall be no interference in the grant, the same blessing and anathema, and essentially the same corroboration. In both the king's subscription has the same form. The similarity between these two charters suggests three possibilities. They could support each other, and show that the basic formulation is contemporary. One may be genuine and the other modelled on it (any fabrication would have to take place in or after the eleventh century, when the Minster charters entered the St Augustine's archive). Finally, neither charter may be authentic in its present form. In his discussion of these two texts, Scharer (*Königsurkunde*, pp. 63–5, 78–83) argues that some of the shared formulation, particularly the blessing and anathema, points to a model of the later eighth century, and would be out of place in a seventh-century charter. This conclusion may be mistaken (see commentary to **6**). The relationship between **6** and **40** remains rather mysterious, but it is probably better explained as a consequence of contemporaneity than as an indication of the joint-reworking of the two charters.

There are also close links between **40** and **42**, a charter of King Oswine granting ten hides in Sturry to Æbba. The correspondence is most noticeable in the graceful list of appurtenances, with its string of paired items. There is also repetition of other short phrases, particularly those relating legal matters (*ius monasteriale, ius ecclesiasticum, tantum in dominio*). As in **40**, the assessment in **42** is expressed in hides (*manentes*) instead of the usual Kentish sulungs (see also **43** and **46**, and discussion pp. lxxviii–lxxix). In **42** the dating material is inserted, not directly after the superscription, but after a brief motivation clause. Once more the date is expressed in terms of regnal year, indiction and calendar date, the latter intrduced by the phrase *sub die*, found not only in **6** and **40**, but also in **10**, Wihtred's grant of privileges to the Kentish churches. It is interesting that both Swæfheard in **40** and Oswine in **42** claim blood-relationship with Æbba; in Swæfheard's case, the relationship probably derives from the sixth-century marriage between the sister of King Æthelberht (Æbba's great-grandfather) and the father of King Sæberht of Essex (see Bede, *HE*, ii.3). Scharer condemns **42** as well as **6** and **40**.

The witness-list of **40** begins with the king's subscription, followed by those of eleven laymen and King Sebbi. The position of Sebbi's subscription may indicate corruption of an arrangement in columns. These subscriptions are in the objective form, which was considered appropriate for lay witnesses in early charters (see S 8, and p. lxxxv). Most of these laymen attest other charters of the period: Gumberht (**41**, S 8); Gebred (**46**, S 8, 233); Osfrid (**6**, **8**, **42**, S 8); Hagona (**10**, S 8, 19/21); Egisa (S 233); Bernhard (**10**, **44**, S 8, 19/21); Ecca (**6**, **8**, **10**, **41**, **42**, **43**, S 22, 233); Gudhard (**46**, S 8). See further, Whitelock 1976. The lay subscriptions are followed by those of Archbishop Theodore and Abbot Hadrian of St Augustine's.

Æthelred's confirmation of the charter, which is probably in part a note added by a Minster scribe (see above), is said to have occurred at a place called both *Mirafeld* and *Stapulford*, which seems odd (and may be the contribution of the Minster scribe, perhaps here condensing a longer record). The best identification of these two places is with Marefield and Stapleford in Leicestershire, which are about seven miles apart. Æbba had presumably taken her charter(s) to Mercia in order to acquire Æthelred's confirmation. The inclusion of an incarnation year here requires some comment. Bede has generally been credited with the popularizing of dating by this method, but it has been recognised that the incarnation year was in limited use in England in the pre-Bedan period. Several of the earlier instances are in documents associated with Wilfrid and his followers, or from areas where Wilfrid had influence, particularly Mercia (Harrison, *Framework*, pp. 62–75; Sims-Williams 1988; and see above, p. lxxxiv).

41

Suabertus, *king of the men of Kent, grants two sulungs* (aratra) *in Sturry and three at Bodsham, Kent, to Abbess Æbba.* [*c.* A.D. 690]

F. BL Cotton Julius D. ii, 102r: copy, s. xiii[1]
   Rubric: Suabertus rex de Sturei et de Bodesham.
H. PRO E 164/27, 77v: copy, s. xiii
   Rubric: De Stureia et de Bodesham.
N. Cambridge, Trinity Hall, 1, 49rv: copy, s. xv[1]
   Rubric: Carta eiusdem Suabherti eidem Æbbe abbatisse de terris in Sturrigia et Botdesham.
Ed.: a. Lewis, *Tenet*, p. 58, from N
   b. Kemble 15 from N
   c. Hardwick, *Elmham*, pp. 234–5, from N
   d. Birch 41 from N
Listed: Sawyer 11
Edited from F, H and N

In nomine saluatoris. Ego Suabertus*ᵃ* rex Cantuariorum, miserationum Domini memor quas erga me exercuit, ideo ergo*ᵇ* rectum iudicaui ut pro

eterna salute anime mee atque meorum aliquid munusculum Domino im-
penderem, id est^c terram que sita est in Sturige .ii.^{d} aratrorum atque .iii.^{e}
aratrorum in loco qui^f dicitur Botdesham^g monasteriali potestati atque
regulariter uiuentibus subicerem. Quod hodierna die Domino auxiliante
compleui dedique uenerabili abbatisse Eabbe^h ut ibi seruientium Deo preces
protelentur atque pro uita mea sine defectu in conspectu Dei effundantur.
Et ad confirmationem donationis istius signum sancte crucis expressi^i necnon
et principes meos ut similiter facerent rogaui sicque fecerunt, ut si aliquis
ausu nefarie temeritatis aliquid ex ea auferre uel minuere uoluerit, nouerit
se alienatum a Deo in resurrectione iustorum.

+^{j} Signum Suaberti^k regis.^{l}
+ Signum Gumberti.^{m}
+ Signum Æcci.
^{n}+ Ego Oswynus rex consensi et subscripsi.^{n}

^{a} Swabertus H ^{b} Probably for ego ^{c} idem F ^{d} duorum H ^{e} trium H
^{j} que F ^{g} Bodesham H ^{h} Rabe F ^{i} expressi + H ^{j} F omits cross
^{k} Swaberti H ^{l} F ends here ^{m} Cumberti H ^{n} ... ^{n} Omitted N (see commentary)

The donor of **41** may be the Swæfheard (*Suebhardus*) of **40**, who is said by Bede to
have been ruling with Wihtred in July 692. The post-Conquest historians were
certainly of the opinion that the two charters were issued by the same man, and the
spelling of the name in the rubric to Elmham's text (*Suabhertus*) seems to support
the suggestion that the form of the name in **41** could be corrupt. However, Swæfberht
is an acceptable Anglo-Saxon name, and the possibility does remain that this
was another contemporary king, presumably of East Saxon origin and perhaps
Swæfheard's brother. See further discussion in Appendix 3. **41** was attested by King
Oswine, as was **40**. Two of Oswine's charters (**42**, **43**) are attested by Swæfheard,
while in the third (**8**) a witness named *Gabertus* may be a corruption of *Sabertus*,
who could be Swæfberht (*Suabertus*). It is unfortunate that in distinguishing these
names we can rely only on later manuscripts which do not seem reliable.

Elmham claimed to have taken his texts of **40** and **41** directly from the *originales*,
and remarked that they were superior to the copies in the cartularies (Hardwick,
Elmham, pp. 237–8). In the case of **40** it can be shown that the readings of the
cartulary copies are to be preferred to those of the 'original', which suggests that
Elmham was using a pseudo-original, a later fabrication on a single sheet. In **41** the
discrepancy between the two versions again seems to support the cartulary reading.
Here the issue centres on the subscription of King Oswine, found in the witness-list
in PRO E 164/27 and apparently in the cartulary copies which Elmham consulted,
but missing from his 'original'. Elmham approved the absence of this subscription
on soberly historical grounds; Oswine could not attest this charter because he had
died some years before. Unfortunately, this conclusion is based on the mistaken
identification of Oswine of Kent with the infinitely more celebrated Oswiu of

Northumbria (see p. cii). The Kentish Oswine certainly attests **40**, while Swæfheard attests Oswine's charters. It is to be presumed that a pseudo-original of **41** had been created in which Oswine's subscription was deliberately or mistakenly omitted. It is likely that in this pseudo-original the witness-list of the original charter had been curtailed. Elmham usually copied out the full witness-list of his sources, so in this case the source would appear to have had only two subscriptions apart from that of the donor; the copy in PRO E 164/27 adds Oswine's subscription, making a total of four. Original charters surviving from this period have a much larger number of witnesses (see S 8, 19; also **10**).

  41 is a simpler and shorter text than **40** and there is no real difficulty in accepting it as an essentially genuine seventh-century charter, although Scharer (*Königsurkunde*, p. 84) is correct to point out that it is not usual to find a single charter granting land in two widely separated places. The brief verbal invocation is the same as that in **7** and conforms to the usual pattern of Kentish invocations. There is no proem. The royal style is followed by an oblique statement of pious motivation, comparable to those in **42**, **43** and **44** (see also **10**, S 19); some of the wording is repeated in **42**. The donor makes a double grant, of two sulungs in Sturry, a regional name (see the commentary to **3**), and three at Bodsham. The wording of the disposition is comparable to that in contemporary charters; the use of the phrase *monasterialis potestas* recalls similar references to ecclesiastical jurisdiction in **6**, **40** and **42**, while the verb *subiecerem* resurfaces as *subieci* in the same context in **43**. The construction of the disposition is rather unusual in that the donor states that he has contemplated making the grant to the Church and that today he has completed the transaction and granted the land to Abbess Æbba. In return her community is to pray for the king's life; there is a similarly-worded request in **46**, and a comparable prayer condition in **9**, **47** and **48**. The corroboration, request for witnesses and sanction are economically combined. The formulation here seems acceptable; *expressi* is used in this context in a number of charters (see, for instance, S 8 and 19), and the request addressed to the witnesses is a standard feature of Kentish charters at this time. The wording of the first clause of the anathema recalls that of the prohibition against interference in **40**. For the forms of the subscriptions see p. lxxxv. The two non-royal witnesses are Gumberht and Ecca; for their subscriptions in other Kentish charters, see the commentary to **40**. **41** is now undated, perhaps because the dating clause was lost in the course of transmission (it may have been deliberately omitted if it was felt to conflict with the mistaken identification of Oswine with Oswiu). It was probably issued at around the same time as **40** and the three charters of Oswine. Scharer (*Königisurkunde*, p. 84) suggests that the absence of an archiepiscopal subscription could imply that the charter was issued during the vacancy after Theodore's death, but this is hardly conclusive, since the witness-list has probably been curtailed and it was anyway at this date not unknown for a charter to have no ecclesiastical subscriptions (see S 8).

  This is one of three Minster charters relating to land in Sturry, then a name for the region north of Canterbury rather than a simple place-name (see the commentary to **3**). The spelling here seems early, for it preserves the archaic *-ge* element, also found in Lyminge and in early forms of Eastry. In **40** a *curtis* or vill of twelve hides at Sturry is mentioned (the incorporated historical passage has a reference to ten hides at Sturry and in the Reculver area). **42** records a grant of ten hides in Sturry.

In 1086 St Augustine's manor at Sturry was assessed at five sulungs and estimated to have land for twelve ploughs (GDB 12r). If it is assumed that the sulung was equivalent to two hides (see p. lxxviii n. 26), then the total area in Sturry granted in **40**, **41** and **42** was thirteen sulungs (or twenty-six hides); there may be a rough correspondence between this figure and the twelve ploughs of the Domesday entry (for other examples of such a link, see Witney 1988, pp. 104–9; and above, p. cxi n. 79). The eleventh-century St Augustine's manor at Sturry may then represent mainland property inherited from Minster (see further, Tatton-Brown 1992, pp. 85–7).

41 also covers land at Bodsham in the Downland, near Hastingleigh in the lathe of Lyminge. St Augustine's had a manor there assessed at a sulung in 1086, but this was probably land acquired from Æthelric Bigga in the Confessor's reign (see **38**). There is some slight possibility that Æthelric gave the land to the abbey in settlement of a dispute, perhaps as a result of the abbey's claim to Bodsham through Minster.

42

Oswine, king of the men of Kent, grants ten hides (manentes) *in Sturry, Kent, to Abbess Æbba.* A.D. 690 (27 January)

F. BL Cotton Julius D. ii, 102r: copy, s. xiii[1]
  Rubric: Oswinus rex de Stureie.
H. PRO E 164/27, 77v–78r: copy, s. xiii
  Rubric: Item Oswynus de Stureia.
N. Cambridge, Trinity Hall, 1, 48r: copy, s. xv[1]
  Rubric: Carta eiusdem Oswyni de terra in Sturreya quam dedit Æbbe abbatisse de Menstre.
Ed.: a. Lewis, *Tenet*, pp. 54–5, from N
     b. Kemble 8 from N
     c. Hardwick, *Elmham*, p. 229, from N
     d. Birch 35 from N
     e. Pierquin, *Recueil*, pt 1, no. 8, from Birch
Listed: Sawyer 13
Edited from F, H and N

In nomine Domini Iesu Christi saluatoris. Ego Oswinus*[a]* rex Cantuariorum aliquod munusculum pro Deo destino dare ut sit refrigerium anime mee inperpetuum et uigilet mea memoria cum sanctis in sublime. Anno secundo regni mei, indictione autem tertia, sub die .vi. kalendarum Februarii, pro remedio anime mee et absolutione peccatorum meorum, ecclesiastico iure concedo quandam terram que dicitur Stureie,*[b]* id est decem manentes ex ea, cum siluis et campis ac paludibus, cum fluminibus ac fontibus, cum pratis ac pomariis*[c]* et cum omnibus utensilibus, in ipsa quantitate sicut principes a regibus antiquitus perdonatum possederunt, alme*[d]* Æbbe*[e]* abbatisse atque carnali propinquitate proxime in Deoque matri monasteriali*[f]* iuri*[g]* dono perpetuo trado, quatinus habeat possideatque proprio arbitrio et cuicumque uoluerit uiuens uel moriens habeat integram facultatem condonare tantum in domino.[h] Istud autem territorium a me modo commemoratum ac pro Deo perdonatum in presentia principum meorum qui ad presens haberi possunt, hoc est Cantuariorum quos iure ac propria nostra potestate adipiscimur, pro testimonio confirmationis ad subscribendum ac ad consentiendum mihi huic donationi conduxi in hunc locum qui dicitur Dorouernis. Confirmamus stabiliter in euum ut quisquis hanc donationem meam mente maliuola[i] disrumpere temptauerit, sciat se coram Deo et sanctis angelis eius eterno anathemate reum. Quisquis uero bene addendo custodierit sit benedictus in secula.

+[j] Theodorus gratia Dei archiepiscopus rogatus a rege subscripsi.
+ Ego Osuuinus[k] propria manu subscripsi ac consensi.[l]
+ Ego Suebhardus[m] consensi et subscripsi.
+ Ego Adrianus abbas indignus subscripsi.
+ Signum manus Ecca.[n]
+ Signum Osfridi.[o]

[a] Oswynus H   [b] Sturrie F, H   [c] pomeriis F, N   [d] aliene F   [e] Eabbe H
[f] monasteria ei H   [g] iuri F, H, N; *for* iure   [h] domino F, H, N; *for* dominio
[i] maliuolo F
[j] *No crosses except one added by the rubricator after Oswine's subscription* F; *crosses after the subscriptions* H   [k] Oswynus H, N   [l] *F ends here*   [m] Suebardus N   [n] Ecci H
[o] Hoffridi H

Oswine is also the donor of **8**, in favour of St Augustine's, and **43**, another grant to Minster. His reign began at some point in the year before 27 January 689, and for some time he was joint-ruler with King Swæfheard and perhaps also with another king named Swæfberht (see Appendix 3); Oswine and Swæfheard/Swæfberht regularly attested each other's charters. All three of Oswine's surviving charters include a statement stressing his legitimate right to rule in Kent, presumably because his position was less than secure; in **42** this claim is inserted into the corroboration, and there is probably a similar significance in the reference to his blood-relationship with Abbess Æbba, a member of the Kentish royal dynasty.

The construction of **42** is mildly eccentric, but this need not condemn a charter of so early a date. The oddest feature is the position of the dating clause, which breaks the flow of the dispositive section. Several early charters from Minster and St Augustine's have dating information placed at or near the beginning of the text, and this has been seen as a sign of fabrication or tampering (Scharer, *Königsurkunde*, pp. 63–4 n. 9), but it is possible that this is simply experimentation (perhaps based on Italian models, where a dating clause might be found in a similar position), and such a feature may be compatible with authenticity (see further, p. 28). In general the formulation of **42** seems acceptable. The verbal invocation is of the regular Kentish type, and the superscription is followed by a statement of pious motivation, such as is found in **10, 41, 43, 44** and in S 19 (see p. lxxvii); the wording here is similar to that in **41**. There is a particularly close relationship between **42** and **40**. They have the same long list of appurtenances, and share several short phrases; in **40** the dating information appears after the superscription, and consists (as here) of regnal year, indiction and calendar date (introduced by the phrase *sub die*). The authenticity of **40** is not beyond question (it certainly seems to have been reworked at some stage), and the correspondences have been taken as reason to condemn **42** (Scharer, *Königsurkunde*, pp. 74–5); but this conclusion is probably unjustified. Another formula in **42** seems to confirm that the text is at least based on an early document; the statement of powers is almost word-for-word the same as that in a seventh-century charter from Much Wenlock in Staffordshire (S 1798), and probably derives directly from an Italian model. The anathema is slightly unusual, but not suspiciously so; the verb *disrumpere* is also used in **6** and **40**. It was not usual at this date for a Kentish charter to include a blessing (although there are examples from the first half of the eighth century: see p. lxxxii). Again there are possible parallels in **6** and **40**, which may represent a legitimate alternative strand of Kentish diplomatic, and it is worth mentioning that blessings appear in early charters from Essex and Wessex. The formulation of the sanction in **42** does not seem overtly suspicious in any way. There is no good reason not to accept this as a genuine seventh-century charter.

The witness-list as it stands contains only six subscriptions, and may have been abbreviated. Archbishop Theodore subscribes in exactly the same terms in **6**; he died in September 690, which is compatible with the implied date of **42**. Abbot Hadrian's subscription is also the same in **6**; it incorporates a 'humility formula' which is occasionally associated with him (see further discussion in the commentary to **10**). For other subscriptions of Ecca and Osfrid, see the commentary to **40**.

42 is concerned with a grant of ten hides in Sturry (for the use of a hide-assessment in some Minster charters, see pp. lxxviii–lxxix). Sturry was a regional name at this time (see the commentary to **3**), and this seems to be reflected in the awkward wording of the dispositive section; the draftsman first treated Sturry as a simple place-name, using the regular formula to refer to an estate, and then qualified the initial statement with the phrase 'that is, ten hides from it'. For Minster lands in Sturry, see the commentary to **41**.

43

Oswine, king of the men of Kent, grants eighteen hides (manentes) *in Thanet to Abbess Æbba.* [*c.* A.D. 690]

F. BL Cotton Julius D. ii, 102rv: copy, s. xiii[1]
   Rubric: Oswinus rex de Taneto.
H. PRO E 164/27, 78rv: copy, s. xiii
   Rubric: Item carta Oswyni de Thaneto.
N. Cambridge, Trinity Hall, 1, 48rv: copy, s. xv[1]
   Rubric: Carta eiusdem Oswyni de terra .xviii. manentium in Thaneto quam dedit eidem Æbbe abbatisse de Menstre.

Ed.: a. Lewis, *Tenet*, pp. 55–6, from N
   b. Kemble 10 from N
   c. Hardwick, *Elmham*, p. 230, from N
   d. Birch 40 from N
   e. Pierquin, *Recueil*, pt 1, no. 10, from Birch
Listed: Sawyer 14
Translated: Ward 1938, p. 61
Edited from F, H and N

In nomine Domini nostri Iesu Christi. Ego Osuuinus*a* rex Cantuariorum gratias refero miserenti*b* Deo omnipotenti qui confirmauit me in regno patrum meorum et dedit mihi domum cognationis mee. Quamobrem placuit mihi ne ingratus beneficiis*c* Domini uiderer,*d* et terram que sita*e* est in insula Tenet,*f* .xviii. manentes continentem, quam aliquando Irminredus*g* possidebat, (et aliqua pars ipsius archiepiscopi erat, ipso tamen consentiente *h*et aliam a nobis accipiente*h*)*i* monasteriali seruituti subieci; nuncque in presentia*j* adiuuante Domino perpetraui*k* sub manus Christicolarum, gubernatrici Æbbe*l* perpetuali donatione redegi, ut teneat, possideat ipsa semper, successoresque eius incommutabili decreto defendant; atque ad confirmationem istius*m* cartule cespitem terre supradicte sacro altari superposui, ut omnis quicumque ausus fuerit aliquid ex ea temerare aut minuere uel etiam transmutare sine uoluntate possidentium, sciat se alienum a participatione regni ecclesiis*n* effici et a cetu fidelium segregatum, nisi*o* regulariter emendauerit.

+*p* Signum sancte crucis propria manu expressi.*q*

+ Signum manus Oswyni regis.

+ Ego Suebhardus*r* consensi et subscripsi.

+ Signum manus Acce.*s*

---

a Oswynus H, N   *b* miseranti N   *c* *For* beneficiorum
d 'Therefore it was my wish not to seem ungrateful for the Lord's favours'
e terra inquisita H   *f* de Thanet H; Thanet N   *g* Yrminredus N   *h* … *h* *Omitted* H
i *This section may be an intrusion into the dispositive section, although the grammatical confusion could equally well be the fault of the draftsman, who does not seem to be fully in control*   *j* *Presumably for* in presenti   *k* *The object of the verb is* terram
l Eabe F; Eabbe H   *m* huius H   *n* ecclesiis F, H, N; *probably for* celestis
o *Omitted* H   *p* F *omits cross*   *q* F *ends here*   *r* Swabertus H   *s* Ecci H

This is the third charter of Oswine in the archive (see also **8, 42**); like the others it includes a statement bolstering Oswine's claim to rule legitimately in Kent. It is attested by (King) Swæfheard, who was Oswine's co-ruler (see Appendix 3). The land granted to Æbba is located vaguely in Thanet, and more precisely through its previous owner, Irminred, who is presumably Æbba's father Eormenred, scion of the Kentish dynasty (see Rollason, *Mildrith Legend*, pp. 37–8); the fact that this relationship is not underlined in **42** confirms the general impression of its authenticity. There is a slight problem in the following sentence, which remarks that part of the land had previously belonged to the archbishop and that he had been compensated. This does not agree grammatically with the surrounding material, which suggests that it could be an interpolation (? after a dispute settlement), but it is not impossible that the original draftsman simply had difficulty in fitting this information into a model. For the use of a hide assessment in Minster charters, see pp. lxxviii–lxxix.

The construction of the dispositive section is a little odd, but closely comparable to the corresponding formulation in **41** and **42**. In all three charters the draftsman has introduced a statement of pious motivation after the superscription (in **43** this is twisted into a statement of legitimacy); some of the wording of this part of **43** resurfaces in two slightly later charters of Wihtred (**9, 44**). In **42** and **43** the draftsman seems to have experienced some difficulty in combining the statement of motivation with the dispositive section proper, and has been forced to start a new sentence (in **43** this is introduced by an exposition). The transaction in **43**, as in **41**, is presented as a two-fold procedure; the king conceived the idea of subjecting the land to monastic control, and has now (today) carried out that intention. The formulation of the statement of powers in **43** is similar to that in S 8. In a brief corroboration Oswine states that he has placed a sod of earth from the estate on the altar; for references in other charters to a similar ceremony, see p. lxxxiii. The wording of the sanction was partly revived in **9** and **44**; for the 'escape clause', see **46**. The curious phrase which precedes the king's subscription may be part of a formula introducing the witness-list (as in S 8, 19). Perhaps a later copyist mutilated this section, although it is also possible that the original draftsman here corrupted his or her model. There are only three subscriptions, which suggests that the witness-list has been curtailed at some stage. For other subscriptions of Ecca, see the commentary to **40**.

44

Wihtred, king of Kent, grants four sulungs (aratra) *at* Humantun *to Abbess* Æbba. A.D. 694 (17 July)

F. BL Cotton Julius D. ii, 102v: copy, s. xiii[1]
  Rubric: Wytredus rex de Taneto.
H. PRO E 164/27, 78v–79r: copy, s. xiii
  Rubric: Item carta Withredi regis de Thaneto.
N. Cambridge, Trinity Hall, 1, 61rv: copy, s. xv[1]
  Rubric: De carta Wihtredi regis pro terra iiii aratrorum in Thaneto Æbbe abbatisse de Menstre eidem anno quo Brithuualdus in archiepiscopum fuerat ordinatus cuius carta tenor iste est.
Ed.: a. Spelman, *Concilia*, i. 192–3, from N
  b. Lewis, *Tenet*, pp. 58–9, from N
  c. Wilkins, *Concilia*, iv. 746, from Spelman
  d. Kemble 37 from N
  e. Hardwick, *Elmham*, pp. 288–9, from N
  f. Birch 86 from N

Listed: Sawyer 15
Edited from F, H and N

In nomine Domini Dei saluatoris. Ego Uuihtredus*a* rex Cantie una cum
coniuge mea Kinigitha*b* regina, referens gratias*c* largitori bonorum Domino
qui dilatauit terminos nostros iuxta paternam antiquitatem, in commune
pertractauimus aliquam partem terre nobis conlate*d* ad uicem impendere,*e*
ne ingrati beneficiis*f* uideremur largitoris nostri. Qua de re a presenti die et
tempore tibi religiose Æbbe*g* abbatisse*h* Deoque dicate femine terram iuris
nostri que sita est in insula Teneti,*i* que quondam appellata est Humantun,*j*
aratrorum .iiii., contulimus inperpetuum possidendam, ut cum omnibus ad
eandem pertinentibus, pratis, campis, fontanis, siluis, piscariis, fluminibus,
marisco et quicquid ad supradictam terram pertinet, a .iiii. partibus, orientis,
occidentis, aquilonis et meridiei, tuo usui dicionique subicias,*k* teneas,*l* possideas, dones, commutes, uenundes uel quicquid exinde facere uolueris
liberam habeas potestatem successoresque tui defendant inperpetuum.*c*
Numquam me heredesque meos contra hanc cartulam descriptionis nostre
aliquando esse uenturos.*m* Ad cuius cumulum etiam affirmationis*n* cespitem
huius*c* supradicte terre super sanctum altare posui*o* et propria manu pro*p*
ignorantia litterarum signum sancte crucis in hac cartula*q* expressi. Sed et
Kinigitha*r* id ipsum fecit principesque meos ut pari modo propriis manibus
facerent rogaui, quorum nomina subtus annecta sunt. Si quis*s* quod absit
contra hanc cartulam*t* a me factam uel heredes mei contraire presumpserint,
nouerint se*u* a participatione corporis et sanguinis Domini nostri*v* Iesu Christi
esse alienos et a cetu fidelium segregandos hic*w* et in eternum. Quam
sepedictam cartulam scribendam dictaui et tibi Eabbe*x* abbatisse tradidi
conseruandum. Actum .xvi. kalendas Augusti, indictione .vii.,*y* anno regni
nostri tertio.*z*

+ Signum manus Wihtredi*a2* regis.
+ Signum manus Kinigithe regine.
+ Signum manus Bernhardi.
+ Signum manus Alhuuardi.

a Withredus H; Wythredus N   *b* Kynigitha N   *c* Omitted H   *d* collate H, N
e rependere F   *f* For beneficiorum   *g* Eabbe F, H   *h* abbatissie F
i Thaneti H; Thanæti N   *j* Humantiun F, H
k The object of this and the other verbs in the statement of powers is (hanc)
terram   *l* teneat F
m This is a common formula (see commentary), which requires an introductory phrase
(compare 7, where it is preceded by Sicut donatum est manere decerno)
n affirmitationis F   *o* posuit H   *p* per H   *q* kartula F   *r* Kynygytha F, N

˟ quid F   ˡ kartulam F   ᵘ *Omitted* F   ᵛ Domini nostri *omitted* H   ʷ huic H
˟ Eabe F   ʸ .uiia. H   ᶻ F *ends here*   ⁴² Withredi H; H *ends here*

When considered on its own terms, **44** seems entirely acceptable as a seventh-century charter. It is presented as the record of a joint-grant by Wihtred and his queen Cynegyth. In later charters Wihtred is associated with an Æthelburh and afterwards with a Werburh; Cynegyth may have been his first wife. Wihtred's queens seem to have enjoyed a remarkably high status, to judge from their attestations and other references to them in his charters (see commentary to **9**). The regnal year in the dating clause of **44** indicates that Wihtred came to power in the year before 17 July 692, which is consistent with the dating information in **10**, although it diverges from Bede's calculation (see further discussion in the commentary to **10**). The discrepancy is probably due to the confused beginning of Wihtred's reign in a period of joint-kingship with the usurper Swæfheard (see Appendix 3); the regnal years in **10** and **44** are probably reckoned from the date at which Wihtred achieved sole power in Kent. It is tempting to see a connection here with the statement of pious motivation that follows the superscription, in which Wihtred thanks God for extending his boundaries to their ancient limits. This clause corresponds with anxious statements of legitimacy in the charters of the usurper Oswine (see **8**, **42**, **43**). The wording of this section of **44** is in some respects similar to that in **43** and **46**, and there are also links between the sanctions of **44** and **46**.

44 is notable in diplomatic terms for the inclusion of a number of formulas which seem to have been borrowed almost directly from Italian models. The list of appurtenances (very similar to that in S 8) is rounded off by a curious reference to the four cardinal points; it may have been a formula of this type which inspired the typical Kentish boundary clause of the eighth and ninth centuries (see **17**, **18**, **19** etc., and p. lxxx). After this comes a statement of powers which has close counterparts in continental charters (see pp. lxxx–lxxxi n. 30), and then a formula binding the donor and his heirs not to infringe the grant, which occurs nearly verbatim in several other early charters (**7**, and S 1165, 235, 100, 56; see p. lxxxi). The corroboration begins with a formula with Italian antecedents (see **10**, **11**), continues with a reference to the ceremony of placing a sod on the altar (see **43**, and p. lxxxiii), and concludes with an apology for the donor's illiteracy, a fossil from late Roman legal documents (see further, p. lxxxiii). Finally, the sanction is followed by a corrupt version of an Italian *rogatio* clause. This was first noticed by Chaplais (1968, pp. 335–6 [pp. 86–7]), who suggested that it reflected forgery on the basis of the *Liber Diurnus*. In view of the other Italian formulas preserved in **44**, it seems reasonable to conclude that the draftsman was directly adapting an Italian model or models, and that the use of the formula here is legitimate.

The dating clause is expressed in terms of a full calendar date, an indiction and a regnal year; this arrangement is found in other Minster charters (see **40**, **42**, and p. lxxxiv). The witness-list has probably been abbreviated. The subscriptions of the king and queen are followed by those of two layman; the first of them, Bernhard, attests other contemporary charters (**10**, **40**; S 8, 19).

Doubt is thrown on the authenticity of **44**, not as a result of any internal deficiency, but because of its mysterious relationship with two charters in the Christ Church archive. S 156 supposedly records a grant in 799 by King Coenwulf and his Queen

Cenegitha of four sulungs at Wootton and Giddinge to the archbishop (unnamed) and the Christ Church community; it is extant as a single-sheet copy, written probably in the later tenth or eleventh century. S 156 an evident forgery, for it is attested by Archbishop Theodore and Abbot Hadrian. Apart from the details of the donor, beneficiary and estate, and the witness-list, the Christ Church charter is almost identical to **44**; it even has the same dating clause with the same calendar date. The close connection is underlined by the retention in S 156 of a redundant phrase *Deoque dicte*, corresponding to the *Deoque dicate femine* in **44**. A further complication is generated by S 1610, a summarized and standardized version of a charter in which Cædwalla of Wessex, with his wife Kenedritha, grants Wootton and Giddinge to Archbishop Theodore; towards the end of the text the donor's name is given as Cenuualh.

A simple explanation would be that **44** (or a copy of it) became available to the Christ Church scriptorium, at some point before the eleventh century, and that it was the model for the charter underlying S 1610; the forgery itself was then used for the fabrication of S 156 (the relative order of production is indicated by the appearance of subscriptions of Theodore and Hadrian in the witness-list of S 156). It would then be necessary to explain how a Minster charter came into the Christ Church archive, but this is by no means impossible. In the ninth century Archbishop Wulfred won control over Minster-in-Thanet (see p. xxviii), which may have entailed the (perhaps temporary) transfer of documentation; it is also possible that the Minster charters passed through Christ Church to St Augustine's after St Mildrith's community was broken up in the early eleventh century. Another possibility is that two identical charters of Wihtred were drawn up on the same day, one for Minster and one for a different beneficiary, and that it was the latter which came into the possession of the Christ Church scriptorium (see Brooks, *Church of Canterbury*, pp. 102–3). A difficulty here is that the model for the Christ Church forgeries was apparently in favour of a female religious (hence the phrase *deoque dic[a]te*), and it is rather a coincidence that two identical charters should be issued on the same day in favour of two different nuns. It might be suggested, however, that two charters in favour of Abbess Æbba were drawn up in exactly the same terms; **47** and **48** show that Minster draftsmen were not averse to repeating formulation almost verbatim (see also **49** and S 88). In this case, the second charter may have come to Christ Church as the title-deed for part of the Minster endowment which did not pass into the possession of St Augustine's, perhaps even via Lyminge, which was effectively combined with Minster in the later eighth and early ninth centuries (see pp. xxvii–xxviii).

But one factor weighs against such a simple explanation of the relationship between **44** and the Christ Church documents. Chaplais (1968, pp. 335–6 [pp. 86–7]) points out that the calendar date common to both S 156 and **44** (17 July) is the feastday of St Kenelm (Cynehelm), son of King Coenwulf, who attests S 156. Kenelm was buried and culted at Winchcombe; his sister Cwoenthryth was abbess of both Winchcombe and Minster-in-Thanet in the ninth century. Chaplais argues that both **44** and S 156 are forgeries, and suggests that the fabrication may have taken place at Winchcombe in Cwoenthryth's time. This suggestion has been taken up and expanded by Scharer (*Königsurkunde*, pp. 86–9), who treats **44**, S 156 and S 1610 as a *Fälschungenskomplex*, produced at Winchcombe between 812 (the date of Kenelm's death) and 825 (when Cwoenthryth finally ceded Minster to Archbishop Wulfred).

This complicated hypothesis is difficult to accept. It rests upon the assumption that Kenelm's cult was being promoted immediately after his death by the sister reputed to have killed him; independent evidence suggests that the cult did not become important until the latter part of the tenth century, when Kenelm's name began to be included in calendars (Levison, *England and the Continent*, p. 249). Another detail that strains belief is the suggestion that the hypothetical Winchcombe forger introduced the name of Offa's wife (Cynethryth) into the three forgeries; apart from the fact that the name in **44** and S 156 is actually Cynegyth, it does seem unlikely that Abbess Cwoenthryth would have countenanced the invention of a fictitious wife for her father in S 156. The whole Winchcombe connection is probably a red herring. It is important to remember that the single-sheet copy of S 156, the only one of the three documents which overtly suggests a link with Kenelm, belongs to the late Anglo-Saxon period, the time when his cult was becoming more popular. Instead of arguing that the calendar date in **44** is a suspicious feature and must reflect tampering (why should a forger contrive such a detail in a charter of Wihtred?), it is easier to suggest that **44** was indeed dated 17 July, and that it was this circumstance which prompted the forger of S 156 to use that particular text (or a duplicate or copy) as his model for a charter of Coenwulf. It does not seem unreasonable to consider **44** as entirely authentic, calendar date and all.

The Thanet estate with which **44** is concerned is *Humantiun* in the thirteenth-century cartularies and *Humantun* (a better version) in Elmham's history (the reading *Humeratun* in earlier editions results from a slightly misplaced suspension mark in the Trinity Hall manuscript). The first element is a personal name *Huma* (perhaps a corruption of Huna), evidently that of a previous owner of the property; the charter implies that this place-name was no longer in use, which explains why it cannot be traced in later sources. Sprott (BL Cotton Tiberius A. ix, 112r) gives the name as *Humantune* and remarks: 'nunc uero per corrupcioni nominis uocatur Upmantone et Ledene'. If he is justified in this statement, the estate would have been located in the region of Manston and Lydden in the east of Thanet, and would have formed part of the later manor of Minster (GDB 12r).

45

Wihtred, king of the men of Kent, grants privileges to Abbess Mildrith.
A.D. 696 (February)

i. *Charter version*

N. Cambridge, Trinity Hall, 1, 61v: copy, s. xv[1]
   Rubric: Carta eiusdem Withredi regis de defensione hominum et rerum Mildrede abbatisse in Thaneto et successorum eius qui fuerint in regimine monasterii illius.
Ed.: a. Lewis, *Tenet*, p. 61
     b. Kemble 39
     c. Hardwick, *Elmham*, pp. 289–90
     d. Birch 88
Listed: Sawyer 17 (MS 1)

In nomine Domini nostri saluatoris. Ego Wythredus rex Cantuariorum, anno quinto regni nostri, cum concilio[a] Brithuualdi archiepiscopi, Adriani abbatis et omnium ecclesiasticorum graduum una cum Gebmundo Rouesciestre episcopo, dabo et concedo propinque mee Mildrythe abbatisse et suis successoribus futuris in regimine monasterii sui in Thaneto, ut defensio eius in hominibus et in omnibus rebus sit sicut regum antecessorum nostrorum fuerunt.[b] Si quis autem hanc donacionem meam minuerit, sciat se separatum esse a societate sanctorum omnium. Actum est hoc in loco qui dicitur Berkamystede, indiccione nona, anno regni nostri .v., in mense Februarii.

+ Signum manus Withredi regis donatoris.
+ Signum manus Brithuualdi archiepiscopi.
+ Signum Adriodi.
+ Ego Adrianus abbas indignus subscripsi.
+ Ego Gemundus expressi.

[a] *For* consilio   [b] *For the construction and meaning of this clause, see commentary*

ii. *Narrative version*

F. BL Cotton Julius D. ii, 86r: copy, s. xiii[1]
  Rubric: Wihtredus de defencione Taneti
Ed.: a. Birch 845
      b. Scharer, *Königsurkunde*, p. 91 n. 26
Listed: Sawyer 17 (MS 2)

Regnante rege piissimo Cantuariorum Wihtredo, anno .v. regni eius, consilium factum fuit in loco qui dicitur Bergamystede, presente archiepiscopo Brehtuualdo et episcopo Rouesciestre Gebmundo, cum consilio omnium ecclesiasticorum graduum. Ibi concessum fuerat a piissimo rege propinque eius Mildrithe ut defensio eius in hominibus uel in omnibus rebus sit sicut regis, et eorum qui successores eius fuerint in regimine monasterii illius. Si quis autem hanc donationem meam minuerit, sciat se separatum esse a societate sanctorum omnium.

This is the only Minster charter which seems to be an outright fabrication. Difficulty is signalled immediately by the naming of Abbess Mildrith as beneficiary. Mildrith succeeded her mother Æbba as abbess, but the latter was still alive and in office in 696; she is the beneficiary of **46** from 697 and she was present at the *Cilling* synod in 699 (**10**). Mildrith probably became abbess between 699 and 716 (see pp. xxv–xxvi). **45** does not otherwise compel confidence. It is extant in regular charter form, but also in a narrative version (concluding with a subjective sanction). The charter version has its own peculiarities: a repeated regnal year, and a consent clause naming three ecclesiastics who also attest. It has been suggested that the date and other details of **45** were adapted from the introduction to Wihtred's lawcode (Liebermann, *Gesetze*, iii. 24–5). This tells of the convening of an assembly at *Berghamstyde* in the fifth year of Wihtred's reign in the month of *Rugern*, and notes the presence of Archbishop Berhtwald, Bishop Gebmund and members of all the ecclesiastical orders. The only detail in **45** which differs is the month, here given as February (perhaps because the later forger did not understand *Rugern*). The first sentence of the narrative version of **45** is closer to the beginning of the lawcode than the charter version, which bears upon the question of priority. It seems best to conclude that the forger of **45** used either the lawcode or a lost synodal document issued at the same meeting, and that he supplemented the details drawn from this source with a brief invocation and sanction, and with a witness-list. He may have modelled the witness-list at least in part on a lost charter: note the mixture of subjective and objective subscriptions, the inclusion of *donator* in Wihtred's subscription (compare S 8, 19) and the humility formula associated with Abbot Hadrian (see **6, 40**). *Adriodus* may be a corruption of Aldhodus, the name of one of the witnesses to S 8.

The nature of the privilege supposedly conveyed by **45** is not at all clear, in part because the language of the relevant clause is confused. In the charter version Wihtred seems to be granting to Mildrith and her successors in Minster-in-Thanet that her *defensio* (or the *defensio* of the monastery) over her or its men and all things should be the same as it was under the kings his predecessors. It is difficult here to decide the force of *eius*. In the narrative version this problem does not arise: Wihtred grants to Mildrith that her *defensio* over men and things should be (? the same as) the king's; the following phrase (from *eorum*) seems to extend the privilege to Mildrith's successors at Minster. Here the narrative version seems to have the more acceptable reading (although it is not wholly clear), which might be another reason to think that it has priority over the charter version. The privilege granted seems to be one of jurisdiction over Minster property and men. No early royal diplomas are concerned with such issues, but it is a constant preoccupation of late Anglo-Saxon writs (compare **35**). It may be that **45** was forged at St Augustine's towards the end of the Anglo-Saxon period in order to boost the community's control over Thanet (as the heir to St Mildrith). The wording of the narrative version seems significant here; the reference to 'eorum (note the masculine form) qui successores eius fuerint in regimine monasterii illius' could be understood to extend to the St Augustine's community.

46

Wihtred, king of the men of Kent, grants forty hides (manentes) *at* Hæg *to Abbess Æbba.* A.D. 697 (April)

H. PRO E 164/27, 79r: copy, s. xiii
  Rubric: Carta Withredi regis de Hegh'.
N. Cambridge, Trinity Hall, 1, 62r: copy, s. xv[1]
  Rubric: Carta eiusdem Withredi regis Eabbe abbatisse de terra uocata Hæg .xl. manentium.
Ed.: a. Lewis, *Tenet*, p. 60, from N

b. Kemble 42 from N
c. Hardwick, *Elmham*, pp. 291–2, from N
d. Birch 96 from N
Listed: Sawyer 18
Edited from H and N

Ego Wihtredus*ᵃ* rex Cantuariorum, consenciente regina Ædilburga,*ᵇ* atque ⟨Berhtuualdo⟩*ᶜ* gratia Dei archiepiscopo non solum consenciente sed eciam persuadente, una cum omnibus prouincialibus principibus, anno regni mei .vi.,*ᵈ* secunda*ᵉ* feria Aprilis, terram nominatam Hæg, .xl.*ᶠ* manencium, pro anima mea atque meorum, absolutam ab *ᵍ*omnium secularium dominorum in*ʰ* Dei tributum*ᵍ* abbatisse Eabbe in propriam possessionem atque monachilem regulam perhenniter perdonaui, ut Deo seruiencium preces sine mutacione pro uita mea protelentur. *ⁱ*Qui autem ausus fuerit*ⁱ* aliquid aut auferre aut transmutare sine licencia possidencium quod absit, reddet racionem Christi genitricis Marie in die iudicii, in cuius suffragio perdonaui. Quam perdonacionem cum signo crucis ornatam*ʲ* omnium presencium manus adfirmant, ut qui sine uoluntate Dei refregerit audax, crux Christi super eum in uindictam ueniat nisi regulariter emendauerit.

+ Archiepiscopi Bertualdi.*ᵏ*
+ Agesmundi.
+ Wihtredi regis.
+ Germani.
+ Wihtgari.
+ Gefredi.
+ Cynyadi.
+ Guhtardi.

ᵃ Withredus H   *ᵇ* Ethilburga H
ᶜ *Supplied (both MSS omit the archbishop's name)*   *ᵈ* sexto H   *ᵉ* .ii. H
ᶠ quadraginta N   *ᵍ ... ᵍ This passage seems corrupt (see discussion in commentary)*
ʰ ni H   *ⁱ ... ⁱ Repeated H*   *ʲ* ornate H   *ᵏ* Berthwaldi H; H *ends here*

46 is not without difficulties and may not be authentic in its present form, but it is probable that a genuine charter underlies the extant text. The deficiencies which are common to both manuscripts (the omission of the archbishop's name in the consent clause and a corrupt or deficient passage in the dispositive section) suggest that the text may have been reworked at an early date. The charter lacks a verbal invocation, which is unusual in an early Kentish charter but can be paralleled in **9**, a charter of Wihtred that probably dates from 696 (where the invocation is replaced by a brief statement of pious motivation): see also **50**, and S 89 from Mercia. The association of Queen Æthelburh in the grant is a contemporary feature (see commentary to **9**).

The date is expressed in terms of a regnal year and calendar date, and this information is placed after the consent clause; the position is unexpected but not necessarily suspicious, for there seems to have been no fixed convention at this period (see p. lxxxiv). The use of a hide-assessment can be paralleled in other Minster charters, and may be an indication of Minster involvement in drafting (see pp. lxxviii–lxxix). The wording of the prayer-condition is close to that in **41** (and see also **9**, **47** and **48**). The text concludes with two sanctions, the second developing out of the corroboration. In the first place the transgressor is threatened with punishment at the hands of the Virgin Mary, to whom the minster was dedicated; there is a similar personification of Mary as the beneficiary in S 24, a rather later charter from Lyminge. The second sanction rather chillingly promises a visitation from an avenging Cross; the word *uindictam* recurs in two Minster charters from the 720s (**47**, **48**), and the 'escape clause' is paralleled in **43**. The witness-list certainly derives from a contemporary charter. An unusual feature is the omission of the word *Signum* before the names of the beneficiaries. The position of Wihtred's subscription suggests that the order of the witnesses has become confused; it is possible that the subscriptions were at one stage arranged in two columns of four, and that a copyist read across instead of down. Wihtgar and Cyniath both attest **10**; Gefred and Guthard both attest **40** and S 8, while Gefred also appears in the witness-list of S 233. Agesmund can perhaps be identified with the Egisa/Egera who subscribes **40** and S 233 (although there was also an Egisberht attesting in this period: see S 19, 22).

The main textual difficulty is the apparently corrupt passage in the dispositive section which is concerned with a reference to exemption. An ablative noun is needed to qualify *absolutam ab* and *omnium secularium dominorum*. It is possible that a word such as *seruitute* has dropped out, but an alternative explanation is suggested by the pendant phrase *in* (or *ni*) *Dei tributum*. It may have been the case that the land was originally said to be 'absolutam ab omnium secularium dominorum tributo', and that this was later glossed *ni Dei* (*tributo*), with the intention of stressing that the exemption did not extend to ecclesiastical dues; perhaps a subsequent copyist tried to incorporate the gloss, transforming it into *in Dei tributum*. No certainty is possible, but an initial exemption from secular tribute would have the important effect of suggesting a connection with the first provision of Wihtred's lawcode, issued only two years previously, which states that the Church is to be free from taxation (*gafola*; Liebermann, *Gesetze*, i. 12). Scharer (*Königsurkunde*, p. 92) regards such a connection as suspicious, and also points out that the first immunity clause in a wholly acceptable charter occurs in S 23 from 732; in his view this passage condemns the charter. But this conclusion may be too rigorous. The lawcode shows that exemption for Church lands was a current issue in the late 690s, and in 699 Wihtred saw fit to confirm this with his grant of privileges to the Kentish minsters, stressing that they were to be free *ab omni exactione publici tributi* (**10**). It may be incorrect to treat the passage in **46** as a formal immunity clause; it is possible that the draftsman simply decided to mention that the land was exempt. Scharer also objected to the phrase *in propriam possessionem*, which first appears in original Anglo-Saxon diplomas *c.* 800; again this may perhaps be explained as an independent coinage by the draftsman, rather than a formula governed by strict diplomatic rules. On balance, it seems justifiable to regard **46** as essentially an authentic seventh-century charter rather than an outright forgery. It certainly appears corrupt, and it may be even be the case that certain details of the dispositive section have been tampered with and perhaps rewritten.

46 is concerned with a grant of forty hides at *Hæg*, which cannot be identified with confidence. The chronological table prefixed to Elmham's *Speculum* states that it was located in Thanet (Hardwick, *Elmham*, p. 7). The name presumably derives from OE *gehæg*, 'enclosure, meadow'. Hayne, perhaps from the dative plural *gehegum*, is quite common as a minor place-name (*DEPN*, p. 228). Wallenberg (*KPN*, pp. 24–5) identifies the estate of **46** with Haine, near Manston on Thanet, but this must be regarded as debatable. A thirteenth-century St Augustine's register (BL Cotton Faustina A. i; see p. lxi) mentions two Thanet tenants with the surname *de Hag(h)e*, of whom one paid her church dues to St Peter's, Broadstairs (Turner and Salter, *Black Book*, pp. 89, 529). Turner (*ibid.*, p. xxxvii) observed that the forty-four hides of **40** were equivalent to the forty hides of **46** plus the four sulungs of **44**, and went on to argue that the latter two charters refer to the same area as **40** (with some further implications for the connection between the place-names *in Sudaneie* and *Hæg*). But it is a difficulty that the sulung was not exactly equivalent to the hide (see p. lxxviii n. 26); the four sulungs of **44** are likely to represent eight hides, which upsets the calculations.

47

Æthelberht, son of King Wihtred, grants one sulung (aratrum) *by the River Limen and three yardlands* (iugera) *at* Hammespot, *Kent, to Abbess Mildrith and her familia.* A.D. 724 (11 July)

F. BL Cotton Julius D. ii, 131rv: copy, s. xiii[1]
  No rubric
H. PRO E 164/27, 79v–80r: copy, s. xiii
  Rubric: Carta Ethelberti de terra iuxta Lymene.
N. Cambridge, Trinity Hall, 1, 63rv: copy, s. xv[1]
  Rubric: Carta Ethelberti filii regis Wythredi de terra unius aratri circa flumen Limene.
Ed.: a. Lewis, *Tenet*, pp. 61–2, from N
    b. Kemble 72 (and iii. 377 for list of dens), from N
    c. Hardwick, *Elmham*, pp. 298–9, from N
    d. Birch 141 from N
Listed: Sawyer 1180
Edited from F, H and N

In nomine Dei saluatoris nostri Iesu Christi. Quoniam[a] spes Christianorum hominum his mercedem pollicetur eternam,[b] qui pro intuitu pietatis[c] seruis et ancillis Dei aliquod temporale subsidium misericorditer tribuunt, idcirco ego Æthelbertus[d] filius gloriosi regis Wihtredi,[e] cum consensu illius, terram unius[f] aratri circa flumen Limenæ,[g] quam dudum possiderant[h] qui in Ieccham[i] pro tempore habitabant, cum omnibus ad se pertinentibus rebus, et tria iugera prati in loco qui dicitur Hammespot,[j] dedi et do Mildrithe[k] religiose abbatisse et uenerabili familie eius inperpetuum possidendam, a quibus id premium potissimum quero, ut memores mei assidue sint in orationibus suis posterisque earum precipiant hoc ipsum sedulo agere. Quisquis igitur successorum heredumque meorum hoc tantillum et primitiuum donum meum integrum illibatumque esse permiserit, mercedem beniuolentie sue et ipse a Deo, qui largissimus non tantum piorum[l] actuum uerum etiam et uoluntatum bonarum remunerator est, habeat. Si quis uero non permiserit,[m] ipse ab eodem Domino, qui iustissimus[n] impiorum et uoluntatum et operum ultor est, uindictam percipiat, nisi preuenerit debitum[b] illius iudicium cum correctione dignissima. Actum die .xi. Iulii mensis, anno .xxxiii. regni regis Wihtredi, indictione .vii.[o] Ego Aethelbertus presentem donationem meam[b] signum sancte crucis scribendo firmaui testesque quorum nomina subter digesta sunt ut subscriberent[p] petii.

+[b] Ego Wihtredus[q] rex Cantuariorum rogatus a dilectissimo filio meo Æthelberto presentem donationem illius consensi et subscripsi.
+ Ego Berhtuualdus[r] gratia Dei archiepiscopus expetitus ab inclito Æthelberto hanc donationem illius subscripsi.
+ Ego Eadbertus ad petitionem karissimi germani mei Æthelberti presentem donationem ipsius consensi et subscripsi.
+ Signum[s] manus Putan testis.

Hec sunt pascua porcorum, Brentingesleag on Limenþearapalde,[t] Þeoccing[u] peorrocas, Hlossanham, on Oxnaiea[v] anum prede,[w] Brunesbeam on Þeoperapealde 7 on Blean anum prede 7 on Bocholte[x] anum prede.

[u] quas H [b] omitted H [c] caritatis N [d] Eathelbertus N [e] Withredi N
[f] huius H [g] Liminae F; Lymene H [h] possederant H, N [i] Ieccaham F, N
[j] Hammesspot F, H [k] Mildrethe H [l] priorum F [m] promiserit H
[n] iusticimus H [o] F ends here [p] scriberent H [q] Withredus H [r] Berthwaldus H
[s] et signum H [t] Limenþeapalde H [u] Þeoccyng H [v] Oxenaeya H [w] preðe N
[x] Bokholte H

47 records the details of a grant of land made by Æthelberht shortly before the death of his father, King Wihtred, and with his consent. Other early Anglo-Saxon charters concern land-grants made by royal kinsmen (the most celebrated are S 1164 and S 1171), and there is no particular difficulty in believing the details of the transaction in **47**; a forger would probably have made this a grant by Wihtred himself. There is a full dating clause, with calendar date, regnal year and indiction (for the use of calendar dates in early Kentish charters, see p. lxxxiv); the implied date is 11 July 724. The regnal year seems to agree with Bede's calculation for the beginning of Wihtred's reign; by contrast, the draftsmen of **10** and **44** seem to be calculating from a slightly later date, perhaps from the time when Wihtred achieved sole control over the kingdom (see commentary to **10**, and Appendix 3). This discrepancy need not throw doubt either on **47** or on **10** and **44**, since we cannot reckon on consistency in these matters; in the diplomas of Athelstan's reign, for instance, the regnal year is calculated at first from the king's consecration in September 925 and later from a date at the beginning of the year (see **26**).

47 has to be considered alongside **48**, a charter of Æthelberht's brother Eadberht which is dated 727. The formulation of the two charters is nearly identical; they differ only in the specific details of the dispositive section, dating clause and witness-list. This extreme similarity could reflect particular procedures for charter-production at Minster. There are grounds for thinking that in the period before the mid eighth century the individual minsters in Kent might play an important part in the drafting of charters of which they were the beneficiaries (see pp. lxxvi–lxxxv). At Minster it seems that charter-scribes were not averse to producing near duplicates of existing diplomas. The similarity of **47** and **48** is paralleled in the case of **49**, which shares much of its formulation with a Rochester toll-privilege (S 88); in addition, there is a possibility that a duplicate of **44** was at one point in existence and was later used by the Christ Church scriptorium as a model for two fabrications (see commentary to **44**). These few instances suggest that Minster charter-scribes may have had the habit (unusual in early Anglo-Saxon England) of simply reproducing a model, without introducing variations or changes. There seems to be a good case for accepting **47** and **48** as separate documents on their own terms.

The formulation of **47** (and, of course, **48**) includes some important new departures for Kentish diplomatic. There is a brief proem (apparently tailored for a double monastery, for it includes the phrase *seruis et ancillis Dei*) and an elaborate sanction, with a paired blessing and anathema. Scharer (*Königsurkunde*, pp. 103–6) sees the appearance of such formulas in Kentish charters as a development of the later eighth century, reflecting the influence of the formulation of ship-toll privileges (which he regards as emanating from London); he consequently treats both **47** and **48** as fabrications. These charters certainly have a great deal in common with **49**, and, consequently, also with S 88; these two toll-privileges include a proem, and a paired blessing and anathema which are very similar indeed to the corresponding formulas in the sanctions of **47** and **48**. But a good case can be made that the Kentish toll-privileges were essentially drafted by the beneficiaries, not in a London scriptorium (see pp. lxxxv–xc), and we may wish to regard **47** and **48** as early representatives of new developments in Kentish diplomatic, which were shortly afterwards reflected in **49** and S 88, and also in S 24, a Kentish land-charter of 741 which includes a proem and a paired blessing and anathema. In this context it should be remembered that there is a dearth of comparative material from the first quarter of the eighth century; there are no surviving Kentish land-charters from the period between 697 (**46** and S 19) and 724, the date of **47** (unless **9** and S 19, which are dated by the indiction, belong to the later rather than the earlier part of Wihtred's reign; this seems unlikely). Therefore it is not surprising that **47** and **48** should reflect some development from the norms of the later seventh century. It may be significant that two earlier charters (**6**, **40**) also include a proem and a paired blessing and anathema; an odour of fabrication or rewriting clings to both documents, but it is possible that they represent an alternative aspect of the Kentish diplomatic tradition which became more popular in the eighth century.

Apart from the inclusion of a proem and blessing, **47** and **48** conform quite closely to earlier Kentish conventions. The invocation is of the usual Kentish type. There is a prayer-condition, as in **9**, **41** and **46**. The dating clause as usual begins *Actum*, with no qualifying verb. The formulation of the witness-list in **47** is rather unusual. The subscriptions of Æthelberht, of his father and brother, and of the archbishop are all surprisingly lengthy. That of Æthelberht doubles as a request to the witnesses, while the other three subscriptions include a reference to Æthelberht's request. There is a parallel to this in S 23 from 732, where the subscriptions of both the ecclesiastical witnesses refer to King Æthelberht's command (and see also **11** for a parallel for the donor's subscription); the ultimate source for this formulation must have been an Italian model (see Tjäder, *Papyri*, i. 306 etc.). The final witness is a layman named Puta, who does not occur elsewhere; the witness-list has probably been curtailed.

There seem to be reasonable grounds for accepting **47** as an authentic charter of the implied date, although the list of seven swine-pastures at the end is almost certainly an addition. This list is of interest for its references to the *Limenwearawald* and the *Weoweraweald*, that is, the Wealden commons of the people of the Lyminge and Wye lathes; the attachment of dens in these commons to private estates represents the break-up of the traditional system (see Witney, *Jutish Forest*, pp. 78–103). The swine-pastures listed in **47** seem to be scattered, for they include dens in two different Wealden commons, on the Isle of Oxney (south of Tenterden) and in Blean Forest, to the north of Canterbury. For speculative identifications, see Wallenberg, *KPN*, pp. 33–4, and Witney, *Jutish Forest*, p. 272. The estate to which these swine-pastures were allegedly appurtenant consisted of a sulung by the river *Limen* (thus in the vicinity of Romney Marsh), previously held by those who were living in Ickham *pro tempore* (? seasonally). Ickham lies just north-east of Canterbury, so the sulung conveyed in **47** was presumably a detached piece of land, perhaps a seasonal pasture, which had been associated with the settlement at Ickham but was now being placed in separate ecclesiastical ownership. There is some reason to believe that this land lay in the vicinity of Ruckinge, known to have had a later association with Ickham (G. Ward, 'The River Limen at Ruckinge', *AC* xlv (1933), pp. 129–32; Brooks 1988, p. 96). Wallenberg (*KPN*, p. 224) suggests that *Hammes(s)pot* is a corruption of *hamm(e)fleot*, and connects it with *ham fleot* in the bounds of S 1203. An alternative possibility is that it is a corruption of *ham(m)espynd*, to be linked with the *flothamespynd* of S 1617; the second element here is *pynd*, 'dam, embankment', and the first *hamm*, 'meadow, dry piece of ground in a marsh' (for *hamm* names in Romney Marsh, see Brooks 1988, p. 102).

48

Eadberht I, king of the men of Kent, grants a half-sulung (aratrum) *in* regione qui dicitur bi Northanuude *to Abbess Mildrith and her* familia.
A.D. 727 (14 October)

F. BL Cotton Julius D. ii, 86rv: copy, s. xiii[1]
    Rubric: Donacio regis Eadberti de dimidio aratri in bi northanuude.
H. PRO E 164/27, 79rv: copy, s. xiii
    Rubric: Carta de Northanuude.
Ed.: Birch 846 from F
Listed: Sawyer 26
Edited from F and H

In nomine Domini Dei saluatoris nostri Iesu Christi. Quoniam[a] spes Christianorum[b] hominum his mercedem pollicetur eternam, qui pro intuitu pietatis seruis et ancillis Dei aliquod temporale subsidium misericorditer tribuunt, idcirco ego Eadbertus rex Cantuariorum terram dimidii aratri quam dudum habuit Aescuuald[c] in regione qui dicitur bi Northanuude, cum omnibus ad se pertinentibus rebus, dedi et do Mildrithe[d] religiose abbatisse et uenerabili familie eius inperpetuum possidendam, a quibus id[e] premium potissimum quero, ut memores mei assidue sint in orationibus suis posterisque eorum precipiant hoc ipsum sedulo agere. Quisquis igitur successorum heredumque meorum hoc tantillum et pietate plenum donum meum integrum inlibatumque[f] esse permiserit, mercedem beniuolentie sue et ipse a Deo, qui largissimus non tantum piorum actuum uerum etiam et uoluntatum bonarum remunerator est, habeat. Si quis uero non permiserit ipse ab eodem Domino, qui iustissimus[g] impiorum et uoluntatum et operum ultor est, uindictam percipiat,[h] nisi preuenerit debitum illius iudicium cum correctione dignissima. Actum pridie idus Octobris, anno ab incarnatione Domini .dccxxvii.,[i] indictione .x. Ego Eadbertus rex presentem donationem meam signum hoc sancte crucis scribendo firmaui testesque quorum nomina subter digesta sunt ut subscriberent petii. Anno regni mei tertio.[j] Signum manus Balthardi. Signum Bynnan. +[k].

    a quondam H   *b* H *adds* omnium   *c* Escuald H   *d* Mildrethe H   *e* *Omitted* H
    f illibatumque H   *g* iusticimus H   *h* precipiat H
    i This could read either .dccxxvii. *or* .dccxxiiii., *but the former is preferable (see commentary)*   *j* .iii. H   *k* F *omits cross*

Eadberht's charter does not seem to have been known to Sprott or Elmham. It is the only Minster charter not mentioned by Elmham and (with the exception of **15**) the only one of the abbey's muniments dated before 805 that he has missed. This neglect may be due to the very close relationship between **47** and **48**, which are couched in almost identical formulas; a careless reader might easily take **48** to be a duplicate of **47**. The two charters differ only in the name of the donor, the details of the donation, the dating clause and witness-list (in both charters the witness-list has been abbreviated). This extreme similarity has been seen as suspicious (see Scharer, *Königsurkunde*, pp. 115–16), but it may simply be the result of particular procedures for charter-production at Minster; **47** and **48** are best considered as separate documents, both fundamentally authentic (see the commentary to **47** for a more detailed discussion). Proper assessment of **48** has been hindered by minor dating difficulties. The charter is dated by an incarnation year, the earliest example of this in a wholly Kentish diploma (the incarnation year in **40** is associated with a Mercian confirmation); for further discussion of the introduction of this dating method in Kentish charters, see p. lxxxiv. To agree with the indiction and the regnal year (which is given as part of the king's subscription) the incarnation year should be 727, which is a possible reading of the manuscript copies (in each case the number ends with four minims, which can be taken as *uii* or *iiii*). In his edition Birch opted for the reading 724, partly on the basis of similarity with **47**, which has an implied date in that year. But, as far as we know, Eadberht did not become king until his father died in 725, so a charter issued solely in his name in 724 would need much explanation. There is no particular problem in preferring 727, which fits the rest of the dating information, and would be appropriate for a charter of Eadberht. Eadberht and his brother Æthelberht seem to have ruled jointly in Kent from 725 until Eadberht's death in 748, with Æthelberht primarily responsible for East Kent and Eadberht taking responsibility for the western section of the kingdom (see Appendix 3). A Rochester charter issued in 738 or before (S 27) indicates that Eadberht's charters required confirmation from Æthelberht, so it seems worth noting that there is no reference to Æthelberht in **48**; but it is probably unwise to place too much emphasis on this, given the unsatisfactory and probably abbreviated condition of the witness-list. Only two subscriptions are preserved apart from that of the king; a Baltheard and a Bynna also attest S 23, and Baltheard appears in the witness-list of S 24 as well.

The *regio* called *bi Northanuude* is to be associated with the area between Canterbury and Whitstable, and thus presumably with Blean Wood (see Wallenberg, *KPN*, p. 167). A den in Blean belonging to St Mildrith's community is mentioned in S 535 (see pp. xxix–xxx). In the narrative passage inserted into **40** is a reference to Minster property in a *regio* called *ad aquilonis siluam*, at a place called *Mæccanbrooc* (Makenbrook (lost) in Herne: see Gough 1992, pp. 93–4, map pp. 98–9); this can probably be identified with the land granted in **48**. The entry for **48** in the charter-list in PRO E 164/27 (Appendix 2, no. ix) adds the detail that the land was *in Swalcliue* (Swalecliffe). In the immediate post-Conquest period the St Augustine's manor of Sturry, assessed at five sulungs, included detached property at Swalecliffe (see commentary to **28**). There is a very good chance that the Sturry manor represented land inherited by St Augustine's from Minster (see p. cxiii and commentary to **41**); the Minster property at Makenbrook (Swalecliffe) presumably passed to the abbey at the same time and was reckoned as part of the same manor. The Æscwald who is named as the previous owner of the land could be the priest of that name who attended the Bapchild synod, probably in 716 or just before (see S 22).

49

Æthelbald, king of the Mercians, grants remission of toll on one ship at the port of London to Abbess Mildrith. A.D. 716 or 717 [? *for c.* 733] (29 October)

F. BL Cotton Julius D. ii, 131v: copy, s. xiii[1]
   No rubric
N. Cambridge, Trinity Hall, 1, 64v–65r: copy, s. xv[1]
   No rubric
Ed.: a. Lewis, *Tenet*, pp. 63–4, from N
   b. Kemble 97 from N
   c. Hardwick, *Elmham*, pp. 306–7, from N
   d. Thorpe, *Diplomatarium*, pp. 30–1, from N
   e. Birch 149 from N
Listed: Sawyer 86
Edited from F and N

In nomine Domini Dei saluatoris nostri Iesu Christi. Si ea que quisque pro recipienda a Deo mercede hominibus uerbo suo largitur et donat stabilia iugiter potuissent durare, superuacaneum uideretur ut litteris narrarentur ac fulcirentur. Sed dum ad probanda donata ad conuincendumque uolentem donata infringere nihil prorsus robustius esse uidetur quam donationis manibus auctorum ac testium roborate,[a] non immerito plurimi petunt ut que eis prestita dinoscuntur paginaliter confirmentur. Quorum postulationibus tanto libentius tantoque promptius consensus[b] prebendus est, quanto et illis qui precatores sunt utilior res secundum hoc uisibile seculum nunc impertitur et illis qui concessores existunt pro impertito opere pietatis uberior fructus secundum inuisibile postmodum tribuetur. Quamobrem ego Aethelbaldus[c] rex Merciorum presentibus apicibus indico me concessisse atque donasse pro anime mee salute Mildrithe[d] religiose[e] abbatisse eiusque uenerabili familie que una cum ea conuersatur in insula Tanet[f] totam exactionem nauis earum mihi et antecessoribus meis iure publico in Lundoniensi portu prius conpetentem,[g] quemadmodum mansuetudinem nostram rogarent. Que concessio atque donatio ut inperpetuum firma et stabilis sit, ita ut nullus eam regum uel optimatum uel theloneariorum uel etiam iuniorum quilibet ipsorum in parte aut in toto in irritum presumat ut possit adducere, manu propria signum sancte crucis subter in hac pagina faciam testesque ut subscribant petam, proculdubio sperans quia sicut ego quod poposcerunt libenter concessi, sic ille quod promiserunt erga orationes pro me ibidem celebrandas implebunt fideliter. Quisquis igitur id quod pio animo donaui ita ut donatum est illibatum permanere permiserit, habeat communionem beatam cum presente Christi ecclesia atque futura. Quisquis autem non permiserit, separetur a societate non solum sanctorum hominum sed etiam angelorum, manente hac donatione nostra in sua firmitate coram uniuersis qui recta diligunt et custodiunt. Actum est die .iiii. kalendarum Nouembris, anno .i.[h] regni mei, indictione .xv., in loco qui dicitur Willanhalch.[i]

+ Ego Ædbaldus rex Merciorum hanc donationem meam firmaui et subscripsi manu mea.

+ Signum manus Wori.

+ Signum manus Cottan.

+ Signum manus Cinrici.

+ Signum manus Wilfrid

+ Signum manus Lullan.

+ Signum Cuthredi.

+ Signum manus Oban.

[a] *This phrase appears deficient (perhaps supply* cartula *and read* quam cartula donationis ... roborata); *the proem of S 88 has the same faulty reading, which may be an error of the original author of the proem*   [b] concensus F   [c] Athelbertus F   [d] Myldrithe F
[e] regiose F   [f] Thænet N   [g] conpetente F
[h] .xxii. *written on an erasure, probably of a single minim* N (*see commentary*)
[i] F *ends here*

This appears to be the earliest of the five toll-privileges in the Minster archive (but see below). It records the grant to Mildrith and her community by King Æthelbald of exemption from the customary ship-toll levied by his agents in the port of London. The privilege seems to be connected with a particular ship belonging to the community, and the terms of reference suggest that this may have been the only vessel which Minster owned at that time; other charters in the archive show the acquisition of more ships later in the century, one being purchased in about 748 (**51**) and another constructed in the minster itself in about 763/4 (**53**). For further discussion of this type of privilege, see pp. lxxxv–xc and Kelly 1992.

Two aspects of **49** are of particular importance. In the first place, it is almost identical to S 88 (A.D. 733), in which King Æthelbald grants a toll-exemption in London to the bishop of Rochester; the Rochester charter was confirmed by Berhtwulf of Mercia in the ninth century, and survives as a single-sheet copy apparently made at that time. It is necessary to consider how it came about that diplomas in favour of beneficiaries in different dioceses came to be drafted on the same model. The second problem concerns the date of **49**, and this can profitably be addressed first. The copy of the charter in BL Cotton Julius D. ii (MS F) puts it in Æthelbald's first year (716/17), which agrees with the given indiction but seems remarkably early. The Trinity Hall manuscript (MS N) also originally dated the charter to Æthelbald's first year, but a later revisor (perhaps Elmham himself) has altered the minim to *xxii* (thus 737/8). This regnal year does not agree with the indiction, so modern commentators (unaware that *xxii* was written on an erasure of *i*) have suggested emending *xxii* to *xvii* (733/4). This new date has the advantage of agreeing with that of S 88, but it is a problem that it still conflicts with the indiction, which would be appropriate for 732. Moreover, emendation of *xxii* may be inappropriate, in view of the fact that it was itself substituted for another numeral.

An important aspect of this dating confusion is the fact that **49** shares its dating clause and witness-list with **50**, another charter of Æthelbald granting toll-exemption to Abbess Mildrith. **50** is preserved in MS F, where the text breaks off before the witness-list and dating-clause, and in MS N, where it occurs after the copy of **49**, separated from it by material taken largely from Bede, *HE*, v. 23. The implication of the arrangement in the later manuscript is that Elmham, when he was compiling this section of the *Speculum*, did not believe that **49** and **50** were contemporary. The dating clause of **50** is in most respects similar to that in **49**, but there are two significant differences. In the first place, the regnal year is *xxii* and it is not written on an erasure. Secondly, there is no reference to an indiction, so there is no reason here to emend the regnal year: **50** can be dated to 737/8. It seems possible that the revisor of the Trinity Hall manuscript, who substituted *xxii* for *i* in the copy of **49**, took the figure of *xxii* from **50**.

But this is far from a complete solution to the problem of dating **49**. It is necessary to consider why **49** and **50** should have essentially the same dating clause (mentioning a place of issue) and witness-list, with the difference that **50** was apparently issued in Æthelbald's twenty-second year and **49** in the first year of his reign. In the most recent examination of these documents (Scharer, *Königsurkunde*, pp. 200–1), **50** is condemned as a forgery, which suggests a simple solution: the forger borrowed the dating clause and witness-list from **49**. But the case against **50** is by no means watertight; there are reasons to believe that it may well be an authentic document (see the commentary to **50**). And so the problem of the shared dating clause remains. It is an interesting point that **50** contains material which suggests that it may belong to the very beginning of Æthelbald's reign; in it the king gives thanks to God for raising him to a high position after so many years of humble and troubled life (a reference to the period of his exile in Middle Anglia). Yet it is **49** which apparently claims to have been issued in 716/17.

The dating problems of **49** and **50** are clearly very complex indeed, and it seems likely that this is in large part due to the repeated attentions of the later medieval revisors of the muniments. There is no obvious straightforward explanation of all the various difficulties, but the following scenario is put forward as as a possible solution of the problem. There seems to be a reasonable chance that **50**, if it is authentic, was indeed issued in the first year of Æthelbald's reign. The probability is that the dating clause and the witness-list common to **49** and **50** both originally belonged to **50**; the regnal year was given as *i* (the original reading in both copies of **49**) and the indiction was *xv*, which is consistent. The privilege conveyed in **50** is less closely defined than in the other surviving ship-toll privileges, which usually specify a port at which the exemption was to apply; this may be because **50** belongs to an earlier period when the procedures for collecting tolls and granting exemption were not yet fully organised. By contrast, **49** is aligned with the other Mercian toll-privileges in that it is specifically concerned with toll-immunity at London; its formulation is far more elaborate, and seems to reflect a later stage in the development of this type of charter. It can probably be assumed that **49** is later than **50**. So why does it have the same dating clause? One possibility is that **49** was at some point found to be deficient, lacking a dating clause and witness-list; and so these were borrowed from **50**. Perhaps this was the result of physical damage, but it may also have been the case that the later medieval monks of St Augustine's for some reason had access only to an incomplete draft of the document, without the details of its ratification. Whatever the explanation, the probability seems to be that the dating clause and witness-list of **50** were later borrowed and added to **49**, and that at one stage both documents were dated to the first year of Æthelbald's reign. Subsequently, the medieval students of the St Augustine's archive began to emend the regnal years, in pursuit of some chronological chimera. It is possible that there was then available some external information, no longer extant, which pointed to a later date for these charters; it may be significant that the chronological table prefixed to Elmham's *Speculum* refers to **49** and **50** under the year 732 (Hardwick, *Elmham*, p. 9), which is broadly compatible with the dating of S 88 but seems to have little relation with the various regnal years supplied in the texts (except that 732 was also the fifteenth indiction).

The relationship between **49** and **50** having been considered (if not resolved to complete satisfaction), it becomes necessary to turn to the relationship between **49** and S 88 from Rochester. The two charters are identical, apart from the central portion of the dispositive section and the dating clause and witness-list (**49** also includes a prayer condition, such as frequently occurs in Minster charters: compare **41**, **46**, **47**, **48**). The most noticeable feature is a very long proem, on the theme of the desirability of written records; the second half was reused by a Rochester draftsman in the later eighth century (S 37). The corroboration incorporates an injunction directed against those who might challenge the exemption, including toll-collectors and their *iuniores*; similar formulas are found in **51** and S 1788. The sanction consists of a paired blessing and anathema, very similar indeed to those in **47** and **48** from the 720s.

In his discussion of the toll-privileges issued in the name of King Æthelbald, Scharer (*Königsurkunde*, pp. 195–211) explains the diplomatic links between the various texts, in particular between **49** and S 88 and between **51** and S 1788, as the result of common production in the episcopal scriptorium in London. He argues that certain aspects of their formulation, such as the inclusion of a proem and of a blessing in the sanction, were alien to the Kentish diplomatic tradition and were introduced into Kent as the result of influence from these London-drafted toll-privileges; he disputes the authenticity of **47** and **48**, which appear to reflect earlier use of such formulas in Kent. But in the introduction to this edition (pp. lxxxv–xc) and in the commentaries to **47** and **48**, it has been shown that the evidence can be interpreted in a very different way. **47** and **48** seem to be authentic, and therefore their diplomatic features can probably be accepted as part of a current Kentish tradition; there is nothing which demonstrates that this kind of formulation is necessarily to be associated with the London episcopal scriptorium. It was probably the case that beneficiaries usually played a major part in the drafting of toll-privileges, as they did in the production of land-charters. But because this type of document was new and still relatively unfamiliar, the charter-scribes in the various minsters were more inclined than usual to use and reproduce available models. If there were none available in their own archives, they may have borrowed them from elsewhere; and this could be the explanation for the similarity between **49** and S 88 (and for the links between other toll-privileges for different archives). The direction of the borrowing between Minster and Rochester is now difficult to determine, in view of the poor condition of the text of **49**. It is tempting to see a possible conection between the use of borrowed models and the fact that **49** at some stage seems to have lacked a dating clause and witness-list; it is possible that **49** originated as a simple copy of the Rochester privilege which was later the basis for a fabrication in the name of Abbess Mildrith, produced either at Minster or St Augustine's.

For the witness-list, see commentary to **50**.

50

Æthelbald, king of the Mercians, grants remission of toll on one ship to Abbess Mildrith. A.D. 737 or 738 [? for 716/17] (29 October)

F. BL Cotton Julius D. ii, 131v–132r: copy, s. xiii[1]
No rubric
N. Cambridge, Trinity Hall, 1, 65v–66r: copy, s. xv[1]
No rubric
Ed.: a. Lewis, *Tenet*, pp. 64–5, from N
    b. Kemble 84, from N
    c. Hardwick, *Elmham*, pp. 310–11, from N
    d. Thorpe, *Diplomatarium*, pp. 25–6, from N
    e. Birch 150 from N
Listed: Sawyer 87
Edited from F and N

Ego Æthilbaldus rex Merciorum Deo omnipotenti gratiarum actiones in quantum possum persoluo, qui me ad tantum sublimitatis gradum eligere dignatus est de tam humili et inquieta uita quam per tot annorum spacia transegi. Idcirco pro remedio anime mee mihi in potestatem redacta et pro munificentia sanctarum orationum seruorum et ancillarum Dei, largifica munera summi saluatoris Domini nostri Iesu Christi libenter ecclesiis Dei impendo et tibi Mildrithe abbatisse singulariter et ecclesie tue nauis onuste transuectionis censum, qui a theloneariis nostris tributaria exactione inpetitur, perdonans attribuo, ut ubique in regno nostro libera de omni regali fisco et tributo maneat. Si quis hanc donationem a nobis perdonatam infringere uel in maximo uel in modico temptauerit, sciat se alienum a nostra communione et maxime a cetu sanctorum manere.[a]

+ Signum manus Æthilbaldi.
+ Signum manus Cuthraedi.

+ Signum manus Selerædi.
+ Signum manus Worres.
+ Signum Cottin.
+ Signum manus Cynrices.
+ Signum manus Wlfridi.
+ Signum manus Lullan.
+ Signum manus Oban.

Actum est die .iiii. kalendarum Nouembris, anno .xxii. regni nostri, in loco qui dicitur Willanhalch.

^a F *ends here*

In this charter Æthelbald seems to be exempting a Minster ship from liability to toll throughout the Mercian kingdom. Presumably this is the same ship granted toll-immunity in London in **49**. **50** may represent an extension of this grant, or perhaps an earlier grant which did not apply to London and which was extended in **49**. Offa confirmed **50** at some point between 761 and 764 (**52**).

In the Trinity Hall manuscript **50** has essentially the same witness-list and dating-clause as **49** (it is unfortunate, and possibly significant, that the other copy breaks off before the first subscription). The dating clause causes extraordinary problems, which are discussed in more detail in the commentary to **49**. At present both texts are associated in the Trinity Hall manuscript with the twenty-second year of Æthelbald's reign (737/8). But there is clear evidence that the regnal year in **49** has been altered; *xxii* is written on an erasure of a single minim, and the earlier cartulary copy also assigns **49** to Æthelbald's first year (716/17). The dating clause in **49** is supplied with an indiction (there is none in **50**), and this would be appropriate for 717 but not for either 737 or 738. It seems therefore that **49** should properly be dated to 717, and the alternative regnal year rejected as a substitution by a later revisor. For **50** the case is rather different; the regnal year of *xxii* is not written on an erasure, and no indiction is included to contradict it. So it appears that **50** can be dated to 737/8. But clearly both versions of the dating clause cannot be accepted, especially in view of the shared witness-list. Either both documents were issued on the same occasion (which in view of their pronounced differences seems unlikely) or in one case the dating clause and witness-list were borrowed from the other text.

The question of priority depends upon one's view of the authenticity of the two charters. Scharer (*Königsurkunde*, pp. 200–1) dismisses **50** as a fabrication; if this is correct, it can be assumed that the forger took the witness-list and dating clause from **49**. But these suspicions of **50** may not be justified. Scharer rejects **50** because it does not conform to his rather rigid conception of what a toll-privilege should look like, because the dating clause appeared to have been taken from **49** and because he saw difficulties in **52**, which is Offa's confirmation of **50**. On the first point, it should be noted that the newly-discovered toll-privilege from St Paul's (S [Add.] 103a; for this see Kelly 1992) demonstrates that such documents did not necessarily follow a conventional pattern. Moreover, Scharer's objections to Offa's confirmation do not appear to be well-founded (see commentary to **52**). And it is by no means established that the dating clause and witness-list should rightly belong to **49**.

It is certainly the case that **50** is unlikely to belong to 737/8. Mildrith is not an appropriate beneficiary in a charter of that date; she was probably succeeded by Eadburh before 735/6 (see pp. xxv–xxvi). But **50** would fit very well in the context of 716/17, the first year of Æthelbald's reign and the date to which the earlier version of the dating clause in **49** refers. In **50** Æthelbald thanks God for placing him in such a high position after so many years of difficulty, presumably a reference to the period of troubled exile which preceded his reign. Generally such a reference to specific political circumstances in an Anglo-Saxon diploma would be a signal for keen suspicion. Yet there are precedents in earlier Minster charters. In **44** Wihtred gives thanks to God for extending his boundaries to their ancient limits, which is obviously to be connected his achievement of sole rule in Kent after a period of joint-kingship with an invader. Similarly in **43** Oswine is grateful for the divine aid which gave him the kingdom of his ancestors. There appears to be a valid background for a passage of this type in an early charter with a Minster connection. If we take it as its face value, **50** implies that Æthelbald made this concession to Minster soon after he became king in 716. There is a possible context for this. Æbba had a Mercian connection through her former husband, Merewalh of the Magonsæte, and it was perhaps this which in 691 prompted her to apply to Æthelred of Mercia for the confirmation of the most important title-deeds for the Minster endowment; **40** implies that she took or sent her charters to the Mercian heartland for this confirmation. The Mercian connection continued through Æbba's daughter Mildrith, and may have entitled Minster to a special consideration from the new Mercian ruler. The dating clause (if it correctly belongs to **50**) implies that this charter was brought to central Mercia for ratification, either to Willenhall in Staffordshire or the place of the same name in Warwickshire.

In terms of its formulation, **50** seems to be an acceptable product of the Minster scriptorium. The lack of any preliminary matter before the superscription is paralleled in **46**. The form of the king's name is early (see also **51**, **52**, **53**). The motivation clause in which the king gives thanks to God is another feature found in earlier Minster charters (see above). The participle *perdonans* (see also *perdonatum*) echoes *perdonaui* in **46**. The wording of the sanction has close links with those in **43** and **44**. It could be argued that **50** stands in a line of development from Minster charters of the 690s, which would be expected in a privilege of 716/17. A text of that date could not be expected to conform to any fixed pattern for the formulation of toll-charters; indeed, it seems unnecessary to suppose that any rigid rules governing charter composition were in operation in the first half of the eighth century. Finally, in connection with the relative claims of **49** and **50** to the dating clause and witness-list, it should be remarked that there is an extra subscription in **50**, that of a certain Selered, who may possibly be the king of Essex who died in 746 and is believed to have succeeded in about 709 (B. Yorke, 'The Kingdom of the East Saxons', *Anglo-Saxon England* xiv (1985), pp. 1–36 at 23).

There can be no doubt that the witness-list common to **49** and **50** derives from a genuine charter of Æthelbald. Some of the witnesses occur elsewhere in contemporary Mercian charters: Cynric (S 84), Wilfrid (S 85, 95, 97, 101–3), Oba (**51**; and S 85,

88–90, 94–5, 97, 101–3). Oba (or Ofa) was a companion of Æthelbald before he became king: see *Felix's Life of St Guthlac*, ed. B. Colgrave (Cambridge, 1956), pp. 139–41; he was unfortunately long-lived and was still attesting in 748 (**51**), so his presence is not necessarily a sign that the witness-list belongs to the early part of Æthelbald's reign. The other charters attested by Cynric and Wilfrid cannot usually be dated precisely, but they seem mostly early. Wor is perhaps the bishop of Lichfield and Leicester, otherwise known as Aldwine, who was appointed between 716 and 727 and died in 737; if so, the order of the witnesses in **49**, where Wor attests after Æthelbald, may be preferable.

49 and **50** present enormous problems of interpretation, in large part due to later chronological interference at St Augustine's. The solution which is suggested here is by no means entirely satisfactory, and various other complex possibilities could be put forward (for a very different understanding of the issues, see Scharer, *Königsurkunde*, pp. 195–201). But there does seem to be a reasonable case for accepting **50** as a genuine document of the very beginning of Æthelbald's reign, probably drawn up at Minster itself and then taken to Mercia for Æthelbald's approval. The text implies that the community was already engaged in trading activity at this date.

51

Æthelbald, king of the Mercians, grants remission of half the toll due on one ship to Abbess Eadburh. A.D. 748 (May)

N. Cambridge, Trinity Hall, 1, 66v–67r: copy, s. xv[1]
  Rubric: Carta Ethelbaldi regis Merciorum Edburge abbatisse qua donauit eidem dimidium uectigal unius nauis et tributum quod sibi de iure spectabat.
Ed.: a. Lewis, *Tenet*, pp. 65–6
    b. Kemble 98
    c. Hardwick, *Elmham*, pp. 314–16
    d. Thorpe, *Diplomatarium*, pp. 31–3
    e. Birch 177
Listed: Sawyer 91

In nomine Domini saluatoris nostri. Omnem hominem qui secundum Deum uiuit et remunerari a Deo sperat et optat, oportet ut piis precibus assensum ex animo hilariter prebeat, quomodo certum est tanto facilius ea que ipse a Deo poposcerit consequi posse, quanto et ipse libencius hominibus recte postulata concesserit, quod tunc bonorum omnium largitori Deo acceptabile fit, cum pro eius amore et utilitate famulancium ei peragitur. Quocirca ego Æthilbaldus ⟨rex⟩[a] Merciorum iuxta peticionem uestram tibi Eadburge abbatisse tueque familie conuersanti in monasterio beate Dei genetricis Marie quod situm est in insula Taneti, necnon in monasterio apostolorum Petri et Pauli quod tu ipsa non longe a predicto monasterio construxisti, unius nauis quod a Leubuco nuper emisti dimidium uectigal atque tributum quod meum erat, pro intuitu superne mercedis et amore consanguinitatis religiose abbatisse Mildrede cuius uenerabile corpus a priori sepultura translatum in ipso monasterio apostolorum decenter posuisti, accipiendum possidendumque eterna donacione concedo. Et cuicumque uolueritis heredum successorumque uestrorum seu quolibet hominum hoc ipsum de iure in re uestra perdonare liberam habeatis potestatem. Hinc igitur precipio ac precor in nomine Dei omnipotentis patriciis, ducibus, comitibus, theloneariis, accionariis ac reliquis publicis dignitatibus ut hec inoffense[b] donacio per presentes ac posteros percurrat. Si autem contigerit ut nauis ista disrupta ac confracta sit uel etiam uetustate detrita aut omnino quod absit naufragio perdita, tunc quoque ad cumulum huiusce donacionis hoc addo et concedo, ut alia in huius donationis locum et condicionem construatur et habeatur. Et hoc non solum me uiuente in hac uita, sed etiam post obitum meum per succedentes semper generationes precipio et per Christum Iesum iudicem omnium postulo fieri. Quisquis uero heredum successorumque meorum uel aliorum quilibet hominum siue secularium siue ecclesiasticorum huic pie donationi nostre in aliqua re contraire quoquo tempore fuerit ausus, nouerit se quisque ille sit audaci malicie sue racionem esse redditurum coram omnipotente Domino nostro qui iudicabit orbem terre in equitate, reddens unicuique secundum opera sua, Iesus Christus filius Dei filiusque sancte Marie semper uirginis, cuius scilicet in prefato monasterio sacris atque magnificis indesinenter die noctuque frequentatur et adoratur precibus, iudex seculi Iesus Christus Dominus noster, Amen. Igitur manente hac cartula in sua semper firmitate quam propria manu sacro signaculo roborare curaui et testes nonnullos ut id ipsum consencientes agerent feci quorum nomina infra tenentur. Actum[c] mense Maio in ciuitate Lundonia, indiccione .xiiii., anno ab incarnacione Christi .dccxlviii.

+ Ego Æthilbaldus rex Merciæ suprascriptam donacionem meam signo sancte crucis in hac cartula expresso diligenter confirmaui.
+ Ego Ædbeortus rex Cantie testis consenciens subscripsi.
+ Signum manus Cuthberti archiepiscopi.
+ Signum Milredi episcopi.
+ Signum Ecguulfi episcopi.
+ Signum manus Obani ducis.
+ Signum manus Kyniberti.
+ Signum Eoppani.
+ Signum Friðurici.
+ Signum Ealhmundi.
+ Signum Panti thelonearii.

ª Supplied   *ᵇ For* inoffensa   *ᶜ* Act' N

In **51** Æthelbald grants to Abbess Eadburh and her community exemption from half the *uectigal atque tributum* due on the ship which they have recently purchased from someone called Leubucus, who may have been a Frank (see Kelly 1992, p. 7). The restriction on the immunity is strong support for the text's authenticity, since a forger would presumably have claimed immunity from the whole toll. It may have been the acquisition of an additional ship that prompted an application for a new exemption; in the 760s the construction of another vessel brought a request to the Kentish king for further immunities (see **53**). The charter was issued in London, which is probably where the toll-exemption was supposed to apply. Eadburh was Mildrith's successor and was remembered at Minster for having expanded the community by building a second house near Æbba's original foundation, to which she transferred the greater part of the community and Mildrith's relics (see p. xxvi). **51** refers in detail to these events, which could indicate later interpolation. Alternatively, there may have been direct Minster involvement in drafting the charter, leading to an airing of present preoccupations. A Minster scribe was presumably also responsible for the extraordinary extension of the sanction into a statement about the energetic worship of Christ and St Mary by the community.

51 seems to be an authentic text of the given date. Its formulation reflects a development of the new departures seen in S 88 and **49**. There is a particularly close connection with S 1788, a St Paul's toll-privilege datable only to between 716 and 745 (for a new and fuller text of this charter, see Kelly 1992, pp. 27–8). The relationship lies primarily in the technical formulas of the dispositive section; both include a clause providing for the transfer of the privilege to a new vessel in case of shipwreck or other disaster (for the significance of this, see p. lxxxvi). The two texts diverge markedly in the proem and sanction, which supports the argument that in this case draftsmen in different communities were using similar models which they adapted in their own way, retaining mostly the technical formulas (see further p. lxxxviii). The proem in **51**, of modest length compared to that in **49** and S 88, reappears in three Kentish charters of the later eighth century, from Reculver and Rochester (S 31, 32, 131); it also occurred in the mid-eighth-century diploma which was the model for the forgery of **1**. In **51** the injunction directed at various royal officials is longer than that in S 1788, and contains some vocabulary which suggests that it may ultimately be based upon the address in a Frankish toll-privilege (see Kelly 1992, p. 19). The 'shipwreck clause' in **51** incorporates the phrase *ad cumulum huiusce donationis*, which is an adaptation of a late Roman formula sometimes found in the corroborations of early Kentish charters (see **10, 11, 44**; and p. lxxxiii). This supports the argument that **51** was drafted in Kent, not London, as does the inclusion after the sanction of another fossilized antique formula, an ablative absolute phrase beginning *manente*, which is particularly associated with Kentish charters (see pp. lxxxii–lxxxiii); the dating clause is also in the usual Kentish form (see p. lxxxiv).

The witnesses are consistent with the given date. The bishops are Cuthbert of Canterbury (740–60), Milred of Worcester ([743 × 745]-774) and Ecgwulf of London (745-[766 × 772]). Most of the lay witnesses attest elsewhere: Oba (**49, 50**; and S 85, 88, 89, 90, 94, 95, 97, 101–3; see also *Felix's Life of St Guthlac*, ed. B. Colgrave (Cambridge, 1956), pp. 139–41), Cyneberht (S 89, 90, 92), Eoppa (S 92, 96, 97),

Frithuric (S 90, 92), Ealhmund (S 92, 96). The exception is *Pantus*, described as a toll-collector; his name seems odd, and may be corrupt. The charter is also attested by a king of Kent named Eadberht, who should be Eadberht I, king in West Kent between 725 and 748 (see Appendix 3). It was to this king that the two toll-charters issued by Eadberht II in the 760s (**53**, S 1612) were mistakenly assigned, so it is remarkable that he should witness a toll-charter of Æthelbald.

52

Offa, king of the Mercians, grants to Abbess Sigeburh the toll-exemption
which King Æthelbald had granted to Abbess Mildrith (**50**) [A.D. 761 × 764]

N. Cambridge, Trinity Hall, 1, 68rv: copy, s. xv[1]
Ed.: a. Lewis, *Tenet*, p. 67
    b. Kemble 112
    c. Hardwick, *Elmham*, pp. 321–2
    d. Thorpe, *Diplomatarium*, p. 37
    e. Birch 188
Listed: Sawyer 143

In nomine regnantis inperpetuum. Ego Offa rex Merciorum illam don-acionem quam rex gloriosus Ethilbaldus, Deo omnipotenti graciarum per-soluens acciones, Mildrithe abbatisse de nauis onuste transueccionis censu qui a theloneariis exigebatur conferre uoluit, pro remedio anime mee et pro munificencia oracionum sanctarum tibi Sigeburge eiusdem monasterii abbatisse condonans attribuo. Ad hanc condicionem signum saluatoris nostri propria manu firmaui et testes ut subscriberent rogaui.

+ Ego Bregwinus archiepiscopus consensi et subscripsi.
+ Signum Tottan episcopi.
+ Signum Milredi episcopi.
+ Signum Egwlfi episcopi.
+ Signum Eardulfi episcopi.

This is a confirmation of the privilege granted by Æthelbald in **50**, which involved toll-exemption for one of the community's ships throughout the Mercian kingdom. The subscription of Archbishop Bregowine dates it to between 761 and 764. It appears to have been issued at a synod (as were many of Offa's charters dealing with Kent; see p. xci), for the remaining witnesses in the truncated witness-list are all bishops: Torhthelm (Totta) of Leicester (737–64), Milred of Worcester ([743 × 745] -774), Ecgwulf of London (745-[766 × 772]) and Eardwulf of Rochester (747-[765 × 772]). All are consistent with the implied date, as is the name of the abbess (see **53**) and the diplomatic of the text, so far as can be determined; the unusual verbal invocation is a slightly shorter version of that in **13** (762 or 763), and the corroboration seems contemporary (compare S 105 from 764). The awkward construction of the dispositive section is partly due to the incorporation within it of phrases taken directly from **50**, which is not a suspicious feature in a confirmation dealing with a type of privilege with which the charter-scribe may not have been familiar. There is no particular difficulty in accepting **52** as an authentic document, in which Offa reinstates a privilege which had perhaps lapsed during the period of civil war in Mercia; S 88 shows that Mercian kings might confirm toll-privileges issued by their predecessors. Scharer (*Königsurkunde*, p. 201) rejects **52** because he believes **50** to be a fabrication and because he has misidentified Bishop Totta with a non-contemporary bishop of Selsey.

53

Eadberht II, king of Kent, grants to Abbess Sigeburh remission of toll on two ships at Sarre and on a third at Fordwich and Sarre.

[*c.* A.D. 763 or 764]

F. BL Cotton Julius D. ii, 86v: copy, s. xiii[1]
    Rubric: De transuectione duarum nauium ad Sarre.
H. PRO E 164/27, 150r–151r: copy, s. xiii or xiv
    Rubric: De transuectione duarum nauium ad Serre.
N. Cambridge, Trinity Hall, 1, 68v–69r: copy, s. xv[1]
    Rubric: Carta regis Edberti Cantie de eiusdem nauis transueccione.
Ed.: a. Lewis, *Tenet*, pp. 1–2, from N
    b. Kemble 106 from N
    c. Hardwick, *Elmham*, pp. 322–4, from N
    d. Thorpe, *Diplomatarium*, pp. 35–6, from N
    e. Birch 189 from N
Listed: Sawyer 29
Edited from F, H and N

Regnante inperpetuum Domino nostro Iesu Christo. Unicuique mortalium uite sue terminus omnipotentis Dei dispensatione incertus esse dinoscitur. Uenit enim Dominus ad uisitandum seruum suum in die qua non sperat et hora qua non putat. Qua de re ego Eadbertus*ᵃ* rex Cantie, anno secundo*ᵇ* regni nostri, una cum consensu et consilio*ᶜ* archiepiscopi Bregwini et principum meorum, pro eterna redemptione anime mee, aliquid ex his que mihi idem ipse Dominus et saluator noster cunctorum bonorum largitor tribuerit*ᵈ* statuens donare decreueram, id est duarum nauium transuectionis censum qui etiam iuris nostri erat in loco cuius uocabulum est ad Serrae,*ᵉ* iuxta petitionem*ᶠ* uenerabilis abbatisse Sigeburge*ᵍ* eiusque sacre conuersationis familie in monasterio sancti Petri, quod situm est in insula Tenet,*ʰ* sicut a regibus Merciorum Æthilbaldo*ⁱ* uidelicet clementissimo et rege Offan longe ante concessum est tributum in loco cuius uocabulum est Lundenwic. Alterius uero, quod nuper edificatum est in monasterio eiusdem religiose Dei famule, omne tributum atque uectigal concedimus quod etiam a theloneariis nostris iuste impetitur publicis in locis que appellantur Fordwic^j et Seorre.^e Hinc igitur precipio et precor in nomine omnipotentis Dei patriciis, ducibus, comitibus, theloneariis, actionariis, publicis dignitatibus, ut hec nostra concessio in Dei donatione eternaliter sit confirmata, ita ut nec mihi nec alicui successorum meorum regum siue principum seu cuiuslibet conditionis dignitatibus nefario temeritatis ausu de supradicta donatione nostra aliquid fraudare uel minuere liceat. Si autem contigerit ut nauis ista rupta et confracta sit uel nimia uetustate consumpta siue etiam quod absit^k naufragio perdita, ut alia in loco illius ad utilitatem ibidem Deo seruientium famulorum Christi et famularum construatur, ad hanc uidelicet conditionem, ut quicquid in suis mercimoniis in diuersis speciebus adquirere possint, nobis fideliter inoffense offerre debeant simul cum ipsa naui ad locum qui appellatur Fordwik.^l Et quicumque de hac donatione nostra, quod etiam specialiter omnipotenti Deo firmiter concessum est, aliquid nefario caliditatis ausu abstrahere uel minuere temptauerit, sciat se a consortio sanctorum omnium separatum et cum diabolo et angelis eius inperpetuum esse dampnandum, quoniam sanctum locum istum dehonestare conatus est, in quo primi apostolorum principis Petri intercessio orationibus assiduis et elemosinis floret pro omni populo Christiano. Iccirco uiuens benedictione Dei carebit et moriens maledictioni debite subiacebit, nisi digna satisfactione emendauerit quod inique studuit deprauare. Quicumque uero hec augenda custodierit sit benedictus inperpetuum et beatissimam uocem audire mereatur cum sanctis, Uenite benedicti patris mei.[1]

+^m Ego Edbertusⁿ rex hanc donationem a me factam propria manu signo sancte crucis roboraui.^o

+ Ego Bregowinus archiepiscopus ad petitionem Edberti^p regis signum sancte crucis expressi.

+ Signum manus Iaenberti^q abbatis.

+ Signum manus Daene abbatis.

+ Signum Brůuni^r abbatis.

+ Signum manus Baltheardi comitis.

+ Signum Eathelhun principis.

+ Signum manus Redfridi.

+ Signum manus Budda.^s

+ Signum manus Athelberti.^t

+ Signum manus Headda.^u

+ Signum manus Egesasi.
+ Signum manus Aldredi.[v]

^a Aldbertus F; Aðelbertus H   ^b .xxxvi. N (see commentary)   ^c concilio H, N
^d tribueret F   ^e Serre H   ^f peticioni H   ^g Segeburge F   ^h Thanet H; Tanæt N
ⁱ Ætilbaldo H   ^j Fordwicht H; Fordwik N   ^k Omitted H
^l Fordwich H; Fordewik N   ^m Cross omitted F   ⁿ Aldbertus F; Adelbertus H
^o F ends here   ^p Adelberti H   ^q Iamberti N   ^r Bruni N
^s This subscription omitted H   ^t Eathelberti H   ^u Eadda N   ^v Aldred N

[1] Matt. 25: 34

The donor of this charter seems to have been the successor and probably the son of Æthelberht II, and to have ruled for a few years from 762 (see Appendix 3). He was also the donor of **13** and S 1612, and he attested S 32 in 762. In the thirteenth-century cartulary copies, **53** is attributed to Eadberht's second year, and **13** to his first; in Elmham's history the regnal year of both charters has been altered to thirty-six, in an attempt to identify the donor with Eadberht I, son of Wihtred, who died in 748. **53** belongs without question to the early 760s. It is attested by Archbishop Bregowine (761–4), and by Abbot Jænberht of St Augustine's, who was elected in about 762 and succeeded Bregowine as archbishop in 764. Most of the other witnesses occur in Kentish charters of the 760s. Eadberht II's toll-privilege for Reculver (S 1612), which survives only in an abbreviated form in the Christ Church cartularies, also includes an internal reference to Archbishop Bregowine, although it has been given the date 747, no doubt through the same confusion with Eadberht I that prompted revision of the muniments at St Augustine's.

The two toll-privileges of Eadberht II are the only surviving examples of such a concession by a Kentish king, and they may represent a new development; in **53** the king says that he is imitating earlier grants made long before by Æthelbald and Offa in respect of the port of London. The reference to Offa in this context requires explanation, for he could hardly have made such a grant 'long before' the early 760s. It seems probable that the passage from *Æthilbaldo uidelicet* to *Offan* is a later interpolation, inserted by a copyist who knew of the other toll-privileges in the archive; the original reference may simply have been to 'Mercian kings' who had made this concession. The nature of the privilege in **53** is not entirely clear, but the best interpretation seems to be that the concession applied to three separate ships. In the first place two ships are given immunity at the Kentish port (or toll-station) at Sarre on the Wantsum, such as Æthelbald (and Offa) had granted at London. These two ships may be the community's original vessel (covered by **49, 50** and **52**) and the vessel purchased in the 740s (**51**); Eadberht would then be extending the existing immunities of these trading-ships. If these two ships regularly travelled to London from Minster, they would need to pass Sarre each time, so a toll-exemption there would be useful. The dispositive section then deals with a ship recently built at Minster, which is to be exempt from toll at both Fordwich (the port just downstream from Canterbury) and Sarre. It seems best to regard this as a third ship, rather than one of the two previously mentioned (although the wording is ambiguous); this makes more sense in terms of the concessions being granted. Later in the charter the king imposes a condition, which seems to apply to the third ship only; this seems to involve pre-emption rights over the merchandise (of all kinds) which the ship brings to Fordwich. This passage is welcome and explicit evidence that the vessels to which the toll-privileges applied were actually engaged in some kind of commercial activity, not simply the transport of the community's produce. Abbess Sigeburh seems to have been particularly concerned with the Minster trading-ships. She apparently petitioned King Eadberht for the privileges granted in 53, and acquired a confirmation of one of Æthelbald's toll-privileges from King Offa (52). Abbot Deneheah of Reculver also acquired a toll-exemption at this time, covering a single ship at Fordwich (S 1612). Both Deneheah and Sigeburh may have been taking advantage of the relative weakness of Eadberht's position.

The diplomatic is compatible with the implied date. The verbal invocation is of a type associated with Mercian rather than Kentish charters at this time, but there is good evidence for its occasional use by Kentish draftsmen in the early 760s (see S 105, and the hybrid versions in 13 and 52; and discussion, p. xci). The theme of the proem is the transitory nature of human life, which is not a common emphasis at this period but was to become a staple of later Mercian diplomatic (see S 114, 139 etc.); this may be another reflection of Mercian influence. For the position of the regnal year, see pp. lxxxiv, 28. A very similar consent-formula appears in S 1612, and in S 105 there is a close parallel for the desire to redistribute gifts given by the *largitor bonorum*. The beneficiary, Abbess Sigeburh, is associated only with the minster dedicated to St Peter founded by her predecessor (see 51 and p. xxvi), which may imply that Æbba's original foundation had been abandoned by this date. Some of the formulation of the dispositive section shows the influence of earlier toll-privileges in the archive: 50 (note the phrase *transuectionis censum*) and, to a much larger extent, 51. The injunction directed at various officials and the 'shipwreck clause' were apparently adapted from 51; the prayer-condition in the earlier charter has been replaced by the passage about pre-emption rights. The sanction has some points in common with that of 51, particularly in the stress on worship of the patron saint (in this case Peter) by the community; the phrase about dishonouring the minster recalls a section of the anathema in an earlier Lyminge charter (S 24), which also has a blessing incorporating the same quotation from Matthew (see also S 31, 33). There are additional verbal links with the sanctions of S 1612 and 33. The forms of the subscriptions are contemporary (compare S 33).

APPENDIX I
Lost charters and benefactions mentioned in post-Conquest sources

i. S 1648 and S (Add.) 1648a (Cambridge, Trinity Hall, 1, 52v; Hardwick, *Elmham*, pp. 249–50). Elmham knew of two charters of King Hlothhere which appear to have been versions of **40** and **41** in which the name of Hlothhere had been substituted for that of Swæfheard/*Suabertus*. Elmham did not give the full texts, but he described how they differed from **40** and **41**. The first of the charters was identical to **40**, except for the name of the donor, the regnal year (which he gives as four), the references to payment and the donor's kinship with the beneficiary, and the references to the consent of Kings Æthelred and Sebbi. This probably implies that the lost charter did not include the second part of **40**, the section which appears after the (possibly interpolated) passage on the earlier history of the estates. Kemble 989 purports to be the text of the document known to Elmham. This has no manuscript authority; Kemble or his clerk would appear to have reconstructed the charter on the basis of Elmham's remarks, the indiction being calculated from **6**, the previous charter in the history (and thus not representing independent evidence for the dating of Hlothhere's reign; see the commentary to **6**). Birch used Kemble's text, citing also BL Harley 686, a straightforward transcript of the Trinity Hall manuscript, which has no additional information about the lost charter. The second of the documents seen by Elmham seems to have been identical to **41**, with the name of the donor changed. Elmham interpreted S 1648 and S (Add.) 1648a as Hlothhere's confirmation of grants by Swæfheard. In fact Hlothhere preceded Swæfheard on the throne on Kent by well over a decade (see Appendix 3). The two lost charters were probably forgeries, perhaps intended to associate the donation of important Minster estates with the well-known Hlothhere rather than the 'usurper' Swæfheard, or perhaps simply misjudged 'confirmations', designed to strengthen the documentary record. There is further discussion in the commentaries to **6** and **40**.

ii. S (Add.) 1651a (BL Cotton Tib. A. ix, 115v; Twysden, *Scriptores*, col. 1777; Davis, *Thorne*, p. 35). Sprott, followed by Thorne, mentions that the St Augustine's community sold land at Willesborough to Eadwulf, son of

Eadweald, for two thousand pence, with the implication that this transaction took place in the late ninth century. Eadweald himself had granted Willesborough to the abbey (see S 332 endorsement, and discussion, p. xxxiii n. 57). It would therefore appear that the donor's son redeemed the estate from the abbey with a money payment. Sprott presumably acquired his information from a separate document recording the alienation (perhaps the abbey's copy of a duplicate charter or chirograph) or from estate records. The PRO charter-list mentions an Old English charter for Willesborough (Appendix 2, no. xxxvii) which may have been a record of the sale (but see also below, no. iii).

iii. S 1652 (BL Cotton Tib. A. ix, 115v; Twysden, *Scriptores*, col. 1777–8; Davis, *Thorne*, p. 35). Sprott, followed by Thorne, refers to the will of Æthelferth, *minister abbatis*, which involved a bequest to the abbey of land at *Atelesworthe* in Willesborough and at Hinxhill, with an implicit date in the later ninth century. Sprott notes that the Hinxhill estate had been usurped by Hugh de Montfort after the Conquest, but that the land at *Atelesworthe* was still bringing in an annual return of ten shillings, reckoned under the total for Kennington; St Augustine's held four sulungs at Kennington in 1086 (GDB 12v). Æthelferth also bequeathed to St Augustine's five marks of gold, two oxen, two cows in calf, a horse, ten pigs, ten sheep and ten goats. The PRO charter-list mentions a vernacular charter for Willesborough and another for Hinxhill (Appendix 2, nos xxxvii, xxxviii); on this basis Sawyer ·suggested that Æthelferth's bequest was treated as two separate documents (see S 1652). But the former entry is more likely to refer to a document connected with the sale of Willesborough to Eadwulf (see above, no. ii). If so, the Old English charter for Hinxhill may have been Æthelferth's will.

iv. (BL Cotton Tib. A. ix, 115v; Twysden, *Scriptores*, col. 1777; Davis, *Thorne*, p. 34) Sprott and Thorne have a note that Egelred (Æthelred) of Fordwich offered his son to St Augustine's as a monk, and along with him six tenements (*hagas*), three acres and part of a meadow to the south of Fordwich. Sprott had no date for the grant, but placed it in his account of late-ninth-century donations. In one manuscript of his history (BL Cotton Tiberius A. ix) this notice was immediately followed by a reference to a grant by Edward of Combe, which was later deleted, presumably because the same grant appears later in the manuscript, dated 997 (see below, no. vii). It is possible that the notice of Æthelred's grant was also misplaced in the narrative and that it belongs to the later tenth or eleventh century, when St Augustine's was acquiring other property at Fordwich. Thorne follows Sprott and has no information to add. There is no entry in the PRO charter-list. Sprott may have derived this information from records relating to gifts made by or on behalf of postulants, or perhaps from a lost charter.

v. S 1653 (BL Cotton Tib. A. ix, 116rv; Twysden, *Scriptores*, col. 1779; Davis, *Thorne*, pp. 37–8; Hardwick, *Elmham*, p. 22). A grant to St Augustine's in 974 by a woman named Wynflæd of one hundred acres at Mongeham is mentioned by Sprott (followed by Thorne) and in the chronological table prefixed to Elmham's history. Sprott says that the grant was made at Kingston with the permission of King Edgar and witnessed by Dunstan and others, so it seems likely that he had access to a lost charter recording the benefaction. He describes the land given by Wynflæd as stretching from the northern part of the abbey's great manor of Northbourne eastwards towards the parish of Little Mongeham, but says that it was not actually located at Little Mongeham itself. The hundred acres may have been reckoned under either the manor of Northbourne or that of Mongeham, both of them being held by St Augustine's at the Conquest; there is some reason to believe that mutual boundary of the two manors was adjusted at some stage (see p. 55).

vi. S 1654 (BL Cotton Tib. A. ix, 116v; Twysden, *Scriptores*, col. 1780; Davis, *Thorne*, pp. 38–9; Hardwick, *Elmham*, p. 23). In 991 a port-reeve named Bruman made a grant of two tenements and a meadow at Fordwich to Abbot Wulfric I (*c.* 985–1006), on condition that he was received *in fraternitatem domus* and allowed to retain the property during his lifetime at an annual rent of seven shillings and a penny, the property reverting to the abbey after his death. It is possible that Bruman is to be identified with the *praepositus* called Brunman who unjustly levied tolls on foreign merchants on St Augustine's property (GDB 2r: see W. Urry, *Canterbury under the Angevin Kings* (London, 1967), p. 83). Since the Domesday Brunman rectified his abuses after the Conquest, it is unlikely that he was operating as early as 991; Sprott and Elmham could have been mistaken about the date of Bruman's grant, perhaps as a result of confusion between Abbots Wulfric I and Wulfric II (1045–61). The abbey acquired two-thirds of the borough of Fordwich in the reign of Edward the Confessor (**39**), and the remaining third after the Conquest (GDB 12r).

vii. S 1655 (BL Cotton Tib. A. ix, 116v; Twysden, *Scriptores*, col. 1780; Davis, *Thorne*, p. 39; Hardwick, *Elmham*, p. 23). At around the same time as Bruman's grant, according to Sprott (followed by Thorne), a certain Edward of Combe, whose son Leofhard was a monk at St Augustine's, bequeathed to the abbey his land at Combe in Brabourne. The PRO charter-list (Appendix 2, no. xxxv) has the entry: *Item alia [carta in anglico] Eadwardi de terra de Cumbe et Broke* (perhaps Brook near Brabourne). A reference to this bequest is inserted in the chronological table prefixed to Elmham's history, under the year 997.

viii. S (Add.) 1655a (BL Cotton Tib. A. ix, 116v; Twysden, *Scriptores*, col 1780; Davis, *Thorne*, p. 39). Sprott (followed by Thorne) mentions that a certain Brihtric bequeathed to the abbey his land at Wateringbury (*Woderyngbourne*), during the abbacy of Wulfric I (*c.* 985–1006). The PRO charter-list (Appendix 2, no. xxxvi) refers to a vernacular charter relating to Wateringbury, and an entry for it appears in Elmham's chronological table under the year 999. In 1086 Wateringbury was held by Odo of Bayeux and the Domesday entry remarks that it had previously belonged to King Edward (GDB 8v).

ix. S 1656 (BL Cotton Tib. A. ix, 118r; Twysden, *Scriptores*, col. 1781; Davis, *Thorne*, p. 40; Hardwick, *Elmham*, p. 24). Sprott, followed by Thorne, has a notice of a bequest by a certain Godwold of a hundred acres in the northern part of *Sturtune* (unidentified); Elmham's chronological table suggests that this took effect in 1009. The PRO charter-list mentions a vernacular charter concerned with the estate (Appendix 2, no. xxxiv), presumably Godwold's will or a record of the bequest.

x. (BL Cotton Tib. A. ix, 118rv; Hardwick, *Elmham*, p. 24). Sprott notes that a matron named Elfgiva (Ælfgifu) granted a food-render to the community, at around the same time as the Viking sack of Canterbury in 1011. He goes on to say that, on the day in which she was received into the *fraternitas* of the abbey, she gave fifty pounds sterling to the community and twenty shillings to each monk. Elmham's chronological table refers to this benefaction under the year 1019. It is possible that the generous matron was Ælfgifu/Emma of Normandy, wife of Æthelred and subsequently of Cnut. Thorne mentions that Emma gave many gifts to St Augustine's, including precious palls for the house saints (Twysden, *Scriptores*, col. 1784; Davis, *Thorne*, p. 45).

xi. S 1657 (Hardwick, *Elmham*, p. 26). In the column of Elmham's chronological table devoted to royal grants to St Augustine, under the year 1045, there is a note: *Carta de Sellyng et Conybroc sive Kennington*. This charter is otherwise unknown, and is not mentioned by Sprott, Thorne or the PRO charter-list. In 1086 the abbot of St Augustine's held land assessed at six sulungs in Selling and four in Kennington (GDB 12r, 12v).

xii. S 1657a (PRO E 164/27, 18r; Ballard, *Inquisition*, pp. 4–5). The manor of Badlesmere was disputed between St Augustine's and Odo of Bayeux in the reign of the Conqueror. Domesday Book lists Badlesmere among the estates which Ansfrid held from Odo, but notes that the abbot claimed the manor because he had held it TRE; it goes on to say that the hundred bore witness for the abbot, but *filius hominis* (presumably the son of the Domesday tenant) stated that his father could turn where he wished (i.e. choose his own lord), a claim which the monks denied (GDB 10r). At the end of the list of the abbey's holdings there is another reference to the affair, to the effect that the shire testified that the abbot held the land TRE and had jurisdiction over the tenant (GDB 12v). Further information comes from a Kentish satellite survey included in PRO E 164/27 (see pp. cvi–cvii), which states that the monks claimed Badlesmere through the charter and seal of King Edward: 'Badlesmere manerium tenuit Godrich Wisce de rege Edwardo et defendit pro uno solino et modo tenet illud Anfridus de episcopo Baiocensi et est appreciatum iiii libras. Hoc idem manerium reclamant monachi sancti Augustini per cartam et sigillum regis Edwardi' (Ballard, *Inquisition*, pp. 4–5). It is possible that Badlesmere was one of the estates leased out by the last Anglo-Saxon abbot, Æthelsige, which were lost to the abbey around the time of the Conquest (see p. cx).

xiii. S 1658 (BL Cotton Tib. A. ix, 120r; Twysden, *Scriptores*, col 1785; Davis, *Thorne*, p. 47). Sprott , followed by Thorne, has a note that Abbot Æthelsige (1061-*c.* 1070) gave the land of *Dene* in Littlebourne to Blakemann, Drithred and Agelred, sons of Drihtmer. *Dene* was part of the estate at Littlebourne given to the abbey by Archbishop Eadsige between 1042 and 1050 (**37**; see **36**). The PRO charter-list mentions a vernacular charter concerning *Dene* which is probably a record of the lease in gavelkind (Appendix 2, no. xlv).

APPENDIX 2
A charter-list from PRO E 164/27 (3v–6v)

The main cartulary section of the PRO cartulary is prefaced by a collection
of preliminary material which includes a list of benefactions (see p. lii). The
entries appear to be summaries of pre- and post-Conquest charters, some
no longer extant. In certain instances a considerable part of the formulation
has been reproduced (for example, nos xviii, xix); sometimes, especially
when the source was a vernacular document, the entry is nothing more than
a brief rubric (see nos xxxiv–viii). The list seems to be organised on a largely
topographical basis, with documents covering properties in the same area
usually grouped together (although there are inconsistencies): nos v-xvi are
Minster charters; nos xvii and xviii cover appurtenances in the Weald;
Plumstead, Lenham and Sibertswold charters are grouped together (nos
xxi-ii, xxiii-vi, xxvii-viii); and so on. The entries for the vernacular charters
and writs appear together at the end of the collection. There is a complex
relationship with the order of charters in BL Cotton Julius D. ii (see further,
pp. xlvi–xlvii). The charter-list in PRO E 164/27 is unlikely to be a compilation
drawing directly on surviving single-sheets, but it may perhaps be a summary
of texts in an earlier cartulary. The entries often conclude with a reference
to the archbishop in whose reign the transaction took place; in two instances
(nos vi, xviii) the wrong archbishop is cited. It is possible that the compiler
of the charter-list was drawing on an exemplar in which the texts had been
organised on the basis of archiepiscopal sequence, or in which this detail
had been highlighted for some reason.

 i. Edbertus 'rex' dedit Moningham 'vi aratrorum' abbati Iamberto, tempore Bregowini archiepiscopi. (**13**)

 ii. Rex Ethelbertus dedit Mertone 'id est tria aratra' Wernodo abbati anno
Domini .dcccxl., tempore Cialnothi archiepiscopi. (**22**)

 iii. Egbertus rex dedit terram unius aratri que nominatur on Scirdune et
ante pertinebat ad regalem uillam Dorouernie cum siluis que appellantur
Daiborne et Hussing denn, anno uidelicet Domini .dcccxxxvi., tempore
Cialnothi archiepiscopi. (**18**)

 iv. Anno Domini .dcclx. Dunwaldus minister regis Ethelberti dedit sancto

Augustino uillam unam que iam ad Quengatum urbis Dorouernis in foro posita est, tempore Bregwini archiepiscopi. (12)

v. Aelbertus (*for* Eadbertus) rex Cancie dedit Sigeburgge abbatisse eclesie sancti Petri in Thaneto, tempore archiepiscopi Bregwini, duarum nauium transueccionis sensum (*for* censum). (53)

vi. Item Aethilbaldus rex Merciorum dedit sancte Mildrede abbatisse in Thaneth sue nauis transueccionis sensum (*for* censum), tempore Bregwini archiepiscopi. (50)

vii. Item Aethelbertus (*for* Æthelbaldus) 'et scilicet Edbaldus' rex Merciorum dedit beate Mildrede abbatisse libertatem super exaccionem thelonei nauis sue. (49)

viii. Item Etelbertus rex filius Witredi regis dedit gloriose Mildrede terram unius aratri circa flumen Limenea quam (MS liminearum) dudum possiderant qui in Ieccaham pro tempore habitabant et tria iugera prati in loco que dicitur Hammespot, tempore Bretwaldi archiepiscopi. (47)

ix. Item Eadbertus rex dedit beate Mildrethe abbatisse terram dimidii aratri quam dudum habuit Aescuuald in regione qui dicitur bi Northyandune in Swalcliue. (48)

x. Item Withredus rex dedit terram nominatam Haeg quadraginta manentium abbatisse Eabbe, tempore Brithwaldi archiepiscopi et anno regis sexto. (46)

xi. Item rex Withredus anno eius .v. omnes terras et homines beate Mildrethe in Thanet in parliamento suo in loco qui dicitur Berghamstede concessit esse liberos et defensos. (45)

xii. Item Withredus rex Cancie Eabbe abbatisse terram que quondam appellata est Humancium aratrorum quatuor in Thanet, anno regni sui tercio, cum campis, siluis, piscariis, fluminibus, marisco et quicquid ?pertinet a quatuor partibus, orientis, occidentis, aquilonis et meridiei. (44)

xiii. Item Edwynus (*for* Oswynus) rex Cantuariorum dedit Eabbe abbatisse terram que sita est in insula de Thanet .xviii. manentes continentem quam aliquando Irminredus possidebat, et aliqua pars ipsius archiepiscopi erat, ipso tamen concenciente (*for* consentiente) et aliam a nobis accepiente. (43)

xiv. Item Oswynus rex Cantuariorum dedit terram que dicitur Stureie, id est .x. manentes ex ea (MS a), cum siluis, campis, paludibus, cum fluminibus ac fontibus, pratis ac pomeriis, alme Eabbe abbatisse propinque sue, tempore Theodori archiepiscopi. (42)

xv. Item Suuabertus rex Cantuariorum dedit Eabbe abbatisse terram que sita est in Sturige duorum aratrorum atque terram trium aratrorum in loco qui dicitur Bodesham, tempore Oswini regis. (41)

xvi. Item Suuabertus rex Cantuariorum, anno Domini .dcxci. et anno regni sui secundo, cum consensu Sebbe regis patris sui dedit terram Eabbe abbatisse que dicitur in Sudenaie intra insulam de Thanet, que et continet antiquo iure .xliiii. manentes et curtem id est curiam .xii. manentes habentem ultra insulam in loco qui dicitur Sturegh cum siluis et paludibus, cum fluminibus, fontibus et pratis, pomariis et omnibus aliis rebus ad eandem pertinentibus, in ipsa quantitate sicut antiquitus principes a regibus sibi perdonatam habuerat. (**40**)

xvii. Oswinus rex Kancie dedit sancto Augustino terram unius aratri in qua mina ferri habere cognoscitur, que pertinebat ad cortem que appellatur Liminge, que etiam coniuncta est terre presbiteri uenerabilis Brithwaldi abbatis a parte meridiana, tempore Adriani abbatis. (**8**)

xviii. In nomine Domini nostri Iesu Christi. Possessio quedam est terre in regione que uocatur Cherd monasterii beati Petri et Pauli apostolorum quod situm est ad orientem ciuitatis Dorouernensis. In hac autem terra habetur molina cuius quippe semis utilitas, id est dimidia pars molendine, a possessoribus prefati monasterii ac terre huius ad uillam regalem que nominatur With tradita est, pro hac uidelicet condicione atque comutacione, ut homo ille qui hanc terram in qua molina est tributario iure teneret unius gregis porcorum pascuam atque pastinacionem in saltu Andoredo iugiter haberet. Hanc autem comutacionem (MS comutacioni) Ethelbertus rex Kancie ut rata in perpetuum existat, signo dominice crucis roborare curauit, tempore Cuthberti archiepiscopi. (**11**)

xix. Item Eadricus rex Kancie quandam terram iuris sui dedit sancto Augustino pro .x. libris argenti, que terra coniuncta est terre quam sancte memorie Clotharius quondam rex beatus Petro donasse cognoscitur, que terra determinatur, ex una parte habet uadum quod appellatur Forstreta publica indirectum, et a parte alia fluuii quod nominatur Stur, omnes terras sacionales, tam pratis, campis, siluis, fontanis uel mariscum quod appellatur Stodmerche, cum omnibus ad predictam terram trium aratrorum pertinentibus, tempore sanctorum Theodori archiepiscopi et Adriani abbatis. (**7**)

xx. Item Withredus rex Kancie cum coniuge sua Athelburga dedit sancto Adriano abbati terram iuris sui .v. aratrorum que appellatur Littelbourne. (**9**)

xxi. Edgarus rex dedit sancto Augustino terram quatuor aratrorum que nominatur Plumstede. tempore sancti Dunstani. (**29**)

xxii. Item Willelmus rex Anglorum dedit sancto Augustino terram que dicitur Plumstede a predicto sancto antiquitus possessam et postea a Godwyno comite ui et fraude et iniuste ablatam et Dostic (*for* Tostic) filio suo datam quam tum rex Edwardus postea sancto reddiderat. Sic uariis euentibus possessa et ablata restituta tandem predicta uilla per Willelmum regem confirmata est, tempore Odonis episcopi Baiocensis. (Hardwick, *Elmham*, pp. 350–1)

xxiii. Ethelwlfus rex occidentalium Saxonum et Cantuariuorum dedit Wernodo abbati pro eius humili obediencia et peccunia, .c. mancas et duo milia argenti, terram .v. aratrorum in loco qui nominatur Lenham, uidelicet anno Domini .dcccxxxviii., tempore Ceolnothi episcopi. (**19**)

xxiv. Item Cunewlf rex Merciorum et Cudred rex Kancie dederunt Wernodo (MS Wernodoro) abbati terram .xx. aratrorum in loco qui nominatur <Len>ham et omnibus pertinentibus iuxta antiquos terminos sicut antecessores eius comites habuerunt, et .xiii. denberende on Andrede ad illam terram pertinencia, anno Domini .dccciiii., tempore Athellardi archiepiscopi. (**16**)

xxv. Item Kenwlf (*for* Æthelwulf) rex occidentalium Saxonum dedit Wernodo abbati .xl. cassatos in uilla que uocatur Lenham, cum omnibus pertinenciis et utilitatibus et locum in quo (*supply* sal) adipisci potest et cum ingressu trium carrorum in silua que uocatur Blen, anno Domini .dcccl., tempore Ceolnothi archiepiscopi. (**21**)

xxvi. (Henricus rex Anglorum testatur per litteram suam de terra de Eaytune iuxta Lenham ita finitum esse in curia sua quod recognitum est quod ipsa terra est de feodo sancti Augustini. Et episcopus Lincolniensis debet eam de abbate tenere.)

xxvii. Eadmundus rex Anglorum dedit Sigerigo abbati sancti Augustini terram duorum aratrorum in loco qui dicitur Siberdeswalde et successoribus in perpetuum, anno Domini .xliiii. (*for* .dccccxliiii.), tempore fratris eius Eadredi et Odonis archiepiscopi. (**27**)

xxviii. Etheldredus rex dedit Sigeredo ministro suo quandam particulam telluris, id est duorum cassatorum in loco quem silicole (*for* solicole) Siberdeswelde uocant, cum omnibus rebus ad ipsam pertinentibus, anno Domini .dccccxc. et tempore Siggerici Cantuar'. (**30**)

xxix. Item Ethelstanus rex dedit sancto Augustino terram .xiiii. aratrorum in insula de Thanet que appellatur Werburginland, que rapta fuerat iniuste per multos annos, sed rex Ethelstanus predictam illam terram sancto Augustino restaurauit, cum consensu Aldelmi archiepiscopi Cant' et aliorum principum suorum, anno Domini .dcccxxv. (**26**)

xxx. Item Wlfredus archiepiscopus tribuit Wernodo abbati aliquantulum territorium, id est .vi. iugera in loco ab incolis Doddingland nominatur, pro uice mutua illius terre que Ealdenford appellatur eiusdem mensure atque magnitudinis, anno Domini .dcccxxvi. (**17**)

xxxi. Edwardus rex dedit sancto Augustino et abbati Elfstano et successoribus suis in perpetuum Thanathos insulam quam Egbertus rex iure hereditario concessit uenerabili regine Domneue, matri sancte Mildrethe, quantum cerua posse cursu suo lustrauerat, pro interempcione duorum fratrum eius quos iussu eiusdem principis Deo odibilis Tunor iniqua strauit, sed et omnes donaciones possessionum uel facultatum quas prisco siue moderno tempore predecessores sui reges eidem contulerunt. (**34**)

xxxii. Edwardus rex tradidit et concessit Eadsino archiepiscopo quandam (*supply* terram) unius aratri cui incole eius prouincie Littelbournan nomen indiderunt. Hanc autem terram id est Littelbournan idem Edsuinus (*for* Edsinus) sancto Petro et Paulo apostolorum principi et sancto Augustino Anglorum apostolo donacione perpetua concessit cum concensu (*for* consensu) eiusdem regis. Anno Domini .mxlvii. (**36, 37**)

xxxiii. Eadredus rex Anglorum dedit cuidam homini suo nomine Hersige mansam et dimidiam ubi ruricole nomen imposuerunt Swalcliue et omnibus ad se rite pertinentibus. Et idem Heresi regis minister cum concensu (*for* consensu) regis et regine et eius optimatum monasterium apostolorum Petri et Pauli atque sancti Augustini predicta donacione ditauit. Hec donacio prima anno Domini .dcccxlvi., Oda archiepiscopus. (**28**)

xxxiv. Item carta in Anglico Gudwoldi de terra de Sturtune. (S 1656; Appendix 1, no. ix)

xxxv. Item alia Eadwardi de terra de Cumbe et Broke. (S 1655; Appendix 1, no. vii)

xxxvi. Item alia in Anglico Saxonico Brichtrich de Worderrongebeorn'. (S [Add.] 1655a; Appendix 1, no. viii)

xxxvii. Item similis carta de Wyuelesberge. (S [Add.] 1651a; Appendix 1, no. ii)

xxxviii. Item alia de Engselle. (S 1652; Appendix 1, no. iii)

xxxix. (Item bulla de terra de Natyndone.)

xl. (Agreement between Abbot Hugh and Luvia, wife of Odo, *miles*, concerning land at *Sudtune* and *Heyham*.)

xli. Etelwlfus rex occidentalium Saxonum et Cantuariorum dedit Wineher abbati sancti Augustini quandam partem terre iuris sui in orientali parte Kancie, id est unum aratrum in illo loco qui ab incolis Linchesore nominatur, anno Domini .dcccxlv. et tempore Ethelstani regis. (**20**)

xlii. Eadbald dedit Winemundo amico suo aliquam (*supply* partem) terre iuris sui pro eius pecunia quod ab eo accepit, hoc est .viii. hunt peniga, in loco qui dicitur Berewaremersch alf seata, de consensu Ethelwlfi regis et Ceolnothi archiepiscopi. (**23**)

xliii. Et idem Winemundus eandem terram dedit sancto Augustino (**23A**) xliv. Item carta in Anglico Aelburge de terra de Baburne (*for* Braburne), id est Hortune. **(24)**

xlv. Item alia in Anglico. Dene. (S 1658; Appendix 1, no. xiii)

xlvi. Cnutus rex dedit sancto Augustino corpus sancte Mildrethe cum terra tota sua de Thanet et extra cum omnibus consuetudinibus ad suam ecclesiam pertinentibus. **(33)**

xlvii. Carta Eadwardi regis in Anglico et alia in Latino de sacca et soccna et aliis libertatibus. **(35)**

xlviii. Item Eadwardus rex dedit Fordwik per cartam in Anglico. **(39)**

(The remaining entries refer to post-Conquest charters)

APPENDIX 3
The Kings of Kent

The chronological contamination of the abbey's pre-Conquest muniments at the hands of medieval scholars (see above, pp. xcvi–cv) has generated considerable confusion about the chronology and sequence of the kings of Kent. Most of the difficulties can be resolved by a closer consideration of the textual history of the individual charters.

The first Christian king of Kent was Æthelberht, who died on 24 February 616 (Bede, *HE*, ii. 5); for the date of his accession (probably *c.* 580 × 593), see N.P. Brooks, 'The Creation and Early Structure of the Kingdom of Kent', in *The Origins of Anglo-Saxon Kingdoms*, ed. S. Bassett (Leicester 1989), pp. 55–74, 250–4, at 65–7. From Bede it is also possible to discover the dates of Æthelberht's five successors: Eadbald, 616–40 (*HE* iii. 8); Eorcenberht, 640 to 14 July 664 (*HE* iii. 8; iv. 1; v. 24); Ecgberht, July 664 to July 673 (*HE* iv. 1, 5; v. 24); Hlothhere, July 673 to 6 February 685 (*HE* iv. 5, 26); Eadric, February 685 to the summer or autumn of 686 (*HE* iv. 26). It is on the question of the date of Hlothhere's accession that the evidence of the St Augustine's charters first comes into conflict with Bede's testimony. **6** is a charter of Hlothhere datable to 1 April 675, said to be his first year; this would indicate that Hlothhere became king in the year after 2 April 674, which is difficult to reconcile with Bede's implication that Hlothhere directly succeeded Ecgberht on the latter's death in July 673. It has been argued on the basis of **6** that there was a brief interregnum in Kent after Ecgberht died (D.P. Kirby, 'Bede and Northumbrian Chronology', *English Historical Review* lxxviii (1963), pp. 514–27, at 517). But **6** is not very secure evidence. Its authenticity is debatable, and it has been preserved only in the fifteenth-century manuscript of Elmham's history, where other regnal years have become contaminated. A motive for interfering with the dating material in a charter of Hlothhere is suggested by the decision of certain St Augustine's scholars to reassign to the early 670s a number of charters from *c.* 690 in the names of Kings Swæfheard and Oswine, as the result of a mistaken identification (see **8**, **40-3**, and Hardwick, *Elmham*, p. 6); there seems to have been an effort to place the reigns of these two 'intruders' between those of Ecgberht and Hlothhere. The confusion caused by this decision is evident in the chronological table prefixed to Elmham's history (Hardwick, *Elmham*, p. 6; the printed text of the *Chronologia Augustiniensis* is misleading here, for Hardwick has tidied up a complex pattern of entries spread over three columns in the table, with several additions). The note *Vacavit* after Ecgberht's death in the table appears to reflect Elmham's editorial decision respecting the validity of the rule of Swæfheard and Oswine, rather than any definite knowledge of events in 673. It has been suggested that support for the implied dating of Hlothhere's accession in **6** is to be found in the text printed as Kemble 989. But this text has no manuscript source and seems to be Kemble's reconstruction of a lost document on the basis of remarks made by Elmham (Hardwick, *Elmham*, pp. 249–50); the indiction was probably calculated from **6**, the preceding text in Elmham's manuscript, and has no independent value (see Appendix 1, no. i). Consequently Kemble 989 cannot confirm the aberrant regnal year of **6**, which is not in itself sufficiently trustworthy to support the theory of an interregnum in Kent from 673 until a point in 674.

Hlothhere was killed and succeeded in 685 by his brother's son Eadric, who in turn reigned for a year and a half (*HE* iv. 26). Eadric's position was probably insecure, and it seems significant that a charter in his name in the St Augustine's archive (**7**) includes a statement of legitimacy, such as is found in the charters of the slightly later usurper Oswine (**8, 42, 43**); see also **44**, from the early years of King Wihtred. Bede mentions that Eadric's own death was followed by a period in which 'reges dubii uel externi' ruled in Kent, before Eadric's brother Wihtred established himself (*HE* iv. 26). One of these foreign usurpers was Mul, imposed on Kent in 686 by his brother, Cædwalla of Wessex, and killed by the people of Kent in the following year; this information comes from the *Anglo-Saxon Chronicle*, which also mentions that in 694 the people of Kent paid compensation to King Ine for Mul's death. A narrative section in **40** refers to Mul as king; at St Augustine's, where he was supposed to have been buried, later sources refer to his royal status (Goscelin, *Translatio S. Augustini*, p. 434).

Another of the invaders was Swæfheard, said by Bede to have been ruling jointly with Wihtred when Archbishop Berhtwald was consecrated in July 692 (*HE* v. 8). Swæfheard (*Suebhardus*) is the donor of **40**, in favour of Abbess Æbba of Minster-in-Thanet, from which it can be discovered that he was the son of King Sebbi of the East Saxons, and that he acknowledged the overlordship of Æthelred of Mercia. Confirmation of his connection with Sebbi comes in S 233, a charter relating to the Kentish minster at Hoo which was preserved in the Peterborough archive; the document as it now stands appears to represent the rewriting and conflation of a series of early

Hoo charters from the last two decades of the seventh century, one of them in the name of Swæfheard and attested by Sebbi. **40** provides the crucial evidence for the dating of Swæfheard's reign. The texts of the charter in the thirteenth-century cartularies state that **40** was issued by Swæfheard on 1 March in his second year and in the second indiction, and that it was confirmed by Æthelred on 8 January 691, in the fourth indiction; from this it can be calculated that Swæfheard's initial grant took place on 1 March 689, and that his reign must have begun in the year before the end of February 688. In Elmham's text of **40** the dates have been contaminated; Æthelred's confirmation has been redated to 676 and the indiction in the main text has been altered from two to four. The incarnation year has evidently been tampered with in order to connect Æthelred's confirmation of **40** with his invasion of Kent in 676, which is mentioned by Bede (*HE* iv. 12; v. 24). As well as **40**, the Minster archive includes a coeval but undated charter in the name of a King *Suabertus* (**41**). This *Suabertus* may have been a separate king Swæfberht, presumably related to Swæfheard (Sebbi certainly had another son named Swæfred), but it is also possible that the name is a corruption of *Suebhardus* (via *Suabhertus*, the spelling in Elmham's rubric to **41**). The later St Augustine's historians clearly assumed that the donors of **40** and **41** were the same man, and the PRO cartulary assigns both texts to a King *Swabertus*. On balance, it seems unlikely that two separate East Saxon princelings ruled in Kent at around the same time. Swæfheard was still king in July 692, when he was ruling jointly with Wihtred (*HE* v. 8). He appears to have died or been been ousted before July 694, when Wihtred issued **44** without reference to a co-ruler. It may have been the case that he predeceased his father, since he is not named by Bede among the sons who succeeded Sebbi (*HE* iv. 11); Sebbi was still alive in 693, for he was consecrated a monk by Bishop Waldhere of London, who was appointed in that year (*HE* iv. 11).

Both **40** and **41** were attested by a King Oswine, who is the donor of three surviving charters: **8** in favour of St Augustine's, and **42** and **43** in the Minster archive. **42** was issued on 27 January in the third indiction (690), which is said to have been in Oswine's second year; thus he came to power in Kent at some point in the year before 27 January 689. All three of his charters include a statement proclaiming the legitimacy of his ancestral claim to the kingdom, but he seems to have relied on Mercian support; **8** refers to the consent of Æthelred of Mercia to the land-grant. Swæfheard/*Suabertus* in turn attested Oswine's charters, which indicates that the two (or three) kings were co-rulers around the year 690. In the later medieval period St

Augustine's scholars imaginatively identified Oswine with Oswiu of Northumbria, which formed an additional reason for reassigning the interconnected
charters of Oswine and Swæfheard to an earlier date than the 690s (see
above, p. cii). Oswine had apparently disappeared by July 692, when
Swæfheard and Wihtred were ruling together (*HE* v. 8).

By 694 Wihtred seems to have become sole ruler of Kent (**44**). Bede says
that when he died in April 725 he had been ruling for thirty-four and a half
years (*HE* v. 23), which implies that his reign was understood to have begun
in the autumn of 690. But other evidence suggests that the beginning of his
reign might be calculated from a rather later date, in the summer or autumn
of 691. **10** was issued on 8 April in the twelfth indiction (699) and Wihtred's
eighth year, which indicates that the reign length was being calculated from
a point in the year before 8 April 692. Similarly, **44** was issued on 17 July
in the seventh indiction (694) and in Wihtred's third year, implying that he
became king in the year before 17 July 692. The evidence of the dating of
Wihtred's lawcode is ambiguous, since it is not clear whether *Rugern* refers
to August or September (a crucial matter when an indiction is in question).
On the other hand, Wihtred's regnal year in **47** does seem compatible with
Bede's calculation. It is possible that the uncertain beginning of Wihtred's
reign, in a period of joint-rulership with Swæfheard, led to some later
confusion about calculating reign-length.

Wihtred died on 23 April 725 and was succeeded by three sons, Æthelberht,
Eadberht and Alric (Bede, *HE*, v. 23). Alric seems to have been the son of
Queen Werburh, probably Wihtred's third wife, who is associated with him
in the genuine witness-list from the Kentish synod at Bapchild (*c.* 716)
attached to the spurious S 22 (see discussion in commentary to **9**). Alric is
likely, therefore, to have been the younger half-brother of Æthelberht and
Eadberht, which probably explains why he immediately disappears from the
record; William of Malmesbury (*GR*, p. 18) credits him with a reign between
the death of Æthelberht in 762 and the 'accession' of Eadberht Præn in 796,
but this is evidently fantasy, inspired by a desire to account neatly for the
three brothers mentioned by Bede. Æthelberht appears to have been the
oldest, and he issued at least one charter before his father's death (**47**). His
death is mentioned in the *Anglo-Saxon Chronicle* under the year 762, which
also has an obit for Eadberht in 748. A series of charters, largely preserved
in the St Augustine's archive, constitutes the only other evidence for the
reigns of Æthelberht and Eadberht, but the dating information in these has
been considerably complicated by the attentions of later medieval scholars.
Two factors created difficulty. In the first place Æthelberht and Eadberht
seem to have ruled at the same time, an arrangement unfamiliar to the later

historians, who assumed that they were successive kings of Kent, Eadberht being succeeded by Æthelberht in 748. The second difficulty arose because when Æthelberht died in 762 his successor was a second king named Eadberht, probably his own son. Eadberht II is the donor in three extant charters, one each in favour of St Augustine's, Minster-in-Thanet and Reculver (**13, 53** and S 1612); he also attested in 762 a charter of a King Sigered, apparently his co-ruler at that time (S 32). In all three charters in the name of Eadberht himself the dates were tampered with because the donor was wrongly identified with Eadberht I, son of Wihtred. The two charters in the St Augustine's archive (**13, 53**) had their regnal years altered from (respectively) one and two to thirty-six at some point between the thirteenth and fifteenth centuries. The revisor intelligently based his calculation on two factors: Bede's date for the death of Wihtred and the accession of Eadberht I, and the apparent date of the two charters (both are attested by Archbishop Bregowine, who was in office between 761 and 764); but he was apparently unaware of the Chronicle's obit for Eadberht I in 748. In the case of the Reculver charter, preserved at Christ Church (S 1612), a cartularist who did know of the obit saddled the text with a date of 747, incompatible with the internal reference to Archbishop Bregowine. The whole situation becomes much clearer when it is realised that all three charters belong to the period 762–4, and that the donor is not to be identified with Wihtred's son (see further, Scharer, *Königsurkunde*, pp. 120–4).

Æthelberht and Eadberht appear to have ruled together between 725 and the latter's death in 748. Four charters survive from this period, two of them in the name of Eadberht. **48** is datable to 14 October 727 and grants to Minster-in-Thanet land in the area called 'Northwood', which lay north of Canterbury; no reference is made to Æthelberht, but it is possible that a confirmation has been omitted by the cartularist, who radically curtailed the witness-list. The second charter is S 27 from Rochester, which records Eadberht's grant to the bishopric of land at Stoke in Hoo. It has an addition dated April 738 in which the beneficiary explains that he had not realised that the grant should have been confirmed by the archbishop of Canterbury and the king (i.e. Æthelberht), and states that this has now been done *in metropolitano urbe* (Canterbury), under the supervision of Eadberht, the donor. It has been suggested on the basis of this charter that there had been by 738 an effective division of the kingdom between the two brothers, with Æthelberht, the elder, taking control in Canterbury and East Kent, while Eadberht ruled in West Kent; the additional passage would imply that Æthelberht was the senior ruler, confirming his brother's charters. A single document is not very strong evidence for this hypothesis (and **48** certainly suggests that no such division had taken place immediately after Wihtred's death). There is no reference to Eadberht in either of Æthelberht's charters from this period (S 23, 24). But some later charters do contribute to the impression that there was a territorial division of some kind in Kent during the eighth century (on this aspect, see below, and also discussion by B. Yorke, 'Joint Kingship in Kent c. 560 to 785', AC xcix (1983), pp. 1–19; note that Yorke has misunderstood the evidence for the succession of kings in the central decades of the eighth century).

On his death in 748 Eadberht I seems to have been succeeded by his son, Eardwulf, who is the donor of S 30 and S 31. The former is in favour of Rochester, while the latter grants land in the vicinity of Rochester to the minster at Reculver; this seems to confirm that the power-base of Eadberht and Eardwulf was in West Kent. Neither of the two charters can be precisely dated. S 30 does have a dating clause, which assigns it to 762 and supplies the correct indiction for that year, but 762 is impossible for Archbishop Cuthbert (740–60), who appears among the witnesses. A suggested emendation to 747 on the basis of the indiction seems unwise, since the indiction also fits the given year, 762; in addition, 747 would appear to antedate Eadberht I's death and Eardwulf's succession. It seems possible that the Rochester community, as well as St Augustine's and Christ Church, was tempted to emend the dates of its charters to make them agree with a mistaken chronological framework for the eighth century. Here again the influence of the 762 obit for Æthelberht in the Anglo-Saxon Chronicle may have been crucial, leading a Rochester cartularist to assume that Eardwulf was Æthelberht's successor. If so, the decision was obtuse, since a subscription of Æthelberht appears in the witness-list of S 30; this implies that Æthelberht and Eardwulf were co-rulers, as Æthelberht and Eadberht I had been. Yet Eardwulf's second charter, S 31, makes no reference to Æthelberht. This survives as an apparent original, but lacks any kind of dating clause. In theory its dating limits are provided by King Eardwulf's presumed succession in 748 and the death of Bishop Eardwulf of Rochester between 765 and 772, but the fact that King Eardwulf does not appear in any of the relatively large number of Kentish charters issued between 762 and 765 makes it probable that his rule came to an end in 762 or before. Scharer (Königsurkunde, p. 127) argues that the fact that S 31 was not confirmed by Æthelberht suggests that it was issued in 762, soon after Æthelberht's death and before his successor had time to establish himself.

King Æthelberht died in 762, according to the Anglo-Saxon Chronicle. He appears to have been succeeded by another Eadberht, probably his son, who granted land in East Kent to St Augustine's in his first year (13) and in his second year made a grant to Minster of toll-exemption in the East Kentish ports of Fordwich and Sarre (**53**); Reculver received a similar privilege relating to Fordwich at some point between 762 and 764 (S 1612). None of these charters refers to a co-ruler, but it does appear that Eadberht II shared power with a king named Sigered, established in West Kent. The Rochester archive preserves two charters of Sigered (S 32, 33). S 32 records a grant of Bishop Eardwulf of land at Rochester and is dated 762; a subscription of Eadberht appears in the witness-list. S 33 is a grant to the same beneficiary of land near Rochester, undated but datable to between 761 and 764 on the basis of a subscription by Archbishop Bregowine. This has no reference to Eadberht, but was confirmed instead at some point before 765 by a King Eanmund. We can probably assume that in *c*. 762 Eardwulf was replaced as the ruler of West Kent by Sigered, whose name indicates a probable East Saxon background. Sigered ruled jointly with Eadberht II for a year or so. Before 765 Eadberht II was replaced in East Kent by a King Eanmund. The rapid turnover continued, for a charter of 765 (S 34) has a King Ecgberht granting land in Rochester to Bishop Eardwulf, with confirmation by a King Heaberht.

It appears from the charter evidence that the death of the long-reigning King Æthelberht in 762 ushered in three years of political confusion in Kent, which saw the end of the dynasty of the *Oiscingas*. In West Kent Æthelberht's nephew, Eardwulf, disappeared in 762, to be replaced by an unknown king of possibly East Saxon ancestry. Eadberht II, who was probably Æthelberht's son, hung on in East Kent for at least a year, but in 763 or 764 was displaced by an otherwise unknown Eanmund. By 765 the wheel had turned again, and there were two more kings in Kent, Ecgberht and Heaberht. The background to these rapid permutations was the increasing Mercian pressure on the kingdom. In 764 Offa issued a charter which made a direct grant of land in Kent, without reference to any native king (S 105); this was apparently a restatement of a grant made shortly before by Sigered (S 33). At some point between 765 and 772 Offa confirmed a charter of Ecgberht, at the request of the beneficiary (S 34). Two charters of 774 in which Offa grants land to Archbishop Jænberht (S 110, 111) are not authentic, although the witness-list found in both clearly derives from an authentic charter of Offa from the 770s.

The next Kentish charters to be preserved are all in the name of Ecgberht, with no reference to any co-ruler. S 35 and S 36 are from 778 and 779 respectively; S 37 is undated, but probably belongs to approximately the same period. All three are in favour of Rochester and concern land in West Kent. The lack of any reference to Offa's overlordship in these three charters has been seen as evidence that the battle of Otford which took place between the Mercians and the Kentishmen in 776 (*ASC*) was won by the latter and led to a brief period of Kentish independence from Mercia (see Stenton, *Anglo-Saxon England*, p. 207). The moving spirit behind the rebellion would seem to have been King Ecgberht. It is likely that he had died or been deposed by 784, the date given to an edited text in the Christ Church cartularies which records a grant by a certain King Ealhmund to Reculver (S 38). There is some reason to believe that this Ealhmund may have been the father of King Ecgberht of Wessex (802–39), who had some hereditary claim to the kingdoms of the south-east (see *ASC s.a.* 825, and 855 for the genealogy naming Ecgberht's father). The circumstances under which Ealhmund became king in Kent must remain obscure. It is possible that he was a West Saxon ætheling who was able to establish himself briefly after the death of Ecgberht.

Kentish independence had been snuffed out by 785, when Offa issued the first of a series of direct grants of land in Kent without reference to any native king (S 123). Kent by this stage had been effectively annexed into the Mercian kingdom. A Kentish revolt broke out on Offa's death in 796, led by a certain 'King' Eadberht Præn; two years later Coenwulf bloodily reimposed Mercian rule on the province, capturing and mutilating Eadberht (*ASC*). It seems likely that Eadberht Præn had some hereditary claim to the Kentish kingdom; his name suggests that he may have been the last representative of the *Oiscingas*, a kinsman of Eadberht I and Eadberht II. There is some reason to think that he may be identified with the priest named Odberht who was sheltering from Offa's wrath at Charlemagne's court in 796 (Letter of Charlemagne to Offa: see Whitelock, *EHD*, no. 197).

After the suppression of Eadberht Præn's revolt, Coenwulf set up his brother Cuthred as sub-king of Kent (see **16**), presumably to placate local feelings. When Cuthred died in 807, Coenwulf ruled Kent without an intermediary until his own death in 821. He was succeeded by another brother, Ceolwulf, who followed the same policy until he was deposed in 823 (S 186, 187). Beornwulf, the next Mercian king, may have revived the idea of establishing a kinsman as sub-king of Kent; at any rate, when the West Saxons invaded Kent in 825/6, they drove out a King Baldred (*ASC*, S 1438). The West Saxon King Ecgberht made his son Æthelwulf king of Kent and the other south-eastern counties, and various sons of Æthelwulf later took on the same role (see **22**). This arrangement came to an end after the death of Æthelbald, when his surviving brothers made a pact not to divide the West Saxon realm (see Alfred's will, S 1507; and commentary to **22**).

Summary

Æthelberht I (*c.* 580 × 593 to 24 February 616)
Eadbald (616–40)
Eorcenberht (640 to 14 July 664)
Ecgberht (July 664 to July 673)
Hlothhere (July 673 to 6 February 685)
Eadric (February 685 to summer or autumn 686)

reges dubii uel externi

Mul, brother of Cædwalla of Wessex (686–7)
Swæfheard, son of Sebbi of Essex (accession: between 1 March 687 and 28 February 688. Death or deposition: between July 692 and 694). Joint-ruler with Oswine and then with Wihtred.
Suabertus = Swæfheard ?
Oswine (accession: between 27 January 688 and 26 January 689. Death or deposition: after 27 January 690 and before July 692). Joint-ruler with Swæfheard.
Wihtred (accession: probably autumn 691. Death: 23 April 725). Joint-ruler with Swæfheard, July 692. Sole ruler by 17 July 694.

East Kent	West Kent
Æthelberht II (725–62)	*Eadberht I* (725–48)
	Eardwulf (? 748 – *c.* 762)
Eadberht II (762 – *c.* 764)	*Sigered* (*c.* 762 – *c.* 764)
Eanmund (*c.* 764)	*Ecgberht* (*c.* 765 – ?)
? *Heahberht* (*c.* 765)	

c. 778/9: Ecgberht apparently king of the whole of Kent.
784: Ealhmund (? the father of Ecgberht of Wessex) ruling in East Kent.
c. 785: Offa imposes direct Mercian rule on Kent.
796–8: 'King' Eadberht Præn leads the Kentish rebellion.
c. 799 to 807: Cuthred, brother of King Coenwulf, sub-king in Kent.
825/6: King Baldred, probably a Mercian sub-king, ruling in Kent.

APPENDIX 4
The Abbots of St Augustine's

There are three main sources for the names and sequence of the abbots of St Augustine's in the Anglo-Saxon period. The earliest is a thirteenth-century list found in BL Cotton Julius D. ii (fo. 2v), which originally terminated with Abbot Hugh III (1220–4) but was brought down to the fifteenth century by a number of later scribes. This list is not of great value; comparison with other sources demonstrates that in its early reaches it is corrupt and incomplete (for example, it omits Jaenberht, one of the better-known of the early abbots). A more accurate sequence, together with many precise dates, can be pieced together from the related histories of Sprott and Thorne, but this is overshadowed by the information in the chronological table prefixed to Elmham's history, which appears to provide the names and dates of all the abbots from the seventh-century foundation until the early fifteenth century (Hardwick, *Elmham*, pp. 1–73). Elmham's material on the pre-Conquest abbots can sometimes be checked against entries in the *Anglo-Saxon Chronicle* and by cross-reference to the abbots' charter-subscriptions, and this exercise reveals major difficulties. For instance, in 985 or 986 an abbot of St Augustine's named Sigeric was appointed bishop of Ramsbury; in 990 he was translated to Canterbury, where he remained in office until his death in 994. According to Elmham's table, Sigeric was abbot from 980 until 988, which could be interpreted as indicating that he retained the abbacy for some years after his appointment to Ramsbury; but faith in Elmham's dates is undermined by his information that Sigeric was archbishop from 1000 to 1005, which is a decade out. Considerably more worrying is Elmham's information about an earlier Abbot Sigeric, whose period of office is said to have stretched from 942 until 955. This Abbot Sigeric was entirely fictional; he was brought into existence as the result of tampering with a charter in the archive in favour of a thegn named Sigeric (**27**) in order to create a direct grant to the abbey. Sprott and Thorne assign the period 942 to 971 to an Abbot Ælfric, but this is again contradicted by an original Canterbury will of 942 × 958 (S 1506, probably 958), which is attested by an Abbot Eadhelm, identified as the head of the St Augustine's community. Eadhelm is mentioned by none of the historians and does not appear in the list of abbots in BL Cotton Julius D. ii. It appears that the preoccupation of later medieval scholars at St Augustine's with precise chronology for the pre-Conquest period led them to re-arrange and tidy up their information about the early abbots, just as they altered the muniments to adapt them to an incorrect chronological framework. All such interference was of course cumulative, since one adjustment could well throw out another calculation, forcing further emendation. Evidently all the post-Conquest sources for the early abbots must be treated with a high degree of scepticism, and Elmham's dates are certainly not entirely trustworthy (although they are of some use in assessing relative chronology).

In the following pages I consider the evidence for the Anglo-Saxon abbots, using these abbreviations: Sp (Sprott), Th (Thorne) and E (Elmham). The material is divided into three periods: from the foundation to *c.* 866; from *c.* 866 to 942; and from 942 until 1066.

a. *The foundation to c. 866*

1. *Peter*

The first abbot was a priest named Peter, drowned in the Channel while on a mission to Gaul (Bede, *HE*, i. 33). He was probably the monk of that name whom Augustine had sent back to Rome with news of the mission (*HE*, i. 27); presumably he returned to England with Mellitus's group in 601/2. Sprott, Thorne and Elmham place his death in 607, but this seems to be too early, for an Abbot Peter attests the acts of the 614 Synod of Paris, together with Bishop Justus of Rochester (C. de Clercq, *Concilia Galliae, A. 511 – A. 695*, Corpus Christianorum Ser. Latina cxlviiiA (Turnholt, 1963), p. 282). He probably drowned on his return from attending the synod.

2. *John* (607–18; Sp, Th, E)

The beginning of his abbacy must be shifted to 614; the date of his death cannot be checked. He was probably the John who travelled to England with Mellitus (*Liber Pontificalis*, ed. L. Duchesne, 3 vols (Paris, 1886–1957), i. 312).

3. *Ruffinianus* (618–26; Sp, Th, E)

Bede (*HE* i. 29) includes him among Mellitus's companions.

4. *Graciosus* (626–38; Sp, Th, E)

The historians state that he was a Roman.

5. *Petronius* (638–54; Sp, Th, E)
All the historians mention that he was not consecrated until 640.

6. *Nathanael* (654–67; Sp, Th, E)

[Vacancy 667–9]

7. *Benedict Biscop*

In the *Historia Abbatum* (Plummer, *Bede*, i. 366–7), Bede says that Benedict Biscop accompanied Theodore on his journey from Rome to England and, on arrival in Kent, was made abbot of the Canterbury monastery, a position which he held for two years, before leaving once more for Rome. Bede dates Theodore's arrival precisely to 27 May 669 (*HE* iv. 2); the date is rather suspicious, since that was exactly a year from the day on which he was supposed to have left Rome. This would seem to imply that Benedict was abbot of St Augustine's until at least the end of May 671. There was no memory of him at St Augustine's; indeed Elmham dismisses the rumour of his abbacy as a malicious fabrication (Hardwick, *Elmham*, p. 186). The St Augustine's historians seem to have relied on the slightly different account in the *Historia Ecclesiastica*, which omits any reference to Benedict and states that Hadrian was made abbot as soon as he arrived in England (*HE* iv. 1). Benedict may have been appointed a temporary caretaker of the monastery, for the period of Hadrian's detention in Gaul.

8. *Hadrian* (669 or 670 to 708; Sp, Th, E)

Hadrian set out from Rome with Theodore in May 668, but was detained in Gaul as a suspected spy for an unknown period; immediately after his belated arrival in England he made abbot of the Canterbury monastery (*HE* iv. 1). This seems incompatible with the statement in the *Historia Abbatum* (see above) that Benedict Biscop remained abbot for two years, for it is unlikely that Hadrian was so long delayed. It may be that in the *Historia Ecclesiastica*, relying on new information from his informant Abbot Albinus, Bede was correcting his earlier chronology (he may originally have added the year's journey from Rome to the period of Benedict's abbacy). Elsewhere Bede implies that Hadrian arrived in England two years after setting out in 668; his death is said to have taken place thirty-nine years after his arrival in England and forty-one years after being entrusted with the mission by the pope (*HE* v. 20). This calculation suggests that Hadrian died in 709; but other evidence points to 710 (see Plummer, *Bede*, ii. 329).

9. *Albinus* (708–32; Sp, Th, E)

709 or 710 would be a more acceptable date for Albinus's election and consecration. He attended a synod of *Clofesho* in 716 (see the spurious S 22, which has a genuine witness-list), and attested S 23, issued on 20 February 732. Bede refers to him in the preface of the *Historia Ecclesiastica* (731).

10. *Nothbaldus* (732–48; Sp, Th, E)

No other appearances.

11. *Aldhun* (748–60; Sp, Th, E)

An abbot of this name attests S 32, dated 762, and the historians' dates for the next abbot seem to be two years too early, so it seems likely that Aldhun remained abbot until at least 762.

12. *Jaenberht* (760–2; Sp, Th, E)

Jaenberht is mentioned as the abbot of St Augustine's in **11** (A.D. 762), **12** (A.D. 762) and **13** (A.D. 762 or 763), and he attests as abbot **53** (A.D. 763 or 764) and S 33 (A.D. 764). Since his predecessor attests S 32, also from 762, Jænberht was probably not elected until at some point in that year. The historians put Jaenberht's election to the archbishopric in 762 instead of 764, no doubt following a version of the *Anglo-Saxon Chronicle* with dislocated chronology for the period. They also imply that Jaenberht did not consecrate his successor as abbot until he received his pallium in 766 (they have the uncorrected *ASC* date, 764).

13. *Æthelnoth* (762–87; Sp, Th, E)

The date of his election should probably be 764 and he may not have been blessed until 766 (see above). He is the beneficiary of **14**, a forgery which is difficult to date, but he does not attest any other charters.

14. *Guthheard* (787–803; Sp, Th, E)

Sprott and Thorne are uncertain about the date of Guthheard's death, but note that his successor was blessed by Archbishop Wulfred in 803. There is a problem here (see below). Guthheard does not attest any surviving charters.

15. *Cunred* (803–22; Sp, Th, E)

Sprott and Thorne state that Cunred was consecrated by Archbishop Wulfred in 803, although Wulfred did not become archbishop until 805 (the uncorrected *ASC* date is 803). He received his pallium in 806 and attests as *electus* until then, so it is unlikely that he would have consecrated an abbot until 806. Cunred does not attest any charter between 803 and 822. He is the beneficiary of Elmham's text of **16** (804), but this was originally a grant to a layman in which the name of the beneficiary has been altered. Other versions of **16** name Abbot Wernoth as beneficiary, and an abbot of that name attests a number of charters from 805.

16. *Wernoth* (822–44; Sp, Th, E)

Wernoth first occurs as a priest in the entourage of Archbishop Æthelheard at the 803 synod of *Clofesho* (BCS 312). As abbot, Wernoth appears in Kentish charters between 805 and 838: he attests S 39 (A.D. 805), 40 (A.D. 805), 161 (A.D. 805), 1439 (A.D. 810), 1264 (A.D. 811), 1265 (A.D. 813), 1434 (A.D. 824), is mentioned in **17** (A.D. 826), and is the beneficiary of **19** (A.D. 838); his name has been substituted for that of a lay beneficiary in some versions of **16** and **21** (it is possible that **19** represents another substitution, in which case his abbacy may not have extended as late as 838; see further discussion of Beagmund below). Brooks (*Church of Canterbury*, pp. 163–4) suggests that Wernoth may initially have been an abbot of the Christ Church community, who later transferred to St Augustine's; this suggestion is based on the fact that Wernoth was the only abbot to attest S 1265 (A.D. 813), Wulfred's grant of a new constitution to Christ Church, which implies that he was connected with the community. It would be easier to accept this hypothesis if there was some evidence of Cunred's existence between 805 and 822. In view of Wernoth's prominence and Cunred's absence during this period, it seems simpler to assume that Wernoth was abbot of St Augustine's from *c.* 805 until at least 826 and perhaps as late as 838 or 844. Wernoth's subscription to S 1265 can perhaps be explained by the unusually close links between the two Canterbury communities (see pp. xiii–xiv).

17. *Dryhtnoth* (844–64; Sp, Th. 844–63; E)

An Abbot Dryhtnoth attests **24** (*c.* A.D. 850) and seems to be the beneficiary of **22** (A.D. 861). A priest named Dearnoth/Drihtnoth appears in several earlier Kentish charters: S 1264 (A.D. 811), 1265 (A.D. 813), 1436 (A.D. 826/7), 291 (A.D. 842). The priest, probably a member of the Christ Church community, may well later have become the abbot of St Augustine's, but there is reason to think he was not Wernoth's immediate successor (see below). The similarity between the latinized name forms Wernodus and Diernodus seems to have led to confusion between the two. In what seems to be the earlier manuscript of Sprott's history (London, Lambeth Palace, MS 419) the charters of which Wernoth was the beneficiary were placed in the abbacy of Dryhtnoth (*Diernodus*). It seems later to have been realised that Dryhtnoth's supposed successor, Wynhere, was the beneficiary of a charter dated 845 (**20**); consequently, in the second manuscript of Sprott's history (BL Cotton Tib. A. ix, 115r) the date of Dryhtnoth's death has been altered from 864 to 844.

18. *Wynhere* (864–6; Sp, Th. 863–6; E)

Wynhere, *presbyter abbas* and clearly abbot of St Augustine's, is the beneficiary of **20** (A.D. 845). He also attests S 296, an original charter of the same year. From this it would appear that Wynhere preceded Dryhtnoth as abbot of St Augustine's.

b. *From c. 864 until 942*

For the period between the death of Abbot Winhere and 942, Sprott and Thorne have virtually no information about the abbots of St Augustine's, apart from their names and sequence. They provide a list of fifteen names and note that the last on the list, Beornhelm, died in 942. Elmham's chronological table has the same sequence of names, but also provides full dates for each abbot. The details are as follows:

Beahmundus (Sp)/Beadmundus (Th)/Bewmundus (E)	866–74
Kynebert	874–9
Etans/Etaus	879–83
Degmund	883–6
Alfred	886–94
Ceolbert	894–902
Beccanus	902–7
Athelwold	907–10
Tilbert	910–17
Eadred (I)	917–20
Alchimundus (Sp)/Alchmund (Th)/Alcherindus (E)	920–8
Guttulf	928–35
Eadred (II)	935–7
Lulling	937–9
Beornhelm	939–42

Checking this sequence proves very difficult. Abbots named Beagmund and Dægmund attest a number of ninth-century Kentish charters, but these subscriptions cannot be reconciled with Elmham's dates:

Beagmund.

He attests S 286 (A.D. 838) as abbot, and S 1268 (A.D. 825 × 832), 1510 (A.D. 837, ? for 845 × 853), 1438 (A.D. 838) and 287 (A.D. 839) as *presbyter abbas*. A priest of the same name attests S 1482 (A.D. 833 × 839; in this case the style may be an error for *presbyter abbas*) and S 1197 (A.D. 843 × 863), and an individual, rank unspecified but perhaps a member of the Christ Church or St Augustine's communities, attests **24** (*c.* A.D. 850), S 328 (A.D. 858) and S 332 (A.D. 863). It is likely that these subscriptions are those of at least two different men, an earlier abbot active in the 830s and perhaps the 840s, and a later cleric of lesser rank active in the 850s and and 860s. We might speculate that the last individual became abbot of St Augustine's for a brief period in the later 860s, which would fit Elmham's dates, but an alternative possibility would be to fit the abbot who was attesting in the 830s into the sequence of St Augustine's abbots at that period. Abbot Wernoth appears in charters up to 826, and then as the beneficiary of **19** from 838 (see above); there is a chance that his name has been substituted for that of a layman in the last document, which might indicate that he was already dead by the 830s. After this, there is no firm evidence until the appearance of an abbot named Wynhere in two documents of 845. It is possible that Beagmund succeeded Wernoth as abbot of St Augustine's at some point after 826, and ruled the abbey until *c.* 845. This may seem an arbitrary suggestion, but the evident confusion in the sources for the ninth-century abbots means that the traditional sequence is by no means sacrosanct and that we should be looking instead to the charter-attestations for firm evidence.

Dægmund.

A *presbyter abbas* named Deimund attests S 1196 (? A.D. 859) and 332 (A.D. 863). A Dægmund *diaconus* subscribes S 1436 (A.D. 825) and a *presbyter* of that name attests S 1268 (A.D. 825 × 832), 1197 (A.D. 843 × 863) and 1439 (A.D. 844). It is difficult to believe that a man who was a deacon in 825 could have become abbot of St Augustine's as late as 883 and ruled until 886. If Elmham's dates have any basis in reality, then his Abbot Dægmund cannot be linked with this attesting cleric.

The historians' list implies a very rapid turnover of abbots during this period. The seventy-eight years between 866 and 942 apparently saw fifteen abbots, none of whom remained in office for more than eight years (the average term was five years). By contrast, there seem to have been only about eighteen abbots in the two and a half centuries between the foundation of the monastery and 866, while for the better-documented period between 971 and 1066 there were only seven abbots. The relatively large number of abbots between 866 and 942 is suspicious, and it is possible that the list of names given by Sprott (and provided with dates by Elmham or a predecessor) was taken wholly or in part from an alien source, perhaps from a confraternity book or a list of ninth-century abbots from another Kentish monastery. If so, then Elmham's dates would be fictitious. It is worth noting that Thorne copied out Sprott's list of fifteen abbots for the period 866–942, but drew on another source for the information that the fifteenth, Beornhelm, was the abbot of that name who took Alfred's alms to Rome in 890, as mentioned in the *Anglo-Saxon Chronicle* (Twysden, *Scriptores*, col. 1777; Davis, *Thorne*, p. 34). Thorne also received from somewhere the impression that Beornhelm was elected abbot in 869 (thus consigning his fourteen predecessors to 866–9). A Beornhelm, *abbas or presbyter abbas*, attests Kentish charters from 867 to *c.* 890: S 338 (A.D. 867), 319 (confirmation, A.D. 870 × 888), 1200 (A.D. 867 × 870), 1202 (*c.* A.D. 871), 1203 (A.D. 875), 1508 (A.D. 871 × 889); an abbot of that name also occurs in S 1288 (A.D. 924, ? for 890, 905 or 920). This Beornhelm could have become abbot of St Augustine's in the later 860s (? in succession to Dryhtnoth) and may indeed have been the Alfredian abbot mentioned in the *Chronicle*, but his abbacy certainly did not extend as late as 942.

In conclusion, it would appear that in the later medieval period knowledge of abbatial succession between 866 and 942 was deficient, and that the extant list represents an attempt to plug the gap; by the fifteenth century these men had been equipped with fictitious dates.

c. *From 942 to 1066*

From 942 onwards the historians' information about the post-Conquest abbots seems to improve, although there is initially confusion. Sprott and Thorne state that an Abbot Ælfric was in office from 942 until 971, while Elmham inserts the abbacy of the fictional Abbot Sigeric between 942 and 955, restricting Ælfric's rule to the years 955–71. Neither version seems to be correct. A Wigstan, identified as abbot of St Augustine's, attests **28** from 946, and a certain Eadhelm attests a Kentish will of *c.* 958 (S 1506; A.D. 942 × 958, probably 958) as abbot of the monastery. The latter was almost certainly the Abbot Eadhelm who witnessed the grant of Reculver minster to Christ Church in 949 (S 546), and he may also have been the witness to S 556 and 557, two charters of 951 covering land in Huntingdonshire and Staffordshire (although there seems to have been another contemporary abbot of the same name, who was murdered at Thetford in 952: *ASC* D). It seems then that the community may have been ruled by an Abbot Wigstan in the mid 940s and by an Abbot Eadhelm from *c*. 949 until *c*. 958. This conclusion would agree with with the evidence of Abbot Ælfric's subscriptions. An Abbot Ælfric attests on several occasions between 959 and 970, although the existence of contemporary abbots with the same common name name at Glastonbury, Malmesbury and St Albans makes it difficult to be entirely confident about the consistent identity of this witness. It would appear that Ælfric was the successor of Eadhelm and that his period of office was much shorter than the historians believed. But the cessation of his (presumed) subscriptions coincides quite neatly with the traditional date of 971 for his death.

From this point it appears that the historians' information about the abbots is reasonably reliable, although sometimes the given dates may be wrong by several years The available information is summarized clearly in *HRH*, pp. 35–6.

APPENDIX 5
The rotating 'chancellorship'

According to a passage in the twelfth-century compilation known as the *Liber Eliensis*, from the time of King Æthelred until the Norman Conquest St Augustine's shared with the abbots of Glastonbury and Ely, on a rotating basis, the honour of sending a representative to carry out what is described as *cancellarii . . . dignitatem* at the king's court:

Statuit vero atque concessit [rex Æthelredus], quatenus ecclesia de Ely ex tunc et semper in regis curia cancellarii ageret dignitatem, quod etiam aliis, Sancti videlicet Augustini et Glestonie, ecclesiis consitutit, ut abbates istorum cenobiorum vicissim adsignatis succedendo temporibus annum tripharie dividerent, cum sanctuariis et ceteris ornatibus altaris ministrando. Abbas quoque Elyensis cenobii semper in die purificationis sancte Marie ad administratorium opus procedebat in ipso Februarii mensis initio et sic ipse abbas, vel quem de fratribus destinaret, quantum temporis ei suppetebat per iiii menses, tertiam videlicet anni partem, cum summa diligentia illic officium reverenter supplevit, deinde alii, quos diximus, residuum anni per adsignata sibi tempora explicabant. (*Liber Eliensis*, ed. E.O. Blake, Camden Third Series xcii (London, 1962), pp. 146–7; cf. also p. 153)

This account is so circumstantial that it is difficult to believe that it has no basis in reality. Chaplais (1966, pp. 165–6 [p. 49]) finds it suspicious that the arrangements resemble those which King Alfred had made for the rotation of the personnel of his court (*Asser's Life of King Alfred*, ed. W.H. Stevenson (Oxford, 1959), pp. 86–7), but this feature could also be regarded as a sign of authenticity. The diplomatic evidence provides no basis for the suggestion that the abbots of these three houses had a role which involved the drafting of charters or the supervision of royal scribes (see Keynes, *Diplomas*, pp. 151–2); in other words, there is no good reason to think that they carried out duties similar to those of the post-Conquest *cancellarius*. The compiler of the *Liber Eliensis* clearly thought of the service carried out by the representatives of the three abbeys in terms of caring for sanctuaries and altars, and so it seems significant that there is some evidence that in late Anglo-Saxon England the word *cancellarius* might be equated with *scriniarius*, which could mean 'custodian of relics' (see Keynes, *Diplomas*, pp. 146–7, and comment by P. Chaplais, 'The Royal Anglo-Saxon "Chancery" of the Tenth Century Revisited', *Studies in Medieval History presented to R.H.C. Davis*, ed. H. Mary-Harting and R.I. Moore (London, 1985), pp. 41–51 at 42). It seems probable that the representatives of St Augustine's, Glastonbury and Ely attended the royal court on a four-month rotation in order to perform duties which involved caring for the king's collection of relics and the altars of the royal household, not to act as royal 'chancellors'.

INDEXES

In these indexes *w* is substituted for *p* and *uu* and *th* for *ð* and *þ*. The forms of personal names occurring in the texts are followed as far as possible, but normalized forms have been used when a common name occurs in one or more variant forms, and when it is mentioned in the introduction and commentaries. All variants are given except for *Æ*, *Ae* and *E* in both initial and medial positions. Square brackets [ ] enclose editorial comment. Charters are referred to by their numbers, in bold type; other references are to the pages of the introduction or the commentaries.

I. INDEX OF PERSONAL NAMES

This is an index of names and titles, rather than of individuals. References to laymen with the same name and rank are normally grouped together. Ecclesiastics have been identified where possible.

2. INDEX OF PLACE-NAMES

All places mentioned are in Kent, unless otherwise stated.

3. WORDS AND PERSONAL NAMES USED IN BOUNDARY CLAUSES

abbod, 'abbot'. *abbudes mearce* **14**; *abbates land* **22**

æcer, 'field, cultivated land'. *lectan* (or *leccan*) *æcer* **27**

ælf, 'elf'. ? *helfesdene* **27** (or **hielfe**)

Ælfwold (pers. n.) *Ælfwoldes mearke, Ælwoldes mearke* **28**

æsc, 'ash-tree'. *æschurud* or *æschurnd* **18**

teninge faledun. See index 2, Teynham

tun, 'enclosure, farm'. *beringtune* **21**

ufeweard, 'upward, higher up'. *ufewyrde* **27**

weg, 'way'. *hegewai* **14**; *tafinguueg*, ? *cornuug* **20**; *ealdanweg*, ⁊*lang weges* **27**

wicingas, 'people of the *wic*'. *wykenge mearce* **2** (see index 2, *Wyke*)

Wilcume (pers. n.) or **wilcuma** 'welcome guest', *wiltunam ninhinga* **21** (see index 2, *Welcumeweye*)

wrede, wreðe, 'flock'. **48**

wudunga, 'wood-gathering privilege'. *widumga* **21**

wudurǽden, 'wood-gathering privilege'. *wudureden* **28**

4. LATIN GLOSSARY

The following abbreviations are used: n. = noun; v. = verb; adj. = adjective; adv. = adverb; p.p. = past participle.

actionarius (n.) **[51, 53]**: agent, official

adfirmo (v.) **[40]**: to confirm

adstipulatio, astipulatio (n.) **[22, 34]**: confirmation

affirmatio (n.) **[44]**: confirmation

agellulus (n.) **[23]**: land

agellus (n.) **[17, 18, 23]**: land

aggeratim, aggregatim (adv.) **[30]**: corruption for *aggregatus*

agius (adj., from Greek ἅγιος) **[5, 27, 29]**: holy

alimonia (n.) **[15]**: nourishment, refection, entertainment

allodiarius (n.) **[32, 35]**: holder of land by allodial tenure (post-Conquest term)

anathema (n.) **[23A, 42]**: accursed object, curse

apex (n.) **[49]**: letter, writing

aratra (n.) **[27]**: for *aratrum*

aratrum (n.) **[6, 7, 13, 16, 18, 19, 20, 22, 26, 27, 29, 36, 41, 44, 47, 48]**: sulung (a unit of land-assessment peculiar to Kent)

archiepiscopatus (n.) **[5]**: archbishophood

archipresul (n.) **[3]**: archbishop

armilcaisia (n., for *armilausa*) **[3]**: cloak

astipulatio, see *adstipulatio*

astipulor (v.) **[5]**: to confirm

astriferus or *astrigerus* (adj.) **[21]**: starry

baro(n) (n.) **[35]**: baron

calumpnia (n.) **[34]**: charge, accusation

camisia (n.) **[3]**: shirt, gown

canonice (adv.) **[11]**: in due ecclesiastical order

caraxo (v., ultimately from Greek χαράσσω) **[20]**: to write

carrus (n.) **[13, 21]**: two-wheeled wagon

cartula (n.) **[6, 7, 8, 14, 30, 43, 44, 51]**: charter

cassatus (n.) **[21, 30]**: a measure of land, a hide

cedula (n., for *scedula*) **[20]**: charter

census (n.) **[15, 50, 52, 53]**: tax

Christicola (n.) **[2, 43]**: Christian, worshipper of Christ

circumcingo (v.) **[1, 2, 20, 23, 27, 30]**: to surround, enclose

circumgiro (v.) **[28]**: to bound, enclose, encircle

cirographum (n.) **[22]**: charter. writing

commutatio (n.) **[11]**: arrangement

condono (v.) **[30, 42]**: to grant

confauo (v.) **[5]**: to support, agree

consecratio (n.) **[26]**: royal anointing, consecration

consigno (v.) **[5, 27, 28]**: to endorse

copula (n.) **[5]**: wife

cors or *cortis, curtis* (n., from *cohors*) **[8, 40]**: vill

decima (n.) **[34]**: a tithe

defensio (n.) **[45]**: ? jurisdiction

dehonesto (v.) **[53]**: to treat disgracefully, to insult

denbera, denberende (n. pl., from OE *denbær*) **[18, 21, 28]**: swine-pastures

ditatio (n.) **[28]**: endowment, enrichment

elimosina (n.) **[50]**: alms

emulator (n., see *aemulator*) **[36]**: enemy, envious man

episcopium (n.) **[4]**: bishopric, diocese

ether (n., see *aether*) **[29]**: heaven

excommunicatorius (adj.) **[4]**: excommunicative, pertaining to excommunication

exiliatio (n.) **[34]**: exile

exinanitus (p.p.) **[27, 28]**: immune, free

fiscus (n.) **[50]**: tax

forum (n.) **[12]**: market-place

gramen (n.) **[27]**: ground, earth, sod

grauedo (n.) **[21]**: burden

gressus (n.) **[21]**: (right of) entry, passage (? for *ingressus*)

hereditas (n.) **[36]**: inherited property

idolatra (n.) [2]: idolater
iduma (n., from Hebrew) [30]: hand
impendo (v.) [44, 50]: to grant
incola (n.) [13, 17, 30]: local inhabitant
indesinenter (adv.) [51]: incessantly
interminatio (n.) [4, 5]: a threatening, ? punishment
iugum (n.) [17, 47]: unit of land, a yoke

larcitor (n., for *largitor*) [22]: bestower, dispenser
legatarius (adj.) [4]: legatine
libellus (n.) [12, 37]: 'little book', charter
libitum (n.) [36]: will, desire
ligamen (n.) [27]: chain, bond

maceria (n.) [12]: wall, enclosure
mancipium (n.) [3]: slave
mancusa (n.) [18, 19, 20, 22]: mancus (a gold coin, or its equivalent in gold and silver, with a value of thirty silver pence)
manens (n.) [14, 40, 42, 43, 46]: unit of land, a hide
mansa (n.) [28]: unit of land, a hide
mariscum (n.) [7, 44]: marsh
metropolis (n.) [4]: principal city
mina (n.) [8]: mine
missurium (n., for *missorium*) [4]: serving-dish
monachilis (adj.) [46]: monastic
monarchus (n.) [29]: monarch
montana (n.) [19]: hill
munusculum (n.) [41, 42]: small gift

obedibilis (adj.) [22]: obedient
oloserica (adj., for *holoserica*) [4]: silken
optimas (n.) [2, 3, 22, 28, 29]: magnate, prominent man in the realm

paginaliter (adv.) [49]: in writing
paginula (n.) [11]: (little) page, document
palestra (n., ultimately from Greek παλαίστρα) [30]: wrestling ground
pantocrator (n.) [30]: the all-powerful one (God)
pastinatio (n.) [11]: pasture
pastio (n.) [32]: feeding, hospitality
patrocinator (n.) [4]: protector, defender
patricius (n.) [7, 53]: important man, magnate
penninus (n.) [28]: winged
perpetro (v.) [43]: to execute, bring about
pertica (n.) [12]: unit of land, a perch
piscarium (n.) [21, 44]: fishery
pomarium, pomerium (n.) [40, 42]: orchard
prefectus (n.) [11, 16]: reeve
prepositus (n.) [16, 32]: reeve
primitiae (n.pl.) [34]: first fruits

prot(h)odoctor (n.) [5]: first teacher (applied to St Augustine)
prouidentia (n.) [10]: ? provision

referendarius (n.) [1, 2, 3]: referendary, chancery official
refrigerium (n.) [42]: refreshment, consolation
ruricolus (n.) [28]: countryman, local inhabitant

sabaoth (n.) [29]: the Lord of Hosts
saca (n.) [32, 35]: sake, a privilege of jurisdiction
saltus (n.) [11]: wood-pasture
satago (v.) [27, 30]: to endeavour
sationalis (adj.) [7]: sowable, suitable for cultivation
scapton (n., from Greek σκάπτον, equivalent to σκῆπτρον) [3]: sceptre, staff
sertus (adj.) [27]: twisted, plaited, interwoven
socna (n.) [32, 35]: soke, a privilege of jurisdiction
solicola (n.) [27, 30]: local inhabitant
suapte (adv.) [30]: in one's own way (*sua* and enclitic *-pte*)
subarro (v.) [27]: to pledge, to endorse
suffragium (n.) [46]: support, aid

tauma (n., ultimately from the Greek letter *tau*) [29]: +, sign of cross
tenatura (n.) [28]: tenure, holding (post-Conquest)
terrula (n.) [17]: a small piece of land
teter (adj., for *taeter*): offensive, foul, loathsome
thelonearius (n.) [49, 50, 51, 52, 53]: toll-collector
theloneum (n.) [32, 35]: tax, toll
thesaurizo (v.) [34]: to lay up treasure
thesaurus (n.) [34]: treasure
transuectio (n.) [50, 52, 53]: a passing through, a transporting past (*in the phrase* transuectionis census, *perhaps meaning* 'a toll on the transit of merchandise')
tropheum (n.) [5, 27]: sign, mark
tyrannis, -ide (n.) [4]: tyrant

uectigal (n.) [51, 53]: toll, tax
uenatio (n.) [19]: a hunting-ground
uendicare (v., for *uindicare*) [4, 8]: to lay claim to
uicissitudo (n.) [17]: an exchange
uicus (n.) [13]: a vill
uirga (n.) [12]: a unit of land, a rod

xenium (n., from Greek ξένιον) [3]: gift, donation

DIPLOMATIC INDEX

1. *Verbal Invocations*

In nomine almo trino diuino **18**
In nomine altithroni regis eterni **20**
In nomine Dei celi **23A**
In nomine Dei saluatoris nostri Iesu Christi **47**
In nomine Domini **24, 25**
In nomine Domini Dei et saluatoris Iesu Christi **6**
In nomine Domini Dei nostri et saluatoris Iesu Christi **8**
In nomine Domini Dei saluatoris **44**
In nomine Domini Dei saluatoris nostri Iesu Christi **10, 48, 49**
In nomine Domini Dei summi saluatoris Iesu Christi **22**
In nomine Domini Iesu Christi saluatoris **42**
In nomine Domini nostri Iesu (Christi) **11**
In nomine Domini nostri Iesu Christi **1, 2, 12, 17, 31, 43**
In nomine Domini nostri Iesu Christi saluatoris **40**
In nomine Domini nostri saluatoris **45**
In nomine Domini saluatoris nostri **51**
In nomine Iesu Christi saluatoris mundi **15**
In nomine patris et filii et spiritus sancti **5**
In nomine redemptoris mundi **16**
In nomine regnantis inperpetuum **52**
In nomine regnantis inperpetuum Domini nostri Iesu Christi ac cuncta mundi iura iusto moderamine regentis **13**
In nomine saluatoris **41**
In nomine saluatoris cuius pietate regimen assecuti sumus ... **7**
In nomine saluatoris Dei Iesu Christi conditoris nostri **19**
In nomine sancte et indiuidue trinitatis **3**
In nomine sancte trinitatis **27**
In nomine trino diuino Dei celi **23**
In nomine trino diuino regi regnanti inperpetuum Domino Dei Sabaoth **29**
Regnante inperpetuum Domino nostro Iesu Christo **14, 21, 28, 53**

2. *Proems*

Conditor celi terreque Deus uniuersitate totius creature **34**
Fortuna uolubilis infortunii fallax sibi iugiter **30**

Imminentibus uite caducis terminis qua in nos **28**
Omnem hominem qui secundum Deum uiuit **1, 51**
Quamuis decreta pontificum et uerba sacerdotum **27**
Quamuis igitur sermo solus catholicorum Dei seruorum **22**
Quamuis parua et exigua sunt que pro admissis peccatis offerimus **13**
Quoniam spes Christianorum hominum his mercedem pollicetur **47, 48**
Sacre nos catholicorum patrum per quos Dei spiritus est locutus **36**
Si ea que quisque pro recipienda a Deo mercede **49**
Unicuique mortalium uite sue terminus omnipotentis Dei dispensatione **53**

3. *Dispositive Words*

(a) *Past tense*
condonaui **30**
contuli possidendum **8**
contulimus ... possidendam **44**
dedi **41**
dedit **26**
largitus sum **21**
optuli **3**
perdonaui **46**
possidendam optuli **13**
redegi **43**
tradendo concessi **27**
tradidi **2, 36**

(b) *Present tense*
concedimus **16, 53**
concedo **28, 42, 51**
condonans attribuo **52**
perdonans attribuo **50**
possidendam attribuo **12**
possidendam perdonamus **40**
tradimus possidendam **9**
trado **34, 37, 42**

(c) *Paired verbs*
concedimus et confirmamus **6**
concedo et ... do **5**
dabo et concedo **1, 18, 19, 20, 22**
dedi et do **47, 48**
do et concedo **14, 23, 23A, 29**
donaui et dono **7**

4. *Royal Styles*

	(A) *Dispositive clause*	(B) *Subscription*
Æthelberht **1**	rex Cantie	rex Kancie
Æthelberht **2**	Dei gratia rex Anglorum	rex Anglorum
Æthelberht **3**	rex Anglorum	
Eadbald **5**	rex	
Hlothhere **6**	rex Cantuariorum	rex Cancie
Eadric **7**	rex Cantuariorum	rex
Oswine **8**	rex Cantie	rex Cantie
Wihtred **9**	rex Cantie	rex et donator
Wihtred **10**	rex Cantie	rex Cantie
Æthelberht II **11**	rex Cantie	rex
Eadberht II **13**	Dei dispensatione ab uniuersa prouincia Cantuariorum constitutus rex et princeps	rex
Offa **14**	rex Merciorum	rex Merciorum
Offa **15**	rex Merciorum	
Cenwulf **16**	rex Merciorum	rex
Cuthred **16**	rex Cantie	rex
Ecgberht **18**	rex occidentalium Saxonum	gratia Dei rex occidentalium Saxonum
Æthelwulf **19**	rex occidentalium Saxonum et Cantuariorum	
Æthelwulf **20**	gratia Dei rex occidentalium Saxonum necnon et Cantuariorum	rex
Æthelwulf **21**	occidentalium Saxonum rex	rex
Æthelwulf **22**	occidentalium Saxonum necnon et Cantuariorum rex	
Athelstan **26**	rex Saxonum et Anglorum	
Edmund **27**	rex Anglorum ceterarumque gentium in circuitu persistentium gubernator et rector	rex Anglorum
Eadred **28**	rex Anglorum ceterarumque gentium in circuitu persistentium gubernator et rector	rex Anglorum
Edgar **29**	rex Anglorum	Anglorum monarchus
Æthelred **30**	rex Anglorum	rex Anglorum
Cnut **32, 33**	per Dei misericordiam basileus	
Edward **34**	regis regum gratia rex et Anglorum princeps	

Edward **35**	king Dei gratia rex Anglorum	
Edward **36**	regis regum Dei predestinatione Anglorum rex	
Edward **39**	cyng	
Swæfheard **40**	rex Cantuariorum	rex Cantie
Suabertus **41**	rex Cantuariorum	rex
Oswine **42**	rex Cantuariorum	
Oswine **43**	rex Cantuariorum	rex
Wihtred **44**	rex Cantie	rex
Wihtred **45**	rex Cantuariorum	rex
Wihtred **46**	rex Cantuariorum	rex
Wihtred **47**		rex Cantuariorum
Eadberht I **48**	rex Cantuariorum	rex
Æthelbald **49**	rex Merciorum	rex Merciorum
Æthelbald **50**	rex Merciorum	
Æthelbald **51**	[rex] Merciorum	rex Mercie
Eadberht I **51**		rex Cantie
Offa **52**	rex Merciorum	
Eadberht II **53**	rex Cantie	rex